A HISTORY OF
THE AMERICAN DRAMA

A HISTORY
OF THE
AMERICAN DRAMA

From the Beginning to the Civil War

BY

ARTHUR HOBSON QUINN

*John Welsh Centennial Professor of History and English Literature,
University of Pennsylvania*

Second Edition

APPLETON-CENTURY-CROFTS, INC.
NEW YORK

TO THE UNFADING MEMORY OF
MY MOTHER

CONTENTS

vii

CONTENTS

CONTENTS

CONTENTS

PREFACE TO THE FIRST EDITION

In the histories of our literature, there has been one notable omission. The failure to treat the drama has sprung primarily from the rarity of the printed plays, which were usually issued in perishable form and whose very popularity proved to be their doom. Many of the stage successes, both of the past and the present, have been kept from publication by the protective instinct of the producing manager, who feared for his property rights and to whom the literary reputation of the playwright was of secondary importance. Conditions are much better now, however, in this regard than they were in the days when the researches began whose result is this volume. The old plays are coming from their hiding places and the universities are beginning to recognize the importance of obtaining specimens of our dramatic literature. The most significant of our dramas are becoming more accessible in printed collections, but there still remains much to be done before a complete body of dramatic material is generally available to the student. It is comforting to note the steady increase in the publication of modern plays and the growing habit of reading plays as our drama is being rediscovered. It had been my first intention to complete the account of the drama in America before issuing any portion of it, but it became evident that a different treatment must be accorded to the early and to the later drama. No convenient date presents itself as one in which a sudden change took place, for the progress of our playwriting has been continuous, and the roots of our modern drama lie deep in the early days. It has been found possible, however, to treat the drama before 1860 with a completeness that is forbidden to the historian of the period since the Civil War. When one realizes that the list of plays copyrighted in the United States since

1870 includes over 56,000 titles, it becomes apparent that such a wealth of material will have to be approached in a different manner from that which has been attempted in this volume. It seemed best, therefore, to publish first the record of our drama up to 1860, including, however, for the sake of completeness plays by men like Boker and Boucicault which fall beyond that limit. For reasons which are given in detail in the final chapter, the history of our drama up to the Civil War can be considered not as a fragment but rather as a work complete within itself. All necessary bibliographical material has therefore been furnished and a List of Plays arranged for ready reference has been appended. The form of these is explained in the appropriate places.

In the absence of a chart, the method of treatment of the material becomes important and the writer has been guided rather by his desire to present a helpful survey than by any worship of mere uniformity. Certain of the playwrights have their special significance, but as the subject develops, the type of play becomes usually of more importance than the individual playwright. A compromise has been effected, by which the work of the most significant dramatists has been made the center of a group of plays of similar nature. Thus while the greater dramatists have been treated as a unit, the minor playwrights may appear in more than one chapter, depending upon the nature of their contributions.

The drama has been considered throughout as a living thing. No attempt has been made to treat the unacted drama except incidentally, and except for the Revolutionary satires, attention has been concentrated upon the plays which actually reached the stage. From another point of view it has not been so easy to define the limits of our theme. The term American Drama presupposes native origin, and yet the interwoven threads of our early stage history make this term uncertain if we are to observe the spirit rather than the letter. It has seemed best to include those playwrights who, while born abroad, remained here and became identified with our stage and whose work has

PREFACE

taken its place, however humble, in the progress of our drama. When, like Boucicault, they have become vital forces in that development, it is easy to select for discussion those plays which were written in this country, leaving the balance to their proper position in British drama. In the case of playwrights like Burton and Brougham, where their plays remained largely foreign in spirit and indeed were frequently revamping of earlier plays, the distinction is not made so easily, but it has seemed best to disregard their contributions unless they come definitely under one of the types into which our native drama runs. On the other hand, the work of men like Ralph and Bernard, who were born in America but who became identified with the stage in England, seems to lie outside our province. It is the nature of the play and the circumstances of its production that determine the nationality of drama and not the accident of birth.

So generous and so courteous has been the assistance rendered me that recognition becomes a real pleasure. The very extent of that help, however, proves an embarrassment, and special mention seems invidious. The work would have been impossible had it not been for the establishment of the Clothier Collection of American Plays in the Library of the University of Pennsylvania and for the continued support of the generous donor. The endowment of a fund for a similar purpose by my fellow members of the class of 1894 has been one of the most encouraging episodes of the progress of the work. The constant interest of both authorities and attendants in the University Library has been invaluable, and indeed the expert assistance of Miss K. S. Leiper, now unfortunately no longer in charge of the Collection, cannot be overestimated. Among the many other libraries which I have laid under tribute, that of my friend Dr. F. W. Atkinson has been of the greatest service. He has placed at my disposal not only his remarkable collection but also his wide knowledge of the field itself, and the pages of this volume constantly reflect our many conversations. It is to be hoped that he will soon publish his

PREFACE

Bibliography of American Plays, to which only a few fellow workers have had private access. Miss J. L. Farnum of the Library of Congress, Mrs. L. A. Hall of the Shaw Theatre Collection, Mr. T. Franklin Currier of the Harvard Library, Mr. H. L. Koopman of the Brown University Library, Mr. Ernest Spofford, of the Historical Society of Pennsylvania, and Miss P. H. Fowle of the Boston Athenæum have been of great service to me, either upon the ground or through correspondence.

It is with especial pleasure that I acknowledge here the generosity and courtesy of the descendants of playwrights and actors. Mrs. George Boker has not only placed at my disposal the manuscripts of her father-in-law, but also has confirmed by her testimony the results of my study of them. Miss Helen Tyler Brown has interrupted her own labors upon her memoir of Royall Tyler to loan me unpublished manuscripts and to establish dates of performance. To Mrs. Laura E. Richards I owe the privilege of reading unpublished manuscripts of Julia Ward Howe, and to Mr. Murdoch Kendrick the opportunity of examining the prompt books of James E. Murdoch. Here again must be recorded, too, the debt of the the University of Pennsylvania and the writer to Mr. Robert Montgomery Bird for his splendid gift of the entire manuscript collection of his grandfather to the playwright's alma mater.

The encouragement of my colleagues has been most gratifying. Naturally, I have turned to Professor Schelling for counsel, which has been given with unfailing sympathy and with discrimination born of his wide experience. Professor Baugh's unsparing effort is reflected in the Bibliography and the List of Plays. Professor Crawford has been of great service in connection with the sources of our drama in France. Among my friends in other universities, the advice and encouragement of Professor Brander Matthews has been most stimulating, coming as it does from one who knows the field so well. I am only one of many who have experienced the generosity of a scholar who is never too busy to perform a graceful action.

PREFACE

His comments upon the proof as well as those of Dr. Atkinson and Professor Crawford, have been invaluable. Professor Odell of Columbia and Professor Snowden of South Carolina have been cordial in their response to inquiries concerning the New York and Charleston stages. The greatest service of all, however, came from my wife who through many seasons has read to me the forbidding typography of the early drama, when my work would otherwise have been at a standstill.

A. H. Q.

University of Pennsylvania
March 1923

PREFACE TO THE SECOND EDITION

Since the publication of the First Edition in 1923 there has been a great deal of scholarly activity devoted to the history of the American Theatre. Dr. Odell's monumental *Annals of the New York Stage*, the *Histories of the Philadelphia Stage* by Dr. Pollock, Dr. James and Dr. Wilson, and *The Theatre of the Frontier*, by Dr. Carson, to mention only a few of the contributions, have been published, and I have reflected their new information concerning the theatre in my revision of this record of the drama.

For practical reasons, the text has not been completely reset. It proved not to be necessary to alter the general plan of the *History*, but by resetting some pages and many individual lines it has been possible to correct errors and to add vitally necessary information.

Fortunately it has been possible to revise completely the Bibliography and the Play List, and they have been entirely reset. In making these revisions, I have had the advantage not only of the new printed sources already mentioned but also of unpublished monographs which the courtesy of their authors has permitted me to see in advance of printing. Mr. Julius Tolson's *Life of Dion Boucicault*, Dr. William S. Hoole's *History of the Charleston Stage* and Dr. Nelle Smither's *History of the New Orleans Stage* have been of particular value. Four hundred and fifty additional plays have been recorded in the Play List.

It has been a source of great satisfaction to me to know of the interest taken in this revision by scholars in the field. It would not be possible to thank every one of my correspondents, but I am especially grateful to Dr. William Van Lennep, Curator of the Harvard Theatre Collection, Dr. S. Foster Damon, Curator of the Harris Collection of American Poetry at Brown University, Dr. Zoltán Haraszti and Miss Harriet Swift of the Boston Public Library, Director Clarence S. Brigham of the American Antiquarian Society, Mr. George Freedley, Curator of the Theatre Collection at the New York Public Library, Mr. Barrett H. Clark, Dr. Oral S. Coad of the New Jersey College for Women, Dr. Roger A. Law of the University of Texas, Dr. Arthur H. Wilson of Susquehanna University, and for the Portland Theatre Mr. James Moreland of the Oswego State Teachers' College. The continued interest of Mr. Seymour Thompson, Librarian of the University of Pennsylvania, and of his associates in maintaining the Collections of American Drama has of course been invaluable and among my colleagues Dr. Alfred Harbage and Mr. E. B. Heg have been of great service in checking the *Play List*.

A. H. Q.

University of Pennsylvania
August, 1942

A HISTORY OF
THE AMERICAN DRAMA

CHAPTER I

The Drama and the Theatre in the Colonies

WHEN the first play written by a native American to be performed by a professional company was put on the stage of the Southwark Theatre in Philadelphia in 1767, the Colonial period was almost over. In our native literature there had been produced chronicles of adventure, histories and diaries, essays of many kinds, some lyric and narrative verse, but no novel or short story. That the drama was delayed so long in its coming was due partly to the literary dependence upon the mother country, which postponed creative writing of all kinds, but in the case of the drama there were special reasons which prevented its growth. These were connected with the prejudice against the theatre, rather than against the drama, but since there could be no real drama until there was a theatre, the result was the same. It is the custom to attribute this hostility to the prevailing religious tone of the different colonies, and to point out that while Puritan New England, Huguenot New York, and Quaker Philadelphia were inhospitable to the playhouse and all it stood for, Episcopalian Virginia and South Carolina and Catholic Maryland welcomed the first traveling companies and even antedated their efforts. It was only natural, of course, that the church out of whose ritual the drama grew and the church under whose shadow the great age of English drama had flowered should show no hostility to the theatre. It was to be expected also that the Puritan, who grouped the drama, together with the kindred arts of painting and music, with his dearest foe, Anti-Christ, should oppose the playhouse where it was performed. But the reasons for the opposition were deeper and were temperamental rather than theological, and were woven out of the social and economic constitution of the people.

1

HISTORY OF THE AMERICAN DRAMA

The Puritan and the Quaker were accustomed to abstract thinking, and the symbol was to them repugnant if not unnecessary. They associated it with monarchical forms in politics as well as religion, and they had no use for it. To the race that discoursed earnestly about the existence of witchcraft in the soul of man, and the race that felt the direct influence of the Spirit in their daily lives, the mimic representations of the stage may have seemed trivial.

The motives of those who opposed the theatre were mixed. They had little to do with freedom of conscience, as is often stated, for the Quaker was one of the most intolerant so far as the theatre was concerned and the Virginia cavalier who welcomed it was tolerant only of those who agreed with him. The Puritan and the Quaker were opposed to the theatre on account of the expense. They were averse to providing a livelihood for "profane shows" and in this thrifty feeling they were joined by the Dutch burgher of New York, who might have been indifferent to their antisymbolic objections. How strong was this feeling may be shown by the necessity felt by more than one manager of the time of publishing his expenses and receipts and by the resolution of Congress which finally closed the colonial theatre.

When Governor Hunter, of Pennsylvania, allowed Hallam's Company to act in 1754 it was with the distinct understanding that "nothing indecent or immoral" was to be performed. It was this general reputation of being connected with loose living that had descended from Restoration times, during which many of the ancestors of the colonists had left England, that hurt the theatre most in New England and Philadelphia. Between the standard of morals prevailing in the theatrical profession in the days of Charles II and of George II there had undoubtedly been improvement, but there was still room for more. Hallam's Company seems to have been composed for the most part of decent, hard-working people, but when one remembers that half a century later it was still possible for the manager's wife to appear on the stage of the Park Theatre in New York

2

in a state of intoxication, he has to confess that the prejudices of the respectable members of society had at least some foundation. Certainly anyone who has been handicapped in his researches in theatrical history of the time by the casual, not to say kaleidoscopic, changes in the marital relations of the leading men and women, cannot deny that the standards of that life were not the ordinary ones. The standards of right living may not have been any lower in Virginia or South Carolina than in New England, but personal derelictions on the part of the players would certainly have been more easily condoned, provided the latter contributed to the pleasure of their audiences. For the social constitution of the Southern colonies provided in its scope more liberally for public amusement. Despite the absences of large towns—there were none in Virginia when the first company came—the race courses had accustomed the gentry to travel long distances for their entertainment. For them entertainment was a necessary part of life; they were willing to pay for it, since their money came easily to them, and they saw no reason why the theatre was at all illegitimate.

When all the difficulties under which the theatre labored are considered, the wonder is, not that it was handicapped in its development, but that it survived at all. That there was a real appreciation of good acting in this country is proved not only by the favor of the Southern colonies, but also by the determined stand taken by the friends of the playhouse, largely of the same temperament, in Philadelphia and New York. In the eloquent words of the first historian of our theatre:

A large portion of the inhabitants, however, saw no offence to morality or religion in any of the colours which diversify and beautify the works of creation; or any of those innocent amusements which bring men together to sympathize in joys or sorrows, uniting them in the same feelings and expressions, with a brotherly consciousness of the same nature and origin.[1]

[1] Dunlap, William. *History of the American Theatre.* I, 27-8.

And that the creative drama had its birth was due likewise not to the patronage of the cavaliers in the South, but to the artistic sense of a young Philadelphian, under the personal inspiration of a great lover of the arts. After all, when we remember that it was but ten years after the first regularly organized company of actors performed in this country until the first American play was written and that it antedated by thirty years the first American novel, the appeal and the vitality of the drama as a form of art in colonial America may be regarded as established.

Unlike the novel, the first American drama had a respectable ancestry and inspiration. It was the study of Shakespeare, of Beaumont and Fletcher, of Dryden, of Ambrose Philips and Nicholas Rowe that inspired Thomas Godfrey to write *The Prince of Parthia*. But it must not be forgotten that it was as an actable play that Godfrey planned his work, and it was definitely for the company of players whom he had seen in Philadelphia that he wrote it. He was prompted also by his association with the amateur production of masques, odes, and dialogues in the College of Philadelphia, and since the beginnings of any art have an intrinsic interest it will be necessary before the first drama is itself discussed to trace the development of these two strains of influence, professional and amateur, which culminated in Godfrey's work.

The first theatrical performance in what is now the United States seems to have been given in Spanish on April 30, 1598, on the Rio Grande River below El Paso. The author was Captain Marcos Farfán de los Godos, and the play, which has not survived, is said to have been a *comedia* dealing with the march of the soldiers under Juan de Oñate. The same expedition on July 10, 1598, performed an anonymous drama, *Los Moros y los Cristianos*, which is still played throughout the Southwest. There was much theatrical activity even earlier in the Spanish provinces in North and South America, and a French masque, *Le Theatre de Neptune en la Nouvelle-France*

DRAMA AND THEATRE IN THE COLONIES

by Marc Lescarbot was given on November 14, 1606, at Port Royal in Acadia.[1]

The first record of a play in English concerns the performance of *Ye Bare and Ye Cubb*, a play written by William Darby, a landholder in Accomac County, Virginia, on August 27, 1665. He was assisted in the production by Cornelius Watkinson, another landholder, and Philip Howard, a servant. The court to which they were reported as offenders, inspected the play, meanwhile keeping the playwright in jail, found them "not guilty of fault" and required the plaintiff, Edward Martin, to pay the costs.[2] In 1702 there is a mention of a "pastoral colloquy" which was recited by the students of William and Mary College before the Governor, perhaps the earliest record of the college drama.[3] The atmosphere of the college and the colony was friendly to plays and players. Governor Berkeley himself wrote plays. The statement,[4] however, that "in 1690 Harvard students gave a performance of Benjamin Colman's tragedy, *Gustavus Vasa*, the first play written by an American acted in America," is not supported by satisfactory evidence.

Probably the first professional performance in America of a play written in this country took place in 1703, when Anthony Aston, a strolling English player, tells us in his journal: "We arrived in Charles-Town, full of Lice, Shame, Poverty, Nakedness and Hunger. I turned Player and Poet and wrote one Play on the Subject of the Country."[5]

---

[1] For references, see Bibliography, Chapter I.

[2] See Bruce, Philip A. *Social Life of Virginia in the Seventeenth Century*, Richmond, 1907. Chap. 13. The original court records are to be found in his *Accomac County Records*, Vol. 1663-66, folio p. 102, reprinted by J. C. Wise in *Ye Kingdom of Accawmacke, or the Eastern Shore of Virginia in the Seventeenth Century*, Richmond, 1911, pp. 324-27. See also account by J. F. Evans, *Washington Star*, August 17, 1941.

[3] Tyler, Lyon G. *Williamsburg, the Old Colonial Capital*, Richmond, 1907. See excellent chapter on the Theatre, pp. 224-231.

[4] Arthur Hornblow. *History of the Theatre in America*, I, 30.

[5] *The Fool's Opera; or, the Taste of the Age. Written by Mat Medley and performed by His Company in Oxford. To which is prefix'd A Sketch of the Author's Life, Written by Himself.* London. [1730?] Printed for T. Payne.

See Sonneck, O. G. *Early Opera in America*, pp. 5-7 for discussion of the date of Aston's journey. Also C. P. Daly, *First Theater in America*, 1864, p. 16, rep. in *Dunlap Society Pub.* Series 2, Vol. I, 1896.

Aston's play was not printed and the first printed play that has survived was not acted. On the one existing copy of *Androboros, A B[i]ographical Farce in Three Acts, viz: The Senate, The Consistory and The Apotheosis*, there are written the words "By Governour Hunter," and it has been attributed to Robert Hunter, Governor of the Province of New York from 1710 to 1719. The play was printed in New York, in 1714. Hunter was an Englishman and the play has, therefore, only an historical interest. It is a clever satire on the Senate, and on Lieutenant Governor Nicholson, who is represented, according to the key written in the unique copy in the Huntington Library, under the name "Androboros," or "man eater." Nicholson being determined to lead an attack against the Mulomachians (the French), the Senate generously votes "Negen Skillingen and Elleve Pence" for the expenses of the expedition and also passes a resolution that "he has behav'd Himself on the said Expedition with Courage, Conduct and Prudence." When the keeper, who is Hunter himself, asks why this resolution is passed before the expedition, "Aesop" replies, "By all means, lest when it is over you should have less reason for this Resolve."

Had there been any attempt made to perform *Androboros*, it would have been hard to find a theatre. He would indeed be rash, in view of the many occasions on which "the first theatre in America" has been discovered, who would attempt to fix finally a date for that event.[1]

One would have first to define what is meant by the word "theatre." We know these early ones only by reference, and it may be doubted whether they were more than public halls with some slight attempt at stage fittings. Williamsburg, the capital of Virginia, seems to have had such a theatre, built about 1716 and referred to in letters and at least one contemporary publication. Hugh Jones

[1] See Daly, C. P. *First Theater in America*, 1864. Reprinted by Dunlap Society, Series 2, vol. I, 1896.
Tyler, L. G. Williamsburg, *the Old Colonial Capital*, 1907, p. 224.

DRAMA AND THEATRE IN THE COLONIES

in his *Present State of Virginia*, in describing Williamsburg, says:

Near the middle stands the Church. Near this is a large octogon Tower, which is the Magazine or Repository of Arms and Ammunition, standing far from any House except James Town Court-House: for the Town is half in James Town County, and half in York County. Not far from hence is a large Area for a Market Place: near which is a Play House and good Bowling Green.[1]

No record has come down to us of the plays produced until September 10, 1736, when the *Virginia Gazette* contains this notice:

This evening will be performed at the Theatre by the Young Gentlemen of the College, the Tragedy of "Cato," and on Monday, Wednesday and Friday next will be acted the following Comedies by the young Gentlemen and Ladies of this Country—"The Busybody" and "The Recruiting Officer" and "The Beaux Stratagem."

It is interesting, in view of the recent revival of dramatic interest in American colleges, to note the production of Addison's tragedy by the students of William and Mary. It would be interesting, too, to know whether the "Young Gentlemen and Ladies of this Country" were amateurs or professionals. Contemporary letters, quoted by Mrs. Stanard, would indicate the former. The social constitution of Virginia, based upon desire for enjoyment and the rather easy terms of intercourse among social equals, would argue for their amateur status, together with the lack of evidence of the existence of any troupe of professionals in that region. It might, however, be made an argument for professional production that *Cato*, *The Busybody*, *The Beaux Stratagem*, and *The Recruiting Officer* were acted both by this company and by a troupe

---

[1] Hugh Jones, *The Present State of Virginia*, London, 1724. Reprint N. Y. 1865, pp. 30-31. The first players, under the management of Charles and Mary Stagg, teachers of dancing, were probably amateurs. Stagg died in 1735 and Mary Stagg resumed her "dancing assemblies." It was probably to this company that Governor Alexander Spotswood referred in a letter of June 24, 1718, to the Board of Trade, in which he says, "These eight counsellors would neither come to my house or go to the play w'ch was acted on that occasion." See *Coll. Virginia Hist. Soc.*, New Ser., II, 284.

7

which performed in New York City in 1732 and 1733 at the "New Theatre" near the junction of Pearl Street and Maiden Lane. But the fact that the part of "Worthy" was acted in New York by a barber points to a somewhat easy transfer from amateur to professional status.

This mingling of amateur and professional is reflected also in an advertisement in the *South Carolina Gazette* for May 3, 1735, which states that "any persons that are desirous of having a share in the Performance thereof, upon Application to Mr. Shepheard, shall receive a satisfactory Answer."[1] This refers to the troupe which acted Otway's *Orphan* on January 24, 1735, in the courtroom at Charleston, S. C., and which on February 18th produced the first opera to be advertised by title in America—*Flora or Hob in the Well.*[2] It may, indeed, have been the same company, en route from New York to Williamsburg. They were the occasion for the erection of a theatre, for on January 24, 1736, the *South Carolina Gazette* contained this notice:

On Thursday, the 12th of February will be opened the New Theatre in Dock Street, in which will be performed the comedy called "The Recruiting Officer." Tickets for the pitt and boxes will be delivered at Mr. Charles Shepheard's on Thursday, the 5th of February. Boxes 30s. Pitt 20s and tickets for the gallery 15s. which will be delivered at the theatre the day of playing.

Performances were given throughout 1736 and as late as May, 1737. New York, too, saw occasional plays in 1739, but it was in Philadelphia that the first company of which we have any real knowledge began its career. In August, 1749, a troupe headed by Thomas Kean and Walter Murray produced Addison's *Cato*, and probably other plays in a playhouse constructed out of a warehouse belonging to William

[1] See Law, R. A. *Notes on Colonial Theatres of Charleston, S. C.*, reprinted from *Nation*, April 23 and Sept. 3, 1914.

[2] Sonneck, O. G. *Early Opera in America*, p. 12.

[3] Daly, *First Theater in America*, p. 53, quoting from *New York Times*, December 15, 1895, an article on Charleston Theatre.

DRAMA AND THEATRE IN THE COLONIES

Plumsted on Water Street, below Pine Street.[1] They had evidently been playing since January, for the Recorder of the city protested to the Common Council against their performance at that time.[2] They then went to New York City, according to the following note:

New York, February 26.

Last week arrived here a company of comedians from Philadelphia, who we hear, have taken a convenient room for their purpose in one of the buildings lately belonging to the hon. Rip Van Dam, Esq., deceased, in Nassau Street; where they intend to perform as long as the season lasts, provided they meet with suitable encouragement.[3]

Among the twenty-four plays[4] given in New York were *Richard III*, Congreve's *Love for Love*, Dryden's *Spanish Friar*, Addison's *Cato*, Gay's *Beggar's Opera*, Lillo's *George Barnwell*, Otway's *Orphan*, and four of Farquhar's dramas. Their season lasted from March 5, 1750, to July 8, 1751. Murray and Kean then went to Virginia, where they organized the so-called "Virginia Company of Comedians" which played at Williamsburg and Annapolis in 1751. In fact, a theatre was built by them in Williamsburg, at which in October, 1751, they presented *Richard III*. They seem to have acted again in the spring of 1752 at Williamsburg, Fredericksburg, and other places[5]—later going on to Annapolis.

Interesting as the speculations concerning this company may be, especially in their later career when they seem to have disputed the Southern territory with "the American Company," it is really with the coming of Lewis Hallam's company in 1752 that our theatrical history begins and more truly our

[1] See manuscript diary of John Smith, son-in-law of James Logan, agent of William Penn, in volume covering period from Third month, 20th, 1749, to Tenth month, 19th, 1749.

"6 mo. [August] 22.3. Jos: Morris & I happened in at Peacock Biggers, & drank Tea there & his daughter being one of the Company who were going to hear the Tragedy of Cato Acted it Occasioned some Conversation in w'ch I Expressed my sorrow that any thing of the kind was encouraged."

This quotation is furnished by Dr. A. C. Myers, who has had access to the privately owned manuscript.

[2] Watson, John F., *Annals of Philadelphia and Pennsylvania*, I, 471.

[3] *Pennsylvania Gazette*, March 6, 1750, No. 1108, p. 2.

[4] See Seilhamer, I, 7, for complete list.

[5] Ford, P. L. *Washington and the Theatre*, 1899.

9

dramatic history. Much discussion has raged between Dunlap, Seilhamer, and others over the Hallam family, but the records of the English stage as given in Genest's *History* provide them at least with a respectable theatrical lineage. William Hallam, who was probably manager of the "Wells Theatre" in Lemon Street, London, and who conceived the idea of sending a company to America, and Lewis Hallam, his brother, who headed that company, were sons of Adam Hallam, a member of the company at Covent Garden from 1734 until about 1741—then at Drury Lane and later at "the Wells." At this theatre, which was not a very prominent one, Lewis Hallam played leading comedy parts and his wife seems also to have been a leading woman. She is not to be confused with Mrs. Adam Hallam, the stepmother of Lewis and William, who as "Mrs. Parker," "Mrs. Berriman," and "Mrs. Hallam" was a prominent member of the company at Lincoln Inn Fields and later at Covent Garden, from 1723 to 1740.

The company that invaded America consisted of Lewis Hallam, his wife, ten other adult members and three children of Hallam, Lewis, Adam, and a daughter. The latter, under the name of "Beatrice," became the heroine of one of the most interesting novels of our literature, John Esten Cooke's *The Virginia Comedians*.

Having obtained the Governor's permission and altered the theatre, Hallam's Company opened at Williamsburg on September 15, 1752,[1] in *The Merchant of Venice*, with Hallam as Launcelot, Malone as Shylock, and Mrs. Hallam as Portia. *The Anatomist* was given also. The company remained in the colony of Virginia for eleven months and then went to New York. Here Hallam built a theatre on the east side of Nassau Street, between Maiden Lane and John Street. The opposition to the theatre continuing, he prepared an address to the people of New York, pleading quite manfully and rather deftly for

---

[1] Ford, P. L. *Washington and the Theatre*, p. 14. Tyler, L. G. *Williamsburg, the Old Colonial Capital*, p. 227, shows the photographic facsimile of the issue of the *Virginia Gazette*, containing the announcement of the play. This evidence settles the date, which is usually incorrectly given, as September 5th.

public support from a city "so polite as this" and dwelling upon the instruction that the plays in his repertoire afforded. There is something very appealing about the plea of this actor-manager, in a strange country, for leave to live by his art. It was a first-class repertoire he provided, too, and it is of especial interest to us as it tells us what plays the American public were to see, and what influences an aspiring dramatist might encounter. Combining the list they were prepared to play when leaving England and the plays whose performance has been recorded in New York and Philadelphia, we find *King Lear, The Merchant of Venice, King Richard III, Romeo and Juliet, Hamlet,* and *Othello,* Rowe's *Fair Penitent, Jane Shore,* and *Tamerlane,* Henry Jones's *Earl of Essex,* Ambrose Philips's *The Distressed Mother,* Lillo's *George Barnwell,* Moore's *The Gamester,* Banks's *Albion Queens,* Lee's *Theodosius,* Farquhar's *The Beaux Stratagem, The Recruiting Officer, The Twin Rivals, The Inconstant,* and *The Constant Couple,* Addison's *The Drummer,* Congreve's *Love for Love,* Cibber's *The Careless Husband,* Hoadley's *The Suspicious Husband,* Vanbrugh's *The Provoked Husband,* Steele's *The Conscious Lovers,* Howard's *The Committee,* Bullock's *Woman's a Riddle,* Baker's *Tunbridge Walks,* and Gay's *Beggar's Opera.*

There were also twelve farces or operatic afterpieces including three by Garrick, *Lethe, Miss in Her Teens,* and *The Lying Valet;* Fielding's *Mock Doctor, The Virgin Unmasked,* and *Tom Thumb,* and Cibber's *Damon and Phillida.*[1]

It is interesting to note that the tragedies hold their own better than the comedies. One can still read with admiration *The Distressed Mother, The Fair Penitent, Jane Shore, Tamerlane,* and *George Barnwell,* but while *The Beaux Stratagem, The Recruiting Officer, The Suspicious Husband,* and *The Careless Husband* are amusing, they fail by sheer lack of sincerity, which is the touchstone of art. It was to tragedy that Godfrey turned, not to comedy.

Hallam's company next came to Philadelphia, against vig-

[1] Dunlap, I, 8; Seilhamer, I, pp. 46-47.

orous opposition on the part of the Quakers. Governor Hamilton favored their claims, however, and there was a strong party in the city who supported him. On April 15, 1754, the company opened in a brick warehouse, owned by William Plumsted, three times mayor of the city and a trustee of the College of Philadelphia. This was the building in which Murray and Kean's Company had acted in 1749, and was on Penn or Water Street, below Pine Street. It remained standing until 1849. Rowe's *Fair Penitent* and Garrick's *Miss in Her Teens* formed the bill, and Mrs. Hallam recited an epilogue which answered wittily the arguments of the opposition. That this opposition was carried far may be proved by a dispute which evidently took place in the Board of Trustees of the College of Philadelphia, for whose charity school a benefit performance was given June 19th. The minutes of the Board for August 13, 1754, state:

It being represented that a Company of Comedians in this City had lately acted a Play for the Benefit of the Charity School, and that upwards of an Hundred Pounds raised thereby was lodged in the Hands of Mr. John Ingles; A Majority of the Trustees present were of Opinion that the Treasurer should receive the same of Mr. Ingles for the said Use.

This item is of especial interest in its revelation of the amount taken in by the company at one performance. It was a benefit, of course, and may not have been the average amount. But it is at least significant that as large a sum as one hundred pounds was received.

The season had been limited by the Governor of Pennsylvania to twenty-four performances. So on June 27, 1754, the company bade adieu to Philadelphia, going first to Charleston, then to Jamaica,[1] where Lewis Hallam died and the organization was disbanded. The reason of his departure may have been the plague which was then raging or the lack of support due to the opposition to the theatre. Before the company left,

---

[1] Daly, *First Theater in America*, p. 57.

12

however, it had inspired the first American dramatist to write a play.

In 1758 Mrs. Hallam, the widow of Lewis Hallam, returned to this country as the leading woman of a company managed by her second husband, David Douglass, whom she had married in Jamaica, and who for many years was to be the directing force of what became the "American Company." He seems to have been an able manager, and to have actually profited by his theatrical ventures. As leading man young Lewis Hallam, then eighteen years of age, was selected, and he and his younger brother Adam, together with a Mrs. Love, were the only members of the former company who returned with Mrs. Douglass to the colonies. The company opened December 28, 1758, in New York City, with Rowe's tragedy *Jane Shore*, and *The Mock Doctor*, by Fielding, after Douglass had placated the authorities, whose permission he had neglected to secure. He built or altered a temporary theatre on Cruger's wharf, but after a brief season lasting till February 7, 1759, he departed for Philadelphia. During the New York season, *Douglas*, by John Home, was first given.

In Philadelphia he was more discreet and secured the permission of Governor Denny to play in the province, while he avoided conflict with the authorities of the town itself by building a theatre just outside the city limits, at the southwest corner of Vernon and Cedar Streets. Cedar, afterward South Street, was the limit of the town, and it is interesting to see how theatrical history parallels itself, for Shakespeare himself had to seek refuge on the Bankside. This building was used as a theatre for only one season, and soon after, three houses were erected on the site, then finally the brick structures that now stand there, one of which is a pawnbroker's establishment.[1] But the enemies of the theatre were not dismayed, and petitions from the Quaker, Lutheran, Presbyterian, and

---

[1] The proprietor insists that the foundations of the party wall formed a portion of the proscenium wall of the theatre. If this be true, we have here the oldest surviving fragment of a theatre in the United States.

Baptist congregations brought about the passage of a bill in the General Assembly prohibiting theatrical entertainments. The bill was set aside by the King in Council in September, 1760, but it placed a limit to the term in which Douglass could play, so that the season lasted only from June 25 to December 28, 1759. As we shall see, this may have prevented Godfrey's play from being performed in 1760, instead of 1767. Douglass opened with *Tamerlane*, by Rowe, and five of Shakespeare's tragedies were acted, *King Lear, Richard III, Hamlet, Macbeth*, and *Romeo and Juliet*, in which Lewis Hallam acted Romeo to his mother's Juliet.

From Philadelphia Douglass went to Annapolis, where the theatre was a welcome institution, but where as usual he had to build a home for his company. This season is noteworthy for the insertion in the *Maryland Gazette* of what is probably the first printed theatrical criticism in America.

Critique: Monday last the Theatre in this city was opened when the tragedy of Orphan and Lethe (a dramatic satire) was performed in the presence of his Excellency the Governor to a polite and numerous audience who all expressed their satisfaction. The principal characters both in the play and entertainment were performed with great justice, and the applause which attended the whole representation did less honor to the abilities of the actors than to the state of their auditors. For the amusement and emolument of such of our readers as were not present we here insert the Prologue and Epilogue, both written by a gentleman of this Province whose poetical works have rendered him justly admired by all encouragers of the liberal arts.[1]

Otway's *Venice Preserved* was acted this season. Then after a short season at Upper Marlborough the company went to Williamsburg, playing there during the winter of 1760-1. In the autumn of 1761 Douglass invaded New England, taking with him a recommendation from the Governor of Virginia as to his character and the skill of his company. Notwithstanding this provision he played *Othello* under the disguise of a

[1] Seilhamer, I, 115. The notice in the *Charleston Gazette* in 1737 contains no criticism.

14

"Moral Dialogue." The parts of each player are described quaintly; for example:

Mrs. Morris will represent a young and virtuous wife, who being wrongfully suspected, gets smothered (in an adjoining room) by her husband.
"Reader, attend; and ere thou goest hence
Let fall a tear to hapless innocence."

Douglass made a visit to New York in the same winter, building a theatre on the south side of Chapel or Beekman Street, a little below Nassau Street. Douglass was limited to a two months' season in New York City by the authorities, which he stretched to five months, and his net profits for the two months were about $1500 for the whole company. It is important to note that some of the opposition to the theatre was due to a belief that people spent too much money upon it, and it was to answer this criticism that Douglass published his receipts and expenses. Some of the objection to the theatre was due also to the character of the rough mob who collected outside of it. There was still a custom of crowding the stage with auditors, for we find the management giving public notice on December 31, 1761, that "it will be taken as a particular favor if no gentleman will be offended that he is absolutely refused admittance at the stage door, unless he has previously secured a place in either the stage or other boxes."[1]

The opposition becoming warmer, Douglass left New York City for at least five years. First he tried Newport again in 1762, then Providence, Rhode Island. The players were probably in Williamsburg in 1762-1763 and they were certainly in Charleston from December, 1763,[2] to May 10, 1764, from a notice which speaks of them as "The American Company" and also of the erection of a theatre "75 feet by 35 feet." After another visit to New England in 1765, Douglass played in Charleston from January 17 to April 16, 1766.

[1] Dunlap, I, 46-7.
[2] See Law, *Notes*, p. 13, Sonneck, p. 33, and Eola Willis, *The Charleston Stage in the XVIII Century*, pp. 52-53.

Then Douglass went to England, returning in October, 1766. He began his attack upon prejudice this time in Philadelphia, building the first permanent theatre in America on South Street, above Fourth Street. It was called the Southwark Theatre, and was a rough brick and wood structure, painted red. The stage was lighted by oil lamps without glasses, and the view was interrupted by the pillars that supported the upper tier and the roof. Yet it was an improvement on the temporary structures that had previously been erected, and it remained in use for theatrical purposes until the beginning of the nineteenth century. It was partly destroyed by fire in 1821, and some time after was rebuilt, being used for many years as a distillery. It was demolished finally in 1912.

On November 12, 1766,[1] the theatre was opened with the play of *The Provoked Husband*, and a musical piece, *Thomas and Sally*. The season was a long one, lasting till July 6, 1767, but its most interesting feature was the production, on April 24th, of Thomas Godfrey's *The Prince of Parthia*, the first play written by an American to be produced upon the American stage by a professional company of actors. The advertisement which appeared in the *Pennsylvania Journal and the Weekly Advertiser*, Thursday, April 23, 1767, runs as follows:

BY AUTHORITY

NEVER PERFORMED BEFORE
By the AMERICAN COMPANY,
At the NEW THEATRE, in *Southwark*,
On *FRIDAY*, the *Twenty-Fourth* of *April*, will be
presented, A TRAGEDY written by the late ingenious
Mr. *Thomas Godfrey*, of this city, called the
PRINCE *of* PARTHIA
The PRINCIPAL CHARACTERS by Mr. HALLAM,
Mr. DOUGLASS, Mr. WALL, Mr. MORRIS,
Mr. ALLYN, Mr. TOMLINSON, Mr. BROADBELT,

---

[1] *Pennsylvania Journal and the Weekly Advertiser*, No. 1248 (November 6, 1766). 3. Advertisement.

DRAMA AND THEATRE IN THE COLONIES

Mr. GREVILLE, Mrs. DOUGLASS,
Mrs. MORRIS, Miss WAINWRIGHT, and
Miss CHEER
To which will be added, *A Ballad Opera,* called
The CONTRIVANCES.

To begin exactly at *Seven* o'Clock.   *Vivant Rex and Regina.*

There is no record of any other performance, and, as was usual in those days, there is no after criticism of the play. It was probably not given again until March 26, 1915, when the Zelosophic Society of the University of Pennsylvania performed it in Philadelphia. It proved a very actable play, not withstanding the handicaps of the revival, in which the women's parts had to be taken by men.

Thomas Godfrey was born in Philadelphia, December 4, 1736. He was the son of Thomas Godfrey, the inventor of the sea quadrant, and was brought up in modest circumstances. His father dying when he was thirteen years old, he was apprenticed to a watchmaker, but through the efforts of Provost William Smith[1] of the College of Philadelphia, he was released from his indentures, and received further education under the Provost's direction. It was not only education he received, however; it was the introduction to a companionship that is one of the most significant in the history of art in America. In John Galt's *Life of Benjamin West*[2] we read that

Provost Smith introduced West, among other persons, to four young men, pupils of his own, whom he particularly recommended to his acquaintance, as possessing endowments of mind greatly superior to the common standard of mankind. One of these was Francis Hopkins[on], who afterwards highly distinguished himself in the early proceedings of the Congress of the United States. Thomas Godfrey, the second, died after having given the most promising indications of an elegant genius for pathetic and descriptive poetry.

[1] See Smith's account of Godfrey, *American Magazine,* Sept., 1758, pp. 602-4.
[2] Galt, John. *The Life and Studies of Benjamin West, Esq.* Phila., 1816, p. 52.

It is pleasant to speculate on what must have been the companionship of Francis Hopkinson, the first poet-composer,[1] Benjamin West, the first painter, and Thomas Godfrey, the first dramatist in our history, all responding to the stimulating powers of one of the greatest teachers of his time.[2] Knowing their interest in drama, we can be certain that both Hopkinson and Godfrey attended the performances of Hallam's company in 1754, and in the winter of 1756-7 this inspiration bore definite fruit. Dr. Smith decided that it was time to produce a dramatic piece at the College of Philadelphia, and during the Christmas holidays of 1756-7 he carried out his plan. His account of the production, given in the columns of the *Pennsylvania Gazette*[3], has a strong appeal, since it is almost certain that Godfrey saw it and may even have taken part. Moreover, it is the first native dramatic effort, containing original material and known to have been produced on the stage, that has come down to us, and it is a forerunner to the hundreds of college dramatic exercises that are an important chapter in our dramatic history.

The piece selected was *The Masque of Alfred*, originally written by Thompson in 1740 and revised by Mallet in 1751, with music by Arne. The original version was acted at Clifden and the second at Covent Garden, with Garrick in the part of Alfred. The masque deals with the rescue of England by Alfred from the Danes. Dr. Smith's own words are so quaint that they deserve reproduction in abstract:

"The Youth having from Time to Time delivered proper Speeches and acted Parts of our best dramatic Pieces, before large Audiences with great Applause," [they, therefore, wished to perform one entire piece, and selected the Masque of Alfred, by Thompson—altered in 1751 by Mallet.] "There is through the Whole, a Love of Liberty and a Concern for the Commerce and Glory of Great Britain, scarce

[1] See Sonneck, O. G., *Francis Hopkinson, the First American Poet Composer*, Washington. 1905.

[2] There is evidence that West painted Godfrey's portrait, but it has apparently not been preserved. There is a pencil drawing in the Historical Society of Pennsylvania which may be Godfrey, but it is not at all certain. No other portrait is known to exist.

[3] Jan. 20, 27; Feb. 3, 10, 1757.

18

equalled by any Thing in our Language." [It was, however, thought improper to include the meeting between Alfred and Eltruda in the Second Act.] "To obviate this Difficulty, the Writer of this Account undertook to alter the Piece, to leave out all the Womens parts, or to put their words into other Mouths. Thus, instead of bringing in Ivar to carry off Eltruda, he is brought in searching for Alfred's sons, as standing between him and the Throne of England; and just as he finds them, and is ready to slay them, Alfred, with the Shepherd, appears to rescue them, and kill the Ruffians. This produces a tender Scene of meeting and such as has never failed to draw Tears; especially as Alfred is immediately forced to leave his children, whom he has just rescued, and commit them to the Care of a Hermit, while he proceeds on his Expedition. His Absence gives an Opportunity to introduce the Hermit, conversing with the Children concerning Education, etc., all which Circumstances render this Act extremely instructive to the Youth who are the Speakers, and sufficiently interesting to the Hearers.

"These alterations, together with the Introduction of some new Hymns, and Pieces of Music, instead of some necessarily left out, and the extending the Hermit's Prophecy of the future greatness of England, so far as to include these Colonies, have occasioned near 200 new Lines, besides a new Prologue and Epilogue."

After some modest remarks upon his own portion of the performance, he gives the Prologue (by him).

It was spoken, in part, by "W. Hamilton," who is pushed off the stage by "S. Chew," who acted the Danish King "in a student's garb," and gives expression to lines like:

"In every Scene the Moral is divine,
And Truth and Mercy breathe in ev'ry Line.
No Thought to spread a Blush on Virtue's cheek;
No Word but what an Anchorite might speak."

The scene is laid in the Isle of Athelney in Somersetshire. The representation opens with shepherds who have found Alfred—also a shepherdess who bewails her lover. Dr. Smith writes some reflections of Corin on the maid's unhappiness. Alfred and the Earl of Devon enter and describe the devastation of the Danes. Here there is inserted a song by Dr. Smith, with music by Hopkinson, sung by the Genius of Britain.

Dr. Smith says it was necessary to enlarge the plan of the

original performance so far as the first scene of Act II went, and to insert a hymn by Milton, and the music by Handel— sung over the cave where Alfred and the Hermit are together. An example of Dr. Smith's blank verse may be selected from Act II. Corin is speaking to an airy form:

"*Corin:*   'Tis gone! but sure,
     Such moving melting Sounds, mine Ear, till now,
     Was never blest with. As they pass'd along,
     In measur'd Cadence, thro the dusky Air,
     Darkness forgot to frown; and ancient Night
     Wore, on her rugged Brow, a transient Smile;
     While Silence, bending o'er his dreary Throne,
     Did listen, and was pleas'd! What think ye, Friends?
     'Twas sure no mortal Hand, nor mortal Tongue,
     That struck these Notes, and swelled the Diapason."

England is saved, of course, the victory is told about by Devon, and Alfred returns, the Hermit winding up by telling him that the way to keep his country safe is by building up a navy. When the Danish King boasts that his son still lives and will revenge him, he is told of Ivar's fall and

"the Mother of Ivar and Wife of the Danish King, supposed to be seen behind the scenes, sings the famous Italian Desperata over the dead Body of her Son. . . .
          'Figlio ascolta! ah! giace estinto!' etc.,
which as she is a Foreigner, comes with Propriety from her, and greatly heightens the Distress."

The Epilogue, spoken by Jacob Duché, afterward Chaplain to Congress, who acted the part of Alfred, refers to the dangers from the Indian attack.

     "Then hear, oh hear, your murder'd Brethren's cries:
     And rouz'd by Pity, and by Vengeance rise,
     Pluck every seed of Discord from your Breast.
     Be *brave!*—*be one*—and Heaven shall do the rest!"

Inspired, therefore, by taste, inclination, and example, Thomas Godfrey wrote *The Prince of Parthia*. It is a romantic tragedy, laid in Parthia, in a time about the beginning of the

Christian era. Historical events, however, had little influence in shaping the plot of the tragedy, which is almost entirely of Godfrey's invention. Arsaces, the son of King Artabanus, is returning in triumph after his victory over the Arabians. His general favor incites envy in the heart of his brother, Vardanes, which is aggravated by the success of Arsaces in winning the love of Evanthe, a captive maiden, whom Vardanes loves and who excites the passion also of the King. Vardanes plots with his tool, Lysias, to inflame the King's mind against Arsaces by suggesting that the latter has designs upon his father's life. Artabanus is easily made suspicious, and when Arsaces asks as a reward for his labors that Evanthe become his bride, the King adds jealousy to his other emotions. The Queen, Thermusa, second wife of Artabanus, hates Arsaces because he has killed Vonones, her son, and she visits him in prison, where the jealousy of the King has sent him, with the intention of killing him. She is prevented from doing so by the apparition of the King, who has been murdered by Lysias out of revenge for insults, and also by a softer feeling, which suddenly comes to her, for Arsaces. Arsaces is freed by his youngest brother, Gotarzes, who with his troops enters the city and defeats Vardanes. Vardanes has been making violent love to Evanthe in the meanwhile and has been repulsed. By an ancient tragic device, Evanthe does not view the battle scene herself, but depends on the word brought to her by her companion, Cleone. Cleone mistakes Arsaces for another, who is killed, and informs her mistress that Arsaces is dead. Evanthe takes poison and the lovers meet only to say good-by. Arsaces kills himself and Gotarzes reigns to restore order in the kingdom.

The Prince of Parthia is not to be judged by modern standards. While it is perhaps not quite worthy of all the praise accorded it by Professor Moses Coit Tyler,[1] it certainly does not deserve the strictures which have been meted out to it by historians of the theatre who probably have not read it at all.

---

[1] Tyler, M. C. *History of American Literature during the Colonial Period*, N. Y. 1878, II, pp. 244-51.

It is a noteworthy fact that while the play was printed in 1765, after Godfrey's death, with his other poems, and that no second edition was called for, it was reprinted three times during the years 1917-18.

The tragedy is based upon real human emotion. The passions of love, jealousy, hatred, and revenge, the sentiments of loyalty, pity, and terror, are fundamental and the main motive of the play, shaped from these elements, the love of Arsaces and Evanthe, is naturally interwrought with the motive of self-preservation through the danger to the lives of both. These two motives, love and self-preservation, are the two motives of widest appeal to an audience, and Godfrey, with the instinct of a dramatist, selected them for his play. The counter motives of the King's lust for Evanthe, the jealousy of the Queen, Vardanes's love and jealousy, form a sufficiently strong combination to overwhelm the main motives of the drama, and thus, while the actual death of Evanthe is an accident, the failure of the love of hero and heroine is practically inevitable. Thus the play is conceived along true tragic lines. The characters of Arsaces, Artabanus, Vardanes, Thermusa, Evanthe, and Bethas, her captive father, are well drawn. The language is dignified, the blank verse is flexible and at times rises to distinction. A few lines may be quoted from Act I, Sc. 5:

"*Bethas:* True, I am fall'n, but glorious was my fall,
The day was brav'ly fought, we did our best,
But victory's of heav'n. Look o'er yon field,
See if thou findest one Arabian back
Disfigur'd with dishonourable wounds.
No, here, deep on their bosoms, are engrav'd
The marks of honour! 'twas thro' here their souls
Flew to their blissful seats. Oh! why did I
Survive the fatal day? To be this slave,
To be the gaze and sport of vulgar crouds,
Thus, like a shackl'd tyger, stalk my round,
And grimly low'r upon the shouting herd."

and from Act II, Sc. 2:

DRAMA AND THEATRE IN THE COLONIES

"*Lysias:* My Lord, forget her, tear her from your breast.
  Who, like the Phoenix, gazes on the sun,
  And strives to soar up to the glorious blaze,
  Should never leave Ambition's brightest object,
  To turn, and view the beauties of a flow'r."

Provost Smith secured Godfrey a commission as ensign in the Pennsylvania militia in May, 1758, and he joined the expedition against Fort Duquesne, receiving a commission as lieutenant while attached to the garrison at Fort Henry. In the spring of 1759 he left for Wilmington, North Carolina, having been offered a position as factor there. He had evidently been at work on his tragedy for some time, for in a letter to a friend, probably the Provost, dated November 17, 1759, he says:

> By the last vessel from this place, I sent you the copy of a Tragedy I finished here, and desired your interest in bringing it on the stage; I have not yet heard of the vessel's arrival, and believe if she is safe, it will be too late for the Company now in Philadelphia.[1]

It was too late: Douglass closed his season on December 28, 1759. Godfrey remained in Wilmington about three years and returned for a brief time to Philadelphia. No opening for him presenting itself, however, he returned to North Carolina in the early summer of 1763. Here on August 3, 1763, he died, of a violent fever brought on by becoming overheated while riding. He did not live, therefore, to see his tragedy either in print or on the stage.

The Prince of Parthia is to be considered not only on its absolute merits, but also in comparison with what was being done or rather what was not being done, in England at that time. It was a bright time in the history of the English theatre, the age of Garrick and Peg Woffington, with the older tradition still lingering in the person of Quin, but in the drama there was a dead calm. Sentimental comedy was the prevailing mode and the new era was not to be ushered in till Goldsmith's *Goodnatured Man* was put on at Covent Garden in 1768, almost

[1] Introduction, p. 5, to Evans's ed. of Godfrey's Poems, 1765.

23

a year after Godfrey's play saw the light at the Southwark Theatre. For models Godfrey turned to an earlier period, and it is of interest to note the English dramas which influenced him. His plot was practically original; from sources in Parthian history he took merely proper names, such as Artabanus, Vardanes, Vonones, Gotarzes, Thermusa, and Arsaces, which was a generic term for the ruler of Parthia, and also the general fact of the rivalry of the sons of the king for their father's throne.[1]

It is idle to speculate upon the possibility of Godfrey's witnessing the plays of Murray and Kean in 1749, for a boy of thirteen would hardly have attended the theatre. But even if he did, the plays of that company would not have greatly affected his work. We do not know what their repertoire in Philadelphia may have been, but of the plays mentioned in New York, *Richard III* and *The Distressed Mother*, of Ambrose Philips, are the only two that could have prompted any of the lines in *The Prince of Parthia*, and both of these belonged to the later repertoire of Hallam's Company in 1754. Here we are on firmer ground. Godfrey must surely have seen this company, whose repertoire has already been given. The record of the plays given in Philadelphia is probably not complete, but among them is Rowe's *Tamerlane*. The mention by Tamerlane of "My Parthian horse" among his forces, the opening scene in which a conquering hero is awaited, and the "captive maid" who is the daughter of a rival king, remind one of the opening of *The Prince of Parthia*. The other tragedies that were surely played in Philadelphia, Moore's *Gamester* and Rowe's *Fair Penitent*, could have had no influence, but in the absence of certain information we may assume that any of the plays in the repertoire of the company may have been given. Ambrose Philips's *Distressed Mother*, which is an adaptation of Racine's *Andromaque*, contains in the speech of Orestes after the murder of Pyrrhus, Act V, Sc. 1, lines which

[1] See Henderson, Archibald. Introduction to his edition of *The Prince of Parthia*, pp. 57-60.

are strikingly like one of the speeches of the Queen in *The Prince of Parthia.*

"*Orestes:* I shiver! Oh I freeze! So Light returns;
    'Tis the grey dawn—See Pylades! behold!—
    I am encompassed with a sea of blood!—
    The crimson billows! Oh!—my brain's on fire.

    Pyrrhus, stand off!—What wouldst thou?—
        How he glares!
    What envious hand has clos'd thy wounds? Have at thee!

    I blaze again! See there—Look where they come
    A shoal of furies."

Compare with Act IV, Sc. 5 of *The Prince of Parthia.*

"*Queen:* Oh all my brain's on fire—I rave! I rave!—
    Ha! it comes again—see, it glides along—
    See, see, what streams of blood flow from its wounds!
    A crimson torrent!

    I'm all on fire—now freezing bolts of ice
    Dart thro' my breast—oh! burst ye cords of life—
    Ha! who are ye? Why do ye stare upon me?
    Oh! defend me from these bick'ring Furies!"

It was, however, to Shakespeare that Godfrey owed the most. The appearance of the ghost of the King in Act IV, Sc. 5, which is invisible to Arsaces but visible to the Queen, is at once referable to *Hamlet*, where the Ghost is visible only to the Prince. There are verbal similarities, too, in this scene to the scene in *Hamlet*, Act III, Sc. 4, where the Ghost appears to Hamlet.

In the same scene from *The Prince of Parthia*, there is a similarity to *Macbeth*, when Queen Thermusa cries, "Why dost thou shake thy horrid locks at me?" and to *Richard III*, Act V, Sc. 3, where the ghosts of the victims of Richard rise one after the other and bid him "despair and die!" The ghost of Artabanus likewise bids the Queen, "Think, think of Artabanus! and despair!"

The situation in Act V, Sc. 1, in which Vardanes offers to

save Arsaces if Evanthe will yield herself to him, reminds one of *Measure for Measure*.

The description by Gotarzes of Arsaces's rescue of Vardanes, (Act I, Sc. 1) is like that by Cassius, in which he tells of his rescue of Cæsar from the river Tiber in *Julius Cæsar* (Act I, Sc. 2). And the error of Evanthe in taking poison, with her lover's consequent suicide, cannot help suggesting *Romeo and Juliet*.

Of even more striking a nature is the similarity of the heroine's name, "Evanthe," to that of Beaumont's heroine "Evadne," in *The Maid's Tragedy* and the situation in which a king loves the maiden who is beloved by another, is alike in the two plays. The despair which seizes Arsaces when he hears of the King's passion, is like that of Amintor when he becomes aware of his wife's relations with the king. There are verbal likenesses, too, in the Queen's raving in Act IV, Sc. 5, of *The Prince of Parthia* to Nourmahal's mad speech in Dryden's *Aurungszebe*.

These similarities prove that Godfrey must have read widely in the dramatic literature of England, for while he could probably have seen *Richard III, Hamlet, Romeo and Juliet*, and possibly *Tamerlane* and *The Distressed Mother* on the stage in 1754, he could not have witnessed *The Maid's Tragedy*, or *Aurungszebe*. That plays were frequently read is proved by more than one reference in letters of the time.[1]

It was in a good school that Godfrey studied, and it is to his credit that he assimilated what he borrowed and did not slavishly copy plot, characters, or language. In fact, nearly all of his verbal echoes are compressed into one scene. It must be remembered, too, that Godfrey hastened the completion of the tragedy to send it to Philadelphia before the theatrical season of 1759 was over, and that some of the weaknesses of the last act might have been overcome. A more serious criticism of *The Prince of Parthia* has been its foreign quality, and it is true that the first American play would have been of more

---

[1] Singleton, E. *Social New York under the Georges*, p. 387.

DRAMA AND THEATRE IN THE COLONIES

interest to us had its scene been laid in Godfrey's native land. But this criticism forgets that the literary fashion in tragedy was to place it in a remote scene and time, and, indeed, in view of the existence of *Othello* and *Hamlet*, the criticism is beside the point. Moreover, there are interesting signs that Godfrey was becoming affected by democratic ideas. He makes Bethas say to Artabanus:

> "*Bethas:* Welcome my dungeon, but more welcome death.
> Trust not too much, vain Monarch, to your pow'r,
> Know fortune places all her choicest gifts
> On ticklish heights, they shake with ev'ry breeze,
> And oft some rude wind hurls them to the ground.
> Jove's thunder strikes the lofty palaces,
> While the low cottage, in humility,
> Securely stands, and sees the mighty ruin.
> What King can boast, tomorrow as today,
> Thus, happy will I reign? The rising sun
> May view him seated on a splendid throne,
> And, setting, see him shake the servile chain."

The last speech of Gotarzes also echoes this sentiment, while a reference to slavery shows Godfrey's innate sympathy with freedom.

The Masque of Alfred was not the only college dramatic exercise that has come down to us. At the public Commencement of the College of Philadelphia, May 23, 1761, there was delivered *An Exercise consisting of a Dialogue and Ode Sacred to the Memory of His late Gracious Majesty, George II.* The dialogue was by Provost William Smith, and the ode was by Francis Hopkinson. A similar exercise on the accession of George III was performed at the public Commencement of May 18, 1762, the epilogue being written by Jacob Duché, Hopkinson's classmate, and later Chaplain to Congress. On May 17, 1763, the exercise was on the occasion of the Peace, and was written by Nathaniel Evans, of the class of 1762, who was later to edit Godfrey's poems. This custom was continued as late as 1790. Nor was it confined to the College of Philadelphia. On September 29, 1762, at the Anniversary Com-

mencement held in Nassau Hall, in Princeton, there was performed "by the late candidates for a Bachelor's Degree" *The
Military Glory of Great Britain*, in which there were more than
two speakers, though it is not clear that they were on the stage
together. There is no indication of an author. Nor is there
any evidence of dramatic authorship at Yale or Harvard,
though there was theatrical interest at the latter as early as
1758.[1] Of the still earlier theatrical interest at William and
Mary College, we have already spoken. This activity in the
College of Philadelphia had its direct effect on the work of
Hopkinson and Godfrey. The general interest had its indirect
result in providing a newer generation, to look with favor on
the theatre and to nullify the effect of prohibiting legislation
and bigoted intolerance.

Although *The Prince of Parthia* was the only play of American origin that was actually performed on a native stage during
this period, before the Revolution, it was not the only product
of the dramatic impulse. In 1764 there was printed anonymously in Philadelphia *The Paxton Boys*, described on the title
page as "translated from the original French by a native of
Donegal." It is an argument in dramatic form concerning the
conduct of those inhabitants of the frontier who came to
Philadelphia to demand protection against the Indians. The
attitudes of the Presbyterian, the Quaker, and the Episcopalian are contrasted. The drama is satiric and it is hard to
tell the author's position. Despite its vigorous language, it
could hardly have been produced on the stage. The relations
between the Indians and the whites were treated from another
point of view by Major Robert Rogers in 1766. His drama,
Ponteach, or the Savages of America, published in London, is a
fairly readable tragedy, the first to be written upon a native
subject. Ponteach, the Indian chieftain, is the central figure,
and when the end of the play finds him with his children dead
and his schemes against the English brought to naught, he

---

[1] Matthews, Albert, "Early Plays at Harvard." *Nation*, XCVIII, 295. March
19, 1914.

rises to a real greatness in his last soliloquy. Curiously enough, Major Rogers himself became a character in a drama on the Pontiac theme, written in 1826, by General Alexander Macomb.

The next play to be printed, *The Disappointment*, was a comic opera, based upon a trick played by Thomas Forrest, afterward a colonel in the Revolutionary army, upon an old Dutchman in Philadelphia who was searching for buried treasure. Thomas Forrest is now generally regarded as the author of the play, which was published in 1767 under the *pseudonym* of Andrew Barton. It came near to performance and was advertised in the *Pennsylvania Chronicle*, of April 6th to be given on April 20, 1767, by the American Company. The issue of the *Pennsylvania Gazette* of April 16th, however, informs the reader that "The Disappointment (that was advertised for Monday), as it contains personal reflections, is unfit for the stage." Had it not been for those qualities it might have been the first American play, for it was four days later that *The Prince of Parthia* was acted. The "personal reflections" are certainly definite enough, and the play seems draggy in any case. It achieved the honor of a second edition, however, in 1796, with references to the President and Congress interpolated. One of the songs in the original edition is to be set to the tune of "Yankee Doodle," thus proving the falsity of the theory that this song was of British authorship in the Revolution.

Such a play as *The Sister* by Charlotte Lennox, which was performed in London at Covent Garden in 1769, seems to have remote connection with our subject, since Mrs. Lennox, while born here, is identified entirely with England in her dramatic and novelistic work. She was a friend of Oliver Goldsmith, who wrote an epilogue for the play. It was not a success, though the speeches read with a certain crispness and the social satire is not uninteresting. For another reason, *The Conquest of Canada*, which was written by an Englishman, George Cockings, derives its connection with our native drama merely by the fact that it was composed in Boston and played in

Philadelphia February 16, 1773, at the Southwark Theatre and repeated on one occasion. The scene, however, is foreign, the point of view entirely British, and the piece is essentially undramatic in structure. As printed, the lines are made up of that curious mixture of prose and verse which distinguishes many of the plays of the time.

It is in a real sense fortunate that none of these dramas disputes with *The Prince of Parthia* the honor of being the first American play. It is not only the relative superiority of Godfrey's play both as a piece of literature and an acting drama that makes it fitting that the honor of priority should belong to it. It was a product of the dramatic impulses of the time, deliberately written not only for the stage but also for the company that performed it, and it remains, therefore, in a special sense the representative play of its period.

That period was drawing to a close. At the end of the Philadelphia season in November, 1767, Douglass took his company to New York City, where a theatre had been built for him in John Street, near Broadway, which was opened on December 7, 1767, with Farquhar's *Beaux Stratagem*. The company was strengthened by the advent of John Henry, later to be the leading man of the American Company, but the season was not successful. The opposition to the theatre still continued, and many protests were published in the newspapers of the time against the support of such a degrading institution. Douglass made another venture in Philadelphia in October, 1768, and then returned to New York, where he continued to play until June, 1769. Notwithstanding the difficulties of his situation, he made a brave effort to produce worthy plays, among them *King John*, Lee's tragedy of *Alexander the Great*, and Steele's *Tender Husband*.

During the Philadelphia season, which opened November 8, 1769, it appeared for a time that the fortunes of the company were reviving. Their reputation seems to have been established, and the number of new plays included *The Tempest*,

Goldsmith's *The Good Natured Man,* and Shirley's *Edward the Black Prince.*

Then Douglass took his company to Annapolis and, after a period in which their movements are uncertain, returned to that city and built in 1771 a brick theatre with a capacity of six hundred. This city was much more hospitable to the theatre than the northern towns and the one critic whose words have come down to us, lavished praise upon Miss Hallam, the leading lady, for her performance of Imogen in *Cymbeline.*[1] After a brief revisit to Williamsburg, the company stopped at Annapolis on their way to Philadelphia, where they reopened the Southwark Theatre October 28, 1772, and played until March 31, 1773. It was a brilliant season if one can judge from the repertoire, which, as Seilhamer truly remarks, included "the best of the English dramatists from Shakespeare to Kelly and Cumberland." *Hamlet, Romeo and Juliet, Richard III, Cymbeline, Taming of the Shrew, Henry IV, Othello, The Tempest,* and *The Merchant of Venice,* were performed, a record surpassing the seasons of to-day.

On April 14, 1773, the American Company revisited New York, after an absence of four years. During this season Milton's *Comus* and Goldsmith's *She Stoops to Conquer* were produced for the first time. On August 5th the comedy was repeated and the season ended. After brief visits to Annapolis and Philadelphia, Douglass opened in Charleston, December 22, 1773, in the new theatre he had built, which seems to have been of a more ambitious character than any before erected. The repertoire was worthy of it, for seventy-seven plays, including operas, were given. Fourteen of Shakespeare's plays were performed, including the first production of *Julius Cæsar.* Plays of Dryden, Congreve, Otway, Addison, Farquhar, Cibber, and Goldsmith were on the list. There was apparently a native play, to judge by the title *Young America in London,* which, however, is known only by name. The season lasted until May 16, 1774. It must have been a pleasure to the players

[1] See *Maryland Gazette,* September 6, 1770, quoted in Seilhamer, I, pp. 278-9.

to contrast their reception in Charleston with that accorded in New York City. There the theatre was still tabooed by many of the better elements of society, especially by the feminine portion of it. In Charleston, often as many as two hundred and fifty ladies were found in the audience, and it was distinctly the smart thing to do to attend the theatre. Douglass was evidently planning to continue in this friendly atmosphere for a series of years, but the approach of the Revolution forbade the accomplishment of this program. According to the *South Carolina Gazette* of May 30, 1774,[1] Lewis Hallam was to sail for Europe to select additional players, and we know that he induced Thomas Wignell, his cousin, to come to this country. Douglass visited New York and Philadelphia, where Mrs. Douglass died, and he was evidently making elaborate plans for the strengthening of the company for the ensuing season. But the approach of war put a stop to amusements. On October 20, 1774, the Continental Congress passed the following resolution:

We will, in our several stations, encourage frugality, economy, and industry, and promote agriculture, arts, and the manufactures of this country, especially that of wool; and will discountenance and discourage every species of extravagance and dissipation, especially all horse-racing, and all kinds of gaming, cock-fighting, exhibitions of shews, plays, and other expensive diversions and entertainments.[2]

Congress had no real authority to enforce this mandate, as such power belonged to the states, but it was generally respected. Douglass and the rest of the American Company departed for the West Indies, February 2, 1775, and the first period in the history of the American drama and theatre was closed.

[1] Quoted, Seilhamer, I, 333.
[2] *Journals of the Continental Congress 1774-1789. Edited from the Original Records in the Library of Congress* by Worthington Chauncey Ford, Chief, Division of Manuscripts. I, 78. Washington, 1904.

CHAPTER II

The Drama of the Revolution

WHEN the native drama which had made its tentative beginnings in the work of Godfrey was banished from the stage, it gave evidence of its perennial vitality in the plays, verse and prose, which on one side expressed the patriotism of the writers and their resentment against the actions of Great Britain and the Tories, and, on the other, their hatred of independence and their loyalty to the King.

These dramatic satires were invariably published anonymously, for obvious reasons, but external and internal evidence have contributed in some cases to the establishment of their authorship. Since the Revolution began in New England, it was natural that the earliest of the satires should have their origin there. Mrs. Mercy Otis Warren, the author of at least two of them, was the sister of James Otis, the patriot statesman and writer. She was born in Barnstable, Massachusetts, September 25, 1728, and lived there until her marriage to James Warren, a young merchant of Plymouth, in 1754. She was an ardent sympathizer with her brother in his great part in the early history of the Revolution, and when the tragedy of his mental alienation came upon him in 1769, she alone had the power to soothe him. Her husband's share in the Revolution was less brilliant, but was consistent and useful. At the death of Joseph Warren, he became President of the Provincial Congress, and while the American Army was in Cambridge was Paymaster General. Mrs. Warren herself was in touch with events, corresponded with Samuel and John Adams, Jefferson, Dickinson, and others, and the letters that passed between her and Mrs. John Adams record a friendship between "Marcia" and "Portia" (as they called each other) and their respective husbands which forms a very attractive picture set against the dark background of war. While her husband and her friends were moulding the Revolution, she wished to do her share. In fact, we find her urged to the task by John Adams in a letter written to James Warren on December 22, 1773, in which he speaks of the destruction of the tea and hopes to see it "celebrated by a certain poetical pen which has no equal that I know of in this country."[1] This praise was probably inspired by her first satire, *The Adulateur*, which had been published in 1773. It is described on the title page as "A Tragedy, as it is now acted in Upper Servia." Mrs. Warren evidently placed her scene as far from actual surroundings as possible, trusting that her readers' ignorance of geography would be as great as her own, for in the very first line of the play Brutus asks Cassius—

"Is this the once fam'd mistress of the north?"

It may, of course, have been only the quick flinging aside of the disguise, for the events are those which had been filling the hearts of the people of Massachusetts with indignation.

The chief satire of the play is directed against Thomas Hutchinson, who had held at once the three offices of member of the Council, Chief Justice, and Lieutenant Governor, and who finally became Governor of the Colony. He is known as Rapatio. He was a native of Massachusetts, and for that reason his duplicity was more keenly resented by his fellow citizens. His character has been painted imperishably by Bancroft.[2] Untrue even to his employers, he pretended to deny the right of Great Britain to tax America, and handed about patriotic letters to be read, which he never sent. The immediate inspiration for the satire was the publication of letters from Hutchinson, the Governor, and Andrew Oliver, the Lieutenant Governor, to Thomas Whately and others, in England. These had come through the agency of a member

[1] *Works of John Adams*, IX, 335.
[2] *History of the United States of America*, III, 358.

of Parliament into the hands of Franklin in December, 1772, and by him had been transmitted to the speaker of the House of Assembly of Massachusetts, of which he was the agent. The letters, which urged the British Government to declare martial law in the colonies, to make the judges absolutely dependent upon the Crown, to suppress the charter of Rhode Island, and in many other ways to nullify the rights of the citizens, were published, with the natural result of fomenting hatred against the fellow countryman who had betrayed them. In the first scene, Brutus, Cassius, Junius and Portius, who represent James Otis, John Adams, Samuel Adams, and John Hancock, declare their intention to strike for liberty. Read superficially, it seems that the characters are so united in their sentiments that they are hardly sufficiently characterized, but read with a better understanding of the various functions of the leading patriots of that early period, one notices first, the peculiar quality of enthusiasm that was Otis's great contribution, and which his sister here represents. Samuel Adams, as Junius, speaks as an older man:

"*Junius:* When Brutus speaks, old age grows young.
Whatever right I've lost!—I've still a dagger,
And have a hand to wield it—'tis true it shakes—
With age it shakes: Yet in the cause of freedom,
It catches vigor. You shall find it strike
The tyrant from his Throne.[1]

Hutchinson is then represented as longing for the day when he shall, through the fall of his predecessor, Bernard, really be governor, in order that his revenge may be taken for the indignities he suffered during the Stamp Act agitation.

In Act II, the killing of a boy of eleven by an informer, Richardson, is described by Cassius. Then Governor Rapatio conspires with Bagshot, the chief of the Janizaries, who represents Captain Preston of His Majesty's Twenty-ninth Regiment of Infantry, to fire on the people and in consequence the Boston Massacre occurs. This is represented off the stage, but

[1] Act, I Sc. 1.

the author describes in vigorous language the killing of unarmed men and children by the troops. The language naturally is a bit bombastic, but such a speech as that of Junius rings with a real sincerity across the years.

> "*Junius:* Her sighs?—and hear them tamely? never—never—
> Who knows the secrets of my soul,
> Knows 'tis on fire, and bursting for revenge.
> What tho' I totter with a weight of years,
> And palsied age relaxes every nerve,
> Yet such foul deeds have rouz'd the genial current,
> That long had lag'd—this life by nature's laws,
> Like an old garment must have soon been drop'd:
> And never could I, had I liv'd to ages,
> Have dy'd so well as now—to die at ease,
> And drop into the grave, unheard, unknown,
> This is but common fate—
> He, who bleeds in freedom's cause, expires illustrious.
> He falls, but catches immortality.
> While greatful millions croud around,
> And with a generous tear bedew his urn."[1]

The scene in Faneuil Hall in which the town determined upon the withdrawal of the troops and the conference between Hutchinson and his Council are then given, but the most dramatic episode of all, that in which Samuel Adams told Hutchinson in no uncertain terms what he must do, is not used by the dramatist. Up to this point in the *Adulateur* there had been little real satire—it was mostly forcible and direct description, but with the introduction of the character of Meagre, under which name Foster Hutchinson, the Governor's brother appears, the satirical touch becomes evident. Meagre introduces himself thus:

> "*Meagre:*   Bravely spoke!
> And here's a soul, like thine, that never linger'd,
> When prompted by revenge—If thirst of power;
> A spirit haughty, sour implacable,
> That bears a deadly enmity to freedom,
> But mean and base; who never had a notion

[1] Act II, Sc. 3.

Of generous and manly; who would stab,
Stab in the dark, but what he'd get revenge;
If such a soul is suitable to thy purpose,
'Tis here."[1]

Rapatio does not seem to be altogether satisfied with the result of his efforts and there is almost a real note of tragedy in his last soliloquy in which he cries out,

"I dare not meet my naked heart alone."

The play ends with a speech of Brutus in which the author, through her brother, sounds a note of prophecy:

"*Brutus.* Yes, Marcus, poverty must be thy fate,
    If thou'rt thy country's friend—Think upon it
    When I'm gone, as soon perhaps I may be.
    Remember it—those men whose crimes now shock,
    May close their measures—Yes, the wish'd for period
    May soon arrive, when murders, blood and carnage,
    Shall crimson all these streets; when this poor country
    Shall loose her richest blood, forbid it heaven!
    And may these monsters find their glories fade,
    Crush'd in the ruins they themselves had made,
    While thou my country, shall again revive,
    Shake off misfortune, and thro' ages live,
    See thro' the waste a ray of virtue gleame,
    Dispell the shades and brighten all the scene,
    Wak'd into life, the blooming forest glows,
    And all the desert blossoms as the rose.
    From distant lands see virtuous millions fly
    To happier climates, and a milder sky.
    While on the mind successive pleasures pour,
    Till time expires, and ages are no more."[2]

The characters of the play became well known, especially in the circle which had made Mrs. Warren's home in Plymouth a center of political discussion. We find John Adams writing to her husband in April, 1774, a very appreciative criticism of her poem on the "sea-deities," and then checking his ardor by

[1] Act III, Sc. 4.
[2] Act V, Sc. 3.

remarking, "But I am almost in the strains of Hazlerod."[1]
Hazelrod was the name in which Peter Oliver had been made
to pay his servile homage to Rapatio in *The Adulateur*.

That the statesmen of the country depended upon Mrs.
Warren's judgment is shown in such a sentence as this from
another of John Adams's letters to James Warren, written in
June, 1774, before he left for Philadelphia to attend the session
of Congress:

> I must entreat the favor of your sentiments and Mrs. Warren's
> what is proper, practicable, expedient, wise, just, good, necessary to
> be done at Philadelphia.[2]

Between the appearance of Mrs. Warren's two satires many
great events had happened. In March, 1774, the British
Parliament had passed the Boston Port Bill, designed to
starve the colony of Massachusetts into submission, had
abrogated the charter of the colony, and in its efforts to prevent
the colonists from governing themselves, had made it certain
that Great Britain would never rule them again. General Gage
was sent over in April, 1774, with four regiments, to quell any
possible opposition. At once the other colonies flew to the
support, moral and physical, of Boston, and on September 5,
1774, the First Continental Congress met in Philadelphia and
the Union was an accomplished fact. This body forbade all
trade with Great Britain, and passed those resolutions of protest and appeal which Lord Chatham truly described as the
wisest state papers that the world had ever seen. They belong
to our literature. But the next Parliament, which had been
elected in 1774, was no wiser than its predecessor and, in fact,
it consisted of much the same men, was honeycombed with
corruption, and was unrepresentative of the people of England.
By a great majority its members rejected the advice of Burke,
of Chatham, of Fox, of Rockingham and Richmond, and determined to rule or ruin their fellow citizens in the colonies. The
colonists meantime were arming for the unavoidable conflict.

[1] *Works of John Adams*, IX, 336.
[2] *Works of John Adams*, IX, pp. 339-40.

THE DRAMA OF THE REVOLUTION

The Group was probably written in the first months of 1775. John Adams, writing in 1814, said that "the 'cawing cormorants' in the 16th page, and Novanglus and Massachusettensis, in the 20th page, prove that it was written during the flickering between those two scribblers; but as no allusion is found in it to the skirmishes of Concord or Lexington, it must have been written and printed before the 19th of April, 1775."[1] In fact, it may have been a passage in one of John Adams's letters to James Warren, March 15, 1775, which inspired her to write, for he says:

My most friendly regards to a certain lady. Tell her that God Almighty (I use a bold style) has intrusted her with powers for the good of the world, which in the course of his Providence he bestows upon very few of the human race: that instead of being a fault to use them, it would be criminal to neglect them.[2]

Massachusettensis was the Tory, Daniel Leonard, a graduate of Harvard in 1760, who published in the *Massachusetts Gazette and Post Boy* from December, 1774, until April, 1775, a series of letters, in which with great skill and eloquence he tried to defend the cause of the British Ministry. He appears in *The Group* as Beau Trumps. John Adams had replied to these letters in the *Boston Gazette*, over the signature "Novanglus," in vigorous language which was reprinted in England and translated into Dutch in 1782. Certainly, whether he directly inspired the writing of *The Group* or not, he contributed to its wide publication. On May 21, 1775, he wrote to James Warren from Philadelphia, where he was attending the Second Continental Congress:

One half The Group is printed here, from a Copy printed in Jamaica.[3] Pray send me a printed copy of the whole and it will be greedily reprinted here.

[1] *Works of John Adams*, X, pp. 99-100.

[2] *Ibid.*, IX, 356.

[3] Despite wide search by American collectors, no trace of the Jamaica edition has been found, but in addition to the original edition, printed in Boston, in 1775, editions appeared in Philadelphia and New York, abridged by the omission of two scenes of the second Act.

The Group is built around the abrogation of the charter of Massachusetts and the appointment by the King of a Council, the upper house of Massachusetts, through a royal mandamus instead of through election by the Assembly. This action was deeply resented by the people. Their charter was to them their most sacred possession, and the tradition of their resistance to its abrogation under Charles II and its triumphant recovery was a glorious spot in their annals. Everyone who accepted the appointment to the Council was by that fact an enemy of the people, and Mrs. Warren's satire needed no "key" when she pilloried the "group" which had sold their birthright for office.

In order to understand the satire of *The Group* it is necessary to visualize the situation in Massachusetts which the sharp logic of events was shaping, and to distinguish clearly the personalities of the actors and the reasons for their fidelity to the royal cause. Read without this interpretation the satire has little meaning, but read in the light of the intense feeling which separated the community into hostile classes and even broke up the ties of family, it becomes a vital document in the history of our national progress. The list of characters was printed, of course, without any interpretation, but is here given with what is believed to be the correct key.

Lord Chief Justice HALZEROD [Hazelrod]	[Peter Oliver]
Judge MEAGAE [Meagre]	[Foster Hutchinson]
Brigadier HATEALL	[Timothy Ruggles]
HUM HUMBUG, Esq.	[John Erving, Jr.]
Sir SPARROW SPENDALL	[William Pepperell]
HECTOR MUSHROOM	Col. (John) [*Murray*]
BEAU TRUMPS	[*Daniel Leonard*]
DICK, the Publican	[*Richard Lechmere*]
SIMPLE SAPLING, Esq.	[Nat(haniel) Ray Thomas]
Monsieur de FRANCOIS	[*James Boutineau*]
CRUSTY CROWBAR, Esq.	(*Josiah*) [*Edson.*]
DUPE,—Secretary of State,	[Thomas Flucker]
SCRIBLERIUS FRIBBLE,	[Harrison Gray]
COMMODORE BATTEAU	(Joshua) [*Loring*]

THE DRAMA OF THE REVOLUTION

Collateralis, a new-made Judge   (William) [*Brown*[e]]
[Sylla]   [General Gage] [1]

By the time *The Group* appeared, Governor Thomas Hutchinson had fled to England, but he still lives in the satire by the remarks of his former associates. The chief mantle of dislike fell upon his brother, Foster Hutchinson, who is represented as possessing a mean and timeserving disposition. He was a judge of the Supreme Court of the province, and a Mandamus Councillor until his flight to Halifax in 1776.

Certain characteristics all these gentlemen shared. They were believers in the royal prerogative, in the right of the King to take away the freedom of the people of Massachusetts. They were of a conservative tendency, usually had property, and most of them held office or wished to do so. All but Oliver and Loring were Mandamus Councillors. They were educated men and well bred, and nine were graduates of Harvard College. They represented the feudal system that was beginning to grow up in New England to a larger degree than is generally realized, and to which the Revolution put an end. They were by their very position natural leaders, and *The Group* voiced the resentment of the people against those who should have led rather than betrayed them.

But there were differences, also, which are represented in the degrees of dislike with which Mrs. Warren viewed them. Naturally those most hated were drawn best and become, from the dramatic point of view, most interesting. Some of the characters are but lightly touched. Joshua Loring, whose inhumanity as Commissioner for the Whig prisoners had not yet begun, does not even speak. Harrison Gray, whose daughter had married Mercy Warren's brother Samuel, is lightly flicked. For those who seem to have been rather genial

---

[1] The list is based upon a comparison of the three copies in the Boston Athenæum, in each of which there is a written key. The three differ among themselves, and also from the key given in Jared Sparks's copy, now in the Cornell Library. The best list is the one in the handwriting of John Adams, and this has been taken as a basis, with necessary corrections, based upon the actual historical facts and the internal evidence of the play.

gentlemen, living contentedly on their large estates and enjoy-
ing personal popularity, like Sir William Pepperell and Judge
William Browne, she shows no special rancor. Pepperell's
name, through his grandfather's valiant services at the fall of
Louisburg, was among the most respected in the commonwealth. He inherited great wealth from this source, and
changed his own name of Sparhawk to his maternal grandfather's in consequence. Hence the name of "Sir Sparrow
Spendall." His later career when, exiled in England and his
estates confiscated, he shared his British pension with his less
fortunate fellow loyalists, shows him to have been a man of
feeling. He had the melancholy distinction of becoming the
principal figure of another "group," that of the loyalists in
Benjamin West's painting, "The Reception of the American
Loyalists by Great Britain in 1783." Boutineau and Lechmere
were representative of that class of men, who at first resented
the encroachments of the ministry but later recanted when
separation seemed the logical result of continued action. They
had signed in 1760 the first memorial against the crown officers,
and this relapse from grace is described in *The Group* by the
words put into Boutineau's mouth:

"*Monsieur:* Could I give up the dread of retribution,
The awful reck'ning of some future day,
Like surly Hateall I might curse mankind,
And dare the threat'ned vengeance of the skies.
Or like yon apostate—[*Pointing to Hazelrod, retired to
a corner to read Massachusettensis.*]
Feel but slight remorse
To sell my country for a grasp of Gold,
But the impressions of my early youth,
Infix'd by precepts of my pious sire,
Are stings and scorpions in my goaded breast."[1]

Mrs. Warren had a personal grudge against him also. His
son-in-law John Robinson was found guilty in 1772 of a violent
assault on her brother, James Otis, and Boutineau acted as his
attorney.

[1] Act II, Sc. 1.

She reserved her finest rage for a select few of the characters. For the office-holding class, which Peter Oliver, Foster Hutchinson, and Thomas Flucker represented, she had the most contempt. To Timothy Ruggles, on account of his rough and violent nature, and his action when as delegate from Massachusetts to the first American Congress in 1765 he refused to sign the resolution of union, she gives a large share of attention as Brigadier Hateall. The title refers to his rank in the French and Indian War, and he was later one of those Tory generals who led the "Loyal Militia" against their countrymen. His sentiments are thus represented in the play:

"Hateall: Curse on their coward fears, and dastard souls,
            Their soft compunctions and relenting qualms,
            Compassion ne'er shall seize my stedfast breast
            Though blood and carnage spread thro' all the land;
            Till streaming purple tinge the verdant turf,
            Till ev'ry street shall float with human gore,
            I Nero like, the capital in flames,
            Could laugh to see her glotted sons expire,
            Tho' much too rough my soul to touch the lyre.

"Simple: I fear the brave, the injur'd multitude;
            Repeated wrongs arouse them to resent,
            And every patriot like old Brutus stands,
            The shining steal half drawn—its glitt'ring point
            Scarce hid beneath the scabbard's friendly cell
            Resolv'd to die, or see their country free.

"Hateall: Then let them die—*The dogs; we will keep down—*
            While N——'s my friend, and G—— approves the deed,
            Tho' hell and all its hell-hounds should unite,
            I'll not recede to save from swift perdition
            My wife, my country, family or friends.
            G——'s mandamus I more highly prize
            Than all the mandates of th' etherial king."[1]

Peter Oliver, though not a lawyer, had been made Chief Justice of Massachusetts in 1756. As he describes himself in the first Act of *The Group:*

[1] Act I, Sc. 1.

"Hazelrod: Resolv'd more rapidly to gain my point;
I mounted high in justice's sacred seat,
With flowing robes, and head equip'd without;
A heart unfeeling, and a stubborn soul,
As qualify'd as e'er a *Jefferies* was;
Save in the knotty rudiments of law,
The smallest requisite for modern times,
When wisdom, law and justice, are supply'd
By swords, dragoons, and ministerial nods,
Sanctions most sacred in the pander's creed,
I sold my country for a splendid bribe."[1]

In the first Act the characters reveal themselves. In the second, they gather in a scene whose stage directions are of interest:

The scene changes to a large dining room. The table furnished with bowls, bottles, glasses, and cards. The group appear sitting around in a restless attitude. In one corner of the room is discovered a small cabinet of books, for the use of the studious and contemplative; containing Hobb[e]'s Leviathan, Sipthrop's Sermons, Hutchinson's History, Fable of the Bees, Philalethes on Philanthrop, with an appendix by Massachusettensis, Hoyle on Whist, Lives of the Stewarts, Statutes of Henry the eighth; and William the Conqueror, Wedderburn's speeches, and Acts of Parliament, for 1774.

In this Act the situation is further developed, the results of Governor Hutchinson's actions are outlined by Leonard, who speaks of the uselessness of patriotism:

"But 'twas a poor unprofitable path
Nought to be gain'd, save solid peace of mind."

In the third scene the most dramatic quality of the play develops with the appearance of General Gage. He is drawn in quite a favorable light compared with the "Group," and the keenness of Mrs. Warren's pen shows in the discussion about the quartering of troops upon the inhabitants. Dupe asks who will harbor them and Meagre replies:

[1] Act I, Sc. 1.

"None but the very dregs of all mankind,
  The Stains of nature,—the blots of human race,
  Yet that's no matter, still they are our friends,
  'Twill help our projects if we give them aid."

'*Simple Sapling:* Though my paternal Acres are eat up,
  My patrimony spent, I've yet an house
  My lenient creditors let me improve,
  Send up the Troops, 'twill serve them well for Barracks.
  I somehow think, 'twould bear a noble sound,
  To have my mansion guarded by the King.

"*Sylla:* Hast thou no sons or blooming daughters there,
  To call up all the feelings of a Father,
  Least their young minds contaminate by vice,
  Caught from such inmates, dangerous and vile,
  Devoid of virtue, rectitude, or honour,
  Save what accords with military fame?
  Hast thou no wife who asks thy tender care,
  To guard her from Belona's hardy sons?
  Who when not toiling in the hostile field,
  Are faithful votaries to the Cyprian Queen.
  Or is her soul of such materials made,
  Indelicate, and thoughtless of her fame:
  So void of either sentiment or sense,
  As makes her a companion fit for thee!"[1]

The moment nearest **to** real drama is occasioned by the
struggle in Gage's breast between his realization of the justice
of the colonial cause and his duty as a soldier, culminating in
the words:

"*Sylla:* And shall I rashly draw my guilty sword,
  And dip its hungry hilt in the rich blood
  Of the best subjects that a Brunswick boasts,
  And for no cause, but that they nobly scorn
  To wear the fetters of his venal slaves!
  But swift time rolls, and on his rapid wheel
  Bears the winged hours, and the circling years.
  The cloud cap'd morn, the dark short wintry day,
  And the keen blasts of rough[e]ned Boreas' breath,

[1] Act II, Sc. 3.

45

Will soon evanish, and approaching spring
Opes with the fate of empires on her wing."[1]

The rest of the play is anticlimax, but we close it with a sense of the strong feeling which it represents, the outcry of democracy against oligarchy, of liberty against prerogative, of the descendant of the Puritans against the upholders of kingcraft and oppression. From the dramatic point of view, both Mrs. Warren's satires are conversations rather than plays. There is no evidence that they were performed, although on the title page of *The Group* we read:

As lately acted, and to be reacted to the wonder of all superior intelligences, nigh headquarters at Amboyne.

Mrs. Warren also wrote, some years after, two carefully constructed tragedies in verse, *The Sack of Rome* and *The Ladies of Castile*, which were published in 1790. She sent the former to John Adams while he was in London in 1787, asking him to find a producer for it, but there was no opportunity. Indeed, these tragedies could hardly have been played.

Two more of these early satires have been attributed to Mrs. Warren, due probably to that tendency in literary history to credit any anonymous work to an author already known to have composed a work of a like nature. One of these, *The Blockheads, or the Affrighted Officers* is a prose farce, published in 1776, vigorous but coarse in language, and consisting mainly of conversation between British officers and Tory refugees, lamenting their starvation in Boston. It was inspired by General Burgoyne's farce, *The Blockade*, which was performed in Boston in the winter of 1775-6 and was evidently a farce, ridiculing the patriot army then blockading the city. This was not printed. The coarseness of *The Blockheads*, especially the scene between Simple and his wife, indicates that the play is not by Mrs. Warren, for that element is not found in her known works. That the satire was prompted, however, by her work is certain, for some of the names used by her reappear.

[1] Act II, Sc. 3.

They represent different living persons, however, Captain Bashaw becoming Admiral Graves; Meagre, Harrison Gray; Simple, probably Josiah Edson; and Dupe, "who you please."[1]

The play centers about the abortive attempt on the part of General Howe to take the fortifications on Dorchester Heights, which Washington had seized. Contrary winds drove back the attacking party under Lord Percy and, the city becoming thereby untenable, the British Army left Boston, taking with them the Tory refugees. The confusion in the city is vividly described by one of the soldiers:

Sol. Nothing can be more diverting, than to see the town in its present situation—all is *uproar* and *confusion—carts, trucks, wheelbarrows, hand barrows, coaches, chaise,* are driving as if the very devil was after them. Our *generals* look as wild as stags, when pursu'd by the hounds; they are startled at every noise; they think the *rebels* are just upon them.—Orders are given for *blocking* up the streets, that the rebels may break their shins, if they pursue us—we have also a parcel of *stuff'd images,* looking like devils behind the *pope,* to be fix'd up as *senteries;* a fit emblem of ourselves—*Burgoyne* could not have contriv'd a *prettier satyr*—our *ambuseirs* are fill'd with *wooden guns;* d—m such *wooden headed* commanders—to crown the whole, they should have had an effigy with a *barber's block-head,* as *engineer.*—Oh Briton! your disgrace makes my very blood dance the hornpipe.—The poor *yankee refugees,* run backwards and forwards,

---

[1] The characters as given by the author, together with the "key" written in the copy in the Clothier Collection of the University of Pennsylvania are as follows:

DRAMATIS PERSONAE

Captain Bashaw	A——l	[Graves]	
Puff	G——l	[Howe]	
L——d Dapper	L——d P——y		
Shallow,	G——t	[Grant]	Officers
Dupe,	Who you please		
Meagre,	G——y	[Gray]	Refugees
Surly	R——s	[Ruggles]	and
Brigadier Paunch,	B——e	[Bratels]	Friends
Bonny,	M——y	[Murry]	to the
Simple	E——n	[Eaton]	gov't.
Jemima,	Wife to Simple		
Tabitha	Her Daughter		
Dorsa	Her Maid		

like a parcel of cats let out of a bag—I would give half my pay, that some droll blade was here to describe the ludicrous scenery.[1]

The most ambitious, as it is certainly one of the most interesting, of the patriot dramas, is *The Fall of British Tyranny, or American Liberty Triumphant. The First Campaign. A Tragi-Comedy of Five Acts as lately planned at the Royal Theatrum Pandemonium, at St. James's. The Principal Place of Action in America.* It has been attributed to John or Joseph Leacock,[2] of Philadelphia, where it was published in 1776, but comparatively little is known of him, and thus the personal interest which irradiates the lines of *The Group* is lacking. It is atoned for, however, by the scope of the drama, which aspires to the dignity of a chronicle play.

It shows in its beginning that the author realized, as Bancroft and Trevelyan have since proved, that the Revolution began in the contests in the English Parliament for place and profit. The Earl of Bute, who appears under the title of Lord Paramount, is represented as plotting the return of the Stuart dynasty, and Lord North, rather appropriately named Catspaw, aids Governor Hutchinson (Judas) in misleading the Cabinet as to the strength and purpose of the Americans. Contrasted with these, in Act II, Pitt and Camden, Burke and Wilkes represent the friends of the colonies, with a good deal of plain speaking. The scene then changes to Boston, where General Gage (Lord Boston) arrives and there is a vigorous argument between a Whig and a Tory. Leacock's ability in dramatic writing is shown in the next scene, in which the battles of Lexington and Concord are vividly described.

Enter a messenger in haste.

I bring your Excellency unwelcome tidings—
Lord *Boston:* For heaven's sake! from what quarter?
Messenger: From Lexington's plains.

[1] Act III, Sc. 3.

[2] John F. Watson, in his *Annals of Philadelphia and Pennsylvania,* I, 104, ed. 1850, quotes a statement from "J. H. J. of Cheriot, Ohio," who had been a resident of Philadelphia, that "Joseph Lacock, Coroner, wrote a play with good humor, called British Tyranny."

Lord *Boston:* 'Tis impossible!

Messenger: Too true, Sir.

Lord *Boston:* Say—what is it? Speak what you know.

Messenger: Colonel Smith is defeated, and fast retreating.

Lord *Boston:* Good God!—What does he say? Mercy on me!

Messenger: They're flying before the enemy.

Lord *Boston:* Britons turn their backs before the Rebels!—The Rebels put Britons to flight?—Said you not so?

Messenger: They are routed, Sir;—they are flying this instant;—the Provincials are numerous, and hourly gaining strength;—they have nearly surrounded our troops. A reinforcement, Sir—a timely succour may save the shatter'd remnant. Speedily! speedily, Sir! or they're irretrieveably lost!

Lord *Boston:* Good God! What does he say? Can it be possible?

Messenger: Lose no time, Sir.

Lord *Boston:* What can I do?—O dear!

Officer: Draw off a detachment—form a brigade; prepare part of the train; send for Lord Percy; let the drums beat to arms.

Lord *Boston:* Aye do, Captain; you know how better than I. [*Exit Officer*] Did the Rebels dare to fire on the king's troops? Had they the courage? Guards, keep round me.[1]

After a pastoral interlude, in which two shepherds tell of Lexington, Clarissa, the wife of Warren, has news of his death broken to her. Then we are taken to Virginia, where Lord Dunmore kidnaps the negroes, whence we are brought back to Boston to a British Council of War, preparatory to a visit to Montreal to the prison of Ethan Allen. The last scene is laid at the camp at Cambridge, and introduces Washington, Charles Lee, and Putnam at a conference. It seems to be the first appearance of Washington in the drama.

The conversations are vigorous, the characters are fairly well drawn, and Leacock understood the value of contrast in art, for the actors do not talk alike by any means. This is shown especially in the Council of War in scene seven of Act IV, in which General Gage, Admiral Graves, General Howe, General Clinton, and others upbraid each other for the failure of the royal cause, the admiral's language being especially picturesque.

[1] Act III, Sc. 4.

The negro character in scene four of the same act talks with some resemblance to reality.

There is quite a contrast between the length and variety, so far as scene is concerned, of *The Fall of British Tyranny* and the unity of the two plays in which Hugh Henry Brackenridge (1748-1816) seized two moments of the early struggle and expressed them in dramatic form. Brackenridge, like Mrs. Warren, had a career in literature outside of the drama and his significance in the history of the novel is a real one. He was a classmate of Madison and Freneau at the College of New Jersey and shared with the latter the authorship of a college dialogue, *The Rising Glory of America*, in 1771. He wrote his two plays for production in the Maryland Academy in which he was a master, so that the first[1] and probably the second had at least amateur performance. In *The Battle of Bunkers Hill*, published in 1776 in Philadelphia, the sentiment of love of country is well and not theatrically displayed. The drama is carried on through conversation, first between the American leaders, Warren, Putnam, and Gardiner. There is no satire here; it is the expression of one great quality, that of courage. As Gardiner says:

> "The free born spirit of immortal sire[s]
> Is stranger to ignoble deeds, and shuns
> The name of cowardice. But well thy mind,
> Sage, and matur'd by long experience, weighs
> The perilous attempt, to storm the town,
> And rescue thence, the suff'ring citizens.
> For but one pass to that peninsula,
> On which the city stands, on all sides barr'd,
> And here what numbers can supply the rage,
> Of the all devouring, deep mouth'd cannon, plac'd,
> On many a strong redoubt; While on each side,
> The ships of war, moor'd, in the winding bay,
> Can sweep ten thousand from the level beach,
> And render all access impregnable."[2]

[1] Memoir of Brackenridge. 1855 Ed. of *Modern Chivalry*, p. 154.
[2] Act I, Sc. 1.

Even when we turn to the British side, and witness the deliberations of Gage, Howe, Burgoyne, Clinton, and Lord Pigot, the tone is serious. The British are represented as not very anxious to fight. General Howe speaks of the friendships which his brother, Lord Howe, had made during the French and Indian War with the very colonists he is now sent to attack. There is no doubt that Brackenridge represented Howe's sentiments correctly, and he gained in dramatic effectiveness by having the very enemy contribute to establish the motive of the drama, the courage and ability of the American troops.

The verse of Brackenridge is flexible and dignified, and the speeches of Warren and Gardiner as they lead their men to the attack reveal the spirit of the "times that try men's souls."

"Gardiner, leading up his Men to the Engagement:

> "Fear not, brave soldiers, tho' their infantry,
> In deep array, so far out-numbers us.
> The justness of our cause, will brace each arm,
> And steel the soul, with fortitude; while they,
> Whose guilt, hangs trembling, on their consciences,
> Must fail in battle, and receive that death,
> Which, in high vengeance, we prepare for them,
> Let then each spirit, to the height, wound up,
> Shew noble vigour, and full force this day.
> For on the merit, of our swords, is plac'd,
> The virgin honour, and true character,
> Of this whole Continent: and one short hour,
> May give complexion, to the whole event,
> Fixing the judgment whether as base slaves,
> We serve these masters, or more nobly live,
> Free as the breeze, that on the hill-top, plays
> With these sweet fields, and tenements, our own.
> Oh fellow soldiers, let this battle speak,
> Dire disappointment, to the insulting foe,
> Who claim, our fair possessions, and set down,
> These cultur'd-farms, and bowry-hills, and plains,
> As the rich prize of certain victory."[1]

[1] Act V, Sc. 2.

The Death of General Montgomery was written in 1777, and
by that time Brackenridge had become a chaplain in the Army.
He showed his confidence, at a dark time in our history, by
stating in the introduction that he believed the publication of
the drama might be more helpful to the colonial cause than
"hereafter when the foe is entirely repulsed and the danger
over." The play opens with the explanation of the plan of
operation by General Montgomery, to Arnold, in which there
is quite an exact description of the circumstances of that brave
but ill-starred attack, on a snowy night, upon the fortress of
Quebec. There runs through several of the speeches the note
of impending disaster, well expressed in the words of Captain
Cheeseman, of the New York militia:

> "The hour is dreary, and all Nature dark;
> But yet, Macpherson, there is something more;
> In melancholy, and a mind o'ercast:
> In this presentiment of some sad change,
> This throb of heart, that bodes fatality,
> And is not cowardice, but God himself,
> That in the knowledge, of the future ill,
> Doth touch the mind, with apprehension strange,
> And feeling sensible of its approach."[1]

Montgomery's death is only indicated in the speech of
Aaron Burr, an eloquent tribute to the dead leader and his
companions. Brackenridge departs from his cherished unities
to bring in the ghost of General Wolfe, who reproaches the
King and Parliament in good round fashion. The play con-
tinues with Arnold's attack, in which it is interesting to note
that the Pennsylvania militia carried a flag representing

> "With thirteen streaks of ivory and blue
> The extended provinces."

The play ends with a note of bitterness toward General
Carleton, the British commander. This is the more remarkable since Carleton was a noteworthy exception to the general

[1] Act II, Sc. 1.

rule and seems to have treated the American prisoners with real consideration.

Brackenridge's dramas are better than the other Revolutionary plays from the point of structure and expression, even if they have not the vigor of action of Leacock's one effort or the sharp satire of Mrs. Warren's plays. It is interesting that he chose defeats for his celebration, but they were defeats that were greater than victories, for they revealed the triumph of character.

How potent the influence of Montgomery was may be estimated from a reading of *A Dialogue between the Ghost of General Montgomery, Just arrived from the Elysian Fields; and an American Delegate in a Wood near Philadelphia*, published in Philadelphia in 1776 and attributed to Thomas Paine. The author of *Common Sense* and *The Crisis* makes the hero of the Canadian campaign a vehicle for arguments in favor of complete independence of Great Britain.

The usual arguments of the moderate Whigs are disposed of, one by one, by the direct and vigorous statements of Montgomery, whose supernatural powers fathomed even the peculiar ramifications of English politics, to prove to the delegate that the opposition to the King was due rather to desire for political advantage than to love of the colonies. The dialogue is brief but telling and, as was usually the case with Paine, he uses direct argument rather than satire.

Last of the surviving plays with a clearly patriotic note is a satire published in Boston in 1779, attributed to Mrs. Warren, although the author speaks of himself as "he." *The Motley Assembly, a Farce. Published for the Entertainment of the Curious* ridicules that element in Boston which believed that hearty support of the Revolution was incompatible with secure social standing. The principal characters are Esq. Runt, "a short fat old fellow: fond of gallanting the Ladies;" Turncoat, one of the managers of the Assembly; Mrs. Flourish, Mrs. Taxall, Mrs. Bubble, Miss Flourish, Miss Taxall, women of supposed fashion who preferred the scarlet coat to the blue, and, contrasted with them, Captain Aid, of the American Army and Captain Careless of the Navy.[1] There is little plot, but the conversation is well done, especially in the scene in the house of Mrs. Flourish, when Captain Aid proposes a toast to General Washington and Mrs. Flourish says:

"I believe Mr. Washington, or General Washington, if you please, is a very honest, good kind of a man, and has taken infinite pains to keep your army together, and I wish he may find his account in it. But doubtless there are his equals—so say no more," and Captain Aid replies:

"If you meant that as a compliment, madam, it is really so cold a one, that it has made me shiver."

The satire is keen, and reflects the indignation of one who loved his country and had no apologies to make for that affection, at that half-hearted allegiance which animated a certain section of society in Boston,

The play closes with the words:

> ——"see they crowd the place
> Stain to their country—To their Sires Disgrace;
> Hell in some hearts; but pleasure in each face;
> All—all are qualified to join this tribe,
> Who have an hundred dollars to subscribe."

One of the most striking characteristics of the Revolutionary satires is their intense partisanship. They were written by ardent patriots or ardent royalists. But there was one author who represented the more neutral attitude which at the beginning was probably that of a majority of the people of the colonies. Colonel Robert Munford, of Mecklenburg, Virginia, was the author of two plays, *The Candidates* and *The Patriots*, published together in 1798. *The Patriots* was also published in 1776 in Philadelphia.

The Candidates must have been written before the conflict,

---

[1] According to the manuscript key in the copy belonging to Dr. F. W. Atkinson, the "Flourishes," "Taxalls," "Bubbles" and "Turncoats" represent members of the DeClois, Sheafe, Swan, and Hubbard families, while Captain Aid symbolizes T. Cartwright and Captain Careless, Amiel.

for there is no reference to the war, and the expression, "I am very sorry our good late Gov'r Botetourt has left us" has the same implication, for Governor Botetourt died October 15, 1770. *The Candidates* is a satire on the methods of conducting elections for the Assembly, and is appropriately conducted mainly at a race course. It introduces in Ralpho probably the first negro character in the American drama.

The Patriots is a much more significant piece. In the first place, it has more plot than any other of the Revolutionary satires. But of even more importance is the attitude taken by the author. Colonel Munford was a soldier who took his part in the Revolution. Yet the tone of the play is decidedly pacifist. The American soldiers are represented as being braggarts or cowards. The Whig Committee is composed of men ignorant and intolerant, and suspicious in a mean way of those who differ with them. Trueman and Meanwell are clearly the characters with whom the author sympathizes. They are moderate in their views and they deprecate war. In the words of Trueman, "I detest the opprobrius epithet of Tory, as much as I do the inflammatory distinction of Whig." In consequence, they are the objects of suspicion, and Trueman's suit for Mira, daughter of Brazen, is opposed by her father.

Tackabout, a Tory masquerading as a Whig, attempts to play double by informing on Trueman and Meanwell, while at the same time telling the former, "You know I'm a Tory." Trueman replies, "Then you are the base villain I always found you to be." The Committee, overhearing these words, release Trueman and Meanwell, who incidentally do not commit themselves. All ends happily in due course, including a subplot of attempted seduction which bears little real relation to the rest of the play. The types of character are better drawn than was usual, and the play is much more than a series of dialogues. It probably represented the sentiments of thousands of the author's countrymen, who were uncertain just where their duty lay, but who, after the decision had been made, fought valiantly for their country. There is no definite proof that either of Colonel Munford's plays was acted, but a prologue to *The Candidates* in 1798 seems to indicate it.

It was only to be expected that the Tory view of the situation in the colonies should also be represented in the drama. Probably the earliest of these is an anonymous work, *A Dialogue Between A Southern Delegate and His Spouse on His Return from the Grand Continental Congress. A Fragment Inscribed to the Married Ladies of America, By their most sincere and affectionate Friend and Servant Mary V. V.* It was printed in 1774.[1]

This is a brief but pointed tirade by a wife against the Continental Congress, of which her husband is a member. He begs her to keep her temper.

> "Pray, for God's Sake, my Dear, be a little discreet,
>   As I hope to be sav'd, you'll alarm the whole street;
>   Don't delight so in scolding yourself out of breath;
>   To the neighbors 'tis sport, but to me it is Death."

She suggests that it would have been much wiser to send women.

> "Wou'd! instead of Delegates, they'd sent Delegates Wives;
>   Heavens! we couldn't have bungled it so for our Lives!
>   If you had even consulted the Boys of a School,
>   Believe me, Love, you cou'd not have play'd so the Fool:
>   Wou'd it bluster, and frighten, its own poor dear Wife,
>   As the Congress does *England!* quite out of her Life?"

The best defense he can make is the old one to mind her own business, which she steadfastly declines to do. She objects particularly to the non-importation act.

> "Your Non-Imports, and Exports, are full fraught with Ruin.
>   Of thousands, and thousands, the utter Undoing:"

The satire is an amusing one, and of especial interest is the attitude of fear lest the Congress may be an instrument of

---

[1] No place of publication is given, but the copy in the Clothier Collection at the University of Pennsylvania has stamped on the binding "(New York)." This copy, purchased from a London bookseller, has the name of "Captain Payne, Royal Irish Reg't." written on the title page.

tyranny even if the colonies are successful in avoiding ruin.
The wife concludes with the advice to

"Make your Peace:—Fear the King:—The Parliament fear."

It is to be noted that several authorities, who have evidently
not read the dialogue, have attributed it to Thomas Jefferson.

The next Tory satire is not nearly as well written, although
it has been ascribed to the well-known Tory, Jonathan
Sewall (1728-1796) of Massachusetts,[1] a Harvard graduate,
who was Attorney-General of the colony from 1767 until his
departure in 1775 for England. He was a great friend of John
Adams, and is supposed to have at first inclined to the patriot
cause. Nothing of this attitude, however, or of his eloquence
is exhibited in *The Americans Roused in a Cure for the Spleen,
or Amusement for a Winter's Evening. Being the Substance of a
Conversation on the Times over a Friendly Tankard and Pipe
between Sharp, a Country Parson, Bumper, a Country Justice,
Fillpot, an Innkeeper, Graveairs, a Deacon, Trim, a Barber,
Brim, a Quaker, Puff, a late Representative. Taken in short-
hand by Sir Roger de Coverly.*

It was published apparently in 1775 in New England and
reprinted by Rivington, in New York. Tory views are expressed
by Sharp, Bumper, and Trim, while Puff and Fillpot are made
to represent the colonial side with halting utterance and evident
ignorance. The conversation is not bad at times, as Trim's
statement that "one-half the world lives by the follies of the
other half" may witness. But it has been difficult for later
readers to echo Dunlap's high praise of the piece as drama.[2]

A Royalist farce, clever at times but extremely scurrilous,
was the anonymous *Battle of Brooklyn*, published by Rivington,
the well-known New York Tory. It is further described as
*A Farce in Two Acts, As it was performed on Long Island, On
Tuesday, the 27th Day of August, 1776. By the Representatives
of the Tyrants of America, Assembled at Philadelphia.* The con-

---

[1] Not to be confused with Jonathan Mitchell Sewall, a patriot, to whom the play
has been attributed incorrectly.

[2] *History of the American Theatre.* I, 91.

duct of the battle by the patriot army is made the subject of ridicule, and while no student of military history would care to defend the execution of the plans of the American defence on that ill-fated day, the characters of Washington, Putnam, Sullivan, and Stirling bear no resemblance to those sketched by the author of the satire. By the introduction of the scene between Lady Gates and Betty, her maid, the author introduces a vileness of slander against Washington, that is absent from any of the other dramas upon either side.

A play which appeared late in the war, being published, according to the London reprint in 1782, is *The Blockheads*; *or, Fortunate Contractor, An Opera in Two Acts as it was Performed at New York. The Music entirely new, Composed by several of the most eminent Masters in Europe.* This drama is concerned with the differences of opinion in the colonies at the close of the war, relative to a closer union with France or with England. The sympathies of the author were evidently with the English party, so that it may be classed among the Tory pamphlets. There is a curious mixture of symbolic characters like Americana (America Personified), Liberta (Liberty Personified), and Amita (Friendship Personified), with members of Congress, English and French physicians, American warriors, and old and young Whigs.

In the first scene Liberta and Amita bewail the discord and approaching war in the country. Then old Shaver chats about the wigs which he has for sale. There is evidently a play on the name "Whig," for old Shaver says of two of these articles:

This is a simple head of hair, not indebted to nature for a curl: the wearer was suspected of less courage than he possessed; he was provident in his principles and sought for an independence.

The next head had a good deal of good nature and wore it upon all occasions, but at last, influenced by the habit of the time, resolved on a change.

Old Shaver becomes a contractor, and in his own words, "thrived till I turned Parliament man; but the devil take the luck, I must either be turned out of doors, or give up my contract," which sentiment reflects the fate of many of his country-men whose commercial instincts rose superior to their patriot-ism. There is an interesting scene in Congress in which the President of that body expresses the opinion that France has fixed her eye on the provinces of Maryland and Virginia. Americana finally decides to cast her lot with England again. The drama represents the confusion of political ideas at the end of the Revolution, but it hardly reflects any widespread sentiment for England. In fact, the first edition, supposed to be printed in New York, has not appeared, and the drama may be simply a bit of Tory propaganda, with its origin in England.

The dramatic satires of the Revolution were naturally more frequent in the earlier stages of the war. The scene soon shifted from Boston, and the occupation of New York City and Philadelphia cut off the possibility of ready publication, for the patriot satires, at least. There were probably other Tory satires written which have not come down to us, since the theatrical activities of the British soldiers in Boston, New York, and Philadelphia reveal an interest in the stage that would naturally have demanded material for its expression. It was usually satisfied, however, with the English plays then being performed by professional companies. They are not con-nected with our subject except as they affected William Dunlap, and their interest has been largely personal, such as that inspired by the association of Major André with scene painting in New York and Philadelphia. The most striking incident occurred during a production of Burgoyne's *Blockade* on January 8, 1776, in Boston. The farce had hardly begun when a sergeant appeared and announced, "The Yankees are attack-ing our work on Bunker's Hill." At first it was thought that the lines belonged to the play, but the orders of General Howe, who was present, soon showed that the report was the result of the attack under Major Knowlton upon the British lines in Charlestown, and the performance was broken up.[1]

[1] Seilhamer. II, 18.

The American officers also relieved the camp tedium by producing plays. According to a letter from William Bradford, Jr. to his sister Rachel [1] from Valley Forge, May 14, 1778; "The Theatre is opened—Last Monday [May 11] Cato was performed before a very numerous & splendid audience. His Excellency & Lady, Lord Stirling, the Countess & Lady Kitty . . . were part of the Assembly. The scenery was in Taste—& the performance admirable—Col. George did his part to admiration. . . . If the Enemy does not retire from Philad[a] soon, our Theatrical amusements will continue—The fair Penitent with the Padlock will soon be acted. The 'recruiting officer' is also on foot." These festivities were part of the celebration of the new French alliance. In May, 1928, on the anniversary of this historic event, a performance of *Cato* was again given at Valley Forge. In view of these performances by the officers, it may be that the statement on the title page of *The Group* has more validity than has generally been supposed, and that the play was actually performed at the American camp.

Viewed from an absolute standard the artistic quality of these dramas of the Revolution may not be high, but it is noteworthy that the more closely they are studied in relation to their inner meaning, the greater their significance becomes. In them not figments of the fancy but real people live and move. Being drama they represent the feeling of the time in its most intense moods, and the hopes, fears, and agonies of that great period are mirrored in a glass that is most interesting when it reflects the nature of human beings who are emotionally under stress. The great strife that separated families, brought ruin to a few and liberty to all who believed in freedom, lives again in a peculiarly vigorous form in these few rare old volumes which preserve all that is left of the drama of the Revolution. Of their significance, therefore, as social history there can be no shadow of doubt.

[1] *Pennsylvania Magazine of History and Biography.* XL (1916) 342-343.

CHAPTER III

THE COMING OF COMEDY

THE prohibition by Congress of "shews and plays" was not sufficient to prevent altogether the production of drama. After the British left Philadelphia the Southwark Theatre was opened for a brief period in September and October, 1778, but Congress objecting, the performances were stopped. On January 1, 1782, however, a more determined effort was made by Messrs. Wall and Lindsay, the former a member of the old American Company, to open a theatre in Baltimore. This company succeeded in holding together until February, 1783, when Dennis Ryan reorganized it, and he even invaded New York in June, remaining till the evacuation by the British. That he returned to the Southern circuit, where, although he died in 1786, his company continued to serve the needs of Charleston and Baltimore for some months,[1] is of interest to us mainly as showing the gradual return to toleration of the theatre after peace was declared. Of this change of attitude the descendants of the old American Company soon took advantage. Under the management of Lewis Hallam and John Henry they had been playing in the West Indies. In January, 1784, Hallam petitioned without success for a repeal of the Act of 1778 by the Assembly of Pennsylvania. Yet he succeeded in reopening the Southwark Theatre and delivered there a *Monody to the Memory of the Chiefs who have fallen in the Cause of American Liberty*, thus linking the drama again to the progress of national events. There was probably a general agreement to let the law remain a dead letter, for we find Hallam cautiously offering drama under disguised forms, and then on August 11, 1785, reopening the John Street Theatre

[1] See Sonneck, *Early Opera in America*, pp. 60-3.

in New York City. John Henry brought several of the former players up from Jamaica and, joining forces with Hallam, re-established the old American Company. This company had practically a monopoly of the principal theatrical towns—New York, Philadelphia, Baltimore, and Annapolis—for several years, during which the attitude of the public became steadily more favorable. The law against the theatre in Pennsylvania, was repealed March 2, 1789, and in the Middle States, the criticism of the theatre as an institution passed from a searching scrutiny of its morals to a rather unsympathetic analysis of its quality.

The drama naturally felt the rising tide of interest in the stage. The return of peace was the occasion of the recitation of odes and dramatic spectacles, most of which have been lost. A typical utterance was John Parke's *Virginia, a Pastoral Drama on the Birth-Day of an Illustrious Personage and the Return of Peace, February 11, 1784.* Washington, who is named as "Daphnis," is accompanied by shepherds and nymphs, in whose company he appropriately remains mute. Whether this "pastoral drama" was performed is uncertain, but if so, it was by amateurs, as was also the case with *The Mercenary Match*, a domestic tragedy in blank verse by Barnabas Bidwell, with the scene in Boston. This was performed by Yale students and published in 1784, the year before that in which its author graduated. Its main interest lies in the continuance of interest in the college drama, although the leading character, Mrs. Jensen, is rather well portrayed as a restless woman whose dissatisfaction leads finally to murder of her husband, death for herself, and the gallows for her accomplice.

Better written than either of these dramas, though it was not performed on the stage, was *The Patriot Chief* by Peter Markoe, who was born in Santa Cruz in 1752 and lived from 1783 to his death in 1792 in Philadelphia. *The Patriot Chief* is laid in "Sardis, the capital of Lydia," and is concerned with the rebellion against the rule of the King, Dorus. He is saved by the young noble, Araspes, who believes he is preventing the schemes of his reputed father, Otanes, while in reality he is preserving the life of his own father, the King. The author tells us that his motive in writing was to call attention to the dangers of an aristocracy, which, in his judgment, forms "the most odious and oppressive of all modes of government." This drama illustrates the early use of that form in the warm disputes that arose between those who favored a strong centralized federal government and those who believed in states' rights and democracy. But *The Patriot Chief* is worth reading for its own sake. It follows the orthodox lines of classical tragedy, but there is a vigor at times that borders on the dramatic and certainly it could have been placed on the stage as well as many of its contemporaries. Markoe was the author of *The Reconciliation*[1] (1790), one of the few operas written in this country in the eighteenth century, which seems to have been accepted by the American Company but was not produced.

It is fortunate, in view of the influences that shaped the beginning of the novel in 1789, that it was not to models of a similar character that the author of the first American comedy turned. It will be remembered that already among the satires of the Revolution the note of contrast between the affectation of British manners and the sturdier reliance upon native worth had been treated in such a drama as *The Motley Assembly*. In 1785 this theme was repeated in *Sans Souci, alias Free and Easy, or an Evening's Peep Into a Polite Circle*. This has been attributed to Mercy Warren, but there is no direct evidence of her authorship. One of the characters is "Mrs. W——n," who is not satirized and whose speech in the first scene may express her opinions as given to the "Republican Heroine." The satire holds up to ridicule foreign affectations and card playing for money in public, especially at a form of entertainment called "Sans Souci," which takes place in "the Metropolis of Massachusetts." The dialogue is clever at times and is inter-

---

[1] It was founded on Gessner's *Erastus*. Markoe made two acts out of one and added songs, producing a didactic domestic opera libretto "modeled to suit the American ear."

esting as revealing the Puritan expression of the national point of view. It is of more than usual significance that our first professional comedy, *The Contrast*, should have continued to express that New England point of view, modified by a liberal attitude toward the theatre and with so little provincialism in its tone that it created in its chief comic character a caricature of the New England Yankee that has been a prototype for over a century.

Royall Tyler, the author of *The Contrast*, was born in Boston, July 18, 1757. His father, a merchant, had been a member of the King's Council until his death in 1771, and Royall Tyler graduated from Harvard College in July, 1776, having the degree of Bachelor of Arts conferred on him by Yale College in the same year. He became one of the group of young men, of whom John Trumbull was perhaps the leader, who were interested in the arts. He·joined, too, the Independent Company of Boston, and in 1778 served as aid to General Sullivan, with the rank of Major, in the attack on Newport. On August 19, 1780, he was admitted to the bar, and practiced law at Falmouth (now Portland), Maine, and later at Quincy (then called Braintree), Massachusetts. Here he became engaged to be married to Abby, the daughter of John Adams. The marriage never took place, however, for the bride to be went abroad with her mother, and while there returned his letters and put an end to the romance. Tradition and indeed, written evidence in the possession of his descendants, indicate that it was because of the excessive "gaiety" of Tyler's nature, but certainly the refusal plunged him for months in a gloom which even interrupted his practice of law. He was consoled, however, by the friendship he contracted for little Mary Palmer, who afterwards became his wife, and by another opportunity for military service. Shays' Rebellion broke out, and he served again with the rank of Major as aid to General Lincoln, taking a prominent part in the pursuit of the fugitives in Vermont. This pursuit led him later to New York City, where he arrived March 12, 1787. He seized the opportunity to visit the theatre, becoming acquainted with Thomas Wignell, the leading comedian of the American Company, and it was at the John Street Theatre, on April 16, 1787, that *The Contrast*, the first native comedy to be produced by a professional company was performed. The cast was as follows:

Col. Manly	Mr. Henry
Dimple	Mr. Hallam
Van Rough	Mr. Morris
Jessamy	Mr. Harper
Jonathan	Mr. Wignell
Charlotte	Mrs. Morris
Maria	Mrs. Harper
Letitia	Mrs. Kenna
Jenny	Miss Tuke

Tyler gave the copyright to Wignell, and he published the play in Philadelphia in 1790 by subscription, the list being headed by George Washington, and including four Cabinet members.

The play was a success, being repeated in New York five times in 1787 and once in 1789. It was played in Baltimore in 1787 and 1788, in Philadelphia in 1790, in Boston in 1792 and 1795, in Charleston in 1793, and in Richmond in 1799. The prejudice against the theatre in Boston is indicated in this advertisement from the Boston *Independent Chronical* [sic] *and Universal Advertiser*, of October 18, 1792: "New Exhibition Room. Board Alley. To-morrow evening (the 19th Oct.) will be presented A Moral Lecture in five parts. . . . called the Contrast, delivered by Messrs. Harper, Morris, Mrs. Murry, Miss Smith, and Mrs. Morris." [1]

[1] Dates and supporting advertisements have been furnished through the courtesy of Miss Helen Tyler Brown. According to her introduction in the Wilbur edition of 1920, modern revivals of the complete play have taken place as follows:

By pupils of the American Academy of Dramatic Arts, New York, 1894.

By townsmen, in Brattleboro, Vermont, at the Brattleboro pageant, June 6, 7 and 8, 1912.

By the Plays and Players of Philadelphia, under the auspices of the Drama League in co-operation with the University of Pennsylvania, January 16 and 18, 1917.

By the Drama League of Boston, April 7, 1917. [Since then many times.]

To those who have had an opportunity to see the play there can be little surprise at its success. The play reads well, but in the hands of a competent company the old comedy actually comes to life upon the stage. Tyler wrote it in three weeks, but he had before him good models and he had a natural talent for conversation. From the very beginning Charlotte and Letitia, the frivolous girls of the period, wake a quick interest in audiences who recognize the essential permanence of the types Tyler satirizes. The first Act begins:

Letitia: And so, Charlotte, you really think the pocket-hoop unbecoming.

Charlotte: No, I don't say so. It may be very becoming to saunter round the house of a rainy day; to visit my grand-mamma, or to go to Quakers' meeting: but to swim in a minuet, with the eyes of fifty well-dressed beaux upon me, to trip it in the Mall, or walk on the battery, give me the luxurious, jaunty, flowing, bell-hoop. It would have delighted you to have seen me the last evening, my charming girl! I was dangling o'er the battery with Billy Dimple; a knot of young fellows were upon the platform; as I passed them I faultered with one of the most bewitching false steps you ever saw, and then recovered myself with such a pretty confusion, flirting my hoop to discover a jet-black shoe and brilliant buckle. Gad! how my little heart thrilled to hear the confused raptures of. . . . *"Demme, Jack, what a delicate foot!"* *"Ha! General, what a well-turned ——"*

Letitia: Fie! fie! Charlotte (*stopping her mouth*), I protest you are quite a libertine.

Charlotte: Why, my dear little prude, are we not all such libertines? Do you think, when I sat tortured two hours under the hands of my friseur, and an hour more at my toilet, that I had any thoughts of my aunt Susan, or my cousin Betsey? though they are both allowed to be critical judges of dress.

Letitia: Why, who should we dress to please, but those who are judges of its merit?

Charlotte: Why, a creature who does not know Buffon from Souflée— Man!—my Letitia—Man! for whom we dress, walk, dance, talk, lisp, languish, and smile. Does not the grave *Spectator* assure us that even our much bepraised diffidence, modesty, and blushes are all directed to make ourselves good wives and mothers as fast as we can? Why, I'll undertake with one flirt of this hoop to bring more beaux to my feet in one week than the grave Maria, and her sentimental circle, can do, by sighing sentiment till their hairs are grey.

Then they dissect the character of their friend Maria, who is engaged to Dimple, the Anglomaniac. He is flirting with Charlotte and Letitia and is, of course, in time discovered. Colonel Henry Manly, Charlotte's brother, visits the town, and he and Maria fall in love with each other. His servant, Jonathan, is the shrewd, half-educated Yankee whose humor is one of the attractions of the piece. Dimple's servant, Jessamy, tries to initiate him in the follies of the town, but Jonathan has himself experimented, and the scene in which he tells Jessamy and Jenny, the maid servant, about his visit to the theatre is of great interest in more than one connection:

Jenny: So, Mr. Jonathan, I hear you were at the play last night.
Jonathan: At the play! why, did you think I went to the devil's drawing-room!
Jenny: The devil's drawing-room!
Jonathan: Yes; why ain't cards and dice the devil's device, and the play-house the shop where the devil hangs out the vanities of the world upon the tenter-hooks of temptation? I believe you have not heard how they were acting the old boy one night, and the wicked one came among them sure enough, and went right off in a storm, and carried one-quarter of the play-house with him. Oh! no, no, no! you won't catch me at a play-house, I warrant you.
Jenny: Well, Mr. Jonathan, though I don't scruple your veracity, I have some reasons for believing you were there: pray, where were you about six o'clock?
Jonathan: Why, I went to see one Mr. Morrison, the *hocus pocus* man; they said as how he could eat a case knife.
Jenny: Well, and how did you find the place?
Jonathan: As I was going about here and there, to and again, to find it, I saw a great croud of folks going into a long entry that had lanterns over the door; so I asked a man whether that was not the place where they played *hocus pocus?* He was a very civil, kind man, though he did speak like the Hessians; he

lifted up his eyes and said, "they play *hocus pocus* tricks enough there, Got knows, mine friend."

Jenny: Well—

Jonathan: So I went right in, and they shewed me away, clean up to the garret, just like a meeting-house gallery. And so I saw a power of topping folks, all sitting round in little cabbins, "just like father's corn-cribs;" and then there was such a squeaking with the fiddles, and such a tarnal blaze with the lights, my head was near turned. At last the people that sat near me set up such a hissing—hiss—like so many mad cats; and then they went thump, thump, thump, just like our Peleg threshing wheat, and stampt away, just like the nation; and called out for one Mr. Langolee—I suppose he helps act the tricks.

Jenny: Well and what did you do all this time?

Jonathan: Gor, I—I liked the fun, and so I thumpt away, and hiss'd as lustily as the best of 'em. One sailor-looking man that sat by me, seeing me stamp, and knowing I was a cute fellow, because I could make a roaring noise, clapt me on the shoulder and said, "You are a d——d hearty cock, smite my timbers!" I told him so I was, but I thought he need not swear so, and make use of such naughty words.

Jessamy: The savage!—Well, and did you see the man with his tricks?

Jonathan: Why I vow, as I was looking out for him, they lifted up a great green cloth and let us look right into the next neighbour's house. Have you a good many houses in New York made so in that 'ere way?

Jenny: Not many; but did you see the family?

Jonathan: Yes, swamp it; I see'd the family.

Jenny: Well, and how did you like them?

Jonathan: Why I vow they were pretty much like other families;—there was a poor, good-natured curse of a husband, and a sad rantipole of a wife.

Jenny: But did you see no other folks?

Jonathan: Yes. There was one youngster; they called him Mr. Joseph; he talked as sober and as pious as a minister; but, like some ministers that I know, he was a sly tike in his heart for all that. He was going to ask a young woman to spark it with him, and—the Lord have mercy on my soul!—she was another man's wife.

Jessamy: The Wabash!

Jenny: And did you see any more folks?

Jonathan: Why, they came on as thick as mustard. For my part, I thought the house was haunted. There was a soldier fellow, who talked about his row de dow, dow, and courted a young woman; but, of all the cute folk I saw, I liked one little fellow—

Jenny: Aye! who was he?

Jonathan: Why he had red hair, and a little round plump face like mine, only not altogether so handsome. His name was—Darby—that was his baptizing name; his other name I forgot. Oh! it was Wig—Wag—Wag–all, Darby Wag–all,—pray do you know him? I should like to take a sling with him, or a drap of cyder with a pepper-pod in it, to make it warm and comfortable.

Jenny: I can't say I have that pleasure.

Jonathan: I wish you did; he is a cute fellow. But there was one thing I didn't like in that Mr. Darby; and that was, he was afraid of some of them 'ere shooting irons, such as your troopers wear on training days. Now, I'm a true born Yankee American son of liberty, and I never was afraid of a gun yet in all my life.

Jenny: Well, Mr. Jonathan, you were certainly at the play-house.

Jonathan: I at the play-house!—Why didn't I see the play then?

Jenny: Why, the people you saw were players.

Jonathan: Mercy on my soul! did I see the wicked players?—Mayhap that 'ere Darby that I liked so was the old serpent himself, and had his cloven foot in his pocket. Why, I vow, now I come to think on't, the candles seemed to burn blue, and I am sure where I sat it smelt tarnally of brimstone.

Jessamy: Well, Mr. Jonathan, from your account, which I confess is very accurate, you must have been at the play-house.

Jonathan: Why, I vow, I began to smell a rat. When I came away, I went to the man for my money again. You want your money? says he; yes, says I; for what? says he; why, says I, no man shall jocky me out of my money; I paid my money to see sights, and the dogs a bit of a sight have I seen, unless you call listening to people's private business a sight. Why, says he, it is the School for Scandalization. The School for Scandalization!—Oh! ho! no wonder you New York folks are so cute at it, when you go to school to learn it; and so I jogged off.

This scene reveals directly—and indirectly—the models upon which our first comedy was written. As had been the case with our first tragedy, the main source lay in the best English playwriting of the type. Tyler tells us that *The School for Scandal*[1] was one of his models and the relation of Dimple to Joseph Surface is not hard to see. He had an opportunity to witness the play between March 12 and April 16, 1787, but it is not necessary to limit the influences upon him to the plays which were performed between those dates. Darby Wag-all, to whom he refers so enthusiastically, is a character in John O'Keeffe's *The Poor Soldier*, which was a very popular comic opera. It had been performed eighteen times the previous season, and is recorded as having been given on February 2[2] and 23,[3] 1787. It was published in 1787 in Philadelphia. Darby is a comic character, who is made a butt by the other characters, but he is an amiable soul, which may have given rise to Tyler's remark. The reference to his being afraid of powder is to his lack of desire to fight a duel with Fitzroy. Tyler's reference to the family whose private life he was witnessing—that "they were pretty much like other families—there was a poor, good-natured curse of a husband, and a sad rantipole of a wife" may refer to *The School for Scandal*. It may also refer to Vanbrugh's *Provoked Husband*, for the use of the rare word "rantipole" and the name "Manly" in both plays, together with the plot of *The Provoked Husband*, point in this direction. It is possible, too, that John Moody, the servant, with his dialect may have suggested Jonathan. Vanbrugh's play was produced March 29, 1787, so that Tyler could have seen it.

The Contrast ends happily, of course, since Dimple loses Maria and Manly wins her, while Charlotte gives evidence of being somewhat reformed through her experience. But it is not the plot which makes *The Contrast* significant. It is the character portrayal, and above all it is the way in which it meets the test of drama, namely, that it shall act better than it reads. Those who were privileged to see the performance in Philadelphia in 1917, which was staged under the supervision of Mrs. Otis Skinner, will not forget Charlotte, Letitia, Jona-

[1] It was first performed in this country by the Ryan Company, Feb. 3, 1784, in Baltimore.
[2] Sonneck—table opp. p. 76.
[3] Brown, I, 8.

70

than, Jessamy, and Dimple—to speak only of the actors and actresses who make these parts a delightful memory.[1]

Tyler followed *The Contrast* with a comic opera, *May-Day in Town, or New York in an Uproar*, which was performed at the John Street Theatre, May 19, 1787.[2] He then returned to Boston, where he wrote in 1797 *A Georgia Spec, or Land in the Moon*, a comedy in three acts which ridiculed the mania for speculating in the Yazoo country. It was first played at the Haymarket Theatre, in Boston, October 30, 1797,[3] and then in New York at the John Street Theatre, December 20 and 23, 1797, and later, February 12, 1798.[4] Contemporary criticism praises these plays, especially *May-Day*, which, according to William Grayson,[5] "has plott and incident and is as good as several of the English farces; it has, however, not succeeded well, owing I believe to the author's making his principal character a scold. Some of the New York ladies were alarmed for fear strangers should look upon Mrs. Sanders as the model of the gentle-women of this place."

May-Day and *The Georgia Spec* have not survived. According to the memoir of Tyler, written by his son, Rev. Thomas P. Tyler, now in manuscript in the Vermont Historical Society,

[1] Much discussion has arisen concerning the authorship of the "Song" in Act I, Sc. 2. McKee in his edition of *The Contrast* expressed his belief in Tyler's authorship, but unfortunately apparently contradicted himself by stating that the song appears in a play entitled *New Spain or Love in Mexico*, published at Dublin, 1740. This date is a misprint, the play being given at the Haymarket and being printed in London in 1790. "The Death Song of a Cherokee Indian" was published in January, 1787, in *The American Museum or Repository of Ancient and Modern Fugitives*, I, 90, anonymously. In an edition of this volume of the *Museum*, reprinted in 1790, the poem is attributed, p. 77, to "P. Freneau." Freneau never claimed it. In *The Songs of Tammany* (1794), from the opera by Ann Julia Hatton, the song appears as a duet, much changed. Later appearances do not, of course, affect the question of authorship. My colleague, Professor F. G. Speck, tells me that "Alknomook" or "Alknomock" (*Museum*), is of Algonquin origin. As the Algonquin confederacy was located chiefly in New England, this evidence would point to Tyler's authorship. I see no reason to attribute it to anyone else.

[2] *Daily Advertiser*, N. Y., May 19, 1787.

[3] *Boston Gazette*, Oct. 30, 1797.

[4] Dunlap, in his manuscript diary, XV, 47, under this date, calls the play "A Good Spec," and an advertisement in the *Time Piece* of New York, for Dec. 20, 1797, shows that it was played in New York under that title.

[5] Quoted, by H. T. Brown, in Int., xxxi. Wilbur Edition.

Tyler also wrote *The Farm House, or The Female Duellists*,[1] a farce, and *The Doctor in Spite of Himself*, founded evidently on Molière. Four manuscript dramas remain by which we may judge of Tyler's work. *The Island of Barrataria* [sic] is an amusing farce in three acts, based upon Chapters 44, 45, 47, 49, 51 and 53 of the Second Part of *Don Quixote*. Sancho Panza becomes Governor of Barataria, and despite his ravenous hunger, he is forced through the rigor of form and precedent to postpone his dinner until he has presided at a court of law. Tyler takes the opportunity to satirize the proceedings of his own profession by contrasting the verbiage of the lawyers and the shrewd common-sense with which Sancho decides the cases. One of these provides a love story, partly of Tyler's own invention, which forms the subplot of the farce. Tyler quickens the action, allowing Sancho only one day of rule, and he selects cleverly from the narrative, the most dramatic incidents. The farce reads as though it would act well, though it seems doubtful that it saw the stage. On the title page of the manuscript appears the note: "As the Author is informed there is a farce in print—on the same subject—and perhaps with the Title first proposed[2]—the following is suggested as a Substitute—Tantalization, or The Governour of a Day. A Farce in Three Acts, never before performed on any Stage— by a Bostonian." The three "sacred dramas," *The Origin of the Feast of Purim, or The Destinies of Haman and Mordecai, Joseph and His Brethren*, and *The Judgement of Solomon* are written in blank verse of a flexible and at times distinguished quality. The characters of Esther, of Joseph, and of Zernah

---

[1] H. T. Brown, Bibliography, 118-20, Wilbur Edition. According to the *Independent Chronicle* of Boston, May 5, 1796, a farce entitled *The Farm House or the Female Duellist* was announced for May 6 at the Boston Theatre. Comparison of the cast with that of Kemble's farce of that name, played at Drury Lane, .ay 2, 1789 (Genest, VI, 539), shows them to be the same. Kemble's play was itself an alteration of *The Country Lasses* (1715). Tyler may have altered Kemble's farce for his brother, the manager of the theatre, who, however, had resigned in April, 1796. T. P. Tyler states positively that "The Dualists [sic] was performed and was especially popular." See *Argus and Patriot* New Series XXIX (Nov. 5, 1879), p. 1.

[2] Probably refers to Pilon's adaptation of D'Urfey's farce, *Barataria, or Sancho Panza Turned Governor*, which was played at the John St. Theatre, on Oct. 5, 1789.

and Maachah, the two mothers in *The Judgement of Solomon*, are well conceived.

Tyler also wrote a novel, *The Algerine Captive* (1797), which purported to be the adventures of a certain Dr. Updike Under-hill, and was really founded in part upon the experiences of a great-uncle, who had been captured by the Algerian pirates and never returned. The novel is amusing, especially the early portion, which satirizes the medical profession of his day. He was a voluminous writer of essays and verse of a humorous character, and his *Yankey in London* (1809) is an interesting series of letters which were supposed to be written from London to his friends. Tyler's dramatic sense is shown in both these imaginary experiences, which deceived the readers of his day. The remainder of Tyler's career lies outside our special interest. He became a successful lawyer, being Chief Justice of the Supreme Court of Vermont from 1807 to 1813, and Professor of Jurisprudence of the University of Vermont (1811-1814). He died in Brattleboro, Vermont, August 26, 1826.

The Contrast had no small influence both as a printed book and as a play. Notwithstanding the rarity of extant copies, it seems once to have been widely read, for Major Tyler, when on a horseback trip through the State of New York in 1792, found an inhabitant of New Lebanon who had a well-worn copy which he had practically memorized.[1] Indeed, its present rarity is probably due to its wide popularity at the time. Most important, however, was the influence of the play upon the first author-manager, William Dunlap.

NOTE TO SECOND EDITION. A minor character, "Jonathan," a Yankee servant, appeared in *A Match for a Widow*, by Joseph Atkinson [?] produced in Dublin, April 17, 1786, but not published until 1788 in London and Dublin. There is no evidence of influence on Tyler. See Marston Balch, "Jonathan the First," *Modern Language Notes*, XLVI (May, 1931) 281-288, and Albert Matthews, "Brother Jonathan Once More," *Trans. Colonial Soc. of Mass.*, XXXII (December, 1935) 374-386.

[1] H. T. Brown, Int., p. xxvi.

CHAPTER IV

William Dunlap, Playwright and Producer

DURING the last decade of the eighteenth century and the first of the nineteenth, the dominating force in the American drama was the interesting figure of William Dunlap. From the pages of his *History of the American Theatre* and his *Arts of Design* emerges a real personality, an artist to his finger tips—enthusiastic, temperamental, and proud of his craft, whether it be that of the dramatist or the painter, yet capable of smiling even at his own performances, which never reached the shining level of his desires. Especially keen was his sense of the impertinence of patronage, and in his sojourn in England he had seen a good deal of it. Therefore, to him America was the hope of the artist of the future where, unhampered by caste or the dead hand of prestige, the painter, the writer, the musician could develop on the firm basis of his intrinsic worth. His belief in democracy as a stimulant of art is expressed with a hopefulness that not even the bitter experience of years could quite disillusion, for he saw, beyond the accomplishment of democracy, the great principle that survives even the hard disappointments of fact.

Born in Perth Amboy, New Jersey, February 19, 1766, he grew up with little regular education, but with a love for Shakespeare and Pope and the romance of history. His early life was colored by his impressions of the British Army stationed at his native town, and, indeed, his father had been an officer in "Wolfe's Own" regiment and had been wounded at Quebec. Later, in 1777, when his family removed to New York City, he attended the plays given by the British officers and gained his first love for the theatre. In June, 1778, while he was at play, his right eye was cut by a piece of firewood and

74

its sight totally destroyed. This accident put an end to his schooling, desultory as it had been, but it seems not to have discouraged his determination to become a painter. With that portion of his career, we have only incidental interest, but the account he gives of his early efforts, the expression of his delight at the opportunity to paint General Washington in 1783, the narrative of his journey to London in 1784 and the description of his experiences there as a pupil of Benjamin West—all are told with that sense of the dramatic which animates all his writing. He learned little from West and he worked little, having a pleasant time and going to the theatre. Here he saw "all Shakespeare's acting plays" and also some of the best contemporary comedy, including *The School for Scandal* and *The Critic* in their author's own theatre. He witnessed, too, the acting of Charles Kemble and Mrs. Siddons, and he secured in London a sense of dramatic and theatrical values which was of inestimable service in later years, when the responsibility of choosing and directing the plays of the American Company fell to his lot.

In August, 1787, he returned to America. The success of *The Contrast* was still fresh in the minds of those interested in the theatre, and Dunlap wrote a comedy. *The Modest Soldier or Love in New York* has not survived, but the author's description shows that it was based on *The Contrast*, for it contained "a Yankee servant, a travelled American, an officer in the late revolutionary army, a fop, . . . an old gentleman and his two daughters."[1]

Dunlap brought his play to the managers of the American Company, Lewis Hallam and John Henry, and they praised it politely, but, to the author's surprise, the production was constantly postponed. Finally, the mystery was explained—there was no good part for the manager, Henry, and worse yet, there was no part suited to the manager's wife, and "she was another efficient manager." But Dunlap learned fast. Soon another comedy was written, this time with a part built to suit Henry's talents and with the "lively lady evidently inferior to the charac-

[1] *History of the American Theatre*, I, 147.

ter assigned to the manager's lady." Thus from its inception the drama in this country has adapted itself, for good or ill, to the practical necessities and the personal interests of the managers.

The Father, or American Shandyism, the second comedy by a native American to be performed on the professional stage and the first so performed to be printed, was put on at the John Street Theatre on September 7, 1789. According to Dunlap it was "received with great applause by the citizens," and as the author is equally frank in recording his failures, we may assume that the play was well received. It was performed seven times, which was in itself a sign of success. It was printed at New York, September 14, 1789, was reprinted in Halifax, and in the *Massachusetts Magazine.*[1]

The Father merits attention, both from the historical and the absolute points of view. In the words of the Prologue, spoken by the great comedian, Wignell,

> "The comick muse, pleas'd with her new abode,
> Steps forth in sportive, tho in moral mode:
> Proud of her dwelling in our new made nation
> She's set about a serious reformation
> For, faith, she'd almost lost her reputation."

This combination of purpose, to amuse and instruct, was characteristic of the century, but, to Dunlap's credit, he did not overdo the moral lecture. Nor did he appeal to the morbid by dishing up contemporary scandal, sugar coated with moral reflections, as did the author of the first American novel, which also saw the light in 1789. One has only to read *The Power of Sympathy* and *The Father* to realize how superior were Dunlap's standards to those of his anonymous rival. The plot of *The Father* is fairly conventional, but from the opening of the first scene, which discloses Mr. and Mrs. Racket at breakfast, there is a sense of reality in the portraiture. Racket is a gay young merchant whose wife is consoling herself for his neglect with the attention of Ranter, masquerading as a British officer, but really the servant of Captain Haller, of

[1] For Oct. and Nov., 1789, I, pp. 620-9, 649-55.

the United States army, who is supposed to be dead. Ranter has his eyes on Caroline Felton, Mrs. Racket's sister, or rather on her fortune. Colonel Duncan, the guardian of both girls, arrives in time to save the situation with the aid of the revived Haller, who turns out to be the Colonel's son, left in Edinburgh in infancy to be brought up by a friend. Haller has met Caroline in Canada and they have become betrothed. There is an amusing doctor, "Quiescent" or "Tattle" as he was variously named on the stage, in whom the medical science of the day was satirized. Wignell played the part. The play is lively: it reads well even to-day, for the conversation is bright at times and rarely stilted, and it leaves room for action. Of course, it was based on Dunlap's knowledge of other plays, and the most obvious dependence, that on *Tristram Shandy*, is acknowledged in the subtitle. Colonel Duncan is provided with a servant, Cartridge, to extol his virtues, as Corporal Trim had lauded those of Uncle Toby. In 1806 Dunlap reprinted the play with additions and changes of names as *The Father of an Only Child*.

Wignell having asked Dunlap to write a play for his benefit, the latter took as inspiration the character of Darby in John O'Keeffe's *Poor Soldier*, and wrote an interlude, *Darby's Return*, in which that popular person returned to Ireland and described his travels, especially in America. The interlude was first performed November 24, 1789, and gained especial interest on account of the fact that Washington witnessed the performance and heard himself described as

> "A man who'd fought to free the land from woe,
> *Like me* had left his *farm a-soldiering* to go;
> But having gain'd his point, he had, *like me*,
> Return'd his own *potatoe ground* to see.
> But there he couldn't rest; with one accord
> He's called to be a kind of—not a lord;
> I don't know what: he's not a great man, sure,
> For poor men love him, just as he was poor!
> They love him like a father or a brother."

Dunlap tells us the President looked grave at this, but when Mrs. Morris as Kathleen continued, "How look'd he, Darby? Was he short or tall?" and Darby replied:

"Why sure I didn't see him. To be sure,
As I was looking hard from out the door,
I saw a man in regimentals fine,
All lace and glitter, botherum and shine;
And so I look'd at him till all was gone,
And then I found that he was not the one,"

Washington burst into a hearty laugh.

Dunlap's next venture, *The Miser's Wedding*,[1] was unsuccessful, and the author dismisses it in this fashion, "The piece was murdered (it deserved death) and never heard of more." *The Fatal Deception, or the Progress of Guilt*, played first on April 24, 1794, was much more successful, and deservedly so. It was published in 1806 under the title of *Leicester*, and was wrongly stated in the preface by Dunlap to have been "the first American tragedy produced upon the stage." Perhaps the wish was father to the thought, or he may have really been in ignorance of the prior production of *The Prince of Parthia*. *Leicester* is a well-conceived if unrelieved tragedy. Twenty years before Scott treated the Kenilworth motive in fiction, Dunlap drew the character of the Earl as an ideal figure of romance. His heroine was, however, of sterner mould than usual, and while the author defends himself in advance from charges of plagiarism upon the character of Lady Macbeth, he acknowledges that Matilda is modeled upon Clytemnestra. Dudley Cecil and his wife Elwina, attacked by robbers in their flight after Dudley's murder of his brother, are brought to Kenilworth, where Matilda is living as the paramour of Henry Cecil, Dudley's younger brother, whom Dudley has also wronged. Matilda urges Henry to kill Leicester, and Henry enters the room in which Leicester is supposed to be asleep, but in which Dudley is really sleeping. Henry's hesitation is

---

[1] Dunlap says the play was produced "early in June," but Ireland gives it, with the cast, as May 20th (I, 102), and the theatre closed June 14, that season.

well done, and the following scene afforded scope for effective acting, of which John Hodgkinson and Mrs. Melmoth took advantage:

"*Matilda:* Why dost thou not go in?
Henry: 'Tis light.
Matilda: (*in great terror*)   Henry!
Henry: I dare to do, but dare not see it done.
Matilda: Ruin!
Henry: O no, Matilda! I cannot do
A deed of darkness in the face of day!
                    (*Throws down the dagger.*)
Matilda: I will not urge thee further, Henry Cecil:
If thou wouldst give me up, why should I live?
Henry: Nay, nay; but then to see him when I do it:
Think, think of that: to look upon his face—
Upon the face of him so lov'd, so injur'd;
And plunge yon weapon in the honest heart
Which teems with thoughts to serve me!
(*She covers her face with an action of despair and horror.*)
                              Look not so.
I'll do it. (*Takes up the dagger wildly.*) Do thou but only
    shut the light,
And, when his heart beats upward to my hand,
I'll meet it with my dagger.
Matilda: Hold thee firm.
But one small window dimly lights the room;
That from within the castle I can reach;
All unperceiv'd.
Henry: (*with the eagerness of despair*) I pr'ythee do it then.
Matilda: When I shall knock twice on the window-board, . . .
        (*Faultering.*)
Then—Henry—then—   [*Exit.*]
Henry: Yes. I *will* go on.
Repentance and retreat are now denied me;
Hell has ensnar'd—by Heaven I am forsaken.
'Twas not a wayward fancy led me from
My brother's roof, and happy native fields;
Alas! all innocent, was I driven forth
To fate, a lamb-like victim, mark'd for destruction,
Doom'd before my birth to horrible perdition!
Dudley: (*in the room as in sleep*) O, Cecil!"

The scene in which Elwina goes mad after having discovered Dudley slain and, coming out, accuses herself of the deed, is extremely well done. Matilda stabs herself and Henry throws himself upon Leicester's sword, and Leicester having pardoned all his fellow sinners, as was appropriate in the romantic tragedy, departs in peace. On the same evening, April 24, 1794, an interlude called *Shelty's Travels* was put on for Hodgkinson's benefit. It has not survived, but from contemporary accounts it seems to refer to the Algerian troubles, which would constitute the first allusion to those matters on the stage.

Dunlap's enthusiasm for art and letters was not merely individual, nor can he be said to have been a voice crying in the wilderness. He tells us of the formation of a club which seems to have risen from the ashes of a still earlier association, the Philological Society, of which Noah Webster had been a member. The new "Friendly Club" had Charles Brockden Brown, Elihu H. Smith, and Samuel L. Mitchill among its local members, while Theodore Dwight, Richard Alsop, and Mason Cogswell came from Connecticut to its meetings. The club "projected many literary works and executed some." A magazine was supported and a review published, and the stimulus that comes from association fired Dunlap's ardor, so that "he thought only of future triumphs, and tragedies and comedies, operas and farces, occupied his mind, his time, and his pen." This group prepared the way for the Irving-Cooper group. Indeed, it was as early as 1796 that we find the beginning of dramatic criticism in New York City of a very interesting character. Dunlap tells us how John Wells, Elias Hicks, Samuel Jones, William Cutting, Peter Irving, and Charles Adams (son of John Adams) met after visiting a play, wrote critiques, and secured their publication in the daily press. They were really the precursors of the Drama League Committees of to-day.

Dunlap next turned to Gothic melodrama for his inspiration, and from Mrs. Radcliffe's *Romance of the Forest* developed a play in which all of the accompaniments of that phase of romance, the ruined abbey, the dagger, the dusty manuscript, played their parts in establishing a mood of terror. *Fontainville Abbey* was performed on February 16, 1795, and was well received. It is the story of one LaMotte, who, pursued by crimes and creditors, repairs to an abbey with his wife and Adeline, who has been forced upon him by DuBose at a lonely house. LaMotte robs the Marquis de Montalt, who, having LaMotte in his power, makes him his pander with Adeline; then, finding she is the daughter of his older brother and, therefore, heir to his estates, persuades LaMotte to kill her. LaMotte's better nature triumphing, however, he denounces the Marquis and, with the help of Adeline's discoveries in the mansion and DuBose's testimony, carries the day against him. The play is, of course, stilted and unnatural as the mode to which it belonged, but the transformation in LaMotte's nature is not badly done and the blank verse is at times quite forcible.

It would be interesting to know whether the French Revolution subconsciously affected the choice of Dunlap's next play, but he turned from Gothic romance for the moment to the theme of liberty. Being asked to adapt an English play, *Helvetic Liberty*, for the stage he found it "incorrigible," but liking the subject turned to the study of Swiss history and produced *The Archers, or Mountaineers of Switzerland* on April 18, 1796.[1] It is an opera in three acts. In the Prologue he pays his respects to the anarchy which results from the wrong kind of liberty, and it may well be that he had the license of the French Revolution in mind. Tell is, of course, the main character and was played by Hodgkinson. Dunlap gives his sources in the history of Switzerland, and seems to labor hard to preserve historical accuracy as far as possible, though he violates chronology cheerfully in making Winkel-

---

[1] A play called *The Patriot, or Liberty Asserted* was performed in New York in 1794. One or two characters seem to have the same names as in *The Archers*. See Ireland, I, 115.

reid's heroic act precede Tell's shooting of Gessler and the murder of the Emperor Albert. The play is interesting, but not one of his best. The chronicle element is uppermost and, as in nearly all operas, the songs interfere with the dramatic action. There is a good deal of fighting and, of course, the incident of the arrow is not omitted. The comic relief is afforded by Conrad and Cecily, who open the opera in a way that points forward to *Pinafore*, especially in the song, "Who'll buy my baskets?"

Before his next play was performed Dunlap had undertaken the managerial task which was to be his undoing. Things were going badly in the old American Company. In 1791 Hallam and Henry had lost the great comedian Thomas Wignell, who went to England in 1792 and recruited a company for his proposed new theatre in Philadelphia. This was built on the north side of Chestnut Street above Sixth Street. It was begun in 1791, but, owing to the yellow fever epidemic of 1793, it was not opened until February 17, 1794. When the "New Theatre" began its career, a company was assembled there which formed the nucleus of the American Company's first successful rival. Mrs. Oldmixon, the singer, James Fennell, and Mrs. Whitlock, the sister of Mrs. Siddons, in tragedy, John Harwood in high comedy, and Susannah Haswell Rowson, herself a dramatist and novelist, were the leaders of a company headed by Wignell himself, the first low comedian in the country. The theatre which housed them was itself a novelty. It was a copy of the Royal Theatre at Bath, and held about two thousand people, nine hundred in the boxes. The exterior dimensions were ninety by one hundred and thirty-four feet, and the general effect of the two projecting wings, connected by the Corinthian columns of the main building, set back from the street, seems to have been impressive.

To meet this competition John Henry had gone abroad and returned with a number of players, chief among them being John Hodgkinson. This actor soon outdistanced both Hallam and Henry in public favor, and it was not long before Henry retired from the management and the company, leaving Hallam and Hodgkinson to carry on the business. This they seemed unable to do in amity. Into the purlieus of their relations and that of their wives, Dunlap and Hodgkinson take us sufficiently, but they are now of little interest, except as they led to the proposition made to Dunlap by both contending parties that he should purchase one-half of Hodgkinson's share and act as manager. The articles of agreement between the three partners were signed in June, 1796, and provided that Dunlap should decide all questions concerning the casting of plays, Hallam and Hodgkinson reserving the parts they already were accustomed to play. Hallam retained one-half interest, Dunlap and Hodgkinson each having one-quarter interest in the property.

Dunlap took up his office at a time both favorable and unfavorable for success. The theatrical situation in the country was practically under the control of two companies, the American in New York and Wignell's in Philadelphia. The prejudice against the theatre was slowly disappearing, and even Boston was beginning to be a fair field for the actors. The American Company had been strengthened by the advent of Joseph Jefferson, the first of the name in the country, a comedian of high merit, to be the progenitor of a line of distinguished comedians. Mrs. Johnson, another addition, was a capable actress, upon whose beauty and refinement Dunlap comments with enthusiasm. But on the other hand the jealousies of the Hallams and the Hodgkinsons were a source of constant danger, and were enough to wreck the fortunes of any manager or company.[1]

The first play by the new manager to be produced under his own direction was again a Gothic romantic drama. *The Mysterious Monk*, performed with success on October 31, 1796, with Hodgkinson as Ribbemont and Mrs. Melmoth as the

---

[1] For the articles of agreement, see John Hodgkinson, *A Narrative of his Connection with the Old American Company From the fifth [of] September, 1792, to the thirty-first of March, 1797*. N. Y. 1797, pp. 20-22.

Countess, is in blank verse which at times is quite effective. The motive is revenge taken by a vassal for injuries inflicted by his feudal lord, who is led to a belief in his wife's infidelity, and to the supposed murder of his best friend, Narbonne, in consequence. Narbonne is not dead, however, and he conceals the Countess. At the right moment, when the proud spirit of the Count has been sufficiently tamed by remorse, he produces her, in time to save their son who has killed the instigator of the trouble and is, in consequence, under sentence of death. The play was published under the title of *Ribbemont, or the Feudal Baron*, in 1803. It is interesting in its criticism of false standards of honor, which probably was occasioned by the practice of dueling.[1] Dunlap showed again in this play his ability, even in this period of romantic sentimentalism, to write direct blank verse, which afforded an actor an effective medium. A few lines from Act II, Sc. 1 will illustrate this:

Theodore: "Thou dost me wrong;
No reveller am I. Youth's levities
Are dead within, or banish'd from this breast.
My father or my mother have been wrong'd.
And by my eternal soul I'll know no peace
Till I have found and punish'd those who wrong'd them.
Manuel: Seek'st thou them here? lurks guilt within these walls?
Theodore: Monk, well thou know'st there's not that place so holy
Where guilt has not found entrance and protection;
Nor is there any place on earth so sacred,
But the keen vengeance of a son shall follow."

Dunlap's first translation of a foreign play, *Tell Truth and Shame the Devil* was performed January 9, 1797. It was an adaptation of a French farce, *Jérôme Pointu*, by A. L. B. Robineau, which had been performed in Paris in 1781. The adaptation has one original character, but Dunlap adds little to the piece, which owes its interest to the Gallic irony with which the original author represents his characters. A lawyer, Semblance, is a hypocrite who is unmasked by his clerk, who

---

[1] See Act I, Sc. 1. Also see *Modern Honor* by J. B. White (1812).

in disguise visits him and leads him to disclose his vices, incidentally winning his money and his daughter.[1] The language, which is not a slavish imitation of the original, is brisk and the comedy reads well. It was played at Covent Garden, May 18, 1799.

Meanwhile, the trials of managerial life kept on. Mrs. Hallam, who had been forced from the stage on account of habits that rendered her unfit to act, was conducting a campaign to return, and the consequent disturbances even in the midst of performances were distressing to a man who was singularly disposed toward fair dealing himself and objected rightly to the insecure reliance he could place upon his partner's words. His journal and his history reveal his delight in intellectual companionship such as he found in the friendship with Brockden Brown and in his intercourse with Dr. Rush and Dr. Barton, on his visit to Philadelphia as a delegate to the Abolition Convention. His view of abolition is sane and conservative, and determined by the consideration of justice for both slave and slave-holder.

Even in the description of the circumstances of the production of *The Man of Fortitude*, a play given as by Hodgkinson, but really an alteration of a play by Dunlap, *The Knight's Adventure*, which he had left with his partner for examination, he shows his tolerance of others' actions. "We scarcely believe," he says, "the author was conscious of wrong in the transaction, so far as injury to another was concerned." He always speaks with respect of his rival managers, even when they were invading New York as Wignell did and upsetting his plans. Hallam withdrew from active participation in the ownership of the company in May, 1797, and Dunlap and Hodgkinson leased the new house to be called "The Park Theatre" which was to be the center of theatrical performances in New York City for many years. They also rented

---

[1] Dr. Coad, who first discussed the relations of the play and its French original in his life of Dunlap (pp. 194-5), interprets the last speech of Semblance as a refusal, but evidently it is only preliminary to a consent.

the Haymarket Theatre in Boston, and, with that optimism so characteristic of dramatic producers, they looked forward to great returns. The Boston engagement, however, proved a loss. As Dunlap quaintly says: "Mr. Hodgkinson's partner sent on money and advice: the one was taken, the other rejected." Spurred on by the competition of Philadelphia, where Reinagle had developed an orchestra of competent performers in place of the one fiddle or harpsichord that had formerly served the purpose, the New York managers engaged competent French musicians, several of them being gentlemen who had left their native land on account of the Revolution.

Finally, after many delays, the Park Theatre was opened January 29, 1798, with *As You Like It* on the bill. An amusing prelude was written by Mr. Milns, or Milne, as he is variously called, which reflects the difficulties of the stage management of the time. The Park Theatre began auspiciously, but ill fortune set in again, only temporarily checked by the production of Dunlap's first attempt at native tragedy, *André*, which was performed March 30, 1798. John Hodgkinson played André, and the talented young actor, Thomas Abthorpe Cooper, who had been brought over by Wignell, but who had quarreled with him, played the part of Bland, André's friend. The play is easily one of Dunlap's best. Its structure is admirable, especially from the point of view of unity. All the preliminary events have taken place—André has been condemned and the motive of the play becomes the development of the various attempts to save him. The opposition to his execution on the part of American sympathizers is made concrete in the person of young Bland. He goes to extremes in his efforts, and in one case he almost wrecked the play. In the first scene of the third Act, he appealed to Washington to save André, and on being refused he pulled the cockade from his hat and flung it on the ground.[1] Hisses filled the house,

---

[1] The black cockade was adopted generally as the emblem of the Federalist party in May, 1798, at the suggestion of "Peter Porcupine." But undoubtedly the incident at the Park Theatre acquired a double meaning from the party strife of the period. See McMaster, II, 381.

and many wished the play withdrawn. Dunlap modified the
play before the second performance. The second force oper-
ating to save André is the plea of Mrs. Bland, the mother of
the young officer, whose husband is in the hands of the British.
Sir Henry Clinton has threatened to execute Colonel Bland,
who is a prisoner of war, if André is not released, and the scene
in which this message is received by Washington is very
effective. The British officer has presented Sir Henry's message, and Washington speaks.

"*General:* 'Tis well, sir; bear this message in return.
          Sir Henry Clinton knows the laws of arms:
          He is a soldier, and I think, a brave one.
          The prisoners he retains he must account for.
          Perhaps the reckoning's near. I likewise am
          A soldier; entrusted by my country.
          What I shall judge most for that country's good
          That shall I do. When doubtful, I consult
          My country's friends; never her enemies.
          In André's case there are no doubts; 'tis clear:
          Sir Henry Clinton knows it."

While they are speaking a message comes from Colonel
Bland himself:

"*Sergeant:* Express from Colonel Bland.
          (*delivers it and exit.*)
General: With your permission. (*opens it.*)
British Officer: Your pleasure, sir. It may my mission further.
M'Donald: O Bland, my countryman, surely I know thee!
General: 'Tis short; I will put form aside, and read it.
(*Reads*)   'Excuse me, my Commander, for having a moment doubted
          your virtue; but you love me. If you waver, let this
          confirm you. My wife and children, to you and my
          country. Do *your* duty.'
          Report this to your General."

This passage illustrates again Dunlap's ability at writing
direct appealing language, and he gives Washington a more
natural vocabulary than is usually allotted on the stage to
the Father of his Country.

The third force working for André's release appears in the person of Honora, who has come from England to see him, having been separated from him by her father's duplicity. She is based upon a real character, Honora Seward, whom André loved, who married another man, after her engagement to André had been canceled by her parents, and who died four months before André's execution.[1]

The character of André himself is well drawn. As good a case as is possible is made out for him, and he acts with dignity and courage. The play was not a great stage success, since it was not frequently acted, but as a reading play it is well worth study. It represents the Federalist point of view in 1798, the desire to be fair to England and yet not to underestimate the worth of our national heroes. Dunlap felt that it was too near the events to be successful, but it remains one of the best of our early plays.

Owing to the popular demand for patriotic spectacles, Dunlap rewrote *André* in 1803 as *The Glory of Columbia*. The unity of André was destroyed, since the play began with a scene between Arnold and Williams, one of André's captors, and the capture of André is the main incident of the first Act. This act is not badly done. Some of the tragic scenes and the monologues of André are cut out, and in the actual representation, if we are to judge by the prompt copy of William Wood, the manager of the Philadelphia Theatre, they were still further reduced. Songs were inserted freely in *The Glory of Columbia*, and at the end the scene is transported to Yorktown and the captors of André are brought in, with a cheerful indifference to history. Dunlap had the sense of proportion which caused him to say in his *History* that *The Glory of Columbia* is "occasionally murdered for the amusement of holiday fools," but as a spectacle it is above the average.

On April 27, 1798, Dunlap became the sole manager of the company playing at the Park Theatre, Hodgkinson having

---

[1] See "Authentic Documents Relative to Major André" in the edition of *André*, published in New York, 1798, pp. 63-74.

withdrawn. He states in a very frank way his limitations as a manager, but his courage was undaunted, even in the face of financial responsibilities which demanded receipts of over twelve hundred dollars weekly before his own recompense began. For his tragic parts he depended upon Cooper and Mrs. Melmoth; for comedy, Jefferson and Mrs. Oldmixon. Hallam and Mrs. Hallam were still with him, the connecting links with the old American Company which had begun its career in the middle of the century that was just closing. His difficulties began with the yellow fever, which kept him from opening the next season until December 3, 1798.

On December 10th he produced his first adaptation of Kotzebue, *The Stranger*. Previous to this time, the influence of the German drama upon the American stage had been slight. Lessing's *Miss Sara Sampson* had been translated by David Rittenhouse under the title of *Lucy Sampson* in 1789, but it was not performed. It is a prose tragedy, whose main motive is the seduction of a girl, Lucy Sampson, who in pursuit of her lover is killed by another of his mistresses, and dies in the arms of her forgiving father, called rather quaintly by Rittenhouse "Sir Sampson." The play is a moral tract, and hardly could have had any influence. Lessing's *Minna von Barnhelm* was performed at Charleston, South Carolina, in 1795, and in Philadelphia in 1796 under the title of *The Disbanded Officer*,[1] and Schiller's *Die Räuber*[2] was played in 1795 in New York. The former may have played its part in helping on the progress of the domestic drama, while the latter certainly had a large share in the parentage of the "robber play" on the American stage.

The great popularity of August von Kotzebue (1761-1819) is an interesting episode in the history of the drama. Born in Weimar, he was passionately fond of the theatre, and wrote plays from an early age. Much of his life was spent in Russia, and his first works were produced at the German theatres at

[1] Seilhamer, G. O. *American Theatre*, III, pp. 207, 214, 217, 282, 283.
[2] *Ibid.*, pp. 111, 116.

St. Petersburg and Reval. He wrote two hundred and fifteen plays, of which the most popular was *Menschenhass und Reue* (1789), or *The Stranger*, as it was called in the English versions.[1]

The influence of Kotzebue upon the English stage began about 1796, when *Die Negersklaven* was produced in London, and Dunlap was quick to see the availability of the domestic drama of this type for American audiences. It was only natural that the British public should respond to its sentimentality and its glorification of the middle class, and these qualities were also likely to make an appeal to the audiences with which he hoped to throng the Park Theatre.[2] For the vogue of Kotzebue upon the English stage was only a return of a dramatic species to its source. The domestic drama was of English, not of German origin. Lillo's *George Barnwell*, produced first in London in 1731, and Edward Moore's *The Gamester*, first played in 1753, had had an influence in France through Diderot and in Germany through Lessing that resulted in the great vogue of domestic drama, not only in these three countries, but practically all through Europe. Since the audiences of the English theatres were more definitely determined by social standards toward the end of the eighteenth century than in the theatres of France,[3] Germany, or America, the so-called genteel comedy was more popular than the domestic drama. But with the rise of interest in the social reforms of Godwin and Holcroft, the drama felt the impulse, even if it was often academic.

Dunlap's version of *The Stranger* has not been published. He tells us that "having got possession of a wretched publica-

---

[1] See a short autobiography in *The Wild Goose Chace*. N. Y. 1800: also Dunlap, *American Theatre*, II, pp. 82-90; also Rabany, Charles, *Kotzebue: Sa Vie et son Temps*, Paris, 1893; Coad, *William Dunlap*, pp. 205-237; Wilkens, F. H. "Early Influence of German Literature in America," *Americana Germanica*, III (1899), pp. 110-136.

[2] For an accurate list of the plays of Kotzebue which were translated and played in England, see Coad, *William Dunlap*, pp. 208-9.

[3] For interesting discussions of the interrelations of the domestic drama in England, France and Germany, see Gaiffe, F., *Le Drame en France au XVIIIe siècle*. Paris, 1910, II, pp. 35-77.

tion in which the plot and part of the dialogue of Kotzebue's play were given in language neither German nor English, he wrote a play founded on these materials.[1] . . . The success of this piece alone enabled the author to keep open the theatre." The motive of *The Stranger* is the return and repentance of an erring wife, who had deserted her husband and children years before with her lover. Her agony when she finds that her children have naturally forgotten her and she is unable to declare herself to them is a motive that has appealed to thousands of auditors and has been reproduced in plays and stories, of which *East Lynne* is one of the many examples.

Dunlap had begun the study of German even before this time, but the success of the piece led him to improve his knowledge. According to competent critics, his ability as a translator who kept the spirit as well as the letter of his originals is superior to that of his British rivals, who took greater liberties with their material.[2]

After an opera, *Sterne's Maria, or the Vintage*, based on the work of the English novelist, with music by Victor Pellesier, sung on January 14, 1799, Dunlap produced an unsuccessful comedy, *The Natural Daughter*, on February 8th, and a patriotic pageant, *The Temple of Independence*, for February 22d. These are known only by the brief description given by the author, who then turned to Kotzebue again and adapted *Lovers' Vows* from *Das Kind der Liebe*, producing the play on March 11, 1799.

Dunlap says that his version was not published, but in 1814 a play appeared with his name on the title-page and it is probably his. The British version was by Mrs. Inchbald, and was, according to the *Monthly Magazine and American Review*,[3] inferior to Dunlap's as an acting version. He worked on a translation by Anne Plumptre and brightened the dialogue

---

[1] There had been three translations into English of Kotzebue's play besides the version made by Sheridan.

[2] Wilkens. *Americana Germanica* III (1899), p. 124.

[3] Vol. I, p. 96-99. The article is signed "D."

somewhat.[1] The play was quite successful, being based upon
the story of an erring but repentant baron who had in early
life led astray Theodosia, who returns in misery to the neighborhood of her early happiness and who is joined there quite
accidentally by the product of this illicit union, just returned
from war. This amiable youth, Frederick, robs his father, the
baron, to save his mother's life and is nobly forgiven by the
baron, whose daughter by a legitimate union is conducting a
love affair with real skill, for a young person, with her tutor.
The tutor convinces the baron at the point of a sermon, that
he should marry Theodosia and make Frederick his legitimate
heir, which the baron does. Having thus repaired the evil of
his younger days, he successfully patronizes virtue by admit-
ting her to unrestricted access to the aristocracy, and the
audience, it is evident by the popularity of the play, was completely satisfied.

On April 1, 1799, the romantic play of *Count Benyowski*,
another of the Kotzebue adaptations, was presented. We are
told that the costumes of Russia and Siberia were accurately
portrayed and "the snow and ice scenes of Kamschatka would
have been invaluable in the dog days." Dunlap did not publish his version, but he tells us that "the literal translations of
Count Benyowski can give no idea of the drama as prepared
for the New York stage." The writer has before him the
prompt copy used by Warren and Wood in Baltimore in 1813,
and there is a possibility, owing to the close relations that
existed between Dunlap and these Philadelphia managers, that
the version as played by them reflects in some respects Dunlap's
own version. That it does not reflect it entirely is evident
from differences in the names of the minor characters. Count
Benyowski is a Polish noble who has been exiled by the Russian
government. He is made the leader of the exiles through the
efforts of Crustiew, an old man, and excites the jealousy of

[1] When compared in print, Dunlap's version is seen to be closer to the literal translation of Kotzebue than Mrs. Inchbald's, but there are indications, by the usual graphical
signs, that Dunlap cut a good deal of his own version in performance. See later
comparison with Payne's version of *Lovers' Vows*.

Stepanoff, who betrays him to the Governor. The latter has taken a great fancy to Benyowski and engages him to teach his daughter, who falls in love with him. Benyowski is married and at first betrays no desire to change his allegiance, though he uses the affection of Athanasia to assist his plans of escape. These are finally successful, after he has escaped a series of dangers, and Athanasia is about to depart with him despite her father's entreaties when she luckily becomes unconscious and he relinquishes her. The play reads well, and Wood, in whose handwriting the additions and excisions are made, cut liberally and it would seem judiciously.[1]

Count Benyowski was played first by the Philadelphia company in 1804, according to Wood,[2] who gives an interesting account of the real Count Benyowski's residence in Philadelphia, where his wife (not the Athanasia of the play) attained quite a good deal of fame as a player on the harp. It is probable that Kotzebue was himself exiled to Siberia on account of a passage[3] in which Hettman suggests that he become regent of the Aleutian Islands and Benyowski conqueror of California. As the Emperor Paul was suspected of having leanings in the direction of conquest, this passage was considered to be indiscreet, and Kotzebue suffered in consequence.[4]

The play which Dunlap considered to be his best came next. *The Italian Father* was produced April 15, 1799, was received with great applause and was supposed to be by Kotzebue, since it was produced anonymously. When he published the play in 1810, Dunlap called attention to his debt to "old English dramatic literature," and in his history acknowledges his particular indebtedness to Thomas Dekker. *The Honest Whore* was his model, and he took from that play the main

---

[1] There was a translation made by the Rev. W. Render, London, 1798; Boston, 1800. The prompt copy is evidently based on this edition, though there are verbal differences.

[2] *Personal Recollections of the Stage*, pp. 101-103.

[3] Act III , Sc. 2, p. 59 in prompt copy.

[4] See most conveniently *The Most Remarkable Year in the Life of Augustus von Kotzebue, containing an Account of his Exile into Siberia. . . . Written by Himself.* Translated by the Rev. Benjamin Beresford, N. Y. 1802, p. 69.

motive, a father's protecting care, shown in the disguise of a serving man, over the daughter whom he had formerly cast off and who even in her poverty and distress proves to be "mine own girl still." A comparison between the original play and its adaptation is interesting. Dekker has, of course, the supreme advantage of originality, but Dunlap was only following the custom of the Elizabethan playwrights themselves in making use of older material, and from the point of view of unity of construction, of swiftness of movement and stage effectiveness, there can be no question of the superiority of *The Italian Father*. He cut out entirely the tiresome subplot concerning the patient merchant and his tormentors, and he substituted an entertaining hoax played by a fool and a waiting woman upon a gentleman of the court. The part of Leonora was written for Mrs. Oldmixon, and in her hands and those of Jefferson, who played the fool, the result seems to have been very satisfactory to the writer.

Changes, too, were made in the characters of Hippolito and Matheo, fewer in those of Orlando and Bellafront. In Dekker's play, Hippolito, after having reformed the character of Bellafront in the First Part, tries to undo his work in the Second Part by attempting her virtue. In *The Italian Father* he does this not of his own evil promptings, but at the request of the father, Michael Brazzo, as a test of Astrabel's fidelity. Matheo, the husband of *The Honest Whore*, is a worthless fellow who urges his wife to sell herself to bring him money. Beraldo in *The Italian Father* is not of much account, either, but when he suspects that Hippolito is tampering with his wife, he rejects the presents his former friend sends him, and one of the best scenes in the play, that in which he forces his way into the court to demand the satisfaction of a gentleman who has lost everything but honor, is Dunlap's own creation.

The result of these changes is a real gain in the sympathy of the audiences. Dekker built up an admirable character in Hippolito in the First Part of *The Honest Whore;* in the Second Part he destroyed it, and no one cares for Matheo's salvation, for he has forfeited all respect. There are, however, in *The Italian Father* four characters, Astrabel, Michael Brazzo, Beraldo, and Hippolito, in whose fortunes the audience is deeply interested, and the surest test of drama is, therefore, met.

Dunlap next adapted Schiller's *Don Carlos*, and produced it on May 6, 1799, "much shorn of its beams." According to Ireland,[1] a play by Kotzebue, *Die Indianer in England*, was adapted by Dunlap under the title of *The Indians in England, or the Nabob of Mysore*, and played June 14, 1799. Dunlap does not mention it in the body of his history, but gives it in the list at the end of the volume. It seems not to have been successful. On July 4th, Dunlap varied his German adaptations with one from the French, *Le Déserteur*, a domestic tragedy by Louis Sébastien Mercier, played under the title of *The School for Soldiers*. The French play had been put on first in 1771, and in 1783 John Henry adapted it for the American Company in Jamaica. On April 24, 1788, John Henry's adaptation was produced in New York. This was printed.[2] Dunlap's version was not, but casts as given in Odell show that Dunlap had borrowed somewhat from Henry. In order to suit the patriotic occasion, Dunlap changed the scene to the American Revolution and saved a young deserter from execution on the eve of his marriage.

Notwithstanding financial loss, Dunlap faced his second season bravely, even though yellow fever again postponed his opening. He spent the time at Perth Amboy translating Kotzebue's *Falsche Scham* and *Der Wildfang*, and being cheered a bit by the fact that his plays, *Count Benyowski* and *The Italian Father*, were being played in Boston with some success. He mentions also receiving a letter from Kotzebue, expressing his pleasure that Dunlap was introducing his plays to the American stage and offering to let him have (for a consideration) his manuscripts ahead of publication.

[1] I, 187.
[2] In Kingston, Jamaica, 1783. Copy is in the Huntington Library.

The last season of the eighteenth century opened on November 18th, with John Hodgkinson and his wife back in the company, taking leading parts. Dunlap brought on the stage on December 11, 1799, his translation of Kotzebue's *False Shame, or the American Orphan in Germany*, which, according to him, "without scenery or decoration, by plain dialogue and natural character, supported the theatre through this season." In this case Dunlap seems not to have used the British translation published anonymously in London in 1799, and reprinted in Charleston and New York in 1800. The manuscript copy of his version in the Library of Brown University shows a close following of the original.[1] *False Shame* is a rather complicated play, with a strong appeal to good morals and sentimentality. The complications arise through failure on the part of Flachsland to explain to his young second wife the necessity of economy; fear on the part of his daughter Adelaide to explain to her lover a slight physical malformation; the hesitation of Captain Erlach, who has saved Emma, a young American girl, from the attack on Charleston by the Hessians, to reveal to her his real feelings. All these troubles are brought about by a false sense of delicacy.

After an unsuccessful adaptation from Boutet de Monvel's *Clémentine et Désormes* (1780) under the title of *The Robbery*, Dunlap made a successful adaptation from Kotzebue's *Der Wildfang* in the form of an opera called *The Wild Goose Chace*, which was first performed January 24, 1800, and printed the same year. It is one of the most entertaining of Dunlap's plays, and he seems to have improved the original both in construction and dialogue. The sentences are crisp, the repartee sparkling, and while the whole thing verges on farce, it has a lightness of touch and a characterization rare in the farce of the period. The comedy is concerned with the adventures in an inn of Baron Frederick, who is in quest of Nannette. He goes through various disguises in order to deceive her mother, a flighty, vain old woman who is being courted by Squire Piffle-

---

[1] See Coad. *William Dunlap*, p. 217. Also his edition of the play, 1941.

berg for her money. After a number of such adventures Frederick comes in the middle of the night disguised as a woman, and is sent by the Baroness to her room, from which he escapes with Nannette. Nannette refuses to go further with him, however, and he puts her under the protection of Mr. Felix, his tutor, who is really Nannette's father. All ends happily, of course.

The Force of Calumny, from Kotzebue's *Die Verläumder*, was not printed, so that we have only the statement of Dunlap that it was successful and the cast as given in Odell, for February 5, 1800. The motive of the play is the mischief caused by lying. *The Count of Burgundy*, attributed by various authorities to Dunlap, and played March 3, 1800, was another adaptation from Kotzebue, which was probably the translation by C. Smith. Dunlap does not mention it in his *History*.

The Virgin of the Sun was brought out March 12, 1800, "at great expense, with splendid scenes and dresses, and [was] attractive throughout the season." This play of Kotzebue was one of the first to lay its scene in South America, destined to become on the American stage a country associated with romance. It is laid in Quito at a time not mentioned. Cora, a virgin of the Sun, has become the wife of Alonzo, a visiting Spaniard, and according to the laws of the Incas, is subject to death by interment alive. Rolla, a native chief who loves her, organizes an insurrection to save her, but Cora persuades him to give up his arms, and they are all pardoned.

Dunlap, in his version printed in 1800[1], reveals in an appendix the fact that Kotzebue himself acted in the play when it was first produced at Reval in 1789. He took the part of Diego, a mildly comic character, played by Jefferson in New York and

---

[1] According to G. C. Baker, Kotzebue's play was based upon Marmontel's novel of *Les Incas*. Coad (p. 223), gives reasons for believing that Dunlap acted Plumtre's version, much altered by himself, and afterward printed his own. Wood's prompt copy, in the Clothier Collection at the University of Pennsylvania, shows how liberally this version was itself cut in representation at Philadelphia, and gives the New York and two Philadelphia casts. Rolla was acted by Hodgkinson, Cooper, and Wood, Cora by Mrs. Hodgkinson and Mrs. Merry.

Blissett in Philadelphia. Dunlap also indicates his omissions from Kotzebue's original.

The play may be looked upon as an expression of the general theme, so popular in the eighteenth century, of the "noble savage." Love, fidelity, self-sacrifice, and general forgiveness on the part of rulers were painted feelingly for European audiences, who lived under barbarous penal laws and customs dedicated to the preservation of the sanctity of property, as opposed to human life. These idealistic stage pictures pleased audiences in America as well, even though not so sharply contrasted with their own state.

Pizarro in Peru, or the Death of Rolla followed quickly on the success of *The Virgin of the Sun*, of which it is a sequel, being performed on March 26th. It is a better play than its predecessor, being full of action, if less of a unit. Pizarro, returning to Peru, attacks the Peruvians led by Alonzo and Rolla. The Peruvians win, but Alonzo is captured, and Elvira, Pizarro's mistress, vainly begs for mercy for him. Rolla gains access to Alonzo's prison, substitutes himself for Alonzo, and then, at Elvira's suggestion, goes to Pizarro's tent, where he refrains from killing Pizarro, although he is in his power. Pizarro frees him, but Rolla, finding that Cora's child has been captured, risks his life in escaping with it. He is shot while doing so, and fights his way to Cora with the child safe before he dies.

Four translations of this play had appeared in England in 1799, including Sheridan's version, acted at Drury Lane in the same year, with Kemble as Rolla and Mrs. Siddons as Elvira. It is interesting to compare Dunlap's version with Sheridan's. Sheridan had altered Kotzebue's play by cutting out one scene, shortening the scene relating to Rolla's death, and adding a scene of single combat between Alonzo and Pizarro, in which the latter is killed. Dunlap wisely restored the original version and dropped the last scene of Sheridan's which detracts from the real motive of the play, the generous love of Rolla. Interesting, too, is the detailed comparison of certain scenes, for example, the dialogue between Pizarro and Orozembo, a Peruvian prisoner, in Act I, Sc. 1. In Dunlap's version the sentences are more crisp and telling, everything unnecessary is rigidly excised, and the defiance of Orozembo is expressed in epigrams that must have been very effective upon the stage, especially in the mouth of Jefferson. Hodgkinson acted Rolla. *Pizarro* became a permanent attraction, and was by far the most enduring of Dunlap's plays.[1]

The Corsicans, attributed to Dunlap, was probably not by him, but he acknowledges some share in the adaptation of *Die edle Lüge* as *The Stranger's Birthday*, on April 23, 1800. In this extraordinary play of Kotzebue's, "The Stranger" tries to make his reformed wife more comfortable by pretending to her that he has betrayed their servant. This extreme of false sentiment seems not to have been successful.

Fraternal Discord, which began the season of 1800-1 on October 24th, was from *Die Versöhnung oder der Bruderzwist* of Kotzebue, and in Dunlap's own opinion "was perhaps the most meritorious of the many translations and adaptations which came from his pen."[2] Two brothers, Philip and Captain Frank Bertram, have been separated for fifteen years over a lawsuit about a certain garden. They have been kept apart by the machinations of Semblance, an attorney, and Mrs. Grimkin, the Captain's housekeeper. This pair provide most of the comedy element, assisted by Jack Bowlin, a sailor, who routs them both. The brothers are reconciled by the efforts of Dr. Bloomfield, who incidentally wins Charlotte, Philip's daughter. It is not hard to see why this play appealed to popular audiences. To be sure, the speeches of Charlotte and her father are representative of a convention, perhaps better a delusion, of the time, that the quality of persecuted virtue conferred upon the speaker certain lofty eloquence and a vocabulary exclusively of Latin origin. But the sincere and

---

[1] Coad notes two hundred performances in forty years, though these may include British versions.

[2] *American Theatre*, II, 134-5.

straightforward expression of the affection between Captain Bertram and Jack Bowlin is even yet worth reading—Dunlap tells us "nothing ever was finer of the kind than Jefferson's sailor except the gouty captain of Hodgkinson." And the scene when Bowlin carries Mrs. Grimkin off must have brought down the house.

Dunlap broke away from Kotzebue to produce an opera, *The Knight of Guadalquiver*, on December 5th, but it was not approved by his audience. To make amends, he scored a success with *Abaellino, the Great Bandit*, which was performed for the first time in English on February 11, 1801. It was from the German of Johann Heinrich Daniel Zschokke, a writer of great popularity in Germany, about whom Dunlap seems to have known little, though he was the first to translate Zschokke into English. The original play had been published in 1795.

His example was imitated widely, for *Abaellino* was translated into French, Spanish, Danish, and Polish, and brought out under various names on many stages.[1] In this country it was also widely popular, being played in all the principal cities in the East, and holding the boards for a quarter century. Dunlap's version, first published in 1802, was reprinted at least five times.

Abaellino, the Great Bandit, is a romantic melodrama, laid in Venice. The central character is that of a noble, who, for patriotic purposes, disguises himself as a bandit, Abaellino, and in this way gains the confidence of a band of patrician conspirators who are seeking to overthrow the Republic. Meanwhile, as Flodoardo, he wins the confidence of the Doge, and the love of his niece Rosamonda. In a scene which must have been theatrically effective, he exposes the conspirators, and wins his reward. The play is blood and thunder, but is skillfully put together, and has been the prototype of many other such plays.

---

[1] See Hoskins, J. P., *Parke Godwin and the Translation of Zschokke's Tales*. Pub. Mod. Lang. Association of America. New Series, XIII, No. 2, pp. 283-4.

WILLIAM DUNLAP, PLAYWRIGHT AND PRODUCER

A patriotic piece, *The Soldier of '76*, was produced for Washington's Birthday, on February 23, 1801. The next play of Dunlap's, *The Abbé de l'Epée*, was a translation from the French of Jean Bouilly's *L'Abbé de l'Epée* (1799). This drama was based on the life of Charles-Michel, Abbé de l'Epée, a humanitarian, who is represented as aiding one of his own pupils, who is deaf and dumb, to regain his property. Kotzebue had translated the French play, as had Holcroft and Thompson in England, but Dunlap worked with the French original. His own version, which was not printed, was performed on March 9, 1801.

Dunlap was having troubles again with Hodgkinson, and for the summer season of 1801 he brought Mrs. Merry from Philadelphia. With her as a star and Cooper and Hodgkinson to support her he struggled to recoup himself, and gave *Romeo and Juliet* and *Much Ado About Nothing*, which were a welcome change after so much German adaptation. Nevertheless, he produced a farce, *Where is He?* from the German, on December 2, 1801, *The Merry Gardener*, an opera from the French, February 3, 1802, and a play upon a Revolutionary theme, *The Retrospect*, on July 5th. These are known only by title, and only the first was successful.[1]

The next of his adaptations that has survived is *Peter the Great*, an historical romance, from the German play, *Die Strelizen*, by Joseph Marius Babo. It was performed on November 15, 1802, and was not very successful, though it was revived in 1815. However, the piece reads well, and the character drawing is above the average. Peter dominates the play, whose motive is the way in which he meets the various situations caused by a revolt of the Strelizes, his former body-guard, whose leader, Suderow, he has exiled. The best scene is the one in which he visits the meeting place of the conspirators alone and dominates the situation by the force of his personality. It was one of the earliest plays on the American stage

[1] *Bluebeard* and *Fiesco,* sometimes attributed to him as adaptor, seem not to be his at all.

to have as a central figure a real historical character from continental sources.

Dunlap, as usual, was looking for novelties, and turned next to the French drama. *The Voice of Nature*, an adaptation from *Le Jugement de Salomon*, by L. C. Caigniez, was given first on February 4, 1803, and became a favorite. Dunlap prepared his version in five days, and worked from the original, although he imitated the title and names of characters from the English version of Boaden, who had changed the scene from Jerusalem to Sicily. This play illustrated the ever-recurring cycle of fashion in the theatre. It was the first example in this country of an adaptation of the French *mélodrame*, a dramatic species which had a continuous influence upon American playwrights for many years. The French *mélodrame* developed out of the pantomime with dialogue and the *scène lyrique*, a combination of spoken words and music, during the last two decades of the eighteenth century. It was in its inception a movement on the part of the popular theatres of the boulevards to bring the drama closer to the people. As is usually the case with dramatic forms, the species existed before the name was applied to it and, indeed, to speak of the melodrama as being a new thing in 1798 when Guilbert de Pixerécourt brought out his *Victor, ou l'enfant de la forêt*, at the Ambigu Comique, is to neglect the history of the stage. The essence of melodrama is its freedom from the observance of the strict dramatic law of cause and effect, its intensification of sentiment and exaggeration of passion. To supply the appeal which true feeling and natural motive make instantly to the audience, melodrama calls in the aid of musical accompaniment to incite emotion and thus weaken, even momentarily, the critical judgment and the appeal of reason.

Melodramas were present on the British stage, whatever they were called, long before the production of Holcroft's *Tale of Mystery* in 1802, and on the American stage they are not clearly to be distinguished at times from the domestic drama or the Gothic romance. The French stage, with its more definite standards emanating from the Thêâtre Français, established certain forms, even laws, for the melodrama. According to Pixerécourt there were four essential characters, a villain, an unhappy virtuous woman, a good man who becomes her protector, and the comic character, who helps the good man rescue the heroine. This neat and compact arrangement was not followed, of course, universally and the principal element which the French *mélodrame* contributed to our stage was its freedom from restraint. This very freedom made the plays easy of adaptation to foreign soil, while the great political interest in France certainly aided in preparing for the melodrama a wide popular approval.[1]

An interlude, *The Good Neighbor*, "altered from a scene of Iffland's" was played February 28, 1803, and published in 1814. The play is a trifle, revealing the persuasive powers of an elderly man who persuades his neighbor to allow the marriage of his daughter and the man who loves her. Dunlap's last translation from the German, *The Blind Boy*, from *Das Epigram* of Kotzebue, was played March 30, 1803. It was well received by a "thin audience," but the vogue of the Kotzebue drama was passing.

The season closed with *The Glory of Columbia*, already described, which delighted the manager by its receipts. It was played again during the next season, usually with popular approval. On December 19, 1803, Dunlap produced a farce, suggested by a newspaper, called *Bonaparte in England*, whose motive was the mistaken consideration given to an Italian Jew, Shadrach, who was taken for Jerome Bonaparte. Shadrach seems to have done his best to live up to the part. This farce was revived in 1833 at the benefit given to its author.

For some reason at which we can only guess, Dunlap did not print this original play or the next, his comedy of *The Proverb, or Conceit Can Cure, Conceit Can Kill*, which first appeared on

[1] For discussion of the French *mélodrame*, see Ginisty, Paul, *Le Mélodrame*, Paris, n.d. [1910]; Mason, James F., *The Melodrama in France from the Revolution to the Beginning of Romantic Drama*, Baltimore, 1912 (Chapter 1 printed); Hartog, W. G., *Guilbert de Pixerécourt*, Paris, 1913.

February 20, 1804. The plot as given by him[1] consisted of a picture of mountebank quackery, such as was familiar to European scenes but not to this country. He bravely kept up his fight against adverse circumstances, even the weather, by producing another original comedy, *Lewis of Monte Blanco, or the Transplanted Irishman*, on March 12th. The hero was evidently a military Irishman, written for John E. Harwood, who had come over from Philadelphia, and it was "repeatedly played with increasing applause."

The last of his plays to be produced this season, on April 4, 1804, was *The Wife of Two Husbands*, an adaptation from *La Femme à deux Maris* of Pixérécourt, a very popular French melodrama,[2] in which Dunlap made use of the two earlier English translations by James Cobb and Mrs. Gunning. While the principle of suspense is used not uncleverly, there seems little justification for the success of the play, which is as stilted in language and sentiment as any of the domestic dramas. The Countess Belflor, through a trick of her villainous first husband, has married again, and the first consort turns up. He is finally killed by an accomplice through a device of the stage Irishman, who had already developed into that conventional character, as remote from life as he could well be, who misrepresented his nation on the American stage for a century.[3]

Nina, an opera from the French *Nina ou la Folle par Amour*, by Joseph Marsollier, was produced unsuccessfully on December 31, 1804, and twice repeated in February, 1805. On February 22, 1805, Dunlap closed his theatre, a bankrupt. No account of his difficulties could be more effective than his own words:

---

[1] *American Theatre*, II, 207.

[2] This melodrama of Pixérécourt illustrates the "laws of the melodrama" as given by him. The four "essential characters," are represented in the Countess, her first and second husbands and the Sicilian concierge. It had 451 representations in Paris and nearly a thousand in the provinces. Ginisty, *Le Mélodrame*, p. 71.

[3] These adaptations of *La Femme à deux Maris* illustrate again the return of inspiration to its source, for there can be little doubt that the main situation was taken by Pixérécourt from Thomas Southern's *Isabella, or The Fatal Marriage* (1694), which the genius of Mrs. Siddons had doubtless made international in reputation.

WILLIAM DUNLAP, PLAYWRIGHT AND PRODUCER

After a struggle of years against the effects of yellow fever, and all those curses belonging to the interior of an establishment, badly organized when he found it, the manager's health yielded to disappointment and incessant exertion.

Dunlap failed honorably. He gave up his property of every kind. He had found the theatre bare, he left it well furnished, and the performers whom he had been unable to lead to success reopened it with the advantages of his properties and his manuscripts.

On leaving the theatre, Dunlap returned to his profession of portrait painting, but in April or May, 1806, he accepted the position of Assistant Manager to Thomas Abthorpe Cooper, the actor, who had taken a lease of the Park Theatre. In the meantime John Hodgkinson had died of yellow fever, and one of the most able and versatile actors was lost to the early stage. Cooper declined to engage Lewis Hallam and his wife, who were constant sources of trouble, and Hallam died soon after in Philadelphia, November 1, 1808. He was the last surviving link between the stage of the nineteenth century and that company of actors who had come to America in 1752 under his father's leadership. The theatre was passing into new hands. Cooper had taken into partnership Stephen Price, and toured the "eastern circuit," playing in New York, Philadelphia, and Charleston, S. C.

Dunlap began in 1806 a project which, to the great regret of all historians of our drama, he was not able to carry out. This was the publication of his works in a uniform edition, in ten volumes. Of these only one was actually revised and published, in Philadelphia, in 1806. Volumes two and three appeared in New York in 1816, but they were simply individual plays bound together, with different dates and paginations.

One of the most interesting items in Dunlap's *History* records the engagement in September, 1809, of Mr. and Mrs. David Poe. Mrs. Poe played Angela in M. G. Lewis's *Castle Spectre*, Mr. Poe taking the part of Hassan. Edgar, their son, had been born in January of the same year in Boston.

After acting as traveling companion and guardian to the gifted but unreliable English tragedian, George Frederick Cooke, Dunlap gave up his managership in 1812 and again turned to miniature painting, varied with literary pursuits, such as the publication of an unsuccessful magazine. In 1814 he became Assistant Paymaster of the New York State Militia, which post he held until 1816.

His play writing during this period is not of a great deal of significance. In his list of plays by himself, given at the end of his *History*, he includes *Rinaldo Rinaldini*. A play by this name was published in 1810 "by an American and a citizen of New York," made, as Wilkens correctly describes it, "by the very simple process of copying out the dialogue from Hinckley's translation of Vulpius's prose romance *Rinaldo Rinaldini*."[1] It would be an act of cruelty to ascribe this version to Dunlap. It is possible that he may have adapted another version for the stage from the original, but of the queer mixture of prose and verse in which this play is written the author of *André* would have been incapable. The introduction included a definite statement that the author did not have an opportunity to present the play upon the stage. Dunlap could, of course, have produced it at the Park Theatre, since he was its manager at the time.

Dunlap's patriotic feeling is evidenced in his interlude, *Yankee Chronology*, originally produced September 7, 1812, which is an account of the victory of the *Constitution* over the *Guerrière* on August 19th, news of which could hardly have reached New York before August 31st. Ben Bundle, a sailor who has been on the *Constitution*, tells his father, Old Bundle, about the fight, and then sings a song which retails in rather vigorous verse certain events in American history of which that generation was proud; with a tenth stanza devoted to the last naval victory. The interlude was frequently repeated, and Dunlap more than once added stanzas celebrating such events as the anniversary of the evacuation of the British in

[1] Wilkens. *Americana Germanica.* III, 135, also 192.

1783, and naval victories such as those of Jones, in the *Wasp* and Bainbridge in the *Constitution*. Printed with this is his song, "The Freedom of the Seas," sung first July 4, 1810, which has a vigor and a rhythm that make it not an unworthy rival of its original. The last of his patriotic plays was *The Battle of New Orleans*, which may have been produced at the Park Theatre, but the evidence is doubtful. It has not been printed.

The final dramatic period of Dunlap's life began in 1827, when he was asked by the management of the new Bowery Theatre to provide plays. He began with a version of *The Flying Dutchman*, which was produced on May 25, 1827, and proved a rival to the version by Fitzball, which had been popular at the Park Theatre. He tells in the *History* that his next play, performed at the Bowery Theatre, February 22, 1828, *Thirty Years, or the Life of a Gamester*, was faithfully translated from the French, and was generally well played.[1]

The French original, *Trente Ans ou la Vie d'un joueur*, was by Prosper Goubaux and Victor Ducange. The pen name of the former, "Dinaux" appears on the manuscript as one of the authors. The play is a real melodrama. The first Act, which takes place in 1790, discloses George St. Germain as a gambler who is to be married to Amelia. He loses at a gaming house through his evil genius Warner. In Act II, which takes place in 1805, we see the misery of Amelia, since George is gracefully divesting her of all her money. He kills her supposed lover, not the real one, who remains to be disposed of in a mountain near Munich fifteen years later. George also kills himself, but Amelia survives.

Of his last play, Dunlap speaks thus: "The last piece I wrote for the stage was a farce called *A Trip to Niagara*, the main intention of which was to display scenery." There is little to be said in its favor. An Englishman named Went-

---

[1] The manuscript of this play, at the Yale Library, begins with the first Act, then follows the third and finally the second Act. The last seems to be in Dunlap's handwriting, not the "first 50 pp." as given by Wegelin. On the Ms. is written the name of "A. Gilfert." Mrs. Gilfert played the heroine.

worth and his sister Amelia are traveling in this country. He dislikes everything he sees, and is as rude as possible. Another Englishman, John Bull, in order to win Amelia's hand, disguises himself as a Frenchman and as a Yankee, and cures Wentworth by so maligning the country to an Irishman that Wentworth takes up the cudgels in its defense. In the second Act a diorama shows the scenery from New York Harbor to Catskill Landing. Perhaps the only real interest in the play lies in its introduction of five caricatures that are found in earlier and in many later plays—the Yankee, French, English, Irish, and negro types. It is to be noted that the Yankee and the French characters are assumed and in the Introduction Dunlap tells us that the reason he cures the Englishman through one of his own countrymen is to avoid any "disagreeable nationalities." To the last, Dunlap preserved his unbiased attitude toward his own work, and when he thought it was weak he said so.[1]

Dunlap died September 28, 1839. Seven years before his death, he published his invaluable *History of the American Theatre*, the first record of our stage. It is not only a mine of information about the beginnings of our theatre and our drama, it is a fascinating autobiography of a man who accomplished much through more than one failure. It was a fitting tribute, paid to him on February 28, 1833, when the citizens of New York arranged a great benefit performance for him, at which Charles and Fanny Kemble and Edwin Forrest appeared. *Venice Preserved* was acted, and his own farce, *Bonaparte in England*. The proceeds, $2,517.34, were welcome, for he had little to depend on but the proceeds of his pen. In 1834 his *History of the Rise and Progress of the Arts of Design in the United States* appeared in two volumes, and was widely circulated. His last years, though passed in ill health, were cheered by the friendship of men like Irving and Cooper, and were

---

[1] *Forty and Twenty*, and *Robespierre*, which are given in Dunlap's *History* by title only, are unknown as to date of publication or performance. *Blue Beard* and *The Africans*, which he also gives in his bibliography, are probably Colman's plays, with only slight changes. See Coad, p. 179.

faced with that courage which remains the most salient quality of William Dunlap.

Dunlap's achievement cannot properly be estimated by the methods of criticism that have hitherto been employed. He produced more than fifty identified plays,[1] twenty-nine of which were entirely or partly his own. He was not provincial, and he was acquainted with the dramatic literature of England, both of an earlier time and of his own day. He kept himself informed of the current movements in French and German drama, and he selected with some discrimination from among all these foreign sources material for adaptation. That he had no contemporary masterpieces to select from was after all not his fault.

His versatility, too, must at least be noted. He began with the comedy of social life in *The Father*, he experimented with the romantic tragedy of history in *Leicester* and the Gothic melodrama in *Ribbemont*, then rose to his greatest height in the dignified if somber tragedy of American history in *André*, and he continued to reproduce American history on the stage with success. He made use of dramatic impulses of the past in *The Italian Father*, and he adapted with success French and German plays of his own period. The assumption of his necessary inferiority to European dramatists is dispelled at once by an actual comparison of his work, not with that of Shakespeare, but with those plays which were actually being written during the decades 1790-1810. In England Sheridan was done, so far as his great work is concerned, and for his translations, *The Stranger* and *Pizarro*, he turned to the same sources that Dunlap used, the German of Kotzebue. General Burgoyne, Mrs. Inchbald, John O'Keeffe, Matthew Gregory Lewis, Thomas Holcroft, George Colman, John Tobin, Thomas Morton, are names which indicate sufficiently the rivals Dunlap had in England, of whose rivalry he need have no fear in any final judgment.

In this field of the Gothic romance, Dunlap was only following a fashion of his time. When we contrast *Ribbemont* with

[1] It is possible to identify fifty-three with moderate certainty. Nine are doubtful.

its predecessors, like Jephson's *Count of Narbonne* (1781), or its successors like Joanna Baillie's *De Montfort* (1803), we see how well he compares with the favorite plays of this type on the British stage. The use of the name "Narbonne" for the mysterious monk of Ribbemont, and of "Theodore" for the son in each case shows that Dunlap had read the British play, but there is little else in the plot to remind us of *The Count of Narbonne*. Much more has been borrowed from *Ribbemont* by John Tobin in his *Curfew* (1807), where the main motive, that of an injured vassal revenging himself after a lapse of years upon his lord, is introduced in much the same manner. Where the very type is artificial in its conventions, comparison is difficult, but Dunlap loses nothing in directness, vigor of language, or in sheer interest in that comparison.

In the historical tragedy, he had no serious competitor during his active period, for Hannah More's *Percy* (1777) belongs to an earlier time, and Colman's plays, like *The Battle of Hexam* (1789) and *The Surrender of Calais* (1791), are not tragedies but chronicle plays. One may urge that the historical element in *Leicester* is not considerable, but it is to Dunlap's credit that he saw the possibilities of tragic situation in English romantic history when his British rivals were unmindful of it. It is also to his credit that the comedy of English fashionable life, in which General Burgoyne and Mrs. Inchbald did their best work, Dunlap avoided. The most valuable lesson he could have learned from it, the building of characters who reveal much by a glance of the eye or by a gesture, he did employ in *The Father* and *André*, but he realized that if his audiences wished such themes, they could find them easily in the British plays.

On the German stage Kotzebue was the central figure, and Dunlap was quick to realize the theatrical effectiveness of his plays. He did not limit himself to Kotzebue, of course, adapting plays of Schiller and Zschokke and bringing the work of German playwrights on the stage in other translations than his own. That this importation was of unmixed benefit is more than doubtful. The standards of morality of the German domestic drama were not the highest, certainly, and the artistic standard was even lower. But it must be remembered that the morbid quality shown in some of Kotzebue's plays did not often pass Dunlap's censorship, and a scrutiny of the prompt copies, as well as the comparison of his versions with the originals, reveals a real ability at excising the long speeches of the German "moralist for sentimentality only." Dunlap felt no overwhelming sense of Kotzebue's importance. He records with apparent sympathy the evidences of growing popular discontent with the "Dutch School," and he cannot be blamed if, as a losing manager, he staved off for a time the inevitable ruin by giving the public what it wanted—tears and thrills.

In his adaptations from the French, he followed the fashions of the time and chose his models either from the domestic drama or the melodrama. He chose, too, the best-known contemporary authors like Mercier, Caigniez or Pixerécourt, but their influence upon him cannot be said to have had either an absolute or a relative value in advancing the cause of the drama in America.

After all, it is to be remembered that his original plays are his best. In *The Father*, his first acted play, he carried on the healthy impulse to describe real types of native character, and for a beginner succeeded well. In *André* he gave us the first adequate tragedy of American history, a play which can still be read without even implicit apology. *Darby's Return*, though a trifle, has no small merit in its sincerity, and it is a pity that Dunlap did not print all his patriotic plays, of which he composed seven. For one of his most likable qualities is his sturdy Americanism. The son of a British soldier, one who had known London intimately, he loved his own country best, and his comments on Joseph Dennie, the editor of the *Portfolio*, are vigorous and valid.

Of the remaining original plays, *Leicester* and *The Italian Father* are the best. The sense of impending doom that hangs over the Dudley family, the inevitable quality of the tragedy, lifts *Leicester* to a high plane. The character drawing, too, in both plays, especially in *The Italian Father*, where he is matching his strength with one of the Elizabethans, is of a quality that deserves much more than the faint praise accorded to it by those who, we must infer, have allowed the scarcity of his plays to discourage their attempts at first-hand criticism.

Dunlap's blank verse deserves, too, its share of praise. It is dignified, flexible, and straightforward. It must be compared again with the blank verse of his English contemporaries, who suffered also from the overpowering achievements in epic blank verse of the time, which served as an unconscious model. But narrative verse is not dramatic verse, and Dunlap knew the difference. He never thought of being a great poet, but he could put verse into the mouths of characters on the stage and make it seem their natural utterance, which many have tried to do and failed.

He was willing, and even anxious, to give other American playwrights a chance at production. At a time when no copyright laws protected foreign playwrights and gave an opening for native talent, and also at a time when the rewards of the dramatist were limited usually to the receipts of the third night, William Dunlap had that overpowering desire for expression which inspired him to match his strength against foreign reputation and to endure native neglect of native talent, hardest of all to bear. He saw, too, the evils of the commercial standards of the theatre, and in his *History* more than once he points to a stage supported by the state or the nation as the only solution for the conditions which rendered success so dubious. He inveighs also against a custom borrowed from the British stage, which then seemed deep-rooted in ours, of the women of the town being allowed a section of the theatre as their province.

In short, William Dunlap had the soul of an artist and the intrepidity of the pioneer, and his place in our dramatic literature will remain secure.

CHAPTER V

Tragedy and Politics, 1788–1805

DURING the period of Dunlap's creative activity there was growing up, partly under his influence but more frequently entirely outside it, the tentative beginning of a native drama. From 1788 to 1805 we find in romantic tragedy, in the national play, in comedy and farce some interesting examples of these several types and they are more significant as types than as representative of any individual author's work.

From the point of view of literary merit, the romantic plays with a tragic impulse are the most significant. The earliest of these is *The Widow of Malabar*, by David Humphreys, produced by the American Company on May 7, 1790, during their visit to Philadelphia, at the old Southwark Theatre, and repeated next season in Philadelphia and New York. It was played as late as 1798 by Wignell's company in Baltimore for Wood's début. It is based on *La Veuve de Malabar*, by Le Mierre, produced in 1770 and revived with great success ten years later. David Humphreys (1753-1818) was aide-de-camp to Washington, received the captured British standards at Yorktown, and became Minister to Portugal and to Spain. He mentions more than one projected comedy in his letters,[1] and he published one, *The Yankey in England*, in 1815. *The Widow of Malabar*,[2] the only play of his to be performed by professional actors, is a romantic drama, laid in India, and is

---

[1] See Humphreys, F. L. *Life and Times of David Humphreys*, 2 v. 1917, I, 428, and II, 150.

[2] Genest records a performance of *The Widow of Malabar* on May 5, 1790, at Covent Garden. This was possibly the version by Mariana Starke, which curiously enough contains an epilogue "as spoken by Mrs. Henry, at the Southwark Theatre in Philadelphia." This epilogue is Trumbull's, incidentally, though not credited to him.

based upon the custom of widows immolating themselves upon a funeral pyre. Lanissa, the widow, is saved by the French general Monteban, who captures the city. The play is built upon classical French models and is respectably dull. The best lines are in the Epilogue, written apparently by John Trumbull, and spoken by Mrs. Henry.

> "Am I to blame, if this dear life to save
> I lik'd a lover better than a grave;
> And held, retreating from my funeral urn,
> ' 'Twas better far to marry than to burn?' "

Even though it was performed only by amateurs connected with the Humphreysville Manufacturing Establishment, January, 1814, *The Yankey in England* is of special interest. It was probably the comedy of which Dunlap speaks in 1805 as being in manuscript, and it hands on the Yankee tradition of *The Contrast* in no doubtful manner. The Introduction to the play carefully explains the actual basis for the characters in real life, but the characters of the Whig and Tory American officers who have become an admiral and a general since the Revolution, or the French Count and Countess are but a background for the character of Doolittle the "Yankey," who furnishes most of the comedy. He is a servant of the adventuress, Countess St. Luc, and as described in the Introduction, "is made up of contrarieties—simplicity and cunning; inquisitive from natural and excessive curiosity, confirmed by habit; credulous, from inexperience and want of knowledge of the world; believing himself to be perfectly acquainted with whatever he partially knows; tenacious of prejudice; docile, when rightly managed; when otherwise treated, independent to obstinacy; easily betrayed into ridiculous mistakes; incapable of being overawed by external circumstances; suspicious, vigilant, and quick of perception, he is ever ready to parry or repel the attacks of raillery by retorts of rustic or sarcastic, if not of original and refined, wit and humour." Humphreys creates another Yankee, Newman, who is better educated and who

114

proceeds without dialect to straighten out the rather complicated affairs of the characters; especially those of the Countess,
whom he prevents from taking poison after the ill success of
her schemes. Humphreys showed a certain dramatic sense in
laying the main scene in a hotel or gathering place in London,
where, he remarks, almost anyone might meet anyone else!
The play, too, is the first surviving one to take the Yankee
character to England, and the glossary of Yankee terms that
is appended is probably the first of its kind.

The prejudice against the theatre died hard in Boston, but
when the Federal Street Theatre was finally opened on February 3, 1794, the management of Charles S. Powell and later of
J. S. Tyler and J. B. Williamson made an effort to secure the
work of American writers. An early result was a tragedy,
Orlando, or Parental Persecution, by William Charles White,
performed in 1797 at the Federal Street Theatre. It is an
unrelieved tragedy, in which the hero, Orlando, played by
White himself, finally takes poison after a series of misunderstandings and persecutions. The blank verse indicates a fair
ability, but the play is really a series of conversations. The
author left the Boston stage after four months' trial, to reappear in New York, January 19, 1801, with "some promise
of success," according to Dunlap. He is of interest as showing
the unconquerable desire to write, despite lack of great appreciation, since he produced in 1809 in Boston *The Clergyman's
Daughter*, a domestic tragedy based on McKenzie's novel of
The Man of the World, with some influence from Moore's
Gamester, in which a high-born villain, Lord Sindal, lures both
the Annesleys, brother and sister, to the city and ruins both,
one by gambling and one by seduction. It is interesting to
note that White promoted Sir William Sindal from the gentry
to the nobility and brought him to a violent death at the
hands of a companion, Norcross, while McKenzie allowed him
to survive for years, until he finally met his fate at the hands
of Annesley, returned from his exile. White frankly states in
his preface that this character of Sindal was drawn "for no

other purpose than to be detested," and he certainly succeeded in producing that effect. White's prefaces, by the way, are entertaining, sometimes unconsciously. In that prefixed to his "comedy," *The Poor Lodger*, performed in Boston in 1810, he resolutely acknowledges that he may have been mistaken in calling it a comedy, but that "the alternation of comic and serious scenes produces that variety, which in a certain degree, is universally pleasing; and like light and shade in a picture, creates that relief, which is the soul both of painting and poetry; nor will it be denied, that the mixed drama has been found, by long experience, to be the most faithful mirror of nature and of life."[1] Surely melodrama, which was then on its triumphant career over both the French and English stages, must have welcomed this unblushing defense from the shrine of the Pilgrims, had it only been more audible! *The Poor Lodger* is, incidentally, founded on Fanny Burney's *Evelina*, and is even now not bad reading.

From New England came also Dr. Elihu Hubbard Smith, a product of Yale and Pennsylvania, whose opera of *Edwin and Angelina, or the Banditti*, was produced by his friend, Dunlap, on December 19, 1796. It is fitly described by Dunlap as "pure and energetic, but not sufficiently dramatic." It is based on Goldsmith's ballad of "The Hermit," and belongs to the cycle of "robber plays" in which the leader of a band, in this case in northern England, figures as a romantic hero. The author had himself a heroic death, from yellow fever, caused by his devotion to his profession in the epidemic of 1798.

This use of early English history was paralleled by the tragedy of *Edwy and Elgiva*, by Charles Jared Ingersoll (1782-1862), which was performed at the Chestnut Street Theatre in Philadelphia in 1801. The struggle between King Edwy and Bishop Dunstan, representing the conflict of the Church and the monarchy for supreme authority, was a dramatic one and the play, with Cooper as Edwy and Mrs. Merry as Elgiva,

[1] Preface, pp. 4-5. Boston, 1811.

116

seems to have been successful. Certainly the characters of Edwy and Elgiva as lovers are made appealing, and the author did not allow himself to be a slave to historical accuracy. Ingersoll, who was a Congressman and United States District Attorney, and wrote the well-known "Inchiquin's Letters," also wrote a blank verse tragedy, *Julian the Apostate*, published in 1831.[1] It is concerned with Julian's attack upon Ctesiphon and with the relations of a Persian family, who are divided between the patriot side and the Roman. The blank verse at times has a real dignity.

Among the writers of tragedy, however, the most interesting is John Daly Burk. Although not a native, since he was born in Ireland about 1776, his dramatic career is entirely American. He came to this country when he was twenty, and was an editor by profession and a stormy petrel at all times. Having first attracted attention by his *Bunker Hill*, to be mentioned later under the national play, he wrote a tragedy, *Female Patriotism, or the Death of Joan d'Arc*, produced at the Park Theatre in April, 1798, which is one of the bright spots that reward the reader of our early drama. How the author of *Bunker Hill* and the rest of Burk's plays did it is an insolvable puzzle, but he produced an original and a powerful conception of Joan of Arc's character in a play that has at times the real savor of the Elizabethan models he had in mind. He tells us that he copied thirty lines of *Henry VI*, and he gives the lines. But it would seem that, fired by the real love of liberty with which Burk was possessed, and guided by the dramatic inspiration that touched him for a brief moment, he accomplished what in the light of his other performances is almost a miracle. He represents Joan as a simple, direct character. What marks her out from other Joans is her human nature. She is willing to let the divine character of her mission gain her adherents and stupefy the enemy, but she herself is under no illusion. She tells her companions in Act III, Sc. 3,

[1] Dunlap says the play has not been played or printed. Wegelin repeats this misstatement. Roden does not mention it.

"*Pucella:*   Forbear my Lords:
    Let not your praises taste of blasphemy:
    I am no more of heaven than yourselves;
    Nor inspiration do I feel, beyond
    The stretch and compass of the human mind,
    Develop'd by its own innate exertions.
    No visions had I more than one of you:
    I saw no sights but all of you did see:
    France torn by feuds and foul dissentions;
    France desolate beneath a stranger sword.
    I saw the fairest kingdom on the earth,
    The gallantest and proudest people,
    And these my country and my countrymen,
    Groan in the bondage of a meaner state.
    This only was my inspiration;
    And was it not enough—Forbid it heaven,
    The time should ever be, when France doth look
    For a more powerful, sacred call than this,
    To rouze her to resistance."

The womanly feeling that bids her say good-by to her glory is finely expressed in Act IV, Sc. 2.

"*Pucella sola:*   My mission's done!
    Orleans is safe and o'er the better half
    Of this rich land the peasant tills the soil
    In peace and safety, while the shepherd leads
    His flocks to feed or with the pipe and song
    Renews Arcadia's pleasures in our France.
    All this my sword hath done; what's yet to do
    May be atchiev'd without my farther aid.
    Why then remain I longer in this camp?
    I feel 'tis not a place for me; For tho'
    The love of liberty sublimes my soul
    And makes me do such things to compass it,
    As my soft sex would shrink at; Yet I feel
    Those timid, soft, and virgin sentiments
    Play on the silken fibres of my heart,
    Which speaks me all the woman."

Dunlap, in his interesting analysis of this play given in his manuscript Journal,[1] fails to see how much this human quality

[1] Feb. 13 and Feb. 26, 1798. Volume 15, p. 47 and pp. 57-8, in the Historical Society of New York.

adds to the tragedy of Joan's death. In the play her love for Chastel is touched delicately. She puts it by till her mission is accomplished; but when she is abandoned by her own king and her own friends she is left all alone to bear her torture, without the spiritual exaltation of the martyr. That it was Burk's Joan and not the real Joan he was portraying is, of course, evident, but he makes her an appealing character. He allows her, too, a bit of prophecy in her letter to Chastel, in which she foretells the French Revolution, comparatively an easy matter in 1798, but in which she also prophesies that England will join hands with France to resist tyranny, not quite so certain at that time. The feeling against France in 1798 may have prevented the success of the play on the stage. Dunlap attributes the failure to poor acting.

All excellence is relative, but the relativity is rarely so striking as it is when we turn from *Joan of Arc* to *Bethlem Gabor, Lord of Transylvania, or the Man-Hating Palatine,* published in 1807 at Petersburg, Virginia, where Burk was living. A cast is given in the published volume, which corresponds to the company at the Richmond Theatre, and the play was put on also at Petersburg by a "Thespian Company" in 1803 or later, in which performance Burk himself acted Bethlem Gabor.[1] It is a wild melodrama laid in Transylvania, in which ventriloquism and mysterious mirrors are mingled in glorious unconcern with blood and tears. It owed some inspiration to William Godwin's[2] novel, *St. Leon* (1799), and the ventriloquism of St. Leon was suggested probably by Charles Brockden Brown's *Wieland* (1798). With the exception of *Bunker Hill,* Burk's other plays are known only by title.[3]

---

[1] Campbell, Charles. *Memoir of John Daly Burk*, pp. 45-46. These "Thespians" acted under Burk's direction actively, and put on such comedies as *Nolens Volens, or the Biter Bit*, by Everard Hall (1809), which is said by the author to be the first play published in North Carolina. It is a fair comedy with the father and son motive.

[2] B. S. Allen. "William Godwin and the Stage." Pub. of Mod. Language Asso. of America. XXXV (1920), pp. 358-374.

[3] Dunlap gives a list (II, 382), of eight plays by Burk. *Female Patriotism* and *Joan of Arc*, which he indicates separately, are evidently the same play. *The Death of Montgomery* is said to have been published in Philadelphia in 1797, but this is an error

Another editor, this time a native of New England, David Everett (1770-1813), a graduate of Dartmouth, produced an historical play, *Daranzel; or, The Persian Patriot* at the Haymarket Theatre in Boston, on April 16, 1798. It was repeated at the Federal Street Theatre in 1800. While laid in Persia, it evidently represents allegorically the struggle of this country for freedom. In this play the rebellion led by Daranzel is finally successful. While the plot is conventional and the characters are not very distinct, the verse is at times vigorous.[1]

One of the most interesting examples of stage modification is afforded by a play, *Preservation, or the Hovel in the Rocks*, published in Charleston, S. C., in 1800, as by John B. Williamson, the director of the Charleston Theatre. He was an English actor who had been for a brief period (1796-7) manager of the Federal Street Theatre in Boston, so that his work hardly belongs to our subject. But a study of the manner in which he changed Lillo's *Fatal Curiosity* from a tragedy to a play with a happy ending will repay anyone who compares the two plays. The original play is an unrelieved tragedy, in which old Wilmot murders his son unknown to himself, thinking that the boy is a stranger. In *Preservation* the tragedy is avoided by the creation of the character of Malign, a wrecker, who enters Wilmot's house with the idea of murdering him and who is in turn killed by old Wilmot. This allows part of the last act of Lillo's play to be used, since Mrs. Wilmot thinks

caused by confusion with the 1797 edition of Brackenridge's *Death of General Montgomery*. *The Fortunes of Nigel* was probably not by Burk, who was killed in a duel in 1808, but his *Innkeeper of Abbeville* apparently was put on in 1840 in Philadelphia. *Which Do You Like Best, the Poor Man or the Lord?* is probably Dunlap's incorrect ascription to Burk of William Ioor's play, *Independence, or Which Do You Like Best, the Peer or the Farmer?* Burk's *Oberon; or, The Siege of Mexico* was played in Norfolk in 1803.

[1] Everett wrote other dramatic pieces, among which *Slaves in Barbary* appeared in *The Columbia Orator*, a book of oratorical selections, in 1810 and in many successive editions. Everett was the author of the famous "Lines spoken . . . by a little boy seven years old," beginning

"You'd scarce expect one of my age,
To speak in public on the stage. . . .
Large streams from little fountains flow,
Tall oaks from little acorns grow."

that her husband committed a murder when he returns with the bloody sword. The love story remains practically unchanged. The long speeches of Lillo have been cut somewhat to advantage, but, of course, there is lost that sense of impending doom which made the strength of *Fatal Curiosity*. The title page of *Preservation* announces with cheerfulness that the play has been "performed in London and Boston with the most flattering success." If this is true, it is a commentary upon the desire of audiences for a "happy ending."[1]

The earliest of the playwrights to follow Tyler and Dunlap in dealing with national themes was a versatile woman, Susanna Haswell Rowson, whose career was a romance in itself. Born in England in 1762, the daughter of a British officer, she spent most of her girlhood in this country, then returned to England and married in 1786 William Rowson, a band master attached to the Royal Guards in London. She came to this country for the second time in 1793, with the other members of the splendid company Wignell had secured for the opening of the new Chestnut Street Theatre. She had had provincial training in England and had written already her famous novel of sentiment, *Charlotte Temple* (1791), of which over one hundred and sixty editions have appeared.

Her first play, and the only one that has survived, was *Slaves in Algiers, or a Struggle for Freedom*, performed December 22, 1794, at the Chestnut Street Theatre and repeated in Baltimore, in which she herself took the part of Olivia, one of the imprisoned American women. Public opinion was excited over the barbarities practiced upon American citizens captured by the pirates of the Mediterranean, to whom most of the European nations paid tribute, as the best way out of an apparently hopeless situation. In the spring of 1794 the

---

[1] The English domestic drama had other imitators, among them Thomas Pike Lathy, born in England, who came to this country while quite young and whose *Reparation, or the School for Libertines* was published in 1800 and was acted in Boston "with great applause." From the prompt copy it seems also to have been performed in New York. It is an interesting effort to bring the noble seducer to a good end, and is a quickly moving piece of sentimentality.

United States had begun the construction of a navy, realizing that such demands as those made by the Dey of Algiers could be met ultimately only by force.   In the meantime, by a curious coincidence, Colonel David Humphreys, Minister to Portugal, and author of *The Widow of Malabar*, was given charge of the negotiations with the Dey, to be stopped, however, by the refusal of that potentate to deal with any representatives of the United States.   Colonel Humphreys, finally despairing of securing speedy action from Congress, came home, and it was while he was on his way to America that Mrs. Rowson's play was performed.   In April, 1795, he returned and the matter was temporarily settled by a tribute of $800,000, a frigate, and a treaty of peace.[1]

Mrs. Rowson depended partly for the plot upon the story of the captive in *Don Quixote*, but most of it is original.   It is concerned, of course, with the rescue of American prisoners by the methods usually employed in comic opera, but the various disguises, escapes, and recaptures are accompanied by conversation which is clever enough to be readable to-day.   The scene in which Sebastian saves Ben Hassan, a Jewish usurer disguised as a woman, and makes love to the supposed Rebecca, was sufficiently dramatic to be imitated by John Howard Payne in his *Fall of Algiers*.   Remarkable, too, it is to hear abolition sentiments expressed on the stage, and the beginning of the Epilogue deserves reproduction:

"Epilogue
Written and spoken by *Mrs. Rowson*.
Prompter: (*behind*).   Come—Mrs. Rowson! Come!—Why don't you
   hurry?
Mrs. R.: (*behind*).   Sir, I am here—but I'm in such a flurry,
  Do let me stop a moment! just for breath,
     Enter
  Bless me!   I'm almost terrify'd to death,
  Yet sure, I had no real cause for fear,
  Since none but liberal—generous friends are here.

[1] *Life of David Humphreys*, II, 224; McMaster, J. B.   *History of the People of the United States*, II, 589.

Say—will you kindly overlook my errors?
You smile—Then to the winds I give my terrors.
Well, Ladies tell me—how d'ye like my play?
'The creature has some sense,' methinks you say;
'She says that we should have supreme dominion,
And in good truth, we're all of her opinion.
Women were born for universal sway,
Men to adore, be silent, and obey.'"

The Volunteers, Mrs. Rowson's next play, like *The Slaves of Algiers*, was accompanied by music composed by Reinagle. It was performed January 21, 1795,[1] and was concerned with the whisky insurrection in western Pennsylvania. Her feminist activities led also probably to her farce, *The Female Patriot*, produced in 1795 and depending upon Massinger's *Bondman*.[2] Mrs. Rowson joined the company at the Federal Street Theatre in Boston in 1796, and played for one season, then withdrew from the stage and conducted a highly successful school for girls in Boston until her death in 1824. On the occasion of her last appearance in 1797 she produced her comedy of *Americans in England*, whose title and cast make us regret it has not survived. She played Jemima Winship. This was the same play as *The Columbian Daughter*, produced by Hodgkinson, September 10, 1800, at Mount Vernon Gardens, New York. Thoroughly nationalized, she represents the impulse to place contemporary events upon the stage, and her sentiments were always for liberty, especially for her own sex.

While with the Philadelphia Company, Mrs. Rowson took the leading part in a play that is one of the curiosities of the stage. *The Triumphs of Love, or Happy Reconciliation*, a four-act comedy by John Murdock, was performed at the "New Theatre" on May 22, 1795. Murdock seems to have been a barber, and his play is as formless as it well could be. But it was put on, much cut, with a splendid cast and was published in September with a subscription list that took seven hundred

[1] Durang, Series I, Chap. 24.
[2] According to an article by Richard Penn Smith, clipped from a magazine yet unidentified, in the Historical Society of Pennsylvania.

copies. It gives a vivid glimpse into customs of the period, one of the episodes attacking the close corporation in marriage prevailing among the Quakers, and treating that Society for the first time on the stage. Sambo, a negro, was well conceived and was the first native negro character on the American stage.[1] He is freed by his master, George Friendly, in the third Act, which action must in itself have caused considerable comment at that time. The whisky riots and the trouble with Algiers are not forgotten, and the whole play is really a running comment upon the events of the time. So shrewd and penetrating are the comments that it is no wonder that Wignell, who had himself acted the character of Peevish, a caricature of the average citizen, declined to repeat the play. For his own satisfaction Murdock published as an introduction to his *Beau Metamorphized* in 1800 all the correspondence between himself and the management, together with the newspaper criticisms of the play. *The Beau Metamorphized* is a rather tiresome farce, but Murdock had published in 1798 a much more readable production in *The Politicians, or a State of Things*. It is an illustration of the drama used as a political vehicle, for there is no evidence that it was performed. It is also a striking example of the way in which history repeats itself.

The country was torn with dissension on account of the treaty with England in 1794 and the consequent refusal of the French government to receive Charles C. Pinckney, when he succeeded James Monroe as Minister of the United States to France in December, 1796. Murdock was evidently in favor of the action of the government and was a strong supporter of Washington. One scene from the play (Act I, Sc. 1) will indicate the nature of the discussion that ran through it:

(*Enter Mrs. Turbulent and Mrs. Violent.*)

Mrs. Turbulent: Our minister refused! this is the effect of the cursed treaty, (*walks in passion*) I wish—I wish—

---

[1] At least in an extant play. There are Negroes in *The Candidates* (1770) and *The Fall of British Tyranny* (1776), but these pieces were probably not acted, and the characters in Robinson's *Yorker's Stratagem* (1792) are not native Negroes.

Mrs. Violent: What do you wish?

Mrs. Turbulent: I wish the president's hand had withered before he had signed it.

Mrs. Violent: Abominable, wicked wish.

Mrs. Turbulent: Wicked, do you say?—no, he deserves the curses of his country for that one act, he has blasted his name forever; I was told it would come to this.

Mrs. Violent: Ah, who was the sagacious person?

Mrs. Turbulent: Mr. Lisp was the person—Mr. Lisp is a man of penetration—Mr. Lisp is a man of parts—of most extraordinary parts.

Mrs. Violent: He, he, he—Peter Porcupine won't admit that, (*aside*) you really consider him a man of consummate wisdom and parts.

Mrs. Turbulent: I do, but he is not the only one who gave me intimation of what would happen in consequence of that diabolical treaty: I say Mr. Timid and Mr. Anticipate of the Senate, told me we might be certain, that the treaty would draw down upon us the vengeance of the French, and Mr. Timid and Mr. Anticipate have the good of their country at heart.

Mrs. Violent: Their own, rather say; their party have nothing else at heart.

Mrs. Turbulent: The reverse, they are disinterested men, it would be a great saving to the nation if such men as them were at the head of it. They would œconomize.

Mrs. Violent: Excellent patriots—excellent œconomisers! they would œconomize in order to disorganize.

Mrs. Turbulent: You are bitter, very bitter, Mrs. Violent.

Mrs. Violent: I will never be otherwise to your party—a wicked, restless, marplotting set; ever combining to cross the purposes of government, trying every possible means to render President Washington's administration unhappy to him.

Mrs. Turbulent: (*scornfully*) President Washington's administration! He never was equal to the situation he was placed in; vastly has his talents been over-rated; he possesses none beyond that of being overseer to a Virginia plantation, or the superintendance of a horse-stable: he is an excellent judge of horses.

The characters are well drawn and represent all shades of opinion, from the most extreme, like Partial, a friend of France, and Hasty, a friend of England, to Conciliate, who wants to be friends with everybody. The negro characters are again drawn with a skill in which Murdock surpassed anyone else for many a year, and he put into their mouths an amusing argument on the merits of France, England, and America.

Philadelphia did not monopolize the patriotic play. John Burk, the author of *Joan of Arc*, began his career as a playwright with a tragic spectacle, *Bunker Hill*, first produced at the Haymarket Theatre in Boston, February 17, 1797, and later in New York and other places, being revived for years as a Fourth of July play. It is negligible as drama, but it seems to have succeeded largely through the last Act, which staged a real attack on the hill, at the expiration of which Warren delivered a farewell address, having had charge, in cheerful defiance of history, of the entire American operations. The play was several times reprinted.[1] In April, 1797, also at the Haymarket, a play, *West Point Preserved*, by William Brown, placed André and Arnold on the stage and antedated Dunlap's *André* by a year.

Bunker Hill may have been the first play in which battle scenes of the Revolution were actually put upon the stage, but it was not the first play to be laid in the Revolutionary period. Another Boston playwright, Mrs. Judith Sargent Murray, began with a domestic drama with some pretense at striking the note of social comedy, in *Virtue Triumphant*, played once at the Federal Street Theatre, March 2, 1795, under the title of *The Medium*.[2] "Virtue" is symbolized by a maiden of irreproachable manners and morals, who resolutely refuses the man she loves until her social and financial position are established. References are made to France and England, and a neutral policy is advocated. Mrs. Murray's next play, *The Traveller Returned*, is better constructed, and although the plot is not new, consisting of the return of a father who has abandoned his

---

[1] See an interesting account of the play and of Burk in the edition of *Bunker Hill*, by Brander Matthews, prepared for the Dunlap Society, in 1891.

[2] Seilhamer, III, 248, attributes *The Medium*, on purely speculative evidence, to Royall Tyler. He had not access to *The Gleaner*, Mrs. Murray's periodical, in which the two plays are printed, or the persistent attribution of them to the "Reverend John Murray" would have been more clear to him.

wife for twenty years and returns in time to prevent the marriage of their two children who have been brought up in ignorance of each other, it is noteworthy on account of its strong defense of Washington in 1796, when it was produced at the Federal Street Theatre on March 9th. It is laid during the Revolution, but the war is simply referred to and plays no real part in the drama. The treason of Arnold has evidently just occurred. The best dialogue in both plays is placed in the mouths of the servants.

One of the most interesting examples of the masque used as a patriotic spectacle is the elaborate *Americana; or, a New Tale of the Genii*, written during the Revolution, according to a footnote by the unknown author, but not performed until February 9, 1798, when John Sollee, the manager of the City Theatre at Charleston, South Carolina, put it on in an elaborate form. The motive of the masque is the transplanting of Elutheria, Genius of Liberty, from England to America, in order to become the companion of Americana, the Genius of America. She is aided by Galiana, Genius of France, but much more effectively by Fulmenifer, who is clearly intended to represent symbolically Benjamin Franklin. Etherius, the Commander-in-Chief of America's forces, is another potent factor for good, while Typhon, Genius of Tyranny, and Fastidio, Genius of Pride, are the evil forces, which for a time deprive Elutheria of consciousness. The blank verse is adequate, and at times rises to vigor and beauty, and the author treated with some skill the curious mixture of symbolic characters, real people, and mountain nymphs which belonged to an orthodox masque of the period. The masque was prompted by a sincere love of country, which Americana's lines in Act III well represent:

"*Americana:* Immortal Power, who form'd the heart of man,
And interwove throughout the tender texture,
That necessary passion, love of self;
That godlike principle, the love of virtue,
That glorious sentiment, the love of freedom—

How lost. how sunk, how impious must they be,
Who say resistance to a tyrant's will
Is opposition to Thy will divine!"

This masque is represented as being given on the summit of one of the "Allegany Mountains," and the stage directions certainly reveal an inventive mind. For the second scene is thus introduced:

Immediately another scene discovers itself falling between the former scene and the audience. This represents an airy and unbounded prospect, wings and back flat representing a clear sky, light clouds but low and near the floor—by this mean the stage will very naturally represent the summit of the vast rock on which the Masque is represented. N.B.—the smallest appearance of vegetation is not to be seen.

The author was not content with representing Franklin as a demigod of liberty, he employed him also as a scientist. When the day seems darkest, and Fastidio and Typhon have apparently triumphed, this strikingly original scene was introduced:

The moment Fastidio and Typhon have violently drawn Elutheria and Americana to opposite sides, a large black cloud descends between the altar and the triangular scaffolding before mentioned—flashes of lightning—a large luminous aperture opens, and discovers Galiana and Fulmenifer on the top of the scaffolding; Galiana in the attitude of darting a thunderbolt—Fulmenifer with an electrical rod in his hand. All appear amazed; Typhon, Fastidio, relax, thro' astonishment, their violence; but do not loosen their holds—Fulmenifer kneels and puts the rod in Galiana's hand—rises—guides her hand—points it towards Typhon—raises it—lowers it—immediate a stream of electric fluid pours from above upon the head of Typhon—he staggers—falls on one knee—The same is done by Fastidio with the same effect.

Equally progressive was the concluding scene, in which Elutheria was restored to life by placing her feet in direct contact with the prostrate enemies, while the antiseptic qualities of an incense brewed from the fragments of their clipped wings was employed as an accessory. Elizabeth Arnold, afterwards Poe's mother, took the part of a "dancing nymph" in this spectacle.

The use of the unacted drama as a vehicle for political satire is hardly to be estimated in its extent by the few specimens that have survived. The political writers of the period found quicker response to their attacks upon their opponents in the Philadelphia *Aurora* or in the Boston *Gazette*. That there must have been more printed drama of a political character than has come down to us is probable, however, for in no period of our history does there seem to have been such violence of party feeling or such bitter and unscrupulous attacks upon political leaders.[1]

One of the earliest and certainly the most entertaining of these political dramas is *The Politician Outwitted*, written in 1788 and published in 1789 as "by an American." It has been attributed to Samuel Low, who was a Federal office-holder and later connected with the Bank of New York, and who is the certain author of two volumes of poems. Dunlap in his *History*[2] says: "About this time, Mr. Samuel Low, in the Bank of New York . . . wrote a comedy, which was rejected by the managers and published for their justification by the author."

Dunlap is a bit severe, for while *The Politician Outwitted* is not great drama, it is interesting as a picture of social life of the period as well as in its more obvious function as a Federalist tract, a defence of the proposed Constitution. Low treated the matter in true satiric form—he represents Old Loveyet as a servile admirer of Maria Airy and as a railer at the new Constitution. Loveyet's criticisms are so silly that they implicitly create a favorable opinion of the proposed government. The author's real sentiments are expressed by Trueman, when he describes the Constitution in Act IV, Sc. 1, as "a new government which some great and good men have lately contrived, and now recommend for the welfare and happiness of the American Nation." Loveyet turns his son out of the house because of his adherence to the new Constitution,

---

[1] See McMaster, *History of the People of the United States*, II, chaps. 9 and 10 esp.

[2] I, 152.

but in the end Charles Loveyet marries the woman of his choice, and the old gentleman is completely baffled, in love and politics. The drama was evidently modeled, in its social satire and its rougher humor, upon *The Contrast*.

In view of the malignant attacks which embittered the last days of Washington's administration and which covered with abuse the names of Adams and Jefferson, it may be to the credit of the drama that its share was not so large.[1] In the first place, the subjects are not nearly so important as those which the dramatists of the Revolution treated. Then the struggle was for the liberty of the nation, but in the period now under discussion, it was for political office. The passage of the "Sedition Act" on July 4, 1798, evidently had a deterrent effect upon the writers who opposed the Federalist Administration, for there was an increase in the production of such satires in 1801 and 1802, after its repeal.

The Essex Junto, by J. Horatio Nichols,[2] is a sample of the type. John Adams is represented as the Duke of Braintree, which was his residence, Alexander Hamilton as General Creole, Washington as Old Patriot, Jefferson as Monticello, Pickering as Earl of Indigo, the country generally as Virginia. Creole and the Duke of Braintree are conspiring to murder Old Patriot and kidnap Virginia, but she is saved by Monticello and his group. The drama is of value only as revealing the opposition to the centralizing tendencies of the Federalists and a real or supposed dread of a tendency toward monarchical institutions on their part. These fears seem idle now, but the country had just witnessed the foolish persecutions under

---

[1] In 1798 the Chestnut Street Theatre was nightly a scene of rivalry between the two parties, as to which could stir up more enthusiasm for its favorites. It was in the Chestnut Street Theatre that the actor Gilbert Fox, for the first time, on April 25, 1798, sang "Hail Columbia," for which at his suggestion Joseph Hopkinson had written the words to the "President's March." See McMaster, II, 378, from the *U. S. Gazette* of April 26, 1798.

[2] The play was published anonymously in Salem, Mass., in 1802, but on the title page of *The New England Coquette*, Salem, n. d., we find his name as "author of *Jefferson and Liberty, The Essex Junto*, etc. *The New England Coquette* is a negligible dramatization of Hannah Foster's novel, *The Coquette, or the History of Eliza Wharton* (1797).

the operation of the Sedition Law, which through the inevitable reaction had driven the Federalists out of power and elected Jefferson in 1801. Plays like *The Essex Junto* were the froth that rode on a very powerful wave of public indignation.

Even more curious are the dramatic satires which reflect state politics. Such a production as *Federalism Triumphant in the Steady Habits of Connecticut Alone, or The Turnpike Road to a Fortune* (1802), by Leonard Chester,[1] a Yale graduate of 1769, proves conclusively how lost to the interest of one generation is the local politics of another. The same violent attack on the office-holding class, combined with democratic sentiments, is carried through six acts, into whose purlieus it is not profitable to wander.

Far more readable is such a drama as *A New World Planted, or The Adventures of the Forefathers of New England, who landed in Plymouth, December 22d, 1620*, by Joseph Croswell. This is a historical drama in five acts printed in Boston in 1802. It is a blank verse play, not badly written, with a large number of characters. Carver is Governor; Brewster, Standish, and Bradford are the principal characters, and an Indian girl, "Pocohante," is introduced, as the daughter of King Massasoit!

This period saw also the beginnings of the farce, and the beginnings are sufficiently curious. On April 24, 1792, there was produced for the first time a two-act farce, *The Yorker's Stratagem, or Banana's Wedding*. In the preface, the author, J. Robinson, one of the American Company, states that the success of the piece on the stage led to its publication in 1792, and Ireland[2] records the "universal applause" that greeted it. It is conceivable that the rapid interchange of persons and scenes may have gone much better on the stage than in reading, and the central situation, that of a New Yorker who disguises himself as a rural Yankee in order to win the hand of a

---

[1] See Int. to *Catalogue of Harris Collection of American Poetry*, pp. xiii–xiv.
[2] I, 93.

West Indian heiress, has a certain amount of originality. Robinson may have been in the West Indies, but he shared the popular delusion that Creoles were half-breeds, and the part he played himself, Banana, is one of the strangest human beings that any stage has seen. He is to be married to Louisa Fingercash by parental stress, but both revolt and he returns contentedly to his mulatto, Priscilla. The play has, therefore, some significance as introducing negro characters for the first time on the American stage, though the negroes are not, of course, native to the United States.

A much more clever farce and one that has a special interest in our theatrical history was *All in a Bustle, or the New House*, written by William Milns for the opening on January 29, 1798,[1] of the Park Theatre, so long to be the leading theatre in New York. It was repeated at the re-opening of the Federal Street Theatre in Boston, October 29, 1798. The farce is very amusing. It describes the difficulties under which John Hodgkinson labored as stage manager of the new theatre. The jealousy of the actresses as to their dressing rooms is well portrayed, and there is a black wench who, in the intervals of waiting on them, falls on the scenery and wipes it up with her head. Dunlap, Hodgkinson, and Jingle, a poet, are among the characters, and while these and other parts were played by certain of the company, other members represented themselves, a rather startling mixture of types. The following lines are of special interest, in view of the dispute as to Dunlap's authorship of *The Man of Fortitude*. Jingle, the poet, who insists upon reading his plays to the manager while the latter is distracted by the difficulties of preparing for his opening, is asked to leave his plays at the manager's house:

Jingle: Leave them at your house!
> *(stares at him)*
Manag.: Yes, in Fair Street.
Jingle: You wrote *The Launch*, Sir, didn't you?

---

[1] It may have been performed, in a very different form, in London in 1789, but the first American production was given as indicated.

Manag.: I did!
Jingle: And you wrote *The Man of Fortitude?*
Manag.: Yes.
Jingle: And I suppose, after you have detained my plays a month
or two, you would be writing again?

Milns or Milne, as he is variously designated, was, according to Dunlap, an Englishman. Of his other farces, one, *The Comet*, which was performed on February 1, 1797, at the John Street Theatre, in New York, and published in 1817, had previously been played in London. Others, like *A Flash in the Pan*, acted in 1798, have perished. *The Comet*, laid in England, is of nothing like the interest of *All in a Bustle*, but it was frequently performed.

Another early example of this species is *The Man of the Times, or a Scarcity of Cash, a Farce*, written by John Beete, the comedian of the Church Street or City Theatre in Charleston, printed in 1797, and evidently played before publication. Little is known of the author who had been a member of the Philadelphia Company in 1795-6, but the farce expresses a native point of view. It is laid in Philadelphia and satirizes the money lender of the period in Mr. Screwpenny, played by Beete himself. Screwpenny buys property, gives his note in payment, and then employs an agent, Grub, to circulate rumors of his failure, in order that the notes may be bought in cheaply. He is foiled through the action of his son, who overhears Grub's conversation and repudiates the suspicion of his father's bankruptcy, to the disgust of the elder Screwpenny.

Perhaps the most industrious writer of farces was John Minshull, of New York, who claims on the title page of his *Merry Dames, or . . . the Poet in Petticoats* (1804), that it was acted at "the New York Theatre." His plays were indeed produced at the Summer Theatre in Bedlow Street in 1805. But neither this rambling and suggestive play nor his other published works, *Rural Felicity* (1801), *The Sprightly Widow* (1803), or *He Stoops to Conquer* (1804), need detain us, though

[1] Odell, I, 429.

their exclusion from the stage of the Park Theatre raised the deep ire of their author.

The college drama continued to be written in this period. Among its most interesting specimens is *The French Revolution*, played by Dartmouth students in 1790, and also by a company, probably of amateurs, at Windsor, Vermont, in 1791. The Revolution is pictured at its beginning, Louis XVI is represented, and also Lafayette, who is inspiring the Revolution. The love story of Leontine and Matilda which constitutes the main plot is not so interesting as is the quick representation of contemporary foreign scenes upon the college stage. The Epilogue at Windsor contains a criticism of the play for violating the unities. There is much more dramatic construction in this drama than in *The Suicide*, which was exhibited at the Yale Commencement, September 13, 1797. This is a moral argument against suicide. Alphonso Bellamy, acted by the author, Thomas Day, of the class of 1797, tries to kill himself because he has been disowned by his father, but he is restored to a healthier state by a friend.

These college dramas are only another indication of the unquenchable interest in the dramatic form which, indeed, is established by the very existence of the plays recorded in this period. In 1805, when Dunlap retired for the first time from the management of the Park Theatre, he and his fellow playwrights had at least laid the foundations of a national drama. It was, of course, as yet spasmodic, for British plays were easily obtainable and managers were prompted often by personal friendship when they produced the plays chronicled in this chapter.

Theatrical conditions were becoming more definitely settled in Philadelphia, where the management of Warren and Wood succeeded to Wignell on the latter's death. The theatres in Baltimore and Washington were controlled by the Philadelphia management, which except for occasional performances at the old Southwark Theatre, was to have a monopoly in Philadelphia until the advent of the Olympic or Walnut Street

Theatre.   This was built as a circus in 1809 but began to offer legitimate plays in 1811.   It is now the oldest play-house in the United States.   The Boston Theatre was prosperous under Powell's management, during the early years of the century, and for a time the Charleston Theatre was successful.   Green had returned to Virginia and was directing the theatres there. As we shall see later, theatrical prosperity does not necessarily run parallel to dramatic achievement.   But for the encouragement of any drama, settled theatrical conditions must obtain, and while this was not the case in New York City, it was more often the situation elsewhere.   Even in New York better times were coming, and the next period saw the results of the foundations in these early and tentative days.

NOTE TO SECOND EDITION.   The cession of New Orleans to the United States was celebrated by James Workman's *Liberty in Louisiana,* produced first at the Charleston Theatre, April 4, 1804 and repeated in New York in May and in Philadelphia in July.   The comedy, which borders at times on farce, begins on the day before the Americans arrive.   It is conducted through two adventurers, of whom the chief, Phelim O'Flinn, was acted successfully by Hodgkinson, according to a criticism found in the second edition, at the Huntington Library.   The judge, Don Bertoldo de la Plata, who decides cases hurriedly before the American occupation, on the basis of the bribes, and who is being deceived by his wife, was also a stage success. After many intrigues, the American Governor arrives and judges the affairs according to the rules of stage law, concluding with a long speech on liberty.

CHAPTER VI

1805–1825

DURING the twenty years that elapsed from Dunlap's retirement in 1805 to the end of the first quarter century, two figures stand out prominently in our drama, and represent in a striking way the influences of native and foreign inspiration. James Nelson Barker and John Howard Payne stand for these two opposite forces, and around them may be grouped the writers of less significance who contributed to the development of the types the two leaders represented.

Barker's work is significant in terms of its quality rather than its quantity. He wrote only ten plays and of these but five have survived in print. But his last play is so much better than his first as to be almost of a different species and, despite the distraction of public duties, he showed a sense of dramatic values and a gift of expression in verse which cause us to wonder what the result might have been if he had devoted himself, under more favorable circumstances, to the drama as a profession. His energies were turned, however, largely in other directions. He was born June 17, 1784, in Philadelphia, the son of General John Barker, who was Mayor of Philadelphia in 1808 and 1809. General Barker was a strong Democrat, and his son followed his father's career both in politics and in war. In the second war with Great Britain he became a captain in the Second Artillery Regiment and performed gallant service on the Canadian Border.[1] At the end of the war Barker was appointed Deputy Adjutant General of the United

---

[1] See "Journal of Major Isaac Roach, 1812-1824," in *Pennsylvania Magazine of History and Biography*, XVII (1893), pp. 131-143.

States with the rank of Major. He became Mayor of Philadelphia in 1819 and was Collector of the Port in Philadelphia from 1829 to 1838, when he was appointed by Van Buren First Comptroller of the Treasury. With a slight intermission he was connected with the Treasury Department until his death, March 9, 1858.

Barker's choice of American themes was not accidental nor was it parochial. He knew other literatures and he made use of them, but he felt keenly the lack of a native drama and he did his best to fill the lack. Fortunately, we have in his own words, written at the request of Dunlap and published in the latter's *History*, an account of his dramatic career. He began with a play based on Cervantes, which he called *The Spanish Rover*, in 1804, but he afterwards burned this. In 1805 he wrote a masque, *America*, "a brief, one-act piece, consisting of poetic dialogue, and sung by the genius of America, Science, Liberty, and attendant Spirits, after the manner of the mask in the Tempest." This was not performed. After beginning a tragedy on the subject of Attila, he wrote his first play to be acted, *Tears and Smiles*, composed between May 1 and June 12, 1806. It was suggested by Warren, the manager, at a dinner at which Dunlap and Jefferson were present, and Jefferson asked that a Yankee character be put in for him. *Tears and Smiles* was put on with the full strength of the company at the Chestnut Street Theatre, which included Warren, Wood, and Jefferson and Mrs. Melmoth, Mrs. Wood, and Mrs. Jefferson. It was first acted March 4, 1807, to a "brilliant audience and with complete success," according to the author's own account. He then proceeds to describe the attempt on the part of certain political enemies on the second night to interrupt the actors by impertinent remarks from one of the stage boxes, and his own visit to the box to expostulate successfully with the offenders.

Tears and Smiles is a comedy of manners, laid in Philadelphia at the time of writing. It is evidently based on *The Contrast*, for Sydney Osbert returns from naval triumphs over the Mediterranean pirates to win Louisa Campdon's hand from Fluttermore, a fop. It is interesting that Fluttermore in 1807 is an imitator of French fashions and interlards his conversation with Gallicisms, while Dimple in 1787 was a disciple of Chesterfield. Nathan Yank hands on *The Contrast* tradition also, and Jefferson seems to have made the part a stage success. Read to-day, the best parts seem to be those of Rangely, Yank's master, a likeable if inconstant gentleman, and the Widow Freegrace, who frankly goes after Rangely and gets him. The sentimental and moral portions are not so well done as the comedy elements, but the play showed Barker's ability, and he was sufficiently encouraged by its reception to try again. His prefaces to the published versions of *Tears and Smiles* and *The Indian Princess* in 1808 show how keenly an American dramatist felt the attitude of that part of the public which "can never pardon the endeavor to depict our national peculiarities, and yet will listen with avidity to Yorkshire rusticity or New Market slang."

Blissett, one of the comedians of the Philadelphia Company, suggested to Barker a play on the Embargo Bills of December 22, 1807, and February 19, 1808, which forbade American vessels to engage in foreign trade. Barker, being a supporter of the administration, wrote a play which expressed the national resentment at the British and French encroachments upon our commerce, which had made the Embargo Bills necessary. *The Embargo, or What News?* was produced at the Chestnut Street Theatre on March 16, 1808, and though it met with some opposition from the mercantile classes, it was generally well received. Barker says: "I know not what became of the manuscript: Blissett took the piece to Baltimore, where it was performed, and whence it was sent, at the request of Bernard, to Boston. It was never printed." Incidentally, this transfer of plays between managers reveals an interesting phase of the theatrical relations of the time.

The next play that has come down to us, *The Indian Princess, or la Belle Sauvage*, performed for the first time on April

6, 1808, at the Chestnut Street Theatre, is the first surviving play on a theme that became very popular, the romance of Pocahontas. It was also the first Indian play by an American to be performed, since *Ponteach* (1766) never saw the stage. Barker at first planned the play as a regular drama, but at the request of the composer Bray, he wrote songs, and the result was what the authors called "an operatic melo-drame," possibly on account of the popularity of the French *mélodrame*, which it does not resemble to any marked degree. At its first performance almost a riot occurred on account of the opposition to Webster, the singer who was playing Larry the Irishman, and finally the curtain had to be rung down.[1] It had its first New York performance at the Park Theatre, June 14, 1809, and was played, according to the author, in all the theatres in the United States. On December 15, 1820, it was produced at Drury Lane, London, under the title of *Pocahontas, or the Indian Princess*. It was much changed, the British adaptor omitting the comic parts and changing some of the names. Barker doubted that the play bore any relation to his own, but Genest[2] states positively that it was Barker's *Indian Princess*, and evidently had the printed play before him when he made the comparison between the American and British versions. This seems to be the first well authenticated instance of an original American play being produced in London after an initial performance in America.

Barker found his materials, as he tells us himself, in John Smith's *General History of Virginia*, 1624. He took liberties, of course, with history, but he succeeded in producing an entertaining play, with a romantic atmosphere. There are five pairs of lovers, of whom Rolfe and Pocahontas are the chief, and while all the characters are types, they are sufficiently characterized to be individuals as well. Realizing that the most theatrical episode, the saving of Smith by Pocahontas

---

[1] See Barker's account—Dunlap, *History*, II, 313, and Durang, *Philadelphia Stage*, 1st Series, Chap. 41.
[2] IX, 83-4.

comes too early to be the climax if a dramatist is to be faithful
to chronology, Barker makes the love interest the main theme
and unites it with the salvation of the English, through Pocahontas's warning, by having her lead Lord Delaware to the
rescue of Smith and Rolfe at Powhatan's banquet.

The Indians, except Pocahontas, are conventional, and
their language is only a fair attempt to reproduce their rhythmic
utterance. When Pocahontas falls in love she begins to speak
blank verse, but this may be pardoned in Barker, for it gives
him an opportunity to write a love scene between Rolfe and
Pocahontas in Act III, Sc. 2, in which the truest poetry in the
play occurs. Barker understood that what an audience wants
is human nature, not archæology, and Pocahontas reveals her
love simply and tenderly in a flexible verse, in which her
creator was certainly then excelled by none in his native
country and by few, if any, of those who were writing at that
time for the stage in England.

Early in 1812, at the request of Wood, the Philadelphia
manager, Barker dramatized Scott's *Marmion*. *Marmion* was
first played on April 13, 1812, at the Park Theatre, New York,
with Cooper in the title rôle. The play was announced as by
Thomas Morton, the British playwright, as it was feared that
a work by a native author would not be appreciated. According to Ireland[1] it "commanded an extraordinary success," and
when it was brought out in Philadelphia on January 1, 1813,
at the Chestnut Street Theatre, it played to receipts of $1414.00,
about three times the usual amount. Duff played Marmion.
Wood in his *Personal Recollections of the Stage*[2] gives the following interesting account:

The merit of the piece was positive but the old difficulty remained.
I knew the then prejudice against any native play, and concocted
with Cooper a very innocent fraud upon the public. We insinuated
that the piece was a London one, had it sent to our theatre from
New York, where it was made to arrive in the midst of rehearsal, in

[1] I, 283. See also Odell, II, 383-384.
[2] P. 188.

the presence of the actors, packed up exactly *like pieces we were in the habit of receiving from London. It was opened with great gravity, and announced without any author being alluded to.* None of the company were in the secret, as I well knew "these actors cannot keep counsel," not even the prompter. It was played with great success for six or seven nights, when, believing it safe, I announced the author, and from that moment *it ceased to attract.*

This story has become one of the stock anecdotes of the stage, but the most significant portion of it is not true. In Wood's own manuscript diary, now in the Library of the University of Pennsylvania, the receipts of *Marmion* are given as follows:

Jan. 1, 1813, $1414.75; Jan. 2, $357.25; Jan. 3, $483.00; Jan. 11, $578; Jan. 18, $845 (Wood's benefit); Feb. 5, $332; Feb. 15, $466.

If Wood announced the author after "six or seven nights" the play could not have "ceased to attract," for it was not put on after the seventh performance for some time, and it then proved very popular. It was the only play put on for three consecutive nights that season (1812-13), and it led all other plays in popularity at the Baltimore season in the fall of 1813. In 1814, on the occasion of Barker's own benefit, the receipts were $948.00. Durang says "it lost none of its interest after the mask was removed," and the moral of the affair is clearly that there was a lack of courage on the part of the managers who believed that it was necessary to introduce a play as by a British author. *Marmion* held the stage for many years. James Wallack acted in it in 1819; it was played at the Chestnut Street Theatre in 1826 with Duff again as Marmion, and was performed as late as February 26, 1848, at the new Bowery Theatre in New York.[1] It was printed in 1816 and reprinted in 1826.

Marmion fully deserved its popularity. It was no slavish imitation of Scott's poem, and indeed Barker went back to the Chronicles of Holinshed[2] to gain "certain facts and char-

---

[1] See P. H. Musser, *James Nelson Barker*, Phila., 1929, pp. 45-56, for a list of performances and additional analysis of *Marmion*.

[2] Holinshed's *Chronicles of England, Scotland and Ireland.* Reign of James IV, pp. 460-483.

acters"[1] which add greatly to the vigor of the play. But the ability of Barker shows, first, in the way he rearranged or altered the episodes of the story. He saw that the relations of Constance and Marmion were essentially the most dramatic of the themes woven together by Scott, and he introduces us at once to a striking scene, not in Scott's poem, in which Marmion bids farewell to Constance and in which, in verse of fine quality, she fights for her losing cause. For the second Act he selects the dramatic contest between Marmion and the supposed supernatural appearance of DeWilton. For the third, he takes the condemnation scene at St. Cuthbert's Abbey, and while he makes use of Scott's language in a few lines, the best of the verses are Barker's own.

Barker rose to his greatest heights in *Marmion* in Act IV, Sc. 4, which is laid at the banquet over which King James IV of Scotland presides and to which Marmion comes as an ambassador from Henry VIII. Here Barker left Scott, and although he received some help from Holinshed, never of a verbal nature, it is in the light of the situation then obtaining in the United States that the verses to be quoted must be read. In April, 1812, our relations with Great Britain were at the breaking point, and Congress was debating the question of war. Henry Clay was Speaker of the House, and was leading the Democratic party in the direction of vigorous measures, while the Federalists were equally determined to block any move against England. Barker's utterances, therefore, became in a sense an expression of the intense national resentment against the imprisonment of our seamen, the Orders in Council, and the insolence and studied neglect of our remonstrances on the part of the British Government. He placed the words in the mouth of King James, of Scotland, but everyone knew their application.[2]

[1] Preface to Ed. of 1816, p. 3.
[2] See Barker's own statement of historical facts upon which he based the speech, in the Preface to *Marmion* (1816) p. v. The Preface is an energetic appeal for literary independence, voicing ideas which afterward gained wider publicity through Emerson and Lowell.

"James: My lord, the first base step
    Is ne'er the last! the foot that fear but moves,
    Fear still impels. Do you not ask us here
    To throw our armour off, and cower at home,
    Patient, till England find a time to treat?
Marmion: Till Henry come from France.
James: Why went he thither
    But to wage unjust war?
Marmion: Your highness' pardon,
    He went to quell the general enemy,
    Of you, and all.
James: The general enemy!
    Spare me, my lord, the stale, distasteful tale,
    I know it all. The nation the most selfish,
    Presuming, arrogant, of all this globe,
    Professes but to fight for others' rights,
    While she alone infringes every right.
Marmion: I knew before, your majesty was partial
    To those you most mistakenly conceive
    To be your friends and allies.
James: Soul of Bruce!
    Were they not then our allies, when your king
    Sought to enslave us? who of all the world
    Came at our need, but they? by heaven, Lord Marmion,
    England insults us with the trite complaint
    That we are partial; for she shows by this,
    She thinks our senses are too dull and blunt
    To know who wounds us and who gives the balm.
    But let that rest; my country's bloody page
    I will not quote. Its former friend and foe
    Be now forgot; we urge our present griefs.
Marmion: All that you can, with justice, ask of England,
    Henry will grant. But he requires your pause
    Till he return from waging foreign war.
James: Yes: till, like Edward, the flushed conqueror come,
    To bid our blazing cities warm our hurts
    To fresher anguish. 'Twas for this, my lord,
    When on the border our commissions met,
    Each day blushed on some new and poor evasion
    Of your commissioners—who strove at last
    To cloak their shame in rude display of passion,
    As cowards hide their fears with blustering.

Marmion: The subject may have been most intricate,
Your claims involved in doubt.

James: Not so—not so—
Simple as truth they were, clear as the sun.
But what did England during this our parley?
While thus negociating, what did England?
When, trusting in your faith, resentment slept,
And patience stayed your tardy reparation
Of wrongs so long inflicted? It was then—
Even in days of truce! I burn to speak it—
Murder and pillage, England's constant agents,
Roamed through our land, and harboured in our bays!
Our peaceful border sacked, our vessels plundered,
Our abused liegemen robbed, enslaved and slaughtered.
My lord, my lord, under such injuries,
How shall a free and gallant nation act?
Still lay its sovereignty at England's feet—
Still basely ask a boon from England's bounty—
Still vainly hope redress from England's justice?
No! by our martyred fathers' memories,
The land may sink—but, like a glorious wreck,
'Twill keep its colours flying to the last."

Between the time of the New York performances in April,
1812, and January 1, 1813, when the play opened in Philadelphia, much had happened. Madison had proclaimed a state of
war on June 9, 1812, and Barker had gone to the Canadian
border as Captain in the Second Artillery Regiment. According to Durang[1] it must have been a memorable night at the
Chestnut Street Theatre, for when King James finished his
speech, General Barker, the author's father, rose in his box
and waving his cane, led the applause that rocked the theatre.

A play that has not survived, *The Armourer's Escape, or
Three Years at Nootka Sound*, a melodrama in two acts, was
written by Barker for John Jewitt, armorer of the ship *Boston*,
who acted the hero himself. It was first performed March 21,
1817,[2] and according to Wood, much curiosity and some interest

[1] First Series, chap. 51.
[2] Barker states that the play was first performed March 24, but Wood's Diary
shows performances on March 21, 22, and 24 and the playbill at the Pennsylvania
Historical Society gives March 21st.

were excited by such a unique exhibition. The dispute with
England concerning the Northwest Boundary was still unset-
tled and the presence on the stage of one of the intrepid adventurers who had seized and held the outposts of Oregon for
the United States, was an event of real importance.

The playbill is a complete scenario, and reveals almost unlim-
ited possibility of entertainment. The principal characters,
beside the "Armourer," were his companions in captivity,
Thompson, acted by the first Joseph Jefferson; Maquina, the
Chief of the Nootka Indians, by Barrett; Tyee, the Prince,
by "Master J.[ohn] Jefferson;" Machee Utilla, King of the
Klaissats, another Indian tribe, by Thomas Jefferson; Arcomah,
by Mrs. Jefferson, and Yuqua by Mrs. Harris. The scenes
proceed through the treachery of Maquina, the destruction of
the crew, the salvation of Jewitt and Thompson by the Klaissats, and the arrival of the American brig to take them away.
But the most interesting part must have been the representation of the manners and customs of the Nootka Indians.
In Act I, Sc. 4 and Sc. 5, the King, his chiefs and women were
assembled, the funeral ceremonies over the body of a chief
were conducted, the ship was set on fire, an eclipse of the moon
took place, and an attack by the Aychats! In the second Act,
the Nootka Indians paraded in the costumes of the captured
crew, then entered "a Procession of Klaissats, headed by
Machee Utilla, followed by Wykinnish, Esquates, Attizarts,
Cayuquits, and other tribes." It would be illuminating if we
could be told just how the stage manager of the Philadelphia
Theatre differentiated between these tribes! Then followed
the "ludicrous ceremonies of the Bear," then a war dance and
the armorer was compelled to choose a wife—the choice falling on the Princess Yuqua. Next came a dance of young Noot-
kian girls and the chiefs entered masked with heads of animals
to carry them off. The girls were rescued and a general dance
ensued.

In the same year, 1817, Barker wrote one of his best constructed plays, *How to Try a Lover*. On the title page of the

play, published in 1817, the words "as performed at the Philadelphia Theatre" are found, and a cast is given, but Barker
states in his account of his career that the drama "was cast,
studied, rehearsed, and announced; and why it was not acted,
I am unable to say, as it was the only drama I have written,
with which I was satisfied." The play was performed, however,
as *The Court of Love*, March 26, 1836, at the Arch Street
Theatre, in Philadelphia. It is a quickly moving comedy, based
on *La Folie Espagnole*, a novel by Pigault-Lebrun, and laid in
the Spanish province of Catalonia in the thirteenth century.
Carlos, an attractive lover, and his squire, Pacomo, for which
part Jefferson was cast and who is a delightful creation, are
wandering about searching for Eugenia, with whom Carlos has
fallen in love at first sight—his usual practice. Their respective
fathers, Count Almeyda and Count Arandez, concoct a scheme
to bring them together through apparent difficulties, on the
assumption that their love will be stronger if it is opposed.
Carlos and Pacoma gain entrance to the castle vaults, and an
amusing scene follows, at the end of which they are arrested
for trespass and are tried before the Court of Love, an institution of chivalry whose code and laws are used cleverly in the
play. Eugenia presides over the court, and gives her father
and father-in-law elect a bad quarter of an hour in revenge for
their deception, before she awards her hand to Carlos. It is
all fooling, of course, but it is delightful fooling, and the
dialogue is crisp and flies back and forth with the directness
that Barker always possessed. Without change, it could be
placed on the stage to-day, for its humor is of a universal
quality. After Tyler's *Island of Barrataria*, it is also the first
significant example that has survived of that interest in Spanish
themes for stage treatment, which was to become so frequent
in the next period.

Barker took his plot, characters, and even some of the dialogue from his French source, which had been published in four
volumes from 1799 to 1801. It is a picaresque novel, and
Barker has selected with fine dramatic discrimination enough

incidents from the fourth volume to frame out of the loosely constructed romance a unified play. The characters are changed in name and to some extent in nature, especially the squire, Pacomo, whose development out of the utter rascal, Trufaldin, is a proof of Barker's talent. Skillful, too, is his rearrangement of incidents, so as to center our attention on the progress of the charming love affair between Carlos and Eugenia, and his elimination of Lebrun's wanderings among the purlieus of Trufaldin's amours.

With his last and greatest play Barker returned to his native country for a theme, and he found one in Colonial history in 1675. Five years before Cooper used the motive of the regicides of Charles I in *The Wept of Wish-ton-Wish* and eleven years before Hawthorne published *The Gray Champion*, Barker had placed on the stage the dramatic story of the Puritan refugee Goff, issuing from his solitude to lead the villagers to victory against the Indians. With this theme he interwove that of the intolerance of the New England Puritans and their persecution for witchcraft.

Superstition was first acted at the Chestnut Street Theatre, March 12, 1824. Wood says it was received "with deserved applause," and it seems strange that it was not more often performed. F. C. Wemyss, who acted George Egerton in the play, offers an interesting explanation in his *Twenty-six Years of the Life of an Actor and Manager*,[1] when he states that Wood did not put the play on more frequently because Mrs. Duff in the character of Mary outshone Mrs. Wood as Isabella. Truly, "the manager's wife" has had a potent influence in the records of our stage. Wemyss adds, "I have been surprised that no manager ever rescued so good a play from oblivion." The play was printed in Lopez and Wemyss's *Acting American Theatre* in 1826.

Barker states that he took the principal incidents from actual happenings, and surely he has marshaled his facts in such a manner that they present the form of truth. Ravensworth, the

[1] I, 88.

clergyman of the village, is determined to effect the ruin of Isabella and her son Charles Fitzroy, who have offended him by their disregard of his clerical office. They have come recently from England, and Charles has dared to love Mary, Ravensworth's daughter. Charles is returning to the village from college and meets The Unknown, who has sought refuge from the vengeance which Charles II meted out to the judges of Charles I. The Unknown is really Isabella's father and therefore Charles's grandfather, and their meeting is arranged with skill to create an interest in each other without the relationship being discovered. Sir Reginald Egerton and his nephew George have been sent by Charles II on a mission to find the regicide. George attempts to force his attentions on Mary, and Charles rescues her; the result is a duel in which George is wounded. On their return to the village they find the Indians are attacking the place, and at first the colonists fight in vain. Then the regicide appears in their midst, and with the help of Charles and others wins a victory in a scene that must have been effective of its kind. But Charles's valor is immediately turned against him by Ravenworth, for his immunity from wounds and his apparent acquaintance with The Unknown, supposed to be supernatural, are brought forward as evidence of his commerce with the Evil One.

Isabella urges Charles to fly with her, and in a scene that is pathetic through its reserved strength, reveals to him her secret marriage and the cause of her flight with him from England. They are summoned to appear before a commission, on the charge of sorcery. Charles has sought and obtained an interview with Mary in her own room, where he is found by her father and others looking for him to bring him to the court room. Only those who are familiar with similar scenes in the British and American plays of the time, where suggestive language expresses the seduction motive in a hundred ways, can appreciate the reticence and yet the passion of this one love scene of the play, with the shadow of impending tragedy over it. The last scene presents the trial of Isabella and Charles for sorcery. Ravensworth deals at first with generalities of prejudice and superstition. The law which forbade counsel to the defendant places upon Isabella the dramatic duty of self-defense and in a noble speech which certainly gave Mrs. Wood an ample opportunity, she refutes Ravensworth.

> "*Isab.*:   I beseech you
> Let him proceed; let him endeavor still,
> To excite the passions of his auditors;
> It will but shew how weak he deems his proof
> Who lays such stress on prejudice. I fear not,
> But I can answer all his accusations.
> If I intended flight—need I remind you
> Of what your fathers—what yourselves have done.
> It was not conscious guilt bade them or you
> Escape from that, was felt was persecution—
> If I have thought the manner of my worship
> A matter between Heaven and my conscience,
> How can ye blame me, who in caves and rocks
> Shunning the church, offer'd your secret prayers?
> Or does my state offend? Habit and taste
> May make some difference, and humble things
> Seem great to those more humble; yet I have used
> My little wealth in benefits. Your saints
> Climb'd to high places—Cromwell to the highest—
> As the sun seeks the eminence from which
> He can diffuse his beams most bounteously.
> *Raves.*: The subtle power she serves does not withhold
> The aid of sophistry.
> *Isab.*: I pray my judges
> To shield me from the malice of this man,
> And bring me to the trial. I will meet it,
> As it concerns myself with firm indifference;
> But as it touches him whom I exist in,
> With hope that my acquittal shall dissolve
> The fetters of my son."

Ravensworth adroitly shifts his ground to the charge against her son and accuses him of the murder of George Egerton, of attempted rape upon Mary, and of dealing with the devil in the person of The Unknown. Charles, to save Mary from the

distress of being questioned, refuses to plead, and thus condemns himself; for Ravensworth, taking advantage of his
silence and the storm which breaks forth, so works upon the
superstitious fears of the assemblage that he hurries them into
instant execution of Charles, off the stage. Charles is brought
back just as Mary who has broken from her father's grasp
begins to plead for him.

> "*Mary: (Reviving)* Nay, ye shall not detain me—I will go,
> And tell them all. Before, I could not speak—
> My father held me here fast by the throat.
> Why will you hold me? they will murder him,
> Unless I speak for him. He spoke for me—
> He sav'd my honour; Ah! what's here? O Heaven!
> 'Tis he. Is he asleep? No, it is not he.
> I'd think 'twere he, but that his eyes are swoll'n
> Out of their sockets—and his face is black
> With settled blood. It is a murder'd man
> You've brought me to—and not my Charles—my Charles!
> He was so young and lovely. Soft, soft, soft!
> Now I remember. They have made you look so,
> To fright me from your love. It will not do—
> I know you well enough—I know those lips
> Tho' I have never touch'd them. There, love, there,
> It is our nuptial kiss. They shall not cheat us—
> Hark in thine ear, how we will laugh at them.
> (*Leans her head down on the body, as if whispering.*)
> *Sir R.:* Alas! poor maniac."

Sir Reginald enters with a message which reveals Charles as
the King's son and also a pardon for the regicide, who
arrives in time to close his daughter's eyes. Barker explains
that the incident of Charles's speedy execution was based on
actual fact, but anyone who has searched the records of the
witchcraft persecutions will not worry about its probability.
For the tragedy is one of the few in which the catastrophe is
really inevitable. Barker's skill is shown by the way in which
the complicated threads are all woven together naturally, and
in which every honorable impulse, every brave action of
Charles, conspires against him. The sense of impending doom

is apparent almost from the beginning, and we witness one of the most cruel of situations, that in which human beings struggle against an evil fate wrought out of the bitter prejudices of their own kind. Barker closed his dramatic career fittingly with the best play that had so far been written in America.

As a representative of the play with a national and historical interest, probably the most important playwright of this period next to Barker was Mordecai Manuel Noah, who was born in Philadelphia, July 19, 1785, and died in New York City, March 22, 1851. We have his own statement of his career, given in Dunlap's *History*, and to his credit he declines to take his dramatic powers more seriously than his performance warrants. He was engaged in political offices of various kinds, and his life was spent in different cities of the Union. It is entertaining to read of his early efforts with a group of amateur comedians at the old Southwark Theatre in Philadelphia. Interesting, too, was his acquisition of a dramatic library by the original process of exchanging the manuscript of his first play, *The Fortress of Sorrento*, with David Longworth, the New York publisher, for a copy of every play he had published. *The Fortress of Sorrento* (1808), a romantic play based on Bouilly's libretto of the French opera of *Léonore*, was not acted. His first acted play, *Paul and Alexis, or the Orphans of the Rhine*, written in Charleston, 1812, was also on a foreign theme, and will be treated later.

Having engaged in journalism in New York, he wrote for Miss Leesugg, afterward Mrs. Hackett, *She Would be a Soldier, or the Plains of Chippewa*, which was first played at the Park Theatre, June 21, 1819.[1] It is based on the battle of Chippewa, July 5, 1814, at which the American army under General Jacob Brown and General Winfield Scott redeemed the earlier defeats of the Canadian campaign. Christine, played by Miss

---

[1] Title page, edition of 1819. I am unable to find any supporting evidence for the statement in Wegelin's Bibliography, p. 75, that the play was first performed in Philadelphia in 1813. The first Philadelphia performance occurred on December 24, 1819.

Leesugg, leaves her home to avoid a distasteful marriage with a farmer, Jerry, and in male disguise reaches the American camp to find her lover, Lenox, apparently unfaithful to her. She enlists as a soldier and is arrested as a spy while trying to enter the commanding officer's tent to see her lover. Refusing to give any explanation, she is condemned as a spy, but is saved, of course, at the end of the play by Lenox. The battle of Chippewa is described in a remarkable scene in which Lenox calmly narrates to General Brown the operations which he had himself directed! The account of the battle is fairly correct according to historical records, and Noah makes concrete the scorn felt by the army for the militia which had stood idly on the American side and let their comrades fall at Queenstown. The play is below Barker's from the point of view of construction and literary merit, but it moves quickly and it held the stage for many years, being played as late as July 8, 1848, at the Broadway Theatre.[1]

Marion, or the Hero of Lake George, written also for the Park Theatre Company, who performed it on November 25, 1821, is a drama of the Revolution, with a background of the Battle of Saratoga. There is much the same kind of plot as in *She Would be a Soldier*, except that the interest centers upon Marion, a patriotic leader, who is in constant peril from the time the play opens, and whose hairbreadth escapes must have excited an interest similar to that now aroused by the moving pictures. His wife dons male attire to save him from prison, and the surrender of Burgoyne solves a rather difficult situation for all concerned. The play is more direct than its predecessor and was popular for ten years on the New York, Philadelphia, and Boston stages.

The Grecian Captive, or the Fall of Athens (1822), although based upon a foreign theme, was prompted by sympathy on

---

[1] Ireland, II, 500. It is significant that Wood's Diary, for 1819-20, shows that after playing the older English favorites like *Fazio* and *The School for Scandal*, and even Shakespeare to houses averaging $200 to $300, the receipts for Noah's play jumped, on a rainy night, to $435, and, the next day, being fine, to $811.50. The Diary proves conclusively that there was no avoidance of native plays on the part of the public.

the part of an American for a country fighting for its independence. As Noah says in the preface: "If eventually the Greeks should not recover Athens, it will not be my fault; it was necessary to my play and so I gave them possession of that interesting spot with a dash of my pen." As a matter of fact, the characters from Ali Pacha down are as much like Americans as they are like Greeks or Turks.

Another play by Noah that was prompted by national feeling was *The Siege of Tripoli*, which has not been preserved. It was first played at the Park Theatre, May 15, 1820, and was apparently very successful. On the third representation, May 25th, which was the author's benefit night, the house which had been "crowded with beauty and fashion" had hardly been emptied before a disastrous fire laid the Park Theatre in ruins. It is pleasant to record that the dramatist devoted his entire profits, four hundred dollars, to the benefit of the distressed members of the company. The play was repeated in Philadelphia on January 25, 1822, with new scenery and with success, under the title of *Yuseff Caramalli*.

Noah was not the only playwright to follow Mrs. Rowson's example in dramatizing the difficulties with the Mediterranean pirates.[1] James Ellison wrote for the company at the Boston Theatre in 1811 a play, *The American Captive, or the Siege of Tripoli*, which has some merit. It is based on the capture of Americans and their treatment by the Bashaw, together with the interest which Anderson, the chief American, excites in Immorina, daughter of Ali-ben-Mahadi, the ex-Bashaw. This play was revised in 1841 by J. S. Jones. This motive may be seen in its most exaggerated form in *The Siege of Algiers, or the Downfall of Hadgi-Ali-Bashaw, a Political, Historical and Sentimental Tragi-Comedy*, in five acts, by Jonathan S. Smith of Philadelphia, in which city it was printed in 1823. A Prologue and an Epilogue are given, but there is no other accom-

---

[1] This type of play is combined with the Yankee motive in the *Young Carolinians, or Americans in Algiers*, by M. Pinckney, Charleston, 1818, in which Zeikel and Homespun, two rural New England caricatures, appear.

paniment of the play that indicates stage performance. An interesting feature of the drama is the creation of a symbolic character, Christian Monitor by name, who remains invisible but who "in the shape of conscience, issues his timely monitions" to the other characters, some of whom are quite in need of such assistance.

The contemporary expression of dramatic interest in the War of 1812 is hard to judge, since few of the plays have survived. Before Noah had written *She Would be a Soldier*, C. E. Grice had published *The Battle of New Orleans*, in 1815, acted in New York July 4, 1816, at the Park Theatre.[1] It is a rather stilted play, and the language is a curious mixture of prose and verse. General Jackson appears, of course, in an heroic character. Plays like *The Fair Americans*, by Mary Clarke (1815), with its undercurrent of Federalist criticism of the War, seem not to have been acted, and of the plays dealing with the naval victories we have only the records of performance. It is interesting to read in Durang's *History*[2] that on December 8, 1812, there came news to Philadelphia of the capture of the *Macedonian* by the *United States*, and that on December 11th a patriotic sketch, *The Return from a Cruise*, was performed at the Chestnut Street Theatre, including a part for Captain Decatur. Nearly as prompt was the dramatization of the victory of the *Constitution* over the *Guerrière*. The fight occurred on August 19, 1812. Captain Hull reached Boston on August 30th, and by September 7th Dunlap's *Yankee Chronology* was on the boards in New York. On October 2d, a play commemorating the event was on the stage in Boston. According to Clapp,[3] "in the early days of the theatre, every public event of sufficient importance was immediately dramatized, and during the progress of the war the spirit was kept up by the frequent production of pieces in honor of our naval victories."

[1] This has been attributed to Dunlap, but the cast in Ireland, I, 318 is the same as that given in the 1815 ed. of Grice's play.
[2] First Series, Chap. 49.
[3] *Records of the Boston Stage*, p. 134.

But naval victories are not by their very nature susceptible of theatrical representation in any permanent literary form, and except for the Battles of Chippewa and New Orleans our successes on land were not such as to call for celebration.

It was only natural that the Revolution should be preferred to the War of 1812 as material for dramatic treatment. Dunlap's *André* and Noah's *Marion* have already been mentioned. William Ioor's *Battle of Eutaw Springs* was produced at the Charleston Theatre in 1807, in Richmond in 1811, with Mrs. Poe in the cast, and at the Southwark Theatre[1] in Philadelphia in 1813. It is a chronicle play of patriotic text rather than dramatic effectiveness. The central historical character is General Greene, who is visited at times by the Genius of Liberty, which in Charleston was embodied in the attractive person of Mrs. Young. Captain Laurence Manning is the youthful hero, and the humor is furnished largely by a British soldier, appropriately named Queerfish.

Toward the end of this period, examples of the Revolutionary play began to multiply. Samuel B. H. Judah, more frequently a writer of foreign romance, produced in four days *A Tale of Lexington*, which was played at the Park Theatre on July 4, 1822. Judah tells us in his preface that it was received with unbounded applause and it was repeated in 1823, but it is a formless affair and far inferior to the work of Finn and Woodworth in the same field. Finn's play, *Montgomery, or the Falls of Montmorency*, performed first at the Boston Theatre, February 21, 1825, is an example of the introduction of the national note into a domestic comedy. General Montgomery has little to do with the play, which centers about the successful efforts of Sergeant Welcome Sobersides to save Altamah, a half-breed Indian wife of Chevalier LaValle, from the villain, L'Araignée. Sobersides, acted by Finn himself, is an entertaining stage figure and one of the succession of Yankee characters that

---

[1] When the piece was first performed in Philadelphia, it was put on by an independent company under William Twaits. Actors felt the stress of war conditions keenly and so this group, out of employment elsewhere, sought a refuge in the old playhouse.

form a link between *The Contrast* and our present rural drama. Finn had been born on Cape Breton, knew the Yankee and Canadian characters, and formed from them an entertaining, well moving play.[1] He was for a time a student at Princeton College and was an actor of ability in England and America, until his tragic death by fire on the steamer *Lexington* in Long Island Sound in 1840.

Samuel Woodworth, whose play of *The Widow's Son, or Which is the Traitor?* ranks easily next to *André* as the best of the Revolutionary plays of this period, is one of the most significant of the playwrights of the time. His work is an example of the transition which came over the drama at the end of the quarter century. He was born at Scituate, Massachusetts, January 13, 1785, went to Boston at the beginning of the new century, and while there collaborated with John Howard Payne in the publication of a newspaper. He was a literary man-of-all-work in Baltimore and New York, living in the latter town from 1809 to 1842, the year of his death.

His first play, *The Deed of Gift*, was acted at the Boston Theatre, March 25, 1822, and was repeated at the City Theatre in New York on January 21, 1823. It is a domestic drama, laid in Westchester, New York, with the conventional plot of a disinherited younger brother, a villainous elder, and a skillful sweetheart who, through a series of clever disguises, circumvents the villain. It is of interest that George Barton is disinherited because he has left college to go on the stage. Woodworth's career as a playwright lasted from 1822 to 1833, but his methods were generally those of the older school. Yet his *Forest Rose*, to be mentioned later, was the inspiration of a multitude of plays, and his work illustrates the steady devel-

---

[1] It was revived by James H. Hackett, who on account of the success of *Metamora*, wished to combine the interest of the Indian and the Yankee plays. Under the title of *The Indian Wife*, it was put on at the Park Theatre, June 4, 1830, Mrs. Sharpe playing Altamah. Hackett played Sergeant Peabody, evidently based on Sergeant Sobersides. Ireland (I, 629) is, of course, in error in stating that the play was written for Hackett. It was played under its own title in Philadelphia, February 3, 1831.

opment of our playwriting, in whose history, period marks are milestones rather than boundaries.

The Widow's Son, produced at the Park Theatre, November 25, 1825, is based upon one of those domestic tragedies which colored so darkly the Revolutionary period in New York. The line between Whig and Tory was easily passed and it divided families into elements out of which drama naturally sprang. Woodworth seized upon the story of Margaret Darby, the daughter of a British officer living in the State of New York, who had sunk in the social and economic scales until she had acquired the reputation of a witch. Her eldest son, William, had been accused, perhaps falsely, of being a Tory, and had been driven to revenge himself for persecution by treachery to his adopted country. Through his aid Fort Montgomery was betrayed to Sir Henry Clinton, and Darby was rewarded with a captain's commission in the British Army. Margaret grieved so deeply over her son's treason that she offered her services to Washington as a spy, and so skillful was she that she deceived Clinton into the belief that she was devoted to the royal cause. Woodworth took these facts and combined them with the Arnold-André motive in one of the best conceived and constructed plays of its kind. He invents, very properly, the hero, an American sergeant, Champe, who is sent by General Lee into the British lines to capture Arnold. Through a series of probable accidents Arnold's place is taken by John Darby, Margaret's younger son, who, under his masquerade of Dr. Stramonium, furnishes most of the comedy element. Margaret saves William, who was also marked for capture, by taking his place, and she is content in the knowledge that his death, which saves him from dishonorable execution, has been at the hands of an enemy of his country. The characters are natural—the British are human beings, not villains—and the conversations have an inherent interest which makes them very readable to-day. The play pictures well the bustle and confusion that marked the irregular warfare of that period of the Revolution, and the constant danger in which the characters move keeps the interest of the auditor stimulated by a clever use of the motive of self-preservation.

It was this motive also which formed the basis of Woodworth's *La Fayette, or the Castle of Olmutz*, first performed at the Park Theatre on February 23, 1824. It was inspired by the approaching visit of Lafayette to this country and is an illustration of the national impulse in drama, since the hero, Francis Huger, who together with a young German, Bolman, attempts to rescue Lafayette from his imprisonment, was an American and a real person. In 1792, Lafayette was arrested while in Germany and in 1794, the attempted rescue was made. As in *The Widow's Son*, Woodworth had the dramatic sense to let the love interest, provided by Huger and Ellen, become the principal motive and Lafayette remains in the background, but sufficiently in the picture to be important. The play was repeated several times, and on September 9th it was performed with a great deal of ceremony in honor of Lafayette's actual visit. It was also given in Philadelphia and Baltimore. Although others[1] were written, it is the only significant play on the Lafayette motive, and remains as an interesting example of the dramatization of contemporary events.

Of Woodworth's other plays some are known only by name. *Blue Laws, or Eighty Years Ago*, played for a few nights beginning March 15, 1833, at the Bowery Theatre was a farce which evidently satirized intolerance, and *The Cannibals, or the Massacre Islands*, played in the same place in February, was not very significant. *King's Bridge Cottage*, published in 1826 as being "written by a Gentleman of N. York" has been attributed to him, and there is a certain similarity in the language to Woodworth's style, especially in his references to "that god-like hero," which was his usual manner in describ-

---

[1] *Fayette in Prison, or Misfortunes of the Great*, Worcester, 1800 and 1802, in which there are no American characters, and *La Fayette, or the Fortress of Olmutz*, by Walter Lee, Philadelphia, 1824, are much inferior to Woodworth's play. The extent of the interest may be judged from the publication of *La Fayette en Monte Vernon en 17 de Octobre, 1824. Drama en 2 Actos. Por Felix Megia.* Filadelfia, 1825, in which G W. P. Custis is a character!

ing Washington. But if the play was written by Woodworth, it is the poorest that has survived. It is evidently a hasty bit of writing, dealing with the rescue of a girl by her lover, an officer in the American Army, from the assaults of a British officer, and is laid at the close of the Revolution. The characterization, such as it is, is unlike Woodworth's, for the British officer is pictured as a monster, and it is hard to believe the author of *The Widow's Son* to be guilty of the last scene, in which Captain Richardson receives a special dispatch from Washington, announcing to him, with a finer consideration for the feelings of his junior officer than for the facts of history, both the surrender at Yorktown and the evacuation of New York! This play was first performed by amateurs, but was later produced at the Richmond Hill Theatre, February 22, 1833.

The native comedy without definite historical interest continued the expression of general motives on the model, usually, of British drama. Even before Barker wrote *Tears and Smiles*, Charles Breck (1782-1822), a native of Boston but a citizen of Philadelphia, had written for the company at the Chestnut Street Theatre *The Fox Chase*, performed April 9, 1806.[1] In fact, it was the performance of *The Fox Chase* that caused Manager Warren to suggest to Barker that he write a play for the company. *The Fox Chase* is not as truly a comedy of manners as *Tears and Smiles;* it belongs to the class of comedy-melodrama, in which a prodigal returns and plays the hero. The characters have real life in them and there is a special interest in the humor, which is secured mainly through a character, William Heartwell, in whom is satirized the futility of pseudo-science. In the "animated carriage" that never goes, we may even see the first sketch of the automobile. Fox-hunting appears only as a dim background, but it was, of course, much in evidence near Philadelphia, and not merely

---

[1] Duane's *General Advertiser*, April 9, 1806, advt.; Durang, Series I, Ch. 39; Dunlap II 310. *The Mirror of Taste and Dramatic Censor*, in issue of March 3, 1806, gives an account of the play, but the issue was misdated.

an echo of a British custom. Breck's other play, *The Trust*, was not acted. It is a bit complicated and the characters are not so distinct as those of *The Fox Chase*, but Hebe is a more charming soubrette than is usually present at that time on the stage.

Love and Friendship, or Yankee Notions, a three-act comedy by A. B. Lindsley, was produced during the season of 1807-8 at the Park Theatre, where Lindsley was a member of the company. It brings several Yankee characters to Charleston, South Carolina, among them, Seldreer, a lover, Captain Horner, a sailor, and "Brother Jonathan," his man, an echo of *The Contrast*. The humor, which at times is not bad, is provided by the Yankee character and also by a sailor, Jack Hardweather, a negro servant, Harry, and a college fop, Dick Dashaway, probably the first American college type to be satirized on the stage.

The gradation from comedy of this type to farce is easy. *Beaux Without Belles, or Ladies We Can Do Without You*, by David Darling, was produced at the Fredericksburg Theatre and published at Charlottesville in 1820. It is an amusing farce in which the characters are all men, although two of them are at times disguised as women. In the first Act, very pronounced abolitionist sentiments are expressed.

Blackbeard, a farce by Lemuel Sawyer, has a plot which reminds one of *The Disappointment*, the play which in 1776 just missed being the first native drama to be performed. It is an amusing farce, in which two sharpers fool four persons by promising them that the devil will appear and change into much larger amounts sums of money which they have deposited in a bag under water. There is also satire on political conditions of the time. *Blackbeard*, published in 1824 in Washington, while actable, seems not to have been produced. Its author, a native of North Carolina, was also the creator of an amusing novel, *Printz Hall*, in which the early Swedish settlements on the Delaware were introduced. His other play, *The Wreck of Honor*, laid in Paris, introducing an American officer,

Captain Allen, and capitalizing the friendly relations of the two countries, seems not to have been acted. Indeed, it is hard to see how even the broad taste of the time could have tolerated the vulgarity of some of the language.

In this period the dramatic form was still sought for didactic purposes, and novels were placed upon the stage when their popularity gave them value. But these are of interest only as reaffirming the perennial impulse to write in dramatic form.[1] The achievement of the period lay in the successful attempt to dramatize native themes, treated with sincerity and dignity. In the work of Barker, Noah, Woodworth, Finn, and others we see the man of affairs, the writer of all work, or the finished actor recreate the Indian legend, the motive of Puritan intolerance, the self-sacrifice and the patriotism of the Revolution, and make them live upon the stage. As we look upon the portrait of Mrs. Duff as Mary in *Superstition* we realize also that here character was created, with power and with restraint.

But opportunity and encouragement were still lacking. In the carefully kept columns of the diary of William Wood, the Philadelphia manager, from 1810 to 1833, there is one item conspicuously absent, that of remuneration to the dramatist. Occasionally, as in the case of Barker, who had enriched the treasury with a popular play, he seems to have received a benefit. But there was no definite rule about the matter. Later there grew up a custom, more honored in the breach than the observance, of giving the author a benefit on the third night, and theatrical history records the distant fulminations of dramatists who had in their judgment been defrauded of this return by the simple expedient of not having any third performance of the play in question, at all!

The managers, with all the range of the British drama at their disposal and with the opportunity to adapt French and

---

[1] One striking example of enterprise is recorded in Wemyss, I, 149-152. Wemyss secured a copy of *The Red Rover* of Cooper from Carey and Lea, in advance of publication, and S. H. Chapman dramatized it, acting the Rover to Wemyss's Wilder. The novel was published January 9th, and the play was put on February 21, 1828. The Prologue, by R. P. Smith, is given in Wemyss's account.

German successes without payment, were cautious in a time of precarious business. It is interesting to analyze the choice of pieces during relatively successful seasons and note the program that an audience had spread before it. Fortunately we have in Wood's Diary such a carefully recorded list of plays. In the Philadelphia season of 1810-11, extending from November 26th to April 30th, were offered eighty-eight performances. Of these, twenty-two were devoted to Shakespeare, the plays being *Macbeth, Richard III, King Lear, Hamlet, Othello, Romeo and Juliet, Merchant of Venice, Coriolanus*, and *Katherine and Petruchio*. These performances were the most profitable, for Shakespeare, far from spelling ruin, was the main support of the season. Tragedies like *Venice Preserved* and *The Distressed Mother*, comedies like *The School for Scandal*, domestic drama like *The Stranger*, and melodramas like *The Foundling of the Forest* were also played.

During the season of 1811-12, performances were given on 108 nights, and again exactly one-quarter of them, twenty-seven, were devoted to Shakespeare. In addition to the plays offered the previous season, *Much Ado About Nothing, The Merry Wives of Windsor*, and *King John* were put on, and *Coriolanus* was dropped. Imagine the courage of a present-day manager who would provide such a program! Warren and Wood were on the outlook, too, for novelties. On February 19, 1812, Charles Lamb's farce, *Mr. H.*, was played for the first time in America, and was repeated several times although it had been a failure in London. The American playwright, then as now, had as rivals not only the successful European playwrights of his own time, but also the greatest dramatists of the past.

CHAPTER VII

IN sharp contrast with the author of *The Indian Princess* and *Superstition*, John Howard Payne represents in our dramatic history the actor-playwright, the man of the theatre, living the precarious existence of the author of that time who depended upon the fickle favor of the public, as interpreted by the none too able judgment of the professional managers of Drury Lane and Covent Garden. For it was not only that Payne wrote mostly on foreign themes; his life for many years was spent in London or Paris, and his plays were usually first performed in London. He becomes, then, the representative of foreign influence in our playwriting and around him we may group those other playwrights whose impulse led them to select foreign rather than native material.

John Howard Payne was born in New York City, June 9, 1791. At that time his father, William Payne, was the head-master of Clinton Academy at East Hampton, Long Island, the home of Payne's maternal grandfather, a convert from the Jewish faith. In 1796 William Payne was called to the direction of a school in Boston, later to be known as the Berry Street Academy, and the boy grew up in that city. He was a precocious child and, like Edgar Poe, seems to have been of a highly wrought nature, and to have had a fondness and a fitness for the companionship of his elders. Like Poe, too, he was a leader in the athletic sports of his school, and one of his schoolmates tells how as a boy of twelve he was the captain of the "Boston Federal Band," a completely equipped military company. He excelled in the recitation of prose and verse, and this practice, begun by his father to aid his physical development and counteract his nervous tendencies, stimulated Payne's latent interest in the theatre. At the academy he was the leading figure in the performances that took place at the mimic theatre in the school, even borrowing the actual costumes from the Federal Street Theatre nearby. He saw every play he could, and his criticisms even at that early age were welcomed in the newspapers. He became associated, too, with Samuel Woodworth, who was at that time learning the printer's trade, in the publication of a little paper, *The Fly*, and it is pleasant to speculate on the conversations that must have taken place between the two future dramatists and authors of "The Old Oaken Bucket" and "Home, Sweet Home!"

It is interesting to note that, while Payne's father had encouraged him to act at school, he should have been horrified at the thought of his son being associated professionally with the theatre. Payne had been fired by the accounts of the success of the English boy actor, William Betty, in 1804-5 and he ardently desired to begin a stage career, for which indeed his charming personality well fitted him. But the play-house still held the flavor of immorality for Puritan Boston, and Payne was sent to New York in 1805 to enter the mercantile house of Forbes and Payne, to cure him of the taste for the theatre. The repressive measures taken by his guardian had no more effect than those which had been practiced in the Irving household a few years before, and the two boys, Washington Irving and John Howard Payne, both grew up indulging that passion for the theatre which was to cement their later friendship, till it led to their joint authorship of *Charles the Second*. The boy of fourteen was desperately unhappy, and he solaced himself by the publication of the *Thespian Mirror*, which was issued on Saturday evenings from December 28, 1805, to March 22, 1806, with a supplement on May 31st, in which he said farewell. It was intended "to promote the interests of the American Drama; and to eradicate false impressions respecting the nature, objects, design, and tendency of theatrical amusements"—a sufficiently ambitious program, especially in 1805.

The Mirror attracted the attention of William Coleman, editor of *The Evening Post*, and Payne became soon a well-known figure in the social life of New York, which at that time under the influence of Irving, just returned from Europe, of Paulding, Verplanck, and others, had a certain literary atmosphere.

Thus encouraged, he wrote his first play, *Julia, or the Wanderer; a Comedy in Five Acts*, which was acted at the Park Theatre, on February 7, 1806, and published in the same year. The play belongs to the type of melodrama then popular. Frederick, the hero, excites the attention of the heroine, Julia, by saving her from insult by Ranger, the villain. Julia is taken under the protection of Longville, really her father, from whom she had been stolen by her brother in order to secure the family property. The play, however conventional, is remarkable for a boy of fourteen to have written, and, according to Ireland, it was acted with considerable applause. A friend of his brother's, John E. Seaman, then proposed to defray the expenses of Payne's education at college, and Union College was selected. Since he was not prepared to undertake the regular work of the course, he became a private pupil of the president, Eliphalet Nott, intending to enter the sophomore class. Here he published another paper, *The Pastime*, from February 2, 1807, to June 18, 1808.

In 1808 he acted in a play given by the Adelphi Literary Society, but he seems to have been set apart from the usual student life, by his method of instruction and by his heavy financial responsibilities for debts he was vainly trying to repay. Misunderstandings arose with Mr. Seaman; his father became bankrupt, and in November, 1808, he left college for Boston, to prepare for his début as an actor, which took place at the Park Theatre, New York, February 24, 1809. On this occasion he acted Young Norval in Home's tragedy *Douglas*, with distinct success. Dunlap tells us that "he performed Young Norval with credit, and his succeeding characters with an increased display of talent. The applause bestowed on his Norval was very great—boy actors were then a novelty, and we have seen none since that equalled Master Payne." He followed his first success by playing Zaphna in *Mahomet*, Octavian in *The Mountaineers*, Achmet in *Barbarossa*, Tancred, and Romeo. He appeared in Boston at the Federal Street Theatre, on April 2, 1809, with even greater success, as Norval, and then returned to New York, playing Frederick in *Lovers' Vows*, Rolla in *Pizarro*, Hastings in *Jane Shore*, Edgar, and Hamlet. In the fall and winter of 1809-10 he acted in Baltimore, Philadelphia, Richmond, Charleston, Norfolk, Petersburg, and Washington, and yet notwithstanding remarkably successful results, especially in Baltimore, he found it difficult to secure regular engagements in New York.

In 1809 his second play appeared in print, an adaptation of Kotzebue's *Das Kind der Liebe* under the title of *Lovers' Vows*. Payne did not translate Kotzebue, however; he took the English versions of Mrs. Inchbald (1798) and Benjamin Thompson (1800) and combined them into a version in which he himself took the part of Frederick. When he first began to act in his own version is not certain. *Lovers' Vows*, in the versions of Mrs. Inchbald, Anne Plumptre, and William Dunlap had long been familiar to the British and American theatre. But since Payne's version was published in Baltimore in 1809, he was in all probability using it at that time. The first recorded performance is at the Chestnut Street Theatre, September 16, 1811.[1] His adaptation is not in any sense to be looked upon as an original play, but it is interesting as showing his methods of work and also his sense of the theatrically effective. With the versions of Dunlap, of Mrs. Inchbald, of Thompson, and of Payne before us, we can see how Payne seized upon the best parts of the original play which Dunlap and Thompson had preserved and which Mrs. Inchbald had modified, and how, on the other hand, he could appreciate the improvements which Mrs. Inchbald had made on her own account. For example, the scene in which Amelia, the daughter of Baron Wildenham, tells her tutor, Anhalt, that she loves

---

[1] Wood's Diary.

him, is charmingly expressed in the original, and is followed faithfully by all the translators except Mrs. Inchbald. It is quite astonishing to learn from Mrs. Inchbald's introduction to her version that "the forward and unequivocal manner, in which she [Amelia] announces her affection to her lover, would have been revolting to an English audience." So the good lady toned Amelia down and reduced a charming scene to an insipid one. One is lost in wonder why the creator of Lady Mary Raffle and Mr. Bronzeley should have been so squeamish about the sensibilities of her audiences, but perhaps she knew them best. Payne kept her creation of Verdun, the butler in *Lovers' Vows*, since he saw its possibilities in comedy, but more important, he used her conception of Frederick, which is much more vigorous than the original. The character of Frederick remained one of his favorite parts, and contemporary criticism[1] tells us that "his performance was one consistent piece of natural, affecting, and indeed skillful acting." He is said to have altered, also, the translation of Voltaire's *Mahomet*, made in 1755 by the Reverend James Miller. A version printed in 1809 in New York has been attributed to Payne, who acted Zaphna frequently, but in the volume itself there is nothing to prove his authorship.

Partly through a natural reaction against the unusual acclamation that had greeted his appearance as a boy prodigy, and partly through the jealousy of the great tragedian, Cooke, who had been obliged, against his will, to accept Payne as a supporting attraction, Payne continued to find his way blocked in New York. He played in Philadelphia, Baltimore, and Boston in 1811-12, and he seems to have been associated with an effort to organize an opposition to the Theatrical Trust of the day. He shared, too, the general decline of prosperity of the theatrical business at this time, caused by commercial depression, the burning of the Richmond Theatre on December 26, 1811, when seventy-one spectators lost their lives, and the "McKenzie riots" in Philadelphia, which for a time kept

[1] *Mirror of Taste and Dramatic Censor.* Phila., March 1810, p. 221.

the respectable members of that community away from the playhouses. We learn much concerning the conditions obtaining in the theatres from the protests printed in periodicals of the day, which indicate that smoking was still permitted in the seats of the play-houses, and that it became necessary in the New Theatre in Philadelphia to provide an outlet in the ceiling six feet in diameter to take care of the fumes. Vehement also were protests against the custom of allowing loose women ("impures" was the technical term employed) to occupy certain boxes with their escorts. One writer dwells fondly on the past when such customs would have been impossible.[1]

It had long been Payne's dream to go abroad and perfect his art, so that when a purse of two thousand dollars was raised by his friends he gladly set sail for Liverpool on January 17, 1813. As the United States and Great Britain were at war, Payne was imprisoned for a time after landing, but through his friends, Brevoort and members of the Irving family, he was introduced to pleasant acquaintances and he secured an opportunity to act at Drury Lane on June 4, 1813, in the character of Norval. His success was great, notwithstanding the discouraging circumstance that the leading lady, Miss Smith, declined to play Lady Randolph at the last minute and he was introduced to her substitute, Miss Powell, just before he went on the stage. In Liverpool and Dublin he even surpassed his success in London. In Paris, where he arrived during the excitement of the "Hundred Days" after Bonaparte's return from Elba, he lived for a time with Irving and made a friend of Talma, the great actor. Through Talma he received the freedom of the Théâtre Français, and he began that close study of the French drama which was to produce such an effect upon his own dramatic work.

His first translation was *The Maid and the Magpie*, from *La Pie Voleuse*, a *mélodrame* by Louis Charles Caigniez and Jean Marie Théodore Baudouin. It was offered to Douglass Kin-

---

[1] *Mirror of Taste and Dramatic Censor.* Philadelphia, October and November, 1810.

naird, manager of Drury Lane, but that theatre had just accepted another version. Payne's play may have been performed at Covent Garden, the rival theatre, on September 15, 1815.[1] It was not printed until 1940.

Payne established relations with Kinnaird, which sent him back to Paris to observe the plays there and to adapt as quickly as possible the successful ones for Drury Lane. The first fruit of this arrangement was *Accusation, or the Family of D'Anglade*, a melodrama, produced on February 1st at Drury Lane and at the Park Theatre, New York, May 10, 1816. It was adapted from *Le Vol ou La Famille d'Anglade*, by Frédéric du Petit-Méré, a *mélodrame* based on real facts related in *Causes Célèbres*.

It proceeds according to the rules of French *mélodrame*. Adolphus d'Anglade, a wealthy man, is married to a remarkably beautiful woman who is sought by the villain, Valmore. He and his valet, Hubert, conspire to ruin d'Anglade by robbing Valmore's aunt of two thousand louis and then, by purchasing Mme. d'Anglade's diamonds with the stolen and marked notes, throwing the blame on him. The scheme works, aided by the circumstance that Leon de Valency, d'Anglade's cousin, has returned and demands his estates. De Valency, however, turns out to be his real friend, and the villains are frustrated. The play reads well and was successful on the British and American stages. It is important, like *Lovers' Vows*, in showing Payne's ability at adaptation.

In the Robert Gould Shaw Theatrical Collection at the Harvard Library, there is a voluminous manuscript containing the correspondence between Payne and the subcommittee of Drury Lane Theatre, which reveals unfair treatment of Payne at Kinnaird's hands, with regard both to his royalties as an author and his engagements as an actor. The publication of

---

[1] According to Harrison's *Life*, p. 81. The version, by Isaac Pocock, as printed in 1815, announces on the title page "as performed at Covent Garden on Sept. 15, 1815," and Genest gives a cast which fits Pocock's play. The explanation may lie in the fact that Harris, the manager of Covent Garden, reserved the right to make changes in Payne's version. The play bills, in the Shaw Collection, do not contain Payne's name, or, in fact, any name as the author.

Accusation, through Kinnaird's fault, brought Payne nothing, though it netted the publisher £200.[1]

In the midst of his difficulties Harris, the manager of Covent Garden, offered him three hundred guineas for his general services for the season, fifty pounds for each translation of a foreign play, and the usual recompense, about two hundred pounds, if the play was produced. Payne accepted the terms, but for reasons that were then usual in theatrical circles, his début at Covent Garden as Lothair in *Adelgitha* was postponed indefinitely. Consequently, when his tragedy of *Brutus, or the Fall of Tarquin*, was ready, Payne offered it to Drury Lane, where it was first produced, December 3, 1818. It was an immediate success, and was performed during the rest of that season more than fifty times. It is interesting to note that more than a year before Sydney Smith uttered his famous "In the four quarters of the globe who reads an American book or goes to an American play?" the British public was thronging Drury Lane to see one of the most successful tragedies written in English in the nineteenth century. Kean played Brutus. It was at first intended that Payne should play Titus, son of Brutus, but that part was finally taken by D. Fisher. H. Kemble played Sextus; Mrs. Glover, Tullia; Mrs. West, Tarquinia, and Mrs. Robinson, Lucretia. Payne benefited little by the play, however, his financial return being £183, 6s., little more than was frequently received for a successful afterpiece.

Brutus was first played in America on March 15, 1819, at the Park Theatre, with Pritchard as Brutus and Mrs. Barnes as Tullia, and it held the stage for seventy years. Junius Brutus Booth, the elder Wallack, Edwin Forrest, John McCullough, and Edwin Booth were among those who found it a splendid vehicle for their talents in England or America, and Kean played it in Paris.

Perhaps the dramatic sense of Payne shows nowhere so

[1] Letter of John Howard Payne to the sub-committee of Drury Lane Theatre, April 29, 1816, p. 21 Mss.

clearly as in the case of this play. *Brutus* revealed Payne's ability as a moulder of stage characters, as a constructor of effective scenes, and as a selector, from among a wealth of historical tradition and earlier dramatic efforts, of the essential elements in a tragic theme. Brutus, the patriot, is the great character in the tragedy. He is set against a background of lust and tyranny of which the Tarquins, Prince Sextus, Queen Tullia, and Tarquinia, the daughter of Lucius Tarquinius, are the chief representatives. On the side of Brutus, the action is developed by his assumed foolishness, by Sextus's rape of Lucrece, by the vengeance taken by Brutus and Collatinus, her husband, which leads to the establishment of the Republic and the election of Brutus and Valerius as consuls. The tragedy is brought about by the treason of Titus, Brutus's son, who through his love for Tarquinia, aids her escape to the King's army, and is condemned to death by his own father, in his capacity as consul.

Payne stated clearly in his preface that there were seven plays upon the subject of Brutus before the public, only two of which had been played, and he adds, "I have had no hesitation in adopting the conceptions and language of my predecessors wherever they seemed likely to strengthen the plan which I had prescribed."

The five plays from which he derived his main inspiration were *Lucius Junius Brutus, Father of His Country, A Tragedy*, by Nathaniel Lee, produced in 1681 for three nights and then withdrawn owing to its ridicule of monarchy; *Brutus*, a tragedy, by Voltaire, produced December 11, 1730; a translation and adaptation of Voltaire's play, by William Duncombe, under the title of *Junius Brutus, a Tragedy*, produced at Drury Lane, November 25, 1734; *Lucius Junius Brutus, or the Expulsion of the Tarquins, an Historical Play*, by Hugh Downman, not played, but printed in 1779; and *The Sybil* [sic], *or the Elder Brutus; a Tragedy*, by Richard Cumberland, not played, but printed in 1813, among his posthumous works.

It is both interesting and instructive in the technique of

theatrical effectiveness to compare Payne's *Brutus* with the originals, and to note the deftness and dramatic instinct with which the born playwright and actor combined plays which had either had little success on the stage or had even been denied representation into one of the most successful and long-lived tragedies of the nineteenth century, which was played as long as there were great romantic tragedians to play it.

He owed most to Cumberland and Downman, though he seems to have read Lee first. The two main themes, the use by Brutus of Sextus Tarquin's rape of Lucrece to expel the Tarquins, and his condemnation of his own son, belong to mythical history, and are common property. Payne saw that Lee, and Cumberland after him, had combined them, it is true, but not skillfully and in each case had dragged out the tragic situation unbearably. Lee brought in Sempronia, Brutus's wife, and Tiberius, his second son, to add to the misery and Cumberland, by including the later history of Rome, together with Brutus's death at the hands of Sextus, not only changed the myth but dulled the poignancy of the great moment of sacrifice. Cumberland had confused the story also by the introduction of the supernatural element in what he calls "the Sybil," who prophesies events, and Payne eliminated her.

He saw that Downman had visualized quite well the Lucrece episode, and he made use of portions of several scenes, notably those in the camp before Ardea and at the home of Collatinus, where Lucrece shames the prince's mission and by her beauty inflames his passion. Downman does not make use of the Titus theme, so his influence, although it lasts verbally till the fifth Act, does not show in the structure after the third Act. The heavy joviality of Aruns, made much of by Downman, is not used by Payne at all.

While there are verbal similarities between Duncombe's translation of Voltaire's play[1] and Payne's *Brutus*, to the total

---

[1] Payne used Duncombe's translation more frequently than the original, but in three lines he uses words or expressions of Voltaire which are not in Duncombe. He also omits certain interpolations of Duncombe, which indicates that he had Voltaire before him.

amount of thirty-seven lines, the general conception is affected only by the more definite unity of the French tragedy. Voltaire begins his play after the exile of Tarquin, and Lucretia, Sextus, and Collatinus do not appear.

Payne's skill is evidenced quite as much in the handling of single episodes as in his general shaping of the plot. The third scene of the fourth Act may be taken as an example. Tullia, the Queen, is assigned to the Priestess of Rhea for safe keeping. In the temple stands the tomb of her father, Servius Tullius, murdered at her instigation. Cumberland leads her to a couch, where she reclines and awaits the "Sybil," who calls up the ghost of Servius Tullius, to whom she discourses at some length before she expires. Payne's method is much more swift and sure. She is an active, not a passive force—she demands that the vault be opened, and when the statue of Servius Tullius breaks on her view, she believes in her disordered state that it is her father, and with one brief cry, "'Tis he! It is my father!" she falls dead.

Payne makes use of the language of his predecessors with the high courage of the great adaptors. From Cumberland he takes many lines, often verbatim; from Downman he takes largely also, but he more often alters the language. Our admiration of his ability, instead of diminishing as we read, increases while we see him cutting relentlessly the poetic verbosity of a scene of Downman to one-fifth of its original length, and inserting a few lines of his own in just the right places. Or, we note as in Act V, Sc. 1, how he begins with a few lines from Downman and his own intermingled, then builds up the scene from Cumberland, with a few lines from Voltaire or its translation, and fuses the whole into a unified product where no signs of joints are visible. From Lee he took thirty-seven lines, mostly in Act V, Sc. 3. Curiously enough, his own language shows most clearly in the first scene and the last. The second speech of Valerius, describing the Queen's ride over the dead body of her father, shows his ability at striking the note of tragedy:

"High in her regal chariot Tullia came—
The corpse lay in the street. The charioteer
Turn'd back the reins in horror. 'On, slave, on!
Shall dead men stop my passage to a throne?'
Exclaimed the parricide. The gore was dashed
From the hot wheels up to her diadem."

In the last scene the language of Cumberland, Lee, and
Voltaire is so intermingled with Payne's own that quotation is
impracticable, but such lines as

"A little moment
And I am childless."

seem to be his alone.

His sense of verbal effect is seen in the handling of the
climax. In Act III, Sc. 2, he has taken the line from Cumberland, sunk in the middle of a scene,

"Did not the sybil tell you
A fool should set Rome free?"

and has placed it at the end of the powerful scene in which
Collatinus enters with the bloody dagger of Lucrece, and in
which Brutus reveals himself as the leader of the rebels. One
can imagine what Kean made of a curtain speech like

"Summon your slaves and bear the body hence
High in the view, through all the streets of Rome,
Up to the Forum! On! The least delay
May draw down ruin and defeat our glory!
On, Romans, on! The fool shall set you free!"

At Kean's suggestion, Payne now wrote a play on the theme
of Virginius, but it was not performed at this time. A play
by the name of *Virginia* by Payne was produced on February
19, 1834,[1] at the Park Theatre, and is probably his earlier
treatment. It has not survived.

Payne tried his hand at managing the Sadler's Wells Theatre,
but only incurred debts which lodged him in prison. While

[1] Ireland, II, 78.

there he received a package containing two French plays, and seeing the possibilities of *Thérèse ou l'Orpheline de Genève*, by Victor Ducange, which had been performed at the Théâtre de l'Ambigu Comique, November 23, 1820, he adapted it in three days, and it was produced with great success at Drury Lane, February 2, 1821, and at the Anthony Street Theatre, New York, on April 30th.

Thérèse is a typical *succès de larmes* among the French melodramas of the time. Starting out with the reputation of illegitimacy, the heroine is attacked from all sides through the machinations of the villain, Valther, by whose efforts she is accused of forgery and suspected of murder. She is saved through the confession of the real murderer, Valther, who has killed Mme. de Sénange in mistake for Thérèse, and who is so affected by the appearance of his supposed victim that he loses at the same time his senses and the papers necessary to establish her inheritance.

Payne changed the play, altering the name of the villain to Carwin, possibly under the influence of Brockden Brown's novel of *Wieland*. His most significant alteration is the definite charge of murder made against Thérèse, by the magistrate in her presence, while in the original the charge is made while she is off the stage.[1] Payne cut down the long speeches of the French melodrama, usually improving them by the substitution of shorter and crisper sentences. The action was thus made more rapid and the effect heightened. Miss Kelly scored a triumph as Thérèse, and the play proved so popular that the Cobourg Theatre stole it and Covent Garden produced another version on February 23d. In America Forrest frequently played Carwin.

Payne was under no illusions as to the permanent worth of such work as *Thérèse*. In his preface to the first edition, he says:

[1] See *Thérèse*, Act III, Sc. 5 and Sc. 6, most conveniently in *Théâtre Contemporain Illustré*, No. 355. M. Lévy Frères, Paris. Also see Ginisty, pp. 150-3, and T. T. Payne Luquer, "Writing a Play in a Debtor's Prison"—*Scribner's Magazine*, LXVIII (Jan. and Feb., 1921), pp. 66-81, 237-246.

One word to my friends the critics, and I have done. They have honored me with more attention than I have ever coveted, but I wish them to understand that this, like former publications of mine, is a work planned for stage effects exclusively, and printed for managers and actors only. It is so necessary in the production of the modern drama to consult the peculiarities of leading performers, and not offend the restive spirit by means of situations almost panto-mimic and too impatient to pause for poetical beauty, that it seems almost hopeless to look to the stage of the present day for a permanent literary distinction. An actable play seems to derive its value from what is done more than from what is said, but the great power of literary work consists in what is said, and the manner of saying it. He, therefore, who best knows the stage, can best tell why, in the present temper of the audience, good poets should so often make bad dramatists.

In his next play, *Adeline, the Victim of Seduction*, per-formed at Drury Lane, February 9, 1822, and at the Park Theatre on May 1st, Payne continued to seek the inspiration of the French melodrama, and he adapted the work of Guilbert de Pixerécourt, the first noteworthy exponent of the school, whose *Wife of Two Husbands* Dunlap had earlier adapted. *Valentine ou la Séduction* (1810) is quite aptly described as *la pièce la plus sobre de l'infatigable auteur*,[1] for it is the only one of Pixerécourt's many melodramas which has an unhappy ending. Payne followed his model in producing an unrelieved picture of sorrow, and while conventionality of plot, sentimentality, and unrestrained emotion prevent the play from rising to the dignity of tragedy, there is a simplicity about Payne's ending, at least, which in part redeems the play. *Adeline* is a type of the seduction drama which pictures every young and virtuous woman as the natural prey of the titled villain, who, by means of a false marriage, tricks her into momentary happiness and eternal misery. In the pathetic helplessness of the blind father, who tries to fight a duel with his daughter's betrayer, Pixeré-court had a really dramatic motive which Payne was quick to see. Years afterward Steele MacKaye was to create out of a somewhat similar situation the poignant climax of *Hazel Kirke*.

[1] Ginisty, p. 87.

JOHN HOWARD PAYNE AND THE FOREIGN PLAYS

Payne was by this time released from a debtor's prison by the receipts of *Thérèse* and had returned to Paris, where he watched the French stage closely and adapted what he thought fit for a London production. The management of Drury Lane, however, was not sufficiently prompt or enterprising to suit his fancy, so that only a one-act comedy, *Love in Humble Life*, laid in Poland, was produced at that theatre, February 14, 1822. It is based on *Michel et Christine*, by Scribe and Dupin (1821). *Peter Smink, or the Armistice*, another one-act French comedy, was produced at the Surrey Theatre, one of the minor playhouses of London, on July 8th. It contains a truly remarkable situation. Chevalier Bayard, finding himself in the hands of the enemy, calmly signs an armistice, which is conveniently lying near by, and then defies the commanding officer to capture him![1]

The inertia of Elliston and the assumption by Charles Kemble of the management of Covent Garden transferred Payne's services to the rival house, and he furnished it with the adaptation of a two-act French melodrama, *Two Galley Slaves*, on November 6, 1822, a quickly moving play, but one of no special importance.

Ali Pacha, or the Signet-Ring, a two-act melodrama, performed at Covent Garden, October 19, 1822, and in New York, May 8, 1823, may be compared with Noah's *Grecian Captive*, which had been first played in June, 1822. There is a slight similarity in plot, for in both cases Ali has a Grecian maiden in captivity who is sought by her lover. This theme goes back to the French tragedy[2] which is ultimately their common source, but in other respects Noah's play is better constructed and is more entertaining. Payne's was evidently hastily written, and the general destruction caused by the blowing up of the citadel may be looked upon as convenient rather than convincing. There was some basis for both plays in historical

---

[1] Probably derived from a scene in a *mélodrame* of Frédéric du Petit-Méré.

[2] *Mahomet II*, by Lanoue (1739). The immediate source of Payne's play was *Ali Pacha*, by Mm. Hyacinthe and Alfred, played at the Théâtre du Panorama Dramatique, July 9, 1822.

facts, for Ali Pacha, while not a friend to the Greeks, did help their cause by his attack upon the Sultan.

Clari, or the Maid of Milan, which Payne sold to Kemble along with *Ali Pacha* and *The Two Galley Slaves* for two hundred and fifty pounds, owed its great popularity in large measure to the song "Home, Sweet Home," sung by Miss Maria Tree. This song, certainly the most popular ever written by an American, was set to music by Henry Bishop, from a Sicilian air which Payne had heard and with which Bishop was familiar. The play, taken from a French ballet-pantomime, was first called *Angioletta* and produced at the Surrey Theatre, London. After revision and change of name to *Clari*, it was played at Covent Garden on May 8, 1823, and in New York on November 12th. It is a piece of slight texture, with the ancient plot of the mis-guided but virtuous rural maid and the penitent duke who marries her in the end. The song which carried it into success is, however, not an extraneous affair. It is woven into the theme of the drama, for the one sincere note that is struck in the play is the longing for home on the part of Clari which gives her courage to break her "silken ties." The device of having a play within the play by means of which a parallel situation to her own brings Clari to a determination to leave the duke is well done, even though not original. Contrary to the usual statements of theatrical history, *Clari* was frequently repeated, especially upon the American stage.

After another clever but trifling farce, *Mrs. Smith, or the Wife and the Widow*, put on first at the Haymarket Theatre, June 18, 1823, and at the Park Theatre, March 6, 1826, Payne produced his best comedy, *Charles the Second, or the Merry Monarch*, first played at Covent Garden, May 27, 1824, and at the Park Theatre, October 25, 1824. It shared popular favor with *Brutus*, holding the stage for many years, and being selected by such actors as Elliston and Fawcett for their farewell benefits to the stage, in 1826 and 1830. Compact and unified in structure, rapid in action, after the first act, and brilliant in language, it provided that combination of youthful love, family loyalty, and the spirit of adventure that have always delighted audiences of whatever class. There was also the tone of high comedy, so often attempted and so hard to reach. Charles II is to be reformed and, in return for being the amused but able agency of his reformation, the Earl of Rochester is to be rewarded with the hand of Lady Clara. Rochester finds that his protégé, Edward, a court page, under the assumed guise of a music teacher, has fallen honestly in love with Mary Copland, niece of Captain Copp, a retired sailor who keeps the "Grand Admiral" at Wapping. Rochester and the King, disguised as sailors, visit the tavern on one of their night rambles and after an amusing party, in which Copp almost succeeds in singing his song concerning "Admiral Trump," the King is left by Rochester in the lurch with no money to pay the landlord. Copp threatens him with arrest, leaves with the watch that Charles has tried to pawn, and Charles escapes by a window through Edward's connivance and Mary's sympathy. Copp and Mary call next day at the palace to return the watch, which has been recognized by a jeweler as the King's. After some clever byplay, the identity of both Charles and Rochester is disclosed. Mary turns out to be the niece of the late Earl of Rochester, and is married happily to Edward; and Rochester is forgiven by Charles through the astuteness of Lady Clara, who meets the King as he is trying to find his way in without discovery in the morning. She presents him with a pardon, ostensibly for a young author who is being persecuted and he signs Rochester's pardon to secure her silence, truly remarking, "Let him write against me only and they'll never trouble him." The King promises to reform, which is the only improbable note in the play.

Charles the Second has several points of interest to the student of the drama. It was the first of Payne's plays in which he had Washington Irving's help, and when we compare this play with Payne's earlier efforts, it is not hard to notice a certain blitheness, a delicate fancy, that we like to think was due to Washington Irving. Irving had made Payne promise to keep his share of the work secret, so Payne could only refer in his preface to the literary friend to whom he is "indebted for invaluable touches." In the life of Irving by his nephew we read that at the end of November, 1823, Irving transmitted to Payne the manuscript of *Charles II*, and later comes this account of his relation to the play:

> *Charles II*. was produced May 27, 1824, and met with the most decided success. "The piece will grow upon the public on representation," writes Payne to Mr. Irving, "and I am convinced become a stock piece. The points all told amazingly. My notion about Copp's always trying a song, and never being able to get it out, was very effective in representation." The conception and execution of this song, which Payne jestingly speaks of as *my* notion, were his coadjutor's, done, as he once told me, to hit the English taste for broad fun. Some time later, after a series of successful representations, Payne writes in regard to this song: "Charles Lamb tells me he can't get Copp's song out of his head, and is very anxious for the rest of it. He says the hiatus keeps him awake o'nights."
>
> Payne disposed of the copyright for fifty guineas, after Mr. Irving had assisted him in pruning the piece, and reducing it to two acts.[1]

Charles II is an adaptation of *La Jeunesse de Henri V* by Alexandre Duval (1760-1838), one of the leading dramatists of the post-Revolution period in France, of especial interest to us since as a boy he took part in the expedition of aid to the Colonies in the War of Independence. His play, performed at the Théâtre Français, June 9, 1806, was one of his most successful efforts. It is based in its turn on *Charles II, roi d'Angleterre, en un certain lieu,* by Sébastien Mercier, published in 1789 but not represented, which may go back to an English original. The French censor forced Duval to change the hero from Charles II to Henry V, fearing that audiences in 1806 might think of "the Cromwell who then governed France."[2] Duval was driven into anachronisms by this change, and, of course,

---

[1] Irving, Pierre M. *The Life and Letters of Washington Irving.* N. Y., 1883. II, 6.

[2] For an interesting account of Duval's conception of the comedy and his difficulties with the censor, see his *Notice sur la Jeunesse de Henri V* in *Œuvres Complètes d'Alexandre Duval.* Paris, 1822, VI, pp. 71-95. See also Lenient, C. F., *La Comedie en France au XIXe Siècle,* Paris, 1898, I, pp. 130-4.

Payne restored the rightful King to his own.   The main plot and even the names of the principal characters, except that of the heroine, who is "Betty" in the French, are taken from Duval.

It was no slavish translation, however.   There are two scenes instead of one in the second Act, as first played, and the dialogue, especially in the first and last Acts, often differs from the original.   The tone is Anglicized, and Copp is made distinctly British.   Fawcett acted this part admirably.   Such touches as Charles kissing Mary while he leaps from the window and advising her "to tell Uncle Copp to put it in the bill" are original and probably Irving's.   The songs are all original.

The characters of Rochester and of Charles II are, of course, idealized, but Charles Kemble seems to have imbued the part of the King with that innate dignity which even in a ridiculous situation the "merry monarch" could assume as well as his father.   The French ancestry and training of Charles II may have accounted for the ease with which a French dramatist could paint a picture of an English king which an American dramatist interpreted to the delight of English audiences.

An amusing comic opera, *The Fall of Algiers*, was performed at Drury Lane, January 19, 1825, in which a number of English characters are saved, after many vicissitudes, through the attack by Admiral Rockwardine, whose son is rather obviously placed among the characters.   There is quite a likeness between this play and Mrs. Rowson's *Slaves in Algiers* (1794), especially in the scene in which Timothy Tourist is disguised as a woman and is borne off by Cogi, who thinks he is saving Lauretta.   The opera was played in Philadelphia in 1827.

Encouraged by the success of *Charles II*, Payne turned again to Duval for inspiration and adapted *La Jeunesse du Duc de Richelieu ou le Lovelace Français* (1796), which reveals at once by its title the influence which the novels of Richardson had had in France.   The French nobleman took only his casual morality from the English gentleman who was his prototype, and he is the betrayer, not of maiden innocence, but of the honor of a virtuous but indiscreet wife. The character of Richelieu is well drawn by Duval; the picture of the aristocrat with all the vices and some of the virtues of the régime that had just gone down with the Revolution, was an appealing one to the audiences of the new Republic. Duval drew well, also, the tightening chain of circumstances which drive the unhappy Madame Michelin to her ruin, despite her struggles against them and against the promptings of her heart. These circumstances are made concrete in the persons of Armand, the secretary of Richelieu and the friend of the Michelins, and of Madame Renaud, also their friend and the mistress of Richelieu. Madame Renaud is the only character that is changed by Payne. She becomes the Countess Fleury, and is a patroness rather than a friend of the wife. Perhaps Payne thought this made more effective her plea with Armand to save Madame Michelin, her rival, when the latter had been decoyed to Richelieu's house. But the change is not of importance. Of more significance is the attempt to make even less guilty the central character, the wife of the furniture dealer, Madame Dorival, as she becomes in the English version. She does not contribute to the *liaison* by her meetings with the libertine at church; she is sought out from the beginning by the duke in in the disguise of his servant.

In general atmosphere, Payne's *Richelieu* differs from its original in just those ways in which the social and moral standards of England, as interpreted by a dramatist, would naturally differ from those of France. The cynicism and insolence of race are expressed less subtly and also with less heartlessness. Duval's Richelieu, in his crime and his remorse is more callous and also more consistently *le grand seigneur*. At the catastrophe Payne makes him scold his secretary in an exaggerated manner unknown to the original and yet he spares us, with an artistic sense which is rather American than British, the moral utterance with which the French author felt it necessary to bring down the curtain.

Richelieu, a Domestic Tragedy, is dedicated to Washington

Irving, and Payne states in his graceful preface that the aid given him renders it imperative upon him to thank Irving publicly. The play met with misfortune at the outset. A descendant of the "Duc de Richelieu" was the French Ambassador at the Court of St. James, and he objected strongly to the representation of his ancestor in the guise of a villain. Owing to the firmness of Charles Kemble, however, it was produced at Covent Garden, February 11, 1826, as *The French Libertine*, and Kemble played the leading part under the name of "Rougemont." A political cabal having been formed against it, however, it was not successful. In this country it was played for the first time at the Chestnut Street Theatre in Philadelphia under the title of *Richelieu*, the part of the heroine being acted by Mrs. Sloman, who had played it in London. As late as May 4, 1850, at the Broadway Theatre, Mrs. Catherine Farren was acting a version under the title of *Remorse*.

'Twas I, or the Truth a Lie, a clever farce, based on *La Rose et le basier*, was played at Covent Garden, December 3, 1825, and at the Park, May 19, 1826. Equally amusing was a military farce, *The Lancers*, played at Drury Lane, December 1, 1827, and at the Bowery on March 4, 1828. *The Spanish Husband; or, First and Last Love*, put on at Drury Lane, May 25, 1830, and repeated at the Park on November 1, was a wild melodrama, partly in blank verse, and laid in Naples and Barcelona. Much better was a one-act burletta, *Woman's Revenge*, laid in a rural district of England, played at the Olympic in London, February 27, 1832. Though the plot is conventional, the dialogue is crisp and the dominating figure of Miss Flashington is well drawn. *The Solitary of Mount Savage; or, The Fate of Charles the Bold*, a romantic melodrama, played in London in 1822, is less certain of identification as Payne's. The rest of Payne's acted plays, *The White Maid* [or *Lady*], an opera (1827), and *Procrastination*, a comedy (1829), have come down only by title. On July 25, 1832, Payne landed in

New York, and after the alarm of the cholera epidemic had subsided, a testimonial was arranged by leading citizens of New York, in the shape of a dramatic festival, on November 29, 1832.

The plays selected were *Brutus, Charles the Second*, and *Katherine and Petruchio*. The leading actors of the time contributed to make the occasion a memorable one. Charles Kemble played Petruchio to his daughter's Katherine. Forrest played Brutus to Scott's Titus, with Mrs. Barnes as Tullia. Wallack studied Captain Copp especially for the occasion. An address was written by Theodore S. Fay, of the *New York Mirror*, whose father had written the address for Payne's first appearance at the old Park Theatre in 1809. The house was packed, and the proceeds, seven thousand dollars, were presented to him. Payne's responses, both at the theatre and at the public dinner in his honor on December 1st, show him to have been a speaker of real charm and sincere eloquence. At the dinner, verses written by his boyhood friend, Samuel Woodworth, reveal the impression that *Brutus, Charles II, Thérèse, Clari*, and *Richelieu* had made on audiences in the United States, and a late tragedy, *Oswali of Athens*, which was performed at the Chatham Theatre, June 13, 1831, is spoken of by Woodworth with enthusiasm. At the testimonial benefit in Boston, *Charles II, The Lancers, Thérèse*, and *Love in Humble Life* were played. *The Boston Transcript*, in commenting upon the occasion, remarks that an average of twenty-five plays by Payne were performed each season in that city.

Payne might indeed feel that some testimonials were due him. For years his plays had been performed with success in the United States, and yet he had received no return. He took the occasion of a testimonial benefit in New Orleans in April, 1835, in his letter of acknowledgment to the committee of arrangements, to express himself on the subject of international and national copyright for American playwrights. It was a manly, straightforward statement of the fact that in order to be able to live even partially upon his writing for the stage, an American playwright had to leave his own country. Another significant statement was contained in the sentence:

"It was known that much prejudice had been excited against me by a party in England for having so strongly asserted my American principles as to endanger the license of certain plays and to bring down the vengeance of certain critics and I was promised that my own land would sustain me against what I have suffered from the support of sentiments to which I trust no persecution will ever make a citizen of our country false."[1]

It was not accidental that Payne chose Brutus, the republican, for his greatest tragedy, or selected for adaptation those plays of Duval's which represented the republican point of view even at the risk of the imperial censor. This democratic attitude is shown very clearly in his play of *Romulus the Shepherd King*, which was written for Edwin Forrest in 1839 but not played or printed.[2] Romulus emphasizes the spirit of service to all men. In the second Act he says:

"*Romulus:*   Oh should it be
            My destiny to send beyond all this
            To far, far time, the enviable fame
            Of being the beginning of a country
            Where every man untrammel'd may enjoy
            All that the Heavens intend for all alike,—
            Father! forgive me that the very thought
            Should overcome me with its vastness—bring
            The woman into eyes unused to tears——"

It cannot be said, however, that Payne met any material recompense from his own countrymen for his persistence in his democratic sympathies. After his return to his native land, he had the satisfaction of knowing that his plays were continually being performed, but no other reward seems to have come to him. He tried unsuccessfully to found a periodical, to be published in London, and to represent the work of both

[1] *Life*, by Harrison, p. 156.
[2] Ms. in the Shaw Theatrical Collection at Harvard University. Printed 1940.

British and American writers, with a view toward establishing a better understanding between the two countries. His later activities, including his adventures among the Cherokee Indians, belong outside our immediate interest. On August 23, 1842, he was appointed by President Tyler consul at Tunis, which position he filled until 1845, and again from 1851 till his death on April 9, 1852.

Payne's position in our dramatic history is a peculiar one. His most significant work was done abroad and his direct inspiration was foreign. Yet his theatrical training was received in America, and his general attitude, like Irving's, remained materially unchanged by his long residence in Europe. His themes were universal rather than parochial. His industry, like that of Dunlap, whom he somewhat resembles, was prodigious. Over sixty[1] plays have been attributed to him, and though many of these prove on examination to be of doubtful identity, or to be the result of only slight alterations of other plays, the residue is a creditable one. He went to the French drama of his time or a little earlier for much of his inspiration. So did other dramatists in England at that time, and frequently their adaptations were produced simultaneously with his, at rival houses. The difference lies in the fact that Payne usually points out his sources clearly and that his plays were successful. The latter quality brought his work promi-

---

[1] The extant but probably unproduced plays of Payne include *The Boarding Schools; or, Life Among the Little Folks*, a farce; *The Two Sons-in-Law*, a clever comedy from a French adaptation of the Lear story; *Mazeppa; or, The Wild Horse of Tartary*, a spectacular melodrama; *The Last Duel in Spain*, a serio-comic romance on the practice of duelling at the time of Charles V; *The Italian Bride*, a melodrama laid in Baltimore, with complicated marital relations but with rapid action; and *The Black Man; or, The Spleen*, a domestic melodrama laid in France.

The following titles of plays attributed to Payne (arranged alphabetically) are uncertain as to identification or date of first performance: *The Bridge of Kehl* (Chatham, N. Y., October 11, 1848); *Fricandeau, or The Coronet and the Cook* (farce); *Grandpapa; Madame du Barry; Man of the Black Forest; Married and Single; Norah, or The Girl of Erin; Paoli; The Post-Chaise; The Robbers; Tyrolese Peasants* (opera). For additional information see List of Plays.

Nineteen plays appearing in Harrison's List (*John Howard Payne*, 1885, pp. 395-6) are known only by title. Since they are incapable of identification and are in many cases probably not by Payne, they are not included in the List of Plays.

nently before the public, and the first brought charges of plagiarism upon him. No one bothered, obviously, to level charges of borrowing at a failure.

Originality in its greatest sense was not his. His prime characteristic was a capacity for borrowing what would be theatrically effective, and reshaping it to make of it a new thing, and his ability in this direction amounted almost to genius. To have constructed as great a romantic tragedy as *Brutus*, as brilliant a social comedy as *Charles the Second*, as successful a melodrama as *Thérèse*, as popular an opera as *Clari*, is an achievement on which his position may rest secure. But in dramatic history, his reputation grows as we watch the influence of *Brutus* upon later playwrights. Roman history had long been on the stage, but the great vogue of the historical play, in which life was treated not in the rigid manner of the eighteenth century, but with the freedom which Payne had learned from the French *mélodrame*, was due at least partly to him. Kean took *Brutus* to Paris in 1827, and it may well have had an effect upon Hugo and his school. The later American romantic tragedy goes back to him and not to Sheridan Knowles. It is not merely a question of chronology. Knowles's *Caius Gracchus* was played in Belfast in 1815, but Payne could not have seen it until it was performed at Drury Lane in 1823, and *Virginius* was not put on until 1820, two years after *Brutus* had begun its long career. But it is rather in its freedom and vigor of treatment that *Brutus* separates itself from the British school of playwriting of which *Virginius* was in a sense the leader. Knowles made history domestic. Payne kept it heroic, but instead of preserving merely the outline of heroic figures as the eighteenth century had done, he filled them with the life with which romance revivifies history.

While Payne was bringing to our stage his adaptations of contemporary foreign models, a number of playwrights, working at home, were seeking their inspiration in foreign themes, both ancient and modern. One of the most significant groups was to be found in Charleston, South Carolina. Removed by distance from immediate contact with the newer plays produced in New York and Philadelphia, the playwrights of Charleston made a praiseworthy effort to provide their theatre with suitable material. One of the earliest of these plays to be produced on the professional stage was *Independence, or Which Do You Like Best, the Peer or the Farmer?* by William Ioor. It was put on at the Charleston Theatre in 1805, with John Hodgkinson in the leading part of Charles Woodville. The play was based on the English novel, *The Independent*, and contrasts the gentleman farmer, Woodville, with the foppish, dissipated peer, Lord Fanfare. The latter endeavors to seduce Lady Violet, Woodville's sister, under cover of a masquerade ball, and is completely fooled by the substitution of her brother, dressed as Dame Quickly, while Lady Violet, disguised as Ancient Pistol, flirts with Lady Fanfare. The play reads well, for the characters are individualized, and Ioor gave the cast some good theatrical situations. It is one of the earliest examples of social comedy, and was the first native play to treat English life with a real appreciation of its social values. Ioor's *Eutaw Springs* had a native theme, and has already been treated, but the greatest efforts of this school of playwrights were turned into the field of romantic tragedy and comedy.

Fifteen years before Byron published his tragedy of *The Two Foscari*, John Blake White (1781-1859), a young South Carolinian, wrote his *Foscari, or the Venetian Exile*, produced at the Charleston Theatre in 1806, with Mr. and Mrs. Whitlock in the cast. White was the most prolific of the dramatists of the State, and his paintings occupied even more of his attention than his plays. One of his historical paintings, "The Battle of Fort Moultrie," hangs now in the Capitol in Washington. *Foscari* is based on the story of the Doge of Venice, whose son is accused of the murder of Count Donato, father of Almeria, whom he loves. Erizzo, the real culprit, is stabbed accidentally by his tool Policarpo, and confesses his guilt, but the revelation comes too late, for Almeria has gone mad and the younger

Foscari dies of grief.[1] White was writing with the Elizabethans in mind, but Almeria's mad scene, reminiscent of Ophelia as it is, is no burlesque, and the figure of the childless Doge is invested by the playwright with real dignity as he stands unbroken in his sorrow:

> "*Doge:*   It is done:
> My fate is now decisively determined!
> Let then the whirlwind of calamity
> Drive on—Let all the complicated ills
> Of life join in the blast to overwhelm
> Me with despair—; I can defy them all—
> For now I know the honor of my boy
> Stands unpolluted."

White's second play, *The Mysteries of the Castle, or the Victim of Revenge*, was performed at the Charleston Theatre in 1806. It is a Gothic melodrama, laid in Castile, which deals with the robber theme, and is based on the motive of revenge. The touch of inspiration which gave dignity to *Foscari* is rarely present in this play, which is artificial in tone and confused in plot. Fauresco, the villain, for no apparent reason, plunges his friend, Count de Manfrois, into a complication of miseries, growing out of the supposed murder of his wife and her brother. It is not clear even at the end of the play who made the attempt at murder, since both the Count and Fauresco claim the doubtful honor, but the Countess lives for twenty years, to chaperon finally her daughter and the heroine in rather dire straits both as to location and company. The prose is better in the few comedy scenes than in the romantic quarrels and escapes but White shows conclusively that his ability lay in the direction of verse tragedy rather than in that of prose melodrama.

Although White was able to express admirably the sense of personal honor in *Foscari*, he knew false honor from true. In *Modern Honor*, produced at the Charleston Theatre in 1812,

[1] The play seems to have been popular, for a second edition in manuscript exists, revised by the author, in the Clothier Collection. In this edition Policarpo kills Foscari as the latter is about to be exiled.

he drew a vivid picture of the evils resulting from the practice of dueling. The scene is laid "in any part of the civilized world," and the characters are typical rather than local. Forsythe, the villain of the piece, persuades Woodville of the infidelity of his mistress, and Devalmore, her brother, challenges Woodville to a duel through the mistaken idea that it is he who has entered her room by night. Woodville kills Devalmore, and after he has discovered Forsythe's perfidy is killed by him in a second duel. The play is handicapped by its motive and is too highly colored in its tragedy, but it is written with sincerity.

The wisdom of laying tragic scenes in a distant time and country is well illustrated in the superiority of White's earlier work to his tragedy, *The Forgers*, performed at the Charleston Theatre in 1825 and '26 and published in the *Southern Literary Journal* in 1837. It is a didactic play leveled at the evils of drink and gambling. The hero-villain, Mordaunt, is made the victim of the hate of Celestina Ridgeford, to whom he has been false, and her brother leads him through all the dissipation necessary to conduct him finally to forgery, murder, and suicide. The folly of representing people as talking in blank verse in the nineteenth century is well illustrated in this play. Its scene is supposed to be in this country, but the characters are so abstract that it fails to be significant as a representation of American life. White's one play that was based on native feeling, *The Triumph of Liberty* (1819), seems not to have survived.

Another of the Charleston group, Isaac Harby (1788-1828), wrote his first acted play, *The Gordian Knot, or Causes and Effects*, in 1807, and after submitting it to Placide, the manager of the Charleston Theatre, and also to Warren in Philadelphia, he finally had the pleasure of seeing it performed in 1810 in Charleston. His introduction to the printed play in 1810 contains a delightful account of the rehearsals, at which the actors, Green and Sully, read the lines with remarks of their own interlarded, until the author calmly took the manuscript and went home to supper! The *Gordian Knot* deserved a better fate, and apparently it met with adequate interpretation at the hands of the cast which finally played it. It is more strictly a romantic melodrama than a tragedy, for while dark passages, disguised monks and nuns, and long-cherished revenge are intermingled in a plot whose complications forbid retelling, all ends happily except for the villain Ferdinand, when the monk Ubaldo discloses the schemes which would have made Alphonso kill his father the Duke. What distinguishes this play among its fellows is the charm of the love scenes. Marcello and Madalena and, to a lesser extent, Alphonso and Clara are a refreshing departure from the usual lovers of romantic plays of the period, in being almost real.

Harby tells us that his source for the early portion of the play was the *Abbess* by Ireland, which in its turn goes back to the Italian *novella, Secreto Maligno,* but that in making the motives and actions of the characters differ in every point from the novel, he has approached a natural treatment! He concludes by remarking:

Dramatists too often think their task completed, if they have justly described the local manners of man. I have preferred to picture him in his general nature. On that basis has rested the immortality of Shakespeare; and I am proud to own, I write for fame.

Harby, who was an editor and a dramatic critic of some ability, tried another play with the revenge motive in *Alberti,* which was performed at the Charleston Theatre in 1819. The scene is Florence; the time, 1480. He tells us that he has been obliged to invent a story, since the revenge motive has been fully worked out in such characters as Zanga, Bertram, Fitzharding, and Pescara. He, therefore, planned Alberti's revenge to consist in restoring Ippolito, whom he had brought up as his son, to his real father Ridolfo, Alberti's brother and arch-enemy. Unfortunately, Ippolito has fallen in love with Ridolpho's daughter, Antonia, and this restoration would make them brother and sister. This situation is saved, however, by the omniscient friar (without whom the romantic play could scarcely have proceeded) who reveals the fact that Ippolito is Alberti's own son and the cousins are betrothed. The play is easily one of the best of its kind from the point of view of expression. The blank verse is flexible and interesting, and the construction is more unified than in *The Gordian Knot*. It seems a pity that Harby should have died on December 14, 1828, shortly after he went to New York, for he is one of the writers of the time whose work has the touch of inspiration.[1]

As was natural, the romantic figure of Byron was popular in the South, and a dramatization of *The Corsair*, by Edwin Clifford Holland, was played in Charleston in 1818. It has some merit in its unity and compactness of structure. Young played Conrad; Mrs. Young, Medora; and Mrs. Gilbert, Gulvare. It is called "a melodrama," and the music, either "soft and plaintive" or "descriptive of sudden joy," shows the fidelity to the type. Holland drew largely on Byron's language, but changed the rhymed couplet to blank verse with considerable skill.

The plays of this group that actually reached the boards are, of course, of most significance. But it is interesting also to see the attempts to provide material for the company at the Charleston Theatre, which, while they may not have reached the stage, show how strong was the dramatic impulse of that period and place. *A Tyrant's Victims*, for example, by M. Pinckney (1818), is not at all a weak effort. It is a tragedy laid near Carthage. She also wrote *The Orphans*, a five-act social satire upon English life (1818). Both are written with more sense of the stage than the productions of James Wright Simmons, another South Carolinian, whose *Manfredi* (1821) is a tragedy laid in Italy and belonging to the school of terror. Simmons dramatized *The Bride of Lammermoor* under the title of *Valdemar, or the Castle of the Cliff*

---

[1] See *Memoir* in Harby's *Miscellaneous Writings*, Charleston, 1829.

(1822), a gloomy melodrama with many shifts of scene. An anonymous tragedy, *The Female Enthusiast*, "By a Lady," which has been attributed to Sarah Pogson, was published in Charleston in 1807, and is interesting on account of its early date. It dramatizes the murder of Marat by Charlotte Corday, but submerges the tragedy in a confused domestic drama of mediocre quality.

Mordecai Noah, whose work on native themes has been discussed, began his active career as a playwright with an adaptation from the French *mélodrame*. His *Paul and Alexis, or the Orphans of the Rhine*, was written in Charleston in 1812 for Mrs. Charles Young, and while Noah was interested in theatrical matters as a boy in Philadelphia it is significant that his first acted play should have been produced in Charleston during this period of dramatic activity. It was founded on Pixerécourt's *Le Pèlerin Blanc ou les Orphelins du Hameau* (1801),[1] a play which seems to have been the most popular of all Pixerécourt's melodramas, being represented 1533 times. Noah follows his original in the plot, which is concerned with the return of two boys, Justin and Paul de Croisy, to their ancestral estate, Olival, in Provence, and their salvation from the machinations of their cousin, Baroness Olival, by their father, the Count de Croisy, who is disguised and watches over them. The theme of fatherly affection is well worked out and appealed for many years to the sentiment of playgoers. Noah tells us that the play was sent to London by Young, where the "bantling was cut up, altered, and considerably improved." The alterations were probably made by John Kerr, since two editions of a version ostensibly by him have appeared. Between his version and Noah's as printed the differences are so slight as to be negligible. Noah's play, published anonymously in 1821, is in two Acts with three scenes in the third Act, while Kerr frames his third Act out of scenes two and three of the

---

[1] Founded on a romance, *Les Petits Orphelins du Hameau*, by Ducray-Dumesnil, based in its turn on Marsollier's opera of *Les Petits Savoyards*. See W. Hertzog. *Guilbert de Pixerécourt*, p. 95.

third Act of Noah's play. At Covent Garden, on February 24, 1814, it appeared under the title of *The Wandering Boys, or the Castle of Olival*, probably the second play by an American to be performed in England after an initial production in America.[1] On March 16, 1820, it was produced at the Park Theatre under this title, and remained popular for many years.

The Grecian Captive, or the Fall of Athens, was first played at the Park Theatre, June 17, 1822. According to Noah, the incidents were borrowed from a French *mélodrame*. This was *Mahomet II*, by Charrin and Joseph (1820), but Noah did not follow his model slavishly, and his rearrangements of geography and contemporary history are justified by the result, which is interesting and well constructed. *The Grecian Captive* was also rendered noteworthy by the appearance of the hero on an elephant and the heroine on a camel, and by the presentation to each auditor of a copy of the play, as he entered the theatre. "Figure to yourself," the author remarks, "a thousand people in a theatre, each with a book of the play in hand—imagine the turning over a thousand leaves simultaneously, the buzz and fluttering it produced, and you will readily believe that the actors forgot their parts, and even the equanimity of the elephant and camel were essentially disturbed."

The native and the foreign elements of the drama in this period are not always easily distinguishable. *Altorf*, a tragedy by Frances Wright, afterward Madame Darusmont, is laid in Switzerland in the fourteenth century, yet the impulse which caused the young Scottish woman to select the theme was the freedom she had found in her adopted country. She came to New York in 1818, and *Altorf* was produced at the Park Theatre on February 19, 1819. It seems to have been only moderately successful in New York, but in Philadelphia Wood tells us "it was received with general approbation," Cooper appearing as Altorf. It was revived in 1829 in New York and

[1] See p. 139.

was reprinted in London. The play reads well; there is a
nobility in the conception of the characters that reflects the
enthusiasm for freedom which was characteristic of the author,
even if at times she carried that enthusiasm into too radical
an atmosphere. The hero, Eberard de Altorf, is caught in a
web of circumstances in which he has to seem untrue to his
country and to his wife or to abandon Rosina who loves him
and whom he has long loved. Miss Wright was one of the
first advocates of woman suffrage, and she conducted for a
time a settlement for freed slaves near Memphis, Tennessee.
Her preface contains some interesting comparisons between the
British and American stages.

I know not if my wishes influence my judgment, but I cannot help
believing that this country will one day revive the sinking honour
of the drama. It is I believe generally felt and acknowledged, by the
public of Great Britain as of America, that the dignity of English
Tragedy has now degenerated into pantomime; and that rapid
movements, stage tricks and fine scenery have filled the place of
poetry, character, and passion. The construction as well as the
management of the London Theatres perhaps present insurmountable
obstacles to any who might there ambition to correct the fashion of
the stage. No such difficulties exist here. But this is not all: America
is the land of liberty. Here is the country where Truth may lift her
voice without fear;—where the words of Freedom may not only be
read in the closet, but heard from the stage. England pretends to
an unshackled press; but there is not a stage in England from which
the dramatist might breathe the sentiments of enlightened patriotism
and republican liberty. In America alone might such a stage be
formed; a stage that should be, like that of Greece, a school of
virtue;—where all that is noble in sentiment, generous and heroic in
action should speak to the hearts of a free people, and inspire each
rising generation with all the better and nobler feelings of human
nature.

It is probable that the substitution of Cooper for Wallack
who had played first in *Altorf* may have accounted for the
success of the play in Philadelphia after its comparative failure
in New York. Cooper was the inspiration for more than one
dramatist. John Neal, the strange apostle of passion in fiction,

who just missed genius, wrote for Cooper a tragedy, *Otho*, in 1819, which has all the author's characteristic incoherence and yet at times a real dignity in its blank verse. It seems not to have been acted. Some dignity lies, too, in the verse of *Alexis the Czarewitz*, by Alexis Eustaphieve, which was played at the Boston Theatre in 1814. The author was the Russian consul in Boston at the time, but is allied to our stage by his artistic interest.

As might be expected, the melodrama of the minor writers of this period falls far below the level of the tragedies or comedies. Joseph Hutton, a native of Philadelphia, a schoolmaster and later an actor both in Philadelphia and with Caldwell in New Orleans, had two of his productions staged at the Chestnut Street Theatre, *The School for Prodigals*, in 1808, and *The Wounded Hussar, or Rightful Heir*, in 1809. The first is laid in England, though it might have been laid anywhere a high-road was available, and the second is a musical afterpiece of a trifling nature. He published also a Gothic melodrama, *The Orphan of Prague*, in 1808, which is delightful in its impossibility. It is not certain that this was performed, and his one native comedy that has survived, *Fashionable Follies*, was not played, although it was cast and put in rehearsal. This play, laid on the borders of Lake Champlain just after the War of 1812, has some amusing moments.

John D. Turnbull, who played at the Park Theatre in 1802, and after a stay in Boston and Charleston, reappeared in New York at the Chatham Theatre in 1825, wrote a very popular melodrama, *Rudolph, or the Robbers of Calabria*, which was first performed in New York in 1804 and published in 1807.[1] While not the first it was an early example of the adaptation of a French *mélodrame*, being based on *La Forêt périlleuse, ou les Brigands de la Calabre*, by Loaisel de Tréogate, played at the Théâtre de la Cité in 1797, which in its turn goes

[1] Owing to an error in the catalogue of the Harris Collection of American Poetry at Brown University, which gives an edition of 1799, some attention has been drawn to *Rudolph* as the earliest example of the melodrama from French sources. The first edition was that of 1807.

back, of course, to Schiller's *Robbers*. It is an active melo-drama, laid in Sicily, in which Count Albert and his betrothed, Rosolia di Borgia, fall into the clutches of the bandit, Rudolph, who is finally circumvented by the cleverness of a Sicilian officer who has wormed his way into the confidence of the bandit chief. The stage directions are interesting as showing the use of musical accompaniment. When Rudolph and his lieutenant are examining the cavern we have "music expressive of suspicion," then later "music expressive of agitation." Turnbull refers rather pathetically in his preface to his obscure position in the theatre which prevented his obtaining a benefit, and the plight from which the kindness of General Jacob Morton rescued him. *Rudolph* was republished more than once, and it is to be hoped that the proceeds went to the dramatist, whose struggles probably reflect a tragedy too common in those days. His daughter, Mrs. Pritchard, was more successful, being for a time the leading actress of the Albany Theatre. Turnbull also produced *The Wood Dæmon, or the Clock Has Struck, a Grand Romantic Cabalistic Melo-drama, Interspersed with Processions, Pageants and Pantomime*, in 1808, founded on M. G. Lewis's play of the same name. The opening scene which represents the Wood Dæmon about to stab a child was mercifully omitted, apparently, "owing to the great expense," rather than to any artistic qualms on the part of the manager. But *The Wood Dæmon*, like *Rudolph*, was vastly popular, and as one of the principal dancers we find David Poe, the father of Edgar.

Samuel B. H. Judah, whose *Tale of Lexington* has already been mentioned, produced two melodramas. *The Mountain Torrent*, performed at the Park Theatre, March 1, 1820, treats the theme of a daughter's betrothal to save her father from ruin in a way which makes it interesting to compare with *The Banker's Daughter* of Bronson Howard, for Judah's plays follow the French melodrama in its path of improbability. His *Rose of Arragon* [sic] (1822), is even worse, but one cannot help wishing that the last scene, in which Rosaline stabs the villain,

Laranda, then rushes into Aurelio's arms while Benorio stretches his hands in benediction over them and the "characters are formed in a picturesque manner" might be reproduced at least once, for the delight of posterity.

It would be fruitless even to name some of the other wild and improbable melodramas which, frequently of foreign origin, were adapted for the American stage. The plays based on native conditions have their values as social history, but those founded on foreign themes must stand the test of absolute merit and even here they fall below the plays upon American themes. Payne's best work delighted thousands and has, therefore, its secure place; the work of the Charleston group has a real significance and at times an actual merit. Noah's plays deserved more recognition perhaps than they received, but for the rest there is not much to urge. It was only natural that such should be the case. When the playwrights turned to foreign themes, nearly all of them were dealing with unfamiliar scenes and social customs known to them superficially. Only occasionally did they touch upon the universal passions or borrow the dignity of great historical figures. For these our stage had to wait for the genius of Bird and Boker.

CHAPTER VIII

From Melodrama to Tragedy

AT the beginning of the second quarter of the nineteenth century, a change began in the nature of the drama. This change became more apparent after 1830, but the causes that underlay the change were beginning to operate for some time before they became really effective. They were based partly on the condition of the theatres, partly on the advent of certain actors like Edwin Forrest, and they were due partly to the general social, political, and economic condition of the country.

By 1825 improvements in transportation had brought Boston within two days of New York, New York only eleven hours from Philadelphia, and Philadelphia fifteen hours from Washington.[1] The rapid growth which this condition made possible was revolutionizing industry and bringing to the front a group of people who before this were outside the consideration of purveyors of dramatic art. While banks, insurance companies, canals and turnpikes, mills and factories were springing up on every hand, openings were found for thousands who passed with prosperity from the class who worked without hope to those who not only hoped but demanded reward and enjoyment in addition to a bare livelihood. This class did not at once come into the theatre; in fact, the reduction in 1823 in prices of tickets to seventy-five, fifty, and twenty-five cents seems to have had no favorable result, so far at least as the Philadelphia theatres were concerned. But there is evidence in the building of theatres in New York, Philadelphia, Boston, and Washington in the period 1820-30 that the managers anticipated a demand which came, but came more

[1] McMaster, V, 83.

slowly than they had expected. The accounts of this transition period as given by the theatrical managers of the time are confused and at times contradictory. They are swayed, too, by personal feeling and the embittered memories of rivalry that spelled ruin for themselves and their companies. We are concerned not with these ancient feuds, but with the effect upon the drama exercised by the shifting theatrical conditions of this period.

In 1822 the supremacy of the Park Theatre in New York was threatened, first by the erection of the Chatham Garden, to become in 1824 the Chatham Garden Theatre, with a company that included Joseph Jefferson. The Lafayette Theatre which, like the Chatham, was for a time under Henry Wallack's management, was built in 1825 and burned in 1829. These two theatres proved to be only temporary rivals of the Park, but in 1826 the Bowery Theatre began a career, checkered it is true, but in time destined to be a great one. It is interesting to remember that it was built to house an audience which, on account of its location, was expected to be fashionable, and that on the contrary its palmy days were those when, under Hamblin's management, it became the stronghold of democracy. The evidence of the public appeal is shown indirectly by the change in scale of prices. At first the charges were fifty cents for the boxes and the pit and twenty-five cents for the gallery. But "a few nights' experience proved that to keep a portion of the house free from admixture with the vulgar and unrefined, it would be necessary to discriminate between the boxes and the pit, and the admission was raised to seventy-five cents for the former, and reduced to thirty-seven and one-half cents for the latter, which soon produced the effect desired."[1]

At the beginning of the decade 1820-30, the theatrical metropolis of the country lay in Philadelphia. The Chestnut Street Theatre Company, under the management of Warren and Wood, with its fine theatre, its well-balanced company,

[1] Ireland, I, 522.

headed by the managers and containing also Mr. and Mrs. Henry Wallack, the first Joseph Jefferson, Mrs. Jefferson, Mrs. Wood, Mrs. Darley, Mrs. Entwistle, to say nothing of Burke. Francis, John and Thomas Jefferson, formed an organization which, especially in comedy, had no rival in the country. Francis Courtney Wemyss, the English light comedian who came to America in 1822, and who was nothing if not critical, compares his impression of the troupe at the Park Theatre, "which was certainly the worst company I had ever seen in a metropolitan theatre," with the Philadelphia company, which "had such an array of talent that every part was filled with an actor fully competent to sustain the reputation of the theatre."[1]

At this time the Philadelphia managers practically controlled the situation in Baltimore. They would open in Baltimore in September or October, play until November, when the Philadelphia season opened, to last until April, when a spring season would be resumed in Baltimore, lasting until July. A summer season would sometimes be conducted at Washington and even Alexandria, Virginia, thus holding the company together. Not only in the personnel of the company but also in matters of theatrical appointments, the management of "Old Drury," as the Chestnut Street Theatre was called, were foremost. They installed gas lighting in November, 1816,[2] for example, nine years before it was introduced in New York City at the opening of the new Chatham Theatre on May 9, 1825. By 1828 this situation was completely changed. Dissension and outside interference led to Wood's withdrawal from the managership; the rivalry between the Walnut Street, Arch Street, and Chestnut Street Theatres resulted in the disintegration of the splendid company and financial bankruptcy followed. Five companies failed in Philadelphia from October 1, 1828, to May 27, 1829.

It was not only the disasters of the Philadelphia theatres that brought the primacy to New York. The year 1825

---

[1] *Twenty-six years of the Life of an Actor and Manager*, p. 70 and p. 74.
[2] Wood's Diary.

marked the beginning of a new era for the Park Theatre, and owing to the temporary nature of her rivals' efforts she kept the leadership. This season saw the first successful attempt at the introduction of Italian opera, and brought Mme. Malibran to the beginning of her great career. Of much greater importance, a strong company was organized, including Mrs. Barnes, in tragedy and a combination in comedy of Hilson, Barnes, Placide, Mrs. Wheatley, and Miss Kelly, which was augmented for the first time by the ability of James H. Hackett, who began his famous imitations of Yankee dialect. This season saw also the first appearance of Thomas S. Hamblin, whose long subsequent career as manager of the Bowery Theatre made him a potent force on the American stage.

By the year 1830 this priority of New York was well established, and the excellence of the light comedy company at Niblo's Garden, built in 1830, added to its prestige. Better theatrical conditions began to prevail in Philadelphia also in 1831–2 and in Boston, where, in addition to the Federal Street Theatre and the Washington Street Theatre, the Tremont Theatre had been built in 1827.

But of all the causes which led to the priority of New York, her geographical position as the greatest port of entry was the most potent. To her came first the foreign stars, and their influence upon our theatre and upon our drama was great. Wood speaks of the "star system" with bitterness, attributing the decline of the theatre to this cause, and he had reason, when he compared the prosperous, well-ordered days of his company from 1810 to 1820 with its later disaster. Galling indeed it was to pay stars more than the receipts they brought in to the theatre, and surely human sympathy must go out to the members of the stock company who witnessed a star like Miss Lydia Kelly, taking her nightly sum in cash, before she left the stage, with the knowledge that the balance did not provide their own modest salaries. Yet that the stars did attract in general much larger audiences than the regular companies is proved by the relentless testimony of Wood's own account books, and the mistake lay in paying the extortionate amounts which the foreign actors seemed able to demand from managers who lost, in their desperate rivalry, a proper sense of proportion. Wood's attitude was colored, too, by local feeling. He foresaw in 1821 what happened a little later—that the coming of the stars first to New York would make the theatres in other cities tributary to the metropolitan management that first secured them.

Beginning in 1820, a succession of great actors and actresses visited the American stage—Edmund and Charles Kean, Charles Mathews, Junius Brutus Booth, William Charles Macready, Charles and Fanny Kemble, to mention only the greatest, but with the exception of Booth, they contributed almost nothing to the encouragement of our drama. It was not that they were hostile to it, they were simply indifferent. They had their own plays and they saw no reason to adopt new and untried parts. But the very fact that these foreign stars acted first and most frequently in New York, while it added to that city's theatrical prestige, hindered the development of a native drama there. In Philadelphia, on the other hand, which welcomed the stars less frequently, and where theatrical rivalry spurred on the respective managers to provide attractions, there grew up a number of playwrights whose work became widely known both at home and abroad. Settled theatrical conditions are, of course, necessary to the encouragement of the drama, but full houses do not always mean prosperity to the native playwright, while theatrical failure sometimes spells success for him. The season of 1921-22 is a glittering example in which history repeated itself after a century. Too many theatres may bring ruin to producers, but they may give the American dramatist his long-awaited opportunity.

While the foreign stars, therefore, were on the whole indifferent to the native drama, the case was far different with the two native actors whose careers began in the decade from 1820 to 1830—Edwin Forrest and James H. Hackett. Forrest was born in Philadelphia, March 9, 1806. Against family opposition and with no enthusiastic welcome from the management, he made his début at the Walnut Street Theatre, November 27, 1820, as young Norval in Home's tragedy of *Douglas*, the character chosen by Payne for his first appearance. He showed real ability, but no opening presenting itself in Philadelphia, he was advised to acquire experience in the West, and he spent some years in Pittsburgh, Lexington, Cincinnati, New Orleans, and Albany, reappearing in Philadelphia in May, 1826, and acting Othello in New York in June. He soon was established in popular favor as a star, and it is to his credit that he stimulated American playwrights to produce plays suited to his ability. John Augustus Stone, Richard Penn Smith, Robert Montgomery Bird, Robert Conrad, and George H. Miles were among those who wrote plays for him or were encouraged by his performance in their plays. Of his relations with them it will be more appropriate to speak when we are discussing the work of the dramatists themselves, but the group of Philadelphia playwrights who were stimulated by a great Philadelphia actor remains a significant landmark in the history of our drama.

Through his interest and support he almost restored Philadelphia to her theatrical prestige. In 1831-2, under the management of James, Duffy, and Forrest, the Arch Street Theatre had a brilliant season, according to Durang "the first legitimate American management in the large Atlantic Cities" and certainly with Edwin Forrest's help, which was freely given to his brother's theatre, the season which witnessed the first production of *The Gladiator*, *De Lara*, and *Conrad of Naples*, and revivals of *Metamora* and *Sertorius* was a promising one for the American playwright. It was also a profitable venture for the manager. While Maywood at the Chestnut Street Theatre was losing money through his policy of employing foreign stars imported by the Park Theatre, the Arch Street management had a most profitable season. Real results might have followed if this experiment of pitting an American actor with American plays against a theatre with the policy of producing foreign importations, could have continued.

FROM MELODRAMA TO TRAGEDY

James H. Hackett was born in New York City, March 15, 1800. His first appearance in 1826 was not successful, but his renderings of Yankee characters made him famous, and his own dramatic contributions will be treated under that head. The success of James K. Paulding's *Lion of the West* in which Hackett acted Nimrod Wildfire was due in large measure to his performance, and he supplies one of the links in the long development of *Rip Van Winkle*. Forrest and Hackett were not alone, of course, in their encouragement of native play-wrights. Naturally, actors were looking for the proper vehicles for their talents, and managers were willing to risk something in a business whose very foundation is the unstable quality of public favor. That they were not willing to risk enough, is evidenced by the solid profit which came to Edwin Forrest from *Metamora*, *The Gladiator*, and *Jack Cade*, but this object lesson was yet to be brought to their attention in 1825, the year in which Longfellow chose for his graduation oration an appeal for better appreciation of "Our Native Writers"!

As a people we had almost no artistic courage, and even the dramatists turned, as Payne had done, too frequently, to foreign inspiration. A typical playwright of this transition period, 1825 to 1830, was Richard Penn Smith. He was born in Phila-delphia, March 13, 1799, the grandson of William Smith, first Provost of the College of Philadelphia, who had been the patron of our first playwright. Richard Penn Smith was well educated, and his library, sold at his death, contained many volumes, the largest group next to that containing his legal volumes being devoted to English and French drama. He was editor of the *Aurora* for a time, but his principal profession was that of law. A significant passage from his son's biography of the Reverend William Smith[1] reveals the dramatic associations of the time in Philadelphia:

Well do I remember how proud I was of him: he took me with him wherever he went, and his associates and companions (child as I was) became mine. James N. Barker, Robert M. Bird, Joseph C.

[1] Smith, Horace W. *Life of Reverend William Smith*, II, 529.

HISTORY OF THE AMERICAN DRAMA

Neal, Edwin Forrest, James Goodman, Edgar A. Poe, Louis A. Godey, William E. Burton, Robert T. Conrad, Joseph C. Chandler, and Morton McMichael were the literary magnates of Philadelphia, and of all that intellectual coterie my father's star was the brightest, his wit the gayest, and his sarcasm the most cutting; as a writer he was admired; as a dramatist, at that day the most successful in the country, and with some fame as a poet, he was beloved as a companion and a gentleman.

Some allowance must be made for filial feeling, and the calm critic would not place Penn Smith, as he was usually called, in such a relatively high position among the group of Philadelphia dramatists, but his work is important not only for itself but also because it illustrates the tentative experimenting in dramatic forms in which a playwright of transition is apt to indulge. Romantic tragedy and comedy, national historical plays, domestic drama, melodrama, and farce, based both on native and foreign inspiration, were constructed by him, always with a view to stage presentation. He wrote twenty plays, of which fifteen were performed. He seems to have begun dramatic composition in 1825, with a farce, *The Pelican*, and with *The Divorce*, a tentative effort at romantic comedy, later to be rewritten successfully as *The Deformed*. On May 27, 1828, his first acted play, *Quite Correct*, was put on at the Chestnut Street Theatre. It is an attractive comedy, in which a hotel keeper, Grojan, whose object in life is to be "quite correct," provides a meeting place for a separated couple to be reunited, and two lovers to be joined. It was based on a story, *Doubts and Fears*, by Theodore Hook, contained in his collection, *Sayings and Doings* (1826-9), in the volume entitled *The Man of Many Friends*. This story was in its turn founded on a French comedy by Désaugiers (1772-1827) and Gentil, *L'Hôtel garni ou la Leçon singulière*,[1] a one-act verse comedy, performed in 1814 at the Théâtre Français,

---

[1] See Lenient, *La Comédie en France au XIXe Siècle*, I, p. 218 and p. 228. Ireland attributed a play by the same name, performed on September 18, 1826, at the Park Theatre, to Poole, but is probably in error, as the cast is exactly the same as that of an English play, *Quite Correct*, by Caroline Boaden, which had proved very popular at the Haymarket Theatre in 1825. (Genest IX, 315.)

of all Désaugiers's work probably the most truly a piece of literature. Smith follows the story of Hook quite closely as to incident and characters. The conversation is clever and yet natural, and the play could be produced to-day without much change.

Smith next turned to American history for material, and produced *The Eighth of January*, played first at the Chestnut Street Theatre on January 8, 1829. It celebrated ostensibly Jackson's victory at New Orleans in 1815, but in reality it celebrated his triumph of 1828, and was consequently of deeper significance. Andrew Jackson had just been elected President of the United States, and, to a great majority of the people, he was the champion of popular government as opposed to the class government of which the "Adams dynasty" was the symbol. The play represents, therefore, the dramatization of political feeling and belongs to social history. In the preface Penn Smith tells us that:

The Eighth of January was merely intended to serve the occasion on which it was produced, and so little time was allowed for its composition, that it was sent piecemeal to the theatre to be copied, and the last act was not written until after the piece was announced, and within a week of its performance. This much is stated that those who expect a finished drama may be undeceived at the outset; but as its success on the stage far exceeded anticipation, the writer is induced to throw it before the public, trusting that what merit it appeared to possess in action, may not wholly evaporate on closer examination. The difficulty of introducing a distinguished living character on the stage without offence to propriety, can be duly estimated by those alone who have attempted it; and if the writer of the following drama escape this censure, he will be satisfied; but should it attach itself to him, he can only plead in extenuation, that it is time that the principal events in the history of our country were dramatised, and exhibited at the theatres on such days as are set apart as national festivals, and that there are few more deserving of commemoration than that herein slightly touched upon.

The Eighth of January contrasts Charles Bull, the American soldier who is willing to sacrifice himself for his chief, with his father, John Bull, who as a loyal Englishman will not fight against either his native or his adopted country. Joseph Jefferson played the comic character, Billy Bowbell. General Jackson avails himself of the extraordinary device, used before by Payne in *Peter Smink*, of signing an armistice in the presence of the enemy, thereby preventing his own capture. In this and a few other features he derived assistance from a French melodrama, by Frédéric du Petit-Méré (1787-1827).

Smith's plays can be studied most profitably in their types rather than in accordance with strict chronology. His next historical play, produced at the Walnut Street Theatre on December 25, 1829, was an attempt to dramatize the figure of William Penn, and to carry on the interest in Indian themes, already being kindled by the success of Stone's *Metamora* ten days before. Two manuscripts of William Penn exist. One, lacking three scenes, has been printed. The scene is laid on the banks of the Delaware River, and the play deals with the rivalry of the Shakamaxon and Sanhiccan tribes, the rescue of Oulita, the Indian heroine, by Lenape, who kills her assailant, the demand of the Sanhiccans for his blood, and the proffered sacrifice of his father, Tammany, to save his son. The arrival of William Penn rescues Tammany and after he succeeds in reconciling the tribes, he departs. The play reads well, despite the curious language which the Indians speak on the stage and there only. *William Penn* was played as late as January 1, 1842, by William E. Burton at his National Theatre in Philadelphia.

The best of Smith's historical plays was *The Triumph at Plattsburg*, based on the victory of McDonough's fleet on Plattsburg Bay in September, 1814. It was put on January 8, 1830, at the Chestnut Street Theatre, with considerable scenic effect, to judge from the program, which promised "a view of the Arrival and Capture of the British Fleet." The fight, however, is really kept in the background, and the main interest lies in the escape of Major McCrea from the British soldiers. This is brought about by a clever comedy scene, in which

Andre Macklegraith, a Scottish miller, is represented by his mother and sweetheart as being half-witted, in order that McCrea, who has disguised himself in Andre's clothes, may escape his pursuers. Elinor McCrea, the major's daughter, is searching for her husband, Captain Stanley of the British Army. McCrea is about to attack him for deceiving her when he learns that Stanley has been acting throughout in an honorable way. This avoidance of the villain, clad in a scarlet coat, is characteristic of Smith's work, and his emphasis upon the human interest in the motive of self-preservation shows his knowledge of his audience.

The greatest quantity, although not by any means the highest quality, of Penn Smith's work, is to be found in the adaptation of French comedy or melodrama. His first venture in this field was *The Disowned, or the Prodigals*, whose initial performance took place at the Holliday Street Theatre, Baltimore, March 26, 1829. Wemyss, who was managing the Chestnut Street Theatre Company, acted the part of Malfort, the villain, who desires to gain the fortune of Pauline Duval. Gustavus, who is intended by his uncle for Pauline, falls in love with a young widow, Amelia, and Malfort, with the aid of his hired accomplice, Bertrand, tries to hasten the marriage of Amelia and Gustavus in order to clear his path to Pauline. Bertrand, who turns out to be Amelia's brother, agrees to kill Gustavus's rich uncle, but Amelia herself receives the blow of her brother's dagger. Crime is punished and there is evidence that Pauline and Gustavus will be reconciled. Smith founded his play upon *Le Caissier*, a three-act drama published in 1826, by Jouslin de la Salle, known as Armand François (1797-1863). He changed the plot, however, especially at the end, and his reasons as given in the preface, are interesting in the revelation of his technique. In the original, Amelia retired to a convent, and Bertrand remained unrepentant. Smith observes: "The termination was without a climax, for Amelia is still alive, and the man to whom she is so devotedly attached is given in marriage to another. Besides, a blemish is unnecessarily thrown upon the moral character of Amelia, which diminishes the interest awakened by her situation. The result proved the alterations to be judicious, and the powerful acting of Mr. Rowbotham [in the character of Bertrand] never failed to rivet the attention, and elicit the unqualified applause of the audience." The withdrawal of Amelia to the convent and the marriage of Gustavus to Pauline while Amelia is alive, presented, of course, no such obstacles to a French audience as they did to the American, and Smith's endeavors to awaken the sympathy of the audience by making more secure the moral quality of Amelia is paralleled all through the history of our adaptations from the French, even down to Mr. Belasco's translation of *Kiki*. Smith's best change was undoubtedly in the character of Bertrand, for Wemyss and others bear testimony to Rowbotham's fine acting in the part. Wemyss changed the name to *The Disowned* to avail himself of the popularity of Bulwer's novel, and he further tells us that the play was afterward performed in London.[1] It was certainly repeated in April and on December 22, 1829, when Durang tells us that "it was acted with approbation."

Smith's next play, *A Wife at a Venture*, produced at the Walnut Street Theatre, July 25, 1829, was a confused comedy-melodrama laid in Bagdad, in which a variety of complications ensue in consequence of a law promulgated by the Caliph to the effect that everyone must marry, enlist, or pay a fine. The manuscript bears the dates 1828 and 1829, both erased, and it is evidently an early effort, worked up hastily for the summer season of that disastrous theatrical year.

A better adaptation from the French was *The Sentinels, or the Two Sergeants*,[2] played in December, 1829, at the Walnut

---

[1] I, 171.

[2] The manuscript (in a later hand) gives the date as 1832 at the Chestnut Street Theatre, but then follows a cast, which includes S. Chapman, Manager of the Walnut Street Company, who died May 16, 1830. His death was caused by a cold contracted while visiting with his stage artist, Turner's Lane, the scene of a recent robbery which he was dramatizing for the theatre under the title of *The Mail Robbers*. Surely theatrical realism deserved a better fate! See Durang, Series Three, Chap. 37, for a detailed account.

Street Theatre. This is a dramatization of the Damon and Pythias story. Two sergeants are condemned to death for allowing a woman from the yellow fever district to pass. Robert is engaged and Felix is married. One is to be executed by lot, and the die turns against Felix. Robert takes his place while Felix visits his wife on the Isle of Roses. After several adventures he returns to prevent the execution of Robert, and the General pardons both. The play deserved its apparent success, for it is well constructed, the conversation is lively and, while the audience knows perfectly well that all must end happily, the sympathy is so well evoked for the two friends that a real interest is maintained.

Smith was a constant student of the English drama, and the best of his plays that has come down to us in complete form owes its inspiration to Thomas Dekker. In 1825 he wrote a play, *The Divorce, or the Mock Cavalier*, which was not performed and in 1830 he revised this as *The Deformed, or Woman's Trial*, played at the Chestnut Street Theatre on February 4, 1830. It was repeated on several occasions, including the author's benefit on February 11th. *The Deformed* owes its sub-plot to the second part of Dekker's *Honest Whore* and its earlier adaptation, Dunlap's *Italian Father*, to both of which Smith acknowledges his indebtedness. The motive of a father watching over a daughter whom he has abandoned and of a nobleman pretending to seduce the daughter in order to test her fidelity are introduced in a manner which forms an interesting basis for comparison in the methods of the three dramatists. The relation of the plays of Dekker and Dunlap has already been discussed,[1] but in that case the dependence is much closer than in the present one. Only six of the fifteen scenes of *The Deformed* owe inspiration to either *The Honest Whore* or *The Italian Father*, and even these are radically changed. Such speeches as that of Beraldo in Act II, Sc. 4, "There is as much rejoicing in this world upon the falling off of a sinner, as we are told there is in the next over his repent-

[1] Pp. 93-95.

ance," will show the quality of Smith's interpolations. But the main plot owes nothing to either Dekker or Dunlap. Smith created as the central character Adorni, a man misshapen but worshipping beauty all the more on that account, who is married to Eugenia, the sister of Astrabel, the reformed courtesan in the earlier plays. Pathetic is his self-loathing:

"*Adorni:* I look abroad, and all that strikes mine eye
    Is beautiful. E'en things inanimate
    That were created but to live a day,
    And die; the flower we tread upon
    Betrays the labor of the skillful hand
    That fashioned it. The sky is glorious
    Passing all wonders. The birds that cleave the air,
    Are beautiful in plumage and in form.
    The living sea, when warring with the sky,
    Making its weapons of the works of man,
    That float upon its bosom, is sublime.
    . . . .

    Nature has lavish'd with unsparing hand,
    The choicest gifts upon her meanest works;
    But, in her boundless prodigality,
    Not one has fallen here. I—I alone,
    Move through this world of vast variety,
    A species in myself—disown'd by all!
    As 'twere a foil to set off all beside;
    The sport of nature and the scoff of man."

He tortures himself with wonder that his wife should love him, and urges his friend Claudio to test her fidelity. Then when the latter agrees, Adorni, insanely jealous, has him condemned to death and divorces Eugenia. Being convinced later, however, of her truth, he takes upon himself the sentence of Claudio, to be saved in his turn by the Duke. Smith wrote his original scenes in blank verse of a vigorous and varied texture, and drew well not only Adorni's craving for affection, but also Claudio's loyalty to his friend and Eugenia's fidelity, expressed with true womanliness throughout the trial scene till, after the adverse judgment, she concludes:

FROM MELODRAMA TO TRAGEDY

"I bow to your decree.   Farewell, Adorni.

I ask but this—
When my fair name is thrown among the crowd,
Stained with the poison of corrupted minds,
Give me a sigh, and struggle to forget,
That this fond heart ne'er harbored yet a thought
Unworthy of the matchless love it bore you."

Durang speaks highly of the acting of Maywood as Adorni and of the favorable reception given the play, which was acted as late as March, 1839, and seems to have also been performed in London.[1]

The facility of Penn Smith seemed to be constantly in demand for the holiday season, as on December 25, 1830, his dramatization of Cooper's novel of *The Water Witch* was played at the Chestnut Street Theatre.   It has not been preserved.   Wemyss tells us that "the piece passed off with éclat and then passed on to the manager's shelves."   He was called on to play the leading part of Tom Tiller at the eleventh hour because Young thought the part too long to commit, and then Wemyss found that he had to prompt the rest of the company! There were at least two other versions of *The Water Witch* produced soon after Penn Smith's attempt.   Among the Smith manuscripts there is a blank verse dramatization of Cooper's *Bravo* which was written in 1836 and produced as a five act tragedy, *The Venetian*, at the Arch Street Theatre, in 1849.   A letter from J. W. Wallack, dated December 4, 1836, urges Smith to have Maywood produce the play for him in May, 1837.

It is greatly to be regretted that *Caius Marius*, probably Smith's greatest play, has not been preserved even in manuscript.   It was written before 1828, for in that year it was offered to Wemyss, with the intention of presenting Southwell in the leading rôle.   Fortunately for the author, however, it was not produced at that low-water mark in theatrical history, but waited for the genius of Edwin Forrest to interpret the

[1] See account of Smith by his friend Morton McMichael, reprinted in *The Miscellaneous Works of the late Richard Penn Smith* by H. W. Smith, 1856, p. 11.

character of Marius. Forrest had made his great triumph with *Metamora* in 1829 and was looking for other American plays, with which to vary his Shakespearean program. He produced *Caius Marius* at the Arch Street Theatre on January 12, 1831, repeated it in New York on May 9th at the Park Theatre, and played it on his southern trip in the fall of 1831. Durang speaks of the dramatic construction, the vigor of language, and the harmony of versification. In one sense, however, Penn Smith was unfortunate in the association with Forrest, whose selfish policy forbade the publication of any of the plays he controlled, lest they should be acted by others. Consequently nothing has been preserved of *Caius Marius* but fragments found in newspapers or in theatrical histories. One of these shows Marius in the decline of his great powers, boasting of his triumphs and trembling at the approach of Sylla. Smith implies artistically the effect on the plebeian soldier of the patrician prestige, against which he had fought bravely but which he could not ignore either in his triumph or in his despair. A few lines from Act V, Sc. 5, will illustrate these qualities:

"*Marius:* Fill up your goblets, till the rosy wine
Sparkle like Sylla's blood.   Drink to the shades
Of the Ambrones and the Cimbrii; drink
To those whom Marius vanquished.   See, they come;
The yelling spirits of the savage Teutons,
And mad Jugurtha, foaming 'neath his chains,
Arise to join the pledge.   Drink deep, I say,
To th' enemies of Rome, for they are now
The friends of Marius.

Enter *Granius*.

Marius: How now, my son!   So pallid, wo-begone,
Thou look'st like a tenant of the grave.
Granius: I would I were.   I have just left the dead.
Marius: True, death rides forth in purple glory now:
His chariot wheels run axle-deep in blood,
What bring you, boy—what news?

Granius: Sylla, with all his forces, is before
The city walls.
Marius: So soon!
Sulpitius: He changes color,
And at the name of Sylla, his whole frame shook.   [Aside.]
Marius: More wine. An icy chilliness creeps around my heart.
The infirmities of age are coming o'er me—
Wine, wine, I say, to melt the ice within.
How stand our forces?
Granius: Lost in mad excess.
Marius: Ha! ha! ha! They live like devils, but they'll die like
gods!"

Smith reacted from the tragic treatment of Roman history
to the lightness of comedy and farce. *My Uncle's Wedding*,
which was produced at the Arch Street Theatre, October 15,
1832, as an afterpiece to Bird's *Oralloossa*, and which was
evidently a successful comedy, has not survived. *Is She a
Brigand?* acted first at the Arch Street Theatre, November 1,
1833, and printed in 1835, is a farce-comedy, based on the
idea of mistaken identity. Clara, Countess D'Albi, is hasten-
ing to the home of Colonel Herman, her former lover, to prevent his marriage. She is mistaken for a brigand in a Swiss
hotel and, to avoid delay, assumes that character and is conducted to Herman's château under the plea that she will discover the other members of the band. The farce was adapted
from *Clara Wendel; ou, La Demoiselle Brigand.*

Smith's one attempt at the domestic drama, *The Daughter*,
was published in 1836, produced at the Walnut Street Theatre
on May 21, 1836, and repeated as late as 1850. It was a fairly
literal adaptation of *Clara, ou le Malheur et la Conscience*, by
Hubert [Laroche] played in Paris in 1808. Clara, who is
really the daughter of Count Rosenberg, believes herself to
be the daughter of Montalban and, knowing that he has killed
the child of Valmore, the French Ambassador, suffers herself
to be accused of the murder. Although Montalban has committed the crime with an eye to her interests by marrying her
to Valmore, he decides to be rid of her, and she is saved only

by the energy of a cottager who has a prejudice, which he expresses in fitting terms, against the triumph of crime over virtue. The play might have given an actress a sentimental opportunity in the part of Clara.

In what was probably Smith's last acted play, *The Actress of Padua*, he drew upon the newer French impulse, the romantic drama of Victor Hugo. The play was performed for four successive nights beginning June 13, 1836,[1] at the Walnut Street Theatre, then called the American Theatre, the third night being the author's benefit. E. S. Conner played Angelo, and Miss Waring, Thisbe.

This play of Smith's exists not in dramatic form, but as a narrative.[2] In the preface, dated April, 1836, the author tells us that:

The Actress of Padua is an attempt to throw into the form of a tale, a drama by Victor Hugo entitled *Angelo, Tyran de Padoue*. He is among the most distinguished of the modern French dramatists, still his productions are not very familiar to the American public. *Angelo* was produced last year, and its popularity in Paris prompted the present attempt to clothe it in an English dress. Victor Hugo belongs to the high pressure romantic school, and *Angelo*, with all its extravagance, is the most rational of his dramas. It was the translator's first intention to have adapted this production to the American stage, but as experience has taught him that few go to witness the performance of dramas of this description, and no one reads them when printed, he concluded to submit it to the public in its present shape, believing it to possess sufficient interest to repay the trouble of a perusal.

It would be of interest to know what caused Smith to change his mind and write the play. It proved to be the longest lived of his plays, for Charlotte Cushman acted in it during the season of '51-'52, appearing as La Thisbe on September 29th at the Lyceum Theatre; on December 10, 1851, at the Chestnut Street Theatre; and on May 8, 1852, at the Broadway Theatre. Lucille Western revived the play on February

[1] *North American Gazette*, Advertisements.
[2] *The Actress of Padua and Other Tales.* Phila., 1836.

16, 1860, at the New Bowery Theatre, played it in 1863 at Breslin's New Theatre, and there is a record of its performance as late as November 8, 1873, at Daly's Broadway Theatre with Virginia Vaughan as Thisbe.[1]

The story is powerful, if melodramatic. It is laid in 1549 in Padua, where Angelo is the tyrant, the deputy of Venice. He is insanely jealous of his wife, Catharina, though he does not love her, and also of Thisbe, an actress whom he does love. Thisbe and Catharina both love Rodolpho, and he has loved Catharina even before her marriage, for state reasons, to Angelo. This situation provides the opportunity to portray the working of strong passion set against the background of good and evil, which Hugo loved to paint. A spy of the Council of Ten, in revenge for a slight placed upon him by Catharina, introduces Rodolpho to her room at midnight, but also gives Thisbe the key. Hearing her approach, Rodolpho hides, but she demands him of Catharina, waking Angelo by her outcries. Then she suddenly recognizes by a crucifix in the room that Catharina has saved her own mother years before, and she saves Catharina by quick wit from the situation. But Angelo learns, through the spy, of his wife's lover and condemns her to die. Thisbe has made up her mind to save Catharina, though she is insanely jealous of her, and so Hugo makes use of the apparent poison and actual sleeping draught of *Romeo and Juliet* to save Catharina. Thisbe is stabbed by Rodolpho, who believes she has betrayed Catharina, and the actress dies in his arms after having made his flight with her rival secure. It is impossible to tell how closely Smith followed Hugo in the play, but he preserved the atmosphere quite accurately in the story.

Among the manuscripts are plays which were apparently

[1] Among the Smith manuscripts are playbills of the performances by Charlotte Cushman on December 10, 1851, and Lucille Western (undated). On one of the Lucille Western playbills appears "Written by Rd. Penn Smith," in his own hand. Ireland (II, 594), 600 and Brown (I, 456; II, 191, 392), do not give any author's name, and the play has been attributed to John Brougham. Neither play has survived, and we may conclude that Brougham, finding Smith's manuscript, retouched it, as was his frequent custom.

not performed. *The Bombardment of Algiers,* written in 1829, was based on *Le Bombardement d'Alger ou le Corsaire reconnaissant,* by Frédéric du Petit-Méré. This is one of the best melodramas of the time. The action is rapid and the characters are distinct. The French spirit is well kept and the Algerians are not all villains. *The Last Man, or the Cock of the Village* is an amusing farce, adapted from the French, in which the only remaining male in the village is captured by a trick. *Shakespeare in Love* is an interlude based upon Alexandre Duval's *Shakespeare amoureux ou la Pièce a l'Etude* (1804) which centers upon the truly original idea of having Shakespeare fall in love with an actress who is playing in Richard III! *The Solitary, or the Man of Mystery*, is an unfinished melodrama laid in Switzerland, dealing with Charles the Bold of Burgundy.

These fragments or dramatic trifles are probably early works of Penn Smith, for the steady progress in his dramatic ability is marked. The great difference between *The Deformed* and its earlier form *The Divorce* shows this most concretely. *The Triumph at Plattsburg* is much better than *The Eighth of January.* But of more significance to the historian is the very existence of *The Deformed, Caius Marius,* and *The Actress of Padua*, even if we have two of them only in fragments or a name. Before 1830 Smith was experimenting in comedy, hastily dishing up material from American history for anniversaries or holidays, or imitating French melodrama of a period whose influence, by 1830, was passing. In *Caius Marius* he chose the embodiment of one of the most tragic of themes, the failure of a leader of the people to retain his moral greatness. In this play he allied himself with the drama that was to come in America during the next period. In his choice of Victor Hugo's play for adaptation he showed a quick appreciation of the new romantic figure in France, for the echoes of the struggle of the Romanticists and Classicists of Paris had not resounded very loudly in America. He probably saw *Hernani,* when Kenney's adaptation was produced in Philadelphia during the season of 1831-2. Just as the newer Romanticism in France was represented not only by Hugo, but also by Dumas, and had a parentage in the French *mélodrame* of Pixerécourt and his school, so the flowering of romantic tragedy in America, of which Bird's *Gladiator* is the first example to survive, had its precursor in the author of *Caius Marius* and *The Deformed*. That the latter goes back to the Elizabethans proves only the perennial quality of fine art and the freedom any age has to treat universal passions and emotions. That the former owed its inspiration to Payne's *Brutus* is only another indication of the essentially consistent progress of our drama.

CHAPTER IX

ROBERT MONTGOMERY BIRD AND THE RISE OF THE ROMANTIC PLAY

LITERARY parallels are the temptation of the historian and it would be easy to overemphasize the resemblance between the dramatic movements in France and America which dominate the second quarter of the century.[1] It was not an accident, however, that Alexandre Dumas in 1829 and Victor Hugo in 1830 should have inaugurated a romantic period in French drama with *Henri III* and *Hernani*, and that in 1830-31 Robert Montgomery Bird should have written *Pelopidas* and *The Gladiator*. It was likewise from 1829 to 1832 that Hawthorne and Poe in America, and Balzac and Mérimée in France were forming the model of the modern romantic short story. Romance was in the air. Scott was nearing his end, but his novels were at the summit of their popularity. Cooper's romances were published as soon as written in thirty-four places in Europe, and Byron was still exerting his influence upon European poetry. The visit of Kean, Charles Kemble, and Macready to Paris in 1827, where they played not only Shakespeare but also, at least in Kean's case, romantic tragedy in Payne's *Brutus*, shook the classic tradition of the French tragedy and had much to do with the rise of the romantic school. In France the playwrights took from the melodrama the lesson in liberality it had to offer and the transition from Pixerécourt, Caigniez, and others seems clear. In England, although Shakespeare had so much to give to Hugo and Dumas, there was no corresponding development in practical stagecraft from melodrama to tragedy. As we have seen.

[1] How appreciative the American audiences of that day were of the French opera may be judged by the discriminating article on "The French Comic Opera" in *The Philadelphia Monthly Magazine*, for November, 1827, pp. 92-95.

THE RISE OF THE ROMANTIC PLAY

Sheridan Knowles in his *Virginius* (1820) points back to the limitations of the domestic drama. An occasional success like Miss Mitford's *Rienzi* was a *tour de force* of the closet drama, not a natural development of practical playwriting such as occurred in France and America.

There has probably been no literary term so variously used as "romantic." Much of the consequent confusion has been caused by the employment of the term to describe both the material selected and the method of treatment of that material. If the term "romantic" could be confined to the selection of material and in that field be contrasted with the term "classic," its proper antithesis, while the terms "realistic" and "idealistic" could be applied to the treatment, clarity could be secured and some of our literary tendencies and movements would be better understood. Romantic material may be treated either realistically or idealistically, as *Henry Esmond* and *Ivanhoe* will illustrate, although the latter treatment is more likely to occur. For the type of mind that chooses classic or familiar material is prone to treat it in a realistic manner, while the writer who prefers romantic scenes and characters is also apt to accentuate certain phases of these, rather than to draw a picture of actual life. Curiously enough, when the unusual combination occurs and the romantic material is treated in a realistic manner as in the plays of Shakespeare, or the classic material is treated in an idealistic manner as in the novels of Dickens, we have some of the greatest productions of literature. It would be idle, perhaps, to insist on such a series of definitions, but they will at least call attention to the fact that there is no necessary antagonism between romance and realism. The essence of romance is freedom from restraint. The dramatist or novelist or poet chooses his theme without restriction of place or time. He may choose the large figures of history, but if he does he will invest them with a greatness that is true to the dignity which the past fittingly assumes in the eyes of the present. He may escape from the familiar by placing his characters in a foreign atmosphere, and here he will have the task of remaining faithful to the exotic spirit while at the same time making it intelligible to the sympathy of his audience. When he has to make his choice between verisimilitude to history or foreign custom and a quick appeal to the understanding and emotions of his hearers, the dramatist who knows his art will choose, with Shakespeare, the latter alternative. And the romantic dramatist, realizing that his material has no general appeal to the experience of his audience, will all the more surely be wise if he treats a motive which on account of its universal quality will have as wide an appeal as possible to their imagination. There are certain motives that approach this universal quality: among these are self-preservation, love of sex, family affection, love of country, religious feeling, and personal honor, and it is interesting to note that as the motive grows less general in its appeal, the impulse becomes of a higher nature. It is the touchstone of the skillful dramatist that he can so mingle these motives in a natural development as to bring the largest number into conflict with each other, and that he can so clothe these motives in human guise that the characters will seem to domi-nate the action and bring about a probable conclusion. It is because Robert Montgomery Bird so well understood this fun-damental problem of his art that his plays mark a decided advance in the progress of our drama.

Robert Montgomery Bird was born in Newcastle, Delaware, February 5, 1806. His father, Hon. John Bird, was a man of standing and of some literary taste, and after his early death, Robert was brought up by his maternal uncle, Nicholas van Dyke, in an atmosphere of culture and achievement. He was educated in Philadelphia, attending the Germantown Academy and matriculating in the School of Medicine of the University of Pennsylvania in 1824. He seems to have entered upon the study of medicine without any great fondness for the science, but rather with the idea that a liberal profession was a neces-sary path for one with his traditions to follow. He took his degree in medicine at the University in April, 1827, but although he began practice in Philadelphia with a prospect of success, he deliberately abandoned his profession at the expiration of one year. According to his wife's account,[1] he disliked to accept fees for his services, and gave medicine to his patients free of charge. His circumstances were not such as to make such a career a suitable one, and he relinquished it with relief. That he continued to be interested in science is proved by the many manuscript notes concerning chemistry, botany, and agriculture, and by his later appointment to the chair of the Institutes of Medicine and Materia Medica at the new Pennsylvania Medical College in Philadelphia in 1841. But this interest was only one phase of his quick reaction to intellectual stimulation from all sources, and from our point of view its chief importance lies in the sense of form and of proportion which his plays exhibit and the accuracy with which he examined the sources of his plots. It is seldom in the career of a dramatist that we have the opportunity to trace so fully the steps in his development, but the richness of the manuscript material left by him and the fidelity with which it has been preserved, reveal Doctor Bird as one of the most scholarly and the most versatile men of his time.[2] His notebooks, beginning in 1826, indicate an omnivorous reading in ancient and modern writers, and the abstracts and criticisms prove that Bird was one of those rare souls who read creatively and not merely to forget. They show, too, his acquaintance with Latin, Greek, French, Spanish, and Italian, but of special interest to us is their revelation of his close study and judicial attitude toward the playwrights of the past. He had read the Elizabethan and some of the Restoration dramatists, and he viewed them appreciatively but critically.

The real cause of his abandonment of medicine was his greater love of literature. While he was still a medical student at Pennsylvania he was writing plays, and his first manuscript of any length bears the date of May, 1827. It is a comedy,

---

[1] Among the Bird papers in the University of Pennsylvania is a manuscript biography by Mary Bird, which is the basis for the statements of personal history in this chapter.

[2] See bibliography to Chapter IX for account of the Bird Mss.

'Twas All for the Best, laid in England and imitative of Congreve at his feeblest. Far below any other of Bird's plays in merit, it is interesting in only one particular. The cast bears evidence that it was written definitely with the Chestnut Street Theatre Company in mind, for the parts are assigned to Warren, Wood, and others. Thus, from the very start, Bird wrote with an eye to stage presentation, and this quality makes his apprentice work of much greater significance than if he had been, even in the beginning, a closet dramatist.

Fortunately, he turned aside from imitation of farce comedy to romantic tragedy, for while *The Cowled Lover* and *Caridorf*, dated in June and August, 1827, are more interesting as preparation than as achievement, they yet show traces of that power of imagination and directness of expression which Bird showed later in their fullness. *The Cowled Lover* is laid on Lake Como, and in plot is reminiscent of *Romeo and Juliet*, for Raymond, the hero, meets his fate on account of his love for Rosalia, daughter of his bitter enemy. *Caridorf* takes place in or near Vienna. Caridorf is a gloomy figure, and his suicide ends a complicated series of events, in which his passion for Genevra is the prevailing motive. Both plays savor of melodrama, but there is no attempt at a happy ending, and the tragedy has more of the inevitable quality than is usual at the time. The other romantic plays, *Giannone*, *The Fanatick*, and *Isidora, or the Three Dukes*, are incomplete, but the three acts of the last, laid in Catalonia about 1500, show how rapid Bird's improvement was in style and character drawing. He even succeeds in giving fresh vitality in Basilio to the ancient stage character of the patrician who, lost in infancy, shows his nobility under the disguise of poverty. When Basilio says

> "The immortality that I do covet
> Is in the memory of a loving heart,"

or when in *The Fanatick*, Wieland says:

> "This is 't to be a spirit, mingled with
> The immortal phalanx of the peopled air,"

we know Bird has been studying at a good school. The comedy element in these romantic tragedies is not a mere relief; it is always worked into the plot, as in the amusing scene in *The Cowled Lover* when the servants draw from each other their master's secrets. And in Bird's other plays of 1827 and 1828, which are comedies laid in Philadelphia, he shows, especially in *The City Looking Glass*, a real skill in the manipulation of constant surprises and in the creation of amusing repartee. The play is important, too, as an early example of the treatment of low life in a large city, for Ravin and Ringfinger, the counterfeiters, are fairly real, and old Raleigh, the Virginia squire, although he is reminiscent of Sir Anthony Absolute, is amusing and contemporary in his cross-questioning of his boy's proposed father-in-law as to his views on slavery and the tariff. *News of the Night* is merely farce, but both plays show that sense of proportion and probability that kept the romantic element in Bird's nature from running away with him. He was concerned, too, with principles of dramatic construction. An undated manuscript gives us his views in part in this manner:

The true secret of effect consists in having everything, as well in details as in the general structure, *Epigrammatic or Climacteric;* the story rising to rapidity and closing with power; the chief characters increasing in passion and energy; the events growing in interest, the scenes and acts each accumulating power above their precursors; the strength of a speech augmenting, at its close, and the important characters dismissed at each exit with some sort of point and emphasis. He will ascertain that interest cannot be preserved if it be distracted; and that to have his play truly dramatic (in opposition to epic) the interest and importance must be concentred in the hero—and that every event, character or speech which does not serve to increase our interest in this personage, is superfluous and therefore, detrimental.

Bird was also contributing verse and prose tales to the *Philadelphia Monthly Magazine* during 1827 and '28, and in 1830 he began to see the prospect of his ambition realized when his play, *Pelopidas*, was accepted by Edwin Forrest. Forrest was at the beginning of his successful career. He had the praiseworthy desire to encourage native playwrights and Dr. George McClellan and Doctor Black, mutual friends, brought them together. *Pelopidas* was not written expressly for Forrest, and it was decided by mutual agreement that a new play, *The Gladiator*, which Bird was writing with special reference to Forrest's peculiar abilities, should first be played. Yet *Pelopidas* is certainly one of the best of Bird's dramas. It is an historical play, based upon Plutarch's account of Pelopidas, but modified by a keen sense of the dramatic possibilities attending the revolt of the Theban city against the Spartan tyrants. Bird took from Plutarch the general situation, brought about by the betrayal of Thebes by the oligarchical party headed by Leontidas, Archias, and Philip, but he makes Spartans of the two last, instead of Thebans, thereby differentiating them from Leontidas and from Philidas, their secretary, who becomes one of the chief characters. The surprise of Thebes by the exiles under Pelopidas, the leader of the popular party, is arranged on just such a stormy night as Plutarch describes, and the exiles meet at Charon's house. But here Bird departs from history, to provide a dramatic motive that is to run counter to that of love of country and threaten for a time to defeat it. Pelopidas learns that his wife Sibylla and his son Hylas are prisoners in his own house, and that Leontidas, the renegade polemarch or ruler, is making love to her. Sibylla is repulsing Leontidas, yet is dissembling her real feelings in a clever way. She tells Leontidas

> "To-night I would be with my child alone.
> O my good lord, you know not woman's nature:
> Our humors are the ladders to our hearts;
> And he who would climb into its richest seats,
> Must step them gently, one by one."

Pelopidas breaks his word to the other exiles, and visits his home and is imprisoned by Leontidas. Meanwhile Archias and Philip attend a banquet given by Philidas, who plans to overcome them by wine and the presence of some of the fairest women in Thebes and then to deliver them to the swords of the exiles. Meanwhile the patriotic band in Charon's house are overwhelmed with apprehension when their leader does not appear. Archias is notified by the Athenians that some movement is on foot and he sends for Charon who, in a moving speech, leaves his son as hostage for his good faith. The manner in which Philidas baffles the various suspicions of Archias and Philip at the banquet provides two remarkable stage scenes which, in the hands of a capable actor, would undoubtedly have proved successful. But it would have been a success for the actor who played Philidas, not for the star, and indeed Pelopidas, while he appears constantly, is not the real center of attraction till the end of the play. Leontidas dallies, in his efforts to persuade Sibylla to go with him. Even when Pelopidas has escaped by Sibylla's help and at the head of the exiles has broken into the banquet hall and killed Archias, Leontidas lingers, to provide one of the finest scenes in the play. He demands to know who has freed Pelopidas. Sibylla answers him:

"*Sib.:*   I, Polemarch:
     'Twas I that oped his prison door and gave him
     The blade that won his freedom; I, even I,
     The wretch thou thought'st fit only for dishonour,
     That sent him forth to do the like for Thebes,—
     To break her bonds, to arm her hands, to trample
     Her thrones and tyrants, till she is free as air—
     As free as he is!
Leon.: Thou wert a wife for Mars!
     But triumph not too early. (*To Soldier*) Rank the guards,
     Straight at the portal; and be ready all
     To march to the Citadel.
                   (*Exit Soldier*)
                  I make thee now
     The last of love's persuasive invitations.
     All is not won, nor is all lost; for, with
     A Spartan garrison in the Citadel,
     And Sparta's self behind, you soon shall see me
     Master again in Thebes; her riotous people

Chained in securer bondage; and their chiefs
Again in exile. Think'st thou, thyself I'll yield?
Thou must go with me to the Citadel.

Sib.: Never, vain prince,—Think not I fear thee now,
Pelopidas hard by me! Save thyself. (*Another shout heard*)
Hear'st thou those cries,—the uproar of a nation
Mad for the blood of its oppressors! Hence!
I scorn and hate, but would not see thee slaughtered.

Leon.: Prattle these sarcasms in the Citadel—
There is no time for trifling. What! I ask thee,
Wilt thou go peacefully,—or have my slaves,
With base, defiling clutches, drag thee thither?

Sib.: I fear them not, nor thee. (*She draws a dagger.*) The hand
that aided
Pelopidas can help Sibylla too!

Leon.: The day of Amazons is past. (*He seizes and disarms her.*)
Take the boy from her!

* * * * * * * * * * *

Come with me;
Or (by the gods, you know not how you stir me!)
I'll from the window hurl him—

Sib.:   Ah!

Leon.:   To perish
Upon the lances of the guard.

Sib:.   Oh, man!—
No, no, not man; but fiend! most savage demon!—
Cast him forth, if thou wilt, upon the spears
Of thy base followers; or break and mangle
His innocent limbs upon the flinty stones.

. . . .

Strike through his neck and spot me with his blood;
Do this—do all: thou canst not move me yet
One step more near dishonour!"

Pelopidas comes in time, and the play is not a tragedy, for
the main motive is successful, and the curtain descends upon
the patriots in possession of Thebes, with a denunciation of
slavery which was a bit pronounced in 1830. The characters
of Pelopidas, Philidas, Sibylla, and Archias are well drawn.
The nature of Pelopidas, brave and rash, and that of Philidas,
calm and self-contained, the cynical nature of Leontidas, and

above all, the very feminine character of Sibylla remain clearly in the memory. It is easy to see why Forrest did not produce the play. It does not give him sufficiently the center of the stage. Sibylla really excels him in the sympathy and Philidas in the interest of the reader. But it seems a great pity that *Pelopidas* was not performed. Those who read it were high in its praise, and among the manuscripts is this letter:

J. FROST, Esquire.
 My dear Sir:
   I will produce Pelopidas with all possible splendor and befitting appointments. I will share with the author the proceeds of the house, nightly, the same as with a principal star, deducting the expenses, averaging $250, with a third of the gross proceeds of the seventh night, clear of all deductions for the author's profit, reserving to myself the sole use of the tragedy in the city of Philadelphia, so long as I remain manager, but making no claim for its use in any other city, the profits of said use in other cities to be at the author's own disposal.
   I believe that the production of Pelopidas will answer the purposes of all concerned. I pledge myself that it shall be produced in a superior way, and that the characters shall be well supported.
     I am, my dear Sir, your obed^t serv^t,
                                               W. E. BURTON.
   Nat. Theatre, Phila., Dec. 15, 1840.

   P. S. Should Dr. Bird prefer, I will give him ten per cent. on the gross receipts nightly whenever the Tragedy is played.

Bird had previously declined to allow Burton to produce the play on September 18, 1840, as a counter attraction to Forrest's production of *Jack Cade*, for fear this rivalry would hurt his friend the author, Judge Conrad, and in any case, by 1840 Bird had abandoned the active career of a playwright.

The Gladiator, finished in May, 1831, was performed first on September 26, 1831, at the Park Theatre. Its success was immediate and deserved, for Bird had conceived and perfected a vehicle peculiarly adapted to the talent of Forrest. The manuscript notes reveal how thoroughly Bird prepared himself for the writing of the play. The theme may have been

suggested by the performance of *Caius Marius* of his friend
Penn Smith, in January, 1831, for in the preliminary sketch
Bird remarks that the condition of Rome was favorable to
the insurrection on account of the civil wars of Sylla and
Marius.

Probably no dramatist has so clearly indicated his sources.[1]
He took the main facts as given in the accounts of Plutarch
and Appian, and the histories of Ferguson and Hooke. From
the remaining sources, which are brief summaries, he could
have obtained only confirmation and atmosphere. But Bird
used historic facts only as inspiration. With the true instinct
of a dramatist, he took liberties with history in order to produce
a human document. He selected Spartacus, the leader of the
insurrection of the gladiators, as a representative of the eternal
struggle for freedom against tyranny, and he pitted his hero
against the most powerful tyranny of history. He secured
thereby the sympathy of the audience, for the motive of self-
preservation becomes at once dominant. Spartacus is a Thracian, a free man made slave, an event not unfamiliar in contemporary life in America. One reads the sentiments of the
abolitionist throughout the first Act, in which Spartacus rebels
against the state of slavery, and especially in the climax when,
suddenly confronted with his wife Senona and his boy, he begs
his owner, Lentulus, to buy them and promises to fight for
him in the arena.[2]

In the second Act Bird introduces the two countermotives

---

[1] According to the Ms. they were Plutarch, *Lives of Crassus* [8-11] and *Sertorius;*
Livy, 95-[96-97]; Florus, 3, c. 20; Eutropius (Epitome), 6, c. 20; Villeius Paterculus.
(4B. of Greece and Rome, Epit.), 2 c. 30; Appian [*History of Rome, the Civil Wars*, I,
116-120]; [Adam] Ferguson, *History of* [*the Progress and Termination of*] *the Roman
Republic*, vol. I, chap. 16. [Acc. to ed. Lond. 1783 it appears in vol. II, chap. 2, pp.
27-33]; N. Hooke, *The Roman History from the Building of Rome to the Ruin of the
Commonwealth.* 6 v. Dublin, 1767. Vol. 2, pp. 300-365. Vol. 3, p. 284. [These refer to
servile war in Sicily. He also used the account of Spartacus.] Also various articles
in *Blackwood's Magazine.*

[2] In the preliminary sketch a note is made to insert at this place "an impassioned
and strong dialogue about slavery." The wife of Spartacus is merely mentioned in
Plutarch as a prophetess, but Bird makes no use of this quality. Her name Senona
he derived from Senones, an ancient race of the Celts.

which are finally to bring about the tragedy. The characters who carry on these motives are original with him. The first motive, the love story of Julia, niece of Crassus the prætor, with Florus, the son of Lentulus, is barely indicated in a scene which establishes the situation in Rome, governed as it is for the time by a contractor-politician who keeps the people amused by the gladiatorial combats. The second motive, the brotherly love of Spartacus and of Pharsarius, is revealed in one of the most striking scenes in English drama. Spartacus is brought into the arena to fight and, after killing a Gaul, is told that if he wins the next conflict he and his family will be freed. He revolts when he hears it is a Thracian with whom he is to fight, but the love of his wife and child conquers, and then he finds that his adversary is his brother Pharsarius, captured years before by the Romans. They embrace while Crassus and the audience are at first bewildered, then angry at the delay. The guards are sent for, and the momentary respite gives Pharsarius time to whisper:

"*Pharsarius: (Apart to Spart.)* I know them all—This thing was
        hatch'd before.—
       Might we not fire the town? They wait without,
       Circled by cohorts, but all arm'd for combat.
       Let me but raise the cry of Freedom to them
       And each man strikes his Roman to the earth.
Spartacus: The slaves of Lentulus—they will strike too:
       Let us but reach them, and they rise with us,—
Pharsarius: One moment, princely prætor.
Crassus: Not an instant.
       What, shall our shows wait on the time and pleasure
       Of our base bondmen? Sound the trumpets there—
       What, treachery, ho! Call in the soldiers!—
Pharsarius: Freedom
       For gladiators!
Spartacus: Death to all their masters!—
Crassus: Treachery!
Spartacus: Death to the Roman fiends, that make their mirth
       Out of the groans of bleeding misery!
       Ho, slaves, arise! it is your hour to kill!

> Kill and spare not—for wrath and liberty!
> Freedom for bondmen—freedom and revenge!"
> > (*Shouts and trumpets—The guards and gladiators
> > rush and engage in combat, as the curtain falls*)

The effect of the scene seems to have been tremendous. Wemyss[1] says, "Accustomed as an actor is to striking scenes, I was taken by surprise at the effect produced at the closing of the second Act. The rising of the Gladiators in the arena, and the disposition of the characters as the Act drop fell, I do not believe was ever surpassed in any theatre in the world." Wemyss remarks, however, on the fact that this climax is more powerful than any other scene in the play, and therefore, it was a mistake to place it so early. It was the force of the situation, however, and not the words themselves which carried this scene into favor, and the play moves on from this climax of action to a greater climax of character. Pharsarius demands Julia, who has been captured, as his prize, and Spartacus, at Senona's request, determines to save her. In this scene we have the real climax, for the defection of Pharsarius is the countermotive which brings on the catastrophe.

> "*Spartacus:* Brother, I hope thou hast forgot this folly.
> *Pharsarius:* I claim the captive.
> *Spartacus:* Thou shalt have a thousand
> But not these twain.
> *Pharsarius:* I care not for the boy.
> The girl is mine—captured by mine own hands;
> Therefore, mine own.
> * * * * * * * * * *
> Deny me her, and, by the fates, thou art
> No longer brother of mine. 'Twas I that helped thee
> To this high station; and the troops thou rulest,
> Are but my lending; for that hour I leave thee,
> They leave thee too.
> *Spartacus:* Come look me in the face
> And let me see how bad designs have changed thee—
> *Pharsarius:* I claim the captive.

[1] *Life of an Actor and Manager*, I, 194.

Spartacus: Set thine eyes upon her;
    Look you, she weeps, and she is fatherless.
    Thou wouldst not harm an orphan? What, I say,
    Art thou, whom I have carried in my arms
    To mountain-tops, to worship the great God,
    Art thou a man to plot a wrong and sorrow,
    'Gainst those that have no father left but Him?
    Wilt thou now ask her?

Pharsarius: Ay.

Spartacus: Thou art a changeling!
    My father ne'er begot so base a heart,—
    Brother, I do conjure thee, for I love thee,
    Forget this thing.

Pharsarius: Farewell.

Spartacus: Thou wilt not go?

Pharsarius: Ay, by great Jove, I will. Play thou the tyrant
    On those that follow thee.

Spartacus: My younger brother;—
    Nay, I'll not call thee such,—but a hot fool
    And heartless enemy.

Pharsarius: Call what thou wilt;
    I am a man, not to be mock'd and wrong'd,
    Nor flouted in my counsels. I did ask you
    Now that you had the wind of the fooled prætor,
    Now when rich Rome is emptied by her levies
    Now when the eager troops cry all, *for Rome,*
    To march upon it, ere the joining armies
    Of Pompey and Lucullus should prevent you.
    This I did ask, and this you did deny,
    Though by a former promise, pledged thereto.

Spartacus: I promised not.

Pharsarius: By heaven, you did—*when stronger.*
    This you refuse; and when, forgiving this,
    I ask my captive, you deny me her,
    With many a sharp and contumelious word,
    Such as is fitter for a dog than me.

Spartacus: Forgive me if my anger used such shame,
    I knew not what I said.

Pharsarius: March then to Rome.

Spartacus: It cannot be. We should but set us down
    Under her walls, where the three generals,
    Ere we could force the gates, would hedge us in,

     We cannot stand against them all even here;
     But, when in Sicily, are invincible.
Pharsarius: Rome, or the captive; no more Sicily.
Spartacus: To Sicily:
     There by the ocean fenced, rouse up and gather
     The remnants of those tribes by Rome destroyed,
     Invited to their vengeance. Then will come,
     Arm'd with retributive and murderous hate,
     The sons of fiery Afric,—-Carthaginians
     Out of their caves, Numidians from their deserts;
     The Gaul, the Spaniard, the Sardinian;
     The hordes of Thessaly, Thrace and Macedon
     And swarming Asia—all at last assembled
     In vengeful union 'gainst this hell of Rome.
     Then may we crush, but now we crush ourselves.
     Let us to Sicily.
Pharsarius: Those that will. Farewell.
Spartacus: Will you desert me?
Pharsarius: I did think thee meant
     For the most godlike enterprise of earth;
     Thou fail'st. Farewell; protect thyself.
Spartacus: Mad boy,
     Remember Crixus.
Pharsarius: And his thousand Germans!
     I go with Gauls and Thracians, and fifty thousand—
     A Roman girl was worth this coil! Farewell!"

In the next Act Spartacus, left with only seven thousand men, rejects the offers of Crassus to ransom Julia, and when Jovius, the Ambassador, tells him that "Rome does not war on women," he replies in a speech that was often singled out for comment:

"*Spartacus:* Men do not war on women! Look you;
     One day I clomb upon the ridgy top
     Of the cloud-piercing Haemus, where, among
     The eagles and the thunders, from that height,
     I looked upon the world—or, far as where,
     Wrestling with storms, the gloomy Euxine chafed
     On his recoiling shores; and where dim Adria
     In her blue bosom quenched the fiery sphere.
     Between these surges—lay a land, might once

> Have matched Elysium, but Rome had made it
> A Tartarus. In my green youth I look'd
> From the same frosty peak where now I stood,
> And then beheld the glory of those lands,
> Where peace was tinkling on the shepherd's bell
> And singing with the reapers; or beneath
> The shade of thatch eaves, smiled with grey old men,
> And with their children laughed along the green.
> Since that glad day, Rome's conquerers had passed
> With withering armies there, and all was changed;
> Peace had departed; howling war was there,
> Cheered on by Roman hunters: then, methought,
> Even as I looked upon the altered scene,
> Groans echoed through the valleys, through which ran
> Rivers of blood, like smoking Phlegethons;
> Fires flashed from burning villages, and famine
> Shriek'd in the empty cornfields. Women and children,
> Robb'd of their sires and husbands, left to starve—
> These were the dwellers of the land! Say'st thou
> Rome wars not then on women!"

This mode has passed away, and its faults have had frequent comment, but it also had its strength and its beauty.

The last Act contains the vigorous scene in which Pharsarius returns alone to describe the rout of his army and the crucifixion of those who surrendered.   This execution did not actually take place until after the final rout, but Bird wisely transfers it to this place, for it provides Pharsarius a description of the crucifixion, where

>   "Many lived;
> Some howled and prayed for death and cursed the gods,
> Some turned to lunatics and laughed at horror:
> And some with fierce and hellish strength, had torn
> Their arms free from the beams, and so had died
> Grasping, headlong at air."

Spartacus confides his wife and child to Pharsarius to save and then, hemmed in by Crassus, Pompey, and Lucullus, he forces his way through the prætor's camp. But once more Pharsarius fails him; Senona and the boy are killed, and, with a magnificent gesture, Spartacus sends Julia back to Crassus, kills his horse, and dies in one last attack upon the prætor's camp.

The Gladiator had the virtues and the faults of romantic tragedy, and some of the excellent results of Bird's research were cut relentlessly in the acted version by Forrest, so as to concentrate attention upon himself. Reading after a lapse of years is a severe test for such a play, and yet it meets that test surprisingly. It must be judged, however, in terms of its effect upon the stage. Contemporary criticism was, on the whole, highly in its favor. Bird has himself told of its flattering reception in New York, where apparently the full strength and effort of the company were not put forth, and of the better rendition at the Arch Street Theatre in Philadelphia on October 24th, where J. R. Scott played Pharsarius. Durang tells us that the audience rose to its feet and actually cheered at the end of the second Act. "I never saw in my experience," he says, "any theatrical applause so wildly and impulsively given."[1] Hundreds failed to gain access to the house on the first night, and the play was started on the career that was to make it the most successful so far performed in America.

Forrest selected *The Gladiator* to make his initial appearance in London at Drury Lane on October 17, 1836. He scored an instant success, and the criticisms next day were generally appreciative. *The Courier* stated that "America has at length vindicated her capability of producing a dramatist of the highest order, whose claims should be unequivocally acknowledged by the Mother Country."[2] The London *Times* spoke with discrimination of the play, praising especially the passage describing the Thracian valley, and concluding with "if Forrest acquits himself hereafter as well as he did on this occasion, he will have no reason to be dissatisfied with his voyage." Bunn, the manager of Drury Lane, announced that Forrest would

[1] Ser. 3, Chap. 16.
[2] *Life of Forrest*, by W. L. Alger, I, 299.

repeat the character of Spartacus three times weekly until further notice, on account of the success of the piece.[1]

Forrest in letters home declared that "I did not think they treated *The Gladiator* and my friend Doctor Bird fairly," but it was a severe test for the work of a youth of twenty-five to be played in a repertoire made up almost exclusively of the plays of Shakespeare. And the prompt and generous recognition recorded in this letter is of more significance than Forrest's impression:

Dramatic Authors' Society, London,
October 26, 1836.

Sir:

I have the honor to inform you, that at a general meeting of this Society, you, as the author of the Play of *The Gladiator*, were unanimously elected an *Honorary Member* in token of respect for your talent as a writer, by the English Dramatic Authors.

I have been directed to intimate this to you, through your friend, Mr. E. Forrest, which I do with great pleasure.

I am, sir,

Your faithful servant,
RICHARD BRINSLEY PEAKE,
Secretary and Treasurer.

To Dr. Bird, etc.[2]

Forrest acted *The Gladiator* until his retirement from the stage in 1872. A statement is made among the manuscripts, on the occasion of the one thousandth performance in 1853, that it was the first play written in English that had been played one thousand times within the lifetime of the author. Whether this be true or not, it had a vitality which held the stage until the close of the century. John McCullough played it many times, and on the last night, September 29, 1884, on which, with his mind failing, he bade his tragic farewell to the stage, he acted Spartacus. After his death it was performed by Robert Downing, as late as March 29, 1893, at the Grand Opera House, New York. Robert McLean was also acting in the part during the season of 1892-3.

[1] See Wemyss, I, 111-113, for account of Drury Lane performance.
[2] Bird Mss.

Encouraged by his success, Bird promptly set to work on a new tragedy, and this time selected a theme from South America. His interest in the Spanish American countries was great and continuous, being kindled by the successful revolutions in Mexico and among the South American republics, which had led to the enunciation of the Monroe Doctrine in 1823.

The background in Peruvian history was studied with Bird's usual zeal and industry.[1] He selected one of the most dramatic moments, the insurrection of the younger Almagro, and the assassination of Francisco Pizarro. Not finding a hero, however, in the Almagrist party, he created the character of Oralloossa, the son and heir of Atahualpa, the Inca who had been put to death by Pizarro. Him he made the symbol of the Peruvian desire for freedom, and to him he assigned the actual killing of Pizarro. Diego de Almagro became then the animating force of the countermotive, whose treachery brought about the betrayal of Oralloossa by his own people, his ruin and death. The power of Spain, which finally triumphs, is symbolized by the Viceroy, Vaca de Castro, whom Bird brings on the scene, in disregard of history, to play the part of retributive justice and to punish the double traitor Almagro.

Bird had in mind two objects in this play, "first, the portraiture of a barbarian in which is concentred all those qualities of good and evil which are most strikingly characteristic of savage life; the second, to show how the noblest designs of a great man and the brightest destinies of a nation could be interrupted and destroyed by the unprincipled ambition of a single individual."[2]

Oralloossa has not the force of *The Gladiator* or the propor-

---

[1] He made copious extracts from *A Historical and Descriptive Narrative of Twenty Years' Residence in South America*, by W. B. Stevenson, London, 1825; *Travels in Various Parts of Peru*, by Edmund Temple, London, 1830, and *Travels into Chile, over the Andes*, by Peter Schmidtmeyer, London, 1824, but he used only some few historical facts and the general atmosphere. He refers also to Ranking's *Conquest of Peru*, and a list of 220 works on North and South America is to be found among the Mss.

[2] Bird Mss.

tions of *Pelopidas*. There is too little humanity in the hero, while his weakness, treachery, and deceit, even for a patriot's cause, do not appeal to an audience. He is too much of an abstraction, in short, and while probably truer to nature than Rolla, he had not the romantic glamor of that other opponent of Pizarro. *Oralloossa* has, however, its high spots, especially the banquet murder scene and the fourth scene of Act IV, in which Oralloossa is betrayed and his sister Orallie is doomed to be buried alive. In a manuscript criticism upon the play Forrest suggests that it has been written in some haste. Bird acknowledges that this is true, but defends himself on the ground that "this is an age of steam and railroads."

Oralloossa was first performed by Forrest at the Arch Street Theatre, October 10, 1832, with a sumptuous setting. It ran for five nights against the strong counter attraction of Charles and Fanny Kemble at the Chestnut Street Theatre, and Forrest played it in New York in December with success, according to Ireland. Wemyss did not like it as well as *The Gladiator*, but his opinion was doubtless colored by the unlucky accident by which two of his teeth were removed through Forrest's sword thrust at Don Christoval, in which part Wemyss was playing. Forrest played *Oralloossa* as late as 1847 at the Park Theatre, but gradually withdrew it from his repertoire.

Bird had provided Forrest with two tragedies in which the vigor and power of that actor had been emphasized. With a real understanding of Forrest's capabilities, he next wrote for him a play which permitted the finer qualities of this great romantic actor's art to find expression. *The Broker of Bogota* is easily the best of Bird's plays. The scene is laid in Santa Fe de Bogota; the time is not clearly indicated,[1] but is probably the eighteenth century.

---

[1] After 1718, when Granada became a viceroyalty, and probably after 1739, when that office was re-established.

Among the Mss. are found copious extracts from *A Voyage to South America, describing at large the Spanish Cities, Towns, Provinces, of that Extensive Continent*, by Don George Juan and Don Antonio de Ulloa. Translated from the Spanish. Third Edition, London, 1772. Here are found references to customs and manners and products, like

The great appeal of the *Broker of Bogota* lies in its fidelity to human nature. In his other plays Bird's hero had been a public character and his personal concerns had been frequently, through their counter claims upon his sympathy, the causes of his tragedy. In *The Broker* the situation is a domestic one. Baptista Febro is a money lender, honest and trusted, his two outstanding qualities being his love for his children and his regard for his personal and business integrity. Ramon, his eldest son, he loves best, but in the opening scenes it is made clear that Ramon has been cast off by his father for his dissipation. His temptations are made concrete in the person of Caberero, a profligate hidalgo, whose deviltry, never over-emphasized, but relentless in its cunning, animates one of the finest villains of the stage. Ramon is in love with Juana, to whom he has been betrothed, but her father, Mendoza, repudiates him and Caberero incites him to a plot against his own father, in order that he may have gold enough to win her. Febro's other son, Francisco, is faithful to him, and so is Leonor, his daughter, but she is being wooed by the son of the Viceroy in disguise. Caberero and his tool, Pablo the innkeeper, who is as thorough a rascal as his master, and who provides a low comedy part that is very effective on the stage, concoct a scheme to rob Febro, who has a large sum in his vaults, just deposited by the Viceroy, Palmera. Febro, prompted by love for his son, has tried to bribe Caberero to leave the country, and, maddened by the cool insults and the rapacity of Caberero, Febro denounces him and dares him to rob the vaults so that he may hang. The broker is overheard by a servant, Silvano, and later his speech is twisted into evidence that he was in complicity with Caberero to rob his own vaults and profit by the transactions. With an ingenuity that becomes more apparent every time the play is studied, Bird weaves a net around Febro of circumstantial evidence, which makes his guilt probable. Febro acts in the crisis in accord-

the Chirimoya tree (see Act II, Sc. 1), but no suggestion of the plot or characters is apparent

ance with his character. He has gone to Pablo's den to bring help to Ramon, who is supposed to be held there for debt, and while he is away the robbers break into his vaults. Leonor is eloping with Fernando, and Mendoza the neighbor enters, finds everything in confusion and, with Francisco, seeks Pablo's inn. Ramon has had an affecting interview with Juana, who gives him a week to become reconciled with his father and who touches, with a rare delicacy, the note of a love founded on the friendship of boy and girl, fragrant with many years' affection. But Ramon is only the more spurred on to gain wealth, and Caberero holds him to his purpose when Febro offers forgiveness to his erring son. Then, like a thunder-clap, the news of the robbery and the accusation against him of complicity fall together on Febro's head. Stunned by the blows of circumstance, his silence is used against him, and in the trial before the Viceroy, he defends himself poorly in a court, which, based upon Roman law, requires the accused to prove his innocence. Pablo, claiming he is turning state's evidence, accuses Febro directly of robbing himself and Febro breaks out:

> "Now were Heaven just,
> Thou shouldst die with this slander in thy throat.
> Monster of falsehood! Has it come to this?
> Is't true? Is't possible? A man like me,
> Old—in the twilight of my years, and looking
> Into the dusky midnight of my grave?—
> An old man, that has lived a life whereon
> No man hath found a stain. Oh! you are mad
> To think this thing of me. A fraud! A fraud!
> What, I commit it? With these gray hairs, too?
> And without aim save to enrich that rogue
> Who swears away my life?"

Palmera is inclined to believe him, but the momentary flash of energy is over. Ramon is brought in as a witness and refuses to speak. By his silence he testifies against his father, and Febro is condemned. Then the scenes gather force and intensity. Juana taxes Ramon with his acted lie; he pleads he has done everything for her love. She turns upon him:

> "A word—
> And I have done with thee. Then for what fate
> Heaven has in store:—the altar or the grave—
> I shall not care,"

and by a device, wrung out of the agony of her soul at having to trick her lover into the confession that kills her love for him, she finds out that he knows of Febro's innocence. With a quick change of manner, she calls to her father to take her to the Viceroy.

> "*Juana:* Father!
> Justice! There shall be justice done to all!
> Justice! I tell thee, monster, though I die,—
> Justice! Ho father!
> (*Enter Mendoza from house, Ramon flies.*)
> *Mendoza:* What's the matter, girl?
> That wretched Ramon!
> *Juana:* To the palace father,
> Quick, lead me to the Viceroy.
> *Mendoza:* Art thou raving?
> *Juana:* Father, I have a story for his highness,
> Will make all rave and let me speak it now,
> While I have strength.
> *Mendoza:* Come in, compose thyself.
> *Juana:* The Palace, father, the Palace!
> Curtain."

Learning of his daughter's flight, Febro storms at the Viceroy's palace gate, and finds it is the Viceroy's son who has eloped with her. Then Juana brings Ramon and Caberero before the Viceroy, and the old man's anger turns against those who would accuse his first-born son of having conspired against him. Ramon confesses his guilt and rushes out. Febro is cleared and Fernando begs his father's permission to marry Leonor. The old merchant again seems about to be happy, for with his daughter married to a nobleman all may be well. But Mendoza returns with the news that Ramon, overcome with guilt and remorse, has thrown himself from the balcony and with one cry Febro falls lifeless.

In *The Broker of Bogota*, Bird made domestic drama heroic. For the sentimentality which dominates plays like *The Stranger*, Bird substituted the pathos that springs from the yearning of a father over his erring son, who had been "the first life of his mother," and it is the naturalness of Febro, his simplicity, and the way he remains true to his middle-class standards, that secure our sympathy. When he attacks Caberero, he fights with the weapon of his class, his money. When his daughter is to be the wife of a noble gentleman, he rejoices. Yet he has the pride of his own caste, too, and his dignity never entirely leaves him, even in distress.

The Broker of Bogota was first produced at the Bowery Theatre on February 12, 1834, with Ingersoll as Ramon and Henry Wallack as Caberero. Among the manuscripts is found this letter from Forrest written the night of the performance:

Dear Bird:
I have just left the theatre—your tragedy was performed and crowned with entire success. "The Broker of Bogota" will live when our vile trunks are rotten. You have every reason to congratulate yourself. Will you come to New York immediately upon the receipt of this letter? Start on Friday morning and you will have an opportunity of seeing your last child in "health and spirits."

Forrest produced *The Broker* in Philadelphia on June 11, 1834. It remained one of his favorite plays, was acted on his second trip abroad in 1845, and was performed by him until the last year of his stage appearance. After his death John McCullough acted in it occasionally.

Bird's last dramatic work was the revision of *Metamora*, an Indian play by John A. Stone. Forrest had been acting in Stone's play since 1830 with success, but was not satisfied with it and commissioned Bird to revise it. Bird had been interested in the Indians at an early period and had written a drama which had been read by Stone before he wrote *Metamora*.

Both plays are too fragmentary in the surviving manuscripts to establish any relationship but, according to Mrs. Bird, Doctor Bird stated that Stone had borrowed the idea of an Indian tragedy from him. In any case, he undertook the revision, and delivered the manuscript to Forrest in September, 1836. He had found it impossible to revise the play, and had consequently rewritten it. Forrest claimed in 1856 that he had not used the work of Doctor Bird, and he certainly did not pay for it. But he retained the manuscript, notwithstanding various requests to return it.

That Doctor Bird should have ceased to write plays, after having produced one great popular success in *The Gladiator* and a still greater artistic success in *The Broker of Bogota*, was due to his disappointment at the financial returns from his dramatic work and to his treatment at the hands of Edwin Forrest. His relations with the latter reveal clearly the conditions that discouraged American playwrights of that time. Forrest and Bird were not only actor and dramatist—they were personal friends. In 1833 they journeyed together through the South and West. Doctor Bird had hoped to visit Mexico and South America, whose institutions he had been studying, but owing to a cholera epidemic they went no further than New Orleans. They were in constant and friendly relation until the return of Forrest from Europe. Then in 1837 a demand from Forrest for the payment of a note for two thousand dollars, which Bird believed to have been canceled by royalties due him, precipitated a stormy meeting at which they parted forever. Bird's own statement of their financial relations is as follows:

The state of affairs between us is simply this. I have received from him $1000 on each of my plays, *The Gladiator*, *Oralloossa*, and *The Broker of Bogota*, and $2000 in loans for which he has my note, in all $5000. But he owes me still (if there was a bargain between us, as I supposed there was) $2000 on each of these plays, in all $6000, minus the $2000 loan, that is $4000. He owes me also $2000 for *Metamora*, rewritten, for so much I think it worth.

How did this misunderstanding arise? The account books, manuscript statements, and legal correspondence among the Bird papers make the situation clear. Bird, as a young dramatist, was flattered by Forrest's approval and was glad to sell him *Pelopidas* for one thousand dollars. When it seemed best to substitute *The Gladiator* he agreed orally to take a first payment of that amount, with a later payment of two thousand dollars if the play was successful. No contract was signed, apparently, and Bird supposed the same terms were to apply to *Oralloossa* and *The Broker of Bogota*, and in each case he was paid one thousand dollars for these plays, and no more. For *Pelopidas* and *Metamora* nothing was paid. Some years afterward his friend, Senator Clayton, advised him that since his only witness, Doctor McClellan, was dead, he had no legal redress. There seems to be no doubt that Bird trusted Forrest's word, his sense of justice, and, to a certain extent, his generosity, and that Forrest, having possession of the plays and having paid a minimum sum which Bird had accepted, felt legally safe. That he did not sue on the note shows that he did not wish to make the transaction public. It would not have been to his interest to do so for, while his understanding of the agreement may have differed from Bird's, there can be no question that he treated the playwright unfairly. From *The Gladiator* alone his profits were enormous. By December, 1853, it had been played one thousand times, and never to profits of less than several hundred dollars. From *The Broker* Forrest made many thousands. And for these two plays Bird was paid two thousand dollars! Even on the old benefit system of "third nights" Bird should have received at least $5000 apiece, and we have seen what value Burton attached to *Pelopidas*.

But there is another chapter in which Forrest appears in even a worse light. The American dramatist was unprotected by the copyright laws, and the play having once been purchased by a producer he usually ceased to have any rights that the public or the producer respected. There was still, however, his literary reputation. Forrest steadily refused to allow any play that he controlled to be printed, fearing that it might be performed by some other actor. How far this selfish policy was pursued may be seen from the following letters which passed between Doctor Bird's son, Frederic M. Bird, and Forrest.

Sept. 30, 1869.

Dear Sir:

As the only representative, since my mother's death, of my father, the late Dr. R. M. Bird, I am the guardian of his Mss., and to some sense, of his reputation. I have always regarded it as a duty to be discharged whenever I should be able, to publish his plays and poems. But I remember that when, some years ago, my mother was about to do this, you asserted an exclusive right over *The Gladiator*, etc., and Mr. Redfield, unwilling to risk a lawsuit, declined to issue the volume. I write now, not at all to discuss the question of ownership, on which we probably might not agree, but simply to inquire your views and intentions in the matter. I am not rich enough to contest the point legally, nor do I suppose that any publisher would care to: so that it is probably still in your power to prevent the plays from seeing the light. Will you have the kindness to inform me of your disposition as to this subject? My present residence is in this town, but for the next two weeks I shall be away, part of the time in Philadelphia, and a line sent to 1309 Arch Street will reach me. I am, Sir,

Very respectfully and truly yours,

FREDERICK M. BIRD.

Philadelphia, October 1, 1869.

MR. FREDERICK M. BIRD.
Dear Sir:

The heirs of the late Dr. R. M. Bird have neither right, title, nor any legal interest whatever in the plays written by him for me, *viz:* "The Gladiator," "The Broker of Bogota" and the play of "Oralloossa."

These plays are my exclusive property, by the right of purchase, and for many years by the law of copyright.

Yours respectfully,

EDWIN FORREST.

Bird's withdrawal from dramatic authorship is, therefore, to be understood. He could not support his family by a profes-

246

sion so insecure, and he turned next to producing five novels between 1834 and 1839. *Calavar, or the Knight of the Conquest*, and *The Infidel* are romances of Mexico at the time of the conquest of Cortés. They were pioneers in a new field of romance, and while they are long-drawn-out, according to the fashion of the time, they are rich in color and thronged with characters faithful to history. *The Hawks of Hawk Hollow* is even better. It is laid at the close of the Revolution near the Delaware Water Gap, and in it Bird wove a fascinating romance around the fortunes of a decaying patrician family, who had taken the Tory side. *Nick of the Woods* is, however, the best of all. In it Bird pictured the Indians of Kentucky, not as ideal types but in their true colors. The central character, that of a half-crazed white man whose revenge upon the Indian destroyers of his family is rendered possible by his disguise as a peaceful Quaker, is a real contribution to our character portraiture. And the interest of the story has carried it into many editions at home and abroad, and into the German and Dutch languages. *The Adventures of Robin Day*, a picaresque romance, and the curious psychological study, *Sheppard Lee*, remain outside our province, but it is interesting that *The Infidel* was dramatized by Benjamin H. Brewster and played in Philadelphia in 1835, *Nick of the Woods* was adapted for the stage by Louisa Medina in New York in 1838 and proved very popular, and *The Hawks of Hawk Hollow* was put on the stage in Boston and Portland in 1836 and in Philadelphia in 1843.

Farming, journalism, and politics occupied Bird's attention during the latter part of his life. He was editor and part proprietor of the *North American* in Philadelphia and took an active interest in Whig politics, especially in Delaware, his native state, where his farm lay. He was rich in friendship if not in money, and the many letters among his manuscript papers testify to the unvarying respect and confidence in which he was held by the men of his time. The correspondence with Senator Clayton, Secretary of State under Taylor, reveals interesting sidelights on the political history both men were making. Doctor Bird was a delegate to the National Whig Convention of 1844, and declined nomination to both the House of Representatives and the Senate. He had married in 1838 Mary, the daughter of Reverend Philip F. Mayer, a Lutheran clergyman. Written in her fine hand, a life of her husband reveals indirectly the inspiration she was to him. Their son, Frederic Mayer Bird, became the editor of *Lippincott's Magazine*.

Bird died, literally worn out by his work, on January 23, 1854. His life was a brave struggle for the right to create, and had he lived in a time when the American playwright received fair treatment, it is not easy to put a limit to his possible achievements. For he had a rare sense of dramatic effect, a power to visualize historic scenes and characters, to seize the spirit of the past out of the mass of facts and, in a few brief lines, to fuse those facts into life. Before he was thirty years old he had lifted romantic tragedy to a level higher than it had reached in English since Congreve and had written plays which even to-day can be placed on the stage with effect.[1] Tireless as was his literary energy, one who has lived with him in the intimate relationships revealed by his manuscripts, feels even more the sterling character which faced with unshrinking courage the daily tragedy of an American man of letters in the days that tried the soul of Nathaniel Hawthorne and broke the heart of Edgar Poe.

Notwithstanding the difficulties and discouragements that beset the American dramatist, the impulse to write plays seemed irrepressible. For reasons that have been given, this impulse centered most definitely in Philadelphia, and there arose a group of playwrights who knew each other and who were stimulated to write through the encouragement offered by the rivalry of the theatres. Bird and Penn Smith were the most significant, but there were others of ability who con-

---

[1] On May 21, 1920, the Zelosophic Society of the University of Pennsylvania reproduced *The Broker of Bogota*, and, notwithstanding the obvious limitations of an amateur performance, the merits of the play were apparent.

tributed to the rise of a drama which had as a foundation a real love of literature and a practical knowledge of stagecraft. The best work was done in the field of the romantic play, usually with its roots in history, ancient and medieval. Probably the earliest attempt to place Irish history on the stage was made by Dr. James McHenry, whose tragedy of *The Usurper*, laid in Druidical times, was produced at the Chestnut Street Theatre, December 26, 1827. The blank verse is quite fair and the play, although long-drawn-out, is interesting. It is based on the usurpation by Cartha of the Irish throne and his death at the hands of the priestess of Beal. It was not very successful, although it was afterward repeated at the Arch Street Theatre. Wemyss[1] gives an amusing account of the uproar caused in Philadelphia by his failure as manager to give the author a benefit or third night performance, and the incident reveals the great interest in the affairs of the theatre among a certain element in the population.

Sertorius, or the Roman Patriot, by David Paul Brown, a distinguished member of the Philadelphia bar, was produced at the Chestnut Street Theatre on December 14, 1830, with Junius Brutus Booth in the title rôle. Wemyss,[2] who acted Pompey, says that "Booth played the hero in a manner which would have commanded success for any piece: the beautiful poetry of this play, flowing from his lips, must have gratified the fastidious taste of any author." Durang and Wood also record its success, notwithstanding the fact that Brown had provided copies for his friends and they sat in the front rows and made the actors nervous by turning the pages. Durang also makes the interesting statement that this was "the first time that real drawing room furniture was used on the stage in Philadelphia." It was certainly a triumph of anachronism in this play, which is laid in Spain during the Roman Republic, and is concerned with the victory of Sertorius over Pompey and Metellus and his death at the hands of Persenna and other

[1] I, 141-6.
[2] I, 186-7.

conspirators who are jealous of his great power over the people of Spain. *Sertorius* is based upon Plutarch's life of that hero and is true to history. It has fine passages but lacks action. Booth revived it on February 6, 1832, at the Arch Street Theatre "with perfect success."[1] Brown's romantic comedy, *The Prophet of St. Paul's*, written in 1830, was not played until March 20, 1837, at the Walnut Street Theatre. It is concerned with a royal love story which has more than once been given the dress of romance and in recent times was the inspiration for such a novel and such a play as *When Knighthood Was in Flower*. Brown's excellence can be best appreciated when his work is compared with productions of this character. Mary, the sister of Henry VIII, loves Charles Brandon, Duke of Suffolk, but is compelled to marry Louis XII of France. Before leaving England under Brandon's charge, she has visited the prophet of St. Paul's, who is Brandon in disguise and who naturally makes a prophecy concerning her future career. The Duke of Valois, afterward Francis I, also falls in love with her. At the King's death, Brandon and Mary run away and marry, Francis pursuing them, but finally joining their hands in true romantic fashion. Both Durang and Wemyss speak of the play as being butchered by the company, and it certainly merited better treatment.

John Augustus Stone, who is of most significance in the development of the Indian play, contributed also to the romantic historical drama during his brief career as a playwright, spent in Philadelphia and Charleston. Of his seven known plays only one has survived in complete form, *Tancred, or the Siege of Antioch*, which is a chronicle play, dealing with the Christian attack upon Antioch during the First Crusade (1097). Its merit is far from great and it seems not to have been acted, but, curiously enough, another play by Stone, *Tancred, or the King of Sicily*, of which only a fragment survives, was performed at the Park Theatre, March 16, 1831. Stone wrote for Forrest *The Ancient Briton*, which was played at the Arch

[1] Wood, 363.

Street Theatre, March 27, 1833, Forrest taking the part of Brigantius. It was not printed, but we learn from Durang[1] that it was historical tragedy, the action beginning about A.D. 60, and during its progress Boadicea defeats the Romans. A triumph of archæology was secured by painting the ancient Britons like the Indians in *Metamora*.

Next to Bird and Smith, Robert T. Conrad was the best of the Philadelphia group. His tragedy, *Conrad, King of Naples*, written for a rising star, James E. Murdoch, who produced it successfully at the Arch Street Theatre on January 17, 1832, has not survived. His most important play was *Jack Cade* or *Aylmere*, as it was variously called. It is a tragedy centering upon the Kentish rebellion of 1450, which had Jack Cade for a leader. The revolt had in reality a political rather than a social or economic basis, but Conrad rightly judged that personal oppression of serfs and yeomen would form a better dramatic motive than the struggle for political rights and freedom of elections, which are contained in the historical "Complaint of the Commons of Kent." Jack Cade becomes, therefore, the symbol of rebellion against the arbitrary power of the nobles, represented by Lord Say, while the starvation of the peasants, the attacks upon Mariamne, Cade's wife, and the violent prevention of the marriage of Kate Worthy and Will Mowbray by Lord Say, in order that his tool Courtnay may possess Kate, are transferred from an earlier state of affairs to the time of the play. Cade takes the name of Mortimer and is believed to be the real heir to the English throne. His uprising is successful and he seizes London, Henry VI flying to Kenilworth. Lord Say is stabbed by Cade, but revenges himself by a blow with his poisoned dagger. Mariamne, who has been crazed by grief at the loss of their child and by shock after she has killed Lord Clifford in defense of her honor, dies first, and the play ends with Will Mowbray waving the "charter" which frees the bondmen of England and which existed only on the stage.

[1] Series 3, Chap. 27.

We have the play in both its earlier and in its later form, when it had been rewritten for Forrest, and it is truly a vehicle for a robust actor. Cade is the vehement leader of a rebellion, every incident is painted in vivid colors, and the misery becomes almost unendurable. But there are very powerful scenes and Conrad knew how to use blank verse effectively. Lines like

> "Nothing is trifling that love consecrates"

or

> "When the red hand of force is at their throats
> They know what freedom is."

show his ability in this direction. The career of the play, given in great detail in Wemyss[1] and repeated in many places, illustrates well the dramatic conditions. The play was first written for A. A. Addams, and was announced for the seventh of December, 1835, at the Walnut Street Theatre. At six-thirty o'clock on that evening Addams was too intoxicated to appear, so that the performance was postponed until December 9th, when David Ingersoll played the part. Addams tried it on February 1, 1836, but failed, and Judge Conrad later re-wrote the play for Forrest, who produced it at the Park Theatre, May 24, 1841. It became one of his favorite parts and was played on his second trip abroad in 1868. John McCullough acted *Jack Cade* after Forrest's death, and as late as August 29, 1887, Edmund K. Collier produced it at the Third Avenue Theatre in New York. Record[2] has been found of another play Conrad wrote for Forrest, *The Heretic*, played by Edwin Adams April 13, 1863, at the Arch Street Theatre and evidently a romantic tragedy.[3]

Ugolino, or Blood for Blood, a romantic tragedy, has been attributed to Junius Brutus Booth. Booth, of course, was not

[1] II, 245-52.

[2] Ms. *Hist. of the Philadelphia Stage*, by W. D. Coder.

[3] The Catalogue *of the Library of Edwin Forrest*, compiled by Joseph Sabin, 1863, gives *The Heretic* in Ms. Diligent search in the Forrest Home, however, has met with no result.

born in America, but that he wrote the play at all may have been due to the stimulation given to the playwright by the local situation.

It would be a straining of our imposed limits, also, to include the plays of Fanny Kemble, since her first, *Francis I*, was written before she came to this country in 1832. Her *Star of Seville*, a tragedy laid in Spain, written in England, was published here, and was played at the Walnut Street Theatre, August 7, 1837. It is a close adaptation of *La estrella de Sevilla*, once attributed to Lope de Vega. In Mrs. Kemble's version, the lovers meet their death in the last scene, while in the Spanish version they part forever. Julia Dean put on Mrs. Kemble's adaptation of Alexandre Dumas' *Mademoiselle de Belle-Isle* as *The Duke's Wager*, in 1850. There is record of her *English Tragedy* being played on May 16, 1864 at the New Broadway Theatre. While her work is mainly translation, her style, both in her plays and in her autobiographical accounts, has a real distinction. Her romantic marriage, her divorce, and her subsequent career belong partly to this country, but she remained an Englishwoman at heart.

The writing of romantic drama was, of course, not confined to Philadelphia, but in other places it was more sporadic and had less unity of purpose. The New York editor and poet, James Lawson, wrote for the Park Theatre his *Giordano, or The Conspiracy*, and it was produced there November 13, 1828. It is laid in Florence, and its hero is a villain whose conscience is too tender for him to be thoroughly successful. It is in reality a closet drama placed on the stage, and Lawson, while he wrote other plays, did not have them produced. A comparison of *Giordano* with *Camillus, or the Self-Exiled Patriot*, written by Jonas B. Phillips, an author of popular melodramas, illustrates the greater significance that the work of a practical playwright possesses. Phillips wrote, as a usual thing, plays of the type of *The Evil Eye*, an absurd yet startling production which held the stage from 1831 to 1899. Once in his career he caught the inspiration from Shakespeare's *Coriolanus*, and his

Camillus, played first at the Arch Street Theatre, February 8, 1833, has a real power and dignity. Camillus, the exiled Roman tribune who returns to save his country from the Gauls, is well drawn, as is also Lucius Apuleus, the conspirator against him. The success of *Brutus* and of *Virginius*, and the study of ancient history, more usually an integral part of the school curriculum then than now, probably account for the number of historical heroes placed upon the stage. One of the best, from the point of view of character drawing, occurs in *Waldimar*, by John J. Bailey, of New York, in which Charles Kean acted the part of Waldimar. It was first produced at the Park Theatre, November 1, 1831, and Ireland remarks that "having many passages of rare merit," it deserved more than the four nights' representation. Kean brought it to Philadelphia, however, and it was simply another instance of a fine play being absorbed by a star whose main interest lay elsewhere. *Waldimar* is laid in Thessalonica at the close of the fourth century during the reign of Theodosius the Great. The massacre is a historical fact, used before by Brockden Brown, but the characters and the plot are entirely fictitious. It is quite a distinguished play; the blank verse is flexible, and while the speeches are at times too long, the author has carefully indicated where they may be cut.

Waldimar is pictured as a tyrant, under whom the citizens are restless and who is willing to sacrifice Hersilia, his daughter, to his ambitions. He wishes her to marry the son of Theodosius, the Emperor. She really loves Claudius, a young soldier who has saved Waldimar's life. Rufus, an old warrior, who is devoted to Waldimar and is an admirable character, indicates to him that Claudius has conspired with the Senators to have him removed. Martian, who is the favorite of the people, has incurred the enmity of Rufus, and has, in fact, betrayed his daughter. Rufus urges punishment for him, and Waldimar orders him to be killed. The populace rebels in consequence, and Waldimar is saved only by the determined opposition of a few of his troops under Claudius. The mob frees Martian, and

Waldimar plots and counter plots, until Theodosius himself comes on the scene. Here Waldimar rises to a certain greatness when he has the Emperor in his power and does not kill him. Waldimar is condemned to death, but is pardoned through the efforts of his daughter and Claudius. Among many heroes who are animated by love of the people, Waldimar is noteworthy as representing the tyrant who scorns popular rule.

Teresa Contarini, a tragedy by Mrs. Elizabeth Ellet, produced at the Park Theatre on March 19, 1835, and founded on incidents in Venetian history, is a respectable production. In quality, however, it is far below the work of the man who was easily the most important of the writers who were living in New York during their careers as playwrights. Nathaniel Parker Willis was born in Portland in 1806 and educated at Yale College, but left New England in 1831 to seek his fortune in New York. After five years' travel in Europe and the East, he settled at Glen Mary near the headwaters of the Susquehanna River, but was compelled by financial necessity to return to New York. Here he became probably the most popular American writer of the forties, was next to Irving the best-known abroad, and is a shining example of the price a gifted man pays in terms of lasting fame for contemporary popularity. He is remembered now in the histories of literature as the author of a few lyrics and some admirable nature essays, but his two plays far exceed these in merit. *Bianca Visconti* is a blank verse tragedy, which was written in competition for a prize offered by Josephine Clifton for the best play suited to her peculiar talent. It was played first August 25, 1837, at the Park Theatre, where Miss Clifton made a powerful impression as Bianca. It was well received in Boston and Philadelphia, and after Miss Clifton had ceased to star in it Miss Margaret Davenport revived it in 1852 in Philadelphia.

The tragedy concerns a real character, Francesco Sforza, who married the natural daughter of Philip Visconti and later became Duke of Milan. In the play Bianca and Sforza have been betrothed for some time, but the Duke, her father, has postponed the wedding until forced to agree to it by Sforza's attempted conquest of the city. They are married, and Francesco believes that she does not care for him, although she loves him deeply. Giulio, her page, who is really her brother, sent in disguise from Naples, is accompanied by Sarpellione, who tries to prevent Sforza from becoming powerful in Milan, in order that the throne may come to Giulio. Sarpellione tempts Sforza first of all by offers of power and then Pasquali, a poet, tries to kill Sforza but fails. Finally Bianca, at the Duke's death, takes the throne. Sarpellione bribes Brunorio, his lieutenant, to murder Sforza, and the arrangement is made that he shall do so while Sforza sleeps in the garden. Bianca overhears the plotting and arranges in an affecting scene that Giulio shall take his place. When she finds out she has been the cause of her brother's death, Bianca goes out of her head with grief, and, waking in time to place the crown on Sforza's head, dies of a broken heart.

The real poetic vein that lay in Willis showed in many passages, and the characters not only of Sforza, Bianca, and Giulio, but also the comedy parts, Pasquali and Fiametta, are well conceived. Willis tried to write a native comedy for Miss Clifton, but *The Kentucky Heiress* was performed unsuccessfully on November 29, 1837. Driven back fortunately to the field in which his real strength lay, he wrote another verse play, this time a romantic comedy, which challenges comparison with any contemporary play of its kind in English. As Poe well said:

"Its merits lie among the higher and most difficult dramatic qualities. These merits are naturalness, truthfulness and appropriateness upon all occasions, of sentiment and language; a manly vigor and breadth in the conception of character; and a few ideal elevations or exaggerations throughout—a matter forgotten or avoided by those who, with true Flemish perception of truth, wish to copy her peculiarities in disarray."[1]

[1] *Burton's Gentleman's Magazine*, August, 1839.

Tortesa the Usurer was written for James William Wallack, who produced it at the National Theatre, New York, April 8, 1839. It was very successful, and Wallack considered that in Tortesa he had one of his best parts. When Wallack returned for a time to England after the burning of the National Theatre, he produced *Tortesa* at the Surrey Theatre in August, 1839, and acted the character frequently. The first professional appearance of his son, Lester Wallack, after he arrived at manhood, was made in the part of Angelo, when he supported his father on this tour.[1] In *Tortesa* Willis created the character of a money lender, no longer in his first youth but still vigorous, who determines to marry Isabella, the daughter of Count Falcone. He is attracted by her beauty, but his main interest in her is as a symbol of the rank and refinement which have not been his. Isabella and Angelo, a young painter, fall in love with each other. Zippa, a well-drawn girl of the middle class, loves Angelo also, and in ignorance of Isabella's passion, agrees to help her in a scheme by which the latter will feign death, escape Tortesa and marry Angelo. When she discovers Isabella's love she begs the patrician to give her back her lover in a fine scene of contrasted womanly affections.

> "*Zippa:* You mock me!
> You are a woman, though your brow's a rock,
> And know what love is. In a ring of fire
> The tortured scorpion stings himself, to die—
> But love will turn upon itself, and grow
> Of its own fang immortal!"

Isabella, however, refuses Zippa's plea, takes the sleeping potion, and then tries to return to her father's house, but he refuses her admittance because he thinks she is a ghost. She is then taken to Angelo's house by Tomaso, his servant. Tortesa and officers come to Angelo's studio where he is painting Isabella. They make a search for her, and try to apprehend him, claiming that he has stolen a corpse from the cemetery. Isabella steps within the picture frame and they

[1] Wallack, Lester, *Memories of Fifty Years*. P. 35.

are at first baffled, but a veil of hers is found and Angelo is brought before the Duke. Isabella, who has followed in the disguise of a friar, reveals herself to Count Falcone, who then tries to force her to marry Tortesa. Tortesa now rises to the height of his character as he turns to Isabella:

Tortesa: If my liege permit,
I will address my answer to this lady.
                                   (*Turns to Isabella*)
For reasons which I need not give you now,
Fair Isabella, I became your suitor.
My motives were unworthy you and me—
Yet I was true—I never said I lov'd you!
Your father sold you me for lands and money—
(Pardon me, Duke! and you, fair Isabella!
You will—ere I am done!) I push'd my suit!
The bridal day came on, and clos'd in mourning;
For the fair bride it dawn'd upon was dead.
I had my shame and losses to remember—
But in my heart sat sorrow uppermost,
And pity—for I thought your heart was broken.
(*Isabella begins to discover interest in his story, and Angelo watches
    her with jealous eagerness.*)
I see you here again! You are my bride!
Your father holds me to my bargain for you!
The lights are burning on the nuptial altar—
The bridal chamber and the feast, all ready!
What stays the marriage now?—*my new born love!*
That nuptial feast were fruit from Paradise—
I cannot touch it till you bid me welcome!
That nuptial chamber were the lap of Heaven—
I cannot enter till *you* call me in!
                    (*Takes a ring from his bosom.*)
Here is the golden ring you should have worn.
Tell me to give it to my rival there—
I'll break my heart to do so!
                    (*Holds it toward Angelo.*)

At the same time he offers to give her to Angelo and with her Falcone's land, which has become forfeit to him according to his bond. There is an interesting struggle between Angelo

258

and Tortesa for Isabella's regard in this last Act, and there are indications that Isabella hesitates between them, but she finally takes Angelo. Tortesa comforts himself with Zippa, on the ground that they really are better suited to each other.

The merit of the play lies in the character drawing of the hero, and of Angelo, Isabella, Zippa, and Tomaso, Angelo's servant. They are human beings, not idealistic abstractions, and they are drawn with that reality which adds life to romance. The play is noteworthy, too, for the manner in which Willis has, without making the language stilted, placed such excellent poetry in the mouths of these characters. His plot owes many debts. The resemblances to *Romeo and Juliet* and to *The Winter's Tale* are sufficiently evident. For the episode of Isabella's revival, the play goes back to the Florentine story of Genevra degli Amieri, who was married to Francesco Agolanti, although she was in love with Antonio Rondinelli, and who apparently died and was buried. Reviving in the night, she escaped from the vault and was refused admittance in turn by her husband, her father, and her uncle, each of whom thought she was a spirit. Going to Antonio's house she was tenderly and considerately treated by him. The former marriage being annulled, they were wedded. Willis probably took his suggestion from the Italian story or its translation[1] and not from Scribe's *Guido et Genevra ou la Peste de Florence*, played and published in 1838. This is so different from *Tortesa* that it is unlikely Willis used it as a source. Scribe made Guido a sculptor, but his art plays no part in the drama as it does in the case of Angelo.

The literary fashion which placed the scenes of the romantic play more and more frequently in France, Italy, or Spain, and the way in which a dramatic motive leaps over time and space,

---

[1] The origin of Genevra is to be found in the story of "La Sepolta Viva," included in *La Novella di Grasso Legnaiuolo* by Domenico Maria Manni, Florence, 1744. The Genevra episode is translated in full in Thomas Roscoe's *The Italian Novelists*. London, 1836, second ed., IV, pp. 251-60.

Shelly had used the story in 1821 in his fragments, *Genevra*, and Leigh Hunt afterward made it the theme of his *Legend of Florence* (1847).

are illustrated in a striking manner in the origin and career of *Octavia Bragaldi, or the Confession*, by Charlotte Barnes Conner. The daughter of the well-known Mr. and Mrs. John Barnes, the latter long the favorite *comédienne* of the Park Theatre, Charlotte Barnes was herself an actress and her plays show the technical skill that such training brings.

Octavia Bragaldi was first produced at the National Theatre, New York, November 9, 1837, Miss Barnes herself acting as Octavia. Ireland says "it has been repeated in almost every city of the Union."[1] It is possible that the origin of the play caused some of this popularity. In 1825 in Frankfort, Kentucky, Colonel Beauchamp killed Colonel Sharpe on the discovery that the latter had seduced his wife before Beauchamp had married her. He was convicted of murder, and he and his wife attempted suicide in his cell the night before the execution. Beauchamp was unsuccessful in his attempt and was actually hanged. The case attracted wide attention and soon after began to appear in literature. T. H. Chivers' drama of *Conrad and Eudora* (1834) seems to have been the first published. Next came Poe's dramatic fragment, *Politian*, which clearly reflects the incident, placed in Rome in the seventeenth century. This was published in 1835, though probably written earlier. Miss Barnes evidently had read Poe's scenes, for the similarity of Castiglione, the name of Poe's villain, to Castelli is evident. The most interesting link in this chain, however, lies in the fact that, while Poe and Miss Barnes had so far felt it necessary to change the scene of the tragedy, the novelists placed the story among its real surroundings. William Gilmore Simms wrote his border romance, *Beauchampe*, in 1842 upon the theme and Charles Fenno Hoffman used a suggestion from the situation in *Greyslaer* (1840). By 1858, when John Savage dramatized *Beauchampe* under the title of *Sybil*, he felt it possible to stage his tragedy in Kentucky, and to produce the play in Louisville as well as in St. Louis, New York, and Philadelphia. It is a significant revelation of

[1] II, 240.

the different standards of the stage and of fiction, and of the methods of the romantic tragedy of the thirties, to note the changes Miss Barnes made in the story. Frankfort becomes Milan in the fifteenth century. Octavia has been deceived by Count Castelli by a false marriage, which was not the case in Kentucky. Castelli disappears and Octavia, believing him dead, marries Bragaldi. Castelli marries a rich woman and, not wishing his wife to know of the earlier false marriage, slanders Octavia. Octavia overhears him and begs him to take back the slander, which he refuses to do. She then demands that Bragaldi kill him, in a scene that must have been very effective. Bragaldi, accused of the murder, confesses it and stabs himself while Octavia takes poison. Miss Barnes produced the play in London and Liverpool, and continued to present it as late as 1854, when she and her husband, E. S. Conner, played it at the Bowery Theatre. Of her other plays, *The Forest Princess* will be discussed under the Indian drama, and the rest have come down only by title. She seems to have made a stage success of the play, *La Fitte*, a dramatization of J. H. Ingraham's novel based on the adventures of the pirate of Louisiana. She also adapted French melodramas, among them *A Night of Expectations*, acted, according to Durang,[1] in England and Ireland, and *Charlotte Corday* from Dumanoir and Clairville's play of that name.

In Boston the outstanding figure was that of Epes Sargent (1814-1880), a journalist of distinction. His *Bride of Genoa* was played first by Josephine Clifton in Boston, at the Tremont Theatre on February 13, 1837. The initial success there was repeated in New York, where Charlotte Cushman played Laura to Miss Clifton's Montaldo. The play was printed in *The New World* in February, 1842, as *The Genoese*. It is a romantic drama, laid in Genoa in 1393, and is concerned with the struggles of the patrician and plebeian orders. Montaldo, the son of the former leader of the popular party, is the hero, and he loves Laura Castelli, the daughter of the patrician,

[1] Series 3, Chaps. 98, 102.

Count Castelli. She is also beloved by the Doge, Fiesco. There is nothing unusual about the plot, which proceeds to the imprisonment and rescue of Montaldo in quite an orthodox manner, but there are passages of real beauty, which foretold the improvement in Sargent's next work.

Velasco, his most important play, was produced at the Tremont Theatre, November 20, 1837, with James E. Murdoch as Velasco and Ellen Tree as Izidora. The scene is laid in Burgos, Spain, about 1046, the general action of the piece being based, according to the author, on the career of Rodrigo Diaz, the Cid. When the play opens Izidora is betrothed to Hernando, but Velasco, who has won many victories, reveals his name, he having been in disguise up to this time on account of banishment. Velasco and Izidora have loved each other even as children, and she is given him in marriage by the King. Hernando plots to separate them, and stirs up trouble between DeLerma, the father of Velasco, and Gonzalez, the father of Izidora. These two men fight, and DeLerma, evidently being much older than Gonzalez, has to take the insult, which he asks his son to revenge. Velasco kills Gonzalez. who, in dying, makes his daughter swear to avenge herself for his murder. Izidora learns from Velasco himself that he has been her father's assailant, and the horror of the situation deepens. The King, however, persuades Izidora to forgive Velasco and to go on with the marriage, but Julio, her brother, returns in time to make more trouble. Hernando suggests that he poison the wine which Velasco is to drink at the marriage feast. Izidora overhears them plotting to poison the wine, and tries to prevent her husband from drinking it, but Julio stabs him and she then takes the poison.

The tragedy was successfully played in Philadelphia and New York. When the Marylebone Theatre in London was opened for the season of 1849-50 *Velasco* was chosen as the attraction, E. L. Davenport acting Velasco and Fanny Vining Izidora.[1] It was several times repeated. It deserved its

---

[1] See Mrs. A. C. Mowatt's *Autobiography of an Actress*, p. 309.

success, for the plot is well knit, the tragedy is inevitable, and the language, at times powerful, is always adequate. Sargent drew well the character of the impetuous Spaniard of the eleventh century, with his keen sense of family honor, before whose claims love itself struggled without avail. The scene between Julio and Izidora, when he begs her not to proceed with the marriage, illustrates the stage effectiveness of the romantic play. Of course, the emotions are strung up to the breaking point, but even the cold type cannot conceal the force of Julio's answer when she pleads her plighted word to Velasco.

> "Thy word! 'tis well for thee
> To be so scrupulous—thou who hast kept
> So faithfully thy word unto the dead!"

Sargent's other plays with three exceptions have come down to us only in name. *The Candid Critic* and *The Lampoon* are dramatic trifles, but the former, in which Dionysius insists on reading his poetry and plays to critics who prefer imprisonment and even death to hearing him, is a clever satire. *The Priestess* (1854), a tragedy in five acts, was produced in Boston, in 1855, by Julia Dean Hayne.

The impulse to translate native happenings into foreign settings had a sharp contrast in one of the earliest of the Southern dramas. In 1830, a prize play, *Irma, or the Prediction*, was published. According to the introductory "Remarks" it gained a prize of three hundred dollars, offered by Caldwell, proprietor of the American Theatre in New Orleans. It was first acted in March, 1830, and was played in Cincinnati to "an overflowing house." It was printed anonymously as "the first effort of a very young man," and was written by James M. Kennicott of New Orleans in 1829, while he was teaching school in western New York. Kennicott died in Texas in 1838.[1] But of most interest is the statement that "the play is wrought out of an old Welsh legend, but the author (thinking it perhaps necessary to secure the prize) has altered the scene and laid

[1] See Rees, pp. 94-8, for an extended account of the play.

it in this country, at the early period of the Revolution." It is a blank verse tragedy with some merit in the verses. Irma is pictured as a woman of strong character, who yet allows her life to be shadowed and finally ruined by the prediction of Remington that she will become a murderess. The obsession is one that might well have been developed in a Celtic atmosphere, but among the scenes of the Revolution it is out of place. If any argument were needed in favor of the placing of romantic verse dramas in a place and time distant from the familiar scenes of life, it is furnished by this play.

There was undoubtedly more playwriting in the South than has come down to us. The early theatrical pioneers in Cincinnati, Vicksburg, New Orleans, Mobile, and St. Louis have left many records of their labors, but they belong to theatrical rather than to dramatic history. If there were dramatic activity such as that which flourished in Charleston in an earlier period, it has left only a scant record,[1] but, as a matter of fact, the circumstances were different. Closer communication between the South and the North did away to a certain extent with the opportunity for local playwriting. Just as the Southern novelists and poets published in New York and Philadelphia, the Southern playwrights looked more and more to the North for their opportunity. For example, William Pelby, a Boston actor and the manager of the Tremont Theatre, and later of the National Theatre, offered a prize of five hundred dollars for the best original tragedy. It was won by Mrs. Caroline Lee Hentz (1800-56), a novelist, then living in Kentucky, with her play, *De Lara, or the Moorish Bride*. Pelby apparently could not pay all of the prize, but at least he produced the play in Philadelphia at the Arch Street Theatre on November 7, 1831, and also in Boston at the Tremont Theatre. Wemyss speaks of the play as deserving of a better actor, and Durang praises it highly, but, while there is a certain skill in the way in which Fernando is followed by his father's ghost,

---

[1] Ludlow, in his *Dramatic Life*, records not more than a dozen plays, of a fugitive nature, none of which has survived.

the characters are purely types, and the Moors have none of the verisimilitude that Boker was later to give them. Mrs. Hentz, undiscouraged, provided Pelby with another tragedy, *Werdenberg, or the Forest League,* which he put on at the Park Theatre, March 24, 1832. Rees states that he saw her *Lamorah,* "an excellent Indian play," at Caldwell's Theatre in New Orleans, on January 1, 1833. Neither has survived.

The most prolific of Southern dramatists was Nathaniel H. Bannister, born January 3, 1813, who began his career on the stage in Baltimore at the age of sixteen, and who died in poverty in New York in 1847. The brief outlines of his career indicate a tragic story of an actor, popular in the West but not quite good enough for the East, who wrote many plays, but none quite great enough to be remembered, and who sold his only very successful play, *Putnam,* for fifty dollars! Of the five plays that have survived, four are romantic. *Gaulantus* is a tragedy laid on the frontier of Italy during the conquest of Gaul by the Romans. The blank verse has a roughness that prevents the reader from viewing the play seriously. It seems to have been acted first at the Walnut Street Theatre in 1837, and was put on in New York also. *England's Iron Days* is laid in a rather indeterminate time, when Normans and Saxons were at odds with each other and certainly with history. *The Three Brothers* is a more modern English play, equally impossible in plot, characterization, and expression. *The Gentleman of Lyons,* performed August 16, 1838, at the Walnut Street Theatre, is a play in which the influence of *The Lady of Lyons* is apparent. They are all examples of melodrama and they represent simply hasty imitation of a prevailing mode.

Of a much higher quality was the work of George H. Miles (1824-1871), a lawyer and teacher in Baltimore. His tragedy, *Mohammed,* was written in competition for a prize of one thousand dollars offered by Forrest. The committee was unable to select, from among the eighty plays submitted, one that met the conditions, but Forrest sent the prize to Miles as the competitor who had most nearly fulfilled them.[1] Forrest did not use the play, but it was performed at the Lyceum Theatre in New York, October 27, 1851, with Neafie as Mohammed and Miss Maeder as Cadijah, Mohammed's first wife. Mohammed is conceived as a man who believes in his mission to free Arabia from idolatry, but invents the visions that give him supernatural authority. The blank verse is above the average, the action is fairly rapid, and the characters are distinct.

The romantic play in verse was naturally the medium chosen by many of those who wrote for the reader rather than for stage production. These dramas lie outside our scope, but two plays which in their inception at least were created with a view to performance could in all probability have been as successful as many of their more fortunate rivals. *Athenia of Damascus*, by Rufus Dawes, is a tragedy of considerable power, written, according to Rees, for Mrs. George Jones, but apparently not acted. The final scene in which Athenia, half crazed, leads the mob to ruin and kills her lover under the belief that he is a traitor, might have afforded scope for a tragic actress. It was the first play selected by Colman in his ambitious attempt to publish an "American Dramatic Library," which reached only to the second instalment, Willis's *Bianca Visconti!*

Longfellow began his *Spanish Student* with a view to production, but apparently met with little encouragement, so that it was published first in *Graham's Magazine* in 1842 and later in book form. He has indicated in the preface to the first edition that the theme was taken in part from Cervantes' tale of *La Gitanilla*, and he refers to the Spanish plays and to Middleton's *Spanish Gypsy*, which had also used the theme. The love of a student, Victorian, for Preciosa, the gypsy maiden, is developed charmingly, and the devices by which the Count of Lara's perfidy is foiled are managed skillfully enough to have provided action, rapid in some places and progressing at all times. Considering the vogue of this species it seems an accident that Longfellow's first drama was not acted,

[1] Alger, I, 169.

and it would have been interesting if he, like Irving and Cooper and Mrs. Howe, had been definitely connected with our stage. In a later period he continued to write dramas, but none approached *The Spanish Student* in their theatrical possibilities.

By the middle of the century the romantic play was firmly established and was yet to achieve greater artistic triumphs. To the superficial observer its significance has been obscured by its foreign setting, and to the canon of dramatic art that demands national themes, a canon that has never been applied except to America, it cannot respond, particularly to those who know its masterpieces only by title. But to the historian who reads the plays of this group of writers, especially those who wrote in Philadelphia from 1825 to 1840, with constant reference to the political and social ideals of America in that day, the essentially native flavor of this drama becomes apparent. It was no accident that *Caius Marius* should celebrate the revolt of the Roman populace against oligarchy; *Metamora*, the revolt of the Indians against the encroachments of the whites; *Pelopidas*, the revolt of the Thebans against the tyranny of Sparta; *The Gladiator*, the revolt of the slaves against their Roman masters; *Oralloossa*, the revolt of the Indians against their Spanish conquerors; *The Broker of Bogota* and *Tortesa the Usurer*, the resentment of the merchant class against the oppression of a ruling caste; *The Bride of Genoa*, the revolt of the plebeians against the patrician order; *Sertorius*, the revolt of Spain against Roman rule, and *Jack Cade*, the rebellion of the commons against the tyranny of the English barons. At that time democracy was the dominant political note. The Grecian Revolution of 1829, the revolt of the South American republics against Spain, and the establishment of a constitution in Spain itself, the French Revolution of 1830, the struggle of Poland for freedom, were in the air. But the most vital inspiration was the triumph of democratic institutions at home. The election of Andrew Jackson in 1828 showed the preference of the people of the United States for democracy. It was not, however, a matter of politics in a narrow sense. Smith was a

Democrat, but Bird and Conrad were active Whigs. It was the general sympathy with those who opposed political oppression that caused these plays to be written and made them popular. The native historical plays of the Revolution were many: they are obviously the result of this same feeling, but that it should animate the historical tragedy of earlier days is even more significant. It proves, once more, as *Hamlet* and *The Merchant of Venice* once proved triumphantly, that playwrights need not confine their themes and situations to their own locality, provided the national point of view is preserved.

CHAPTER X

WHILE the romantic tragedy and comedy were engaging the efforts of the most skillful of our dramatists, numerous and industrious playwrights sought to place upon the stage the scenes and characters of their native land. Disregarding opera and pantomime, our stage histories record about one hundred and ninety plays with a historical background between 1825 and 1860. Their general level of excellence fell below that of the romantic play, for several reasons. First, they were often written hurriedly for holidays or other special occasions. Second, they frequently dealt with wars or other well-known events that lent themselves to exaggeration or else confined the playwright's imagination. But in another sense they are of even more significance, for in them we find the roots of a later development of great importance. They handed on, too, the impulse started by Tyler, Dunlap, and Barker, and their study reveals again the continuity of our dramatic impulse. Unfortunately, out of more than one hundred and ninety recorded, fewer than one-third have survived. But enough remain to represent the various types into which they ran, and they are most profitably to be considered as types rather than as the work of individual playwrights.

It was natural that the Indian should be treated frequently at the time. The love of romance found in him a link between the strange and the familiar, which secured freedom of treatment at the same time that it satisfied the desire for a native subject. It was not, of course, a new theme. *Ponteach* had been printed in 1766, and the first Indian play to be acted, an operatic spectacle, *Tammany* by name, written by Anne Kemble Hatton, a sister of John Kemble and Mrs. Siddons, was played at the John Street Theatre, New York, on March 3, 1794. We know it by Dunlap's description, by the songs, and the scenario, which have been preserved, but the real beginning of Indian drama came with Barker's *Indian Princess* in 1808. This seems to have started some interest in the subject, for we find a *Harlequin Panattatah, or the Genii of the Algonquins* produced at the Park Theatre on January 4, 1809. But it was not until 1827 that the Indian plays commenced to multiply.

The honor of introducing the vogue seems to belong to George Washington Parke Custis (1781-1857), the son of John Parke Custis, the stepson of Washington. Custis was a writer and speaker of ability, but, with the instincts of a Southern land-holder, he published little. In 1826 he began in *The United States Gazette* his recollections of the private life of Washington, and an incident related in these became the basis of his first play, *The Indian Prophecy*, produced at the Chestnut Street Theatre, Philadelphia, July 4, 1827. This incident was told Custis by Dr. James Craik, a bosom friend of Washington. In 1770 Washington was visited, while he was in the Kanawha region in Virginia, by an Indian chief who told him that he had been the leader of the Indians at Braddock's defeat and though he and his best shots had tried to kill the Colonial officer, they had failed. The chief decided that the Great Spirit protected Washington for some future service and ordered his braves to desist. Custis built a play with several fictitious characters around this incident, which becomes the climax. An attempt is made to trick the old chief, Menawha, by placing Washington's hat and cloak upon one of the hunters but Menawha knows Washington at once.

Whether John Augustus Stone received the inspiration to write *Metamora, or the Last of the Wampanoags* from seeing or reading *The Indian Prophecy* or from the perusal of Bird's *Sagamore* is a matter of conjecture, though probably both had their effect. In the *Critic* of November 22, 1828, Edwin Forrest offered a prize of five hundred dollars and half the pro-ceeds of the third night for the "best tragedy, in five acts, of which the hero, or principal character, shall be an original of this country." Fourteen plays were submitted to the committee of award, headed by Bryant, and the prize was awarded to *Metamora*. It was first produced at the Park Theatre, New York, on December 15, 1829, and was an instant success, and the performance on January 23, 1830, at the Arch Street Theatre was a triumph for the native actor who had come into national prominence. Forrest played it continually during his entire career and records of its performance by E. K. Collier are found as late as 1887.[1] The author shared in no way in this prosperity. He had begun his career as an actor in Boston, had appeared in New York at the City Theatre in 1822, and acted in old men's parts with varying success in New York and Philadelphia. His contributions to romantic tragedy have been recorded, but in neither the theatre nor the drama did he find any adequate support. In despair he threw himself into the Schuylkill River from the Spruce Street wharf in Philadelphia, May 29, 1834.[2] Forrest erected a handsome tombstone to his memory.

Metamora exists in two incomplete manuscripts, in the Forrest Home and the University of Utah, which were only recently printed. From these and from accounts of the play it is possible to recreate the drama of the last days of Metamora or King Philip, with the prevailing motives of love for his wife, Nahmeokee, and his child, his defiance of the whites, his courage, honesty, and stoicism. The part suited Forrest admirably, for Metamora is a type, not a real Indian, and every admirable characteristic is intensified, and every moment is a tense one. From the first Act, in which he saves the life of Oceana, all through the scenes of alternating triumph and defeat—including his rescue of Nahmeokee from the English—till the last scene, in which he kills Nahmeokee to save her from the hands of the whites and dies defiant from the bullets of the invaders, the interest is preserved by somewhat the same

[1] Brown, III, 227.
[2] Wood's Diary.

devices that animate the moving picture of to-day. The similarity of the death scene of Nahmeokee to the death scene in Knowles's *Virginius* shows the kinship of the Indian play with the romantic tragedy of the time. The language of the play is that mixture of Indian and Ossian which became traditional upon the stage. In Act II, Sc. 3, Metamora says:

> Then would you pay back that which fifty snows ago you received from the hands of my father, Massassoit. You had been tossed like small things on the face of the great waters and there was no Earth for your feet to rest on. Your backs were turned on the lands of your fathers and the son of the forest took ye as a little child and opened the door of his wigwam. The keen blast of the north howled in the leafless woods but the Indian covered you with his broad right hand and put it back.

The author endowed the Indian with that rhythmic antithesis which has been a favorite utterance through all literatures and it is at times effective, as in Act II, Sc. 3:

> Your great Book, you say, tells you to give good gifts to the stranger and deal kindly with him whose heart is sad. The Wampanoag needs no such counsellor, for the Great Spirit has with his own finger written it on his heart.

Curiously enough, the bombast of *Metamora* seems not to have prevented its appreciation by Indian auditors.

Even before *Metamora* reached Philadelphia, Penn Smith had put on *William Penn* at the Walnut Street Theatre, which mingles the motive of Indian self-sacrifice with that of Colonial history. Having written another Indian play, *The Pawnee Chief*, which has survived only by title, G. W. P. Custis next selected the motive of Barker's *Indian Princess* and produced his *Pocahontas, or the Settlers of Virginia*, first played at the Walnut Street Theatre, January 16, 1830, where it ran for the unusually long period of twelve nights. The theatre had been closed for several days, on account of the elaborate preparations that were being made for the performance. It was revived later in New York and Philadelphia. *Pocahontas* employs the usual historical episodes, but with one important change. The story of Captain Smith and Pocahontas has a serious drawback as dramatic material: the climax comes too soon. Barker, although he realized that the salvation of Smith by the Indian maiden was the high point of action, tried to emphasize the love motive of Rolfe and Pocahontas. Custis, with more courage, calmly disregarded chronology and introduced the rescue of Smith into the last scene of the play. The characters of Pocahontas, Powhatan, Smith, Rolfe, and Matacoran, the Indian chief opposed to the English, are well drawn. The speeches are, however, too long and the prompt copy of John Sefton, the manager, shows many cuts.

Notwithstanding the inherent difficulties of the Pocahontas story, its romantic flavor led playwrights to return to it more than once. In 1837 Robert Dale Owen, British by birth but later a member of Congress, wrote his *Pocahontas*, a play in blank verse and prose, which was produced at the Park Theatre, February 8, 1838, with Charlotte Cushman as Rolfe and Emma Wheatley as Pocahontas. Owen tried to introduce a love motive between Smith and Pocahontas, but without much success, and while at times the language is quite effective the play is long-drawn-out and the quarrels of the colonists become tiresome. Charlotte Barnes Conner, in her *Forest Princess*, played first at Liverpool in 1844 and in Philadelphia, February 16, 1848, endeavored to provide a new motive by taking Pocahontas to England, where she dies in a pathetic scene, after Rolfe has been cleared of a charge of treason. The play is in blank verse of a very fair quality, but its tragedy has not the vigor of *Octavia Bragaldi*. Mrs. Conner evidently was inspired to write *The Forest Princess* by witnessing Custis's play, for her mother, Mrs. Barnes, took the part of Pocahontas in the performance at the Park Theatre in 1830. Finally the motive ran to satire in John Brougham's burlesque of *Pocahontas, or the Gentle Savage*, at Wallack's Theatre, December 24, 1855. A late undated play by Samuel H. M. Byers seems not to have been acted.

The Pocahontas series contains easily the best of the plays concerning the North American Indian. Bird's *Oralloossa* has to do with Indians of a different race and he declined to dramatize his Indian story, *Nick of the Woods*, leaving it to be turned by Louisa H. Medina into one of the most popular and most highly colored melodramas of the time. The rage for Indian drama caused an older play with aboriginal characters like Finn's *Montgomery*[1] to be rewritten, and produced as *The Indian Wife* in 1830. It is an interesting example of the mixture of Indian and Yankee themes. Interesting for another reason was *Pontiac, or the Siege of Detroit*, by General Alexander Macomb, who had been in command of the American troops and aided in securing McDonough's victory at Plattsburg Bay. The play was written, according to the preface, in 1826, though it was not published till 1835. It seems to have been acted at the National Theatre in Washington with great success in 1838, the United States Marines being used in the production.[2] Quite appropriately, Major Robert Rogers, who wrote the first *Ponteach* in 1766, takes a principal part and saves the troops after the British have been defeated in a skirmish. A quiet reading indicates that the marine corps must have been the real cause for the success of the play, for it is not constructed with any dramatic effectiveness.

Just as the vogue of the Indian play was losing its hold, George H. Miles wrote one of the most appealing from the literary point of view, in *De Soto*, in which the interest of Colonial history is blended with that of the Indian motive. *De Soto* was written for James E. Murdoch, who produced it at the Chestnut Street Theatre, Philadelphia, April 19, 1852. It has been preserved only in a manuscript, in which De Soto's part is not given, but enough remains to reveal an appropriate treatment of a romantic theme, the conquest and death of the discoverer of the Mississippi. Next to De Soto the interest centers on Ulah, the supposed daughter of Tuscaluza, the chief

---

[1] See Note, Chap. VI, p. 156.
[2] Rees, p. 105. Roden, p. 81.

of the Floridas. She is really a white woman, the child of a murdered survivor of the earlier expedition of Navarez, and her unhappy love for De Soto and her death at the hands of Tuscaluza form an effective scene. *De Soto* was revived in 1857 at the Broadway Theatre, when Mr. and Mrs. E. L. Davenport played De Soto and Ulah.

Stage history records about fifty Indian plays which seem to have been performed between 1825 and 1860, besides others not to be clearly identified. Of these not half have survived. As will be seen from the appended list,[1] the great popularity of this type came in the thirties and by 1847 John Brougham had begun to burlesque the "noble savage." It is not hard to see why the vogue declined. There is a sameness of plot, an exaggeration of motive, and a lack of reality in the treatment of the Indian which soon doomed the aboriginal drama. And, unlike the other national historical plays, it dealt with a vanishing not a coming race.

Colonial history received comparatively less treatment at the hands of the playwrights. Barker's *Superstition* remained unsurpassed in artistic merit during the period now under discussion. *William Penn* and *De Soto* dramatized the interest of the early explorations, as well as the resistance of the Indian to the whites. In 1830, John Kerr and Samuel Chapman put on a play called *Son and Father, or the Dutch Redemptioner,*

---

[1] The plays are arranged by years, so far as possible, in the order of their performance. Those starred have been printed. Those marked † exist in incomplete manuscripts. For details see List of Plays. At least six other unidentified plays seem to be on Indian themes.

(1827) *The Indian Prophecy**; (1829) *The Manhattoes, Metamora**, *William Penn**; (1830) *Naramattah, The Pawnee Chief, The Maid of Wyoming**, *Pocahontas**, *The Indian Wife, The Wigwam, Carabasset**, *Miantanimoh;* (1831) *Last of the Mohicans;* (1832) *Oralloossa**, *The Liberty Tree;* (1833) *Lamorah, Wacousta, The Pioneers;* (1834) *Wacousta, Oronaska or the Chief of the Mohawks, The Wept of Wish-ton-wish**, *Kairrissah, Outallissi;* (1835) *Pontiac**, *The Yemassee;* (1836) *Tecumseh**, *Sassacus;* (1837) *Pocahontas**; (1838) *Nick of the Woods**, *The Indian Girl;* (1840) *Tippecanoe;* (1841) *Osceola;* (1842) *Sharratah;* (1845) *Telula, or the Star of Hope*†; (1846) *Onoleetah, Montezuma;* (1847) *Metamora** (burlesque); (1848) *The Forest Princess**; (1849) *The Eagle Eye;* (1850) *Ouacosta, or the Lion of the Forest;* (1852) *The Star of the West, De Soto*†; (1856) *Silver Knife, Pocahontas** (burlesque), *Hiawatha** (burlesque); (1858) *The Minute Spy* which is said to have been founded on a real incident occurring years before in Philadelphia.

Cornelius Mathews (1817–1889), an editor in New York, employed the Colonial motive twice, first in *Witchcraft, or the Martyrs of Salem*, produced at Philadelphia at the Walnut Street Theatre in 1846 by Murdoch and afterward acted with apparently unusual success in New York, Boston, Cincinnati, St. Louis, and even in California. It was published in London in 1852 and was translated into French.[1] *Witchcraft* is at times fine drama. Gideon Bodish's love for his mother, her arrest for witchcraft, his defense of her, and their death through human intolerance, remind us in their general motive of the story of Charles and Isabella in *Superstition*, but there is great difference in the treatment. Ambla Bodish's nature, gloomy and moody with the memory of her husband's tragedy, fits her to become the object of the Puritan persecution. Mathews had a real inspiration also when he made Susanna Peache, who loves Gideon, testify against his mother because the girl believes that Ambla has bewitched Gideon and forced him to forget his former love for herself. Perhaps the most poignant misery arises from the temporary doubt in Gideon's own mind whether his mother is not really possessed by evil spirits, and the tragedy moves on to its rigorous end. Susanna, despairing of recovering Gideon's love, dies by her own hand and Jarvis Dane, who has loved her truly, but hopelessly, kills Gideon as the cause of her misfortune. The blank verse has a real beauty at times and if the play were actually given as indicated by the prompt copies[2] the author must have suffered extremely at the mutilation his verses received. It was translated into French by Philarete Chasles.

In Mathews's second historical play *Jacob Leisler* he treated the character of the Governor of New York, who was elected by the people and who was dispossessed of his office by King William in 1689. It was first acted by Murdoch on April 15,

[1] Clapp, p. 404.
[2] New York Public Library.

1848, at the Arch Street Theatre in Philadelphia and on May 8, 1848, in New York, but has not survived. Leisler was also made the hero of *Old New York, or Democracy in 1689*, by Elizabeth Oakes Smith. According to the printed play, her journal, and her biography it was produced in New York, and Julia Dean played Elizabeth in New Orleans. Leisler is a tragic figure, being executed for his resistance to the new Governor, William Sloughter, who is also the first husband of Elizabeth, Leisler's wife. The play has little merit, however. It is surprising that the many dramatic situations in our Colonial history should have escaped notice, but it may have been that the robust sense of nationality forbade their selection. In any case, the celebration of Leisler, the representative of democracy, and of the witches who typified the resistance to the ruling theocracy of New England, can hardly be unnoticed.

The Revolution continued naturally to be the most appealing theme. But while out of the score of such plays produced before 1825 fully half were printed, only one-fifth of those that saw the stage between 1825 and 1860 have come down to us. A glance at the list[1] which can be only partially complete, will

---

[1] The identified plays are arranged by years in order of their performance, those printed being starred. For details see List of Plays. (1826) *Briar Cliff, or a Tale of the Revolution;* (1828) *Paul Jones*, or the Pilot of the German Ocean;* (1831) *Washington, or the Savior of His Country, Rake Hellies;* (1832) *Washington, or the Retaliation, The Soldier of the Revolution, The Dream of Christopher Columbus, The Cradle of Liberty, or Boston in 1775*, Washington, or the Hero of Valley Forge;* (1835) *The Spirit of '76;* (1836) *Horse Shoe Robinson* (by Dance), *Boston Boys in '76;* (1840) *The Battle of Stillwater* (Ms.), *West Point, or a Tale of Treason* (acted?)*, *Natalie, or the Frontier Maid;* (1842) *The Death of Nathan Hale*;* (1843) *The Boston Tea Party of 1774;* (1844) *Putnam** (by Bannister), *Putnam* (by Hielge), *1777, or the Times that Tried Us Americans;* (1845) *Anthony Wayne, The Traitor, or the Battle of Yorktown, The Declaration of Independence;* (1846) *The Battle of Germantown, The Irish Yankee** [43-46], *Benjamin Franklin** (Brougham), *The Swamp Fox, Richmond Hill;* (1847) *The Old Waggoner of New Jersey and Virginia, The Witch, or a Legend of the Catskills, Ethan Allen, The Revolution;* (1849) *Three Eras of Washington's Life, Kate Woodhull, Benjamin Franklin* (anon.); (1850) *General George Washington, or the Traitor Foiled, The Swamp Steed, or Marion and His Merry Men of 1776;* (1851) *Harry Burnham, or the Young Continental, Our Revolutionary War, The Patriots of '76, or The Jersey Blues;* (1852) *Rebels or Tories, or the Shoemaker of New York in 1774;* (1853) *The Black Rangers, or the Night Hawks;* (1856) *Horse Shoe Robinson** (by Tayleure), *The Female Privateer, or the Pine Tree Flag of 1773, New York Patriots, or the Battle of Saratoga, The Battle of Brandywine, or the Green Riders of the Santee;* (1857) *Wissahickon, or the Heroes of 1776, The Golden Eagle, or the Privateer of 1776*, Love in '76*;* (1858) *Blanche of Brandywine*;* (1859) *The Miller of New Jersey or The Prison Hulk.**

show how each of the great events from the Boston Tea Party to Yorktown was celebrated. Franklin, Putnam, Morgan, Hale, Marion, Wayne, Ethan Allen were popular figures, but every one else was a bad second to Washington, and it must have taxed the managerial efforts of the time to find actors capable of representing him. John Gilbert of Boston and Peter Richings in New York and Philadelphia seem to have been favorites. The treason of Arnold was a popular subject but, curiously enough, in the closet play. Five plays, Joseph Breck's *West Point, or a Tale of Treason* (1840), Horatio Hubbell's *Arnold* (1847), James R. Orton's *Arnold* (1854), Elihu G. Holland's *Highland Treason* (1852), and W. W. Lord's *André* (1856), only the first of which may have been acted, all illustrate the fate that, since Dunlap's successful attempt, has followed that theme and has driven even such a charming stage picture as Clyde Fitch's *Major André* into oblivion. Four of these five plays are interesting only in their existence, for they are rhetorical and undramatic, and in *Highland Treason* the student of versification will find some of the most curious blank verse ever written. In Orton's *Arnold*, however, we have a sympathetic study of Arnold's physical courage, his impatience of delay, his love of finery and display, and his resentment at his disgrace, which led finally to his fall. It is the only drama which deals with his early career and his term in Philadelphia and, while this makes the play less actable, the development of his character and the natural way in which his downfall is explained through that character makes it the most interesting to read, next to Dunlap's *André*, of all this series of plays. Mrs. Arnold, Beverly Robinson, André, and Gates are also well drawn.

The acted drama of the Revolution that we can now examine contains some popular successes and one fine comedy. Bannister's *Putnam, the Iron Son of '76*, was first put on at the Bowery Theatre, August 5, 1844, and ran for seventy-eight nights. It was produced annually for many years and went into the other principal cities. It is a rather vigorous play in which the principal characters are Putnam, the Indian, Oneactah, and Talbot, the renegade. Washington appears quite frequently in a rather conventional way, and the comedy element is presented by Cabbageall and his wife. The plot is not very important. It consists principally in Putnam's escapes from the British and the Tories, his saving the life of Oneactah's little son, and later of an attempted trick to catch the American officer, which is frustrated by Clara and by Putnam himself. He escapes from Cornwallis by riding down the precipice at Horse Neck Hill. Durang observes that his escape with one hundred and fifty pistol and carbine discharges "will not be without wonder and admiration to the latest posterity!" The wide interest in the play proves how quick is the response to the motive of self-preservation and how the rapidity of a hero's action did not have to wait for the moving pictures to find its way to the favor of audiences. John Brougham's *Franklin* represents him as equally at home as a youth on Market Street, Philadelphia, in a wood near London, in an Indian encampment, in a council chamber in the palace of Saint James, and at the court of Louis XVI. The third scene, in which he baffles Lord Hilsborough, Lord Stormont, and Mr. Pitt, is rather clever. Brougham played Franklin himself, except in the first scene, when the part was taken by an actress!

The best of the Revolutionary plays was *Love in '76* by Oliver Bell Bunce (1828–1890), a writer and publisher in New York. It was put on at Laura Keene's Theatre on February 28, 1857, Miss Keene acting the part of Rose Elsworth, one of the most charming of our stage heroines. The play is concerned with the efforts of Captain Armstrong of the American army to escape from the house of the Tory, Edward Elsworth, Rose's father, and the similarity to Cooper's *Spy* is noticeable. Armstrong is engaged to Rose and when he is surrounded by the British in her father's house, she saves him by her cleverness in outwitting Major Cleveland, the British officer who has offered a reward for his capture. When her pretense that he is another man has failed, she suddenly shifts her ground, pretends to be in love with Captain Arbald of the British army, and secures Cleveland's promise to protect the "captain who is her husband." Cleveland, who hopes to possess her after she has become the wife of his junior officer, decides to bribe Bridget, Rose's maid, to disguise herself as Rose and go through a marriage ceremony with Armstrong. Rose, in a very clever scene, disguised as Bridget, foils him again and when he triumphantly tells her father about the trick he has played on Armstrong, Rose appears with Armstrong to whom she has really been married. And while we are wondering how she is going to hold Cleveland to his promise, she defies him to break it:

If your promise is not observed to the letter, I'll proclaim you through the army. I'll degrade you in the eyes of every English officer and gentleman in the land. You disgrace your sword, sir, by this very hesitation. Your bitter, unsoldierly, and dishonorable hatred and persecution of an honorable prisoner, drove me to an extremity which nothing but a question of life or death could have persuaded me to undertake. My womanly modesty I was forced to outrage. You compelled me to stoop to things which I abhorred. But I have a brother who is an English officer; a husband who is an American one. Be careful, sir, in what way you use my name in connection with this night's work, for, be assured, they will not fail to punish a ribald, a slanderous, or a libertine tongue. Consent to Captain Armstrong's release, and your discomfiture remains a secret; refuse, and with one word, I'll have all our guests upon the spot and a public confession.

It was probably Bunce's study of the earlier English comedy which suggested to him the use of the appeal to the strength of the army's social code. It distinguishes *Love in '76* from the usual play of this type, but of even more importance is the absolute womanly reality of Rose Elsworth, and that wit sharpened by love which has ever proved attractive on the stage. Of Bunce's other acted plays[1] only *Marco Bozzaris* has survived. *The Morning of Life*, produced at the

[1] For his *Fate, or the Prophecy*, see Chap. XII.

Chatham Theatre on June 12, 1848, was evidently a rural comedy according to the cast[1] and was written for the Dennin sisters, who took the parts of a boy and a girl. *Marco Bozzaris*, in which Bunce dramatized recent Grecian history, was played first at the Bowery Theatre on June 10, 1850, J. W. Wallack, Jr., taking the hero's part. It seemed Bunce's fate to have his plays put on just at the end of the season, for in the first case the theatre closed on the next day and in the second on June 24th.

The part of Major Cleveland in *Love in '76* was taken by J. G. Burnett, whose *Blanche of Brandywine*, a dramatization of George Lippard's novel of the same name, was put on at Laura Keene's Theatre, April 22, 1858. Burnett was the stage manager and he was assisted by Joseph Jefferson.[2] In its large cast are representatives of nearly every type of native origin that was then distinguishing the stage. We have Generals Washington and Greene, and Colonel Frazier, the American officer, played by the author. The captures and escapes of Frazier and his adopted daughter Blanche form the main motive of the play, but Washington is introduced at the time of the encampment on Long Island. Sir William Howe, who has lost his way, is brought into the presence of the Commander-in-Chief, in order to give Howe an opportunity to tempt Washington, through an offer of a dukedom, to desert the American cause. In language which is refreshingly human, considering the vocabulary usually allotted to the Father of his Country on the stage, Washington declines the offer and then lets his antagonist depart in peace. The play ends with the victory at Trenton, but before that event occurs we have met Seth Hope, a live Yankee, played by Jefferson, Krout, a patriotic Pennsylvania Dutchman, Gilbert Gates, "a man of Peace," and a negro servant, to say nothing of twenty Continental soldiers, sixteen riders of the Santee, eighteen British soldiers, and ten Hessians!

The student of the Revolutionary play has some moments

---

[1] Ireland, II, 505. Odell, V, 365.
[2] See Jefferson's *Autobiography*, pp. 189-193.

that reward him by their unconscious revelation of the unsophistication of the anonymous playwrights, who were richer in patriotism than in ability. *The Battle of Stillwater, or the Maniac*, which has been attributed to Rufus Dawes but shows no trace of his style, has the ancient plot of a British officer who, having deserted his wife, makes love to her sister on this side of the water, and attempts to kidnap her. When her lover falls wounded in her defense, with his inamorata, apparently, on top of him, the wife, who is crazed, appears clad in a white veil, and exclaims: "Hold! I command you—her false husband doth not call her to the grave!" The curtain descends, and we note on the manuscript this stage direction: "Should Sergeant Bomb's gun not go off, one can be fired from the left wing!"

The interest in the war with the Mediterranean pirates was practically exhausted in an earlier period, but we find record of attempts to combine it with the growth of other types, as in J. S. Jones's *The Usurper, or Americans in Tripoli* (1841), a revision of Ellison's *American Captive* (1811), and it lasted till 1844, when *Naval Glory, or Decatur's Triumph*, afforded an opportunity to blow up ships on the stage. Of the few plays, not more than twenty, that deal during this period with the War of 1812,[1] only two of importance have survived, *The Eighth of January* and *The Triumph at Plattsburg*. G. W. P. Custis wrote, at the request of the manager of the Baltimore Theatre, a play called *North Point, or Baltimore Defended*, which was produced on the anniversary of that battle, September 12, 1833. He also wrote a rival play to Smith's in his *Eighth of January*, which was put on at New Orleans, on December 19, 1831. La Fitte, the pirate of the Gulf of Mexico, was cele-

---

[1] One of the most extraordinary of the historical dramas was *The Patriot, or Union and Freedom*, by George L. Stevens, printed in 1834, and "adapted to be represented in all theatres of the Union," which apparently did not avail themselves of the opportunity. It is laid near Bunker Hill and references are made to the War of 1812 and the victory of the *Constitution*. Henry Wythe, a midshipman on that vessel, is the hero and he marries a daughter of Jack Moreton the "Patriot," son of a hero of 1776. The great feature, however, is a rhymed account of the signers of the Declaration of Independence, which for absurdity would be hard to equal.

brated in two plays by Louisa Medina and Charlotte Barnes
Conner. In 1851 H. J. Conway dramatized Woodworth's novel,
The Champions of Freedom, under the title, *The Mysterious
Chief, or the Heroes of 1812*, and as late as 1859 C. W. Tayleure
put on *The Boy Martyrs of September 12, 1814*, in Baltimore.

Closely allied to the treatment of American history was the
dramatization of contemporary events, and since they expressed
the spirit of the times that inspired them it is again unfortunate
that so few have survived. In 1827 C. S. Talbot, an actor who
came to this country from Ireland in 1820, wrote for his wife
a play of *Captain Morgan, or the Conspiracy Unveiled*. He
called it "a farce in two acts," but it is far from being a farce,
for it dealt with a tragic event which stirred thousands of
people and led to the founding of a new political party. In
1826 William Morgan, a bricklayer then resident in Batavia,
New York, threatened to publish a book revealing the secrets of
the Masonic order. He was arrested on a charge of debt, and
when released he was seized by a number of armed men, forced
into a carriage, taken to Fort Niagara, and never seen again.
Public opinion became aroused and after Morgan's book had
been published and his assailants had been tried, had pleaded
guilty, and had been let off with light sentences, the matter
grew to large proportions. An Anti-Masonic party was
founded, which cast thirty thousand votes in 1829 in New
York alone, and held the balance of power in more than one
State. Talbot published his play early in 1827; it was acted
before publication, for four successive nights, and the cast is
given in the play with Mrs. Talbot as Mrs. Morgan. Morgan
is hardly a hero in the play, for it is indicated that he is thinking
of publishing his work on Masonry for profit. At the same
time, he shows a good deal of courage in defying his captors,
and the sympathy of the reader is with him, for the facts are
followed with reasonable accuracy until he disappears.[1]

In 1833, President Jackson served notice on the United
States Bank that deposits of United States funds would no

[1] See McMaster, V, 109–120 for account of Morgan's abduction.

longer be made, and we find a farce produced on September 7, 1835, at the Bowery Theatre, called *Removing the Deposits*, by Henry J. Finn. Bannister's play, *The Maine Question*, was put on at the Franklin Theatre on February 19, 1839. It referred to the dispute with Great Britain over the Northeastern Boundary, and especially the "Aroostook War," in which serious consequences had been averted only by the prompt action of the Van Buren Administration and the tact of General Winfield Scott, who was in command of the United States troops.[1] Scott became the leading character in the play.

In 1846 the Northwest Boundary dispute caused Joseph M. Field, the prolific dramatist of the Mobile Theatre Company, to stage a rather unique effort in *Oregon, or the Disputed Territory*, in which the territories of Oregon, California, and Texas played their sympathetic parts alongside of more concrete individuals. Only one of Field's plays has survived, but the one which is perhaps most to be regretted from the point of view of literary curiosity is *Victoria*, in which the leading characters were the new Queen of England and James Gordon Bennett of the New York *Herald!*

The struggle between the political parties is reflected in several plays, two of which may be taken as typical. *Whigs and Democrats, or Love of No Politics*, printed in Richmond anonymously in 1839, and attributed to J. E. Heath, was played in 1839 in Philadelphia. It is a clever satire on the methods by which an election was carried on in a rural district in Virginia. The author wrote the play, according to the preface, "to hold up to ridicule the despicable arts of demagogism" then practiced in the country, and he illustrates forcibly the persistence of political institutions in the scene in which "Major" Roundtree, the local boss, sways the votes of his followers by methods which reveal the survival of the feudal system in our democracy. Heath was evidently a Whig, for the better characters belong to that party, and he portrays the inconsistency of General Fairweather, the Democratic candi-

[1] McMaster. VI, 518.

date for Congress, who appeals to the popular judgment for votes but objects seriously to his son's marriage with Catharine Roundtree, the daughter of a tavern keeper, who is his own political lieutenant. Catharine has a reality that is refreshing among the stage heroines of the period.

The Politicians, by Cornelius Mathews (1840), is laid in New York. It seems hardly actable, but is a searching indictment of the methods employed in the local campaigns. Brisk and Gudgeon are the rival candidates for the office of alderman, and the devices they use are neither new nor savory. A love affair is dragged in, but the main interest lies in the fidelity with which both these plays represent that disturbed condition of our mid-century politics, which preceded the war with Mexico and which led to the temporary triumph of the Whig party in 1839 but contributed to its final destruction. *Whigs and Democrats* goes much more definitely to the heart of things than *The Politicians*, but it is a pity that no great dramatist turned to politics for inspiration. At a time when the Democratic party, long intrenched in power, was fighting for its supremacy, when the Whigs, defenders of bank and tariff, were yet depending for their victories of 1839 and 1847 on the popular appeal of "Tippecanoe" and "Old Rough and Ready"; when Van Buren and Clay, in the height of their apparent security, each lost his election by one printed statement of principle—all this period was full of dramatic moments.

The early conflict in Texas which led to the war with Mexico was celebrated in a vigorous if lurid melodrama, *Michael Bonham, or the Fall of Bexar*, by William Gilmore Simms (1806-1870). It was published in 1852 and played at the Charleston Theatre, March 26, 1855. In the version as printed in the *Southern Literary Messenger*, the author states that it was first written with a view to performance, but that he finds it will read better as a story. It is therefore printed in five "parts and scenes," which must have been cut in actual reproduction. Bonham, the hero, was then living in Charleston and seems to have been pleased with the play, which led him, as second in command of the "Texians," through a number of hairbreadth escapes and disguises, to the conquest of the Alamo and the heart of Olivia, the daughter of the Governor, Don Esteban. He is accompanied in these adventures by Davy Crockett, later to be the hero of a much better play, but who was already becoming the literary type of the adventurous pioneer. Simms's other published play, *Norman Maurice, or the Man of the People* (1851), was not acted, though it was put in rehearsal in Nashville, Tennessee, in 1854.[1] It is a tragedy in blank verse, laid in Philadelphia and Missouri, dealing with the attempt on the part of the enemies of Norman Maurice to ruin him. He is a candidate for Senator from Missouri, and politics and love are mingled in a play which is better than *Michael Bonham*, but not of great significance. The climax in which Clarice, his wife, dies is rather effective.

The war with Mexico furnished its quota of plays, one of which has survived. Durang states that the campaign was "on and off all season at the Arch Street Theatre," and the titles of the plays given in Philadelphia and New York, such as *The Siege of Monterey*, *Our Flag is Nailed to the Mast*, *Victory upon Victory*, and *Cerro Gordo*, indicate the nature of their contents. The war continued to be celebrated, however, until quite late, *The Battle of Buena Vista*, the one survivor, being played in New York in 1858.

Toward the close of this period the Mormon emigration, General Walker's invasion of Nicaragua, and the settlement of California find dramatic expression. *The Mormons, or Life at Salt Lake City*, by Dr. Thomas Dunn English, played at Burton's Theatre in March, 1858, is an amusing piece of work. Timothy Noggs, a runaway New York alderman, played by Burton, endeavors to instruct Brigham Young and the other Danites in the latest and best methods of political manipulation, but, after a brief struggle, finds he is a child in the hands of more expert politicians and retires after having had thirteen wives sealed upon him. Doctor English, whose

---

[1] See for both plays Trent, W. P. *William Gilmore Simms*, 1892, p. 199 and p. 214.

lyric, "Ben Bolt," brought him international notice, created farcical names and characters such as "Kneeland Whine," which point forward to the farces of Charles Hoyt. Record is found of other plays of his on contemporary affairs, among them *The Empire of Hayti, or Kingcraft in 1852*, in which he pays his respects to England's attitude. Wallack was not to be outdone by Burton, and in May, 1858, he produced *Deseret Deserted, or the Last Days of Brigham Young*, in which an Irishman, Luny O'Flab, and a fireman, Tom Scott, go out to Deseret in search of their respective maidens. The scene shifts to the "paradise of Mahomet," to which Brigham Young has departed, and becomes a burlesque, including a parody of *The Raven*.

Probably the earliest of the California plays of which we have record was *A Trip to the California Gold Mines*, in which Charles Burke played and which was put on at the Arch Street Theatre, January 10, 1849. It has not survived and the extant California plays, such as *A Live Woman in the Mines, or Pike County Ahead*, by "Old Block", and *Fast Folks, or Early Days of California*, by Joseph A. Nunes, are not nearly as clever as *The Mormons*. *Fast Folks* seems to have been acted by Mr. and Mrs. Wallack in San Francisco and also by John Dolman and Mrs. Drew in Philadelphia in 1858–9, but this national favor is hardly justified by the long-drawn-out comedy with little flavor of the real West about it.

Overshadowing all other human interest, tabooed by the dominating classes alike in the North and the South, and dreaded by the politicians of both parties, the question of slavery was being forced by the abolitionists upon the conscience of the nation. Looking back over that struggle now we can see that the insistent appeal of the writings of Whittier, Lowell, Emerson, Garrison, and Mrs. Stowe was of much more final significance than all the petitions to Congress and the practical politics that were the weapons of the other wing of the abolitionists. Of all these writers Mrs. Stowe made the greatest appeal. *Uncle Tom's Cabin*, from the point of view of structure and characterization, may not be a great novel, but it is more than that; it is a landmark of our national history. Its effect was so great that Lincoln hardly overstated the facts when in meeting Mrs. Stowe for the first time he greeted her with the words, "So this is the little woman who brought on this great war." It would be difficult, of course, to estimate the share of the dramatic versions in this effect. *Uncle Tom's Cabin* was published in book form March 20, 1852. Mrs. Stowe could not protect her dramatic rights and in August, Charles Western Taylor put on a version at Purdy's National Theatre in New York. It was not a success, however, running only eleven nights. G. C. Howard, the manager of the Museum at Troy, New York, believed that his daughter Cordelia could play "little Eva," and at his request George L. Aiken wrote his version which was first played in September, 1852. It was an instant success, running a hundred nights at Troy, then, after a visit to Albany, opening at Purdy's National Theatre in New York, July 18, 1853, and was performed over two hundred times successively, the run lasting until April 19, 1854. During part of the time it was given twelve times weekly and finally eighteen times, the company eating their meals in costume behind the scenes. The acting of Cordelia Howard as Eva and of her mother as Topsy accounted partly for the popularity of the play, but it does not account for its long life in other hands. The original version came to Philadelphia in 1853–4, where Joseph Jefferson acted Gumption Cute, and was seen in Detroit in 1854 and in Chicago in 1858. Another version by H. J. Conway was first seen in Boston on November 15, 1852. In November, 1852, a version called *Slave Life* by Mark Lemon and Tom Taylor was acted at the Adelphi Theatre in London. Two versions were acted in Paris, one by De Wailly and Texier at the Gayety Theatre and one by Dumanoir and D'Ennery at the Ambigu Comique.[1] It has lasted even till to-day in stock and it was one of the most popular revivals produced by The Players (1933). The story is well repre-

[1] See Brown, I, 312-19. Odell, VI, 237-238.

sented in the plot of the play. It is in six acts and begins with the Shelbys in Kentucky, then takes Tom to New Orleans to St. Clair's plantation and brings him to his death under the persecutions of Legree. Eva dies on the stage and is transported bodily by angels to a better world. The play is hopeless from the standpoint of dramatic criticism, and yet in the catalogue of social forces it remains probably the most potent weapon developed by the literary crusade against slavery.

Dred, Mrs. Stowe's second novel of slavery was dramatized several times, C. W. Taylor's version going on the stage of the National Theatre in New York on September 22, 1856, with Cordelia Howard as Tom Tit and her mother as Aunt Milly. It proved fairly popular for five weeks, more so than John Brougham's version which was put on at the Bowery Theatre on September 29. On October 26, 1856, a version by H. J. Conway was played at Barnum's Museum, in which Tom Tit was played by the dwarf General Tom Thumb. But the great sentimental appeal of *Uncle Tom's Cabin* was not present in *Dred*, and it soon ceased to attract.

The tragedy of mixed blood, which was the central theme in *Dred*, had another expression in *Neighbor Jackwood*, by J. T. Trowbridge, who dramatized his own novel of that name for the Boston Museum, where it was played March 16, 1857. The central theme is the pursuit, capture, and rescue of Camille, an octoroon slave from Louisiana, who is protected by a Vermont farmer, Neighbor Jackwood, and is finally purchased, freed, and married by Hector Dunbury. Naturally, Trowbridge had to alter the novel and exaggerate such characters as Enos Crumlett, the Yankee type who assists in the slave's escape and yet is willing to betray her hiding place for money. The play is significant for its representation of the Northern resentment against the Fugitive Slave Law, and while many of the scenes are melodramatic, the domestic comedy of the Jackwood family is redolent of reality. Grandmother Rigglesty is as perfect a picture of ill-tempered old age as one would care to see on the stage, where her success seems to have been gratifying to her creator. *Neighbor Jackwood* had a run of three weeks at its first production and was played for eight years on the Boston stage.

It is surprising that the vogue of *Uncle Tom's Cabin* did not produce a large number of imitations. Perhaps its very success forestalled competition, but the increasing tension of the abolition question may also have made managers cautious. At least one event, however, and that the most dramatic of all, had immediate presentation on the stage. John Brown's raid occurred on October 16, 1859. On December 16, 1859, Mrs. J. C. Swayze's *Ossawattomie Brown* was put on at the Bowery Theatre. The play naturally emphasizes the heroic qualities of Brown and shows, one after another, scenes in which his sons are killed, until finally he is made a prisoner at Harper's Ferry. There is a love story inserted, whose complications are finally solved by the discovery that Alice the heroine is not John Brown's daughter. The play is frankly a melodrama, with a rather amusing maid to introduce the element of comedy. Best of the plays dealing with slavery was Dion Boucicault's *Octoroon* (1859), to be discussed as a portion of his achievement. Part of its merit was due to its lack of the element of propaganda. It simply revealed the situation, one of the most tragic in human history, in which the taint of blood condemns a woman who is loved by one man to be sold as the property of another whom she hates. It was this motive of human suffering which carried *The Octoroon*, even more than its contemporary appeal.[1]

Owing to the comparatively small number of these national

---

[1] Among the unacted plays dealing with contemporary events, *Poltroonius* (1856), attributed to Edward Francis Head, deals with Brooks' attack on Sumner, which is described off stage. Stephen A. Douglas is evidently portrayed under the name of Gigantius Sancho. The satire is at times effective, at times halting. In the collection of Doctor Atkinson there is an apparently unique copy of *The Captured Slave*, a play in three acts, printed for the author in Buffalo in 1815. The type is indistinct and the date may be 1845. If the earlier date is correct, it is a remarkable example of abolition sentiment for the time. Doctor Atkinson has conducted an extensive research, the results of which are not ready for publication, concerning this closet drama, whose theme is the arrest of a white man in New Orleans, his enslavement and escape.

plays that have survived, any comprehensive judgment on their merits has to be abandoned. That they did not engage the efforts of the greatest of the dramatists of the period is obvious, and one is tempted to speculate on what the result might have been if Bird, Conrad, Sargent, Willis, or Boker had visualized our historic past and placed upon the stage the vivid characters with which they peopled other times and scenes. Perhaps the range was too short, and certainly the literary fashion ran counter to such a possibility. Cooper and his followers had already shown the freshness of the native material for fictional use. But history from its very nature is better treated in fiction than in drama, unless that history lies so far in the past that its outlines may be shaped at will into those universal motives which are the only safe material for the playwright.

Note to Second Edition

Judging from the plays which we know only by the newspaper accounts, the drama made its contribution to the effort to preserve the Union.

Distant Relations; or, A Southerner in New York, played on December 16, 1859, at Laura Keene's Theatre, in which the slogan "No North, no South, but Justice and Fraternity" was printed on the program, was evidently an attempt to show through the visit of Mark Smith, a Southern planter, to his son, a farmer in New Jersey, that we were still one people. It ran until December 29.

George Jamieson, who had played Old Pete in *The Octoroon,* produced his own play, *The Old Plantation; or, The Real Uncle Tom,* at the "Old Bowery" Theatre on March 1, 1860, preluding the advertisements with "Union! Union! Union!" The play dealt with the forcible abduction of a quadroon slave by a Yankee abolitionist who is foiled and gets the worst of it. This play ran for a week only, and both of these attempts illustrated the unfortunate fact that peace plays never make the appeal on the stage that war plays are able to secure. Contrast and conflict rather than conciliation are the essence of drama.

CHAPTER XI

American Comedy Types, 1825–1860

IT is not easy to draw a helpful distinction between the plays based upon a patriotic desire to celebrate American history or to catch the interest of contemporary events which have now become historic, and that even larger group of plays which selected native themes for dramatic treatment in comedy. Both tend to become melodrama, and it would perhaps be idle to insist upon too rigid a classification of material which has come down to us so largely by tradition. The stage histories are crowded with names of plays which indicate their light, often trivial, and often imitative nature. As soon as a lucky hit was made by a play or a character, other playwrights and managers hastened to profit by the success of the creator, who was not infrequently drawing himself upon earlier material. Still, out of this dramatic impulse, hasty as it often was, emerged an interesting and significant series of dramatic types which have persisted on the stage even to-day. To the student of the drama who loves to watch an idea, planted perhaps by a mere trifle in the mind of a playwright or an actor, germinate, develop, and finally come to fruition in the creation of a character like Jonathan Ploughboy, Solon Shingle, Mrs. Tiffany, or Rip Van Winkle, this period of our drama will have a special reward.

Unfortunately, some of the most famous of these comedies have not survived, for that fatal paradox in our dramatic history that kept the great tragedies from print kept also the most popular of the comedies, and the danger of reproduction at the hands of rivals led James H. Hackett and others to see that their best plays were kept for themselves alone. It is for this reason in all probability that we know only by tradition the comedy written by James Kirke Paulding for Hackett, known as *The Lion of the West*, which contained one of his most successful characters, Nimrod Wildfire, the man of the frontier. It was written as a prize play for Hackett in 1830, and no trace of it could be found in 1867, when William Irving Paulding edited his father's works. According to his son, James K. Paulding began by creating a "vivid character sketch." This was manipulated by J. A. Stone, the author of *Metamora*, and as a four-act melodrama was produced successfully by Hackett in all the cities in the Union. Subsequently, during his visit to England in 1832–3, it was re-adapted by Bayle Bernard and under the title of *"A Kentuckian's Trip to New York in 1815"* it was produced at Covent Garden in March, 1833, and had a run of several weeks there and of six more at the Haymarket Theatre.[1]

An anonymous writer in *The New York Mirror*[2] states that the play was altered after its first performance at the Park Theatre. He gives a plot, as follows: Lexington, an officer in the British army, is wounded at the Battle of Lundy's Lane. His daughter, Fredonia, an infant, is brought up by a benevolent gentleman, Mr. Peter Bonnybrown. When she grows up, she is sought in marriage by a fortune hunter, known as Lord Luminary. Nimrod Wildfire, a nephew of Bonnybrown, now comes on from Kentucky. He is unpolished, but humorous and generous. He assists in straightening out the complications, which are traditional ones. Trueman Casual, a young gentleman who has just been put out of the inn by Dogwood, the keeper, for lack of money, is, however, paying his court to Fredonia and finally wins her, notwithstanding the machinations of Luminary and his ally Coquinard, a Canadian barber-surgeon, who poses as M. le Comte Rousillon. Luminary and Casual fight a duel, the latter is wounded, and Major Lexington arrives to find his long-lost daughter. The critic states that Casual, Bonnybrown, Luminary, Miss Towertop

[1] Paulding, W. I. *The Literary Life of James K. Paulding*, p. 219. Nicoll, II, 255.
[2] IX, 102. Oct. 1, 1831.

(Bonnybrown's sister), and Fredonia are "additions by Stone, and the Kentuckian remains as originally drawn by the author for Mr. Hackett." If this be true, Stone must have written most of the play, but his part is conventional. Nimrod Wildfire carried the play into fame, and the few samples of his conversation as given in the extract—"he hadn't found a fight for ten days and felt mighty wolfy about the head and shoulders"— or better, at the end of the play when he introduces his intended wife, Miss Patty Snap of Salt Licks, in this fashion, "There's no back out in her breed, for she can lick her weight in wild cats, and she shot a bear at nine years old," show the strength of Paulding's comic invention. The frontier type is met also in the Indian plays, and whatever its eccentricities, it was at least distinctly American.

First in point of time, however, came the "Yankee plays." Royall Tyler in *The Contrast* had created in the character of Jonathan the mixture of homely shrewdness, provincial conservatism, and unfaltering self-respect, which delighted those who saw in the better qualities of Jonathan traits they liked to believe were national, while they were quite willing to laugh at his ignorance, credulity, and uncouthness on the stage. Tyler's Jonathan was imitated by Robinson in *The Yorker's Stratagem* (1792), in Barker's *Tears and Smiles* (1807), and in Lindsley's *Love and Friendship* (1809), but the first[1] of his stage descendants to strike a popular response was Jonathan Ploughboy, in *The Forest Rose*, a domestic comedy with musical accompaniment, first played at the Chatham Theatre, New York, October 6, 1825. It was by that playwright of transition, Samuel Woodworth, who belongs to an earlier period in some respects, but who in this play is the forerunner of so many imitators that he may almost be said to have founded a school of playwriting. The influence of Jonathan in *The Contrast* is obvious, and the acting of Henry Placide in such characters as

---

[1] *The Saw Mill*, by Micah Hawkins, an opera produced at the Chatham Theatre, November 29, 1824, had a Yankee trick in it, but the character of the Yankee was assumed.

Zekiel Homespun in Colman's *The Heir-at-law*, which served to introduce that great comedian at the Park Theatre in 1823, may have been an immediate inspiration to Woodworth. In any event, he took the domestic comedy-melodrama, long familiar on the British and American stage, and placed it in a rural village in New Jersey in the neighborhood of New York City. In Blandford, the wealthy young man who urges Lydia to a secret marriage, in Bellamy, the New York fop who is planning to run off with Harriet, and in William, the honest farmer who wins her, he was simply rearranging a number of stage traditions in slightly different combinations. But in Rose, the negro wench who is made the vehicle of a trick played upon both Jonathan and Bellamy, he provided an opportunity for a broad farcical situation and in Jonathan Ploughboy he created one of those stage characters that are called "lucky hits" by those incapable of constructing them. Woodworth had for some years been writing plays which showed his real ability under discouraging circumstances. Here he indicated his right to be called a playwright, for Jonathan is alive. He is a type and a caricature, to be sure, but he moves among the other conventional characters with a flavor of earth that is the more apparent perhaps for their very conventionality. He is not a fool, either, if he is tricked by Sallie, and in his own clumsy way he helps on the not-too-complicated plot. The dialogue throughout is above the average, the comedy moves quickly, and is interesting to read even to-day. Certainly it provided a vehicle for many a comedian. According to Ludlow, Jonathan was first played by Alexander Simpson as a New Jersey country boy and only later by Henry Placide, G. H. Hill, and Dan Marble with Yankee peculiarities. In the preface to the edition of 1854, the statement is made that J. S. Silsbee played Jonathan in London for over one hundred consecutive nights, and in California Louis J. Mestayer played the part for forty or fifty nights with great success. It held the American stage for over forty years.[1]

[1] Coad, O. S. *The Plays of Samuel Woodworth*, p. 166.

The last piece which Woodworth wrote had a Yankee peddler from Vermont, Zachariah Dickerwell, who according to the analysis of the plot in the *Mirror* of May 18,[1] acts as a long-lost son and also as the savior of the Boston heroine. *The Foundling of the Sea* was written as a prize play for G. H. Hill, and was performed first on May 14, 1833, at the Park Theatre. It was given only four times there, but at least it reached Philadelphia in October. In fact, the committee of award, consisting of Irving, Verplanck, Webb and King decided that none of the written plays submitted was worthy of the prize of four hundred dollars, but Hill paid Woodworth that sum.

One of the first to take advantage of the popularity of the Yankee character was James H. Hackett. His earliest success was made in telling the Yankee story of "Uncle Ben," and in 1827 he took this and other impersonations to Drury Lane. In 1828 he adapted Colman's *Who Wants a Guinea?* (1805), which contained an amusing character, Solomon Gundy, a "French Cockney," by the simple process of transforming him into Solomon Swap, a Yankee. Hackett did not alter greatly the plot or the language of his original, except in those parts in which Solomon Gundy spoke his curious dialect, which gave place to the vernacular of Solomon Swap. This piece he rechristened *Jonathan in England*, in imitation of a play by that name in which Charles Mathews had appeared in 1826 at Drury Lane as "Jonathan W. Doubikins, a real Yankee."[2] Hackett made a great success in this part, which he first performed in America at the Park Theatre, December 3, 1828. On December 10, 1829, he produced *The Times, or Life in New York*, in which he played a Yankee character, Industrious Doolittle, with "great humor and effect." The cast, as given in Ireland,[3] indicates that it was a social satire which may thus have antedated *Fashion* and linked these two types of comedy. Durang believes it was written by Hackett him-

[1] Coad, p. 173.
[2] Genest, IX, 334.
[3] I, 624. See also Odell, III, 448.

self, and he may have had a share in it. One of his most popular characters, Major Joe Bunker, appeared in the sketch *Down East, or the Militia Training*, which he put on at the Park Theatre on April 17, 1830. We have seen how he had altered Finn's *Montgomery* under the title of *The Indian Wife* and, so far as his dramatic work is concerned, it was simply a revamping of older material. His greatest successes came in his acting of Rip Van Winkle, Nimrod Wildfire, or Dromio.

Ireland states that Hackett was surpassed in his interpretation of Yankee characters by George Handel Hill, who was born in Boston, October 9, 1809. Seeing Simpson in Jonathan Ploughboy in *The Forest Rose*, he determined to become a comedian in Yankee parts and found an opportunity in 1826 in Brooklyn, though he retired after his marriage until 1831. His first long trip, taking in Albany, New York City, Philadelphia, and Charleston, shows the sweep of the "circuit" in those days. His real success, however, came at the Arch Street Theatre as Jonathan Ploughboy. He next challenged Hackett by his performance of Solomon Swap in 1832, while the creator of that character was abroad, and so popular was he that Hackett obtained an injunction restraining all persons from using his version. Nothing daunted, Hill inverted the process of adaptation, performed the play under its original English title, *Who Wants a Guinea?* and played Solomon Swap under his old name of Solomon Gundy! Surely the question of dramatic ownership has not frequently been confused more triumphantly.

The other plays Hill produced, like *The Inquisitive Yankee*, *The Foundling of the Sea*, or Stone's *The Knight of the Golden Fleece*, have not survived. The last was one of Hill's most popular plays, the part of Sy Saco being inserted, apparently, from the cast,[1] into a romantic drama of Spain! But the work of one of the playwrights he inspired has come down to us and furnishes interesting material on account of its long life, and of the fact that its author spoke so definitely for his craft.

[1] Ireland, II, 101.

Joseph Stevens Jones was born in Boston, September 28, 1809. He was an active playwright, a manager, and a physician. He began his stage career in Providence, playing Crack, in Knight's *The Turnpike Gate*, and he received his training at the Tremont, Warren, and National Theatres. His first play was a dramatization of *Eugene Aram*. In 1839, after Barry's failure, he leased the Tremont Theatre for eight thousand dollars a year and acted as stage manager for two seasons, and again during its last season, 1842–3, with a company headed by Mr. and Mrs. John G. Gilbert. In June, 1845, the Tremont Theatre, which for sixteen years had been the leading house in Boston, was turned into a church. From the closing speech of the manager[1] it was evidently still true that in Boston the theatre ran counter to the prejudices of an important portion of the community. Jones seems to have left the stage, except for occasional performances in New York and Philadelphia.

His first successful play was *The Liberty Tree, or Boston Boys in '76*, put on at the Warren Theatre, Boston, June 17, 1832, in which he acted the part of Bill Ball, a Yankee type. *The Green Mountain Boy*, written for Hill and first played by him at the Chestnut Street Theatre, Philadelphia, on February 25, 1833, contained the character of Jedediah Homebred, a Yankee servant or general factotum on a farm. His humor consists in saying outrageous things to the other characters, whose stilted language acts as a foil for his very definite expressions. *Moll Pitcher, or the Fortune Teller of Lynn*, played in 1839 at the National Theatre, is not much better. It is an extravagant melodrama, Moll Pitcher being an old witch whom the sailors consult as to their voyages. But in the preface to the edition of 1855 Jones gives expression to the resentment the dramatist felt at the unfair treatment he was receiving at the hands of his countrymen.[2]

[1] Clapp, pp. 382–3.

[2] "I have had objections to publishing my plays; one, that they were written to be acted to the people, and not to be read by them; another that by the publication I lost my ownership, copyright giving no protection against representation upon the

The most famous of his Yankee characters, however, was Solon Shingle, the country teamster of *The People's Lawyer*, which was first acted by Spear and then by Hill at the National Theatre in Boston in 1839. *The People's Lawyer* is a conventional play, in which Charles Otis, who lives in sincere poverty with his mother and sister, is visited by his fellow clerk, John Ellsley, who slips a watch and chain in his pocket in order to incriminate him. Otis is defended by Robert Howard, the "People's Lawyer," who forces Ellsley to confess that he has committed perjury. Solon Shingle has really little to do with the play, but he provided a very amusing character, especially in the court scene when he goes to sleep and wakes up under the impression that Charles is being tried for robbing him of his "apple sarse." Professor Brander Matthews tells us that Hill and Silsbee acted Solon Shingle

stage. As *Moll Pitcher* has been often acted without my leave, no doubt, in time, it would be printed without consent being asked. I, therefore, choose the least of two evils, accord my consent, and in this manner acquaint the critic that the construction of *Moll Pitcher* occupied but two or three days; that it is a stage drama, depending for success more upon what is done, and the manner in which the business of the piece is done, than what is said; that its merits, few or many, depend upon its effect in representation, and they will be readily discovered by those competent to decide, whenever a fair trial is given upon the stage. . . .

"It is often asked why there is no Standard American Drama. One of the best answers is, nobody will pay for it. Some managers of theatres, and some principal performers, while pursuing their vocations, and receiving large sums of money from the public, are willing to avail themselves of the product of the brains of the dramatist, but do not consider it necessary to pay for it. It is not esteemed dishonorable by all, in the way of trade, to use a pirated manuscript, if it can be obtained for less than a true copy from the author could be had. The American dramatic author has no control over his property if printed. *The Carpenter of Rouen* has not only been acted in nearly every theatre in America without consent, but also in many of the theatres of Great Britain. The author has never received one dollar of remuneration, except the sum stipulated in the contract for its original production at the National Theatre. If the law of copyright in plays, and the regulations of a society, similar in some respects, to the Dramatic Authors' Society in London, had force in America as well as in England, we might have a Home Drama which would become creditable to our literature, and profitable to authors, managers, and actors. My personal pecuniary interests in this direction are not now engaged. But for the benefit of a new race of dramatic writers, I hope the subject will receive the attention it merits, and that the works of their pens —the inventions of the playwrights—may be secured to them as property by law, as are the rights of the inventors or improvers of patent corkscrews and 'bottle stoppers.'"

"Respectfully yours,

J. S. JONES."

as a young man, but that Charles Burke first saw the possibilities of making him an old one.[1] He became in Burke's hands, "a simple-minded, phenomenally shrewd old man from New England with a soul which soared no higher than the financial value of a bar'l of apple sass. Until Mr. [John E.] Owens, the last of the Solon Shingles, died, the drivelling old farmer from Massachusetts was as perfect a specimen of his peculiar species as our stage has ever seen."[2] Owens first acted the part in 1854 at the Baltimore Museum, but his great success came in 1864 at the Broadway Theatre and he carried the part back to his native England at the end of the season. Owens's last appearance in New York was in the character of Solon Shingle[3] for he was taken ill during that engagement. He died in 1886.

The last play by Doctor Jones to be printed had a stage life that brings it down to our own day. *The Silver Spoon*, put on first at the Boston Museum on February 16, 1852, was reprinted, "revised and reconstructed" in 1911, which indicates its continued existence, probably in stock. It has the nearest approach to literary quality of all of Jones's plays, and the Yankee character, the Honorable Jefferson S. Batkins, member of the General Court from Cranberry Centre, bears a closer connection with the real plot of the play than in any other of the species. He is the shrewd, none-too-honest, rural delegate, who is made a comic character through his conversation and the tricks the other characters play upon him. These other characters are more true to life, too, than in Jones's earlier plays. Miss Hannah Partridge, to whom "Jeff" makes love, and Glandon King, who provides the plot through his refusal to break his father's will, have individuality of a certain kind. By 1852 the realistic reaction was in the air, and that is why *The Silver Spoon* can live even to-day. The part was created by William Warren, long the leading spirit at the

[1] "The American on the Stage." *Scribner's Monthly*, XVIII (1879), 331.

[2] Hutton, Laurence, *Curiosities of the American Stage*, p. 40.

[3] See "John E. Owens," in *A Group of Theatrical Caricatures*, by L. E. Shipman, Dunlap Society Pub., Ser. 2, vol. 4. 1897.

Boston Museum, who acted in it certainly as late as 1883. Jones's "other manner," of which *Captain Kyd, or the Wizard of the Sea*, played in 1830, *The Surgeon of Paris*, performed in 1838, and *The Carpenter of Rouen*, acted in 1840, are sufficient examples, is frankly romantic melodrama of a wild and strenuous type. These plays, however, were vastly popular, especfally the last, which had a vogue in London.

Another creator of Yankee types, Cornelius A. Logan, seems to have been born in Baltimore and to have first appeared on the stage in Philadelphia in 1825, as Bertram in Maturin's play. He toured principally in the West, but came at times to New York. In 1834 at the Park Theatre, J. H. Hackett appeared in *Yankee Land*, attributed to Logan, in which the character of Lot Sap Sago appeared. Lot is more closely interwoven into the play than was usual, since he turns out to be the natural son of Sir Cameron Ogleby, who finds also a legitimate heir. In fact, pretty nearly everybody comes to this country and in the last act several of them are informed of "the secret of their birth." How important plots were to this species of play, however, can be illustrated by the reappearance of *Yankee Land* in 1846, altered by Leman Rede, under the title of *Hue and Cry*, in which the entire cast differs from the original except in the character of Lot Sap Sago![1]

Logan's other play, *The Vermont Wool Dealer*, a farce in one act, had a wide popularity, in the hands of Danforth Marble and Charles Burke. The former appeared in it at the Bowery Theatre on April 11, 1840, though the play may have begun its life in Cincinnati at an earlier date. It toured the country from Albany to Louisville, and Marble seems to have taken it to London in 1844. Read in cold type, it is hard to see the cause for this popularity. The main character is Deuteronomy Dutiful, who after acting as a guardian to Amanda, while she makes use of him to excite Captain Oakley's jealousy, celebrates their marriage in champagne. Logan himself took the part of Aminadab Slocum in his farce, *Chloroform, or New*

[1] Ireland, II, 451.

301

York One Hundred Years Hence, at Burton's Theatre in 1849. He died in 1852.

Danforth Marble, already mentioned as one of the Yankee actors, began his career in that species in Buffalo in 1836, with his version of *Sam Patch*. He was associated with Logan's plays and in 1846 he offered a prize of five hundred dollars for a Yankee play, which was awarded to J. M. Field, whose *Family Ties*, produced at the Park Theatre, June 19, 1846, was unsuccessful. Among the many other Yankee actors, Joshua Silsbee (1813–1855) was the most important. He added no new characters apparently, but he seems to have developed a more quiet, restrained manner of acting, which pointed forward to the later school. His reception in London in 1850 was enthusiastic.

The Yankee was not confined to his own country or to England. In 1841 Silas S. Steele's *The Brazen Drum, or the Yankee in Poland*, played at the Arch Street Theatre in Philadelphia, took Calvin Cartwheel, "a Drum major in the Varmount Militia—a carter, and a whole team in the cause of Polish Freedom" into the "Polish Revolution of 1831." The play is a melodrama, even to the use of incidental music, but the device of having the Yankee carry off the heroine in the "Brazen Drum" showed at least a certain inventive power in the dramatist, whom Rees praises so highly, but of whose thirty-six plays we have so few printed specimens. In *Miralda, or the Justice of Tacon*, in 1858, M. M. Ballou took the Yankee, Seth Swap, to Cuba, on his way "back home," from the silver mines of Mexico.

Trivial and conventional as the "Yankee Plays" are, they were important in several ways. First, they were successful because they contained one real character, and drama, of course, becomes significant only in proportion as it develops character. Second, this character was native and was usually portrayed by native actors. Third, it grew up from the roots of our own drama, for though it is possible that the English Yorkshire clown may have had something to do with our Jonathan

Ploughboy and Solon Shingle, there is no doubt at all of the influence of the first Jonathan in *The Contrast*, by no means the least of his tribe. Fourth, it led forward to the work of James A. Herne, and Uncle Nat of *Shore Acres* is a descendant of Jonathan. Fifth, it brought to foreign attention a school of American playwriting, which would probably have had little notice given to it, had it not been caricature. Hackett in 1833, Hill in 1836, Marble in 1844, and Silsbee in 1850 captured London, and Hill even went to Paris.[1]

It is rather surprising, unless one remembers how stage characters run in grooves, that the peculiar rural types of other localities were not oftener put on the stage. Probably they were tried and did not succeed. Durang[2] tells us of a play, *The Hoosier at the Circus*, produced at the Arch Street Theatre February 9, 1846, which he says was the "first drama dealing with the mountain whites of North Carolina and Georgia." It is an early treatment of that interesting race and shows again how the drama frequently anticipated other literary forms in treating of American life. For it must not be forgotten that Jonathan antedated Hosea Biglow by many years.

Closely allied to the "Yankee play" in its exaggeration and in its success, was the play dealing with life in the large city. The origin of this type of play is frequently ascribed to the production of *A Glance at New York* in 1848, in which Mose the fireman was the central character. As is usual with dramatic types, however, its creation was not due to the accident of one play, but was the result of years of tentative effort. Then, when American audiences were prepared fully to appreciate the character, it appeared in the hands of an actor whose special ability could carry it across the line which divides toleration from enthusiastic appreciation. The impulse to write of urban life goes back to the Elizabethans, but the immediate origin of our species lies in an English burletta of William Thomas Moncrieff, *Life in London, or the Day and Night Adventures of*

---

[1] Matthews, "'The American on the Stage," *Scribner's Monthly*, XVIII (1879), p. 323.
[2] Series 3, Chap. 83.

Tom and Jerry,[1] which began its career on November 26, 1821, at the Adelphi Theatre in London, and was produced with great success in New York, Philadelphia, and other places in 1823. Corinthian Tom brings up Jerry to London from the country to show him the town and introduces him to Bob Logic. They visit "All Max," the slums, and "Tattersall's" and are cheated at cards by Corinthian Kate and her friends, who thus incidentally secure husbands. Wood speaks with regret of the necessity of putting such a piece on the stage of the Chestnut Street Theatre, but it was not long before the impulse to describe realistically the underworld of the larger cities began to bear fruit in local drama. The insertion of the volunteer fireman into this general framework seems to have occurred on June 12, 1831, at the Arch Street Theatre when *The Fireman's Frolic*, written by a fireman of Philadelphia, was put on. Durang[2] tells us that "the old Diligent fire hose was on the stage filled with water." Realism could surely ask no more!

Dunlap speaks of a play, *Life in New York, or Firemen on Duty*,[3] which means that an ancestor of "Mose" must have been on the stage before 1832. *Life in Philadelphia* was put on at the Walnut Street Theatre, September 11, 1833. *Beulah Spa, or Two of the B'hoys*, which occupied the Bowery Theatre on September 18, 1834, sounds like a play of a realistic nature, while *Fifteen Years of a Fireman's Life*, played at the Franklin Theatre in New York, January 18, 1841, must have given a fairly complete representation of that type. *The New York Merchant and His Clerks*, performed in 1843 with "scenery representing the Battery, Wall Street, Chatham Square, and the Lunatic Asylum," was unquestionably descriptive of actual urban conditions. These plays have not survived, but there can be little doubt that when F. S. Chanfrau made his great

[1] It was founded on a novel by Pierce Egan, *Life in London*, published in July, 1821. By the summer of 1822 ten plays founded on this story were being acted in or around London.

[2] Series 3, Chap. 19.

[3] See Odell, III, 263, for description of the play at the Bowery, in 1827.

success in *A Glance at New York* on February 15, 1848, the public had been prepared to enjoy the type of play he furnished.

The production of *A Glance at New York* had its interesting details. It was written by Benjamin A. Baker, the prompter of the Olympic Theatre, then under the management of William Mitchell, who had succeeded where others had failed, by providing New York audiences with acceptable plays at reasonable prices. Baker had noticed with approval certain imitations of firemen or "B'hoys" given by F. S. Chanfrau, and he saw the essentials of success in the character. The volunteer fire companies were well known institutions. They were not only fire fighters, they were also rude social and political forces, and their methods of dealing with fires were appalling, to say the least. Rivalry was keen between the companies and the first one to reach the scene had to spend time in intrenching its position for a siege before it turned its attention to the fire. Baker offered his play to Mitchell, but the latter declined it on the ground of its quality, in which he was not far wrong. But the clever manager should have seen the possibilities of the play. Baker had copied the character from Mose Humphries, a printer in the *Sun* office, and he carried the real name on to the stage, when the occurrence of his own benefit gave him the right to select the play. The plot is based on the same psychology as that of the modern moving picture, rapid change of scene and vivid action. Harry Gordon and George Parsells land from the Albany steamboat on the Barclay Street dock. Harry has asked George to visit New York, and as soon as he leaves his charge, Mike and Jake, types of "crooks," begin to victimize him, by selling him tickets to the Park and passing off worthless bank notes upon him. Pretty soon Mose, the fireboy, is brought on as an old school friend of Harry's, and the trio visit, like Tom, Jerry, and Bob, the vivid and the seamy sides of city life. Two of the most extraordinary scenes are the visit to the "ladies' bowling club," where presumably respectable women dress in male attire and smoke large cigars, and the trip to the "Loafers' Retreat," a bar and lodging house of the lowest kind, where Mose finally can gratify his cherished desire to fight. A fire scene is, of course, introduced to give him an opportunity to drag the hose across the stage. The printed version which reflects certain changes that were made after the opening night, provides him with his female counterpart in Lize, a shop girl, in whose company he visits Vauxhall Garden.

The appearance of Mose upon the stage of the Olympic Theatre was the signal for a wild ovation. Chanfrau had copied exactly the red shirt, the plug hat, and the turned-up trousers of the fireman, while his own countenance, draped by the "Soap-locks" of the period, reflected the impudence, the conceit, and the physical exuberance of the "Bowery B'hoys," many of whom were constant attendants at the Olympic. The play ran for seventy nights and Chanfrau, who was also the manager of the Chatham Theatre, helped Baker to capitalize the success of his play by producing a companion piece, *New York As It Is*, which was brought out at the Chatham Theatre on April 17, 1848, and ran for forty-seven nights. Chanfrau acted in both plays on the same evening. Ireland says *New York As It Is* excited even more interest than its predecessor and had more variety of characters. It has not been printed, but the cast shows a different support for Mose, who was, of course, the backbone of the piece.

Chanfrau rechristened the Chatham as the National Theatre, and on September 4, 1848, produced *The Mysteries and Miseries of New York*, which, according to Ireland[1], was an adaptation by H. P. Grattan of "Ned Buntline's" novel of the same name. It had twenty-six characters, including not only Mose and Lize but also a Big Lize, and was simply a further development of Baker's play. The temptation to place Mose in different surroundings seemed irresistible. W. B. Chapman brought out *Mose in California* on February 12th and *Mose in a Muss, or a Joke of the Manager's*, on June 27th, while Baker himself continued the motive in *Three Years After*, on June 4,

[1] II, 533.

1849. This series of plays made the new National Theatre prosperous. The contagion spread to other cities. *Mose's Visit to Philadelphia* was played at the Walnut Street Theatre and W. E. Burton put on *A Glance at Philadelphia* at the Arch Street Theatre on June 25, 1848.

While Chanfrau was playing *New York As It Is*, at the Arch Street Theatre in Philadelphia in September, 1849, he found John Owens was playing Jakey in *Philadelphia As It Is* at the Chestnut Street Theatre, and a Philadelphia playwright seized upon some actual events and wrote *The Ship's Carpenter of Kensington*, which was played at the Arch Street Theatre, August 13, 1850. There appeared promptly at the National Theatre in New York during the next season *Nature's Nobleman, or the Ship's Carpenter of New York*, by H. S. Watkins, the stage manager.

In Boston, George Campbell produced in 1848 a local drama in which a scene in a police court was introduced,[1] and S. D. Johnson's *The Fireman* was played at the National Theatre in 1849 with J. B. Booth, Jr., as Frederick Jerome, the Fireman. Baker's *Mose in China*, on June 24, 1850, and *Mose in France*, on November 3, 1851, show how cosmopolitan that gentleman had become.

If there were any doubt of the influence of *Tom and Jerry* upon this type, it would be set at rest by the revamping of that very play by John Brougham in 1856 as *Life in New York, or Tom and Jerry on a Visit*. Corinthian Tom and Jerry Hawthorn are transported to New York, where Bob Logic is waiting for them, and the introductory scene is laid at Canal Street Wharf. Brougham did not hesitate to return the compliment of imitation, for there are elements, even to the words of the opening song, which are clearly inspired by *A Glance at New York*. Kate and Sue follow their husbands to New York and their advent gave Brougham an excuse for taking Tom and Jerry to a ball at the Codfish mansion, thus linking this type of play with the social satire. In the character of James

[1] Clapp, p. 457.

307

Trollop Fidler Dickens Greene, Brougham satirized the English traveler in America who writes a book about the country. But his play, a revision of his earlier *Tom and Jerry in America*, played first in 1844, has not the touch of reality which, in spite of its crudity, Baker's possessed.

The vogue of these plays continued up to and beyond the Civil War, and there is little distinction, so far as type is concerned, to be made between them and such a later play as Augustin Daly's *Under the Gas Light*. Indeed, his very title was anticipated by G. C. Foster's *New York by Gaslight*. Such titles as *The New York Fireman and Bond Street Heiress*, played July 22, 1850, with Perry in the title rôle, or *Democracy and Aristocracy, or the Rich and Poor of New York*, played July 13, 1850, in Philadelphia, show that they became sentimentalized into social contrasts.

The French melodrama was also drawn upon for material. Boucicault's *The Poor of New York* was an adaptation of *Les Pauvres de Paris*, by Brisebarre and Nus, acted in 1856 in Paris at the Ambigu Comique, which had previously been imitated in London as *Fraud and Its Victims*. It was afterwards played in Liverpool as *The Poor of Liverpool*, with great success in 1863; also as *The Streets of London*.[1]

This facility of international adaptation points to one source of the great popularity of this ancestor of the modern "crook play." Human nature is, of course, much the same everywhere, and being less reticent as it descends in the economic scale, it expresses itself more freely, therefore is better material for the stage. Contrasts, too, the very life of drama, are more frequent in the underworld. For the class to which such scenes were revelations, the interest of the unknown was added, while since Mose was usually depicted as a conquering hero, his very compatriots were among the most delighted of his auditors. Literary quality they had not, and it is to be noticed that among all the plays mentioned only four have survived. But the reality of their depiction of life, more faithful at first than

[1] Walsh, T. *The Career of Dion Boucicault*, p. 92.

in the Yankee plays, points forward, even if its fruition was to be of less artistic significance.[1]

Certainly with more pride of ancestry and with a more distinguished achievement, the comedy dealing satirically with the social values in American life presents a vivid contrast to the plays just treated, a contrast epitomized in the relative merits of *Fashion* and *A Glance at New York*. For the ancestry of the social satire of this period we go back once more to *The Contrast*, and again that sterling old comedy suffers much less by comparison with its successors than is assumed by those who have not seen it upon the stage. *The Contrast* was followed by Dunlap's *The Father*, Barker's *Tears and Smiles* and by other plays during the earlier periods, and the impulse to satirize so-called fashionable society seems to have been present more frequently than is generally supposed. For example, one of the prize dramas of J. H. Hackett, *Moderns, or a Trip to the Springs*, played at the Park Theatre in 1831, is evidently from the cast[2] a satirical treatment of the vagaries of a summer colony. A successor to *The Motley Assembly* is to be found in such a closet play as *Scenes at the Fair*, published in Boston in 1833, in which Mrs. Harrison Grey (Mrs. Harrison Grey Otis) presides over a table and her customers represent different types of social caricatures. Miss Fanny Capulet is supposed to have been drawn from Fanny Kemble and there are two other characters from Philadelphia. In the early forties, we find references in the theatrical histories to definite social satires which have not survived—for example we note the production of a "cutting satire upon fashionable life[3]" in the comedy of *Saratoga Springs*, which is said to have been very successful when presented at the Olympic Theatre on Decem-

---

[1] The principal plays have been mentioned. Among other titles that have come down to us are (1851) *Heart of the World, or Life's Struggles in a Great City, The Dry Goods Clerk of New York, The Seamstress of New York, The New York Printer*; (1852) *The Fireman's Bride, or the Chestnut Street Heiress*; (1857) *Fast Young Men of New York and Brooklyn, Life in Brooklyn, Its Lights and Shades, Its Virtues and Vices, A Day in New York, Morning, Noon and Night*; (1858) *The Rag Picker of New York*.

[2] Ireland, I, 648. Odell, III, 501-502, notes scenes at Saratoga.

[3] Ireland, II, 378.

ber 2, 1841. Field's *Such As It Is,* played at the Park Theatre in 1842, was also, evidently from the cast, a social satire.

Fashion, therefore, is not to be spoken of as "our first social comedy." But its quality, its success, and the dramatic career of its author make it perhaps the most significant. Anna Cora Ogden was born in Bordeaux, France, in 1819, the daughter of Samuel G. Ogden, who was tried for his part in the Miranda expedition to liberate Venezuela and Colombia.[1] She was interested in the stage even as a child of five, when she took the part of a judge in a French version of *Othello.* Coming to New York City in her seventh year, she had read all of Shakespeare's plays before she was ten, wrote verse, and put on the stage at her home in Flatbush a translation of Voltaire's *Alzire* when she was fourteen. Next year occurred her romantic marriage with James Mowatt, a New York barrister, who had fallen in love with her when she was thirteen and who persuaded her when she was fifteen to marry him secretly and inform the family afterward. In 1836 she wrote *Pelayo, or the Cavern of Covadonga,* a poetical romance in six cantos, founded on the history of the successor of Roderick the Goth, who in 718 was chosen the first king of the Asturias. It is written in verse of an easy flow, showing the influence of Byron and Halleck, but is interesting chiefly as apprentice work. She was threatened with tuberculosis when she was eighteen, but with her characteristic courage she determined to be well and took the sea voyage to Liverpool, spent a week in London, saw Madame Vestris at the Olympic Theatre, and then went on to Hamburg where she was joined by her sister, a bride, and later by Mowatt, who had come over for medical treatment. Her description of life in the Paris of Louis Philippe is discerning, especially in its analysis of social customs. In a letter to her sister, she scores our imitation of the form of their fashions without conceiving the spirit which dictates them. She illustrates this by our omission of introductions on social occasions. But in Paris "the custom is intended to obviate the ceremon-

[1] The source of this account is her *Autobiography,* published in 1854.

iousness of formal introductions. Everyone is expected to talk to his neighbor, and if mutual pleasure is received from the intercourse an acquaintance is formed. The same fashion in vogue with us renders society cold and stiff. Few persons feel at liberty to address strangers. Little contracted circles of friends herd in clannish groups together and mar the true object of society." It is just this failure to understand the true meaning of social customs that makes Mrs. Tiffany in *Fashion* such a delightful creation. While in Paris, Mrs. Mowatt saw Rachel. After fifteen months' absence, her health restored, she wrote her first play, *Gulzara, or the Persian Slave*, for her intimate group of players at Flatbush, and it was published in *The New World* for 1840. Owing to the limitation of being without male characters, with the exception of a youth of ten, it was not intended for professional performance. Mowatt lost his wealth through speculation, and she began to give public readings in Boston, New York, and other places with great success. Epes Sargent wrote his "Missing Ship" and "The Light of the Lighthouse" for her. Again, in 1842, her health was affected, but she was helped, she states, by hypnotism. The magazines such as *The Columbian, The Democratic Review, Godey's Lady's Book*, and *Graham's Magazine* contain articles by her under the name of Helen Berkeley, some of which were copied into London periodicals, and even translated into German. In fact, she states that she sometimes wrote several articles for the same number under different names! Her novel of *The Fortune Hunter*, which won a prize offered in 1842 by *The New World* had quite a wide sale and was translated into German. It deals with the adventures of a Southerner, Augustus Brainard, who having spent his fortune is introduced into New York society by Ellery, a "man about town," with a view to his making a rich marriage. It has not the vitality of *Fashion*, however. She also wrote *Evelyn*, a domestic tale, but this was not published until after her début in 1845.

At the suggestion of Epes Sargent, she wrote *Fashion*

definitely as an acting play, for the Park Theatre. It was accepted promptly by Simpson, the manager, and Mrs. Mowatt gives in her autobiography an entertaining account of her surprise and joy at the reception of her comedy by the management and of her presence at the rehearsals. It was produced on March 24, 1845, and its success was complete, its three weeks' run being interrupted only by positive engagements of the theatre. It was played at the Walnut Street Theatre in Philadelphia while the New York engagement was still progressing, and Mrs. Mowatt was given an ovation when she appeared in a box.

Fashion deserved its success. It is that rare thing, a social satire based on real knowledge of the life it depicts, but painting it without bitterness, without nastiness, and without affectation. It is true to the manners of the time and place, but it is based on human motives and failings that are universal, and when it is placed on the stage to-day it is as fresh as when it delighted the audiences of the Park Theatre in 1845.[1] The plot of *Fashion* is not important. It is the drawing of character that gives it a right to live. Mrs. Tiffany, the wife of a newly rich business man of New York, is socially ambitious for herself and her daughter, Seraphina. Her husband is ruining himself by her extravagance and has placed himself in the power of his confidential clerk, Snobson, who aspires to the hand of Seraphina. But Mrs. Tiffany has met a Count Jolimaitre, the newest importation from Paris, and she determines to catch him. He is nothing loath, as he is really a valet, so he comes to Mrs. Tiffany's salon, where he meets a number of well-drawn types, T. Tennyson Twinkle, a poet, Augustus Fogg, a "drawing room appendage," and Zeke, a delightful

---

[1] The first Act was played at the matinée performance given by the New York Drama League at the Republic Theatre, January 22, 1917, which presented a series of scenes from historic American plays. When the curtain went down, audible requests were heard that *Fashion* be allowed to go on and that the rest of the program be left out. The complete play was revived at the Provincetown Theatre, New York, February 3, 1924, and after moving successively to the Greenwich Village and Cort Theatres, ran for 235 consecutive performances, until August 30.

colored servant whose conversation with Millinette, the French ladies' maid and social instructor of Mrs. Tiffany, reveals naturally the family relations.

Mil.: Ah, *oui! je comprends.* I am Madame's *femme de chambre*— her lady's maid, Monsieur Zeke. I teach Madame *les modes de Paris*, and Madame set de fashion for all New York. You see, Monsieur Zeke, dat it is me, *moi-même*, dat do lead de fashion for all de American *beau monde!*

Zeke: Yah! yah! yah! I hab de idea by de heel. Well now, p'raps you can 'lustrify my officials?

Mil.: Vat you will have to do? Oh! much tings, much tings. You vait on de table,—you tend de door,—you clean de boots,— you run de errands,—you drive de carriage,—you rub de horses, —you take care of de flowers,—you carry de water,—you help cook de dinner,—you wash de dishes—and den you always remember to do everything I tell you to!

Zeke: Wheugh, am dat all?

Mil.: All I can tink of now. Today is Madame's day of reception, and all her grand friends do make her one *petite* visit. You mind run fast ven de bell do ring.

Zeke: Run? If it wasn't for dese superfluminous trimmings, I tell 'ee what, Missy, I'd run ——

Mrs. Tiffany: (*Outside*) Millinette!

Mil.: Here comes Madame! You better go, Monsieur Zeke.

Zeke: Look ahea, Massa Zeke, doesn't dis open rich! (*Aside.*)
(*Exit Zeke.*)

(*Enter Mrs. Tiffany, dressed in the most extravagant height of fashion.*)

Mrs. Tif.: Is everything in order, Millinette? Ah! very elegant, very elegant, indeed! There is a *jenny-says quoi* look about this furniture—an air of fashion and gentility perfectly bewitching. Is there not, Millinette?

Mil.: Oh, *oui*, Madame!

Mrs. Tif.: But where is Miss Seraphina? It is twelve o'clock; our visitors will be pouring in, and she has not made her appearance. But I hear that nothing is more fashionable than to keep people waiting. None but vulgar persons pay any attention to punctuality. Is it not so, Millinette?

Mil:. Quite *comme il faut.* Great *personnes* always do make little *personnes* wait, Madame.

Mrs. Tif.: This mode of receiving visitors only upon one specified day of the week is a most convenient custom! It saves the trouble of keeping the house continually in order and of being always dressed. I flatter myself that I was the first to introduce it amongst the New York *ee-light*. You are quite sure that it is strictly a Parisian mode, Millinette?

Mil.: Oh, *oui*, Madame; entirely *mode de Paris*.

Mrs. Tif.: This girl is worth her weight in gold. (*Aside.*) Millinette, how do you say arm-chair in French?

Mil.: Fauteuil, Madame.

Mrs. Tif.: Fo-tool! That has a foreign, an out-of-the-wayish sound that is perfectly charming—and so genteel! There is something about our American words decidedly vulgar. *Fowtool!* how refined. *Fow-tool!* Arm-chair! what a difference!

Mil.: Madame have one charmante pronunciation. *Fowtool* (*mimicking aside*) charmante, Madame!

Mrs. Tif.: Do you think so, Millinette? Well, I believe I have. But a woman of refinement and of fashion can always accommodate herself to everything foreign! And a week's study of that invaluable work—"French without a Master," has made me quite at home in the court language of Europe! But where is the new valet? I'm rather sorry that he is black, but to obtain a white American for a domestic is almost impossible; and they call this a free country!

Millinette and "Count" Jolimaitre are old friends, but he persuades her not to betray him. In the meantime he has been making love to Gertrude, a governess, and has been caned by Adam Trueman, a hearty if violent old gentleman from Cattaraugus, New York, a friend of Tiffany and incidentally and secretly Gertrude's grandfather. A love affair develops between Gertrude and Colonel Howard, an officer in the United States army, which is almost ruined by a too-clever device of Gertrude's for entrapping Jolimaitre, by a secret meeting, to reveal himself. They are found together, to Gertrude's discomfiture, but Trueman straightens everything out in the end, even Tiffany's financial trouble and the Count is exposed by Millinette in time to prevent Seraphina's elopement with him. The characters are, of course, types, Mrs. Tiffany being made up of several women, according to the author, who tells us, however, that she drew Adam Trueman from real life, and that the original attended the first performance and heartily applauded it. But the great merit of *Fashion* is the way in which it provides scope for capable acting, and if it is a "shell," as Poe declared in his unsympathetic and not very discriminating review,[1] certainly when the shell is vivified by clever actors it presents a fine counterfeit of life.

Encouraged by the success of *Fashion* and spurred on by necessity, Mrs. Mowatt determined to become an actress. She is one of the few examples of a woman succeeding as a star without long experience and training. She made her début at the Park Theatre on June 13, 1845, as Pauline in *The Lady of Lyons*. Her success was helped by her position and her beauty, but it was also the result of real ability. An unsparing critic like Poe said "we have to speak of her acting only in terms of enthusiastic admiration—let her trust proudly to her own grace of manner—her own sense of art—her own rich and natural elocution."[2] Even the physical weakness which caused Pauline to totter and almost fall in the last act was taken by the audience to be the result of her fine acting in the part of a broken-hearted woman. It was not the only handicap she had to overcome. Crisp, her leading man, came on the stage of the Walnut Street Theatre intoxicated. The audience vented their displeasure by hissing him and, to use her own expressive words, "the theatre seemed suddenly filled with snakes." She was ignorant of the real cause of Crisp's behavior, and thought that the audience was objecting to him as an Englishman. But with that indomitable spirit that carried her frail body through life, she stepped to the front and appealed to their chivalry to allow the play to go on. "Instantaneously," she says, "every seat was resumed. A dead silence prevailed and then applause took the place of hisses." The play was finished. It was during this Philadelphia engage-

---

[1] *Broadway Journal*, March 29 and April 5, 1845. In the latter issue he says he "has been to see it every night since its first production."

[2] *Broadway Journal*, July 19 and 26, 1845.

ment that she first played Gertrude in *Fashion*, and she repeated it in Charleston, Mobile, and New Orleans, but the part was not a favorite with her. After her tour of the United States she began a brilliant season at Niblo's Garden, acting two hundred nights during her first year on the stage. Characters like Juliana in *The Honeymoon*, Lucy Ashton, Katherine in *The Taming of the Shrew*, and even Juliet were added to her repertoire with unwavering success.

Next season E. L. Davenport became her leading man, and she wrote *Armand, the Child of the People*, during the summer of 1847, with his and her capabilities in mind. It was produced at the Park Theatre, September 27, 1847, "with marked favor,"[1] and then taken to Boston. *Armand* is a romantic play, partly in blank verse, laid in the time of Louis XV. It is based on the efforts of the King to secure the person of Blanche, the daughter of the Duke of Richelieu, the nobleman who had been the villain-hero of Payne's *Richelieu*. She is beloved by Armand, who is made the representative of the people, and whose democratic expressions were to meet the unfavorable eye of the British censor. To save her from Louis XV, the Duke gives her a sleeping potion that makes her appear dead. Armand as well as the King is deceived and goes off to the battlefield of Fontenoy, while Blanche is placed in a convent. She escapes through the help of the Duke d'Antin, who wishes to be revenged upon Richelieu for his supposed betrayal of the older Duke's daughter, Adelaide. In reality Richelieu had married Adelaide, and Blanche is the result of their union. So father, grandfather, and lover join in the attack upon the generosity of the King, who finally joins Armand and Blanche in marriage. It is a typical romantic play; the plot is, of course, conventional, but it moves forward rapidly. There are passages such as those in which Armand grieves over the lifeless body of Blanche, which have real beauty, and his defiance of the King, though hardly in keeping with the customs of the court of Louis XV, was quite in tone with the sentiments of America in 1847.

[1] Ireland, II, 485.

AMERICAN COMEDY TYPES, 1825–1860

Mrs. Mowatt sailed for England in November, 1847, appearing at the Theatre Royal in Manchester, December 7, 1847, as Pauline. So favorable an impression did she and Davenport make, notwithstanding the cold reception she was accorded by the company, that they were engaged to act at the Princess' Theatre in London in January, 1848, and at the Olympic, and to take Macready's place at the Marylebone Theatre in London, when he came to America. During this engagement *Armand* was produced January 18, 1849, and ran for twenty-one nights and, to judge from the criticisms, with approval. When *Armand* was produced, its subtitle, *The Child of the People*, proved too democratic for the censor and *The Peer and the Peasant* was substituted. Certain of Armand's speeches had to be omitted, also, as anti-monarchical. These were restored, however, during the later Dublin engagement and were greeted with great applause.

Mrs. Mowatt and Davenport continued to act at the Marylebone Theatre and later at the Olympic Theatre during the season of 1849–50, the opening bill being *Velasco* by Epes Sargent, in which, however, Mrs. Mowatt did not act. *Fashion* was produced at the Olympic Theatre, January 9, 1850, and ran for two weeks. Davenport acted Trueman, Fanny Vining, Gertrude, and Mrs. Marston, Mrs. Tiffany. Criticism was divided—*The Morning Post* made a savage attack on Mrs. Mowatt, for which *Punch* reproved the critic "Jenkins" cleverly, and the *Sun* observed that "last night there was represented at the Olympic Theatre, with the most deserved success, an original American five-act comedy, the scene of which is laid in New York, and which delineates American manners after the same fashion as our Garrick, Colman, and Sheridan were accustomed to delineate English manners, and which as regards plot, construction, character, or dialogue is worthy to take its place by the side of the best of English comedies."[1] Brain fever stopped her career for four months, but in January, 1851, she went to Dublin and she grows en-

[1] Quoted in *Autobiography*, p. 326.

thusiastic over the difference in the treatment she received at the hands of the company from that granted in England. Next she went to Scotland where news of Mowatt's death reached her.

In July, 1851, she returned to America, beginning an engagement at Niblo's Garden in August and then touring the country. An instance of her determination is given in her trip home from St. Louis. She was expected in Philadelphia by December 30th, to stage a performance of *Gulzara* at her sister's home, and on December 10th she left St. Louis. The trip, usually taking seven days, stretched to seventeen owing to the bitter cold weather, but neither the freezing of the steamboat in the Ohio River, the primitive stage coaches of Indiana, nor the railroad delays in Pennsylvania prevented this indomitable person from reaching her destination on time. Mere trifles, such as her horse falling upon her and breaking her rib in March, 1852, in Boston, did not deter her. In May she played Parthenia in Mrs. Lowell's translation of *Ingomar*. In September she opened the Metropolitan Theatre in Buffalo and, notwithstanding the loss of her voice, went as far as New Orleans. Finally in June, 1853, she had to take a holiday and she spent it writing her *Autobiography*, published in 1854, one of the most fascinating books of its kind. In 1854 she retired from the stage and married William F. Ritchie of the Richmond *Enquirer*. Her last appearance was on June 3, 1854, at Niblo's Garden, and she chose the character of Pauline, in which she had made her début. At intervals she published works of fiction, but the most important for our purpose was her *Mimic Life, or Before and Behind the Curtain* (1855), a series of stories dealing with stage life in which her own experiences were often reflected. In the first narrative, appropriately called "Stella," she gives a vivid picture of the trials and triumphs of a novice in her attempts at acting in star parts, with some interesting interpretations of characters in the plays that were then holding the stage, notably in Pauline, Sheil's Evadne and Knowles's Virginia, and in such Shakespearean heroines as

Juliet and Desdemona. The climax of the story in which Stella, while enacting the part of Ophelia, goes mad under the nervous strain is quite dramatic. Mrs. Ritchie usually lived abroad after 1861, and died in London, July 28, 1870.

Real as her contribution to our drama was, her influence upon our theatre was probably even greater. Coming into a life which, notwithstanding the many sterling men and women who pursued it, still suffered from the traditions of loose standards and of the disapproval of the Puritan element in our society, she proved triumphantly that an American gentlewoman could succeed in it without the alteration of her own standard of life. She took into the profession her high heart, her utter refinement, her keen sense of social values, and her infinite capacity for effort, and her effect was a real and a great one. She met the half-concealed jealousy of the British companies with which she acted with that disarming courtesy which the highbred of her nation have perhaps known best how to employ, and her career as retold in the steady sparkle of her *Autobiography* makes any compatriot who reads it thankful that she has lived.

The success of *Fashion* probably caused James K. Paulding to publish in 1847 his *American Comedies*, containing his own play, *The Bucktails, or Americans in England*, and three by his son, William Irving Paulding. *The Bucktails* was written by Paulding shortly after the War of 1812, and is an international satire, laid in England. Jane Warfield, an American girl, is sought in marriage by a number of English types, including Obsolete, the antiquary, Noland, a profligate lord, and Sir Christopher, a physician. Lord Noland tries to elope with her but she is saved by gypsies in order that she may marry the "man from home," Henry Tudor. Frank Tudor, his brother, falls in love with Mary Obsolete, daughter of the antiquary. The comedy is an amusing one, though the speeches are too long. Notwithstanding the success of *The Lion of the West*, *The Bucktails* seems not to have been acted, nor were any of the comedies of the younger Paulding. Of these *The Noble Exile* is a satire on the foreign count and the Boston society which lionizes him. *Madmen All, or the Cure for Love*, is laid in Philadelphia, where Sam Markham, "not overwise but improving every day," is in love with Garafelia Fizgig, daughter of a political speculator and an admirer of the new school of romance. Paulding satirizes through this character the types of romance then prevalent, and in Huskisson Hodgson he makes fun of the Englishman who is in America looking for a wealthy wife. *Antipathies, or the Enthusiasts by the Ears*, contrasts the hater of all modern improvements, Jacob Changeless, with Elihu Goahead, who is a mighty projector of railroads. The comedies are much better reading than many that saw the boards, but the plays of the younger Paulding are not really dramatic, for the satiric intent leads to soliloquy and conversation instead of action.

One of the best of the international contrasts was *Nature's Nobleman*, by Henry Oake Pardey, born in England in 1808, who acted first at the Chatham Theatre in New York in 1848 and died in Philadelphia in 1865. *Nature's Nobleman* was first produced at Burton's Theatre in New York, October 7, 1851, ran twelve nights, and was repeated frequently. It is a comedy laid in Saratoga and in Cape May, New Jersey, and apparently introduces the latter summer resort to the stage. The main characters are the Earl of Lymington, who is traveling under an alias; his servant, Smith, who masquerades as a nobleman; Zachary Westwood, a farmer; Hopkins Crayon, a rich and amateur writer, who is hunting titled Englishmen; Maria Crayon, his daughter; and Caroline Dalton, the heroine. The Earl, who is refreshingly human and not nearly so much of a caricature as he usually is made on our stage, pursues Caroline from Saratoga to Cape May and then to Westwood's farm. Maria has broken with her lover to secure Smith, the supposed lord, but when Lymington finally wins Caroline and announces his real station, Smith has to be satisfied with the cook. The conversation is quite clever and the characters are at times well drawn. Caroline is a real woman and curiously enough,

Pardey represents better than her countrymen usually did the natural attitude an American girl would have taken toward the proposal that she should marry an Englishman.

Some of the most successful of the social comedies have not survived. Among them were a dramatization of George William Curtis's *Potiphar Papers*, under the title of *Our Best Society*, by O. E. Durivage, a Boston actor, played at Burton's Theatre, January 21, 1854, in which Charles Fisher made a hit as the Reverend Cream Cheese. T. B. DeWalden's *The Upper Ten and Lower Twenty*, played at Burton's November 16, 1854, revealed the manager in the serious part of Crookpath and was evidently a social contrast.

Self, a comedy by Mrs. Sidney F. Bateman, first played at Bateman's St. Louis Theatre in 1856, is a satire on New York society and business methods, with much less artistic excellence than *Fashion*. Mrs. Apex is a fashionable lady who is extravagant and whose husband, Apex, is becoming financially embarrassed and is endeavoring to curtail his wife's expenditures. Her son, Charles Sanford, also gets into difficulties, and to save him Mrs. Apex suggests that he forge the signature of his step-sister, Mary Apex, who has about $15,000 of her own money. Her father asks her for this and she says she will lend it to him and gives him a cheque. He finds no funds when he presents the cheque and she does not explain the circumstances, since she does not wish to ruin her brother. Her father, in consequence, turns her out of the house as a selfish girl. Mary retires to a boarding house, accompanied by Aunt Chloe, a faithful old servant. Cynosure follows her and proposes marriage. She is already engaged to a man who does not appear on the stage. She then goes to see her godfather, John Unit, a retired banker, who assists her financially and who insists on the truth being exposed. It was this character of Unit, played first by Burton and later in 1869 by John E. Owens, that distinguishes this play. The lovable quality of this stage uncle and retired banker redeems a play which is otherwise artificial where it is not imitative.

Mrs. Bateman's *The Golden Calf; or, Marriage à la Mode*, played in St. Louis in 1857, was laid in England and in Paris, and satirized snobbery and the love of money, both in American and English types. Her *Geraldine*, played at Wallack's in 1859, was evidently a romantic play, as was also her *Rose Gregorio, or the Corsican Vendetta*, in 1862.

Some of the social comedies came very close to farce. *Young New York*, by E. G. P. Wilkins, played at Laura Keene's Theatre, November 24, 1856, with the old theme of Mrs. Ten Per Cent trying to marry her daughter to Mr. Needham Crawl while she is inclined to Signor Skibberini, shows by its very names the artificial nature of the satire. *My Wife's Mirror* is of the same nature. Slightly better is Brougham's *The Musard Ball*, in which Burton and Brougham must have been amusing, and which had as a background the well-known balls given at the Park Theatre in 1840.

Cornelius Matthews, whose ability lay rather in tragedy, essayed this popular mode in *False Pretences, or Both Sides of Good Society*, at Burton's Theatre, December 3, 1855. He contrasts the Milledollars and the Crockerys, insincere and sincere types, neither of which, however, reveal any deep consciousness of social values. The French barber adventurer who wanders through the play was chosen by Burton as his part. Some variety was introduced into the type by D. W. Wainwright, who laid two scenes of *Wheat and Chaff* in a "fashionable gambling hell." But notwithstanding the strong cast which put on this play at Wallack's Theatre in 1858, it seems to have been a failure.

The most salient criticism which can be leveled at this group of plays is that they really are not social comedies at all, except in a very limited sense. They are satires upon the parvenu, upon those outside of society who are striving to break in through wealth and its attendant publicity. Mrs. Mowatt is the only one of the group who reveals, through her satire of a false standard, any knowledge of the real one, and that is one of the reasons why her work so far surpasses that of her imitators. Of the social comedy in its broadest sense, which develops or reveals character, evolves entertaining situations and problems, and allows an individual to triumph over circumstances, as in other forms of comedy, but which never loses sight of the standards imposed upon the men and women because of their social traditions and relations, this period knew practically nothing. *The Contrast* had had a real sense of this social consciousness, but that model was far away, and our stage left untouched that stratum of society which had its own standards, traveled and read widely and, while appreciating what Europe had to give us, remained content with its own heritage of culture.

One of the cleverest of the comedies, however, approached this standard. *Americans in Paris*, by William Henry Hurlbert, was put on at Wallack's Theatre, May 8, 1858, and proved to be deservedly popular. Hurlbert was an American journalist who was born in South Carolina, in 1827, and died in Italy, in 1895. He was for a time editor of the New York *World*. The play deals with the mistakes consequent upon the relations of Arthur Morris, Dr. Botherer, and their wives, Americans who are living in Paris. Arthur Morris is rather wild and his wife becomes jealous, while Dr. Botherer is almost too attentive to his wife, Annie, according to her statements. The principal action occurs at a masked ball, in which a change of dominoes deludes Dr. Botherer into taking home his own wife, while Mrs. Morris is left at a cabaret to save her husband from an embarrassing situation after she has teased him sufficiently. The conversation is clever and the action rapid.

In creation of a social atmosphere, the titles and other nomenclature of English life make the task much more easy than it is for the American, who must establish social contrasts by the infinitely more difficult task of characterization. This may have been the reason why Oliver S. Leland laid the scenes of his comedies in England. Two of them, *Caprice, or a Woman's Heart*, and *The Rights of Man*, were performed at Wallack's Theatre in 1857, and *Beatrice* at the Arch Street

Theatre in Philadelphia in the same year. They are not of the same significance as the other plays, since they are frankly laid in foreign scenes and adapted from foreign models, but they have amusing plots based on human weaknesses and they analyze the married relation with a skill to which American comedy had not yet aspired.[1]

For similar reasons, the romantic comedy in verse or prose was not of equal significance to the tragedy. The plays of Willis and Boker, described elsewhere, are by far the best. J. W. Wallack was hospitable to the romantic comedy, for his sympathies were foreign. *Romance after Marriage*, by Frank B. Goodrich and Frank L. Warden, played in 1857 at Wallack's Theatre, is a fair example of the late French influence, its source being the romance of *La Clef d'Or*. Lester Wallack's play, *The Veteran*, laid in France and Algiers, was performed at his theatre on January 17, 1859. It is a romantic melodrama, better than the average, which must have been theatrically effective, especially in the last act when Colonel Delmar refuses to betray his country to save his own life and that of his son.[2] Seekers for the curious will be rewarded by a perusal of *Marion, or the Reclaimed*, a product of the Cincinnati stage, where it was played in 1856. The author, J. R. Hamilton, had the courage to make his contemporary characters, distributed impartially between England and America, talk in blank verse.

We have already seen how the comedy types appeared frequently in delightful confusion in the same play, or were inserted into a drama whose main purpose was the representation

---

[1] Among the social satires that apparently were not acted, Edward S. Gould's *The Very Age* (1850) is a vigorous melodrama which might have gone well on the stage, and Henry Clay Preuss's *Fashions and Follies of Washington Life* (1857) is an amusing production, painting a picture of the hotel life and the intrigues of government clerks and Congressmen. *The Young Man About Town* (1854), attributed to Lucien B. Chase, is a feebler effort, which satirizes not only the gilded youth, but also the tippling clergyman, the political policeman, and several other types.

[2] Professor Brander Matthews is authority for the information that it was founded on a novel by James Grant and the comic part of Oflan-Aghan was written by John Brougham, who played it.

of history or of contemporary events. In such a case, clear differentiation or classification is impossible. Some of the social satires became satires also of business and political conditions. The opportunity to contrast the rich and poor was, of course, not lost, and so we find the business man, the honest or dishonest clerk, and the virtuous sewing girl treated perhaps as often as the aspiring lady of fashion, the Yankee, or the fireman. But separate discussion of these types would lead only to repetition. The pervading atmosphere was that which has permeated the domestic drama, a convenient if not very definite term. Even our social satire, as has been seen, was domestic. But there remains a drama which celebrates more strictly the relations of the home and the family, without satiric intent, and of this species *Rip Van Winkle* is the chief representative. In view of Irving's collaboration with Payne, it is interesting to note that, while he had no part in the dramatic versions of the story, he provided a character and a situation which have outlived every other on our stage. So varying and incomplete have been the accounts of its genesis that the essential facts must be given.

The story of *Rip Van Winkle* was published in 1819. On May 26, 1828, what appears to be the first dramatization in America was placed upon the stage of the South Pearl Street Theatre in Albany, New York, the author being "an Albanian" and Rip being played by Thomas Flynn,[1] while Mrs. Flynn played Lowenna, Charles B. Parsons, Derrick, Moses S. Phillips, Knickerbocker, and Mrs. Forbes, Alice.

Noah M. Ludlow, the manager, states that he bought a copy of the play without the name of the author upon it in the summer of 1828 in New York, and produced it in Cincinnati during his season, which lasted through the late summer and early fall of 1829, Charles B. Parsons playing Rip Van Winkle.[2] Since Mrs. Flynn was a member of the Chatham Theatre

---

[1] See Phelps, H. S., *Players of a Century*, Albany, 1880, p. 121. Clapp and Edgett, *Plays of the Present*, p. 228.

[2] *Dramatic Life as I Have Found It*, pp. 390–392.

Company in New York in 1828 when Ludlow was managing it, this version may have been secured through her, or it may have been the Kerr version. Charles B. Parsons, it is to be noted, played in both the Albany and Cincinnati casts.

On October 30, 1829, a version by John Kerr was produced at the Walnut Street Theatre, Philadelphia. Since this is the first version that has survived and is extremely rare, its title page is of interest. *Lenfestey's Edition. Rip Van Winkle; or, the Demons of the Catskill Mountains!!! A National Drama. In Two Acts, by John Kerr. Author of "The Wandering Boys,"* etc. etc. *Printed from the acting copy, with the whole of the stage business as now performed in the London and American Theatres.* Philadelphia. Published by R. H. Lenfestey, No. 53 North Sixth Street.[1] This first edition gives the casts at the Tottenham Street Theatre in London and the Walnut Street Theatre, Philadelphia.[2]

[1] William Winter in his interesting account of the history of *Rip Van Winkle* (see *The Jeffersons* (pp. 186–192) evidently did not know of its existence or many of his statements would have been modified. This edition is not dated, but it was printed earlier than 1835, when the Lenfestey Circulating Library on Sixth Street disappears from the Philadelphia directories.

[2]

	Tottenham St. Theatre London	Walnut St. Theatre Philadelphia
Derrick Van Slous	Mr. Sanger	Mr. Porter
Herman	H. Norton	Mr. Read
Knickerbocker	S. Beverly	J. Jefferson
Rory Van Clump	C. Osborne	Greene
Nicholas Vedder	T. Santer	Sefton
Clausen	Cogan	James
Gustaffe	Master Kerr	Miss Anderson
Lowenna	Miss Kerr	Miss Eberle
Dame Van Winkle	[Mrs.] Porter	Mrs. B. Stickney
Villager	" Harris	Miss Hathwell
Alice	Mrs. W. Hall	Mrs. S. Chapman
Rip Van Winkle	H. Beverly	{ W. Chapman { Mr. Hackett
Dwarf of the Mountains	W. Oxberry, Jr.	Wm. Wells
Demons of the Mountains.		

"In the interim of the two Acts, twenty years are supposed to elapse."

Characters in Act II

The Judge	W. Battersby	W. James
Herman	H. Norton	Read
Knickerbocker	S. Beverly	J. Jefferson
Nicholas Vedder	T. Santer	Sefton

John Kerr was an English actor who, together with his two children, was brought to America by Francis C. Wemyss for the Chestnut Street Theatre Company in 1827.[1] He was a prolific adaptor of plays, especially from the French. His version had evidently been played in London before he left that city, probably in 1825, and it is to be noted that the parts taken by his children were played by others at the Walnut Street Theatre. William Chapman here played Rip and later J. H. Hackett played the character.

All later versions are based on this one by Kerr, though the modifications have been many. Kerr added to the story of Irving, first, the motive of the contract between Rip and Derrick Van Slous, by which Herman, Derrick's son, is to marry Lowenna, Rip's daughter, if Rip does not repudiate the contract within twenty years, and by which Lowenna is to lose her inheritance from her aunt if she fails to carry out this agreement. There is also a love story between Alice, Rip's sister, and Knickerbocker, the ex-schoolmaster. Rip leaves home of his own accord and goes up to the mountain where he meets the dwarfs. In the second act Rip awakens and delivers his monologue. Then in a second scene Lowenna explains that she is in love with Gustaffe, who is away in the navy. Dame Van Winkle and Derrick Van Slous are dead and Knickerbocker has married Alice. Herman insists upon Lowenna carrying out the contract of marriage. Gustaffe returns, of course, to claim her. Rip comes back and at first is unrecognized by the villagers but when he enters the courtroom where

Gustaffe	Atkins	Greenwood
Rip Van Winkl.	H. Beverly	{ W. Chapman { Hackett
Alice van Knickerbocker	Mrs. W. Hall	Mrs. S. Chapman
Lowenna	Miss Eldred	Miss Hammilton
Jacintha	Mrs. T. Santer	Miss Kerr
Villagers, etc.		

It is interesting in view of the third Joseph Jefferson's connection with the play to note that John Jefferson, his uncle, played Knickerbocker, Elizabeth Jefferson (Mrs. S. Chapman), his aunt, played Alice and Miss Anderson, his first cousin, played Gustaffe.

[1] See Wemyss, I, 129, for account of the Kerrs.

the case of Herman vs. Lowenna is being tried, Lowenna recognizes him at once, as does Nicholas Vedder, revived by Kerr for the purpose. But Knickerbocker is dubious until he tries the experiment of giving Rip a drink, when the well-known toast, "Here's your good health and your family's good health and may you all live long and prosper" proves that it is Rip himself. But the Judge declines to give his verdict until testimony is furnished by some one uninterested in the suit. Then Rip forces Herman to acknowledge how his own life had been saved by Rip from a wolf and how Rip had been marked by the beast. Rip then lifts his hair from his forehead and reveals the scar. Lowenna is saved and the play ends with the familiar toast of Rip, which through all changes remains as Kerr's permanent contribution to the play. There are several patriotic speeches in Kerr's play and Knickerbocker's election to Congress is given considerable space in the last Act.

J. H. Hackett played Rip in a modification of this version at the Park Theatre in New York on April 22, 1830.[1] While he was in England he became acquainted with the revision, probably of Kerr's play, which W. Bayle Bernard had already made for Yates, and on September 4, 1833, he played at the Park Theatre in Kerr's version, altered by Bernard. Ludlow says: "I saw Mr. Hackett perform the character of Rip Van Winkle after his return from London and I could discover but very little alteration in either the language or the incidents of the play. This gentleman's copy of the play was nearly if not exactly the same as the one I had produced in Cincinnati.[2]

The next stage in the development of the play is associated with Charles Burke (1822–1854), the half-brother of the

---

[1] Ireland, I, 628. Odell, III, 459-460, gives a criticism from the *Mirror* of May 1. See L. C. Davis, *Lippincott's Mag.* XXIV (1879), p. 60, for description of this version, taken from an old playbill of the Chestnut St. Theatre, Dec. 31, 1830.

[2] *Dramatic Life*, p. 392. But a playbill at the Park Theatre, April 21, 1843, shows Hackett acting in a version that contains new characters, Dick Quockenboss, Baron van Brunt, etc.

third and most famous Joseph Jefferson. Burke acted in a version of *Rip Van Winkle* at the New National Theatre in New York on January 7, 1850,[1] and in Philadelphia on August 16, 1850,[2] at the Arch Street Theatre. This has been printed as *Rip Van Winkle, a Legend of the Catskills. A Romantic Drama in Two Acts, adapted from Washington Irving's Sketch Book, by Charles Burke*, in more than one edition, none, however, dated.

The version by Charles Burke follows the same plot as Kerr's, although there are many changes in language and it is cut in many places. Rip speaks a dialect, of which there is no indication in the Kerr version, although probably the actors assumed one. In the last scene Rip proves his identity by producing the contract but it is at the judge's request, and Lorrenna [sic] recognizes her father first. Rip instead of slyly rejoicing at hearing of his wife's death, says, "So de old woman is dead; well, she led me a hard life—she was de wife of my bosom, she was mine frow for all dat." Hackett, who continued to act Rip after Burke had assumed the part, used this version at the Broadway Theatre in 1855, and it was with this sentence just quoted that he produced his most noted effect. Burke made the character more mellow and lovable, but there is to be noted in his version the tendency, which became more apparent later, to cut down the other parts in favor of the star. The patriotic atmosphere also is somewhat reduced.

The third stage is represented by an English version, *Rip Van Winkle, a Legend of Sleepy Hollow, A Romantic Drama in Two Acts, Adapted from Washington Irving's Sketch Book, by John Kerr, author of Therese, etc., etc. with some alterations by Thomas Hailes Lacy*. London, n.d. Lacy began to publish his series in 1848–9.[3] Although this is attributed to Kerr on the title page, it differs from the first Kerr version even more than that revised by Burke. Many lines which are in Kerr's play

[1] Winter, p. 187.
[2] Durang, Series 3, Chap. 101. Wilson, *Hist. of the Philadelphia Theatre*, p. 421.
[3] See "Lacy, T. H.," *Dict. of Nat. Biog.*

and are retained by Burke are omitted from the Lacy reprint. In Act I, Sc. 2, several speeches have been added and the entire scene has been rewritten. Rip talks in dialect, but there are changes from the dialect of Burke. With Act II the main differences begin. In the Lacy version Dame Van Winkle has been brought to life and married to Nicholas Vedder, who revenges Rip by tyrannizing over her. Nicholas wishes Lowena to marry Herman, while his wife favors Gustave. The patriotic sentiments are also cut out to an even greater extent than by Burke. There is no trial, as in Kerr and Burke, but Herman makes his claim, backed by Vedder, and Rip proves his existence by producing the copy of the agreement. Then Lowena recognizes him and so do Alice and the rest. This version[1] is improved so far as rapidity of action is concerned, but there is no apparent advantage taken of the resuscitation of Dame Van Winkle. She is left in the painful position of having two husbands, neither of whom wants her and she is made ridiculous.

Joseph Jefferson the second (1804–1842) played Rip at times and Joseph Jefferson, the third (1829-1905) had acted Seth Slough, the innkeeper, in his half brother's play in Philadelphia in 1850 and so his statement in his *Autobiography*[2] that the idea of acting Rip came to him in 1859 while reading the life of Irving is rather surprising. He made up, partly from the older texts, a version in three acts, which he produced in Washington at Carusi's Hall in the fall of 1859, but it did not satisfy him. In 1865, on his visit to England, he commissioned Dion Boucicault to rewrite the play. Much has been written upon the method of this revision, but there can be no doubt that Boucicault had Burke's play before him, for the language

---

[1] Mr. Moses, evidently not knowing of the real first edition of Kerr, takes the Lacy or English reprint, calls it the "Kerr version" and in his edition of the play states that "From Kerr to Burke, from Burke to Boucicault" was the progress. He then prints Burke's version and with painstaking effort records the variations from his "Kerr version." Naturally many of his statements that lines are omitted from the "Kerr version" are misleading since they appear in the first edition of Kerr.

[2] Pp. 224–225.

is copied identically in a few places, especially in the last scene. Boucicault, however, followed in one important point the revision of Kerr and Burke which bears Lacy's name, by reviving Dame Van Winkle. He made better use of her than Lacy or whoever else first thought of bringing her to life. In the earlier versions Rip goes out of the house voluntarily, but to Boucicault is attributed the effective scene in which Gretchen turns her husband out of doors.[1] Boucicault continued Jefferson's arrangement in three acts. Jefferson later divided the first act into two, and in fact he made so many changes during the years in which he played the part that the only safe way to describe *Rip Van Winkle* as it now appears in print is to say "as played by Joseph Jefferson." The plot is simpler than in the earlier versions, and Knickerbocker and Alice with their love story and Herman with his marriage contract have been eliminated. There is an agreement between Rip and Derrick that he is to give Derrick his property in exchange for sixteen pounds Derrick hands him in money. Rip does not sign this, however. These changes tend to emphasize the part of Rip for Jefferson as a star. The alterations in the plot, however, are not so significant as the changes in character drawing and language. Mr. Jefferson says in his introduction to his own edition of the play: "From the moment Rip meets the spirits of Hendrick Hudson and his crew, I felt that the colloquial speech and lazy and commonplace actions of Rip should cease. After he meets the elves in the third act, the play drifts from realism into idealism and becomes poetical. After this it is a fairy tale and the prosaic elements of the character should be eliminated and because Rip is a fairy, he neither laughs nor eats in the fourth act." Jefferson also arranged that in his interview with the dwarfs no voice but Rip's was to be heard,[2]

[1] For Boucicault's own account of his writing the play, see *The Critic*, III (April 7, 1883) 158–9, also "Leaves From a Dramatist's Diary," by Dion Boucicault in *North American Review*, CXLIX (1889), 233–4.

[2] In the *Masque of American Drama*, produced at the University of Pennsylvania in 1917, the awakening scene was played in pantomime, as one of a series of scenes from American plays. It was very effective, the tragedy being emphasized by the absence of speech and by Mr. DeKoven's exquisite musical accompaniment.

thus imparting a more lonely and desolate character to the scene.

The version by Boucicault was first acted at the Adelphi Theatre in London, September 4, 1865. It ran one hundred and seventy nights and the triumph was repeated when Jefferson produced the play at the Olympic Theatre, New York, September 3, 1866, and later throughout this country. In fact he became so closely identified with the part that his performances of Bob Acres, Caleb Plummer, and Dr. Pangloss were in danger of being forgotten. Jefferson continued to act Rip Van Winkle until a year before his death, which occurred on April 23, 1905.

Rip Van Winkle was made the theme of an opera produced at Niblo's Garden, September 27, 1855, the libretto being by J. H. Wainwright and the music by George F. Bristow. It is of little significance from the dramatic point of view. Based, according to the preface, on Irving's story, it makes use of Kerr's version at times. Later treatments of the theme fall beyond this period.

Outside of *Rip Van Winkle* the domestic dramas not already treated under their special types are of minor significance. Plays like C. S. Talbot's *Squire Hartley* (1827), or W. E. Burton's *Toodles* or *Ellen Wareham* are British in tone and, indeed, in both cases remain outside our province. George H. Miles's *Mary's Birthday, or the Cynic*, played at Laura Keene's Theatre in New York, in 1857, illustrates the comedy laid in a suburban estate, and while the characters are all well-known types, the return of a prodigal daughter to her father who has waited patiently for her until his mind has faltered, is truly affecting.

One of the most distinctly native of the comedy types was the "stage negro." The first appearance of a real American negro on our stage in a play of native origin seems to have been the character of Sambo in J. Murdock's *Triumphs of Love* at the Chestnut Street Theatre in Philadelphia on May 22, 1795.[1]

[1] See note on p. 124.

Sambo is drawn with some skill and is freed by his master on the stage. The part was played by William Bates, one of the low comedians of the company. Sambo sings and thus at the beginning the negro character is associated with the idea of minstrelsy. In his next play, *The Politicians*, which was not acted, Murdock drew four amusing negroes, Cato, Caesar, Sambo, and Pompey, into whose mouths he put the following conclusive argument concerning the relative claims of France and England in 1797.

Pompey: My massa for France—so I—who you for, Sambo?
Sambo: I go we massa, too.
Pompey: He for France?
Sambo: No.
Pompey: For English?
Sambo: No.
Caesar: Who debil he for den?
Sambo: He for he country!

Laurence Hutton, in his chapter on "The American Stage Negro" speaks of sporadic instances of a negro singer in 1799 in Boston, and Sol Smith states that Andrew Jackson Allen played a negro character in 1815 in Albany in a drama called *The Battle of Lake Champlain*, and sang a song, two stanzas of which Smith gives from memory[1]. But perhaps the most interesting phase of these early attempts at negro characterization is their association with Edwin Forrest. In 1823 Forrest was in Cincinnati and, to help out the desperate fortunes of the Globe Theatre, he acted a negro character, Ruban, in a local farce, *The Tailor in Distress*, written by Sol Smith, the manager. When ready for his part he found that none of the actresses were willing to blacken their faces, so he secured the help of an old negro washerwoman and made a hit in her company.[2] Forrest was not the only great actor whose early efforts were associated with negro minstrelsy. Edwin Booth and John S.

---

[1] *Theatrical Management*, p. 138.
[2] Alger's *Life of Forrest*, I, pp. 108–9.

Clarke, many years afterward, did not scorn to sing and act in negro parts.

As has so often been the case in the theatre, sporadic attempts preceded an individual artist who made the mode his own. Thomas D. Rice, while a member of Samuel Drake's company at the Louisville Theatre in 1828, observed an old and deformed negro singing and dancing in a limping manner, "rocking de heel," and was so much impressed with the stage possibilities of this performance that he paid the negro to teach him the words of the song, the refrain of which was

> "Wheel about, turn about
>   Do jis so,
> And ebery time I wheel about
>   I jump Jim Crow."

Rice was cast for the part of a Kentucky cornfield negro in a local drama, *The Rifle*, by Solon Robinson, and he introduced this song of Jim Crow, with verses of his own and the peculiar limping dances which carried him into fame on two continents. From its inception in Louisville it was very popular and in Cincinnati, in Philadelphia, and in New York, which saw the performance in 1832, he repeated his triumph. In 1836 he sang with great success at the Surrey and other theatres in London, his gait being imitated by the chimney sweeps and apprentices. Rice was not content with merely singing a song. He collected negro melodies, and wove them together with a libretto of his own into such medleys as *Bone Squash* and *Virginny Cupids* and may be said to have created the curious product known as the "Ethiopian Opera."[1]

Rice had been preceded by George Washington Dixon in 1827 in Albany at the Pearl Street Theatre, but his success was not at all equal to that of Rice. He is associated with such songs as "Coal Black Rose" and "Old Zip Coon." Naturally the individual singer soon led to the organization of the negro minstrel troupe, and, as Hutton has shown, the records of this

---

[1] See Hutton, pp. 115–120. Wemyss, I, 206–7. Ludlow, pp. 392–3.

organization are confused and baffling. Charles White and "Dan" Emmett, the possible author of "Dixie," seem to have organized a band of minstrels in 1843 at the Chatham Theatre, and the foundation of the Christy Minstrels is given as 1842. The latter became famous at home and abroad. But their career belongs rather to the history of the theatre than to that of the drama. The main strength of negro minstrelsy lay in its musical and picturesque extravagance, and its significance as drama is slight. Had it been the result of negro initiative it would have been more important, but in its inception it was burlesque rather than sincere imitation, and it has remained for comparatively modern days to see the racial strain of the negro express itself in drama. The dramatic lyrics like "My Old Kentucky Home" of Stephen C. Foster are among the most important contributions of America to art, but they are lyric after all and they have the beauty with which the imagination of the white race endowed the negro.

More important from the dramatic point of view are the negro characters, such as the servant Zeke in *Fashion*, the persecuted negro like Uncle Tom and the comic child type, Topsy, in *Uncle Tom's Cabin*, the loyal negro Pete in *The Octoroon* and, most truly dramatic, the products of mixed blood like Zoe in *The Octoroon* or Camille, in *Neighbor Jackwood*. Considering the popular success of two of these plays, it seems remarkable that the negro type was not more often selected for dramatic expression, but the danger of public disapproval was, of course, evident to the managers.

After all, however, the managers were perhaps not to be blamed if they could not see clearly the importance of cherishing the purely native characters that were presented to them. Many of them, like Wemyss, Burton, Brougham, and the elder Wallack, were British and they did not respond instinctively to the appeal of American themes. Yet despite all discouragement, the very quantity of these native comedies and melodramas shows the demand of the theatrical public for a native drama. Crude as some of these products were, the foundations that had been laid in the earlier period were strengthened in this one. The humor of the Yankee, the rollicking spirit of the fireman, the avid craving of the parvenu, the rough courage of the frontiersman, the melodious eccentricities of the negro, were woven into plays that delighted thousands, without bitterness or morbidity.

By the most acid test of drama, they rise to a real significance in that they provided actors with parts that stimulated the representation of real characters, human to their finger tips, upon the stage. How great was the response, popular and critical, to these performances may be appreciated only when we read the contemporary judgment of those qualified to speak.[1] And the torch was handed on from Woodworth to Herne, from Mrs. Mowatt to Bronson Howard, from Baker to Augustin Daly, as Dunlap and Barker and Payne had handed it to them.

---

[1] See the searching yet enthusiastic analysis of Jefferson in *Rip Van Winkle*, John Sleeper Clarke as Salem Scudder in *The Octoroon*, John E. Owens as Mose the fireman and Solon Shingle, by L. Clarke Davis, editor of the Philadelphia *Ledger*, in the *Atlantic Monthly*, XIX (June, 1867), 750–61.

CHAPTER XII

WE left the romantic verse play striking the note of revolt against oppression and celebrating the hero who typified democracy in its most robust form. Just as the mid-century was reached the romantic play turned in a different direction, and in the work of one of the greatest of our dramatists we find depicted the tragedy of the patrician. It may have been an accident that the year 1848, which saw the Continent of Europe swept by revolution, saw also the first of his plays completed, and the reaction which followed may have caused even the people of America to become more critical of democratic ideals. But there is no doubt that Boker's sympathy was, as a matter of principle, exotic. The advice he gave Richard Henry Stoddard, "Read Chaucer for strength, read Spenser for ease and sweetness, read Milton for sublimity, read Shakespeare for all these things and for something else which is his alone. Get out of your age as far as you can," reveals his philosophy of composition.

He was born in Philadelphia, October 6, 1823, and grew up in an atmosphere of material comfort and cultivated surroundings. The Philadelphia of his boyhood was still fragrant with the Colonial tradition, classic in its white marble steps and wrought-iron balconies, with the touch of romance in the merchant ships that brought the famous Madeira and other exotic goods to the old docks along the Delaware. His dearest friend was Charles Godfrey Leland, whom he introduced to Don Quixote, for already the charm of Spain was upon him. The two boys fed also on Scott's romances together and wove stories of their own of heroes and dragons. Their first separation came when Boker entered the College of New Jersey, as

Princeton was then called, as a freshman, on May 17, 1839. He graduated in 1842, having been one of the founders of the *Nassau Monthly* and a leader among the element that took the narrow curriculum of the thirties and forties as a point of departure for self-education in modern literatures, which were then fighting their way into the college curriculum. His contributions to his college journal show his early acquaintance with the Elizabethan dramatists.

Two years after graduation Boker married Miss Julia Mandeville Riggs, of Georgetown, D. C., a woman whose charm enriched in after years the atmosphere of the American Legations at Constantinople and St. Petersburg. Foreign travel came next and then a decision to devote himself to writing. He had studied law with John Sargeant in Philadelphia, but he had no aptitude for it. If anyone might have felt himself justified in that day in America in choosing a literary career, it was Boker. He felt no pressure from necessity, he had leisure, and Philadelphia was to a certain extent still the publishing center. *Graham's Magazine, Sartain's Union Magazine, Peterson's Magazine,* and even *Godey's Lady's Book* were at their height. But Boker's talent hardly lay in this direction. His first volume of verse, *The Lesson of Life*, published in 1848, contained only a hint of his strength. But when *Calaynos*, his first play, appeared in the same year, it was at once evident that a new and potent force in our drama had arisen. *Calaynos* was first produced in London at the Sadler's Wells Theatre on May 10, 1849,[1] without the author's consent and with considerable alteration. In this version Samuel Phelps played Calaynos and G. R. Dickenson, Oliver. *Calaynos* was first played in this country at the Walnut Street Theatre, Philadelphia, Monday, January 20, 1851, and ran for eleven nights, James E. Murdoch taking the part of Calaynos; Wheatley, Oliver; Peter Richings,

---

[1] This date as well as many others in this chapter have been derived from an examination of the manuscripts of Boker's plays and collateral statements by him. These are in the possession of Mrs. George Boker, daughter-in-law of the dramatist, whose unfailing help and courtesy have been invaluable to me.

Don Luis, and Miss Anderton, Doña Alda.[1] It was played in
Chicago, August 19 and 23, 1851, by Murdoch, who also pro-
duced it three nights in Baltimore and in Albany. On Decem-
ber 1, 1851,[2] G. R. Dickenson, who had played Oliver in the
London production, took this part at the Walnut Street
Theatre, Charles W. Couldock playing Calaynos.

The main theme of the tragedy is the aversion of the Spaniards for Moorish blood. Calaynos is a wealthy nobleman who
lives at a distance from the capital and is summoned by the
King to Seville. His wife, Doña Alda, wishes to go with him,
but he does not allow her to do so, so her maid, Martina, tries to
make her more discontented than she is, and Calaynos is warned
by Oliver, his secretary, and by Friar Gil not to go to Seville,
as they feel that wrong will come of it. In Act II, which takes
place in Seville, Don Luis, a spendthrift, is introduced and
Calaynos, who is his friend, helps him to pay his creditors,
believing him to be an honorable man. Oliver tries to trip up
Don Luis and his creditors, but does not succeed. Calaynos
brings Don Luis home to his castle in Act III, and he falls in
love with Doña Alda and attempts to seduce her. Martina
and Soto, Don Luis's servant, strike up a flirtation also. Don
Luis hears of the Moorish taint in Calaynos, and uses it to try
to persuade Alda to leave him. Don Luis induces her to
meet him in the grand hall of the palace at two o'clock, and
she is so overcome at the revelation of her husband's taint
that she swoons, and Luis carries her off. In the last Act Doña
Alda returns, after some months, to die at the castle. Calaynos
goes to Seville, challenges Luis, and kills him in a duel, Calaynos
being wounded to death, and Oliver arriving in time to see
him die.

Among the Boker manuscripts is a copy of the London
reprint, revised by Boker, with Scene 2 and Scene 3 of Act V
rewritten in Boker's hand. The 1848 edition had concluded
with a duel between Calaynos and Don Luis in a field. Boker

---

[1] Theatrical advertisements in the *Public Ledger* of those dates, where cast is given.
[2] *Durang*.   Third Series.   Chap. 112.

took the idea of ending the play in the banquet hall from the last scene of the London edition, and has altered it considerably. In all the published editions, however, the original scene is preserved. This copy possesses especial interest, since it was the acting version used by Murdoch in the revival in 1851 in Philadelphia. In 1886 Boker revised his plays, evidently with the intention of publication, but the 1891 edition was printed from the old plates. In this revision of 1886 *Calaynos* was extensively changed,[1] and the form was improved from the point of view of dramatic effectiveness. Doña Alda dies on the stage, and Calaynos himself tells Don Luis he is a Moor, which makes the latter's perfidy greater.

The importance of *Calaynos* rests not so much upon the plot as upon the creation of lofty standards of race and conduct, of an atmosphere of inevitable tragedy, clothed in a blank verse already possessed of that distinction which is one of Boker's greatest claims to consideration by posterity.

The next play to be written was *Anne Boleyn*. Boker intended the play for the stage. In a letter to Richard Henry Stoddard[2] on September 5, 1849, he states that he has had overtures from the Haymarket Theatre for the play and that he intends sending early sheets to London. He had assurances, too, from Charlotte Cushman that she would bring it out in this country, provided she believed her powers adapted to it. There are among the manuscripts separate parts for the characters in *Anne Boleyn*, and the play evidently was being considered favorably by some producing manager. It was, however, not performed, and it is doubtful whether it would have had success upon the stage. The central theme, that of a girl queen attacked by a group of cold-blooded noblemen who conspire to ruin her through exciting the king's jealousy, and who are aided by King Henry the Eighth's infatuation for

---

[1] For a detailed statement of the changes and also a comparison between the revisions of Phelps and the later revisions of Lawrence Barrett, see "The Dramas of George Henry Boker," by the present writer, *Pub. Mod. Lang. Assoc. of America*, XXXII (1917), pp. 235-7.

[2] R. H. Stoddard, "George Henry Boker," *Lippincott's Magazine*, XLV (1890), 857.

Jane Seymour, is surely dramatic; for we have the strong motive of self-preservation in conflict with the motives of love and of ambition. The difficulty lies in the fact that there is no real sympathy for Anne; for no matter how false Henry the Eighth, or how base Jane Seymour may be, the thought remains with us that strict justice is being meted out to Anne for her earlier conduct toward Catharine. From the point of view of dramatic structure, too, the play is not the equal of *Calaynos*, to say nothing of the plays that were to come. There is too much monologue and dialogue, and the defense of Anne is weakened by being delivered after the trial is over. She does not rise even to the greatness of remorse when the visions of Catharine, of More, and of others rise to torment her. The only flashes of inspiration come in the second scene of the fourth Act, when Sir Henry Norris defies the King in his efforts to corrupt him, and in the soliloquy of Thomas Wyatt, in the first scene of the same Act, beginning "O coming shape of English liberty."

The Betrothal was the third play to be written and the second to be placed upon the stage. It was composed probably about February, 1850, and was first played at the Walnut Street Theatre, Philadelphia, on September 25, 1850, where it ran for ten nights.[1] Count Juranio was played by Wheatley, Salvatore by Richings, Marzio by Couldock, Costanza by Miss F. Wallack, Filippia by Miss F. Horn, and the Marchioness by Mrs. Kinloch. It was revived in Philadelphia the next year; for in Durang's history we read:

December 5th (1851), Mr. Couldock's benefit—a revival of the popular play of *The Betrothal*, written especially for Mr. E. A. Marshall's theatre by G. H. Boker, Esq., and performed during the last season with as brilliant success as ever greeted any production within the walls of the edifice.[2]

It was played at the Broadway Theatre, New York, from November 18 to November 30, 1850,[3] inclusive, with the excep-

[1] Boker Mss. Also *Ledger* advts.
[2] Series 3, Chap. 112.
[3] Boker Mss.

tion of November 24th, and again from December 30, 1850, to January 3, 1851,[1] inclusive. *The Betrothal* is a delightful comedy, laid in Tuscany in that pleasantly indeterminate time, which may be best described as the age of Romeo and Juliet. The plot is as ancient as human nature, and centers upon the efforts of the Marchioness di Tiburzzi to marry her daughter Costanza to Marzio, a rich merchant, to aid in restoring the family fortunes. Count Juranio falls in love with Costanza and she with him, but she refuses to break her word, given to marry Marzio. Salvatore, Juranio's friend, has Marzio watched and also challenges him and proves his cowardice. The Marquis, who has agreed to the marriage only because he believed Costanza in love with Marzio, begins to suspect that he has been deceived. Marzio bribes his servant, Pulti, to poison Juranio and Salvatore at the betrothal feast, but Pulti tells Salvatore and it is arranged that the apparent poison shall be put in Marzio's own glass. He betrays himself under the influence of the drug, and Salvatore catches him in his own trap, winning Costanza for Juranio and Filippia for himself.

The play is a definite improvement on *Anne Boleyn* and *Calaynos*. It moves more quickly and there is a sense of the characters dominating the situation, especially in the last Act, which makes for real drama. Salvatore and Filippia are not the usual figures of romantic comedy, created for the purpose of receiving the confidences of the hero and heroine. They must have been delightful on the stage and they carry the plot along. The sincerity of the tone is illustrated in this speech of Juranio:

> "*Juranio:* Costanza di Tiburzzi, ere I go,
> Listen. I love you with a single heart.
> I do confess much folly in the deeds
> To which love drew me. Hidden by yon bower—
> While peeping buds unfolded into flowers—
> While infant leaves uncurled their tiny scrolls,
> And, full grown, basked them in the mellow sun—
> While all creation was an active hymn

[1] Boker Mss.

Of ceaseless labor to approving God—
I have stood idly, though the dear time sped,
Waiting to catch the faintest glimpse of you.
Then, happy with that treasure of my sense,
Have hied me home, to fill my waking thoughts
With growing fancies; or through fleeting night
Made my dreams golden with the memory
Of what had blessed my day. I cover nothing;
I have no skill nor wish to circumvent you.
You know the mystery of my presence here;
You know the secret of my love,—ah! yes;
You knew it ere I spoke it."

Durang speaks of the likeness of the play to *Love's Sacrifice*, by Lovell.   There is, however, little in common between the two plays.   There is more similarity between *The Betrothal* and Nathaniel Parker Willis's *Tortesa the Usurer*, played in 1839. But there is not enough likeness in any case to affect the originality of *The Betrothal*.

The Betrothal was played in England in 1853.   Dickenson, of Phelps's company, had played in the second performance in Philadelphia, and must have been impressed by the play.   In a letter from Boker to Stoddard,[1] October 9, 1853, an account is given of its performance and its reception:

I have read the *Times* notice of *The Betrothal*. It is honey to most of the other newspaper criticisms. So far as I can gather the facts from private letters, the play, to begin with, was very badly played: the English playwriters had raised the hue and cry against it. "Hamstring him! Slay him! Cut him down!" was the universal cry of my brother dramatists. Notwithstanding, and taking the accounts of my enemies for authority, the play was unusually successful with the audience on that most trying occasion, the first night. This only added to the gall of my brother dramatists, and increased their exhibition of it in the newspapers; so that after two nights of success with the audience, the manager was so terrified by the howl of the press and by the furious personal applications that he withdrew the play to save himself. I believe I have stated the strict truth, ergo, the play still stands a monument of English injustice. Mark you, it was not prejudice that caused the catastrophe; it was fear lest I

[1] *Lippincott's Magazine*, XLV (1890), 866.

should get a footing on their stage, of which *Calaynos* had given them timely warning.

The next play to be produced was printed only in 1940. It exists in manuscript in three forms.[1] It was put on at the Walnut Street Theatre, Philadelphia, April 21, 1851, and ran for eight nights. The scene of *The World a Mask* is laid in London in 1851. Sir Hugh Blumer has two nephews, Rylton and Galldove. He intends to make Rylton his heir, and Galldove, who is the villain of the piece, plans to bring discredit upon Rylton, and does so by leading him to a gambling house and arranging for a quarrel between him and a gambler. Teresa Crispo, who is passing as the Countess di Crespo, and is apparently Galldove's mistress, aids him in his schemes, although now and then she balks at them. Galldove's plans go to pieces in the last Act on the confession of Captain Fleet, whom he had bribed to quarrel with Rylton at the gaming house. Fernwood is the force that brings about the disclosure. He suspects Galldove all along and is kept from disclosing his plans by his promises to Teresa. Fernwood turns out to be Teresa's brother. The minor characters, such as Garrish, who blurts out whatever he feels like saying, and his sister, Miss Garrish, who has conspired with Lord Row to win £5,000 pounds from Garrish on Lord Row's promise that he will marry her, are not closely woven into the main plot. Galldove was played by Couldock, Rylton by Dyott, Fernwood by Richings, and Teresa by Madame Ponisi.[2]

There is some clever conversation at times, and the play gives one the impression that it would act better than it reads, but it cannot be considered to be a step forward in dramatic technique. It is written in prose, with occasional changes into blank verse, and therefore Boker's great ability in the construction of dramatic verse was of no avail. The play proved,

---

[1] See Bibliography, Chap. XII. Since Boker's autograph statement refers only to his printed plays, even he did not mention *The World a Mask* as having been performed. Among the manuscripts, however, is an account of the receipts of the play when performed at the Walnut Street Theatre.

[2] *Philadelphia Ledger.* Advt. April 21, 1851.

too, that social satire, which is its basis, was not his forte. He did not fail, however, on the side on which so many of our American playwrights have failed: his people seem like ladies and gentlemen. That he himself recognized that *The World a Mask* is not one of his great plays is apparent in his omission of it from his edition of 1856. Yet an enthusiastic criticism in the *Philadelphia Ledger* speaks of the "fine effect on the stage" and analyses sympathetically the character drawing, especially that of Teresa.

The Podesta's Daughter, called by Boker a "dramatic sketch," is simply a dialogue. It was written in 1851 and published in 1852, with other poems, lyric and narrative, all of which have been reprinted in the collected edition. *The Widow's Marriage*, which was written in 1852, was accepted by Marshall, the manager of the Walnut Street Theatre, according to a letter written by Boker, October 12, 1852, to Stoddard,[1] but he was unable to find any actress to impersonate Lady Goldstraw. It is a comedy in blank verse laid in England at the time of George II. The plot is largely concerned with a trick played upon a vain old widow, Lady Goldstraw, who thinks she is married to Lord Ruffler, and who through his treatment of her sees how foolish she has been. She therefore retires and lets her daughter, Madge, have her own opportunity for happiness. The play is an interesting one to read, and a good actress might have made something out of Lady Goldstraw. Here, as before, however, it is in the more serious passages that Boker does his best work. The description of a true hero, put in the mouth of Sir William Travers, in Act II, Sc. 2, is an example in point:

> "Are heroes proven by the knocks they take?
> Is blood the only livery of renown?
> I knew a sickly artisan, a man
> Whose only tie to life was one pale child,
> His dead wife's gift. Yet, for that single tie
> He bore a life that would have blanched the face
> Of armed Hector; bore the hopeless toil,

---

[1] *Lippincott's Magazine*, XLV, 864. That the play was seriously considered is proved by the Mss. made by the copyist of the Walnut Street Theatre in 1852.

That could but scrape together one day's food;
Bore the keen tortures of a shattered frame,
The sneer of pride, the arrogance of wealth;
All the dread curses of man's heritage,
Summed in one word of horror—poverty!
Ay, bore them with a smile. And all the time,
His ears were full of whispers. In his hand,
The common tools of work turned from their use,
And hinted—death! The river crossed his path,
Sliding beneath the bridge so lovingly,
And murmuring— death! Upon his very hearth
The tempter sat, amid the flaming coals,
And talked with him of—death! A thousand ways
Lay open, for his misery to escape;
Yet there he stood, and labored for his child,
Till Heaven in pity took the twain together—
He was a hero!"

Boker returned next to tragedy. On November 14, 1852, he wrote to Stoddard:

I, prolific I, have just finished a tragedy, *Leonor de Guzman*. Her history you will find in Spanish chronicles relating to the reigns of Alphonso XII of Castile, and his son Peter the Cruel. There are no such subjects for historical tragedy on earth as are to be found in the Spanish history of that period. I am so much in love with it that I design following up *Leonor de Guzman* by *Don Pedro*.

Leonor de Guzman was played first at the Walnut Street Theatre, Philadelphia, October 3, 1853, and ran for six nights until October 8th, inclusive. Julia Dean played Leonor; Mrs. Duffield, Queen Maria; Perry, Don Pedro, and Adams, Don Alburquerque.

According to Durang it was received with "warm approbation" and was interrupted only by the engagement of Edwin Forrest. Boker in a letter to Stoddard[1] on October 9, 1853, said:

You need not be anxious about "Leonor," we had her out last Monday and she was as successful as you or I could hope for. Miss Dean, so far as her physique would admit, played the part admirably

[1] *Lippincott's Magazine*, XLV, 866.

and with a full appreciation of all those things which you called its beauties. Doña Maria (the queen) was also well done, but Alburquerque and the other male characters, with the exception of Don Pedro, damnably. For all this the tragedy was triumphant—well noticed by the press and increasing in public favor up to its last night. I feel nothing but gratitude towards you for your part in the business, as it has certainly put my reputation at least one step forward. "Leonor" will be brought to New York during Miss Dean's next engagement there, in November next, if nothing should happen to prevent it.

It was performed at the Broadway Theatre, New York, April 24, 25, 26, 1854,[1] to houses considerably better even than in Philadelphia. Madame Ponisi played Doña Maria in New York. *Leonor de Guzman* is a tragedy laid in Castile, in 1350. The play is concerned with the succession to the throne consequent upon the death of King Alfonso XII. In the first Act the court of Leonor de Guzman is shown, and is represented as being the center of power in Spain. Of her sons, Don Enrique, Don Fadrique and Don Tello, the first two are returning from war and bring news of the death of King Alfonso. At once the courtiers fall away from her and flock to Seville, where Queen Maria, the mother of the new King, Don Pedro, is staying. They are both under the guidance of Don Juan Alburquerque, the prime minister. From here on the play is largely a study of the efforts of this man to retain power for Don Pedro and himself against Leonor and Don Enrique, and of Queen Maria to obtain revenge on Leonor. Queen Maria finally kills Leonor, and there is a subplot concerning the love of Doña Juana Manuel de Villena and Don Enrique. They are married through a trick of Leonor.

Boker took only the liberties with history that are necessary to a dramatist. The characters are all actual personages, and the condition of Spain at the time of the death of Alfonso XII is accurately presented.[2] Leonor was actually killed by the

---

[1] Boker Mss.

[2] For the historical background see most conveniently Prosper Mérimée, *The History of Peter the Cruel*, London, 1849, which indeed was probably Boker's chief source.

orders of the prime minister and not by the Queen in person, but this was a natural change and made the tragedy more effective. The most marked advance in *Leonor de Guzman* lies in the character drawing. Boker has taken these historical figures and endowed them with life. Leonor is represented as being a woman of noble character who had devotedly loved the King and who had been a power in Spain. The sympathy of the writer is with her generally, although one cannot help appreciating the emotions of the Queen who allows all other feelings to be lost in her jealousy and desire for revenge. An evidence of this is given in Act II, Sc. 2.

"*Doña Maria:*   Don Pedro, pardon me.
        The open insult of my fellow-queen—
        She who was reigning while I staid at home,
        To rock your cradle, and to suckle you—
        Moved me a little. And besides, my liege,
        There are some years of suffering on my brow,
        Pray, mark my lady's, it is very smooth—
        And some harsh lines of silver in my hair,
        While hers is glossy with untroubled ease.
        The rose has burned to ashes on my face;—
        Yet lives again in her transparent cheek.
        She can go through her fingers and record
        A loving child upon each dainty tip;
        I have but one, and he forgets to love!"

The Queen's jealousy of the prime minister's hate for Leonor is a strikingly effective invention of Boker's. So all-powerful is her desire for revenge that she cannot share it with anyone. The influence of a ready and unscrupulous mind is well shown in the character of Don Alburquerque, and the title rôle gave a good opportunity to a clever actress to make sympathetic a striking figure.

Before *Leonor de Guzman* had been put on the stage, Boker had started his masterpiece. In a letter to Stoddard on March 3, 1853,[1] he tells of his method of work. He wrote *Francesca da Rimini*, a play of twenty-eight hundred lines, in three

[1] *Lippincott's Magazine,* XLV, 864.

weeks. It was composed literally at white heat. He thought about the work all day and smoked a great deal after he began composing at nine o'clock in the evening. At four o'clock in the morning he would retire for about five hours' sleep. He came to his writing with the plan perfectly matured, so that the rapid composition was only the fruition of a long period of preparation. *Francesca da Rimini* was performed for the first time at the Broadway Theatre, New York, on September 26, 1855.[1] Lanciotto was played by E. L. Davenport, Paolo by James W. Lanergan, Francesca by Madame Ponisi, Malatesta by David Whiting, Ritta by Miss Josephine Manners, and Pepé by Charles Fisher. This cast did not do justice to the play. Davenport's performance on good authority seems to have been "unimaginative, mechanical and melodramatic."[2]

Francesca da Rimini was revived by Lawrence Barrett in 1882, the original performance taking place at Haverly's Theatre, Philadelphia, September 14th. The program of this performance, which is inserted in Mr. Barrett's acting copy of the play,[3] shows that Mr. Barrett played Lanciotto; Otis Skinner, Paolo; Louis James, Pepé; Percy Winter, René; Miss Marie Wainwright, Francesca, and Miss Josie Batchelder, Ritta. The occasion was a great triumph for the playwright in his own city, which had not been overappreciative of his merits as a dramatist in the fifties, and also for the members of the cast.[4] Mr. Barrett continued this play in his repertoire for a number of seasons. In 1885 some changes were made in the cast, Mr. F. C. Mosley taking Mr. Skinner's place as Paolo.

In Lanciotto, Boker provided Barrett with one of the

---

[1] Boker Mss. According to Odell's *Annals of the New York Stage*, VI, 425, the play held the boards till October 4th.

[2] Winter, *The Wallet of Time*, I, 316.

[3] In Boker Mss.

[4] See newspaper accounts, especially the long and enthusiastic criticism in The Philadelphia *Press*, September 15th, but especially Winter's analysis, *The Wallet of Time*, I, 317-322.

greatest characters in his career. William Winter, who helped in the revision of the play for the performance in 1882, states correctly that Lanciotto is "a great soul, prisoned in a misshapen body, intense in every feeling, tinctured with bitterness, isolated by deformity, tender and magnanimous, but capable of frantic excess and terrible ferocity; a being marked out for wreck and ruin and bearing within himself the elements of tragedy and desolation."

On August 22, 1901, Otis Skinner again revived the play at the Grand Opera House, Chicago. It was played throughout the country during the season of 1901-02. Mr. Skinner took the part of Lanciotto, Aubrey Boucicault playing Paolo, and Miss Marcia Van Dresser, Francesca. This performance forms one of the imperishable stage memories of the writer.[1]

The Paolo and Francesca story has been a favorite theme for treatment. Beginning with Dante's description of his meeting with the lovers in the fifth Canto of the "Inferno," human sympathy has often been directed toward the unhappy love story of the brother and the wife of Giovanni, lord of Rimini, who loved each other and who died by his hand. Dante was a man of twenty in 1285, the year of the murder. He knew Paolo and he lived at Ravenna from 1317 until his death. Even though he placed the lovers in hell, one gathers from his lines his belief that Fate was more guilty than they, and his one mention of Giovanni, "Caïna (or the circle of fratricides) waits for him who took our lives," is significant. Dante gives no historical facts—the lovers read of Launcelot and Guinevere and when they came to the passage wherein "he kissed her upon the mouth," "that day they read within that book no more." Beginning with Boccaccio's account in 1373, many commentators have enlarged upon the historical basis for the tragedy, which arose from the stormy condition of Italy during the struggle for power between the party of the Emperor and the greater nobles, called the Ghibellines, on one

---

[1] See Clapp and Edgett, *Plays of the Present*, pp. 115-117, for other revivals by Frank C. Bangs and by Frederick Warde, between the Barrett and Skinner productions.

side, and the party of the Pope, the lesser nobles and the citizens of the towns, called the Guelphs, on the other. Whether the contest between Ravenna and Rimini was a direct offshoot of this larger struggle, or whether both cities were Guelph in sympathy is perhaps not important for our purpose. A marriage of state was made, in any event, between Francesca, daughter of Guido da Polenta of Ravenna and Giovanni, eldest son of Malatesta da Verruchio of Rimini. Giovanni, or Lanciotto, was a brave soldier but was stern and rough in character and was called "il Sciancato," on account of his deformed hip. Consequently his younger and handsome brother, Paolo, was sent in his stead and Francesca believed him to be her intended husband. Paolo was already married, also for political reasons. The wedding of Giovanni and Francesca took place in 1275, and she bore him a daughter, Concordia. His suspicions of Francesca's fidelity became awakened ten years later, and being informed by a servant that Paolo was in Francesca's room, he entered. Paolo in trying to escape caught his cloak upon a hook and Francesca, intervening, received the blow intended for him. Giovanni then slew Paolo. Boccaccio is singularly charitable in his interpretation of Dante's opinion of their guilt, and he implies that if Francesca were guilty, the earlier deception justified her.[1]

The earliest dramatic treatment of the story is to be found in Johann Ludwig Uhland's *Franceska da Rimino*, written in 1807. It is only a fragment and was not, of course, put on the stage. The complete "Plan of the Tragedy" outlined by Uhland included Dante as one of the characters and pictured Lanciotto as not physically deformed, but suspicious of all who expressed affection for him. Paolo is the elder brother and a warrior, and the catastrophe is to be brought on by a jealous lover of Francesca who sows suspicion in Lanciotto's mind. In 1816 Leigh Hunt published his narrative version, in

---

[1] See Dante, *Inferno*, Canto V; Boccaccio, *Il Commento sopra la Divina Commedia*, Capitolo quinto. A good account of the story is given in Charles Yriarte's *Françoise de Rimini dans la légende et dans l'histoire*, Paris, 1883. See also Gertrude Urban, "Paolo and Francesca in History and Literature." *Critic*, XL (1902), 425-438.

which Giovanni is represented as a stern warrior with little emphasis on deformity, and the disclosure of the lovers' guilt is made through Francesca's talking in her sleep.

The first play actually to see the stage was *Francesca da Rimini*, by Silvio Pellico, an Italian dramatist (1789-1854). Here there is no deception of Francesca, but she has met Paolo years before and they have loved each other. They do not marry, for he has killed her brother and he spends years in the eastern wars, where he distinguishes himself. She pretends to hate him, in order to conceal her real feelings from her husband. Lanciotto loves her deeply and offers to allow her to return to Ravenna when he finds she does not love him, but when he suspects the mutual passion of his brother and his wife, he quickly changes to a revengeful husband and kills them both. The play is simple in structure and while slow in the beginning, has some fine moments in the later scenes. Paolo and Francesca declare to Lanciotto and Guido their love for each other, and at the same time their innocence.

Boker was the first to write a play in English on this theme, and he was the first to make the injured husband the central figure without lessening our interest in the lovers. To do this he had, of course, to modify the actual historical facts, but, more important, he had to create by the power of imagination what Francesca called "the noblest heart" in Rimini. Boker owed practically nothing to the plays on this theme that preceded him. A detailed comparison of the later plays, of the German version by Martin Greif, *Francesca da Rimini*, of D'Annunzio's play, written for Eleonora Duse, and of Marion Crawford's French drama, written for Sarah Bernhardt, would lie outside of our scope. Of these D'Annunzio's is most definitely Italian in atmosphere and Crawford's most faithful to actual historical events. But there can be no question that, in English at least, Boker's is surpassed by no other version. The spectator who witnesses Stephen Phillips's *Paolo and Francesca* is presented with a poetic spectacle in which the characters belong to no especial time or place. Driven by fate, they are puppets, not themselves determining factors in the action. Boker places us in the midst of mediæval Italy. The character of Paolo, young, handsome, loveworthy, but a bit of a coxcomb, is contrasted through his own actions and words with Lanciotto, a warrior, misshapen in body but sensitive to a degree and with a love for his brother that embodies not only natural affection but also admiration for that physical perfection that has been denied him. Delicately, too, does Boker depict that craving for affection on the part of a man no longer young, which, when made concrete by being centered upon a young and beautiful woman, becomes one of the most real motives of life and of art. Francesca is introduced to us, not a mere receptive character as in Phillips's play or in Leigh Hunt's earlier narrative version, but alive and with a great capacity for love. She is ready to love Lanciotto, and when she mistakes his deputy, Paolo, for him, she gives her heart. Her girlish attempt to hide her pain, when she discovers how she has been duped, is of the essence of drama, for the words seem wrung out of her soul:

> "I'm glad I kept my heart safe, after all.
> There was my cunning. I have paid them back.
> . . . . On my faith
> I would not live another wicked day
> Here in Ravenna, only for the fear
> That I should take to lying, with the rest.
> Ha! Ha! it makes me merry, when I think
> How safe I kept this little heart of mine!"

Those who have seen *Francesca da Rimini* upon the stage will hardly forget the scene in the third Act when Francesca discovers the cheat and when Lanciotto, misconstruing her apparent willingness to go on with the marriage, believes that she is beginning to care for him. Almost at once, however, he is led to suspicion by the jester, Pepé. Pepé's motive is revenge for insults offered him by Lanciotto and by Paolo, and Boker's conception of the character shows how well he understood the relations between a jester of that period and his master. He was a privileged character and a blow to him was almost unknown. His exemption was due to the old tradition that God had already touched one who was not normal and man should not presume to do so. It is possible that Boker may have received inspiration for Pepé from the character of Bertuccio in Victor Hugo's *Le Roi s'Amuse*, but the natures of the two jesters and their motives for revenge are quite distinct. Pepé is a human instrument and a natural one, by which the catastrophe is brought about. In Hunt's version the murmurs of Francesca in her sleep bring about the revelation. In D'Annunzio's play, she is betrayed by Malatesta, the one-eyed youngest brother. In Crawford's drama, Concordia, the daughter of Francesca, innocently leads to the disclosure. In Phillips's, the prophecies of a blind nurse, aided somewhat by the jealousy of Giovanni's cousin, are the means to the end. The nurse of Phillips is probably due to a suggestion in Boker's play, that a nurse in the Malatesta family has prophesied that some day the blood of Guido da Polenta will mingle with theirs. Boker, however, uses this supernatural suggestion in its proper place, the background. Pepé is human and he is mediæval. He acts quickly, too, and he helps the action on. Lanciotto's absence is naturally accounted for by the incursion of the Ghibellines, and thus the way is left open for the great love scene between Paolo and Francesca. The Francesca of Boker has been at times criticized for the active part she took in sending away Ritta, who scented danger, but Francesca is very human, and, therefore, more appealing. The contrast between the love of Paolo that is shot through with remorse and the love of Francesca that goes joyfully on without thinking of the cost, is masterly.

The final scene rises even beyond this one in dramatic effectiveness. As Boker wrote it and as it was first played it was in the garden. Paolo has decided that he will go away. Francesca reminds him in words that reflect the maturity that sin's experience has brought to her, what waits for her in the future, if he leaves her, a pledge for the security of her native land, to the caresses of an unloved husband. Then Lanciotto enters and after begging them to deny the charge that Pepé has brought to him, kills Francesca and then Paolo. When the two fathers rebuke him he defends himself:

"*Lanciotto:* Be satisfied with what you see. You two
         Began this tragedy, I finished it.
         Here, by these bodies, let us reckon up
         Our crimes together. Why, how still they lie!
         A moment, since, they walked and talked and kissed!
         Defied me to my face, dishonored me!
         They had the power to do it then; but now,
         Poor souls, who'll shield them in eternity?
         Father, the honor of our house is safe;
         I have the secret. I will to the wars,
         And do more murders, to eclipse this one,
         Back to the battles; there I breathe in peace;
         And I will take a soldier's honor back—
         Honor! what's that to me now? Ha! Ha! Ha!
                          (*Laughing*)
         A great thing, father! I am very ill.
         I killed thy son for honor; thou mayst chide.
         O God! I cannot cheat myself with words!
         I loved him more than honor—more than life—
         This man Paolo—this stark, bleeding corpse!
         Here let me rest, till God awake us all!"

The printed version of *Francesca da Rimini* represents Boker's judgment of the best form of the play for reading purposes. It has never been put on the stage exactly as it has been printed. Among the manuscripts is a complete autograph manuscript of the play as it now appears in the collected edition. From this was copied in 1853 an acting version, and some very interesting changes were made, partly by Boker himself.[1] There is also a manuscript with alterations by Boker, of the acting version used by Mr. Barrett in 1882. In this last the speeches of Lanciotto are indicated by cues, so that it is impossible to tell how severely they were cut. The acting

---

[1] In the reprint of *Francesca da Rimini*, in the present writer's *Representative American Plays*, the alterations of the 1853 acting version have been indicated, as well as some of the revisions of 1882.

version of 1853 begins with Act II, Sc. 1 of the printed version. There is a note, in Boker's hand, on the manuscript directing that when Lanciotto is the prominent part, the whole of that scene is to be omitted and the play is to begin as in the present reading version. If the scenes were played in the order of the 1853 manuscript the play would begin in Ravenna instead of in Rimini and the interest would center on Francesca, since Act II, Sc. 1 is concerned with the disclosure of Guido to her that Lanciotto is on the way. The reason for this change is not now apparent. Boker had written *Leonor de Guzman* for Miss Dean, and it may be that he had had her in mind when he was writing *Francesca da Rimini*. The fact that he named the play as he did, and that among the fragments there is a different beginning for the second Act, which represents Francesca among her ladies and gives her the opening speech, would make such an explanation reasonable. As the play is printed, Francesca does not come on until the second Act.

It is the opinion of Mr. Otis Skinner, who acted Paolo in 1882 and Lanciotto in 1902, that the changes made in both Mr. Barrett's and in his own versions were necessary for stage effect. The explanations which Mr. Skinner has been good enough to give me seem justified. Yet there are shrewd comments in Boker's own hand on the acting version of 1882 which were accepted as correcting the stage manager's judgment.

The autograph manuscript of *The Bankrupt* is dated 1853. Whether it preceded or followed *Francesca* in actual composition it is not possible to decide, as Boker does not mention it in his memoranda and no published account has any reference to it.

It was put on at the Broadway Theatre, December 3, 1855,[1] with Julia Dean in the part of the heroine, Amy Giltwood, and Charles Fisher as James Shelvill, the villain. It ran for four nights and the critical comments in the newspapers are surprisingly commendatory. It was played without any mention of Boker's name, and this indicates his doubt as to its merit,

[1] Ireland, II, 641.

for the success of *Francesca da Rimini* at the same theatre in September would have been an asset to the later play. *The Bankrupt* is a prose melodrama, laid apparently about 1850—at least the manuscript bears the inscription "Time and Scene, the Present." The main theme has to do with the return of James Shelvill, who passes under the name of Shorn, and who has been so embittered by bad treatment that he has returned to avenge himself upon his former associates. He tries to ruin Edward Giltwood, who had befriended him, and he also tries to seduce Amy Giltwood, over whom he has a hold through knowledge of a former theft which she had committed. The intervention of Paul Tapeley, a wealthy lawyer, who lends Amy Giltwood enough money to pay off her husband's indebtedness, makes the play end happily. The play is certainly the poorest written by Boker. The language is stilted and the prose at times runs into a curious kind of blank verse, as though the author had not been quite certain in which medium he had intended to write it. There is a certain cleverness in the way in which the web is woven about Amy and in the method used to persuade her husband of her guilt. But the characters are not clearly established and the motives are not well worked out.

Königsmark, published in 1869, but written in all probability before 1857, while a verse drama of interest, was not acted and could hardly have been intended for the stage. It is laid in Hanover in 1694 and is a tragedy, dealing with the revenge of the Countess von Platen, the mistress of the Elector, upon Königsmark, a Colonel of the Guards who had been in love with her and who has transferred his affections to Sophia, the ill-used wife of Prince George, the Elector's eldest son, afterward George the First of England.

With *Königsmark* the first period of Boker's dramatic activity came to an end. During the next few years he turned his attention more definitely to lyric poetry. Already in the 1856 edition of his collected plays and poems he gave evidence of his ability as a sonneteer. We are concerned in this study only with his dramatic work; but there is no doubt that, in this country, at least, Boker's sonnets have never been accorded their proper position. His sonnets on public affairs, especially the one written to America beginning, "What, cringe to Europe?" and his love sonnets form a group worthy of comparison with those of any sonnet writer in English except the very greatest. In 1864 appeared his *Poems of the War*. The best of these is the "Ode to America," written March 6, 1862, in a time of discouragement at defeat at home and fear of foreign intervention, but shot through with the lofty courage of the high heart that would not despair of the Republic. Except for Lowell's great Commemoration Ode, written three years later, there is no poetry wrung out of our great conflict more exalted than the close:

> "There are some deeds so grand
> That their mighty doers stand
> Ennobled, in a moment, more than kings,
> And such deeds, O land sublime,
> Need no sanctity from time;
> Their own epoch they create,
> Whence all meaner things take date;
> Then exalt thee, for such noble deeds were thine!"

On July 20, 1865, Boker read the Phi Beta Kappa Poem at Harvard, his topic being "Our Heroic Themes." In it he paid one of the earliest and one of the most sympathetic of the many tributes to Lincoln.

Boker did not confine his services to the nation to the writing of poetry. When the Civil War broke out, Philadelphia was too near Mason and Dixon's line not to be debatable ground. Across the intricate web of her social, financial, and commercial interests the issue of union or disunion ran in an uncertain line. It was natural that many of her citizens, tied to the South by family relationship, should already feel the agony of decision. It was hard, too, for the man who loved his country, but who felt that no sovereign state should be coerced, to act wisely, for the sharp logic of events was fighting on the side of those to whom right or wrong knows no middle ground. While the mob was attacking the houses of those who were suspected of siding with the South, Boker was exerting his influence in the sphere where it was most needed. At that time probably the oldest and best-established families were adherents of the Democratic party. Boker was a Democrat who had voted for Buchanan, and he belonged also to the patrician element. He saw the party divided, the great majority becoming "War Democrats" and placing their partisan devotion below their devotion to the nation, the minority becoming "Copperheads." So bitter became the divisions in social and business life that long associations were disrupted and families were divided in their allegiance. Boker was one of those to whom the most definite action seemed best. He left his party, joined the Republican, and became one of the most prominent in its councils. With others he formed a club which at first met secretly, then more openly became the "Union Club," and resulted finally in the "Union League." As its secretary he threw the great weight of his social and financial prestige in the scale of his national duty, and he made the club the center of the most uncompromising Union sentiment.

Boker had shown by his services during the war, not only in the ways already indicated but also in his labors with the Sanitary Commission and other war activities, that the poet might also be the efficient man of affairs. He was next to prove his fitness for the more delicate art of diplomacy. On November 3, 1871, he was appointed Minister to Turkey, and in a trying situation he showed his vigor, suavity, and sense of the fitness of things. As a reward for his services during a sojourn which to Boker was somewhat of an exile, he was promoted to the rank of Envoy Extraordinary and Minister Plenipotentiary to Russia on January 13, 1875, though he did not actually leave Constantinople until May. From the day of his presentation to Emperor Alexander II of Russia until his recall in

1878, he seems to have been one of the latter's favorites and proved of great service in improving the aspect of the relations between Russia and the United States. These public services having been completed, he turned his attention again to the stage.

The revival of *Francesca da Rimini* in 1882 undoubtedly encouraged him. First he returned to *Calaynos* and endeavored to adapt it to suit Mr. Barrett, but apparently the dispute which arose between them prevented any final arrangements being made.[1] Boker next turned to a different theme and wrote two plays upon the story of the fall of Pompeii. One of these, *Nydia*, is dated on the title page, 1885. *Glaucus*, the longer play, is dated 1886. It is more than a revision, it is an entire rewriting of *Nydia*. *Nydia* seems to be the stage version. According to the memory of Mrs. George Boker, the play was written for Mr. Barrett. It was evidently submitted to him, from the manuscript notes in Boker's handwriting, and this fact points to a resumption of relations. Both plays follow the main incidents of Bulwer's *Last Days of Pompeii*, leaving out Olinthus and the Christians.

The mutual love of Glaucus, a rich Athenian, and Ione, a beautiful Greek maiden; the passion of Nydia, the blind girl, for Glaucus; the rescue of Ione from the house of Arbaces, the Egyptian, through Nydia's agency; the arrest of Glaucus on the charge of the murder of Apæcides, Ione's brother; the conviction of Glaucus and his sentence of death in the amphitheatre and the eruption of Vesuvius, all are woven into a really dramatic poem, which in the case of *Nydia* at least is eminently suited for stage presentation. Boker's plays owe nothing to the language of Bulwer. The stilted artificial style in which *The Last Days of Pompeii* is written is changed into vigorous and flexible blank verse, among the best that Boker wrote.

---

[1] The formal note found in the Mss. from Barrett's agent returning *Calaynos*, in October, 1883, indicates a continued breach of relations. It grew out of a dispute concerning the amount of royalty to be paid on *Francesca da Rimini*.

As an example of his later work, a passage from *Glaucus* may be quoted. Glaucus and Ione have just parted and Nydia comes upon him while he is thinking upon his happiness:

"*Glaucus:* Can you ask?

Nydia: Ah! then, 'tis not for all, this happiness.
  Thank heaven that gave it to you 'tis so far,
  So very far above the common lot.
  Nor does it always come at love's command:
  Sweet though his gifts be to the fortunate,
  They seem like curses of the angry gods,
  Like the hot arrows of Hyperion's wrath,
  When poured into a heart that cannot share
  Its blessings with another, love for love.

Glaucus: These are strange thoughts to fill your youthful brain.
  Whence were they gathered?

Nydia: From the tree of life.
  We who pass under, shake its fatal fruit,
  Ripened or rotten, at our startled feet.
  A child may do that. Once I knew a maid,
  Humble as I am, and she loved a king!
  O not a king with sceptre, crown and throne,
  The common frippery of royal state,
  But a real king by nature bred and crowned,
  And so acknowledged by a subject world.

Glaucus: She flew too high.

Nydia: But why has love his wings,
  Unless to soar with? Ah! my lord, you talk
  Like all the world; but not like Glaucus.

Glaucus: But of the maiden?

Nydia: I forgot the girl.
  Lost in the splendor of the man she loved,
  Her passion was the secret of her breast:
  She dared not tell it to an earthly thing,
  Lest gossip Echo, from her hollow cave,
  Should spread her story to the jeering land.
  O no, she whispered to the mystic skies,
  Distant and voiceless,—to her mother's soul,
  Silent as death, that stood between their lives,—
  The bitter story which she knew too well.
  Nothing was pitiful. The raging clouds,

With thunder upon thunder, shouted, fool!
Her mother's voice, as fine and thin as songs
Sung to an ailing infant, murmured, fool!
And her own heart—there was the hopeless pang—
Muttered forever, fool! and fool! and fool!"

It is to be regretted that Boker did not publish the complete edition of his works which he was evidently preparing in 1886. For it he had revised *Calaynos*, had prepared *Nydia* and *Glaucus*, had revised *The World a Mask* under the title of *Under a Mask* and *The Bankrupt* under the title of *A Commercial Crisis*. Fortunately, under the editorship of his biographer, the unprinted plays have been published. *Glaucus* was the last of Boker's plays to be written. He died January 2, 1890, in Philadelphia, and the interest excited by his death brought forth enough demand for his work to warrant another reprinting of the edition of 1856 and of the "Poems of the War." No attempt was then made, however, to bring the collected edition up to date.

In the attempt to explain the reasons which have prevented Boker from receiving his proper position in our literature, two have been most frequently presented. The first is that he treated foreign material too exclusively. This criticism, in the light of the existence of *Hamlet* and *The Merchant of Venice*, seems to be beside the point. After an examination of *The Bankrupt*, the only play in which he treated native conditions, and which is by far the poorest, we may be thankful that Boker knew where his own strength lay. His real and strong love for his country rings in the lyrics of the Civil War and in his sonnets to America. His native verse is all the more significant because it has none of the parochial bluster in it. It is the deep and sincere patriotism of one who has known other lands and races, but remains content with our own inheritance and standards. Much as he loved European literatures and peoples, he never hesitated to criticise shortcomings when he saw them, and he had the social courage to love his own country best. Nor is the other explanation that there was no financial encouragement for American playwrights in Boker's time as applicable to him as it was to some others. Boker seems to have received a royalty of five per cent on the gross receipts of each night's performance and as a contribution to theatrical history, the table of returns from the treasurer's offices may be given.[1]

These figures omit at least one series of performances of *Calaynos* and all of *Francesca da Rimini*. It would seem fair to estimate his total royalties from plays up to the time of their publication in 1856 at $1500, and he retained the rights to them. In 1883 *Francesca* was bringing him in $200 weekly.

Perhaps one explanation is to be found in the volume which records the reception tendered him by the Union League in 1871 when he was about to depart for Turkey. The speeches and letters of appreciation were many, but they fall sharply into two groups. The letters from out of town, from Bryant, Holmes, Lowell, Longfellow, Whipple, Aldrich, Stedman, Curtis, and others, all pay their tribute to the poet and dramatist. But to the speakers from his native city and state that sphere of his activity seemed to be almost unknown, except to Bayard Taylor, who paid him a graceful tribute in verse. Aldrich put the whole thing in a nutshell when he wrote: "It is pleasant to see Philadelphia treating one of her own distinguished men of letters as if he were a distinguished man of letters from somewhere else." But Aldrich did not hear the

[1] Calaynos,	Philadelphia,	1851, 9 nights,	$194.08	
"	Albany,	1851, 3 "	17.00	
"	Baltimore,	1851, 3 "	30.00	
"	Chicago,	1851, 2 "	5.80	
				$246.88
The Bethrothal,	Philadelphia,	1850, 10 nights,	$155.92	
" "	New York,	1850, 12 "	185.82	
" "	New York,	1851, 5 "	65.38	
" "	Philadelphia,	1851, 5 "	43.47	
				450.59
The World a Mask,	Philadelphia,	1851, 8 nights,		138.10
Leonor de Guzman,	Philadelphia,	1853, 6 "	$83.33	
" " "	New York,	1854, 3 "	75.76	159.09
		Total		$994.66

speeches at the reception! Nor did he hear the resolutions passed by the Union League at the time of Boker's death in 1890, which, after praising his dramatic work, remarked that it was "an achievement the more remarkable because his labors were voluntary and unaided by the spur of necessity." The appreciation of one's community is after all a great impetus to creative activity! But theatrical conditions, later to be discussed, operated against his plays at the time of their creation, and in an age when so much that is worthless is printed and reprinted it is a grim commentary on our national taste that such plays as *Calaynos*, *The Betrothal* and *Leonor de Guzman* should still be practically unavailable.

During Boker's creative period there were individual efforts at the writing of tragedies, but none that reached his high level. Charles James Cannon's *The Oath of Office*, played March 18, 1850, at the Bowery Theatre, struck with some distinction the note of fatherly love and sacrifice to duty. The play is laid in Ireland near the close of the fifteenth century. James Lynch Fitzstephen, Mayor of Galway, is forced by circumstances to condemn his son to death for murder or to violate his oath. He chooses the latter alternative, although it compels him to perform the execution himself. Cannon's other plays were apparently not acted. The tragedy of Irish history is also treated in *Robert Emmet*, by James Pilgrim, performed in many places after its first production at the St. Charles Theatre, New York, in 1853. *The Italian Bride*, published anonymously in Savannah in 1856, attributed to Samuel Yates Levy, and played at Wallack's Theatre in 1857, has effective passages, descriptive, however, rather than dramatic. Interesting as the work of a practical playwright, whose *Love in '76* has been treated in a former chapter, *Fate, or the Prophecy* (1856), by Oliver Bell Bunce, is a romantic tragedy laid in "Altenburg in the Early Feudal Times." It seems not to have been acted, though it might have been with some pruning, and there are scenes which would have been quite effective on the stage. The characters of Rupert, who is haunted by fear of inheriting his mother's madness, and that of Catherine, who stops at nothing in her desire to be at once his wife and the Duchess of Altenburg, are powerfully conceived.

The most important of these later plays were written by Julia Ward Howe. The life of this distinguished poetess and patriot was in itself dramatic, for it was a constant struggle for the rights of others. Born in New York City, May 27, 1819, she was interested in the drama from childhood, writing a play at nine years of age. But it was not until 1857, when she had long been a resident of Boston, where her husband, Samuel Gridley Howe, was Director of the Perkins Institute for the Blind, that her work saw the stage. *Leonora, or the World's Own*, was first produced at Wallack's Theatre, New York, March 16, 1857. It is a romantic tragedy laid during the early part of the eighteenth century, in a small Italian principality. Leonora, a village beauty, is led astray by Lothair, a nobleman in disguise, and when Leonora finds out that he has been married, she plans a revenge which leads her to become the mistress of the Prince and involves Lothair in ruin through a false charge of treason. The character drawing is fine and, while the play is too long, there are noble passages of poetry, dramatic in their intensity of passion and suffering. The dignity and restraint of the scene in which Leonora meets Lothair and Helen and learns of his perfidy is impressive. E. A. Sothern acted Lothair, and Matilda Heron, Leonora. Contemporary criticism shows that the play was well received, and it was repeated in Boston.

In 1864 Mrs. Howe was asked to write a play for Edwin Booth, and the theme of *Hippolytus* was selected. After some delay, Charlotte Cushman was chosen to play Phædra to Booth's Hippolytus, and rehearsals were in progress when suddenly they were stopped. The reasons given were not convincing to Mrs. Howe or to Booth, and it seems to have been the old story of no satisfactory part for the manager's wife. Discouraged by this failure she abandoned play writing, and *Hippolytus* was not performed until after her death, when

Miss Margaret Anglin produced it in Boston in 1911, playing Phædra to the Hippolytus of Mr. Walter Hampden. *Hippolytus* was not published until 1941 but it contains some of the best of Mrs. Howe's poetry and is composed on a lofty plane of feeling. Phædra's guilty passion for Hippolytus, the son of her husband, Theseus, is the great motive of the tragedy, and when he repulses her love it turns to hate, so that she accuses him to Theseus upon the latter's return. This passage from Act IV, Sc. 1, will show the quality of the blank verse.

"*Theseus:* Dost thou stand speechless there, nor knowest my thoughts
Run on thy blood, thy treacherous blood?
Hippolytus: My father:
If in thine heart no voice of nature speaks,
Strike! I have lived too long, for faith and love
Are dead before me!
Theseus: Wilt thou kneel for grace?
Hippolytus: (*Strides to Phædra*)
Look on me, Madam, and look further on
The heav'ns that see our deeds, whose thousand eyes
Keep the still record of the things we show,
While they attest your word's solemnity,
Speak—do you thus accuse me to my father?
(*Phædra slowly nods assent, supporting herself with the back of a chair.*)
Theseus: Thou art too bold.
Hippolytus: Nay, then, I see it all,
Since thou hast said it, by the fearful oath
Of Jove, I bind thee to unsay it never;
Not though thy heart rose shrieking to thy lips
To loose the hateful burden with a breath;
Not though thy thoughts should envy his repose,
Whose innocent life shall pay the debt thou claimest—
But keep your cunning perfect to the end;
Let Theseus find no hollow in your breast,
Padded with falsehood; let no dream arise
To scare the sleeping husband from your arms.
Keep to your word—walk honoured to your grave,
And with the heart you have, confront the Gods!"

The talent of Mrs. Howe was perhaps more truly lyric than dramatic, as the exquisite songs of the nymphs presaging the death of Hippolytus indicate. But with any real encouragement she could have contributed plays to our stage that would have enriched our literature as well as our theatre.

That encouragement, however, was lacking. It is true that, under the influence of Laura Keene and to a lesser degree of Wallack, the theatre in New York was becoming more hospitable to native plays that had merit as literature as well as possibilities of stage success. But that renaissance was only temporary. The theatre and the drama were both entering upon a transition stage. The individual force that was most potent in bringing about this fundamental change in our drama was largely that of the playwright and actor whose work is to be treated in the next chapter. But general social and economic changes made this transition inevitable. Here again, however, a distinction is to be made. The types of prose comedy survived and had their successors in the next period, but the romantic tragedy and the romantic comedy in verse passed to a great degree from the stage. The classic-realistic reaction in the novel and in other forms of poetry was in the air. But there is no more satisfactory retrospect to the historian of our drama than the steady progress from the *Prince of Parthia* to *Francesca da Rimini*. Perhaps when we are weary of discovering and rediscovering what is base or banal in our civilization we may turn back for comfort to the poets who wrought for the sake of the beauty that is universal and with the art that defies the limitations of time or space. And if that day ever dawns, George Boker and the romantic tragedy of the fifties may come at last into their own.

CHAPTER XIII

The Influence of Dion Boucicault

WE have been concerned in this history with the work of American playwrights. But in the middle of the century there came to this country a foreign craftsman who exercised such a powerful influence upon our drama that he and his work must be considered in any survey that claims to be complete. Dion Boucicault was born in Dublin, Ireland, and it is characteristic of this strange genius that the date of his birth is given variously as either December 26, 1820, or December 20, 1822, and his parentage is disputed.[1] His early playwriting in England, which began in 1837 with *The Old Guard* and had its first success with *London Assurance* in 1841, does not concern us vitally. He showed his ability in the creation of such characters as Lady Gay Spanker and Sir Harcourt Courtly in *London Assurance*, and Jesse Rural in *Old Heads and Young Hearts*. The years 1845 to 1847 were spent in France, where he acquired an intimate acquaintance with the French language and lost his first wife whom he married in 1845. When Boucicault came to New York in September, 1853, he had married Agnes Robertson, long to be identified with the heroines of his plays. His first dramatic efforts on American soil have come down to us only by title. *Apollo in New York* was a satire on woman's rights and the Maine liquor law. *The Phantom* was the revision of the earlier *Vampire* (1820), itself from the French of Charles Nodier and probably nearly all were reworking of foreign material.

The first significant play to be produced here, *Grimaldi, or the Life of an Actress*, was put on at Cincinnati in 1855, with

---

[1] See Townsend Walsh, *The Career of Dion Boucicault*. Mr. Tolson's Ms. (see Bibliography) gives much new material, including the date of the first marriage.

a company that included the Boucicaults, Mr. and Mrs. E. A. Sothern, and J. G. Burnett. It dramatized an appealing theme, the hardships of a young actress, caused by the patronizing and even insulting attitude of the wealthier classes toward the stage. Boucicault's pride of craft showed in the resentment the drama expressed at this attitude. He played Grimaldi, the guardian angel of the young actress, who in true romantic fashion turns out to be an Italian duke, and who proves that his *protégée* is of noble birth.

Boucicault identified himself as soon as possible with the dramatic institutions of his adopted country. He found to his surprise that owing to the lack of a copyright law which would protect the dramatist in the sole right that was valuable to him, the right of representation, the playwrights were loath to print their plays even if allowed to do so by the actors or managers who controlled them. For some years playwrights like Bird and Boker had been laboring with Congress to remove this injustice. Bird had secured the introduction of a copyright law in the early forties, but it came to nothing, and in 1853 Boker had made another attempt to remedy the injustice.[1] In 1856 Boucicault added his efforts and finally the first copyright law was passed, August 18, 1856, which gave the author of a play "along with the sole right to print and publish the said composition, the sole right also to act, perform, or represent the same."[2]

This law has not, as a matter of fact, proved as effective as its sponsors hoped. The difficulties of detecting the violation of its provisions are so great that dramatists have sometimes preferred to proceed without its protection and depend upon a suit in equity to preserve their rights. It would have had a more stimulating effect upon the printing of plays if the law instead of permitting the copyright to be secured by the filing of a title had required the deposit of the complete text. The

---

[1] See the interesting letter from Bird to Boker, describing the difficulties of the dramatist's lot in America, found among the Bird Mss. and printed by C. N. Foust in his *Life and Works of Bird*, pp. 147-150.

[2] *Copyright Enactments of the United States.* Washington, 1906, p. 43.

law placed the playwright, however, in a more respected light. Heretofore he had been the unprotected prey of all who chose to steal the labor of his brains. Now he was the proprietor of his own works and the law was his protector.

After a trifle from the French vaudeville, *Monsieur Jovial* (1827), called by Boucicault *Wanted a Widow*, had been played at Wallack's Theatre in 1857, Boucicault adapted from *Les Pauvres de Paris*, by Edouard Brisebarre and Eugène Nus, which had been acted in 1856 at the Ambigu Comique, one of the most popular of his plays. *The Poor of New York* is not a great play, but it illustrates the sense of theatrical values which Boucicault possessed beyond any of his contemporaries. As it was performed at Wallack's Theatre, December 8, 1857, the first act was laid during the panic of 1837. Gideon Bloodgood, a banker, is about to fail when Captain Fairweather deposits $100,000 with him in the presence of Tom Badger, a clerk. Fairweather returns shortly, having heard that the bank is unsafe, and dies in the office after attacking Bloodgood.[1] Then the play jumps to the panic of 1857, and the sympathy of the audience is excited by the hardships of the Fairweather family while the Bloodgoods are living in luxury on the stolen money. Boucicault followed his model quite closely during the first three acts, including the striking scene in which both the rooms of the Fairweathers and that of Badger are shown with a partition between them, through which the fumes of charcoal penetrate and overcome Badger just as Bloodgood visits him to obtain the coveted receipt for the money Captain Fairweather had deposited. In the fourth act Boucicault left his original and created a lurid fire scene, in which Badger's lodging is set aflame, and which never failed to appeal to the audience. He created, too, throughout the play, a sufficiently local atmosphere, putting in a scene at the Academy of Music and omitting some of the moral reflections and the sentimental soliloquies so frequent in French melodrama. Boucicault readapted the play on his next voyage to England, where it had already been done

---

[1] Note the similarity to Charles Reade's *Hard Cash* (1863).

as *Fraud and Its Victims*, by Sterling Coyne. He renamed it *The Poor of Liverpool* and still later, as *The Streets of London*, it delighted thousands in that city. It belonged, as a matter of fact, to no locality, for virtuous and deserving poverty can find (on the stage) eternal sympathy. The dramatic interest lies in the character of Badger, Planterose in the original, the cool, determined blackmailer, played by Lester Wallack, whom nothing daunts and whose stage realism points forward to the much greater characters of William Gillette.

Agnes Robertson was a Scottish girl, and Boucicault's next play, *Jessie Brown, or the Relief of Lucknow*, provided her with a remarkably successful part in that of the heroine. The stubborn defense of Lucknow was fresh in the popular mind, and the figure of Jessie Brown, the young Scottish girl who kept up the courage of the garrison by her insistence that she heard "the pipes of the Campbells," was a really dramatic one. Lucknow was relieved by General Havelock on September 25, 1857, and *Jessie Brown* began its career at Wallack's on February 22, 1858. So detested was the name of Nana Sahib, the Sepoy leader, that no one could be found to play the part, so Boucicault assumed it himself. *Pauvrette*, a melodrama from Adolphe d'Ennery's *Bergère des Alpes*, and *The Pope of Rome*, likewise from the French, are entertaining but not important.

Boucicault next dramatized *The Cricket on the Hearth*. Dickens' novel had been adapted by Mélesville [Duveyrier] and Léon Guillard and played in 1848 under the title of *Le Marchand de Jouets d'Enfant*. Boucicault may have seen this play, but he seems not to have used it, despite the story that he first adapted the French play in ignorance of the English source. Certainly when the play opened at the Winter Garden, where he and William Stuart had entered into a joint direction, the characters bore Dickens' names and the play was called *Dot*. Agnes Robertson played Dot; Joseph Jefferson, Caleb Plummer; Mrs. John Ward, Tillie Slowboy; and Harry Pearson, John Peerybingle, at the Winter Garden on September 14, 1859. Later in the same season the play ran for two months at the Varieties Theatre, New Orleans, where John E. Owens appeared as Caleb Plummer, Charlotte Thompson as Dot, and C. W. Couldock as John Peerybingle. The statement has been made that the play was written for Jefferson, but an examination of the manuscript prompt copy shows no stellar rôle for Caleb Plummer, and it was probably for this reason that Jefferson later used either in whole or part another version. Boucicault's play opens with a scene in a wood with Titania and Oberon, in which Home enters and indicates that she is driving the fairies away from their haunts and that Home now rules. Then the characters are represented in a vision before they are allowed to assume their earthly forms as Charles Dickens created them. Boucicault at times follows the language of Dickens and at times departs from it. Caleb Plummer provided Joseph Jefferson with his first serious part, and how well Boucicault knew his business as an actor is illustrated by his advice to Jefferson, retold by the latter in his *Autobiography*.[1] "You have acted your last scene first," Boucicault told him. "If you begin in that solemn strain you have nothing left for the end of the play." This was the first of Dickens's books to be adapted by Boucicault. Encouraged by its success he produced a stage version of *Nicholas Nickleby* in November, 1859, in which Boucicault played Mantalini and Jefferson, Newman Noggs, and in which Agnes Robertson scored a great success as Smike.

Next came *The Octoroon*, in which Boucicault showed his keen sense of the dramatic possibilities of an American theme. Notwithstanding the success of *Uncle Tom's Cabin*, it might have been considered a doubtful experiment to produce a play which could inflame the passions of sectional hatred. John Brown's raid had occurred on October 16th and his execution took place on December 2, 1859. But Boucicault had no propaganda in view. He realized that the love of a white man for a colored woman, owned by him, and in danger of being torn from him by his enemy under protection of the law, was

[1] Pp. 209-11.

a dramatic theme of real value. He found his material, as usual, at hand. Mayne Reid had published in New York in 1856 a novel, *The Quadroon*, of which a dramatic version had been produced at the City of London Theatre. In *The Quadroon* an Englishman, Edward Rutherford, saves a beautiful Creole, Eugènie Besançon, from drowning. He falls in love, however, not with her, but with her quadroon slave, Aurore. Yet Eugènie, disguised in male attire, endeavors to save Aurore for Rutherford when she is put up at auction, in consequence of the dishonesty of Eugènie's trustee, Gayarre. After Rutherford has failed to purchase her, through lack of money, he kidnaps Aurore and is about to be lynched when he is saved by the sheriff. It is discovered that Aurore had been freed by her former master and Rutherford marries her.

Boucicault skillfully altered this material and added new characters. Rutherford becomes George Peyton, the young Southern heir to a plantation, which is about to be sold for debt. The Northern contrast is provided by the two New England overseers, Salem Scudder, who has encumbered the estate by his visionary projects, and Jacob McClosky, who has deliberately plotted to obtain possession of it by dishonest means. George loves Zoe, the natural daughter of his uncle, the former owner, and Boucicault's sense of the dramatic is indicated in the very change of title to *The Octoroon*, for the less negro blood runs in the veins of the slave, the more tragic is her situation. Eugènie's place is taken by Dora Sunnyside, a neighbor's daughter, who also loves George. Boucicault added an Indian character, Wahnotee, which he played himself, and which introduces the note of melodrama. McClosky is anxious to intercept the mail which will convey to Mrs. Peyton and her nephew some financial aid. He kills a negro who is carrying the mail and is caught in the act by a self-acting camera. Wahnotee is accused of the murder and disappears. This scene Boucicault took from a contemporary novel, *The Filibuster*,[1] by Albany Fonblanque. The negro

---

[1] London, 1859. See *Life*, by Walsh, p. 68.

characters, headed by Old Pete,[1] were used in a clever fashion. The scene, in which Pete encourages the others to look their best at the forthcoming auction, in order that their old mistress and young master may have something left to live upon, is fine drama. And the humanity of the characters in general is characteristic of Boucicault. Zoe's refusal to allow George to marry her, even though she loves him, Dora Sunnyside's attempt to buy Zoe at the auction, though she knows it means the end of her own hopes, Salem Scudder's whimsical condemnation of himself, are long to be remembered. The slave auction and the burning of the steamer *Magnolia*, on which McClosky has been imprisoned, may have appealed to the theatrical instinct of the audiences, but the sympathy for human suffering carried the play even more surely into popular favor. Jefferson, who acted Salem Scudder, rightly accounts for the approval with which audiences, made up of both parties to the slavery struggle, viewed the play. "The truth of the matter is," he says, "it was noncommittal. The dialogue and characters of the play made one feel for the South, but the action proclaimed against slavery and called loudly for its abolition."[2] It was the dramatic action of *The Octoroon*, far more than the dialogue, which thrilled the hearer of the play. The casual reader of the text can now only dimly sense the effect which the lines produced when recited by that cast in which George Holland played Sunnyside; A. H. Davenport, George Peyton; George Jamieson, Old Pete; Mrs. J. H. Allen, Dora, and Agnes Robertson, Zoe, at the Winter Garden, December 5, 1859. After the play had run a week, Mr. and Mrs. Boucicault withdrew on account of a dispute concerning their share of the profits and it was continued without them. It was played in many places in the United States for years and also in London. In the English version, Zoe, instead of dying

---

[1] An anonymous article in the New York *Mirror*, states that one scene is based on a play, *The Old Plantation* by George Jamieson. But *The Old Plantation* was not produced until 1860. George Jamieson, it will be noted, acted the part of Old Pete, and Ireland says it was his first appearance after a long absence in Europe.

[2] *Autobiography*, p. 214.

of poison, is allowed to live, for to a British audience a happy solution seemed possible.

The Boucicaults now went to Laura Keene's Theatre, where they appeared in his adaptation of *The Heart of Midlothian* under the title of *The Trial of Effie Deans*. This ran fifty-four nights. The next play, *Vanity Fair, or Vain of Their Vices*, not an adaptation of Thackeray's novel, was a failure, and Boucicault, hard put to it for inspiration, was driven into the field where he scored his greatest success, the interpretation of Irish character. There had, of course, been a long succession of Irish characters on the American stage, but they had simply represented types quite familiar to the British theatre and they had been employed almost entirely for the purpose of farce or burlesque. In 1789 Dunlap, borrowing Darby from O'Keeffe's *Poor Soldier*, had given a more sympathetic interpretation of the wandering Irishman's character, but Darby's immediate followers, Patrick, in *The Triumphs of Love* (1795), and Patrick O'Neal in *The Traveller Returned* (1798), are simply the conventional Irish servant with which the stage remained content and who might be fitted into any kind of play.

Efforts were made, indeed, to provide a complete Irish play, and in 1822 Charles S. Talbot produced *Paddy's Trip to America, or the Husband with Three Wives*, a two-act farce acted, according to the author's preface, at "Washington Hall," by a young actor named Ramage, and withdrawn on account of the objection that it was a burlesque on the Irish nation. The author, himself an Irishman, published it for his own vindication. It is a poor affair and those sensitive to its criticism might well have left it to a speedy death. Whalen, the villain, has a wife in Ireland, in New York, and in Philadelphia, and he is confounded by O'Flaherty who has known him in Ireland. Much better were the plays dealing with Irish history, such as McHenry's *Usurper* (1827), already discussed, or George Pepper's *Kathleen O'Neill, or a Picture of Feudal Times in Ireland*, a national melodrama of the fourteenth century, which was first played in New York as early as 1829[1] and revived in Philadelphia in 1831. Pepper also produced *The Red Branch Knight, or Ireland Triumphant*, a national operatic drama, in 1831, at the Arch Street Theatre, and according to Durang they both had great merit on the stage. *Kathleen O'Neill*, at least, has a natural dialogue, and Pepper knew his history. Pepper was an Irishman, the editor of the *Irish Shield*, in which his first play was printed. The tragedies laid in Ireland, like Cannon's *Oath of Office*, or Pilgrim's *Robert Emmet*, have already been mentioned.

Irish plays are usually associated with some well-known actor for whom they were written. Tyrone Power, who seems to have been the most successful in interpreting Irish characters, was a native of Ireland who visited this country in 1833 and later, until his death on the ill-fated steamship *President* in 1841. Barney Williams was popular to a somewhat less degree, and for him and others, playwrights like James Pilgrim and Samuel D. Johnson produced during the fifties many plays, nearly all of a farcical or melodramatic nature. Johnson's *Brian O'Linn* is a clever farce in which a youth chooses his mate by pretending he is dead and overhearing the conversation of his three fiancées over his supposed corpse. One scene of *The Shaughraun* may have been inspired by this play. *Ireland and America*, by James Pilgrim, illustrates the insertion of the Irish character into the local New York drama, and *Irish Assurance and Yankee Modesty* was only one of the many farces in which the Hibernian of Barney Williams and the "Yankee Girl" of his wife shone in combination.

An approach to reality was made by John Brougham in his successful play, *Temptation, or the Irish Immigrant*, put on at Burton's Theatre in 1849, in which an Irish laborer is tested and proves honest under difficulties. The usual caricature of an Irish gentleman is given more semblance to truth in *The*

[1] Durang states that the play was first presented on any stage at the Walnut Street Theatre on June 15, 1831, but the 1832 ed. says "as produced at the Lafayette Theatre" which was burned April 11, 1829.

THE INFLUENCE OF DION BOUCICAULT

Gentleman from Ireland, by the talented Irish-American Fitz James O'Brien, whose death on the battlefield during the Civil War ties him to this country more closely than Brougham, who acted the hero, Gerald Fitzmaurice, at Wallack's Theatre in 1854 and who probably aided in its composition.

Comparatively few of these plays, therefore, were written by native Americans, though men like Brougham and O'Brien became identified to a certain degree with our stage or our literature. They were simply following a British stage tradition in choosing the bizarre features of Irish life, the gentleman in trouble for debt, the servant, or the emigrant, and they rarely placed him on Irish soil. So far as any real interpretation of Irish character is concerned, they are valueless. But when Dion Boucicault began to use the material of his native land in *The Colleen Bawn*, all was changed. He had used Irish characters before in *West End, or the Irish Heiress* (1842), and *Andy Blake* (1854), but in the first he had simply inserted an Irish girl into a sophisticated London society, and in the second he had translated a French play, *Le Gamin de Paris*, by Alfred Bayard, into an Irish situation. Both were done in the traditional manner. How he came to write *The Colleen Bawn* has been variously told, beginning with his own version,[1] but the truth lies probably in the statement of Mrs. Barney Williams that Boucicault had promised to write a play for her husband and herself, and that in the desperate straits in which the Laura Keene management found itself, he transferred the play to that theatre.[2]

Of the source of the drama, Boucicault made no concealment. It is based upon Gerald Griffin's novel, *The Collegians*, itself founded upon actual facts. Eily O'Connor, the daughter of a ropemaker of Garryowen, a suburb of Limerick, was married secretly to Scanlan, a gentleman of some fortune, who tired of her and desired to marry Miss Chute of Castle Chute. First he hired a servant, Stephen Sullivan, to kill her, but

---

[1] "Leaves from a Dramatist's Diary," *North American Review*, CXLIX (1889), 231-2.
[2] Walsh, Townsend. *Career of Dion Boucicault*, p. 72, note.

when Sullivan balked at the deed, Scanlan himself drowned her in a brutal manner. He was hanged in 1820. Gerald Griffin made his villain, Hardress Cregan, much less revolting. He is a weak man, loving Eily but ashamed of her, and he is sincerely devoted to Anne Chute, who is in love with him. Mrs. Cregan, his mother, urges him to the marriage, and he is spurred on also by the rivalry of his college mate, Kyrle Daly. Hardress conceals Eily in a cottage belonging to him. He tells Danny Mann, his devoted servant, whom he has himself crippled in youth, to take her to America, but Danny kills her. The body is found, Hardress is arrested, and Danny betraying him, he is transported.[1]

Boucicault used little of the language of *The Collegians*, and he greatly modified the plot and characters. Hardress Cregan becomes less important. He has married Eily, but to save an estate he makes love to Anne Chute. Anne is in love with Kyrle Daly, and her character, as played by Laura Keene, was that of a very lovable Irish gentlewoman. Agnes Robertson played Eily O'Connor, and for his own part, Boucicault selected the character of Myles na-Coppaleen, the loyal but hopeless lover of Eily, who was rather lightly sketched by Griffin, but who becomes the principal hero of *The Colleen Bawn*. It was not only the desire to shine which prompted this change. Boucicault recognized that loyalty is one of the most appealing motives that the stage knows. Myles frustrates the attempt of Danny Mann, Hardress's servant, to kill Eily. Danny Mann is another triumph for Boucicault. He is the very incarnation of treachery, and, in fact, Charles Wheatleigh, who first played the part, seems to have carried off the

---

[1] The first stage version of *The Collegians, Eily O'Conner, or the Foster Brother*, by J. Egerton Wilks, was produced at the City of London Theatre, July 23, 1831, Ellen Tree playing Eily. It seems to have been a poor affair, but introduced the water-cave scene. See *Plays of the Present*, p. 67. I find a record in Ireland, II, 393, of a play, *The Collegians*, by Louisa Medina Hamblin at the Bowery Theatre on December 26, 1842, when Miss C. Shaw played Eily; Lester Wallack, Hardress Cregan, J. R. Scott, Danny Mann and E. Shaw, Lowery Looby, the peculiar lover of Eily whom Boucicault eliminated. It was repeated at the Chatham Theatre in March, 1843, when Mary Duff acted Eily.

stage honors. Hardress is accused of murder, but is saved by the appearance of Eily and becomes reconciled to the prospect of having her for a wife. Anne Chute marries Daly, and, as she pays off the mortgage on the Cregan estate, all ends happily.

It was not the happy ending, however, that carried *The Colleen Bawn* into its great popularity. For the first time real Irish life was placed upon the stage. Hardress Cregan, Mrs. Cregan, Anne Chute, Kyrle Daly, represented Irish gentlefolk, not of "the garrison" but of the ancient Irish stock, a department of Irish life which made up the backbone of the nation, but which, since it did not lend itself to burlesque, had not been placed upon the stage. Myles and Eily are of a lower social stratum, but are distinctly not peasants. Myles has some property and possesses independence of character. George Sand, in her preface to *Le Pressoir* (1853), draws an interesting distinction between the peasant and the villager, attributing to the first more singleness of mind and fewer but stronger desires, while the latter has greater knowledge and more intercourse with others, and since he analyzes his sentiments is therefore better able to express them. The peasant, she says, loves by instinct, the citizen of great cities by imagination, the villager by both instinct and imagination. While the analogy may easily be strained too far, there is no doubt that Myles and Eily, as well as Conn in *The Shaughraun,* rise above the peasant by just that quality of imagination.

Boucicault understood the Celtic nature, its depths of tenderness, of loyalty, of devotion to a person or a cause, as well as its gusts of passion and weakness, its illimitable patience and hopefulness under misery, and its fatal sense, even in the midst of happiness, of the fingers of fate at its throat. These contrasts provide great opportunities for drama, and Boucicault was able to translate them into terms of real life, as far from the burlesque of his predecessors as it is from the sugary sentimentality of his successors in the romantic Irish play or of the grotesque satire of *The Playboy of the Western World.* *The*

Colleen Bawn was first produced at Laura Keene's Theatre on March 29, 1860.[1] It ran to the end of the season. The Boucicaults took the play to London, where it began, at the Adelphi Theatre, on September 10th, its run of three hundred and sixty consecutive nights in London and the provinces. Needless to say, its welcome in Dublin was enthusiastic, and it was taken in time to Australia. Its revivals continued for many years, the most interesting occurring at the Princess Theatre in London in 1869, when Agnes Robertson played Mrs. Cregan.[2] It was translated into French by Adolphe-Philippe d'Ennery and performed at the Théâtre de l'Ambigu-Comique on October 17, 1861, as *Le Lac de Glenaston*. *The Lily of Killarney*, an opera based on the play, with music by Sir Jules Benedict, was written for Clara Louise Kellogg (1874).

Of Boucicault's experiences in England, including his failure as manager of the "Theatre Royal, Westminster," it is not necessary to speak here. While he was abroad he produced at least twenty-two plays, many of them adaptations. Since they were not written in America, two only need be mentioned, *Arrah-na-Pogue* and *Rip Van Winkle*. The latter has been discussed and Boucicault's part in it assigned as far as was possible. *Arrah-na-Pogue* is of interest as being one of the best of the Irish plays. It was first produced in Dublin, November 7, 1864, and brought out in New York on July 10, 1865. It touched the note of loyalty again in the character of Shaun the Post, played by Boucicault, and in the delightful figure of Colonel Bagenal O'Grady, played by Brougham, the author brought to life one of the most spirited of Irish gentlemen. The play was made the occasion for the revival of the old song, "The Wearing of the Green," to which Boucicault contributed new stanzas. During the English performances, however, the song had to be omitted.[3]

[1] Program in Prompt Copy, New York Public Library, gives March 27. But the *New York Tribune* of March 30 reviews the performance on March 29.
[2] *Plays of the Present*, p. 69.
[3] An anonymous writer in *The New York Mirror*, April 23, 1887, states that a part of this play is from *The Alsatian*, by Eugène Nus, and that so completely had Bouci-

THE INFLUENCE OF DION BOUCICAULT

In 1872 Boucicault returned to America. His first play after his return, *Daddy O'Dowd*, later called by the better title *The O'Dowd*, was played at Booth's Theatre, New York, March 17, 1873. It was based on *Les Crochets du Père Martin*, a domestic drama by Cormon and Grangé,[1] which was produced at the Théâtre de la Gaiété in August, 1858. Again we have an interesting example of Boucicault's methods of adaptation. He took the central idea of a father sacrificing himself to save a prodigal son and resuming the humble occupation with which he had laid the foundations of the fortune that the young man had dissipated. He preserved, too, the effective motive of the concealment of the son's shame from his mother, for he recognized that our illusions are among our most precious possessions. But while in the Gallic original Père Martin assumes the blame and sends his son to Australia to redeem the fortunes of the family, Boucicault lets Mike O'Dowd assume the reparation himself, thus securing more sympathy for the younger man. But this change in no way injured the effectiveness of the characterization of "The O'Dowd." Boucicault took the provincial bourgeois of Havre and glorified him in the change to the Celtic chieftain of Galway, who has won back by hard toil and by personal daring in his fisherman's craft the acres of his ancestors. Then when the money lenders come, he surrenders his hard-won soil to save his son from ruin, in a scene which Boucicault's acting made superb. In the last act, too, he translated the heroic action of young Mike, merely related in the original, into a very dramatic scene. A vessel is in danger off the rocks. No one knows the safe passage except the O'Dowd and his son. Mike goes out to save the ship, and the mind of the O'Dowd, which had given way, returns under the stress of emotion, and thus the action of the son is trans-

cault changed the scene that M. Nus on seeing the play failed to recognize that any of his work was contained in it, and contracted for its adaptation into French. This may be gossip, but M. Nus did translate the play under the title of *Jean La Poste, ou les Noces Irlandaises*, and it ran for one hundred and forty nights at the Théâtre de la Gaiété in 1866.

[1] Pen names for P. E. Piestre and E. P. Basté.

lated to the audience by the words of the father, that find their fitting climax in the cry "My boy! My boy!" One has but to compare this ending with the didactic moral sentiment concerning the virtue of industry, on which the curtain descends in the French play, to appreciate Boucicault's dramatic skill.

He continued his adaptations from the French in *Mimi*, from *La Vie de Bohème*, by Henri Murger and Théodore Barrière, in July, 1873, and on December 6, 1873,[1] *Led Astray*, an adaptation of Octave Feuillet's *La Tentation*, began a long run at the Union Square Theatre. Boucicault changed the names and in two cases the nationalities of the characters. George de Lesparre, the young French poet, who becomes the lover of Armande Chandoce, the heroine and the wife of Rodolphe Chandoce, was in the original of Irish extraction. The most important change, however, lay in making Mathilde, the Héléne of the original, the stepdaughter instead of the daughter of Armande, the heroine. This change made more bitter to the young wife the greater affection which Rodolphe, her husband, felt for his daughter and made more easy of comprehension to American audiences the state of indifference which existed between husband and wife. Rodolphe is divested by Boucicault of some of his more attractive qualities in order perhaps to heighten sympathy for Armande, when she yields momentarily to the advances of her lover. Rodolphe's affair with Miss O'Hara seems more sordid than Gontran's liaison with Madame Dumesnil. The scene between Rodolphe and Armande before the duel which he is to fight with Lesparre, her lover, may have been the origin of a scene in *The Banker's Daughter* of Bronson Howard. *Led Astray* had a remarkable reception in London, where it had four hundred and ninety-eight performances at various theatres.

Although it did not prove successful on the stage, Boucicault's next play, *Belle Lamar*, produced at Booth's Theatre, August 10, 1874, is more important than the foreign adap-

---

[1] Odell, IX, 401. Program, Prompt Copy, New York Public Library, says Dec. 8.

tations, for it dealt with the Civil War. It is one of the earliest of these plays, perhaps too early. Not published until 1933 it exists in manuscript in the New York Public Library. It was laid in the Shenandoah Valley during the spring of 1862, and opens with a very effective scene on the banks of the Black Adder River, with the sentinels singing on either side. Belle Lamar is a Southern girl who has been divorced from her husband, Colonel Philip Bligh, U. S. A., on account of their sectional sympathies. They still love each other, however, as they discover when the fortunes of war bring them together. He is commanding the Union forces and is directed to hold a bridge over the river by which Fremont is to join McDowell and Banks and crush Stonewall Jackson. Belle finds out the plan from Marston Pike, a Union officer, who loves her, and she informs Stonewall Jackson. She is captured with Pike's pass in her possession, while trying to intercept dispatches to Bligh, and at her trial as a spy, Belle, Bligh, Pike, and Stuart, a Confederate officer, all vie with each other in sacrificing themselves for honorable motives. The court martial declines to condemn her, and she is given another pass by Bligh to leave the lines. She gives it to Marston Pike and Stuart to save them and places her husband thereby in a difficult position. Jackson attacks Bligh at White Stone Gap, but Fremont comes in time, and Belle and Bligh are reconciled. The play is too heroic and there are some very curious occurrences in a military camp, but it is difficult to see in view of the success of other war plays why this one did not succeed. The sympathy of the audience is kept for both the North and the South, and Boucicault rightly shows that in a conflict in a woman's heart between love of country and love of man, the latter wins.

The most amazing quality of Boucicault was his fecundity. After nearly forty years of constant labor, he wrote one of the greatest of his plays, *The Shaughraun*, first produced at Wallack's Theatre, New York, on November 14, 1874. The play was founded on an incident that happened in County

Sligo during the Fenian insurrection in 1866. Robert Ffolliott, a young Irish gentleman, is under sentence of death as a Fenian. His sister, Claire Ffolliott, and Arte O'Neal, who is betrothed to him, are living together on the estate of which Robert is heir. Kinchela, who is one of the trustees of Robert, has plotted to win the estate and has had Robert convicted. Captain Molyneux, a young English officer, who is sent out to recapture Robert, falls in love with Claire. Robert is recaptured in a dramatic scene in the cottage of Father Dolan, notwithstanding the efforts of Conn, the Shaughraun, to save him. Kinchela learns of a pardon to be given to the Fenians and urges Robert to attempt to escape so that he will be killed. Robert does escape with Conn's help, and Conn is shot and supposed to be killed by Kinchela. While Conn is lying apparently dead at his wake, he overhears the conversation of two of Kinchela's men and learns where Arte and Claire have been taken by Kinchela after having witnessed Conn's supposed murder. They are rescued and Kinchela is captured. Harvey Duff, the informer, throws himself over the cliff and Molyneux wins Claire.

The rapidly moving succession of dramatic incidents, the constant presence of the powerful motive of self-preservation on the part of Robert and Conn, helped the play to success, but it is the character drawing that gives it permanent value. Conn, the Shaughraun, "the soul of every fair, the life of every funeral, the first fiddle at all weddings and parties," as the program indicated, is one of those creations that belong with Rip Van Winkle, whom indeed he somewhat resembles. Boucicault played the part, and he interpreted to the life the generous, hearty, irresponsible, and none too sober wanderer, ever ready to help others but with little of an eye to his own concerns. According to his biographer,[1] Boucicault coined the name from the Gaelic word to go "a shaughraun,"[2] meaning

---

[1] Walsh, p. 127.
[2] It was not his first use of the word. In *Belle Lamar* the Irish sentinel used it as a countersign in mistake for "Choctaw."

to wander. He is the guiding spirit of the play, aiding Robert
in his escapes, meeting craft with shrewdness, and shamming
death at his own wake to secure the secrets of the enemy. He
is one of those puzzles to moralists who wonder why such a
contradiction in moral values ever touches the hearts of theatre-
goers, but the clever dramatist who created him knew and
shared the weaknesses of human beings as well as their strength.
If Conn is not moral, he helps virtue; if he is careless, it is
always of himself.

The Irish gentlefolk are well drawn, and the British officer,
Molyneux, was a spirited gentleman who loathed the work he
was sent to do. The best drawn characters outside of Conn
were Father Dolan, the parish priest, and Harvey Duff, the
informer. They were the incarnation of the two influences
that have been the hope and the despair of the Irish race for
centuries, and yet they are by no means mere types—they are
real people. Father Dolan, played by John Gilbert, dominates
his people, who recognize that even under great temptation he
must maintain the high standard of his office. When Robert
is in danger Conn may lie, but Father Dolan may not. And
there is a fine climax in Act II, Sc. 4, when Molyneux offers to
take Father Dolan's word that Robert is not in his cottage and
the priest cannot give it, though it nearly breaks his heart.
Harvey Duff, the informer, is another masterpiece. The wily,
treacherous nature which worms itself into the confidence of
others, only to betray them to the authorities, was portrayed
with absolute fidelity. On September 11, 1875, *The Shaughraun* was produced at Drury Lane, the part of Moya being
taken by Agnes Robertson. The play was popular for many
years, and Boucicault derived a fortune from it.

It was, however, the climax of his artistic effort. For a time
he returned to adaptations from the French. *Forbidden Fruit*,
played at Wallack's in 1876, had some success and went to
London in 1880, but it is simply a series of misadventures
attendant upon two husbands endeavoring to elude their
wives and the characters have no importance. *Marriage*

followed at the same theatre in 1877 and *Vice Versa* in 1883. He varied these adaptations from the French with a dramatization of *Clarissa Harlowe* which, despite the services of Charles and Rose Coghlan at Wallack's Theatre in 1878, did not succeed. Better than any of these was his Irish play of *The Amadan*, first performed at the Boston Museum, February 5, 1883. The leading motive, that of the devoted animal-like affection of a half-witted boy for a young girl, who treats him with reciprocal kindness, is a theme that had been treated before in drama, and Boucicault derived some ideas from *Le Crétin de la Montagne* (1861), a French melodrama by Eugène Grangé and Lambert Thiboust.[1] Boucicault played Colley the "Amadan" himself at first and later his son "Dot" assumed the part. While powerfully imaginative, *The Amadan* proved too dark and severe in its tone for popular success. His rewriting of Frank Marshall's *Robert Emmet* was likewise unsuccessful, unfortunately having its premiere on the night of Cleveland's first election, November 5, 1884, at Chicago.

The Jilt, suggested by Hawley Smart's racing story, *From Post to Finish*, was first put on in San Francisco at the California Theatre, May 18, 1885. It is laid in Yorkshire at the county seat of Sir Budleigh Woodstock, and in it Boucicault impersonated Myles O'Hara of Ballinahinch, County Galway, a gentleman rider and prophet of the turf, who loses an exciting race, but wins the heart of Kitty Woodstock through his generosity and self-sacrifice. This play was fairly popular and had a London run. This was his last success. *Fin MacCool*, a revision of *Belle Lamar*, in which he inserted an Irish emigrant boy; *Phryne, or the Romance of a Young Wife*, and *Cushla Machree*, his last Irish play, in which he attempted to put *Guy Mannering* into an Hibernian atmosphere, need not detain us.

Broken in fortunes, he accepted a position as teacher in a school of acting established in connection with the Madison Square Theatre, then under the direction of A. M. Palmer. But his courage did not fail him even in adversity, and he did

---

[1] *Jeannette; or, Le Crétin de la Montagne* was played at the Arch St. Theatre in 1861.

not cease writing until the very end. When he died, on September 18, 1890, he had under way a dramatization of *The Luck of Roaring Camp*.[1]

We have passed far beyond the limits of our period in order to complete the treatment of Boucicault's work. It was, however, in 1860 that he took a step which profoundly affected the drama in America. To him is due the development of the traveling company with one play, an institution which changed the fundamental conceptions of the relation of the play to the company and that of the author to the producer and actor. Throughout our early dramatic history complaint is constant concerning the evils of the star system, but up to 1860 the star was superimposed upon a stock company, which remained fairly constant in personnel and which supported the occasional visiting star in plays of his choosing. Managers in Philadelphia, Boston, St. Louis, Baltimore, or elsewhere maintained stock companies which produced new plays for a week or two, varied by revivals of so-called "stock pieces," consisting of the work of the older dramatists from Shakespeare down. There was thus afforded an opportunity for American playwrights to see their work tried out, whenever the local pride or real dramatic insight on a manager's part caused him to attempt the production of a native play. Inadequate recompense, incompetent criticism, and slovenly production could not wholly discourage the playwrights whose impulse to create resulted in the significant dramatic literature of which this volume is the chronicle.

Curiously enough, it was Boucicault's emphasis upon the play as being of greater significance than the actor which brought about the downfall of the early drama. He had been insistent in his efforts to secure the dramatist's rights in his own work, and about 1860 he conceived the idea that instead

[1] In addition to the plays mentioned in Walsh and other authorities, the Register of Copyrights has the names of these plays: *The Struggle for Life*, a drama in three acts (1873); *Drink*, a drama in five acts (1874); *Free Cuba*, with J. J. O'Kelly (1874); *The Snow Flower*, a romantic drama in five acts (1880). The last was acted by Kate Claxton at the Windsor Theatre, New York.

of sending a star around the theatrical circuit of that day, a second company could be sent out from London or New York in a successful play and the drama could be billed as the attraction. He began in England with *The Colleen Bawn*, and offered a company headed by the elder John Drew, Mr. and Mrs. John Sloane, and Mrs. Hudson Kirby, in this play as an attraction to the managers in other cities. There were obvious difficulties, but the success of the project from a financial point of view led the managers, one by one, to adopt the new idea and the disintegration of the stock companies began.[1] In America the change was not accomplished suddenly nor was it unheralded. The traveling company was, of course, as old as Hallam's day, but the early traveling companies did not limit themselves to one play. They were traveling stock companies with their own repertoire. Dual managements like that of Marshall, who directed both the Broadway Theatre in New York and the Walnut Street Theatre in Philadelphia and moved his plays and players between them at will, were in some ways steps in the direction of centralization and yet, on the other hand, resulted in the production of new American plays. But the changes in methods of transportation which made Boucicault's scheme possible would probably have suggested the plan to some other manager if he had not adopted it. In 1849 there were less than 6,000 miles of railroad in the United States. By the end of 1860 there were 30,635 miles. In 1850 it was impossible to go by direct railway from New York to either Boston or Albany. In 1860 New York had continuous lines reaching west of the Mississippi.[2]

The effect upon the American playwright was obviously unfortunate. If a successful play could fill a New York theatre

---

[1] See Walsh's *Boucicault*, pp. 178-9, based upon Boucicault's account in "Leaves from a Dramatist's Diary," *North American Review*, CXLIX (1889), 232-3. Yet in America Mrs. John Drew organized a stock company at the Arch Street Theatre in Philadelphia in 1860 and Laura Keene started a stock company at the Chestnut Street Theatre in 1869. The stock companies in New York City were, of course, not so vitally affected.

[2] Rhodes, *History of the United States*, III, 18.

for a hundred nights and a second company could tour other cities with the same play, the opportunities for new plays became much more limited. In time, of course, the growth of population and the multiplicity of theatres would tend to off-set this temporary limitation of opportunity. There were advantages, too, from the artistic standpoint, to be later presented. But the historian of our drama cannot help specu-lating on what might have come out of the old stock system with more theatres, with the abolition of social prejudice that was coming, but along with these, the retention of the local pride, the independence of the commercial center, the direct contact of playwright and manager, which had belonged to the old regime.

It so happened that this change coincided with the outbreak of the Civil War. The war conditions were, of course, at first disturbed and hurt the theatre and the drama. But it would be easy to overemphasize this disturbance. The Bowery Theatre was dilapidated by military occupation in 1862, but by that time the theatre generally was again in full swing and the temporary check may be attributed more definitely to local causes, such as the closing of the old Broadway Theatre in 1859 or of Wallack's Lyceum in 1861, which had to do with shifting population rather than war.

Indeed, the fusing of outworn prejudice and of outgrown social instincts in the cauldron of war may have helped the stage in more than one important aspect. The panic of 1857 had hurt the theatre, of course, but the theatre had become accustomed to panics, and the long record of ruin which fol-lowed theatrical managers in this country during the period we have been considering was due to causes more specific and more profound. The appalling list of the theatres destroyed by fire, which Rees compiled in 1845,[1] and which is probably incomplete, shows that twenty-five were burned between 1820 and 1845. Owing to the methods of lighting, to carelessness, and to incendiarism, the theatre was a place of personal danger.

---

[1] *Dramatic Authors of America*, pp. 140-42.

And to a large section of the population, it was even more of a moral danger. The old prejudice against the stage died hard, and during the fifties, when the moral sense of the people was being stirred to the depths by the question of abolition, it revived in full force. A professor in the University of the City of New York told Ampère, the French traveler, that if he went to the theatre, he would be in danger of losing his position.[1] The revival of evangelical religious interest took a definitely hostile attitude toward the theatre. At one of the daily noon prayer meetings which were held in Burton's old theatre in Chambers Street in 1858, "a young man related how, becoming an actor at sixteen, he had played in Burton's Theatre, but that since God had adopted him, he would forsake the stage to embrace the cross." Another man confessed that he had been to see Burton play Aminadab Sleek in *The Serious Family* and had been disgusted with that burlesque on evangelical religion. He was glad to be there under different circumstances among "serious and anxious souls," On another occasion a man in the parquet fervently prayed for Burton that "the Great Father might let him know there was a God." "It is related that Burton was present and was visibly affected at being the subject of so earnest a petition."[2]

Certainly the increase in the volume of theatrical amusement beginning about 1862 is an indication that popular prejudice was subsiding. Theatrical interruptions are usually temporary; dramatic changes are more subtle, and it is necessary again to emphasize the continuity of our dramatic impulse. But, in a real sense, the first period and the first century in the American drama were over. The drama was affected by the literary fashions of the time. Romantic subjects were beginning to attract less strongly; even more definite was the reaction against the idealistic treatment of character that resulted in heroic types or incarnations of evil. Realistic por-

---

[1] Rhodes, *History of the United States*, III, 100.

[2] Rhodes, III, 104, quoting from the New York *Times* of March 23, and the *Independent* of March 25, 1858.

trayal of familiar life was to have its day, in fact had already begun that day in the novel and on the stage. With this keener sense for realism and the passing of romantic tragedy, the vogue of verse plays declined, and the movement that had brought Boker into the dramatic field became in part abortive. But, as has already been indicated, the roots of the later drama of national and local types, the social comedy, and the domestic drama had been laid deep in the traditions of the American stage and were to produce fruit in the future.

But the early drama must not be estimated primarily in terms of its effect upon that future. If this record of its successes and failures has not been able to establish its intrinsic significance, it may perhaps be idle to dwell here upon it. Born in the minds of a few college boys in the mid-eighteenth century, it struggled under discouraging conditions for many years before it received even a tardy recognition. Without the enthusiastic national approval that supported the Elizabethan drama, or the favor of a court which patronized the plays of the Restoration or of the days of Goldsmith and Sheridan, it had to meet almost all the difficulties which the British drama experienced in the nineteenth century. In addition to these, it encountered foreign competition unprotected by the shadow of law. For many years it had to beg for consideration at the hands of managers and actors who, being of foreign birth, were not warmly interested in the encouragement of American art. Hardest of all to bear was the native indifference which distrusted all artistic effort on the part of an American, and the critical stupidity which followed foreign standards in expecting that he limit his themes to his own country, a standard never demanded of any other race.

Yet, notwithstanding these conditions, a devoted band of playwrights treated with skill and sympathy the history of their country, touching with loyal fidelity the great figures that founded the Republic, endowing with romance the aboriginal natives and even transferring, warm from action, the heroic episodes of conflicts with man and nature that were establishing firmly the far-flung limits of the United States. Others brought to the stage the types of character that delighted with their comedy audiences which saw themselves reflected in a mimic world. Others sought in distant lands and loves the freedom of choice which enabled them to depict intense emotions, sublime self-sacrifice, or tender fidelity to a hopeless passion.

As one by one the masterpieces of this drama are drawn from the obscurity where unfavorable copyright laws or managerial cupidity had kept them, their own intrinsic artistic worth and their significance in the social history of America may be revealed to the descendants and successors of the generations whom they delighted upon the stage.

BIBLIOGRAPHY

BIBLIOGRAPHY

THE following works will be of use to the student of the American drama. Owing to the superficial nature of much of the critical material dealing with the drama and stage in this country, the Bibliography has been made strictly selective, and only those works which will be of real service are included. It has seemed inadvisable to distract the attention of the student by references to volumes in which mere passing mention of a dramatist occurs or to fugitive articles which are secondary and of temporary interest. In all cases references have been placed where they will be most useful, either immediately applicable in the shape of footnotes to the text or, if of more general interest, in the chapter bibliographies.

BIBLIOGRAPHIES AND LISTS OF PLAYS

The pioneer of bibliographers on the American Drama was Oscar Wegelin, whose *Early American Plays*, *1714-1830*, published by the Dunlap Society, Series 2, vol. 10, New York, 1900, revised ed. 1905, was invaluable, though subject to revision, especially, in the list of "Plays in Manuscript." R. F. Roden's *Later American Plays*, *1831-1900*, Dunlap Soc. Pub. Series 2, vol. 12, New York, 1900, is not so accurate. The Bibliography published in the *Cambridge History of American Literature*, New York, 1917, I, 490-507, by A. H. Quinn and A. C. Baugh, may be consulted for the authors mentioned in the corresponding chapter in that History. F. W. Atkinson's *Early American Plays*, *1756-1830*, and *Later American Plays*, *1830-1900*, are in MS. at Harvard and the Universities of Chicago and Pennsylvania and at the Huntington Library. In 1934 Frank P. Hill's *American Plays*, *Printed 1714-1830*, *a Bibliographical Record*, Stanford University, California, became the standard Bibliography for that period, including references to the ten chief collections in which the plays are to be found. *Index to Plays*, *1800-1826*, by Ira T. E. Firkins, New York, 1927, and *Dramatic Bibliography*, *an annotated list of books on the History and Criticism of the Drama and Stage*, by Blanch M. Baker, New York, 1933, are useful. They are not limited to American Drama. For special collections, see J. C. Stockbridge, *A Catalogue of the Harris Collection of American Poetry* [in the Brown University Library], Providence, 1886; and D. C. Haskell's *List of American*

BIBLIOGRAPHY

Dramas in the New York Public Library, 1916 (revised). For English performances of American plays, Allardyce Nicoll's *A History of Early Nineteenth Century Drama, 1800-1850*, 2 vols., London and New York, 1930, and Reginald Clarence's *The Stage Cyclopedia*, London, 1909, will be found at times useful, as well as the general bibliographies of American literature, such as Joseph Sabin's *A Dictionary of Books Relating to America*, continued by Wilberforce Eames and R. G. W. Vail, New York, 20 vols., 1936.

PRINTED COLLECTIONS

The first collection including American plays of this period was A. H. Quinn's *Representative American Plays*, New York, 1917, sixth ed., revised, 1938, containing the following:

The Prince of Parthia, by Thomas Godfrey; *The Contrast*, by Royall Tyler; *André* by William Dunlap; *Superstition*, by James Nelson Barker; *Charles the Second*, by John Howard Payne and Washington Irving; *The Triumph at Plattsburg*, by Richard Penn Smith; *Pocahontas, or the Settlers of Virginia*, by George Washington Parke Custis; *The Broker of Bogota*, by Robert Montgomery Bird; *Tortesa the Usurer*, by Nathaniel Parker Willis; *Fashion*, by Anna Cora Mowatt; *Francesca da Rimini*, by George Henry Boker; *Leonora*, by Julia Ward Howe; *The Octoroon*, by Dion Boucicault; *Rip Van Winkle*, as played by Joseph Jefferson; *Hazel Kirke*, by Steele Mac-Kaye; *Shenandoah*, by Bronson Howard; *Secret Service*, by William Gillette; *Madame Butterfly*, by David Belasco and John Luther Long; *Her Great Match*, by Clyde Fitch; *The New York Idea*, by Langdon Mitchell; *The Witching Hour*, by Augustus Thomas; *The Faith Healer*, by William Vaughn Moody; *The Scarecrow*, by Percy Mac-Kaye; *The Boss*, by Edward Sheldon; and *He and She*, by Rachel Crothers. During revisions of this volume were added *Margaret Fleming*, by James A. Herne; *Beyond the Horizon*, by Eugene O'Neill; *Sun-Up*, by Lula Vollmer; *The Silver Cord*, by Sidney Howard; *Paris Bound*, by Philip Barry; and *Winterset* by Maxwell Anderson. Clyde Fitch's *The Girl with the Green Eyes* has been substituted for *Her Great Match*, and to permit the additions, *The Triumph at Plattsburg* and *Leonora* were omitted.

Following this appeared *Representative Plays by American Dramatists*, ed. by M. J. Moses; containing the following:

Volume I (1918): *The Prince of Parthia*, by Thomas Godfrey; *Ponteach*, by Robert Rogers; *The Group*, by Mercy Warren; *The Battle of Bunker's Hill*, by Hugh Henry Brackenridge; *The Fall of British Tyranny*, by John Leacock; *The Politician Outwitted*, by

BIBLIOGRAPHY

Samuel Low; *The Contrast*, by Royall Tyler; *André*, by William Dunlap; *The Indian Princess*, by J. N. Barker; *She Would Be a Soldier*, by M. M. Noah. Volume II (1925): *Fashionable Follies*, by Joseph Hutton; *Brutus*, by J. H. Payne; *Sertorius*, by D. P. Brown; *Tortesa the Usurer*, by N. P. Willis; *The People's Lawyer*, by J. S. Jones; *Jack Cade* by R. T. Conrad; *Fashion*, by Mrs. Mowatt; *Uncle Tom's Cabin*, by G. L. Aikin; *Self*, by Mrs. Sidney F. Bateman; *Horseshoe Robinson*, by C. W. Tayleure. Volume III (1920): *Rip Van Winkle*, by Charles Burke; *Francesca da Rimini*, by George Henry Boker; *Love in '76* by Oliver Bell Bunce; *Paul Kauvar*, by Steele MacKaye; *Shenandoah* by Bronson Howard; *In Mizzoura*, by Augustus Thomas; *The Moth and the Flame*, by Clyde Fitch; *The New York Idea*, by Langdon Mitchell; *The Easiest Way*, by Eugene Walter, and *The Return of Peter Grimm*, by David Belasco.

In 1935 A. G. Halline's *American Plays* duplicated six plays in the earlier volumes and added *The Bucktails* by J. K. Paulding; *The Gladiator*, by Robert Montgomery Bird; *Bianca Visconti*, by N. P. Willis; *Horizon*, by Augustin Daly; *The Danities in the Sierras*, by Joaquin Miller; *The Henrietta*, by Bronson Howard; *Madame Sand*, by Philip Moeller; *You and I*, by Philip Barry; *Ice-Bound*, by Owen Davis; *The Great God Brown*, by Eugene O'Neill; *The Field God*, by Paul Green.

In 1940 and 1941 a series entitled *America's Lost Plays*, under the general editorship of Barrett H. Clark, made available a number of unprinted dramas. The volumes containing plays of this period are:

Volume I, Allardyce Nicoll and F. T. Cloak, Eds.; Dion Boucicault, *Forbidden Fruit; Dot; Flying Scud; Louis XI; Robert Emmet; Presumptive Evidence (Mercy Dodd)*.

Volume II, O. S. Coad, Ed.; William Dunlap, *Thirty Years; or, The Gambler's Fate; False Shame; or, The American Orphan in Germany*.

Volume III, Sculley Bradley, Ed., George Henry Boker, *The World a Mask; Glaucus; The Bankrupt*.

Volumes V and VI, Codman Hislop and W. R. Richardson, Eds.; John Howard Payne, *Trial without Jury; or, The Magpie and the Maid; The Solitary of Mount Savage; The Boarding Schools; The Two Sons-in-Law; Mazeppa; The Spanish Husband; The Last Duel in Spain; Woman's Revenge; The Italian Bride; Romulus; The Black Man*.

Volume XII, E. H. O'Neill, Ed.; Robert Montgomery Bird, *The Cowled Lover; Caridorf; News of the Night; 'Twas All for the Best*.

Volume XIII, H. W. Schoenberger and R. H. Ware, Eds.; Richard Penn Smith, *The Sentinels; The Bombardment of Algiers; William Penn* (Fragment); *Shakespeare in Love; A Wife at a Venture; The Last Man*.

BIBLIOGRAPHY

Volume XIV, E. R. Page, Ed.; J. A. Stone, *Metamora; Tancred;* J. H. Wilkins, *Signor Marc;* H. J. Conway, *The Battle of Stillwater;* Silas S. Steele, *The Crock of Gold;* Joseph M. Field, *Job and His Children;* John Brougham, *The Duke's Motto;* Charles P. Clinch, *The Spy;* J. S. Jones, *The Usurper.*

Volume XV, A. W. Peach and G. F. Newbrough, Eds., Royall Tyler, *The Island of Barrataria; The Origin of the Feast of Purim; Joseph and His Brethren; The Judgment of Solomon.*

Other volumes in the Series contain unprinted plays by Steele MacKaye, James A. Herne, H. C. de Mille, David Belasco, Bartley Campbell, Augustin Daly, Langdon Mitchell and others, belonging to a later period.

HISTORIES OF THE DRAMA AND THE STAGE

The first discussion of the American drama, except as incidental to stage history, was made by James Rees in his *Dramatic Authors of America*, Philadelphia, 1845. This is a valuable source of information concerning individual playwrights, but is not a history and it must be checked, for it is at times misleading. Invaluable for its discussion of certain phases of our drama is Laurence Hutton's *Curiosities of the American Stage*, New York, 1891. *The American Dramatist* by M. J. Moses, Boston, 1911, rev. ed., 1925, is concerned largely with a later period. The first attempt to deal in a systematic way with the plays before 1860 was made in a very condensed form by the present writer in "The Early Drama," Book II, Chapter 2, in the *Cambridge History of American Literature*, New York, 1917. The present volume was first published in 1923. *An Hour of American Drama*, by Barrett H. Clark, Philadelphia, 1930, and *A Short History of the American Drama*, by Margaret Mayorga, New York, 1932, deal principally with a later period.

Much information concerning the drama may be found in the HISTORIES OF THE STAGE, but owing to the hearsay, informal, and often contradictory nature of the information, it has to be received with caution. William Dunlap's *History of the American Theatre*, New York, 1832, or in better form, in two volumes, London, 1833, still remains a source of great value. He was limited in his knowledge, perhaps unavoidably, to New York. *The History of the American Theatre*, by G. O. Seilhamer, 3 vols., Philadelphia, 1888-91, is much more accurate, but not so readable and proceeds only to 1797. *A History of the Theatre in America from its Beginnings to the Present Time*, by Arthur Hornblow, 2 vols., Philadelphia, 1919, the first

BIBLIOGRAPHY

attempt to tell the complete story of our stage, has been largely superseded by *The American Stage*, by O. S. Coad and Edwin Mims, Jr., vol. 14 of *The Pageant of America*, New Haven, 1929. *The Romance of the American Theatre*, Boston, 1913, rev. ed., 1925, by M. C. Crawford, is entertaining but popular. Accurate and thorough is O. G. Sonneck's *Early Opera in America*, New York [1915], an invaluable book for the early theatre. More popular than scholarly is *The American Theatre* by John Anderson, Oral Press, 1938.

Among the LOCAL HISTORIES OF THE STAGE, the most important is George C. D. Odell's *Annals of the New York Stage*, of which thirteen volumes, bringing the record to 1888, have appeared, New York, 1927-1942. This has become the authoritative book in its field, superseding J. N. Ireland's *Records of the New York Stage from 1750 to 1860*, 2 vols., New York, 1866-67, and T. A. Brown's *A History of the New York Stage, from the First Performance in 1732 to 1901*, 3 vols., New York, 1903. The last is not to be confused with Brown's *History of the American Stage*, a series of biographical sketches, New York, 1870. Some vivid pictures are to be found in William K. Northall's *Before and Behind the Curtain, or Fifteen Years' Observations among the Theatres of New York*, New York, 1851.

Of the projected series dealing with the Philadelphia stage, three volumes have appeared, T. C. Pollock's *The Philadelphia Theatre in the Eighteenth Century*, Philadelphia, 1933; R. D. James' *Old Drury of Philadelphia. A History of the Philadelphia Stage, 1800-1835*, Philadelphia, 1932, (which includes a reprint of the diary of William Wood); A. H. Wilson's *A History of the Philadelphia Theatre, 1835 to 1855*, Philadelphia, 1935. These have become the authoritative record of the Philadelphia Stage, second only in importance to Odell's larger work dealing with New York.

Very useful as source material is Charles Durang's *The Philadelphia Stage. From the Year 1749 to the Year 1855. Partly compiled from the papers of his father, the late John Durang; with notes by the editors* [of the Philadelphia *Sunday Despatch*]. It was published in this journal: First Series, 1749-1821, beginning in the issue of May 7, 1854; Second Series, 1822-1830, beginning June 29, 1856; Third Series, 1830/1-1855, beginning July 8, 1860. It was never published in book form. Complete files pasted in bound volumes are to be found in the libraries of the Philadelphia Company, of the Historical Society of Pennsylvania, and the University of Pennsylvania, the last being pasted in six large volumes, each volume extra-illustrated with about three hundred engravings, autograph letters, and playbills. W. B. Wood's *Personal Recollections of the Stage*, Philadelphia, 1855, is a first-hand source of

BIBLIOGRAPHY

information. It is based upon the Manuscript *Diary or Daily Account Book of W. B. Wood*, in nine volumes extending with omissions from 1810 to 1835, in the Library of the University of Pennsylvania. Ed. by R. D. James, in 1932. Francis C. Wemyss' *Twenty-six Years of the Life of an Actor and Manager*, 2 vols., New York, 1847, is an important source of information upon the stage in Philadelphia, New York, and Pittsburgh. Wemyss' other books, *The Chronology of the American Stage from 1752 to 1852*, New York n.d. [1852], and his *Theatrical Biography of Eminent Actors and Authors*, New York [185-], are interesting from a biographical point of view. Information concerning the Philadelphia stage is to be found in John F. Watson's *Annals of Philadelphia and Pennsylvania* and E. P. Oberholtzer's *Literary History of Philadelphia*, Philadelphia, 1906.

A Record of the Boston Stage, by W. W. Clapp, Jr., Boston, 1853, is still the standard work for that city, supplemented by *The History of the Boston Theatre, 1854-1901*, by Eugene Tompkins and Quincy Kilby, Boston, 1908, and Claire McGlinchee, *The First Decade of the Boston Museum*, Boston, 1940. For Maine, see James Moreland, "The Theatre in Portland in the Eighteenth Century," *New England Quarterly*, XI (June, 1938), 331-342. For other localities see H. P. Phelps' *Players of a Century, A Record of the Albany Stage*, Albany, 1880, rep. 1890; Charles Blake's *An Historical Account of the Providence Stage*, Providence, 1868; G. O. Willard's *History of the Providence Stage, 1762-1891*, Providence, 1891. For Washington, see *The New National Theater, Washington, D. C., A Record of Fifty Years*, by Alexander Hunter and J. H. Polkinhorn, Washington, 1885; also two articles by A. J. Mudd, "Early Theatres in Washington City," and "The Theatres of Washington from 1835 to 1850," in *Columbia Hist. Soc. Records*, V (1902), 64-86, and VI (1903), 222-266. For New Jersey, see O. S. Coad's "The First Century of the New Brunswick Stage," *Rutgers Univ. Libr.* V (Dec. 1941) 15-36, Part I.

For the South, *The Charleston Stage in the XVIII Century*, by Eola Willis, Columbia, S. C., 1924, is the pioneer book in that field. For Virginia, see M. S. Stockley, "American Plays in the Richmond Theatre, 1819-1838," *Studies in Philology*, XXXVII, 1940; G. H. Tucker, "Early Norfolk Theatres," *Norfolk Virginian Pilot*, June 30, 1940, E. A. Wyatt, *Three Petersburg Theatres, William and Mary Quarterly*, Ser. 2, Vol. XXI (April 1941) 83–110. For North Carolina, among the many articles by Archibald Henderson, see especially, "Early Drama and Professional Entertainment in North Carolina," *The Reviewer*, V (1925) 47-57; "Early Drama and Amateur Entertainment in North Carolina," *Reviewer*, V (1925) 68–77.

BIBLIOGRAPHY

For the West and Southwest, see Rees, pp. 51-76; Noah M. Ludlow's *Dramatic Life as I Found It*, St. Louis, 1880; and Sol. Smith's *Theatrical Management in the West and South for Thirty Years*, New York, 1868. Much new material is included in W. G. B. Carson's *The Theatre on the Frontier*, Chicago, 1932, and his "Glimpses of the Past—Sol. Smith and Theatre Folk, 1836-1865," Missouri Hist. Society, St. Louis, 1938, and J. S. Schick's *The Early Theatre in Eastern Iowa . . . 1836-1863*, Chicago, 1939. Other pioneer articles are "The Theater in the Old Southwest; The First Decade at Natchez," by W. B. Hamilton, *Amer. Lit.* XII (Jan. 1941) 471-485, "The Theatre in Natchez," by W. B. Gates, *Journal of Mississippi History*, III (April, 1941) 71-129; "The Theater in the Republic of Texas," by W. R. Hogan, *Southwest Review*, XIX (July, 1934), 374-401; "The Beginnings of the Professional Theater in Texas," by E. S. Fletcher, *University of Texas Bulletin*, No. 3621 (June 1, 1936), 3-55.

For the Far West, see Constance Rourke, *Troupers of the Gold Coast*, New York, 1928; G. R. Stewart, Jr., "The Drama in a Frontier Theater," Parrott Presentation Volume, Princeton, 1935, 183-204; Myrtle E. Henderson, *History of the Theatre in Salt Lake City*, Salt Lake City, Utah, 1940, G. R. MacMinn, *The Theatre of the Golden Era in California*, Caldwell, Idaho, 1941; *San Francisco Theatre Research*, W. P. A. in Northern California, 18 vols. San Francisco, 1938-1942.

An important body of DRAMATIC CRITICISM is to be found in the books of William Winter: *The Jeffersons*, Boston, 1881; *Brief Chronicles*, Parts 1, 2, 3. Dunlap Society Publications, Series 1, vols. 7, 8, 10, New York, 1889; *A Sketch of the Life of John Gilbert*, Dunlap Society Pub. Ser. 1, vol. 11, 1890; *Shadows of the Stage*, First Series, 1893, Second Series, 1893, Third Series, 1895; *The Life and Art of Edwin Booth*, New York, 1893; *The Life and Art of Joseph Jefferson*, New York, 1894; *Other Days: Being Chronicles and Memories of the Stage*, New York, 1908; *The Wallet of Time, containing Personal, Biographical and Critical Reminiscence of the American Theatre*, 2 vols., New York, 1913; *Vagrant Memories*, New York, 1915.

Data of value is contained in *Actors and Actresses of Great Britain and the United States from the Days of David Garrick to the Present Time*, 5 vols., New York, 1886, by Brander Matthews and Laurence Hutton. Of great service are the Publications of the Dunlap Society, First Series, 15 vols., 1886-91; Second Series, 15 vols., 1896-1901, and one extra volume, and Third Series, 1902, in which two volumes have appeared. They are indicated under the special subjects treated. Among special treatments of the sources of American drama are *The*

BIBLIOGRAPHY

German Drama in English on the New York Stage, to 1830, by Louis C. Baker, Philadelphia, 1917; *The German Drama in English on the Philadelphia Stage from 1794 to 1830*, by C. F. Brede, Philadelphia, 1918; *American Adaptations of French Plays on the New York and Philadelphia Stages from 1790 to 1833*, by H. W. Schoenberger, Philadelphia, 1924; *American Adaptations of French Plays on the New York and Philadelphia Stages from 1834 to the Civil War*, by R. H. Ware, Philadelphia, 1930; and *The French Drama in America in the Eighteenth Century and its Influence on the American Drama of that Period*, by L. P. Waldo, Baltimore, 1942. *The American Theatre as Seen by its Critics*, Ed. by M. J. Moses and J. M. Brown, New York, 1934, is an anthology of criticism.

The most important accounts of the stage have been indicated, but there remain a number of BIOGRAPHIES OF ACTORS AND MANAGERS in which, from a mass of personal details, some information concerning the early drama may be obtained. They have been arranged alphabetically by subject and the most helpful have been starred:

Retrospections of America, 1797-1811, by John Bernard. *From the Manuscript by Mrs. Bayle Bernard.* Edited with introduction, notes, and index by Laurence Hutton and Brander Matthews, New York, 1887; *The Elder and the Younger Booth*, by Asia Booth Clarke, Boston, 1882; *Life, Stories and Poems of John Brougham*, by William Winter, Boston, 1881; *William E. Burton*, by William L. Keese, Dunlap Soc. Pub. Ser. 1, vol. 14, 1891; the works of Frances Kemble Butler, esp. her *Journals*, 2 vols., Philadelphia, 1835, *Records of a Girlhood*, New York, 1879 (last part), *Records of Later Life*, New York, 1883; *"Frances Anne Kemble,"* by Brander Matthews, in *Actors and Actresses of Great Britain and the United States*, III, 239-258; *Fanny Kemble*, by Dorothy Bobbé, New York, 1931; *Fanny Kemble*, by Leota S. Driver, Chapel Hill, N. C., 1933; *Charlotte Cushman*, by Lawrence Barrett, Dunlap Soc. Pub., Ser. 1, vol. 9, 1889; *Thirty Years Passed among the Players in England and America*, by Joe Cowell, New York, 1844 (Part II deals with this country); *Edwin Loomis Davenport*, by E. F. Edgett, Dunlap Soc. Pub. Ser. 2, vol. 14, 1901; *Mrs. Duff*, by Joseph N. Ireland, Boston, 1882; *Autobiographical Sketch of Mrs. John Drew, with an Introduction by her son, John Drew, with Biographical Notes by Douglas Taylor*, New York, 1899; *The Life of Edwin Forrest*, by James Rees, Philadelphia [1874]; *Life of Edwin Forrest*, by William R. Alger, Philadelphia, 1877; *Edwin Forrest*, by Lawrence Barrett, Boston, 1882; *Edwin Forrest, the Actor and the Man*, by Gabriel Harrison, Brooklyn, 1889; *The Stage Reminiscences*

BIBLIOGRAPHY

of Mrs. Gilbert, edited by C. M. Martin, New York, 1901; **The Autobiography of Joseph Jefferson*, New York, 1890; *Life of Laura Keene*, by John Creahan, Philadelphia, 1897; *Fifty Years of Theatrical Management*, by M. B. Leavitt, New York, 1912; *Memories of an Old Actor*, by W. M. Leman, San Francisco, 1886; the *Autobiography of Clara Fisher Maeder*, ed. by Douglas Taylor, Dunlap Soc. Pub. Ser. 2, vol. 3, 1897; *The Stage, or Recollections of Actors and Acting from an Experience of Fifty Years*, by James E. Murdoch, Philadelphia, 1880; *Letters on the Tremont Theatre*, by William Pelby, Boston, 1830; *Theatrical Apprenticeship*, by Sol. Smith, Philadelphia, 1846; *Personal Recollections of the Drama*, by Henry D. Stone, Albany, 1873; *Leaves from an Actor's Note Book*, by George Vandenhoff, New York, 1860; **Memories of Fifty Years*, by Lester Wallack, New York, 1889; *Life and Memories of William Warren*, Boston, n. d., and in general, *Famous Actor-Families in America*, by M. J. Moses, New York, 1906.

For biographical information, consult in general the articles in the *Dictionary of American Biography*. As practically all the important playwrights have been included, the individual articles have not been indicated in the chapter bibliographies.

LIBRARIES CONTAINING COLLECTIONS OF AMERICAN PLAYS

Students will find collections of American plays of varying degrees of completeness in the following libraries (arranged alphabetically). Those starred are special collections of plays, the others being included in collections of American literature or in the general library.

American Antiquarian Society. Boston Athenaeum. Boston Public Library. Brown University (see Bibliographies). University of Chicago.* Columbia University (Brander Matthews *Dramatic Museum*).* Harvard University (Wendell Collection).* Henry E. Huntington Library. Historical Society of Pennsylvania. Library of Congress. New York Public Library (see Bibliographies). University of Pennsylvania (Clothier and Class of 1894 Collections).* Yale University.

CHAPTER I

THE DRAMA AND THE THEATRE IN THE COLONIES

For the early Spanish and French plays, see A. S. W. Rosenbach, *The First Theatrical Company in America*, Worcester, Mass., 1939; Mary Austin, "Spanish Manuscripts in the South West," *Southwest Review*, XIX (July, 1934), 401-409; Mary Austin, "Folk Plays of the

BIBLIOGRAPHY

South West," *Theatre Arts Monthly*, XVII (Aug., 1933), 599-650; C. E. Castaneda, "The First American Play," *Catholic World* (Jan., 1932), reprinted as Vol. III, No. 1, of *Preliminary Studies*, Texas Catholic Historical Society (Jan., 1936); Winifred Johnson, "Early Theatre in the Spanish Borderlands," *Mid-America*, XIII (Oct., 1930), 121-131; *Los Pastores*, translated by M. R. Cole, *Memoirs of the American Folk Lore Society*, 1907; R. E. Twitchell, "The First Community Theatre and Playwright in the United States," *Museum of New Mexico and the School of American Research*, Sante Fé, XVI (March 15, 1924), 83-87; Marc Lescarbot, *Le Théâtre de Neptune en la Nouvelle-France*, translated by Harriette Tabor Richardson as *The Theatre of Neptune in New France* (Boston, 1927).

For early attempts at censorship of the theatre, see W. S. Dye, "Pennsylvania *versus* the Theatre," *Pennsylvania Magazine of History and Biography*, LV (1931), 333-372. The opposition is represented in *Philadelphia Theatre. Extracts from the writings of Eminent Authors, . . . Representing the Evils . . . of the Stage Plays*, Phila., 1789.

Godfrey's *Juvenile Poems on Various Subjects, with The Prince of Parthia*, Philadelphia, 1765, is now a rarity. The play has been reprinted by A. H. Quinn in *Representative American Plays*, New York, 1917, rev. 1938; by Archibald Henderson in a limited edition, with a very complete and critical introduction, Boston, 1917; and by M. J. Moses in *Representative Plays by American Dramatists*, New York, 1918. *Ponteach, or the Savages of America*, was edited by A. Nevin for the Caxton Club, Chicago, 1914, with a good introduction. The other extant plays treated in this chapter have not been reprinted. *Androboros* exists in an unique copy in the library of Henry E. Huntington. Photostats are in several libraries.

For contemporary accounts of Godfrey, see Nathaniel Evans' introduction to the *Juvenile Poems;* and one by William Smith, in *The American Magazine*, I, 602-604, Philadelphia, 1758. See also for criticism Thomas J. White's "Notes on the Provincial Literature of Pennsylvania," *Proceedings of the Historical Society of Pennsylvania*, Vol. I; Moses Coit Tyler's *History of American Literature during the Colonial Period*, New York, 1878, II, pp. 244-251, and Seilhamer, I, chap. 18, and Archibald Henderson, "Thomas Godfrey; Carolina Days," *Everywoman's Mag.* I (1917) 19-24. *The Life and Works of Francis Hopkinson*, by G. E. Hastings, Chicago, 1926, deals extensively with the *Masque of Alfred*.

For a valuable discussion of the Colonial period in general, see P. L. Ford's *Some Notes Towards an Essay on the Beginnings of American Dramatic Literature, 1606-1789*. Privately printed, Brooklyn,

BIBLIOGRAPHY

1893. This was revised and reprinted in the *New England Magazine*, New Series, Vol. IX (Feb., 1894), 673-87, as "The Beginnings of American Dramatic Literature." See also his *Washington and the Theatre*, N. Y., Publications of The Dunlap Society, 1899 (Ser. 2, vol. 8).

The references for the early theatres have been given in the appropriate places in the text. Durang, Ser. 1, chaps. 1-10. C. P. Daly, *First Theater in America*, 1864, rep. in Dunlap Soc. Pub., Ser. 2, Vol. I, 1896, Odell, Pollock, Seilhamer, Tyler, Law, and Sonneck are the best guides. Mary N. Stanard, in *Colonial Virginia, its People and Customs*, Philadelphia, 1917, gives in chapter 8 an interesting if secondary, description of the colonial theatre in Virginia. Valuable also are three articles by O. S. Coad, "Stage and Players in Eighteenth Century America," *Journal of English and Germanic Philology*, XIX (April, 1920), 1-23, and "The American Theatre in the Eighteenth Century," *South Atlantic Quarterly*, XVII (July, 1918), 190-197, and "The First American Play," *Nation*, CVII (Aug. 17, 1918), 182. A vivid if at times inaccurate picture of the Hallam Company in Williamsburg is given in John Esten Cooke's novel, *The Virginia Comedians* (1854), and the first theatre at Williamsburg appears in Mary Johnston's *Audrey* (1902).

CHAPTER II

THE DRAMA OF THE REVOLUTION

The original editions of the plays treated in this chapter are hard to obtain. *The Adulateur* was reprinted in the *Magazine of History*, Tarrytown, XVI (1918), Extra No. 63. *The Fall of British Tyranny* was reprinted in Brooklyn, 1873. *The Group, The Battle of Bunker's Hill*, and *The Fall of British Tyranny* have been reprinted in *Representative Plays by American Dramatists*, Vol. I. *A Dialogue between the Ghost of General Montgomery and an American Delegate* was reprinted, New York, 1865.

The best critical treatment of the period is in Tyler's *Literary History of the American Revolution*, New York, 1897, II, chap. 32. See also Dunlap, I, chap. 4; Seilhamer, II, chap. 1; Ford, *Some Notes Towards an Essay*, etc. (see Bibliography, Chap. I); Hornblow, I, chap. 7. For Mrs. Warren, see the charming study, *Mercy Warren*, by Alice Brown, New York, 1896, rep. 1903. The letters of John Adams are included in *The Works of John Adams*, ed. by C. F. Adams, 10 vols., Boston, 1856. For accounts of the loyalists, see Lorenzo Sabine's *American Loyalists*, Boston, 1847, or C. H. Van Tyne's *The*

BIBLIOGRAPHY

Loyalists in the American Revolution, New York, 1902. For the question of Leacock's authorship of *The Fall of British Tyranny*, see John F. Watson's *Annals of Philadelphia and Pennsylvania*, ed. 1850, I, 104.

Charles F. Heartman published in New York, 1917, *A Bibliography of the Writings of Hugh Henry Brackenridge Prior to 1825*. A memoir of Brackenridge by his son, H. M. Brackenridge, was published in the edition of his novel, *Modern Chivalry*, Philadelphia, 1846, and has been reprinted in some of the later editions. The standard biography is *The Life and Writings of Hugh Henry Brackenridge*, by C. M. Newlin, Princeton, 1932. For Brackenridge as a novelist see the present writer's *American Fiction*, New York, 1936. The activities of the British soldiers fall outside our province, but students of the theatre will find a detailed account of the Mischianza, the pageant on water and land, directed by Major André, in the *Annual Register*, London, 1778, 264-270.

CHAPTER III

THE COMING OF COMEDY

For original editions of the plays special collections must be consulted. *The Contrast* is rare. It was reprinted in 1887 for the Dunlap Society, Series I, vol. 1, with introduction by Thomas J. McKee; in 1917 by A. H. Quinn in *Representative American Plays;* in 1918 by M. J. Moses in *Representative Plays by American Dramatists;* and in a sumptuous limited edition by James B. Wilbur, Boston, 1920, with an introduction and bibliography by Helen Tyler Brown, a great-granddaughter of Royall Tyler. *The Island of Barrataria, The Origin of the Feast of Purim, Joseph and His Brethren*, and *The Judgment of Solomon* were edited by Arthur W. Peach and George F. Newbrough in 1941 for *America's Lost Plays* Series. They expect to have their edition of the life and works of Tyler ready for publication in 1945, based on the manuscript material in the Vermont Historical Society.

See for first-hand information, Dunlap's account of *The Contrast* and *The Mercenary Match*, I, 135-140. For contemporary criticism *New York Daily Advertiser*, April 18, 1787; *New York Independent Journal*, May 5, 1787; *Philadelphia Universal Asylum and Columbian Review*, V (1790), 117-120, (for *The Contrast*), 46 (for *The Reconciliation*). For Tyler's plays, see Seilhamer, II, 225-239; and Odell, I, 255-257. For biography of Tyler, see *History of Eastern Vermont, from its Earliest Settlement, to the Close of the Eighteenth Century*, by B. H. Hall, New York, 1858, rep. Albany, 1865, pp. 708-718; *Brattleboro, Vermont.*

BIBLIOGRAPHY

Early History, with Biographical Sketches of Some of its Citizens, by Henry Burnham, Brattleboro, 1880, pp. 86-101 (based on unpublished account by T. P. Tyler); "Royall Tyler, Man of Law and Man of Letters," by Frederick Tupper, Proc. Vermont Hist. Soc. (1928, pp. 65-101). For Tyler's relation with Joseph Dennie and their joint productions as Messrs. Colon and Spondee, see *Joseph Dennie and His Circle,* by H. M. Ellis, Bulletin of the Univ. of Texas, No. 40— Studies in English, No. 3, Austin, Texas, 1915. *The Mercenary Match* is discussed by O. S. Coad in "An Old American College Play," *Mod. Lang. Notes,* Baltimore, XXXVII (March, 1922), 157-163.

CHAPTER IV

William Dunlap, Playwright and Producer

Dunlap's plays are hard to obtain in the early editions. The Dunlap Society has reprinted the following: *The Father,* with introduction by T. J. McKee, Ser. 1, vol. 2, 1887; *André,* with introduction by Brander Matthews, Ser. 1, vol. 4, 1887; *Darby's Return,* in P. L. Ford's *Washington and the Theatre,* Ser. 2, vol. 8, 1899. *André* was reprinted also in *Representative American Plays,* 1917, and *Representative Plays by American Dramatists,* 1918. *False Shame; or, The American Orphan in Germany* and *Thirty Years; or, The Gambler's Fate,* were edited by Oral S. Coad in 1940 for *America's Lost Plays* Series. A revised list of Dunlap's plays is included.

The primary authorities for Dunlap's life are (1) his *History of the American Theatre,* (2) his *History of the Rise and Progress of the Arts of Design in the United States,* 2 vols., New York, 1834, and (3) the *Manuscript Memoirs of Wm. Dunlap, or Daily Occurrences,* of which four volumes are in the Library of the New York Historical Society and six in the Yale University Library. These were edited by C. D. Barck, New York, 1930, for the New York Historical Society. Next to Dunlap's own works in value and in some cases of greater accuracy is O. S. Coad's *William Dunlap, a Study of His Life and Works and of His Place in Contemporary Culture,* Pub. of the Dunlap Soc., 1917. A complete list of Dunlap's works is given and thorough research into the sources of his plays has been made. Of value, too, are Oscar Wegelin's *William Dunlap and His Writings,* privately reprinted from *The Literary Collector* (Jan., 1904), and *A Bibliographical Check List of the Plays and Miscellaneous Writings of William Dunlap, Bibliographia Americana,* vol. 1, New York, 1916. See also Bibliography of Dunlap by A. H. Quinn and A. C. Baugh in *Cambridge History of American Literature,* I, pp. 496-499. New York, 1917. References to

BIBLIOGRAPHY

Dunlap in the accounts of Rees, Seilhamer, and Hornblow or in A. R. Marble's "Beginnings of the Drama," in *Heralds of American Literature*, Chicago, 1907, pp. 233-275, will add little information to that given in the above references. Seilhamer's attitude toward Dunlap is unjustified. Interesting letters of Dunlap, concerned with the publication of the *History of the American Theatre* in London, for which Cooper was arranging, are to be found in *Correspondence of James Fenimore Cooper*, edited by his grandson, James Fenimore Cooper, 2 vols., New Haven, 1922. An account of the Chestnut St. Theatre is given in *Voyage aux États-Unis de l'Amérique 1793-1798*, by Moreau de Saint-Mercy, ed. by S. L. Mims, New Haven, 1913, pp. 372-374.

Among the contemporary criticism of Dunlap a comparison of his *Wild Goose Chace* and *The Virgin of the Sun* with the translations by Charles Smith, in *The Monthly Magazine and American Review*, II (March, 1800), 225-237, and II (May, 1800), 365-370, reveal Dunlap's superiority as an adapter of Kotzebue. See also Mary R. Bowman, "Dunlap and the Theatrical Register of the New York Magazine," *Studies in Philology*, XXIV, (July, 1927), 413-425.

CHAPTER V

Tragedy and Politics, 1788-1805

The plays mentioned in this chapter are rare. *Bunker Hill*, by JOHN D. BURK, was reprinted by Brander Matthews for the Dunlap Society, Ser. 1, vol. 15, 1891. For Burk the best authorities are *Some Materials to Serve for a Brief Memoir of John Daly Burk, Author of a History of Virginia*, ed. by Charles Campbell, Albany, 1868, and the introduction to the reprint of *Bunker Hill* by Brander Matthews. See also Clapp, pp. 51-55; Dunlap, I, 371-372; Seilhamer, III, 360-363; and E. A. Wyatt, IV, *John Daly Burk; Patriot—Playwright—Historian*, Charlottesville, 1936. *The Politician Outwitted*, by Samuel Low, has been reprinted by M. J. Moses in *Representative Plays by American Dramatists*, with an introduction in which the editor, evidently following Seilhamer's error, II, 284-285, states that the play "is opposed to the Federal Union." For biography of HUMPHREYS, see *The Life and Times of David Humphreys*, by F. L. Humphreys, 2 vols., New York, 1917. See also Dunlap's account of him in the *American Theatre*, I, 168-169, and the *Biographical Outline of Colonel David Humphreys* in *The Polyanthos*, IV (1807), 145-152. For ELIHU SMITH, see Dunlap, I, 302-4, and Marcia E. Bailey, *A Lesser Hartford Wit, Dr. Elihu Hubbard Smith*, Orono, Maine, 1928. For INGERSOLL, Durang, Ser.

BIBLIOGRAPHY

One, chap. 34. MRS. ROWSON's plays are treated by Durang, Ser. One, chaps. 23, 24, 26; Seilhamer, III, 143, 151, 155-156, 171, 340-341, 351-352; Clapp, 41-42, quoting from J. T. Buckingham's *Personal Memoirs and Recollections of Editorial Life*, Boston, 1852, I, 83-85; Ireland, I, 193; Rees, 114. *A Memoir of Mrs. Susanna Rowson*, by E. Nason, appeared in Albany, 1870, and there is an account by F. W. Halsey in his edition of *Charlotte Temple*, New York and London, 1905. *Susanna Haswell Rowson, the Author of Charlotte Temple, A Bibliographical Study*, by R. W. G. Vail, Worcester, 1933, is of considerable value. For MURDOCK, see Seilhamer, III, 171, 176-8. WORKMAN's *Liberty in Louisiana* seems to exist in print in the unique copy of the second edition, "with additions and corrections" (Charleston, 1804) in the Huntington Library. The first edition has apparently disappeared.

CHAPTER VI

JAMES NELSON BARKER AND THE NATIVE PLAYS, 1805-1825

The plays treated in this chapter are rare. *Superstition* was reprinted by A. H. Quinn in *Representative American Plays*, 1917, and *The Indian Princess* and *She Would Be a Soldier*, by M. J. Moses, in *Representative Plays by American Dramatists*, 1918, Vol. I. *Tears and Smiles* was reprinted in the standard biography, *James Nelson Barker*, by Paul H. Musser, Philadelphia, 1929, which contains also the best bibliography.

BARKER's own account of his dramatic work is to be found in Dunlap's *History of the American Theatre*, II, 308-316. See also Durang, Series I, Chaps. 41, 51, Wood, pp. 186-188, 206; Ireland, I, 258-259, 283, II, 455; Wemyss, I, 88; Rees, pp. 21-24; *American Quarterly Review*, I (1827), 331-357; Odell, II, 318-9, 439.

For sources of *The Armourer's Escape*, see *A Narrative of the Adventures of John R. Jewitt*, New York, 1816; and Jewitt's *Journal Kept at Nootka Sound*, Boston, 1807, and recently reprinted by the Merrymount Press. For *Superstition*, see Thomas Hutchinson's *History of Massachusetts*, 2 vols., Boston, 1795 (Vol. I).

NOAH's account of his plays is given in Dunlap, II, 316-324; for biography see S. Wolf, *Mordecai Manuel Noah*, Philadelphia, 1897; Isaac Goldberg, *Major Noah*, New York, 1937. See also Durang, Series 2, esp. chap. 2; Ireland, I, 356, 396, 402, Rees, pp. 109–111. For an account of Finn, see Clapp, pp. 203-208; Rees, pp. 83-85; Ireland, I, 331-333, II, 150. The best account of WOODWORTH's plays is to be found in O. S. Coad's "The Plays of Samuel Woodworth,"

BIBLIOGRAPHY

Sewanee Review, XXVII (1919), 163-175. For Woodworth's addresses at the opening of the New York theatres see his *Melodies, Duets, Trios, Songs and Ballads*, New York, 1826. See generally Oberholtzer, *Literary History of Philadelphia*, 1906, and for both this and Chapter VII, see "Notes on Some Early American Dramas," by R. A. Law, *University of Texas Studies in English*, No. 5, 1925, 96-100.

CHAPTER VII

JOHN HOWARD PAYNE AND THE FOREIGN PLAYS, 1805-1825

PAYNE's important plays were frequently reprinted, and copies of *Charles the Second, Brutus, Thérèse,* and *Love in Humble Life* can still be obtained in the Samuel French reprints. *Charles the Second* was reprinted in *Representative American Plays* (1917) from the rare London edition of 1824. *Romulus, The Last Duel in Spain, Trial without Jury; or, The Magpie and the Maid, Woman's Revenge, The Spanish Husband, Mazeppa,* and *The Two Sons-in-Law* exist in manuscript in the Harvard College Library.

A number of Payne's plays, both acted and unacted, which had remained in manuscript, have been printed in *America's Lost Plays,* Vols. V and VI, edited by Codman Hislop and W. R. Richardson, Princeton, 1940. Some new information concerning French sources and details of production are given. (See Collected Editions.)

For bibliography by A. H. Quinn and A. C. Baugh see *Cambridge History of American Literature*, I, 502-504; also O. Wegelin's *The Writings of John Howard Payne, reprinted from The Literary Collector*, March, 1905, The Literary Collector Press, Greenwich, Conn., n. d. The standard life of Payne is *John Howard Payne, Dramatist, Poet, Actor, and Author of "Home, Sweet Home,"* by Gabriel Harrison, revised ed., Philadelphia, 1885. *The Early Life of John Howard Payne,* by W. T. Hanson, privately printed, Boston, 1913, is valuable for the first period of Payne's life. An excellent contemporary account, by Theodore S. Fay, which has been a source for later writers, is to be found in the *New York Mirror*, X, pp. 161-163 and 169-173 (issues of Nov. 24 and Dec. 1, 1832). This was reprinted in separate form as *A Sketch of the Life of John Howard Payne,* Boston, 1833. Of some interest also are *Memoirs of John Howard Payne, the American Roscius,* London, 1815; C. H. Brainard's *John Howard Payne: A Biographical Sketch,* Washington, 1885; and "John Howard Payne," by Laurence Hutton, in *Actors and Actresses of Great Britain and the United States,* III, 37-54. See also Rosa P. Chiles, *John Howard Payne* (1930). The relations of Payne and Irving, as indicated in the text, are dis-

BIBLIOGRAPHY

cussed in P. M. Irving's *Life and Letters of Washington Irving*, New York, 1883; in *The Romance of Mary Wollstonecraft Shelley, John Howard Payne, and Washington Irving*, Boston, 1907; and in Stanley T. Williams, *The Life of Washington Irving*, 2 vols., New York, 1935. For a contemporary account of Payne as an actor, see the *Polyanthos*, VI (1812), 62-66. For details of the productions, see Odell, Vols. II and III.

For the CHARLESTON GROUP see Yates Snowden's *South Carolina Plays and Playwrights*, Columbia, S. C., 1909. For HARBY, see *A Selection from the Miscellaneous Writings of the late Isaac Harby, Esq.*, Arranged and Published by Henry L. Pinckney and Abraham Moise— *To which is prefixed a Memoir of his Life.* Charleston, 1829; and the *Biography of Isaac Harby, with an account of the Reformed Society of Israelites of Charleston, S. C.*, by L. C. Moise, Univ. of South Carolina, 1931. From the personal standpoint there is interest in Fanny Wright's *Views of Society and Manners in America, in a Series of Letters from that Country to a Friend in England, during the Years 1818, 1819 and 1820. By an Englishwoman.* New York and London, 1821. An enthusiastic criticism of *Alexis the Czarewitz* appeared in the *Polyanthos*, VI (1812), 222-232. For WHITE, see "The Journal of John Blake White," *So. Carolina Hist. and Gen. Mag.* XLII. (April-July, 1941), 55-71.

CHAPTER VIII

FROM MELODRAMA TO TRAGEDY

For theatrical conditions, Durang, Wemyss, Wood, and Ireland are the best of the older accounts. Much has been added, however, by A. H. Wilson's *History of the Philadelphia Theatre, 1835 to 1855*, and by Odell's *Annals*. *The Life of Edwin Forrest*, by William R. Alger, 2 vols., Philadelphia, 1877, is still the standard, to be supplemented by later accounts such as *Edwin Forrest*, by Lawrence Barrett, Boston, 1882, and by the earlier *Life of Edwin Forrest*, by James Rees, Philadelphia, n. d. [1874].

The published plays of PENN SMITH, *The Eighth of January* (1829), *The Disowned* (1830), *The Deformed* (1830), *Quite Correct* (1835), *Is She a Brigand?* (1835), and *The Daughter* (1836), all printed in Philadelphia, are hard to obtain in original editions. *The Deformed* was reprinted by B. W. McCullough in 1917 (see below) and *The Triumph at Plattsburg* was printed for the first time by A. H. Quinn in *Representative American Plays*, 1917. The following plays are in manuscript form in the Historical Society of Pennsylvania, in Philadelphia: *The Divorce, Quite Correct, The Pelican, A Wife at a Venture, The Sentinels, William Penn* (incomplete), *The Triumph at Plattsburg, Shakespeare in Love, The Bombardment of Algiers, The Solitary, or the Man of Mystery, The Last Man,* and a fragment of *The Bravo.* Several of these have been edited by R. W. Ware and H. W. Schoenberger for Vol. 13 of *America's Lost Plays,* Princeton, 1941 (see Printed Collections). Complete manuscripts of *William Penn, The Venetian, The Daughter,* and *The Witch* have recently come to light at the Harvard Theatre Collection. Act V, Sc. V, of *Caius Marius* has been printed by T. O. Mabbott in "Richard Penn Smith's Tragedy of *Caius Marius,*" *American Literature,* II (May, 1930), 141-156.

The sources of information concerning Richard Penn Smith are the account of Morton McMichael in *The Miscellaneous Works of the Late Richard Penn Smith,* edited by H. W. Smith, Philadelphia, 1856; *The Life and Correspondence of the Reverend William Smith,* by H. W. Smith, 2 vols., Philadelphia, 1879-80, an anonymous sketch of R. Penn Smith in Burton's *Gentleman's Magazine,* V, 117. For contemporary accounts of his plays, see Rees, 127-131; Durang, Series 2, chaps. 51, 55, 56, Series 3, chaps. 4, 10, 25; Wemyss, I, 165, 187-188. The first thorough study, however, was made in *The Life and Writings of Richard Penn Smith, with a Reprint of his Play, "The Deformed," 1830,* by Bruce W. McCullough, Menasha, Wisconsin, 1917.

CHAPTER IX

Robert Montgomery Bird and the Rise of the Romantic Play
1825-1850

For reasons given in the text, Bird's plays were not published during his lifetime. *The Broker of Bogota* was first printed by A. H. Quinn in *Representative American Plays,* 1917. In 1919, Clement Foust published an authoritative *Life and Dramatic Works of Robert Montgomery Bird,* printing for the first time *Pelopidas, The Gladiator,* and *Oralloossa,* and reprinting *The Broker of Bogota.* This work was begun as a thesis at the University of Pennsylvania and was made possible by the generosity of Mr. Robert Montgomery Bird, a grandson of the dramatist, who presented the manuscripts of his grandfather to the University Library.

The City Looking Glass was edited for the Colophon by A. H. Quinn in 1933. *The Cowled Lover, Caridorf; or, The Avenger, News of the Night; or, A Trip to Niagara* and *'Twas All for the Best; or, 'Tis All a*

BIBLIOGRAPHY

Notion were edited by E. H. O'Neill for *America's Lost Plays* Series, Vol. XII, in 1941.

Bird's dramatic manuscripts exist as follows (unless otherwise stated, they are in the University of Pennsylvania): *The Gladiator.* A Tragedy. In Five Acts. Autograph Ms. dated Philadelphia, April, 1831; Ms. copy in hand of Mrs. Bird; another autograph Ms. dated Philadelphia, April, 1831, with pencil notes and corrections; another autograph Ms., incomplete; Ms. (with part of Spartacus only in cues), Brown University. *Oralloossa, Son of the Incas.* A Tragedy. Autograph Ms. dated Philadelphia, Feb., 1832; Ms. copy representing acting version used by Forrest (now owned by Forrest Home, Philadelphia, Pa.), lacking the part of Oralloossa; Ms. copy of the part of Oralloossa only (in Forrest Home, Philadelphia, Pa.); also autograph Ms. of notes and fragments. *The Broker of Bogota.* A Tragedy. In Five Acts. Autograph Ms. lacking Act IV, Sc. 2, 3, and 4; autograph Ms. of first four acts; Ms. copy in hand of Mrs. Bird; Ms. copy representing acting version used by Forrest, containing signature of Forrest on title-page (now in Forrest Home, Philadelphia, Pa.); also autograph Ms. consisting of fragments with introductory and expository matter. *Caridorf, or The Avenger.* A Tragedy. In Five Acts. Autograph Ms. dated Philadelphia, August, 1827. *The City Looking Glass.* A Philadelphia Comedy. In Five Acts. Autograph Ms. dated Philadelphia, July, 1828, with additions and corrections. *The Cowled Lover.* A Tragedy. In Five Acts. Autograph Ms. dated Philadelphia, June, 1827; another autograph Ms. with same title page and date. *The Fanatick.* Autograph Ms. of fragments. *Giannone* (tragedy). Autograph Ms. incomplete. *News of the Night, or A Trip to Niagara.* A Comedy. In Five Acts. Autograph Ms. *Pelopidas, or The Fall of the Polemarchs.* A Tragedy. In Five Acts. Autograph Ms. dated Philadelphia, 1830; another autograph Ms. dated 1830, containing note: "This copy now corresponds with the last written and corrected one"; another autograph Ms. dated "1830-1840"; also autograph Ms. of notes and fragments. *Isidora or the Three Dukes, or The Lady of Catalonia.* Autograph Ms. incomplete, containing astronomical note on inside of cover dated 7 Jan., 1833. Back of first leaf contains note: "In the Drury Lane Company are this season (1832). . . ." *'Twas All for the Best [or] 'Tis All a Notion* (comedy). Autograph Ms. dated "Philadelphia, May, 1827." A selection from Bird's letters was published, edited by Seymour Thompson, entitled "Travelling with Robert Montgomery Bird," in *The University of Pennsylvania Library Chronicle*, VII (March, June, Oct., Nov., 1939) 11-22, 34-50, 75-90; VIII (April, 1940) 4-21.

BIBLIOGRAPHY

For discussion of Bird's plays, see Rees, pp. 29-34; Durang, Series 3, chapters 16, 25; Wemyss, I, 111-13, 194, II, 239, 264. See also Oberholtzer and the Lives of Forrest (Bib., Chap. VI) esp. Alger's *Life*, I, 249-258, 298-303, 350-354. For bibliography of Bird see Foust's *Life*, pp. 161-167.

The plays of the remaining dramatists in this chapter are obtainable only with difficulty in their original editions. Brown's *Sertorius*, Philadelphia, 1830; Conrad's *Aylmere, the Bondman of Kent, and Other Poems*, Philadelphia, 1852; Willis's *Bianca Visconti* and *Tortesa the Usurer*, New York, 1839; and Mrs. Charlotte Barnes Conner's *Plays, Prose and Poetry*, Philadelphia, 1848, are occasionally to be found. *Tortesa the Usurer* has been reprinted in Quinn's *Representative American Plays* (1917, revised, 1938) and *Bianca Visconti* in Halline's *American Plays* (1935). *Sertorius* and *Jack Cade* were reprinted in Moses' *Representative Plays by American Dramatists*, Vol. II.

George Pepper, in *The Irish Shield* for 1830-31, devotes a great deal of space to McHenry's plays. See also Durang, Series 2, chap. 51. The authoritative biography is *James McHenry, Playwright and Novelist*, by R. E. Blanc, Philadelphia, 1939, which includes a full bibliography.

For Brown's plays, see Rees, 24-29, Durang, Series 3, chaps. 4, 48; Wood, p. 359, p. 363; Wemyss, I, 186-187, II, 273. References to Stone are given in Bibliography to Chap. X. For Conrad, see Rees, 39-42, Durang, Series 3, chap. 18; Wemyss, I, 200, II, 245-252; Odell, IV, 460-461. The standard biography of Willis is *Nathaniel Parker Willis*, by H. A. Beers, Boston, 1885, pp. 231-235, but the treatment of the plays is relatively inadequate. See E. A. Poe, *Works*, Virginia Ed., X, 27-30, and XIII, 33-54. See also Rees, 132-137; Ireland, II, p. 215, p. 219; Durang, Series 3, chap. 106; Odell, Vol. IV. For Charlotte Barnes Conner, see Durang, Series 3, chaps. 90, 94, 98, and 102; Ireland, II, 79-80, 239-240 and Odell, IV. Sargent's *Bride of Genoa* is reviewed in the *American Monthly Magazine*, May, 1837, 448-457. See Rees, 121-123; Ireland, II, 219 and 443; Odell, IV; Clapp, 346 and 459. A bibliography of Sargent is being prepared by C. S. Sargent and J. M. Johnson. Mrs. Hentz is discussed by Clapp, p. 295; Wemyss, I, 198; Rees, 88; Ireland, II, 9. All later accounts of Bannister seem to be based on that of Rees, pp. 35-37, who is untrustworthy but voluminous. See Ireland, II, 205, 251, 324, 501, 685; Wemyss, II, 274, 301; Odell, IV. Bannister's place and date of birth were first correctly given by T. F. Marshall, *American Literature*, VIII (Nov., 1936), 306-307.

BIBLIOGRAPHY

CHAPTER X

AMERICAN HISTORY ON THE STAGE, 1825-1860

For the Indian and Revolutionary plays, see Hutton's *Curiosities of the American Stage*, Scenes I and II. A less valuable but interesting account of the general subject is contained in A. E. Lancaster's "Historical American Plays," *Chautauquan*, XXXI (1900), 359-364. Original editions of the plays continue to be scarce. *Metamora* exists in two manuscripts, one with Act IV missing, at the University of Utah, and one containing the part of Metamora only, at the Forrest Home, Philadelphia. These have been edited by Eugene R. Page, for *America's Lost Plays*, XIV, 1941. This may be supplemented by the detailed account of the play in Alger's *Life of Forrest*, I, pp. 237-249. For STONE, see Durang, Series 3, chap. 27; Ireland, I, 404, 454, 647; Wemyss, I, 175; Rees, 119, also his *Life of Forrest;* Odell, III, IV (see Indices). CUSTIS's *Pocahontas* has been reprinted in *Representative American Plays* (1917). An account of Custis is given in *Recollections and Private Memoirs of Washington, by his Adopted Son, George Washington Parke Custis, with a Memoir of the Author by his Daughter* (Mary Custis Lee), Philadelphia, 1861. For his plays, see Durang, Series 2, chaps. 34, 51, 53; Ireland, II, 77; Rees, 39; Odell, III, 494. The Ms. of *De Soto* is in the Library of the University of Pennsylvania. BUNCE's *Love in '76* has been reprinted in *Representative Plays by American Dramatists*, III (1920). The MSS of *Marco Bozzaris* and *Ronmore* are in the Harvard Library. For Bunce's plays, see Ireland, II, 505, 557; Hutton, pp. 20-23; also an obituary notice in *The Critic*, XVI (1890), 262. Rees quotes from McHenry's *Maid of Wyoming*, pp. 105-107. For accounts of Bannister's *Putnam*, see Ireland, II, 417; Brown, I, 121; Odell, IV (see Index). See references in text for the plays on contemporary events. *The Spy, a Tale of the Neutral Ground*, by C. P. Clinch, and *The Battle of Stillwater, or The Maniac*, which may be by H. J. Conway, and *The Usurper, or Americans in Tripoli*, have been printed in *America's Lost Plays*, XIV (1941). For Mrs. Smith, see *Selections from the Autobiography of Elizabeth Oakes Smith*, ed. by M. A. Wyman, Lewiston, Maine, 1925, and *Two American Pioneers*, by M. A. Wyman, New York, 1927.

CHAPTER XI

AMERICAN COMEDY TYPES, 1825-1860

The first general treatment of the topic of this chapter was the valuable article by Brander Matthews, "The American on the

Stage," in *Scribner's Monthly*, XVIII (July, 1879), 321-333. This was based on first-hand information, often oral and now otherwise unavailable. It was amplified by Laurence Hutton, in his *Curiosities of the American Stage*, New York, 1891.

The extant plays of the PAULDINGS are included in *American Comedies*, Philadelphia, 1847, still occasionally to be found. *The Bucktails* has been reprinted in Halline's *American Plays*. For biography see *The Literary Life of James K. Paulding*, by W. I. Paulding, New York, 1867, and *James Kirke Paulding* by A. L. Herald, New York, 1926. See Ireland, I, 648; Odell, III, 502; and *New York Mirror*, IX (1831), 102. For HAWKINS, see Oscar Wegelin's *Micah Hawkins and the Saw-mill*, New York, 1917, and Ireland, I, 455. The 1825 edition of *The Forest Rose* is one of the rarest of Americana, but it was frequently reprinted. See Coad's "Woodworth" (Bib., Chap. VI), and Ireland, II, 50 and 249. For HACKETT's plays, see Ireland, I, 473-475, 594, 628; Wemyss, I, 139-140; Odell, III (index). For the relations of Hill and Hackett, see Ireland, II, 216. *The Life and Recollections of Yankee Hill*, by William K. Northall, New York, 1850, has some value.

The best of J. S. JONES's plays, *The People's Lawyer* and *The Silver Spoon*, have been frequently reprinted, the last in 1911. The introductions to the plays by the author will repay the reader. Rees, pp. 93-94, gives a list of Jones's plays, in some cases obviously incorrect. E. R. Page also gives a list in his edition of *The Usurper*, in *America's Lost Plays*, 1941. See also Ireland, II, 49, 133, 360; Durang, Series 3, chap. 108; Odell, III and IV (indices). For the origin of *Sam Patch*, see Ludlow, 684. Rees, pp. 124-126, gives a list of 36 of Steele's plays, which are included in the Play List of this volume, so far as they can be identified. A partial list is given by E. R. Page in his edition of Steele's *The Crock of Gold* in *America's Lost Plays*, 1941. *The Brazen Drum*, the only other play by Steele to be printed, is rare. For MARBLE, see Ireland, II, 319, 453, 538. Accounts of *A Glance at New York* and successors are given in Ireland, II, 507, 509, 510, 533, 534, 535, 559; Brown, I, pp. 282-284; Durang, Series 3, chap. 94; Odell, V (index). Northall gives quite a different account, pp. 90-92. See for B. A. Baker and Cornelius Mathews, *An Interviewer's Album*, by G. O. Seilhamer, New York, 1881, chaps. IV and XIII.

Fashion was reprinted in *Representative American Plays*, 1917, rev. 1938. MRS. MOWATT's *Autobiography of an Actress, or Eight Years on the Stage*, Boston, 1854, is of great value, not only for her plays, but also for general theatrical conditions. *Her Mimic Life, or*

BIBLIOGRAPHY

Before and Behind the Curtain, Boston, 1856, is also of interest. Poe's criticisms in the *Broadway Journal*, both of her plays and her acting, are found most conveniently in the Virginia Edition of his works, XII, pp. 112-121, 124-129, 184-192. See also "Anna Cora Mowatt," by Lawrence Hutton, in *Actors and Actresses of Great Britain and the United States*, IV, 155-170; Ireland, II, 435-436, 485, 500; Brown, I, 64; Odell, V, VI. Rees, pp. 99-105, gives contemporary criticism of interest. For Mrs. BATEMAN, see Ireland, 661, 689, 701; Brown, I, 453; Odell, VII; and Carson's *Theatre of the Frontier*. *Self* was reprinted in *Representative Plays by American Dramatists*, II. *The Golden Calf* is very rare. For the later social satires, see Ireland, II, 598, 622, 632, 654, 659, 673, 687; Brown, I, 353, 354; Odell, VI, VII (indices). They have not been reprinted.

Rip Van Winkle, as played by JOSEPH JEFFERSON, was published, with an introduction by Jefferson, New York, 1895. It was reprinted in *Representative American Plays*, 1917, rev. 1938. The references to its development through the versions of Kerr, Burke, Lacy, and Boucicault have been given in such detail in the text that it is unnecessary to repeat them. The Burke version was reprinted in *Representative Plays by American Dramatists* (1918). *The Autobiography of Joseph Jefferson*, New York, 1890, and *The Jeffersons*, by William Winter, Boston, 1881, contain the best accounts of Joseph Jefferson and his ancestors. Among critical articles the most helpful are two by L. Clarke Davis, "Among the Comedians," *Atlantic Monthly*, XIX (June, 1867), 750-761; "At and After the Play—Jefferson and Rip Van Winkle," *Lippincott's Magazine*, XXIV (July, 1879), 57-75. Both contain admirable personal criticism of Jefferson's acting. George William Curtis, in the Editor's Easy Chair, in *Harper's Magazine*, XLII (March, 1871), 614-616, analyzes both the play and the acting.

No attempt can be made here at a complete bibliography of NEGRO MINSTRELSY. That belongs to the history of the theatre. The excellent account in Hutton, *The American Stage Negro*, pp. 89-144, and Brander Matthews' article on "The Banjo and the Bones" in the *London Saturday Review*, in 1884, and his "The Decline and Fall of Negro-Minstrelsy" in *A Book About the Theatre*, New York, 1916, will be sufficient for students of the drama in this period. Ralph Keeler's "Three Years a Negro Minstrel," in the *Atlantic Monthly*, XXIV (July, 1869), 71-85, has some personal interest.

BIBLIOGRAPHY

CHAPTER XII

George Henry Boker and the Triumph of Romantic Tragedy

Francesca da Rimini was reprinted in the present writer's *Representative American Plays*, 1917, rev. 1938, in which is indicated the difference between the published version and the acting versions of Davenport and Barrett. *Calaynos, Anne Boleyn, Leonor de Guzman, Francesca da Rimini, The Betrothal, The Widow's Marriage,* and *The Podesta's Daughter* were included in the *Plays and Poems,* Boston, 1856, reprinted in 1857, 1869, 1883, and 1891, but now out of print. *Königsmark* was published in 1869. *Nydia* was edited with Boker's *Sonnets,* by E. S. Bradley, University of Pennsylvania Press, Phila., 1927. He has also edited *Glaucus, The World a Mask* and *The Bankrupt,* with introductions, for *America's Lost Plays* Series, Princeton, 1940. The following manuscripts are in the Library of Princeton University.

Calaynos. Autograph Ms. dated 1848; another autograph Ms. ("This Rehash Begun October 19, 1886—Finished Nov. 25, 1886"); typewritten Ms. dated 1886. *Anne Boleyn.* A Tragedy. Ms. dated 1850 (over 1849); autograph pencil draft, undated; four other pages of autograph pencil draft; some separate Ms. acting parts. *The Betrothal.* A Play. Autograph Ms. undated. *The World a Mask.* A Comedy. This is a Ms. with a large printed title-page to fit. On back of title-page: "Entered according to the Act of Congress, in the year 1851, by George Henry Boker, in the Clerk's Office of the District County, for the Eastern District of Pennsylvania." The Ms. is not in Boker's hand but contains autograph notes. Another Ms. autograph, with title "All the World a Mask. A Comedy," undated. Typewritten copy with title "Under a Mask," dated 1886. *The Podesta's Daughter.* A Dramatic Sketch. Ms. autograph pencil draft, incomplete. *The Widow's Marriage.* A Comedy. Autograph Ms. in pencil; revised Ms. subscribed "Wm. H. Reed. Copyist. Walnut Street Theatre. 1852"; autograph Ms. (revised). *Leonor de Guzman.* A Tragedy. Autograph Ms. undated; Ms. copy; undated. *Francesca da Rimini.* A Tragedy. Autograph Ms. dated 1853; Ms. copy with autograph corrections dated 1853; Ms. copy (Lawrence Barrett's acting copy) with numerous notes in Boker's hand (contains only cues for Lanciotto's part); autograph fragments of first two acts dated 1853. *The Bankrupt.* A Play. Autograph Ms. dated 1853; revised typewritten version entitled "A Commercial Crisis. A Comedy," dated 1886. *Königsmark.* A Tragedy. Autograph Ms. of volume

418

with date April, 1857. *Nydia*. A Tragic Play. Typewritten Ms. dated Philadelphia, 1885, with autograph Ms. notes (Note on Ms. in Boker's hand: "This play was begun on the twenty-sixth of February, and finished on the twenty-first of April, 1885 . . ."). *Glaucus*. A Tragic Play. Typewritten Ms. dated Philadelphia, 1886.

The authoritative biography is *George Henry Boker, Poet and Patriot*, by E. S. Bradley, University of Pennsylvania Press, Philadelphia, 1927, with an excellent Bibliography. Among many articles, largely of a fugitive nature, published at his death, the best are: R. H. Stoddard's "George Henry Boker," *Lippincott's Magazine*, XLV (1890), 856-867; C. G. Leland's "Reminiscences of George Henry Boker," *The American*, XIX (1890), 392-4; [George P. Lathrop] "Some Recollections of Boker," *Atlantic Monthly*, LXV (1890), 427-430. There is an interesting contemporary criticism by Leland in *Sartain's Magazine*, VIII (1851), 369-378, and in William Winter's *Wallet of Time*, I, pp. 312-322. See also Ireland, II, 574, 619, 640, 641, and Odell, VI. Among modern articles may be mentioned the present writer's "Dramas of George Henry Boker," *Pub. Mod. Lang. Assoc. of America*, XXXII (June, 1917), 233-266; "A Little Known American Dramatist," by J. W. Krutch, *Sewanee Review*, XXV (Oct., 1917), 457-468. From the personal point of view, see "George H. Boker," by James Barnes, *Nassau Literary Magazine*, XLVI (1891), 90; "George H. Boker," by George Parsons Lathrop, *The Critic*, IX (1888), No. 224; "George Henry Boker and Angie Hicks," by E. S. Bradley, *Amer. Lit.*, VIII (Nov., 1936), 258-265. From the point of view of national service, see the accounts contained in the *Reception Tendered by the Members of the Union League of Philadelphia to George H. Boker, December 22, 1871*, Philadelphia, 1872, and *The League for the Union* (Twenty-fifth Anniversary), Philadelphia, 1888. For the foreign point of view of Boker, see "Biographie du très-honorable Georges H. Boker, Ministre des États Unis d'Amérique," *L'Orient Illustré*, Constantinople, weekly issues of June 13 and August 22, 1874, and *Journal de St. Pétersbourg*, LIII (1877), 68. *George Henry Boker, Playwright and Patriot*, by the present writer, *Scribner's Magazine*, LXXIII (1923), 701-715, is based upon new material furnished by Mrs. George Boker. Interesting letters are to be found in Elizabeth Robins Pennell's *Charles Godfrey Leland*, 2 vols., Boston, 1906; *The Life and Letters of Edmund Clarence Stedman*, by Laura Stedman and George M. Gould, 2 vols., New York, 1910; *The Life and Letters of Bayard Taylor*, by Marie Hansen-Taylor and H. E. Scudder, Boston, 1884. The extensive correspondence between Boker and Taylor was freely used by Dr. Bradley in his biography. The results of the Boker-Simms correspondence are given in *William Gilmore Simms*, by W. P. Trent, Boston, 1892, pp. 307-308, and by Jay B. Hubbell, in *Pa. Mag. of Hist. and Biog.*, LXII, (Jan., 1939), 66-71. Dr. Hubbell has also edited unpublished letters of Boker, Hayne, and C. W. Stoddard in *Amer. Lit.*, V (May, 1933), 146-165. See also Oberholtzer, *Literary History of Philadelphia*. Boker is treated, though hardly adequately, in the histories of American literature, but neither these accounts nor the many brief and superficial articles in weekly and daily papers will add to the information afforded by the list as given.

Leonora, or the World's Own, was published as *The World's Own* in Boston in 1857, and under the title *Leonore, or the World's Own*, in New York in the same year. It was reprinted in *Representative American Plays* in 1917 and was included until the addition of recent plays caused it to be omitted with regret in the Fifth Edition (1930). *Hippolytus* exists in manuscript in the possession of Mrs. Laura E. Richards and has been edited by J. B. Russak for *America's Lost Plays Series*, 1941. For the life of Mrs. Howe, see her *Reminiscences*, 1899, and *Julia Ward Howe* by Laura E. Richards and Maud Howe Elliott, 2 vols., Boston, 1915. For references to the plays, see Brown, I, 492; Ireland, II, 659; and Odell, VI.

The other plays mentioned in the chapter are long out of print.

CHAPTER XIII

The Influence of Dion Boucicault

The following plays of Boucicault's, produced in America, are available with, however, increasing difficulty, in the reprints of Samuel French: *Jessie Brown, Pauvrette, The Colleen Bawn,* and *Led Astray. The Octoroon* has been reprinted in *Representative American Plays*, 1917, rev. 1938. The New York Public Library contains a valuable collection of prompt books of Boucicault's plays, among them *Belle Lamar*, which was printed for the first time in *Plays for the College Theatre*, ed. by G. H. Leverton, 1933. The manuscript prompt book of *Dot* is in the Library of the University of Pennsylvania. *The Jilt* is out of print, but may be found, with *Forbidden Fruit*, privately printed, in the Library of Congress. *Forbidden Fruit, Dot, Flying Scud, Louis XI, Robert Emmet,* and *Presumptive Evidence (Mercy Dodd)* were edited by Allardyce Nicoll and F. T. Clark for *America's Lost Plays*, 1940.

Boucicault wrote for the *North American Review* a series of articles, forming an important body of dramatic criticism and personal

BIBLIOGRAPHY

reminiscence. Those dealing mainly with the technique of playwriting and acting, are "The Decline of the Drama," CXXV (Sept., 1877), 235-245; "The Art of Dramatic Composition," CXXVI (Jan.-Feb., 1878), 40-52; "My Pupils, CXLVII (Oct., 1888), 435-440; "Coquelin-Hading," CXLVII (Nov., 1888), 581-583; "Shakspere's Influence on the Drama," CXLVII (Dec., 1888), 681-685; "Mutilations of Shakspere, the Poet Interviewed," CXLVIII (Feb., 1889), 266-268; "At the Goethe Society," CXLVIII (March, 1889), 335-343. Those mainly personal are "The Début of a Dramatist," CXLVIII (April, 1889), 454-463; "Early Days of a Dramatist," CXLVIII (May, 1889), 584-593; "Leaves from a Dramatist's Diary," CXLIX (Aug., 1889), 228-236; with a general article on "Theatres, Halls and Audiences," CXLIX (Oct., 1889), 429-436. In "The Future American Drama," *Arena* (Nov., 1890), 641-652, he denounces the situation which he helped to bring about.

The standard biography is *The Career of Dion Boucicault*, by Townsend Walsh, Pub. of the Dunlap Society (1915), Series 3, No. 1. A biography, based on researches in England, by Julius Tolson, is to be published in the future. His Ms. and his list of plays, checked in the Lord Chamberlain's office, has been placed at my disposal through his courtesy. Interesting accounts of individual plays are to be found in *Plays of the Present*, by Clapp and Edgett, Series 2, Extra vol. No. 1, Dunlap Society Pub., New York, 1902. See also "Mr. and Mrs. Boucicault," in *Actors and Actresses of Great Britain and the United States*, V, 77-94; Ireland, II, 621, 633, 691, 692, 698, 700; Ludlow, 704; Odell, Vols. VI to XIII (see Indices). For the relations of *The Octoroon* to its sources, see *The Quadroon, or A Lover's Adventures in Louisiana*, New York, 1856, and *Mayne Reid, a Memoir of His Life*, by Elizabeth Reid, London, 1887, pp. 215-217. *The Collegians*, the source of *The Colleen Bawn*, is available in recent editions.

A LIST OF AMERICAN PLAYS

A LIST OF AMERICAN PLAYS

1665–1860

IN this list are given (1) title, (2) author, (3) place and date of first publication, (4) place and date of first production, in parentheses. The omission of the date of publication or of performance indicates that no such record has been found. For modern reprints see Chapter Bibliographies, through the Index. *A. L. P.* refers to *America's Lost Plays* Series—see Collections.

In the cases of certain theatres, in which no confusion could occur, the following abbreviations have been used.

Arch: Arch Street Theatre, Philadelphia.

Bowery: Bowery Theatre, New York.

Broadway: Broadway Theatre, New York.

[1] Chestnut: Chestnut Street Theatre, Philadelphia.

John St.: John Street Theatre, New York.

Park: Park Theatre, New York.

Walnut: Walnut Street Theatre, Philadelphia.

Since this history deals with the acted drama, no attempt has been made to record completely the unacted plays, except in cases of playwrights whose other work was performed. Certain unacted plays of special significance or of unusual rarity have been given and all plays mentioned in the text have been included.

The principles that have decided which are "American Plays" are stated in the Preface. The year 1860 has been taken as the final date except in the cases of Boker and Boucicault, in which it seemed advisable to include their later work if produced in this country.

---

[1] During this period, the spelling "Chesnut" was used for this theatre. I have modernized it, except for titles of plays in which the word occurs.

A LIST OF AMERICAN PLAYS

In the First Edition, no attempt was made to indicate translations or adaptations. The sources of the most significant plays have been discussed in the text, and are not here repeated. Where poems or novels have been dramatized, the titles usually disclose this fact. However, since this Play List has been completely reset while the text has not, I have taken the opportunity to indicate certain foreign sources, especially from the French, and when the identity of the novels is not apparent, this has been indicated.

Usually only the first production of a play has been given, but later instances have been added if they seemed of special interest, or if they were more definite than the earliest dates. I have never hesitated to give information in one case because it was not available in every instance.

The List has been re-checked with the histories of the theatre which have appeared since the First Edition was published. Dr. William van Lennep has been good enough to read the proof.

Owing to the fugitive nature of the material, this List must still obviously be incomplete, but no pains have been spared to test the information presented. It is hoped that its publication will result in the appearance of plays now believed to be non-extant and in the final establishment of dates of performance. The recorder will welcome such information.

For a list of plays arranged according to authors, see the *Cambridge History of American Literature*, I, 490-507.

Aaron Burr: or, The Emperor of Mexico. W. R. Smith. In *The Bachelor's Button*, Vol. I, Mobile, 1837. In Brown Univ. (Mobile Theatre, May 19, 1837.)

Abaellino, the Great Bandit. Wm. Dunlap. N. Y. and Boston, 1802. (Park, Feb. 11, 1801.)

Abbé de l'Épée; or, Deaf and Dumb. Wm. Dunlap. (Park, March 9, 1801.)

Abbey of St. Augustine, The. R. Merry. (Chestnut, March 20, 1797.)

Accusation; or, The Family of D'Anglade. J. H. Payne. London, 1817. (Drury Lane, London, Feb. 1, 1816; Park, May 10, 1816.)

A LIST OF AMERICAN PLAYS

Actress of Padua, The. John Brougham. (Brougham's Lyceum, Sept. 29, 1851, but see p. 217, note.)

Actress of Padua, The. R. P. Smith. (Walnut, June 13, 1836.)

Adeline, the Victim of Seduction. J. H. Payne. London, 1822. (Drury Lane, London, Feb. 9, 1822; Park, May 1, 1822.)

Adrian Grey: or, The Redemption. C. W. Taylor. (National Theatre, N. Y., Aug. 9, 1852.)

Adulateur, The. Mercy Warren. Boston, 1773.

Advent, A Mystery. Arthur Cleveland Coxe. N. Y., 1837.

Adventure, The; or, The Yankee in Tripoli. J. S. Jones. (Park, Nov. 18, 1835.)

Adventures of a Sailor, The. N. H. Bannister. (American Theatre, New Orleans, March 14, 1835.)

Agnes Robertson at Home. Dion Boucicault. (Pelican Theatre, New Orleans, Feb. 17, 1855.)

Alberti. Isaac Harby. Charleston, 1819. (Charleston Theatre, April, 1819.)

Alberto Albertini; or, The Robber King. Anon. (Park, Jan. 25, 1811.)

Alberto and Matilda. N. W. Eaton. Boston, 1809.

Alexis the Czarewitz. Alexis Eustaphieve. In *Reflections . . . illustrating the Character of Peter the Great.* Boston, 1812. (Boston Theatre, March, 1814.)

Alfred the Great. "By a young gentleman of this city." New York, 1822.

Ali Pacha; or, The Signet-Ring. J. H. Payne. N. Y., 1823. (Covent Garden, London, Oct. 19, 1822; Park, May 8, 1823).

All in a Bustle; or, The New House. Wm. Milns. N. Y., 1798. (Park, Jan. 29, 1798.)

All's Fair in Love. John Brougham. N. Y., [1856]. (New Orleans? Bowery, c. 1856. Cast in play is the company of 1856-57, but the play does not appear in Odell.)

Almachilde. Lorenzo L. da Ponte. N. Y., 1830. (Park, Aug. 11, 1829.)

Almoran and Hamet. William Munford. In *Poems.* Richmond, 1798.

Altorf. Frances Wright (Darusmont). Phila., 1819. (Park, Feb. 19, 1819.)

Amadan, The. Dion Boucicault. MS. Lord Chamberlain's office and Fitzhugh Greene Coll. (Theatre Royal, Richmond, England, Jan. 29, 1883, copyright performance? Boston Museum, Boston, Mass., Feb. 5, 1883.)

A LIST OF AMERICAN PLAYS

Amaldi; or, The Brigand's Daughter. James Rees. (Arch, April 14, 1842.)

Amalek the Arab; or, The Scourge of Algiers. J. S. Jones. (Tremont Theatre, Boston, March 15, 1841.)

Amalgamation; or, Southern Visitors. J. M. Field. (St. Louis Theatre, Oct. 10, 1838.)

Ambroise Germaine; or, The Pet of the Village. John Brougham. (Niblo's Garden, N. Y., July 29, 1850.)

America. J. N. Barker. [See p. 137.]

Americana; or, A New Tale of the Genii. Anon. Balt., 1802. (City Theatre, Charleston, Feb. 9, 1798.)

American Brothers; or, A Visit to Charleston. Hatton? (Charleston Theatre, March 14, 1807.)

American Captive, The; or, The Siege of Tripoli. James Ellison. Boston, 1812. (Boston Theatre, Dec. 11, 1811.)

American Commerce and Freedom. Anon. (Park, Feb. 22, 1813.)

American Naval Pillar, The. Anon. (Olympic Theatre, Phila., 1812.)

Americans Abroad. J. Pilgrim. (Burton's Theatre, N. Y., June 28, 1856.)

Americans in England. S. H. Rowson. (Federal St. Theatre, Boston, April 19, 1797.)

Americans in Paris; or, A Game of Dominoes. W. H. Hurlburt. N. Y. [1858]. (Wallack's Theatre, N. Y., May 8, 1858.)

Americans Roused in a Cure for the Spleen, The; or, Amusement for a Winter's Evening. Jonathan Sewall (?). N. Y. [1775].

American Tar, The. S. H. Rowson. (Chestnut, June 17, 1796.)

American Tars in Tripoli. Anon. (Chestnut, March 27, 1805.)

American Valor; or, Yankee Tars on Hand. Anon. (Walnut, Jan. 27, 1844.)

Ancient Briton, The. John A. Stone. (Arch, March 27, 1833.)

André. Wm. Dunlap. N. Y., 1798. (Park, March 30, 1798.)

André. W. W. Lord. N. Y., 1856.

Andrew Jackson. J. F. Brice. [Annapolis] April, 1828.

Androboros. Richard Hunter. Monoropolis, 1714. Unique copy in library of Henry E. Huntington.

Andy Blake. Dion Boucicault. N. Y., 1856. (Boston Museum, March 1, 1854.)

Angelica and Lizette. R. P. Smith. Fragment in Hist. Soc. of Pa.

Anne Boleyn. G. H. Boker. Phila., 1850.

Anne Boleyn. Thomas Fielding. (St. Charles Theatre, New Orleans, Dec. 27, 1838.)

A LIST OF AMERICAN PLAYS

Annexation of Texas, The; or Uncle Sam's Courtship. Anon. (Union Hall, Portland, Maine, Nov. 4, 1844.)

Anthony and Cleopatra (Burletta). J. M. Field. (Olympic Theatre, N. Y., March 1, 1843.)

Anthony Wayne. James Rees. (National Theatre, Phila., May 5, 1845.)

Antipathies; or, The Enthusiasts by the Ears. W. I. Paulding. In *American Comedies*, Phila., 1847.

Apollo in New York. Dion Boucicault. (Walnut, Nov. 27, 1854.)

Apotheosis of Franklin, The. "Mons." Audin. (City Theatre, Charleston, April 16, 1796.)

Arab Chief, The; or, Pirate of the East. H. J. Conway. (Walnut, Oct. 28, 1835.)

Arasapha; or, The Last of the Delawares. Anon. (Bowery, Feb. 23, 1846.)

Arcade, The. John Brougham. (Chestnut, Jan. 5, 1846.)

Archers, The; or, Mountaineers of Switzerland. Wm. Dunlap. N. Y., 1796. (John St., April 18, 1796.)

Armand; or, The Peer and the Peasant. Anna C. O. Mowatt (Ritchie). London, 1849. (Park, Sept. 27, 1847.)

Armourer's Escape, The; or, Three Years at Nootka Sound. J. N. Barker. (Chestnut, March 21, 1817.)

Arnold. J. R. Orton. N. Y., 1854.

Arnold; or, The Treason of West Point. Horatio Hubbell. Phila., 1847.

Arrah de Baugh. F. C. Kinnaman. Clyde, Ohio, n. d.

Art and Artifice. John Brougham. N. Y., [1859]. Adap. of *Quentin Matsys*. (Burton's Theatre, N. Y., June 20, 1859.)

Artful Dodger, The. J. M. Field. (Bowery, Sept. 4, 1843.)

Atalantis; a Story of the Sea. W. G. Simms. N. Y., 1832.

Athenia of Damascus. Rufus Dawes. N. Y., 1839.

Attack on Fort Moultrie, The. Alexandre Placide. (City Theatre, Charleston, June 28, 1794.)

Avarice and Revenge; or, Virtue Triumphant. D. G. Robinson (Dramatic Museum, San Francisco, Jan. 1851.)

Avenger of Blood; or, Richard Hurdis and the Idiot Girl. Dram. of W. G. Simms' novel. (Walnut, Oct. 10, 1838.)

Avenger's Vow, The. C. P. Clinch. (Park, March 25, 1824.)

Aylmere; or, The Bondman of Kent. R. T. Conrad. Phila., 1852. See *Jack Cade.*

Azael; or, the Prodigal. Dion Boucicault. Adap. Scribe's *L'Enfant Prodigue*. (Gaieties Theatre, New Orleans, Jan. 19, 1856.)

Azendai. J. H. Payne and Washington Irving. MS., ? 1823-24.

A LIST OF AMERICAN PLAYS

Bachelor of Arts. John Brougham. (Chestnut, August 15, 1854.)

Bachelor's Wife, A. Frederick Watson. (Burton's Theatre, N. Y., Jan. 11, 1858.)

Banished Provincial; or, Olden Times. S. E. Glover. (American Theatre, New Orleans, April 29, 1833.)

Bandit Chief; or, The Forest Spectre. Anon. (Eagle Theatre, Sacramento, Oct. 18, 1849.)

Banker, The; or, Fashion and Failure. H. J. Conway. MS. Harvard.

Bank Monster, The; or, Specie vs. Shinplaster. S. S. Steele. (Arch, Sept. 20, 1841).

Bankrupt, The. G. H. Boker. MS. dated 1853. *A. L. P.*, 1940. (Broadway, Dec. 3, 1855.)

Bare and ye Cubb, Ye. William Darby. (Accomac County, Va., Aug. 27, 1665.)

Barnaby Rudge. Anon. Dram. Dickens' novel. (National, Phila.; Sept. 27, 1841; at Chatham, N. Y., same day.)

Batkins at Home; or, Life in Cranberry Centre. J. S. Jones. (Boston Museum, May 10, 1858.)

Battle of Brandywine, The; or, The Green Riders of the Santee. N. B. Clarke. (National Theatre, N. Y., June 30, 1856.)

Battle of Brooklyn, The. Anon. N. Y., 1776.

Battle of Buena Vista, The Yankee Volunteer, The, or, The Heroic Death of Captain Lincoln. John P. Adams. Prompt Copy, Brown Univ. (Concert Hall, Portland, Maine, Dec. 1, 1847.)

Battle of Bunker's Hill, The. H. H. Brackenridge. Phila., 1776. (Acted by students in Brackenridge's Academy, Maryland.)

Battle of Eutaw Springs, The. Wm. Ioor. Charleston, 1807. (Charleston Theatre, Jan. 10, 1807.)

Battle of Germantown, The. Walter Leman. (Walnut, April 10, 1845.)

Battle of Lake Champlain, The. A. J. Allen. (Green St. Theatre, Albany, 1815.)

Battle of Lake Erie. J. S. Jones. (Tremont Theatre, Boston, Oct. 31, 1842.)

Battle of Mexico, The; or, Halls of the Montezumas. Thomas Barry. (Bowery, Jan. 17, 1848.)

Battle of New Orleans, The. Wm. Dunlap. (Park?)

Battle of New Orleans, The. C. E. Grice. Baltimore, 1815. (Park, July 4, 1816.)

Battle of Poictiers, The; or, The Knights of the Garter. Holograph MS. (plot outline only), Harvard. William Barrymore. (Walnut, Feb. 19, 1838.)

Battle of Stillwater, The; or, The Maniac. Rufus Dawes. MS. in N. Y.

A LIST OF AMERICAN PLAYS

Pub. Library. *A. L. P.*, 1941. (National Theatre, Boston, March 16, 1840.)

Battle of Texas, The. Anon. (Greenwich Village Theatre, Dec. 29, 1846.)

Battle of the Frogs, The. See *Blood and Nouns.*

Battle of Tippecanoe, The. S. S. Steele. (Coates Street Theatre, Phila., Aug. 19, 1840.)

Beatrice; or, The False and the True. O. S. Leland. Adap. of *Le Demi-Monde* by Dumas, fils. Boston, 1858. N. Y. and London, n. d. (Arch, Dec. 16, 1857.)

Beau Metamorphized, The; or, The Generous Maid. J. Murdock. Phila., 1800.

Beaux Without Belles; or, Ladies We Can Do Without You. David Darling. Charlottesville, 1820. (Fredericksburg Theatre.)

Belisarius. Margaretta Bleecker Faugeres. N. Y., 1795.

Belle Lamar. Dion Boucicault. N. Y., 1933. See "Collections." (Booth's Theatre, N. Y., Aug. 10, 1874.)

Belle of the Season, The. Maltilda Heron. (Laura Keene's Theatre, N. Y., March 12, 1862.)

Bell Ringer of Boston, The; or, The Dawn of the Stars and Stripes. Anon. (Burton's Theatre, N. Y., July 4, 1854.)

Ben Bolt. Anon. Adap. of poem by T. D. English. (National Theatre, N. Y., Oct. 16, 1854; another adap. at Burton's, N. Y., Oct. 18.)

Benedict Arnold. W. G. Simms. In *The Magnolia Weekly*, Richmond, 1863.

Benevolent Lawyers, The; or, Villany Detected. Mary Clarke. Phila., 1823.

Benjamin Franklin; or, Days of '76. Anon. (Chestnut, Oct. 24, 1849.)

Bennett in Texas. J. M. Field. (St. Charles Theatre, New Orleans, Nov. 18, 1838.)

Bernardo del Carpio. H. F. Harrington. Privately printed, n. p., n. d. Copy in Harvard Library. (National Theatre, Boston, Oct. 31, 1836.)

Bertram. W. G. Simms. With *Norman Maurice* in edition published Charleston, 1852.

Bethlem Gabor, Lord of Transylvania; or, The Man Hating Palatine. J. D. Burk. Petersburg, Va., 1807. (Richmond Theatre, c. 1803.)

Betrothal, The. G. H. Boker. In *Plays and Poems*, Boston, 1856. (Walnut, Sept. 25, 1850; Drury Lane, London, Sept. 19, 1853.)

Better Late Than Never. C. J. Cannon. In *Dramas*, N. Y., 1857.

Better Sort, The; or A Girl of Spirit. Anon. Boston, 1789.

Beulah Spa; or, Two of the B'hoys. Anon. (Bowery, Sept. 18, 1834.)

A LIST OF AMERICAN PLAYS

Bianca Visconti; or, The Heart Overtasked. N. P. Willis. N. Y., 1839. (Park, Aug. 25, 1837.)

Birthday of Freedom, The. John Brougham. Revision of *The Irish Yankee.* (Bowery, N. Y., July 4, 1856.)

Black Agate, The; or, Old Foes with New Faces. Elizabeth Bowers. Dram. of Kingsley's *Hypatia.* Phila., 1859. (Academy of Music, Phila., Sept. 5, 1859.)

Blackbeard. Lemuel Sawyer. Washington, 1824.

Black Knight, The. F. H. Duffee. (Front St. Theatre, Balt., Oct. 7, 1841.)

Black Man, The. J. H. Payne. Auto. MS., Luquer Coll. *A. L. P.,* 1940.

Black Rangers, The; or, The Night Hawks. Anon. (National Theatre, Phila., July 26, 1853.) May be same play as *The Battle of Germantown, q. v.*

Black Schooner, The. Anon. (Bowery, Sept. 1, 1839.)

Blanche of Brandywine. J. G. Burnett. N. Y. [1858]. (Laura Keene's Theatre, N. Y., April 22, 1858.)

Bleak House. John Brougham. (Wallack's Lyceum, N. Y., Oct. 13, 1853.)

Blind Boy, The. Wm. Dunlap. (Park, March 30, 1803.)

Blind Man's Bluff, P. Christin (?). Adap. of *L'Aveugle et son bâton,* by Varin and Laurencin. (Olympic Theatre, N. Y., Dec. 4, 1843.)

Blockheads, The; or, The Affrighted Officers. Anon. Boston, 1776.

Blockheads, The; or, Fortunate Contractor. Anon. London, 1782.

Blondel; A Historic Fancy. George E. Rice. Boston, 1854.

Blud Da Nouns; or, The Battle of the Frogs. T. D. English. (National Theatre, Phila., Dec. 16, 1843.)

Blue and Cherry. O. S. Leland. Boston, n. d. [1871]. (Wallack's Theatre, N. Y., Nov. 18, 1858.)

Blue Beard; or, Female Curiosity. Wm. Dunlap? N. Y., 1802. (Park, March 8, 1802.)

Blue Beard. J. L. Motley. Tr. from the German. *The New World,* Dec. 19, 1840.

Blue Belle. Dion Boucicault. Adap. of *Le Diable à quatre,* by De Leuven and Mazilier. (Burton's Theatre, Nov. 27, 1856.)

Blue Laws; or, Eighty Years Ago. Samuel Woodworth. (Bowery, March 15, 1833.)

Blunders Repaired. "By a citizen of Philadelphia." (New Theatre, Phila., April 15, 1799.)

Boarding-Schools, The; or, Life among the Little Folks. J. H. Payne. Auto. MS., Luquer Coll. *A. L. P.,* 1940.

A LIST OF AMERICAN PLAYS

Bombardment of Algiers, The. R. P. Smith. MS. dated 1829 in Hist. Soc. of Penna. *A. L. P.*, 1941.

Bombardment of Tripoli by the American Fleet. Anon. (Charleston Theatre, March 19, 1805.)

Bonaparte in England. Wm. Dunlap. (Park, Dec. 19, 1803.)

Bone Squash Diavolo. T. D. Rice. (Bowery, Oct. 14, 1835.)

Boston Boys of '76; or, The Battle of Bunker Hill. Anon. (Bowery, Feb. 24, 1849.)

Boston Boys of '76, see *Liberty Tree.*

Boston Tea Party of 1774, The. Anon. (Walnut, May 23, 1843.)

Bourville Castle. J. B. Linn. (John St., Jan. 16, 1797.)

Boy Martyrs of September 12, 1814, The. C. W. Tayleure. Boston, [1859]. (Holliday St. Theatre, Balt., 1859.)

Bozzaris. N. Deering. Portland, 1851.

Bravo, The. R. P. Smith. One act in MS. in Hist. Soc. of Penna. [Revised and produced as *The Venetian*, q. v.]

Brazen Drum, The; or, The Yankee in Poland. S. S. Steele. Phila. and N. Y., n. d. (Arch, Jan. 27, 1841.)

Brazier of Naples, The; or, The Maid of Calabria. J. S. Jones. (Tremont Theatre, Boston, Dec. 19, 1842.)

Brian O'Linn. S. D. Johnson. N. Y., n. d. (Arch, May 12, 1851.)

Briar Cliff; or, A Tale of the Revolution. G. P. Morris. (Chatham Garden Theatre, N. Y., June 15, 1826.)

Bride of an Evening, The. Harry Watkins. Dram. of novel by Mrs. E. D. E. N. Southworth. (Barnum's Museum, March 10, 1858.)

Bride of Death, The. Anon. (N. Orleans Theatre, April 10, 1845.)

Bride of Fort Edward, The. Delia Bacon. N. Y., 1839.

Bride of Genoa, The. Epes Sargent. In *The New World*, IV (1842), 99-103, as *The Genoese*. (Tremont Theatre, Boston, Feb. 13, 1837.)

Bride of Jonah, The. J. S. Jones. (National Theatre, Boston, March 1, 1837.)

Bridge of Kehl, The. J. H. Payne (?). (Chatham Theatre, N. Y., Oct. 11, 1848.)

Brigand's Daughter, The. J. Rees. See *Amaldi.*

Britannia and Hibernia; or, Victoria in Ireland. Charles Walcot. (Olympic Theatre, N. Y., Sept. 10, 1849.)

Broadway and the Bowery. Cornelius Mathews. (Bowery, Nov. 10, 1856.)

Broker of Bogota, The. R. M. Bird. In Quinn, *Representative American Plays*, 209-251. (Bowery, Feb. 12, 1834.)

Brothers of the Pyrenees, The. H. E. Stevens. (Walnut, Jan. 2, 1837.)

A LIST OF AMERICAN PLAYS

Brutus; or, The Fall of Tarquin. J. H. Payne. London, 1818. (Drury Lane Theatre, London, Dec. 3, 1818; Park, March 15, 1819.)

Bucktails, The; or, Americans in England. J. K. Paulding. In *American Comedies*, Phila., 1847.

Bunker Hill; or, The Death of General Warren. J. D. Burk. N. Y., 1797. (Haymarket Theatre, Boston, Feb. 17, 1797.)

Bunker Hill; or, What We Have Done and What We Can Do. Anon. (Walnut, July 4, 1812.)

Bunsby's Wedding. John Brougham. See *Capture of Captain Cuttle.*

Burning of the Frigate Philadelphia in the Harbor of Tripoli. Anon. (Charleston Theatre, March 26, 1806.)

Burning Prairie, The; or, The Buffaloe Hunters. Anon. (Tremont Theatre, Boston, Jan. 24, 1843.)

Bush Whacker. N. H. Bannister. (Walnut, July 24, 1838.)

Busy Bee, The; or, Harlequin in the Hive of Industry. William Barrymore. (Boston Museum, Dec. 25, 1844.)

Cabin and Parlor; or, A Picture on the Other Side of Jordan to Uncle Tom's Cabin. B. Young. Dram. from novel of same name. (Walnut, May 9, 1854.)

Cabin Boy and his Monkey Who Had Seen the World, The. William Barrymore. (Warren Theatre, Boston, Nov. 26, 1832.)

Caecinna. Isaac C. Pray. See *Poetus Caecinna.* (Walnut, June 25, 1851.)

Caius Gracchus. Louisa S. McCord. N. Y., 1851.

Caius Marius. W. G. Simms. With *Norman Maurice* in edition published Charleston, 1852.

Caius Marius. R. P. Smith. See Bibliography, Chap. VIII. (Arch, Jan. 12, 1831.)

Caius Silius; or The Slave of Carthage. N. H. Bannister. (American Theatre, New Orleans, Dec. 29, 1836, [First?].)

Calaynos. G. H. Boker. Phila., 1848. (Sadler's Wells Theatre, London, May 10, 1849; Walnut, Jan. 20, 1851.)

California Gold Mines, The. Anon. (Burton's Theatre, N. Y., Dec. 16, 1848.)

California, Past, Present and Future. D. G. Robinson. (San Francisco Theatre, August 27, 1853.)

Californians' Return, The; or, The Happy Miners. Anon. (San Francisco, May 26, 1856.)

Calmstorm, the Reformer. Cornelius Mathews. N. Y., 1853.

Camillus; or, The Self Exiled Patriot. J. B. Phillips. N. Y. and Phila., [1833]. (Arch, Feb. 8, 1833.)

A LIST OF AMERICAN PLAYS

Campaign of the Rio Grande, The. A. W. Fenno. (Bowery, June 8, 1846.)

Candidates, The; or, The Humours of a Virginia Election. Robert Munford. In *Plays and Poems*, Petersburg, 1798.

Candid Critic, The. See *The Royal Poetaster.*

Cannibals; or, The Massacre Islands. Samuel Woodworth. (Bowery, Feb. 20, 1833.)

Cape May Will. J. H. Conway. (Walnut, Sept. 30, 1842.)

Caprice; or, A Woman's Heart. O. S. Leland. Boston, [1857]. (Wallack's Theatre, N. Y., Oct. 22, 1857.)

Captain Kyd; or, The Wizard of the Sea. J. S. Jones. N. Y., [1856]. (National Theatre, Boston, April 1, 1839.)

Captain Kyd; or, The Wizard of the Sea. F. C. Wemyss. Dram. of Ingraham's novel. May be same as play by Jones. (Walnut, Sept. 2, 1839.)

Captain Lascar, the Pilot of Brest. J. S. Jones. (Harvard Athenaeum, Dec. 17, 1866.)

Captain Morgan; or, The Conspiracy Unveiled. C. S. Talbot. Rochester, 1827. (Rochester, 1827.)

Captain Swift. Dion Boucicault. (Madison Square, N. Y., Dec. 4, 1888.)

Captive, The. Charlotte Barnes Conner. (Arch, March 8, 1850.)

Captured Slave, The. Anon. Buffalo, 1815 [1845?]. Date obscurely printed.

Capture of Captain Cuttle, The, and Bunsby's Wedding. John Brougham. One-act play, episode from *Dombey and Son.* (Burton's Chambers Street Theatre, N. Y., Sept. 7, 1848.)

Carabasset. Nathaniel Deering. Portland, 1830. (Portland Theatre, Feb. 16, 1831.)

Career of Crime, The; or, New York's Inner Life Revealed. Anon. (Brougham's Bowery Theatre, April 15, 1857.)

Caridorf; or, The Avenger. R. M. Bird. MS. dated 1827 in University of Pennsylvania Library. *A. L. P.*, 1941.

Carnival Ball, The; or One Hour on Trial. (Mobile Theatre, April 10, 1846.)

Carnival Revolt. C. P. Ware. (Crisp's Gaiety Theatre, N. Orleans, Dec. 28, 1856.)

Carpenter of Rouen, The; or, The Massacre of St. Bartholomew. J. S. Jones, N. Y., n. d. (National Theatre, Boston, Jan. 9, 1837.)

Casper Hauser; or, The Down Easter. See *Kasper Hauser.*

Cat Changed into a Woman, The. Dion Boucicault. Adap. from Scribe's *La Chatte Métamorphosée en femme.* (National Theatre, Washington, Oct. 26, 1855.)

A LIST OF AMERICAN PLAYS

Catharine Howard. J. M. Field. (St. Charles Theatre, New Orleans, April 29, 1840.)

Celestial Empire, The; or, The Yankee in China. C. A. Logan. (Arch, March 4, 1846.)

Cerro Gordo. Anon. (Arch, June 5, 1847.)

Chameleon, The. Dion Boucicault. (Gaiety Theatre, New Orleans, Dec. 20, 1855.)

Chamooni III. Dion Boucicault. Adap. of *L'Ours et le Pacha* by Scribe. (Winter Garden, Oct. 19, 1859.)

Champion of Cordova, The. S. S. Steele. (Arch, April 26, 1843.)

Change Makes Change. Epes Sargent. (Niblo's Garden, N. Y., Oct. 6, 1845.)

Changes. James Rees. (Chestnut, April 22, 1850.)

Charles O'Malley, the Irish Dragoon. H. J. Conway. Dram. Lever's novel. (National Theatre, Phila., Jan. 20, 1842.)

Charles the Second; or, The Merry Monarch. J. H. Payne and Washington Irving. London, 1824. (Covent Garden, London, May 27, 1824; Park, Oct. 25, 1824.)

Charleston Sailor, The; or, Preparations for a Cruise in the Frigate John Adams. Anon. (Charleston Theatre, March 30, 1801.)

Charlotte Corday. Charlotte Barnes Conner. Adap. from Lamartine's *Histoire des Girondins* and Dumanoir and Clairville's *Charlotte Corday.* (Arch, March 18, 1851.)

Charlotte Corday. H. J. Conway. (Chestnut, Oct. 14, 1852.)

Charlotte Corday. Amos C. Morey. N. Y., 1844.

Charlotte Corday; or, The Assassination of Marat and Death of the Queen of France. Anon. (Charleston Theatre, April 30, 1804.)

Charlotte Temple. Anon. Dram. of novel by Mrs. S. H. Rowson. (Chatham Garden Theatre, N. Y., Feb. 11, 1826.)

Charlotte Temple. James Rees. Dram. as above. (American Theatre, New Orleans, April 25, 1836.)

Charter Oak; or, Old Colony Times. Anon. (National Theatre, Boston, Feb. 21, 1848.)

Child of Feeling, The. George Watterson. Georgetown, 1809.

Children of Love. James Pilgrim. Adap. of novel by Eugène Sue. (National Theatre, N. Y., Nov. 28, 1850.)

Chinese Junk. W. K. Northall. (Olympic Theatre, N. Y., Nov. 1, 1847.)

Chloroform; or, New York One Hundred Years Hence. C. A. Logan (Burton's Theatre, N. Y., May 24, 1849.)

Christmas Gift, The; or, The Golden Axe. William Barrymore. (Boston Museum, Dec. 25, 1843.)

A LIST OF AMERICAN PLAYS

Circe and her Magic Cup. T. C. De Walden. (Burton's Theatre, N. Y., Jan. 11, 1855.)

City Looking-Glass, The. R. M. Bird. MS. dated 1828 in Univ. of Pennsylvania. N. Y., 1933. (Irvine Hall, Univ. of Pennsylvania, Jan. 20, 1933.)

Clairvoyants, The. Nathaniel Deering. MS. (Portland Theatre, July 23, 1844.)

Clandare. S. S. Steele. (Walnut, March 10, 1838.)

Clari; or, The Maid of Milan. J. H. Payne. Adap. of *Clari, ou la Promesse de Mariage* by L. J. Milon. London, 1823. (Covent Garden, London, May 8, 1823; Park, Nov. 12, 1823.)

Clarissa Harlowe. Dion Boucicault. Printed copy in Fitzhugh Greene Coll. (Wallack's Theatre, N. Y., Sept. 10, 1878.)

Clergyman's Daughter, The. W. C. White. Boston, 1810. (Federal St. Theatre, Boston, Jan. 1, 1810.)

Cloud Skiff, The; see *The Brazen Drum.*

Cockneys in California. Anon. (Olympic Theatre, N. Y., April 16, 1849.)

Cold Stricken. J. B. Phillips. (Bowery, Jan. 22, 1833.)

Colleen Bawn, The; or, The Brides of Garryowen. Dion Boucicault. N. Y., [1860]. (Laura Keene's Theatre, N. Y., March 29, 1860.)

Collegians, The. L. H. Medina. (Bowery, Dec. 26, 1842.)

Colloquy on the Necessity of Clergymen in Government, A. Thos. Day. MS., ed. A. E. Morse, N. Y., 1917.

Columbia and Britannia. By a *Citizen of the United States.* New London, 1787.

Columbian Daughter, The; or Americans in England. S. H. Rowson. (Mt. Vernon Gardens, N. Y., Sept. 10, 1800.) See *Americans in England.*

Columbus el Filibustero!! John Brougham. N. Y., [1857]. (Burton's Theatre, Dec. 31, 1857.)

Comet, The; or, He Would Be an Astronomer. Wm. Milns. Balt., 1817. (John St., Feb. 1, 1797.)

Coming Out. J. M. Field. (American Theatre, New Orleans, May 24, 1833.)

Compact, The. C. J. Cannon. In *Poems, Dramatic and Miscellaneous,* N. Y., 1851.

Complete Disappointment, The; or, A Touch at Modern Times. James P. Puglia. MS., Harvard. Printed for the Amateurs, Philadelphia, 1809.

Confidence Man, The. John Brougham. (Burton's Chambers St. Theatre, N. Y., July 23, 1849.)

A LIST OF AMERICAN PLAYS

Congress Hall; or, No Male Visitors Admitted. Anon. (Walnut, Aug. 28, 1835.)

Conquest of Canada, The; or, The Siege of Quebec. George Cockings. London, 1766. (Southwark Theatre, Phila., Feb. 16, 1773.)

Conrad and Eudora; or, The Death of Alonzo. T. H. Chivers. Phila., 1834.

Conrad, King of Naples. R. T. Conrad. (Arch, Jan. 17, 1832.)

Constitution Again, The; or, More American Laurel. Anon. (Chestnut, Feb. 22, 1813.)

Constitution and the Guerrière, The. Anon. (Boston Theatre, Oct. 2, 1812.)

Constitution, The; or, American Tars Triumphant. Anon. (Chestnut, Sept. 28, 1812.)

Contempt of Court. Dion Boucicault. Adap. of Meilhac and Halévy's *Le Reveillon* and Hurlbert's *Americans in Paris.* (Wallack's Theatre, Oct. 4, 1879; Marylebone Theatre, London, Oct. 1, 1879.)

Contrast, The. Royall Tyler. Phila., 1790. (John St., April 16, 1787.)

Convention; or, The Columbian Father. John Henry. (John St., April 7, 1788.)

Coronation of Queen Victoria (Spectacle). F. C. Wemyss. (Walnut, Aug. 10, 1838.)

Coroner's Inquisition, A. A. Oakey Hall. N. Y., n. d. (Burton's Theatre, June 1, 1857.)

Corsair, The. E. C. Holland. Charleston, 1818. (Charleston Theatre, Feb. 18, 1818.)

Cortez, the Conqueror. Lewis F. Thomas. Washington, 1857.

Count Benyowski. Wm. Dunlap. (Park, April 1, 1799.)

Count of Burgundy, The. Wm. Dunlap (?). (Park, March 3, 1800.)

Count of Monte Cristo, The. George H. Andrews. Dram. from novel by Dumas. (Broadway Theatre, Dec. 25, 1848.)

Court of Love, The. See *How to Try a Lover.*

Cousins, The; or, The Dying Requisition. T. B. Logan. Phila., 1848. (Assembly Buildings, Phila., June, 1848.)

Cowled Lover, The. R. M. Bird. MS. dated 1827 in Univ. of Pennsylvania Library. *A. L. P.*, 1941.

Cradle of Liberty, The; or, Boston in 1775. S. E. Glover. Dram. of *Lionel Lincoln.* N. Y., n. d. (Tremont Theatre, Boston, May 21, 1832.) See *Rake Hellies.*

Crichton. "Coleman, of Philadelphia." (Walnut, Aug. 14, 1836.)

Crimson Crimes; or, Deeds of Dreadful Note. W. E. Burton (?). (Arch, March 28, 1846.)

A LIST OF AMERICAN PLAYS

Crockett in Texas; or, The Massacre of the Alamo. Anon. (Chatham Theatre, N. Y., Oct. 12, 1839.)

Crock of Gold, The; or, The Toiler's Trials. S. S. Steele. Dram. of novel by Martin Tupper. *A. L. P.*, 1941. (Boston Museum, Sept. 22, 1845.)

Cuffee and Duffee. J. Hutton. [Cf. Rees.]

Cuishla Machree. Dion Boucicault. MS., Lord Chamberlain's office, as *The Spae Wife.* Printed copies in Fitzhugh Greene Coll. (Hollis St. Theatre, Boston, Feb. 20, 1888.)

Cup and the Lip, The. Maria G. Walcot. N. Y., [1859]. Adap. of *Le Testament de César Girodot,* by Adolphe Belot and Edmond Villetard. (Winter Garden, N. Y., Oct. 7, 1861.)

Cure for the Spleen, A; or, Amusement for a Winter's Evening. See *The Americans Roused in a Cure for the Spleen.*

Custom. J. S. Jones. Warren Theatre, Boston, April 14, 1834.)

Custom of the Country, The. Charles Walcot. (Chestnut, Feb. 11, 1852.)

Czarina, The. O. S. Leland. Adap. of Scribe's *La Czarine.* (Boston Theatre, Nov. 17, 1858.)

Daddy O'Dowd. Dion Boucicault. See *The O'Dowd.*

Dance of the Shirt, The. Anon. (Olympic, N. Y., April 11, 1849.)

Dancing Feather, The. C. H. Saunders. Dram. novel of same title by J. H. Ingraham. (Bowery, Nov. 13, 1843.)

Dandyism; or, Modern Fashions. Martin Smith. (Globe Theatre, Cincinnati, July 16, 1823.)

Dandy Jim of Caroline. S. S. Steele. [Cf. Rees.]

Daranzel; or, The Persian Patriot. David Everett. Boston, 1800. (Haymarket Theatre, Boston, April 16, 1798.)

Darby's Return. Wm. Dunlap. N. Y., 1789. (John St., Nov. 24, 1789.)

Dark Days of the Revolution, The. Anon. (Bowery, April 21, 1856.)

Dark Hour before Dawn, The. John Brougham and F. B. Goodrich. N. Y., [1858]. (By amateurs at Academy of Music, April 18, 1859.)

Dark Lady of Doona, The; or, The Bride's Revenge. W. E. Burton. (Walnut, April 17, 1840.)

Daughter, The. R. P. Smith. In *The Actress of Padua, and Other Tales,* Phila., 1836. Holograph MS., Harvard. (Walnut, May 21, 1836.)

David Copperfield. John Brougham. N. Y., n. d. (Brougham's Lyceum Theatre, N. Y., Jan. 6, 1851.)

A LIST OF AMERICAN PLAYS

David Copperfield. W. K. Northall. (Burton's Theatre, N. Y., Dec. 30, 1860.)

Day in New Orleans, A. John R. Dumont. (American Theatre, New Orleans, May 14, 1835.)

Day in New York, Morning, Noon, and Night, A. Anon. (Burton's New Theatre, N. Y., Nov. 26, 1857.)

Death of Cleopatra, The. W. G. Simms. With *Norman Maurice* in edition published Charleston, 1852.

Death of General Montgomery in Storming the City of Quebec, The. H. H. Brackenridge. Norwich, 1777. (Acted by students in Brackenridge's Academy, Maryland.)

Death of Nathan Hale, The. David Trumbull. Hartford, 1845. (Yale College, 1842.)

Death of Ugolino, The. George Featherstonhaugh. Phila., 1830.

Decatur's Triumph; or, The Destruction of the Philadelphia. Anon. (Bowery, Aug. 24, 1840.)

Deceived, The. George Washington Harby. (St. Charles Theatre, New Orleans, April 1, 1838.)

Decided Case, A. John Brougham. N. Y., [1857]. (Wallack's Theatre, N. Y., April 30, 1857.)

Declaration of Independence, The. John Brougham. (Mobile Theatre, Feb. 27, 1844.)

Deed of Gift, The. Samuel Woodworth. N. Y., 1822. (Boston Theatre, March 25, 1822.)

Deep, Deep Sea, The; or, The American Sea Serpent. Anon. In *The Gentleman's Vade Mecum*, Phila., I, No. 4, Jan. 24, 1835. (Walnut, Jan. 1, 1835.)

Deerslayer, The. Anon. (Bowery, Sept. 23, 1841.)

Deformed, The; or, Woman's Trial. R. P. Smith. Phila., 1830. (Chestnut, Feb. 4, 1830.)

De Lara; or, The Moorish Bride. Caroline L. Hentz. Tuscaloosa, Alabama, 1843. (Arch, Nov. 7, 1831.)

Demetria. J. A. Hillhouse. In *Dramas, Discourses and Other Pieces*, Boston, 1839.

Democedes. J. F. Bryce. [Annapolis], 1827. (Annapolis, Aug. 16, 1827.)

Democracy and Aristocracy; or, The Rich and Poor of New York. (Arch, July 13, 1850.)

Demoniac, The; or, The Prophet's Bride. J. A. Stone. (Bowery, April 11, 1831.)

Demon Lover, The; or, My Cousin German. John Brougham. N. Y., [1856]. (Wallack's Theatre, N. Y., Sept. 21, 1854.)

Deseret Deserted; or, The Last Days of Brigham Young. Anon. N. Y., [1858]. (Wallack's Theatre, N. Y., May 24, 1858.)

De Soto, the Hero of the Mississippi. G. H. Miles. MS. in part, Univ. of Pennsylvania. (Chestnut, April 19, 1852.)

Destruction of Jerusalem, The. N. H. Bannister. (Walnut, Nov. 20, 1837; St. Charles Theatre, New Orleans, Jan. 1837, as *The Wandering Jew.*)

Devil, Ye and Dr. Faustus. John Brougham. (Brougham's Lyceum, N. Y., March 10, 1851.)

Devil's Horse, The; or, The Curse of Ambition. John Brougham. (Bowery, N. Y., May 11, 1857.)

Dialogue, A, etc. Francis Hopkinson. N. p., n. d. (College of Philadelphia, May 30, 1765.)

Dialogue between a Southern Delegate and His Spouse, A. "Mary V. V." [N. Y.], 1774.

Dialogue Between the Ghost of General Montgomery . . . and an American Delegate, A. Thomas Paine (?). Phila., 1776.

Diamond Cut Diamond. J. S. Jones. (National Theatre, Boston, April 30, 1838.)

Dick, the Newsboy. Anon. (Broadway, Oct. 17, 1853.)

Did You Ever Send Your Wife to Harlem? Anon. (Olympic Theatre, New York, May 4, 1846.) . . . *To Germantown,* (Arch, May 13, 1846.) And so on, to many places.

Dion. "Dr. Ware" (Arch?) Cf. Rees.

Disappointment, The; or, The Force of Credulity. Andrew Barton [pseud.]. N. Y., 1767. (Federal Theatre, March 3, 1937, as *The Treasure Hunt.*)

Discarded Daughter, The. J. P. Pirsson. N. Y., 1832. (Richmond Hill Theatre, N. Y., Jan. 17, 1832.)

Discoveries in the Moon. T. D. Rice. (Walnut, Sept. 5, 1835.)

Disowned, The; or, The Prodigals. R. P. Smith. Phila., 1830. (Holliday St. Theatre, Balt., March 26, 1829.)

Distant Relations; or, A Southerner in New York. Anon. (Laura Keene's Theatre, N. Y., Dec. 16, 1859.)

Divorce, The; or, The Mock Cavalier. R. P. Smith. MS. dated 1825 in Hist. Soc. of Penna. (Earlier version of *The Deformed.*)

Dr. Bilboquet. J. M. Field. From the French. (St. Louis, 1851.)

Doctor in Spite of Himself, The. Royall Tyler. See p. 72.

Dolores. C. J. Cannon. In *Dramas,* N. Y., 1857.

Dombey and Son. John Brougham. N. Y., n. d. Prompt Copy, Harvard. (Burton's Theatre, N. Y., July 24, 1848.)

Dombey and Son. Charles Walcot. (Park, Nov. 13, 1848.)

A LIST OF AMERICAN PLAYS

A LIST OF AMERICAN PLAYS

Domestic Folly; or, Old Fools, the Worst of Fools. J. D. Turnbull. (Vaux Hall Garden, Charleston, Aug. 13, 1805.)

Don Caesar de Bassoon. John Brougham. (Burton's Chambers St. Theatre, N. Y., Oct. 24, 1848.)

Don Carlos. Wm. Dunlap. (Park, May 6, 1799.)

Doom of Deville, The. G. L. Aiken. Dram. of novel of same title by E. D. E. N. Southworth. (Barnum's Museum, Nov. 28, 1859.)

Doom of the Drinker. T. D. English. (National Theatre, Phila., April 22, 1844.)

Dot. Dion Boucicault. N. p., n. d. Prompt copy in Univ. of Pennsylvania. Also *A. L. P.*, 1941. (Winter Garden, N. Y., Sept. 14, 1859.)

Down East among the Dead Men. Anon. (Peale's Philadelphia Museum, April 22, 1848.)

Down East; or, The Militia Training. J. H. Hackett (?). (Park, April 17, 1830.)

Down South, or, A Militia Training. J. M. Field. (Park, July 5, 1830.)

Drama of Earth, The. Jerome Kidder. New York, 1857.

Dream of Christopher Columbus, The. W. Barrymore. (Walnut, Feb. 22, 1832.)

Dream, The; or, The Truth Unveiled. S. S. Steele. (Boston Museum, Nov. 17, 1845.)

Dred. C. W. Taylor. (National Theatre, N. Y., Sept. 22, 1856.)

Dred; A Tale of the Great Dismal Swamp. H. J. Conway. N. Y., [1856]. (Barnum's American Museum, N. Y., Oct. 16, 1856.)

Dred; or, The Dismal Swamp. John Brougham. N. Y., [1856]. (Bowery, Sept. 29, 1856.)

Drink. Dion Boucicault. Copy. 1874.

Drumming; or, The Ways of Trade. J. Austin Sperry. (Walnut, March 17, 1853.)

Drunkard, The; or, The Fallen Saved. W. H. Smith. Boston, 1847. (Boston Museum, Feb. 12, 1844.)

Drunkard's Progress, The. Anon. (Arch, Nov. 11, 1842.)

Dry Goods Clerk of New York, The. Anon. (National Theatre, N. Y., Jan. 27, 1851.)

Duellist, The; or, The Source of Sorrow. William Barrymore. (Boston Museum, Dec. 2, 1844.)

Duke of Buckingham, The. Mrs. Ellis. (Park, June 21, 1809.)

Duke of Sacramento, The. Warren Baer. San Francisco, 1856.

Duke's Wager, The. Frances Kemble (Butler). See *Mademoiselle de Belle-Isle.*

Eagle Eye, The. J. H. Hall. (Bowery, March 12, 1849.)

Earning a Living. J. H. L. McCracken. N. Y., 1849.

East and West; or, a Yankee Among the Nullifiers. Anon. (St. Louis Theatre, Sept. 30, 1837.)

East Lynne. Clifton W. Tayleure. Dram. of novel by Mrs. Henry Wood. (Winter Garden, March 23, 1863.)

Easy Joe Bruce. H. H. Weld. (Arch, Jan. 29, 1841.)

Ebenezer Venture; or, Advertising for a Wife. Lawrence La Bree. N. Y., n. d. (Buffalo Theatre, Sept. 18, 1841.)

Edge Hill. [?] Farrell. Dram. from novel by J. E. Heath. (Richmond Theatre, June 2, 1829.)

Edith; or, The Fair Maid of Philadelphia. Anon. (Arch, May 1, 1852.)

Editor with $5000. W. W. Clapp, Jr. (Howard Athenaeum, April 1, 1856.)

Edwin and Angelina; or, The Banditti. Elihu H. Smith. N. Y., 1797. (John St., Dec. 19, 1796.)

Edwy and Elgiva. C. J. Ingersoll. Phila., 1801. (Chestnut, April 2, 1801.)

Egyptian, The. John H. Wilkins. (Broadway, N. Y., Feb. 28, 1855.)

Eighth of January, The. G. W. P. Custis. (American Theatre, New Orleans, Dec. 19, 1831.)

Eighth of January, The. R. P. Smith. Phila., 1829. (Chestnut, Jan. 8, 1829.)

Eighth of January, The. L. A. Wilmer. (Arch, Jan. 8, 1848.)

Elbow Shakers, The; or, A Peep at the Five Points. Anon. (Bowery, Sept. 22, 1830.)

Eliza and Claudio; or, Love Protected by Friendship. Lorenzo DaPonte, N. Y., 1833. ("At the Philadelphia Theatre," Cf. Rees.)

Elopement, The; or, Love and Duty. Robert Morris. Phila., 1860.

Emancipation of Europe; or, The Downfall of Buonoparte. Edward Hitchcock. Greenfield, 1815.

Embargo, The. James P. Puglia. MS., Harvard. Printed for the Amateurs, Philadelphia, 1808.

Embargo, The; or, Every One Has His Own Opinion. Anon. (Chestnut, June 13, 1794.)

Embargo, The; or, The Honest Countryman. "By a gentleman of Charleston." (Charleston Theatre, April 27, 1808.)

Embargo, The; or, What News? J. N. Barker. (Chestnut, March 16, 1808.)

Emilie Plater, the Polish Heroine. S. S. Steele. (Walnut, May 20, 1845.)

A LIST OF AMERICAN PLAYS

Empire of Hayti, The; or, Kingcraft in 1852. T. D. English. (Arch, Oct. 2, 1849.)

Enchanted Harp. Anon. Boston, 1852. (Boston Museum, March 8, 1852.)

England's Iron Days. N. H. Bannister. New Orleans, 1837. (St. Charles Theatre, New Orleans, April 13, 1837.)

English Tragedy, An. Frances Kemble Butler. (Broadway, May 16, 1864.)

Ernest Maltravers. L. H. Medina. Dram. Bulwer's novel. (Wallack's National Theatre, N. Y., March 28, 1838.)

Essex Junto, The. J. H. Nichols. Salem, 1802.

Ethan Allen. N. H. Bannister. (Bowery, March 1, 1847.)

Eugene Aram. J. S. Jones. Dram. Bulwer's novel. MS., Boston Public Library. (Tremont Theatre, Boston, May 17, 1832.)

Eugene Aram. Dr. Ware. [?] (Arch., March 4, 1843.)

Eugene Aram. C. W. Taylor. (Bowery, June 19, 1832.)

Euphemia of Messina. Elizabeth F. Ellet. N. Y., 1834.

Evangeline. Mrs. Sidney F. Bateman. (Winter Garden, N. Y., March 19, 1860.)

Eva, the Lass of the Mill. William Barrymore. (Tremont Theatre, Boston, Aug. 30, 1838.)

Eveleen Wilson, the Flower of Erin. James Pilgrim. N. Y., n. d. (St. Charles Theatre, N. Y., April 4, 1853.)

Evil Eye, The. J. B. Phillips. N. Y., 1831. (Bowery, April 4, 1831.)

Exercise, An, etc. Francis Hopkinson and Jacob Duché. Phila., 1762. (College of Philadelphia, May 18, 1762.)

Exercise, An, etc. Francis Hopkinson and Wm. Smith. Phila., 1761. (College of Philadelphia, May 23, 1761.)

Exercise, An, etc. Thomas (?) Hopkinson. Phila., 1766. (College of Philadelphia, May 20, 1766.)

Exile's Lament, The. Alexander H. Everett. Boston, 1845. Imitated from Virgil.

Expelled Collegian, The. C. P. Clinch. (Park, May 24, 1822.)

Extremes. J. Austin Sperry. (Broadway Theatre, Feb. 25, 1850.)

Fact, The. Andrew Broughton. 1821.

Fair Americans, The. Mary [Clarke] Carr. Phila., 1815.

Fairy Family, The; or, The Three Wishes. William Barrymore. (Tremont Theatre, Boston, Jan. 3, 1842.)

Fairy Star, The. Dion Boucicault. (Broadway, N. Y., Nov. 6, 1854.)

Fallen Angel, A. Dion Boucicault. American title of *Victor and Hortense.* MS. dated 1854, in Fitzhugh Greene Coll.

Fall of Algiers, The. J. H. Payne. London, 1825. (Drury Lane, London, Jan. 19, 1825; Philadelphia, 1826.)

Fall of British Tyranny, The; or, American Liberty Triumphant. John Leacock (?). Phila., 1776.

Fall of Iturbide; or, Mexico Delivered. H. K. Strong. Pittsfield, 1823.

Fall of Kesichack, The. General Harlan. (Chestnut, May 8, 1845.)

Fall of San Antonio; or, Texas Victorious. N. H. Bannister. (American Theatre, New Orleans, Jan. 1, 1836.)

Fall of the Alamo, The. Anon. (German Theatre, New Orleans, Jan. 16, 1840.)

Fall of the Alamo; or, Texas and her Oppressors. Anon. (Arch, May 26, 1836.)

Fall of York, The, and the Death of General Pike. J. Hutton. (Olympic Theatre, Phila., Nov. 17, 1813?)

False and True. John Brougham. Dram. of Cobb's story, *Orion the Goldbeater.* (Bowery, Nov. 29, 1856.)

False Pretences; or, Both Sides of Good Society. Cornelius Mathews. N. Y., 1856. (Burton's Theatre, N. Y., Dec. 3, 1855.)

False Shame; or, The American Orphan in Germany. Wm. Dunlap. MS. in Brown Univ. *A. L. P.*, 1940. (Park, Dec. 11, 1799.)

Family Ties. J. M. Field and J. S. Robb. (Park, June 19, 1846.)

Fanatick, The. R. M. Bird. MS. fragment in Univ. of Pennsylvania. *A. L. P.*, 1941.

Farm House, The; or, The Female Duellists. Royall Tyler. (Federal St. Theatre (?), Boston, May 6, 1796.) See p. 72, note.

Fascination. J. H. Durivage. (St. Charles Theatre, N. Orleans, Jan. 26, 1849.)

Fashionable Follies. J. Hutton. Phila., 1815.

Fashion and Famine. C. W. Taylor. Dram. of novel by Ann S. Stephens. (National Theatre, N. Y., Sept. 11, 1854.)

Fashion; or, How to Write a Comedy. W. E. Burton. (Arch, April 22, 1845.)

Fashion; or, Life in New York. Anna C. O. Mowatt (Ritchie). London, 1850. (Park, March 24, 1845.)

Fashions and Follies of Washington Life. H. C. Preuss. Washington, 1857.

Fast Folks; or, Early Days of California. J. A. Nunes. N. Y., 1858. (American Theatre, San Francisco, July 1, 1858.)

Fast Young Men of New York and Brooklyn. C. W. Taylor. (National Theatre, N. Y., Aug. 3, 1857.)

Fatal Deception, The; or, The Progress of Guilt. See *Leicester.*

A LIST OF AMERICAN PLAYS

Fatal Error, The. A. W. Leland. Pittsfield, 1807. (Williams College, March 25, 1827.)

Fatal Prophecies; or, The Smuggler's Daughter. H. J. Conway. (Walnut, Dec. 5, 1835.)

Fate; or, The Prophecy. Oliver B. Bunce. N. Y., 1856.

Father and Daughter. Anon. Prob. Dram. of Mrs. Opie's novel. (Caldwell's New Theatre, Mobile, Feb. 9, 1841.)

Father of an Only Child, The. Phila., 1806. See *The Father.*

Father Outwitted, The. Anon. Phila., 1811.

Father, The; or, American Shandy-ism. Wm. Dunlap. N. Y., 1789. (John St., Sept. 7, 1789.)

Fauntleroy; or, The Fatal Forgery. John A. Stone. (Charleston Theatre, April 4, 1825.)

Fayette in Prison; or, Misfortunes of the Great. [Samuel Elliot (?).] Worcester, 1800.

Feast of Tabernacles, The. Henry Ware. Cambridge, 1837.

Federalism Triumphant in the Steady Habits of Connecticut Alone; or, The Turnpike Road to a Fortune. Leonard Chester. N. p., 1802.

Female Enthusiast, The. Sarah Pogson (?). Charleston, 1807.

Female Forty Thieves, The. Anon. (National Theatre, N. Y., Oct. 8, 1849.)

Female Patriot, The; or, Nature's Rights. S. H. Rowson. (Chestnut, June 19, 1795.)

Female Patriotism; or, The Death of Joan of Arc. J. D. Burk. N. Y., 1798. (Park, April 13, 1798.)

Female Privateer, The; or, The Pine Tree Flag of 1773. James Pilgrim. (National Theatre, N. Y., Jan. 7, 1856.)

Female Spy, The. J. B. Phillips. (Bowery, Jan. 8, 1828.)

Festival of Peace, The. Anon. (Park, Feb. 20, 1815.)

Fiammina. Matilda Heron. Adap. of *La Fiammina*, by Mario Uchard. (Wallack's Theatre, N. Y., Sept. 7, 1857.)

Fifteen Years of a Drunkard's Life. Anon. (St. Louis Theatre, Oct. 17, 1838. Chatham Theatre, N. Y., May 26, 1841.)

Fifteen Years of a Fireman's Life. Anon. (Franklin Theatre, N. Y., Jan. 18, 1841.)

Fin MacCool. · Dion Boucicault. MS., Prompt Copy in Fitzhugh Greene Coll. (Hollis St. Theatre, Boston, Feb. 3, 1887.)

Fireman, The. S. D. Johnson. N. Y., [1856]. (National Theatre, Boston, 1849.)

Fireman's Bride, The; or, The Chestnut Street Heiress. Anon. (Arch, Dec. 27, 1852.)

Fireman's Daughter. Anon. (Olympic Theatre, N. Y., August 24, 1846.)

Fire Warrior, The. J. S. Jones. (Warren Theatre, Boston, March 31, 1834.)

Fireman's Frolic, The. Anon. (Arch, June 12, 1831.)

First Fleet and the First Flag, The; or, Our Navy in '76. Anon. (Arch, Oct. 18, 1841.)

First Impressions. Lester Wallack. (Wallack's Theatre, Sept. 17, 1856.)

First of May in New York, The; or, Double or Quit. C. P. Clinch. (Park, March 26, 1830.)

Fiscal Agent, The. Park Benjamin. (Park, Feb. 28, 1842.)

Flash in the Pan, A. Wm. Milns. (Park, April 20, 1798.)

Florine; or, The Chateau D'Auray. Anon. (Boston Museum, Oct. 29, 1845.)

Flying Dutchman, The. Wm. Dunlap. (Bowery, May 25, 1827.)

Fontainville Abbey. Wm. Dunlap. In *Collected Works*, Phila., 1806. (John St., Feb. 16, 1795.)

Forbidden Fruit. Dion Boucicault. Adap. of *Le Procès Veauradieux* and *Les Dominos Roses* by Delacour and Hennequin and *Le Premier Coup de Canif,* by Anicet-Bourgeois and Brisebarre. Privately printed, N. Y., 1876. *A. L. P.*, 1940. (Wallack's Theatre, Oct. 3, 1876; Adelphi Theatre, London, July 3, 1880.)

Force of Calumny, The. Wm. Dunlap. (Park, Feb. 5, 1800.)

Foreign and Native. J. M. Field. (St. Charles Theatre, N. Orleans, Jan. 14, 1846.)

Forest Heart, The. Norman H. Brizee. Buffalo, 1855.

Forest of Rosenwald, The; or, The Travellers Benighted. J. Stokes. N. Y., 1821. (Park, April 26, 1820.)

Forest Princess, The; or, Two Centuries Ago. Charlotte Barnes Conner. In *Plays, Prose and Poetry*, Phila., 1848. (Liverpool, Oct. 26, 1844; Arch, Feb. 16, 1848.)

Forest Rose, The; or, American Farmers. Samuel Woodworth. N. Y., 1825. (Chatham Garden Theatre, N. Y., Oct. 7, 1825.)

Forgers, The. J. B. White. In *Southern Literary Journal*, Vol. I, 1837, Nos. 2, 3, 4, 5, 6. Reprinted [N. Y.], 1899. (Charleston Theatre, 1825.)

Formosa. Dion Boucicault. (Boston Theatre, Oct. 18, 1869.)

Fort la Mine; or, The Early Days of Zebulon Pike. S. S. Steele.

Fortress of Sorrento, The. M. M. Noah. N. Y., 1808. (Thespian Society, Union Hotel, N. Y., Oct. 22, 1816.)

Fortunes of Nigel, The. Anon. (Park, June 30, 1823.)

Fortunes of War. Lester Wallack. (Burton's Lyceum, May 14, 1851.)

Forty and Twenty. Wm. Dunlap. See p. 108, note.

Foscari; or The Venetian Exile. J. B. White. Charleston, 1806. (Charleston Theatre, Jan. 10, 1806.)

Foundling of the Sea, The. Samuel Woodworth. (Park, May 14, 1833.)

Foundling, The; or, Yankee Fidelity. R. C. McLellan. Phila., 1839. (Chestnut, March 31, 1840.)

Four Musketeers, The, or, " n Years After. Lester Wallack. (Bowery, Dec. 24, 1849.)

Fox Chase, The. Charles Breck. N. Y., 1808. (Chestnut, April 9, 1806.)

Fox Hunt, The; or, Don Quixote the Second. Dion Boucicault. Ms., Lord Chamberlain's office, London, as *The Fox Chase.* (Burton's Theatre, N. Y., Nov. 23, 1853.)

Francesca da Rimini. G. H. Boker. In *Plays and Poems*, Boston, 1856. (Broadway, Sept. 26, 1855.)

Franklin. John Brougham. N. Y., [1856]. (Chestnut, Jan. 17, 1846.)

Frank McLaughlin. Charles Walcot. (Olympic Theatre, N. Y., Dec. 19, 1849.)

Fraternal Discord. Wm. Dunlap. N. Y., 1809. (Park, Oct. 24, 1800.)

Freaks of Columbia, The; or, The Removal of the Seat of Government. "Timothy Taste." Wash., 1808.

Free Cuba. Dion Boucicault and J. J. O'Kelly. See p. 387, note.

Freedom's Last Martyr. W. M. Leman. (Walnut, July 4, 1845.)

Freedom Suit. Anon. (Portland Theatre, Sept. 26, 1849.)

Freemen in Arms. Anon. (Park, July 5, 1813.)

French Revolution, The. Anon. New Bedford, Mass., 1790. (Dartmouth College, 1790.)

Fricandeau; or, The Coronet and the Cook. J. H. Payne (?). MS., Lord Chamberlain's office, London. (Haymarket, London, Aug. 9, 1831.)

Fridolin; or, The Message to the Forge. J. S. Jones. (National Theatre, Boston, March 19, 1838.)

Frontier Maid, The. M. M. Noah. (Chestnut, Feb. 17, 1840.)

Frontier Settlement, The: Scenes in the West. Alonzo Delano (Old Block). N. Y., 1846.

Gabrielle; or, The Fatal Hazard. J. M. Field. Prob. Adap. of *Mademoiselle de Belle Isle* by Alexander Dumas, père. (Walnut, Sept. 16, 1843.)

G-A-G. J. M. Field. (St. Charles Theatre, New Orleans, Feb. 20, 1841.)

Gambler, The; or, Lost and Won. C. H. Saunders. (Boston Museum, Nov. 4, 1844.)

Gamblers of the Mississippi, The. Anon. (National Amphitheatre, Phila., May, 1850.)

Game Cock of the Wilderness, The. L. Reade. (Tremont Theatre, Sept. 1, 1840.)

Game of Life, The. John Brougham. N. Y., [1856]. (Wallack's Theatre, N. Y., Dec. 12, 1853.)

Game of Love, The. John Brougham. N. Y., [1855]. (Wallack's Theatre, N. Y., Sept. 12, 1855.)

Gammon and Galvinism. T. D. English. (National Theatre, Phila., April 25, 1844.)

Gaspardo the Gondolier. J. Butler. Adap. of *Gaspardo le Pêcheur* by Bouchardy. (Chestnut, March 23, 1839.)

Gasperoni, the Roman Bandit. John Kerr. (Walnut, bet. April 15-25, 1830.)

Gaulantus. N. H. Bannister. Cincinnati, 1836. (American Theatre, New Orleans, March 31, 1836.)

General George Washington; or, The Traitor Foiled. Anon. (Walnut, July 4, 1850.)

Genoese, The. See *Bride of Genoa.*

Gentleman and the Upstart, The. E. [W.?] Ranger. (Caldwell's New Theatre, Mobile, Feb. 8, 1841.)

Gentleman from Ireland, The. Fitz James O'Brien. N. Y., [1858]. (Wallack's Theatre, N. Y., Dec. 11, 1854.)

Gentleman in Black, The. William Barrymore. (Tremont Theatre, Boston, March 29, 1839.)

Gentleman of Lyons, The; or, The Marriage Contract. N. H. Bannister. N. Y., 1838. (Walnut, Aug. 16, 1838.)

Georgia Spec, The; or, Land in the Moon. Royall Tyler. (Haymarket Theatre, Boston, Oct. 30, 1797; John St., Dec. 20, 1797.)

Geraldine; or, Love's Victory. Mrs. Sidney F. Bateman. (Wallack's Theatre, N. Y., Aug. 22, 1859.)

Giannone. R. M. Bird. MS. (incomplete) in Univ. of Pennsylvania.

Giordano; or, The Conspiracy. James Lawson. N. Y., 1832. (Park, Nov. 13, 1828.)

Gladiator, The. R. M. Bird. In C. E. Foust, *Life and Dramatic Works of Robert Montgomery Bird*, N. Y., 1919. (Park, Sept. 26, 1831; Drury Lane, London, Oct. 17, 1836.)

Glance at New York, A. B. A. Baker. N. Y., n. d. (Olympic Theatre, N. Y., Feb. 15, 1848.)

Glance at Philadelphia, A. W. E. Burton. (Arch, April 25, 1848.)

A LIST OF AMERICAN PLAYS

Glaucus. G. H. Boker. MS. dated 1886. *A. L. P.*, 1940.

Glorious Eighth of January, The. Anon. (Walnut, Jan. 8, 1829.)

Glory of Columbia—Her Yeomanry, The. Wm. Dunlap. N. Y., 1817; 1803 incomplete. (Park, July 4, 1803.)

Gold Bug, The; or, The Pirate's Treasure. S. S. Steele. Dram. of Poe's story. (Walnut, Aug. 8, 1843.)

Gold Diggers of 1750; or, The Ancient Miners of California. (Jenny Lind Theatre, San Francisco, January, 1851.)

Golden Age, The; or, The Poet's Vision. Anon. (American Theatre, San Francisco, 1859.)

Golden Calf, The; or, Marriage à la Mode. Mrs. Sidney F. Bateman. St. Louis, 1857. (Wood's Theatre, St. Louis, Aug. 31, 1857.)

Golden Eagle, The; or, The Privateer of 1776. J. B. Howe. N. Y., [1857]. (Bowery, April 6, 1857.)

Golden Legend, The. H. W. Longfellow. Boston, 1851.

Gold Fever, The. Anon. (Olympic Theatre, N. Y., Dec. 21, 1849.)

Gone to Texas. Anon. (Park, Oct. 7, 1844.)

Good Fellow, A. C. M. Walcot. N. Y., [1856]. (Wallack's Theatre, N. Y., 1854.)

Good Neighbor, The. Wm. Dunlap. N. Y., 1814. (Park, Feb. 28, 1803.)

Gordian Knot, The; or, Causes and Effects. Isaac Harby. Charleston, 1810. (Charleston Theatre, May 3, 1810.)

Gotham, or Fast Life Nowadays. Anon. (Bowery, April 25, 1859.)

Grand Canal, The. M. M. Noah. Cf. Rees.

Grandpapa. J. H. Payne. (Drury Lane, London, May 25, 1825.)

Great Attraction, The. O. E. Durwage. (Franklin Theatre, N. Y., Aug. 17, 1840.)

Great Tragic Revival, The. John Brougham. N. Y., [1858]. (Burton's Theatre, N. Y., March 17, 1858.)

Grecian Captive, The; or, The Fall of Athens. M. M. Noah. N. Y., 1822. (Park, June 17, 1822.)

Grecian Gossips, The. Alexander H. Everett. Imitated from Theocritus. Boston, 1845.

Grecian Queen, The. S. S. Steele. Adap. Thomson's *Agamemnon.* (National Theatre, Phila., Feb. 26, 1844.)

Greece and Liberty. Anon. Prompt Copy, Brown Univ. (Park, Jan. 20, 1824.)

Green Mountain Boy, The. J. S. Jones. N. Y., [1860]. (Chestnut, Feb. 25, 1833.)

Green Mountain Boys. Anon. (Park, Feb. 22, 1822.)

Greyslaer. Anon. Dram. Hoffman's novel. (Bowery, Aug. 3, 1840.)

A LIST OF AMERICAN PLAYS

Grimaldi; or, Scenes in the Life of an Actress. Dion Boucicault. Adap.
(in part) of *La Vie d'une Comédienne*, by Anicet-Bourgeois and
Théodore Barrière. New York, 1856. (National Theatre, Cincinnati, Sept. 24, 1855; later as *Violet*, National Theatre, Phila.,
May 2, 1856.)

Griselda; or, The Patient Woman. J. M. Field. Adap. from the German
of Halm via Auguste Waldauer. (Chestnut, Oct. 23, 1854.)

Grub, Mudge and Co. Lucas Hirst. Philadelphia, 1853. (Chestnut,
April 6, 1850.)

Group, The. Mercy Warren. Boston, 1775.

Gulzara, the Persian Slave. Anna C. O. Mowatt (Ritchie). Adap.
Gulnare; ou, L'esclave persane. In *The New World*, 1840. (By
amateurs, Flatbush, L. I.)

Gun-Maker of Moscow, The. John Brougham. Dram. of Sylvanus
Cobb's novel. London and N. Y., n. d. (Bowery, Jan. 19, 1857.)

Gunsmith of Orleans, The. G. Sheridan. (Olympic Theatre, N. Y.,
March 7, 1845.)

Guy Rivers; or, The Gold Hunter. Anon. Dram. of Simms' novel.
(Bowery, Sept. 21, 1834.)

Hadad. J. A. Hillhouse. N. Y., 1825.

Hamlet. James Rush, M. D. Phila., 1834.

Hamlet Travestie. John Brougham. (Chatham, N. Y., Aug. 4, 1847.)

Handy Andy. T. D. English. (National Theatre, Phila., Jan. 1, 1844.)

Happy Results; or, The Hermit of the Rock. J. P. Adams. (Portland
Theatre, Dec. 20, 1847.)

Harcanlack. N. H. Bannister. (American Theatre, New Orleans,
April 9, 1836.)

Hard Times in New Orleans; or, The Gentleman in Black. G. W. Harby.
(American Theatre, New Orleans, April 17, 1837.)

Harlequin and the Ocean Nymph. Anon. (Walnut, July 31, 1843.)

*Harlequin Blue Beard, The Great Bashaw; or, The Good Fairy Trium-
phant over the Demon of Discord.* Anon. N. Y., n. d.

Harlequin Panattatah; or, The Genii of the Algonquins. Anon. (Park,
Jan. 4, 1809.)

Harold; or, The Merchant of Calais. J. A. J. Neafie. (St. Charles
Theatre, N. Orleans, Dec., 1851.)

Harry Burnham; or, The Young Continental. James Pilgrim. (National Theatre, N. Y., March 10, 1851.)

Haunted Man and the Ghost's Bargain, The. John Brougham. Adap.
of Dickens' novel. (Burton's Chambers Street Theatre, N. Y.,
Jan. 10, 1849.)

Haunted Man, The. Charles Walcot [?]. (Olympic, N. Y., Jan. 15, 1849.)

Haunted Man, The. Anon. (Bowery, Jan. 29, 1849.)

Hawks of Hawk Hollow, The. Dram. of novel by R. M. Bird. (Union Hall, Portland, Maine, July 1, 1836.)

Hawks of Hawk Hollow, The. Dram. of Bird's novel. (Arch, Aug. 17, 1843.)

Hawks of Hawk Hollow, The. J. S. Jones. Dram. of novel by R. M. Bird. (Warren Theatre, Boston, March 16, 1836.)

Headsman, The. James Rees. Dram. of Cooper's *Headsman.* (American Theatre, New Orleans, May 17, 1834.)

Heart of the World, The; or, Life Struggles in a Great City. Harry Watkins. (National Theatre, N. Y., June 17, 1851.)

Heaven on Earth; or, The New Lights of Harmony. "Peter Puffem." Phila., 1825.

Helos, the Helot; or, the Messinian Slave. G. L. Aiken. Anon. (Arch, March 24, 1852.)

Henriette. Adapted from the French. E. G. P. Wilkins. (Wallack's Theatre, March 27, 1861.)

Heretic, The. R. T. Conrad. (Arch, Phila., April 13, 1863.)

Herne the Hunter. N. B. Clarke. Adap. of *Windsor Castle* by Harrison Ainsworth. (Bowery, Jan. 28, 1856.)

Heroes of the Lake; or, a Tribute to the Brave. Anon. (Park, Oct. 20, 1813.)

Heroes of the Lakes; or, The Glorious Tenth of September. Anon. (Federal St. Theatre, Boston, Oct. 4, 1813.)

Heroine of the Highlands, The. S. T. Mitchell. (Richmond Theatre, Nov. 12, 1828.)

Hero of Two Wars, The. "W." In *Truth's Advocate and Monthly Anti-Jackson Expositor*, Cincinnati, March-Oct., 1828.

He Stoops to Conquer; or, The Virgin Triumphant. John Minshull. N. Y., 1804.

Hiawatha; or, Ardent Spirits and Laughing Water. Charles M. Walcot. N. Y., 1856. (Wallack's Theatre, N. Y., Dec. 25, 1856.)

Hidden Hand, The. Robert Jones. Boston, n. d. Dram. of novel of same title by E. D. E. N. Southworth. (National Theatre, N. Y., May 9, 1859.)

Highland Treason, The. E. G. Holland. Boston, 1852.

High Life in Philadelphia. Anon. (Chestnut, April 24, 1850.)

Hippolytus. Julia Ward Howe. *A. L. P.*, 1941. (Tremont Theatre, Boston, March 24, 1911.)

Hiram Hireout; or, Followed by Fortune. H. J. Conway. N. Y., [1852]. (Chicago Theatre, 1851.)

History of the Falcos, The. Noah Bisbee. Walpole, N. H., 1808.

Hoboken. Charles Walcot. Dram. of *Hoboken* by T. S. Fay. (Bowery, Aug. 3, 1846.)

Home. John Brougham. (Niblo's Garden, N. Y., May 13, 1850.)

Home in the West. Colonel Bradbury. (Howard Athenaeum, Boston, Nov. 29, 1847.)

Hoosier at the Circus, The. ? Carrol. (Arch, Feb. 9, 1846.)

Hoosier, The; or, The Yankee Outwitted. By "a gentleman of this city." (St. Louis, Feb. 6, 1835.)

Horatii and the Curiatii, The; or, The Fight of the Brothers. W. E. Burton [in part]. MS. Harvard. (Arch, March 21, 1848.)

Horse of the Prairie. Anon. (Arch, May 9, 1849.)

Horse Shoe Robinson. Charles Dance. (National Theatre, N. Y., Nov. 23, 1836.)

Horse Shoe Robinson; or, The Battle of King's Mountain. C. W. Tayleure. N. Y., n. d. (Holliday St. Theatre, Balt., April, 1856.)

Hot Corn; or, Little Katy. C. W. Taylor. Adap. of Solon Robinson's story. (National Theatre, N. Y., Dec. 5, 1853.)

How to Try a Lover. J. N. Barker. N. Y., 1817. (Arch, March 26, 1836, as *The Court of Love.*)

Hue and Cry, The. Altered from *Yankee Land,* q. v.

Hunter of the Far West. J. S. Jones. (National Theatre, Boston, Nov. 14, 1836.)

Hypocrite Unmasked, The. W. Winstanley. New York, 1801.

Ice Queen, The. J. S. Jones. (Warren Theatre, Boston, June 4, 1834.)

Ida Stephanoff. H. J. Conway. (Walnut, Jan. 1, 1836.)

I Dine with my Mother. Charles McLachlan. New York, n. d., c. 1856.

Immola. In *Two Tragedies* by "an American." New York, 1835.

In and Out of Place. S. D. Johnson. N. Y., n. d. (Chestnut, March 15, 1850.)

Independence; or, Which Do You Like Best, the Peer or the Farmer? Wm. Ioor. Charleston, 1805. (Charleston Theatre, March 30, 1805.)

Indian Girl, The. Anon. (National Theatre, N. Y. Oct. 7, 1838.)

Indian Girl, The; or, A Tale of the Revolution. Anon. (Chatham Theatre, N. Y., July 11, 1844.)

Indian Horde, The; or, The Tiger of War. J. S. Jones. (Tremont Theatre, Boston, April 2, 1840.)

Indian Mother, The. J. S. Jones. (Warren Theatre, Boston, Oct. 10, 1832.)

Indian Princess, The; or, La Belle Sauvage. J. N. Barker. Phila., 1808. (Chestnut, April 6, 1808.)

Indian Prophecy, The. G. W. P. Custis. Georgetown, 1828. (Chestnut, July 4, 1827.)

Indian Wife, The. Anon. (Park, June 4, 1830.) Cf. *Montgomery.*

Indians in England, The; or, Nabob of Mysore. Wm. Dunlap. (Park, June 14, 1799.)

Infernal Machine, The; or, The Death of Mortier. J. S. Jones. (Warren Theatre, Boston, Oct. 26, 1835.)

Infidel, The. B. H. Brewster. Dram. of novel by R. M. Bird. (Walnut, Oct. 24, 1835.)

Infidelity. N. H. Bannister. (St. Charles Theatre, New Orleans, Nov. 19, 1836.)

Innkeeper of Abbeville, The. J. D. Burk. (Walnut, July 18, 1840.)

Inquisitive Yankee, The. Anon. (Park, Dec. 4, 1832.)

Intemperate, The; or, A Sister's Love. W. E. Burton. (Arch, March 14, 1835.) Later as *Emigration; or, The Progress of an Intemperate.* (Walnut, April 11, 1840.)

Intolerants, The. Anon. Phila., 1827.

Invisible Witness, The. J. B. Dumont. (Park, May 26, 1823.)

Ireland and America. James Pilgrim. N. Y., n. d. (Broadway, June 28, 1852.)

Ireland as It Is. J. A. Amherst. N. Y., n. d. (Bowery, Aug. 18, 1851.)

Ireland Redeemed; or, The Devoted Princess. George Pepper. (Lafayette Theatre, N. Y., July 1, 1828.)

Ireland's Golden Age. Harry Seymour. (Bowery, Sept. 10, 1858.)

Irish American, The; or, The Lost Keepsake. Anon. (Arch, March 4, 1853.)

Irish Assurance and Yankee Modesty. Anon. N. Y., n. d. (Chestnut, May 4, 1853.)

Irish Emigrant, The. John Brougham. London, n. d. See *Temptation.*

Irish Fortune Hunter, The. John Brougham. (Broadway, Sept. 2, 1850.)

Irish Sibyl and the Rebel Chief. Anon. (Chestnut, Nov. 4, 1854.)

Irish Yankee, The; or, The Birthday of Freedom. John Brougham. N. Y., n. d. (St. Charles Theatre, New Orleans, 1843-46.) Played July 4, 1855 at Broadway as *Battle of Bunker Hill.* See also *Birthday of Freedom.*

Irma; or, The Prediction. J. H. Kennicott. N. Y., 1830. (American Theatre, New Orleans, April 6, 1830.)

Isidora; or, The Three Dukes. R. M. Bird. MS. in Univ. of Pennsylvania.

Island of Barrataria, The. Royall Tyler. *A. L. P.*, 1941. See Bib., Chap. 3.

Is She a Brigand? R. P. Smith. In *Gentleman's Vade Mecum*, No. 2, Jan. 10, 1835; also Phila., 1835. (Arch, Nov. 1, 1833.)

Is the Philadelphian Dead, or Is He Alive and Merry? Anon. (Walnut, Jan. 4, 1840.)

Italian Bride, The. S. Y. Levy (?). Savannah, 1856. (Wallack's Theatre, N. Y., July 2, 1857, as *Venetia; or The Italian Bride*.)

Italian Bride, The. J. H. Payne. *A. L. P.*, 1940.

Italian Father, The. Wm. Dunlap. N. Y., 1810. (Park, April 15, 1799.)

Ivan; or, The Boor of Moscow. William Barrymore. Dram. of Mrs. J. R. Planché's *Sledge Driver* (Act II new). (Lion Theatre, Boston, April 5, 1836.)

I've Eaten my Friend. Anon. (Walnut, Feb. 28, 1852.)

Jack Cade, the Captain of the Commons. R. T. Conrad. London, n. d. (Walnut, Dec. 9, 1835.) Cf. *Aylmere*.

Jack Marlin; or, The Adventures of a Yankee Sailor. Anon. Prompt Copy, Harvard. (Eagle Theatre, Boston, Sept. 19, 1842.)

Jack Sheppard; or, The Life of a Robber. J. B. Phillips. Holograph MS., Harvard. (Bowery, Dec. 30, 1839.)

Jack's the Lad. C. Ferrars. (Walnut, May 18, 1839.)

Jacob Leisler; or, New York in 1690. Cornelius Mathews. (Arch, April 13, 1848.)

Jakey's Marriage. Anon. (Arch, Oct. 28, 1850.)

Jakey's Visit to California. W. Chapman. (Arch, March 14, 1849.)

Jakey's Visit to his Aunts. (Chestnut, Aug. 28, 1849.)

Jane Eyre; or, The Secret of Thornfield Manor House. John Brougham. N. Y., 1856. (Victoria Theatre, London, Jan. 27, 1848; Bowery, March 26, 1849.)

Janet Pride. Dion Boucicault. Adap. (in part) of *Marie-Jeanne*, by Dennery and Mallian. MS. in Lord Chamberlain's office and in Fitzhugh Greene Coll. (Metropolitan Theatre, Buffalo, Aug. 11, 1854; Adelphi Theatre, London, Feb. 5, 1855.)

Jeanie Deans; or, The Heart of Midlothian. Dion Boucicault. MS. Fitzhugh Greene Coll. (Laura Keene's Theatre, N. Y., Jan. 9, 1860.)

Jefferson and Liberty. J. H. Nichols. N. p., 1801.

Jenny Lind in America. MS., Brown Univ. Anon. (National Theatre, N. Y., Sept. 2, 1850.)

A LIST OF AMERICAN PLAYS

Jennie Lind in Charleston. (Charleston Theatre, Apr. 23, 1851.)

Jenny Lind in Philadelphia. "By a Rejected Member of the Dramatic Authors' Society, Philadelphia." Prompt Copy, Harvard. (Arch, April 10, 1850.)

Jessie Brown; or, The Relief of Lucknow. Dion Boucicault. N. Y., [1858]. (Wallack's Theatre, N. Y., Feb. 22, 1858.)

Jesuit, The; a National Melodrama. T. W. Whitely. New York, 1850.

Jesuit's Colony, The; or, The Indian's Doom. "By a Gentleman of Philadelphia." (Walnut, Aug. 8, 1838.)

Jilt, The. Dion Boucicault. N. Y. [Copy. 1909]. (California Theatre, San Francisco, May 18, 1885.)

Joan of Arc. See *Female Patriotism.*

Job and his Children. J. M. Field. *A. L. P.*, 1941. (St. Louis Theatre, Aug 25, 1852.)

Jonah; or, A Trip to Whales. J. S. Jones. (Bowery, Aug. 23, 1841.)

Jonathan in England. J. H. Hackett (?). Boston, [1828]. (English Opera House, Sept. 3, 1824; Park, Dec. 3, 1828.)

Jonathan Postfree; or, The Honest Yankee. L. Beach. N. Y., 1807.

Joseph and His Brethren. Royall Tyler. *A. L. P.*, 1941. See Bib., chap. 3.

Judgment, The: A Vision. J. A. Hillhouse. N. Y., 1821.

Judgment of Solomon, The. Royall Tyler. *A. L. P.*, 1941. See Bib., chap. 3.

Julia; or, The Wanderer. J. H. Payne. N. Y., 1806. (Park, Feb. 7, 1806.)

Julian. J. W. Simmons. N. p., n. d.

Julian the Apostate. C. J. Ingersoll. Phila., 1831.

Julietta Gordini; or, The Miser's Daughter. Isaac C. Pray. N. Y., 1839. (Chestnut, March 20, 1839.)

Jumbo-Jum! T. D. Rice? New York, n. d. (Franklin Theatre, N. Y., Sept. 17, 1838.) "Third time in America."

Jupiter Jealous; or, Life in the Clouds. John Brougham. Revision of *Life in the Clouds.* (English Opera House, July 23, 1840; Mitchell's Olympic Theatre, N. Y., Oct. 3, 1842.)

Kairrissah. L. H. Medina. (Bowery, Sept. 11, 1834.)

Karmel the Scout; or, The Rebel of the Jerseys. John Brougham, with J. B. Howe. Dram. of Sylvanus Cobb's novel. (Bowery, March 2, 1857.)

Kaspar Hauser. H. J. Finn. (Park, Nov. 27, 1835.)

Kasran; or, The Crusaders. S. S. Steele. (Franklin Theatre, N. Y., Aug. 17, 1840.)

Kassimbar. S. S. Steele. (Front St. Theatre, Balt., 1840.)

Kate Aylesford; or, The Refugees. Dram. by C. W. Taylor from Charles J. Peterson's novel of the same name. (National Theatre, N. Y., May 14, 1854.)

Kate Woodhull. C. E. Lester. (Broadway, Feb. 21, 1849.)

Kathleen O'Neill; or, A Picture of Feudal Times in Ireland. George Pepper. Phila., 1832. (Lafayette Theatre, N. Y., May 10, 1827.)

Katty O'Sheal. James Pilgrim. N. Y., n. d. (St. Louis Theatre, 1854.)

Kenneth; or, The Weird Woman of the Glen. N. B. Clarke. Dram. of G. W. M. Reynolds' novel. (National Theatre, N. Y., July 26, 1852.)

Kentuckian, The; or, A Trip to New York. Revision of *The Lion of the West.*

Kentucky Heiress, The. N. P. Willis. (Park, Nov. 29, 1837.)

Kingdom of Woman. By "a gentleman of N. Orleans." (St. Charles Theatre, N. Orleans, Apr. 10, 1845.)

King of Coney Island. T. D. English. MS. (Olympic Theatre, N. Y., July 30, 1857.)

King's Bridge Cottage. Samuel Woodworth (?). N. Y., 1826. (Richmond Hill Theatre, N. Y., Feb. 22, 1833.)

Kit Carson, the Hero of the Prairie. W. R. Derr. (Bowery, Feb. 20, 1850.)

Knave of Hearts, The. E. F. DeNyse. N. Y., 1858.

Knight of Guadalquiver, The. Wm. Dunlap. (Park, Dec. 5, 1800.)

Knight of the Golden Fleece, The. J. A. Stone. (Park, Sept. 10, 1834.)

Knight of the Lion Heart, The; or, Golden Days of Chivalry. J. Foster. (Chestnut, May 1, 1850.)

Knight's Adventure, The. See *The Man of Fortitude.*

Königsmark. G. H. Boker. Phila., 1869.

Konrad of Rheinfeldt; or, The Widowed Bride. F. S. Hill. (Warren Theatre, Feb. 10, 1834.)

Kosciusko; or, The Fall of Warsaw. Anon. In *The Soldier's Wreath and Other Poems.* Charleston, 1828.

Ladies of Castile, The. Mercy Warren. In *Poems, Dramatic and Miscellaneous,* Boston, 1790.

Lad of Spirit, The; or, The Fool of Fashion. R. Fawcett. (Park, April 27, 1798.)

Lady of Irons, The. Burlesque by a "gentleman of New Orleans." (American Theatre, New Orleans, March 25, 1842.)

Lady of the Bed-Chamber, The. W. J. Hoppin. N. Y., n. d. (Wallack's Theatre, N. Y., Nov. 4, 1858.)

Lady of the Lions, The. O. E. Durivage. N. Y., n. d. (Bowery, Oct. 20, 1842.)

La Fayette; or, The Castle of Olmutz. Samuel Woodworth. N. Y., 1824. (Park, Feb. 23, 1824.)

La Fayette; or, The Fortress of Olmutz. Walter Lee. Phila., 1824.

La Fiammina. W. W. Clapp, Jr. Boston, [1857]. (Boston Museum, Sept. 28, 1857.) See *Fiammina.*

La Fitte; or, The Pirate of the Gulf. Charlotte Barnes Conner. Alteration of Medina's *La Fitte.* (Caldwell's New Theatre, New Orleans, 1838.)

La Fitte; or, The Pirate's Home. L. H. Medina. (Bowery, Sept. 19, 1836.)

La Fitte. ? Percival. Alteration of preceding play. (Walnut, Oct. 28, 1836.)

La Fitte, the Pirate of the Gulf. James Rees. (American Theatre, New Orleans, April 3, 1837.)

Lamorah; or, The Indian Wife. "Miss Conway." (National Theatre, N. Y., Nov. 27, 1849.)

Lamorah; or, The Western Wild. Caroline Lee Hentz. (Caldwell's Theatre, New Orleans, Jan. 1, 1833.)

Lamplighter, The. Anon. Dram. of novel by M. S. Cummins. (Bowery, April 17, 1854.)

Lampoon. Epes Sargent. In *Songs of the Sea,* Boston, 1847.

Lancers, The. J. H. Payne. London, n. d. (Drury Lane, London, Dec. 19, 1827; Bowery, March 4, 1828.)

La Perouse. Wm. Dunlap. Adap. Kotzebue.

La Roque, the Regicide. John A. Stone. (Charleston Theatre, Feb. 22, 1828.)

Last Days of Pompeii, The. Charlotte Barnes Conner. Dram. of novel. (American Theatre, New Orleans, May 7, 1835.)

Last Days of Pompeii, The. William Barrymore. (Walnut, March 23, 1835.)

Last Days of Pompeii, The. L. H. Medina. N. Y., 1856. (Bowery, Feb. 9, 1835.)

Last Days of Pompeii, The. J. S. Jones. (Warren Theatre, Boston, Feb. 16, 1835.)

Last Dollar, in Four Quarters, The. J. S. Jones. (Boston Museum, Sept. 16, 1850.)

Last Duel in Spain, The. J. H. Payne. Autograph MS. in Harvard University Library. *A. L. P.,* 1940.

Last Man, The; or, The Cock of the Village. R. P. Smith. Adap. of *Le Coq de Village,* by Décour, Herbert, and T. Anne. MS. in Hist. Soc. of Penna. *A. L. P.,* 1941.

A LIST OF AMERICAN PLAYS

Last Man, The; or, The Miser of Etham. W. R. Blake. (Walnut, Sept. 10, 1839.)

Last of the Kings, The; or, The French Revolution of 1848. J. S. Jones. (Boston Museum, March 27, 1848.)

Last of the Mohicans, The. S. E. Glover. (Camp St. Theatre, New Orleans, March 19, 1831. First?)

Last of the Plantagenets, The. Caroline M. Keteltas. Dram. from romance of that name, by William Heseltine. N. Y., 1844.

Last of the Serpent Tribe, The. Anon. (French Theatre, New Orleans.)

Launch of Columbia, The. G. W. P. Custis. [Cf. Rees, 39.]

Led Astray. Dion Boucicault. N. Y., [1873]. (Union Sq. Theatre, N. Y., Dec. 8, 1873.)

Leicester. Wm. Dunlap. In *Collected Works*, Phila., 1806. (John St., April 24, 1794, as *The Fatal Deception.*)

Legend of the Chestnut St. Theatre, A. Anon. (Chestnut, Jan. 17, 1854.)

Lend Me Your Wife. Dion Boucicault and Sydney Rosenfeld. Adap. from *Prête-moi ta femme*, by Maurice des Vallières. Typewritten MS., Library of Congress. (Boston Museum, Aug. 25, 1890.)

Leoni; or, The Orphan of Venice. T. H. Chivers. MS., Harvard. Printed in *Georgia Citizen*, May 17–June 14, 1851. Macon, Ga.

Leonora. See *The World's Own.*

Leonor de Guzman. G. H. Boker. In *Plays and Poems*, Boston, 1856. (Walnut, Oct. 3, 1853.)

Lewis of Monte Blanco; or, The Transplanted Irishman. Wm. Dunlap. (Park, March 12, 1804.)

Liberty in Louisiana. James Workman. Charleston, 1804. (Charleston Theatre, April 4, 1804.)

Liberty Tree, The; or, Boston Boys in '76. J. S. Jones. (Warren Theatre, Boston, June 16, 1834; as *Boston Boys in '76*, Walnut, July 4, 1836.)

Life in Alabama. Anon. (Chestnut, Feb. 13, 1850.)

Life in Alabama. C. W. Taylor. Prompt copy, Brown Univ. (National Theatre, N. Y., June 19, 1850.)

Life in Brooklyn, Its Lights and Shades, Its Virtues and Vices. Anon. (National Theatre, N. Y., March 23, 1857.)

Life in China. J. M. Field. (New Orleans Theatre, April 2, 1844.)

Life in New Orleans. N. H. Bannister. (St. Charles, New Orleans, May 13, 1837.)

Life in New York. John Brougham. (Chatham, N. Y., Nov. 30, 1844.)

Life in New York; or, Firemen on Duty. Anon. (Bowery, Jan. 24, 1827.)

459

A LIST OF AMERICAN PLAYS

Life in New York; or, The Major's Crime. J. B. Phillips. (Bowery, April 24, 1834.)

Life in New York; or, Tom and Jerry on a Visit. John Brougham. N. Y. [1856]. (Bowery, August 18, 1856.) Revision of *Tom and Jerry in America.*

Life in Philadelphia. Anon. (Walnut, Sept. 11, 1833.)

Life in Philadelphia; or, The Unfortunate Author. N. H. Bannister. (Walnut, Jan. 15, 1838.)

Life in the Clouds; or, Olympus in an Uproar. John Brougham. Revision of *Jupiter Jealous,* q. v. (Chatham Theatre, N. Y., Aug. 2, 1847.)

Life in the West; or, Playing False. J. Austin Sperry. (Walnut, May 1, 1854.)

Life of the Mormons at Salt Lake. C. W. Taylor (?). (National Theatre, N. Y., April 5, 1858.)

Like Unto Like. G. H. Calvert. Boston, 1856. (? Laura Keene's Theatre, N. Y., May 4, 1857.)

Lillian, The Show Girl. W. Barrymore. (Walnut, Feb. 27, 1837.)

Limerick Boy, The. James Pilgrim. N. Y., n. d. (Chicago Theatre, 1848; Broadway, June 24, 1852.)

Linda the Segar Girl. Louisa Reeder. (Bowery, June 1, 1857.)

Lion of the East, The. Anon. (Walnut, May 15, 1835.)

Lion of the Sea, The; or, Our Infant Navy. S. S. Steele. (Front St. Theatre, Balt., Oct., 1840.)

Lion of the West, The. J. K. Paulding. (Park, April 25, 1831.)

Little Katy, the Hot Corn Girl. C. W. Taylor. (National Theatre, N. Y., Dec. 5, 1853.)

Live Woman in the Mines, A; or, Pike County Ahead. [A. Delano] "Old Block." N. Y., [1857].

Logan, the Last of the Race of Shikellemus. Joseph Doddridge. Buffalo Creek, Va., 1823.

Lola Montez in Bavaria. C. P. T. Ware. (Broadway, May 25, 1852.)

Lola Montez, or Catching a Governor. Anon. (Olympic Theatre, Phila., May 27, 1848.)

Lone Star, The; or, The Texan Bravo. Anon. (Arch, March 22, 1845.)

Lord Ivon and His Daughter. N. P. Willis. In *The New York Mirror,* XII (1835), 300-301.

Louis XI. Dion Boucicault. Adap. of *Louis XI* by Casimir Delavigne, from *Quentin Durward.* Charles Kean's MS. Prompt Copy, Corrected by Boucicault, Harvard. *A. L. P.,* 1941. (Princess Theatre, London, Jan. 13, 1855; Laura Keene's Theatre, N. Y., Sept. 7, 1858.)

A LIST OF AMERICAN PLAYS

Love and a Bunch. Frederic S. Hill. (American Theatre, New Orleans, May 13, 1837.)

Love and Friendship; or, Yankee Notions. A. B. Lindsley. N. Y., 1809. (Park, 1807-8, acc. to cast in play. Not in Odell.)

Love and Legislature. J. S. Wallace. (Pearl St. Theatre, Albany, 1832.)

Love and Murder. Anon. (Chestnut, Dec. 29, 1838.)

Love and Murder. John Brougham. N. Y. [1856]. (Olympic Theatre, N. Y., April 17, 1848.)

Love and Poetry; or, A Modern Genius. James McHenry. (Walnut, Dec. 5, 1829.)

Love in All Corners. Frank Dumont. Chicago, 1898. (Le Claire Hall, Davenport, Iowa, Sept. 25, 1858.)

Love in Humble Life. J. H. Payne. London, n. d. (Drury Lane, London, Feb. 14, 1822; Franklin Theatre, N. Y., July 25, 1837.)

Love in '76. Oliver B. Bunce. N. Y., [1857]. (Laura Keene's Theatre, N. Y., Feb. 28, 1857.)

Love of a Prince; or, The Court of Prussia. Charles Gayler. Adap. of *Le Sergent Frédéric* by Vanderburch and Dumanoir. N. Y., [1857]. (Laura Keene's Theatre, N. Y., April 13, 1857.)

Lovers' Vows. Wm. Dunlap. N. Y., 1814. (Park, March 11, 1799.)

Lovers' Vows. J. H. Payne. Balt., 1809. (Balt., 1809?; Chestnut, Sept. 16, 1811.)

Love's Disguises; or, The Daughter's Vow. M. M. Noah. (American Theatre, San Francisco, Feb. 1855.)

Love's Martyr. Mayne Reid. (Walnut, Oct. 23, 1848.)

Lucifer Matches; or, The Modern Mephistopheles. Henry Plunkett, Prompt Copy, Harvard. (Broadway, Nov. 2, 1855.)

Lucretia Borgia. F. Haynes and J. Rees. (New Orleans Theatre, May 4, 1836.)

Lucy Sampson. David Rittenhouse. Phila., 1789.

Luprecaun, The; or, The Fairy Shoemaker. James Rees. MS. Harvard, dated Jan. 8, 1846. (Chestnut, May 3, 1850.)

Mabel, the Child of the Battle Field. James Pilgrim. (National Theatre, N. Y., Oct. 13, 1851.)

Macarthy, The; or, The Peep of Day. Laura Keene. (Laura Keene's Theatre, N. Y., Feb. 22, 1862.)

Macbeth Travestie. W. K. Northall. New York, 1847. (Olympic Theatre, New York, Oct. 16, 1843.)

Madame Anna Bishop in the Provinces. Anon. (Walnut, Jan. 1, 1853.)

Madame du Barry. J. H. Payne (?). (Haymarket, London, Aug. 2, 1831.)

461

Mad Anthony; or, The Pennsylvania Line. Anon. (Arch, Dec. 21, 1844.)

Madelaine, the Belle of the Faubourg. Mrs. Virginia Cunningham. Boston, 1856. (Broadway, Feb. 22, 1850.)

Mademoiselle de Belle Isle. J. M. Field. Adap. from Dumas. (St. Charles Theatre, New Orleans, May 6, 1840; as *Gabrielle; or The Fatal Hazard,* Walnut, Sept. 16, 1843.)

Mademoiselle de Belle-Isle. Frances Kemble (Butler). In *Plays,* London, 1863. (Astor Place Opera House, N. Y., April 29, 1850, as *The Duke's Wager.*)

Madmen All; or, The Cure of Love. W. I. Paulding. In *American Comedies,* Phila., 1847.

Magic Arrow, The; or, The Prince and the Fairy. W. K. Northall. (Olympic Theatre, N. Y., Nov. 4, 1844.)

Magnolia; or, The Child of the Flower. Anon. (Walnut, Sept. 14, 1855.)

Mahomet. J. H. Payne (?). N. Y., 1809. (Chestnut, Dec. 11, 1811.)

Maid and the Magpie, The. J. H. Payne. See *Trial without Jury.*

Maiden Wife, The; or, Romance after Marriage. See *Romance after Marriage.*

Maid of Hungary, The. J. D. Turnbull. (Charleston Theatre, March 26, 1806.)

Maid of Missolonghi, The. Stephen T. Mitchell. (Richmond Theatre, Jan. 17, 1828.)

Maid of Wyoming, The. James McHenry. (Arch, Jan. 28, 1831.)

Maine Question, The. N. H. Bannister. (Franklin Theatre, N. Y., Feb. 19, 1839.)

Major Jack Downing; or, The Retired Politician. Anon. (Park Theatre, May 10, 1834.)

Major Jones' Courtship; or, Adventures on Christmas Eve. William T. Thompson. Savannah, 1850. (Barnum's Museum, Phila., Dec. 22, 1851.)

Manfredi. J. W. Simmons. Phila., 1821.

Manhattoes, The. Anon. (Park, July 4, 1829.)

Manifest Destiny. T. C. De Walden. (Wallack's Theatre, Nov. 14, 1856.)

Man in the Moon, The; or, Harlequin Dog-Star. William Barrymore. (Tremont Theatre, Boston, Jan. 13, 1834.)

Man of Fortitude, The. John Hodgkinson. N. Y., 1807. (John St., June 7, 1797.)

Man of Honor, A. Dion Boucicault. Adap. of *Le Fils naturel,* by Dumas, fils. (Wallack's Theatre, Dec. 22, 1873.)

A LIST OF AMERICAN PLAYS

Man of the Black Forest. J. H. Payne (?). (Sadler's Wells Theatre, London, May 1, 1820.)

Man of the Times, The; or, A Scarcity of Cash. John Beete. Charleston, 1797. (Church St. Theatre, Charleston, April 24, 1797.)

Man without Money. See *News of the Night.*

Man with the Carpet Bag, The. Anon. (Bowery, June 18, 1835.)

March of Freedom, The. Anon. (Chatham Theatre, June 8, 1846.)

Marco Bozzaris. Oliver B. Bunce. MS. Harvard. (Bowery, June 10, 1850.)

Mariner's Tale, The. R. P. Smith. In H. W. Smith, *The Miscellaneous Works of the late Richard Penn Smith,* Phila., 1856.

Marion; or, The Hero of Lake George. M. M. Noah. N. Y., 1822. (Park, Nov. 25, 1821.)

Marion; or, The Reclaimed. J. R. Hamilton. Cincinnati, 1857. (Wood's Theatre, Cincinnati, Dec. 31, 1856.)

Market Street Merchant. W. E. Burton. (Walnut, May 17, 1843.)

Marmion; or, a Tale of Flodden-Field. Mrs. Ellis. (Olympic, March 30, 1812.)

Marmion; or, The Battle of Flodden Field. J. N. Barker. N. Y., 1816. (Park, April 13, 1812.)

Marriage. Dion Boucicault. MS., Lord Chamberlain's, London and Fitzhugh Greene Coll. (Wallack's Theatre, Oct. 1, 1877; as *The Bridal Tour,* Haymarket Theatre, London, Aug. 2, 1880.)

Marriage Contract, The; or, The Restored Son. N. H. Bannister. (American Theatre, New Orleans, Dec. 19, 1835.)

Marriage of Mose and Lize; or, New York in 1855. H. S. Chapman. (St. Charles Theatre, N. Orleans, March 1, 1851.)

Married an Actress. J. M. Field. (Burton's Theatre, N. Y., Dec. 19, 1850.)

Married and Single. J. H. Payne. Adap. of Poole's version from *L'homme à soixante ans.* (Haymarket Theatre, Boston, July 16, 1824.)

Martyr Patriots, The; or, Louisiana in 1769. T. W. Collins. (St. Charles Theatre, New Orleans, May 16, 1836.)

Mary Morton; or, the Shirt Sewer. Louisa Reeder. (Barnum's Museum, Oct. 11, 1855.)

Mary of Mantua. Julia Dean (Hayne). (Broadway, Dec. 7, 1855.)

Mary of Scotland; or, The Heir of Avenel. Anon. N. Y., 1821. (Anthony St. Theatre, N. Y., May, 1821.)

Mary's Birthday; or, The Cynic. G. H. Miles. N. Y., n. d. (Laura Keene's Theatre, N. Y., Feb. 2, 1857.)

Mary Stuart. Frances Kemble Butler. London, 1863.

A LIST OF AMERICAN PLAYS

Mary Stuart; or, The Castle of Lochleven. Anon. (Chestnut, Oct. 9, 1835.) [May be adap. of *Le Château de Loch-leven,* by Pixerécourt.]

Mary Tudor. E. Flagg. (Walnut, June 22, 1842.)

Massacre. S. Woodworth. See *The Cannibals.*

Massacre of Wyoming, The. John F. Poole. (Bowery, Oct. 27, 1859.)

Match Woman of Boston, The. Anon. (National Theatre, N. Y., March 22, 1851.)

Match Woman of Philadelphia, The; or, The Burglar's Stronghold. J. P. Adams. (Arch, Nov. 29, 1849.)

Matricide, The; or, The Cobbler Physician. S. S. Steele. In *Dialogues and Drawing Room Plays,* Phila., 1881, selections only.

Matrimonial Speculation, A. "Mr. Simpkins." (Buckley's Opera House, N. Y., May 14, 1855.)

May Day in Town; or, New York in an Uproar. Royall Tyler. (John St., May 19, 1787.)

May Martin; or, The Money Diggers. C. H. Saunders. (Boston Museum, April 20, 1846.)

Mazeppa; or, The Wild Horse of Tartary. J. H. Payne. Auto. MS., Harvard. *A. L. P.,* 1940.

Medea. Matilda Heron. Adap. of *Medée* by Ernest Legouvé. (Wallack's Theatre, Feb. 16, 1857.)

Medium, The. See *Virtue Triumphant.*

Mental Electricity. Anon. (Peale's Museum, May 28, 1849.)

Mercenary Match, The. Barna[bas] Bidwell. New Haven, [1784]. (Yale College, 1785?)

Merry Dames, The; or, The Humorist's Triumph over the Poet in Petticoats. John Minshull. N. Y., 1804. (Bedlow St. Theatre, N. Y., July 22, 1805.)

Merry Gardener, The. Wm. Dunlap. (Park, Feb. 3, 1802.)

Metamora. John Brougham. Boston, n. d. (Adelphi Theatre, Boston, Dec. 9, 1847.)

Metamora, John A. Stone. *A. L. P.,* 1941. MSS. (incomplete) in Forrest Home, Phila., and in Univ. of Utah. (Park, Dec. 15, 1829.)

Miantonimoh. Anon. Dram. of *Wept-of-Wish-ton-Wish.* (Bowery, Nov. 12, 1830.)

Michael Bonham; or, The Fall of Bexar. W. G. Simms. In *Southern Literary Messenger,* XVIII, Feb.-June, 1852. Richmond, 1852. (Charleston Theatre, March 26, 1855.)

Midnight Murder, The. N. H. Bannister. (American Theatre, New Orleans, May 16, 1835.)

464

A LIST OF AMERICAN PLAYS

Military Glory of Great Britain, The. Anon. Phila., 1762. (Nassau Hall, College of New Jersey, Sept. 29, 1762.)

Miller of New Jersey, The; or, The Prison Hulk. John Brougham. N. Y., [1858]. (Bowery, March 21, 1859.)

Millionaire, The. Walter Leman. (Walnut, Aug. 28, 1848.)

Mimi. Dion Boucicault. MS., Lord Chamberlain's office. Two printed copies Fitzhugh Greene Coll. (Wallack's Theatre, N. Y., July 1, 1873.)

Mina. S. L. Fairfield. Baltimore, 1825.

Miniature, The. James Rees. (American Theatre, New Orleans, May 10, 1834.)

Ministerial Oppression; or, The Grievances of America, with the Battle of Bunker Hill. Author's MS., prob. 18th Cent., at Brown Univ.

Minute Spy, The. T. Law. (National Theatre, N. Y., Aug. 10, 1858.)

Miralda; or, The Justice of Tacon. M. M. Ballou. Boston, [1859]. (Howard Athenæum, Boston, June 8, 1858.)

Miriam, a Dramatic Poem. L. J. Hall. Boston, 1837.

Miser of Philadelphia, The. Anon. (Chestnut, Sept. 8, 1849.)

Miser's Wedding, The. Wm. Dunlap. (John St., May 20, 1793.)

Mistletoe Bough, The. James Rees. (American Theatre, New Orleans, March 17, 1835.)

Modern Chivalry; or, The Days of the Revolution. Anon. (Chatham Theatre, N. Y., Dec. 15, 1845.)

Modern Fashions. See *Dandyism.*

Modern Honor. J. B. White. Charleston, 1812. (Charleston Theatre, March 6, 1812.)

Modern Mistake, The. Barnabas Bidwell. (Yale College, April 3,1784.)

Modern Saint, The. Charles M. Barras. Cincinnati, 1857.

Moderns; or, A Trip to the Springs. Anon. (Park, April 18, 1831.)

Modest Soldier, The; or, Love in New York. Wm. Dunlap.

Mohammed, the Arabian Prophet. G. H. Miles. Boston, 1850. (Lyceum, N. Y., Oct. 27, 1851.)

Moll Pitcher; or, The Fortune Teller of Lynn. J. S. Jones. Boston, 1855. (National Theatre, Boston, May 20, 1839.)

Money Market, The. John Brougham. Adap. of Balzac's *Mercadet.* (Brougham's Lyceum, N. Y., Nov. 10, 1851.)

Monkey Boy, The. T. B. De Walden. (Laura Keene's Theatre, N. Y., Sept. 10, 1860.)

Montezuma; or, The Conquest of Mexico. George Hielge. (Arch, Dec. 23, 1846.)

Montezuma; or, The Future Destinies of Mexico. Anon. (Chatham Theatre, N. Y., Oct. 20, 1845.)

A LIST OF AMERICAN PLAYS

Montgomery; or, The Falls of Montmorency. H. J. Finn. Boston, 1825. (Boston Theatre, Feb. 21, 1825.)

Mora, or the Golden Fetters. Dion Boucicault. (Wallack's Theatre, June 3, 1873.)

Morgan, the Jersey Wagoner. Anon. (Chestnut, Jan. 21, 1850.)

Mormons, The; or, Life at Salt Lake City. T. D. English. N. Y., [1858]. (Burton's Theatre, N. Y., March 16, 1858.)

Morning of Life, The. Oliver B. Bunce. (Chatham Theatre, N. Y., June 12, 1848.)

Morning Visitors; or, A Trip to Quebec. A. B. Lindsley (?). In *The Yankee,* Portland, I (1828), No. 19, 151-152.

Morton's Hope; or, Scenes of the Revolution. J. S. Jones. Dram of Motley's novel. (Tremont Theatre, Boston, Dec. 9, 1839.)

Mose Among the Girls. G. W. Smith. (Adelphi Theatre, N. Y., June 8, 1848.)

Mose and Jakey in Philadelphia. T. W. Meighan. (National Theatre, Phila., Oct. 8, 1849.)

Mose and Jakey; or, The United Fire Boys in Philadelphia. T. B. Johnston. (Arch, Oct. 8, 1849.)

Mose and Jakey's Visit to the Chesnut. Anon. (Chestnut, Nov. 7, 1849.)

Mose and Lize in the Hop of Fashion. (Charley White's Theatre, N. Y., Jan. 31, 1856.)

Mose in a Muss; or, A Joke of the Manager's. W. B. Chapman. (National Theatre, N. Y., June 27, 1849.)

Mose in California. W. B. Chapman. (National Theatre, N. Y., Feb. 12, 1849.)

Mose in China. B. A. Baker. (Chestnut, Nov. 3, 1849.)

Mose in France. Anon. (National Theatre, N. Y., Nov. 3, 1851.)

Mose, Joe, and Jack. (Bowery, N. Y., Dec. 17, 1849.)

Mose, Lize, and Joe at the Market Dance. (Adelphi Theatre, N. Y., June 8, 1848.)

Mose's Dream. (Brougham's Bowery, N. Y., June 15, 1857.)

Mose's Visit to the Arab Girls. (Adelphi Theatre, N. Y., June 1, 1848.)

Mose's Visit to Philadelphia. Anon. (Walnut, June 26, 1848.)

Mother Bailey; or, The Heroine of Connecticut. J. P. Adams. (National Theatre, N. Y., July 4, 1855.)

Mother's Trust, The; or, California in 1849. Mrs. Sidney F. Bateman. (Metropolitan Theatre, San Francisco, June, 1854.)

Motley Assembly, The. [Mercy Warren?] Boston, 1779.

Mountain Torrent, The. S. B. H. Judah. N. Y., 1820. (Park, March 1, 1820.)

A LIST OF AMERICAN PLAYS

Mrs. Smith; or, The Wife and the Widow. J. H. Payne. London, n. d.
(Haymarket, London, June 18, 1823; Park, March 6, 1826.)

Murrell, the Land Pirate; or, Yankees in Mississippi. N. H. Bannister.
(American Theatre, New Orleans, Dec. 7, 1835.)

Musard Ball, The; or, Love at the Academy. J. Brougham. N. Y.,
[1858]. (Burton's Theatre, N. Y., April 29, 1858.)

My Aunt in Virginia; or, Arrivals in New York. John Galt. (Chestnut, Jan. 5, 1830.)

My Christmas Dinner. Fitz James O'Brien. (Wallack's Theatre,
Dec. 25, 1852.)

My Cousin German. See *The Demon Lover.*

My Cousin Tom. O. S. Leland. (Boston Theatre, Oct. 26, 1858.)

My Friend Isaac. Daniel K. Ford. Boston, 1859.

My Friend, the Governor. W. E. Burton (Park, Feb. 7, 1835.)

My Husband's Mirror. William Warland Clapp. New York, n. d.
(Boston Museum, Dec. 22, 1856.)

My Own Cottage Home; or, Love's Young Dream. H. Hastings Weld.
(National Theatre, Boston, Feb. 3, 1837.)

Mysteries and Miseries of New York, The. H. P. Grattan. Dram.
novel by "Ned Buntline." (National Theatre, N. Y., Sept. 4,
1848.)

Mysteries and Miseries of Philadelphia, The. Anon. (Chestnut,
May 31, 1850.)

Mysteries of Paris, The. "Adapted from book of same name by F. C.
Wemyss, James Gann and John Sefton." (National Theatre,
Phila., Nov. 13, 1843.)

Mysteries of Paris, The. C. H. Saunders. (Bowery, Nov. 27, 1843.)

Mysteries of the Castle, The; or, The Victim of Revenge. J. B. White.
Charleston, 1807. (Charleston Theatre, Dec. 26, 1806.)

Mysterious Chief, The; or, The Heroes of 1812. H. J. Conway. Dram.
of *Woodworth's Champions of Freedom.* (National Theatre, N. Y.,
July 21, 1851.)

Mysterious Knockings. Anon. (Burton's Theatre, N. Y., May 16,
1849.)

Mysterious Monk, The. See *Ribbemont.*

My Uncle's Wedding. R. P. Smith. (Arch, Oct. 15, 1832.)

My Wife's Mirror. E. G. P. Wilkins. N. Y., [1856]. (Laura Keene's
Theatre, N. Y., May 10, 1856.)

Naiad Queen, The; or, The Mystery of Lurlei Berg. W. E. Burton.
Adap. of *Lurline, or the Spirit of the Rhine.* (National Theatre,
Phila., Dec. 19, 1840.)

A LIST OF AMERICAN PLAYS

Naramattah. Anon. (Park, Jan. 15, 1830.)

Natalie; or, The Frontier Maid. M. M. Noah. (Tremont Theatre, Boston, May 1, 1840.)

National Defences; or, The Long Shot Cavalry. Anon. (Olympic Theatre, N. Y., March 27, 1848.)

Nationalites; or John, Jean, and Jonathan. J. Oakes Pardey. (Arch, Nov. 28, 1853.)

Native Nobility. L. A. Wilmer. (Arch, May 31, 1847.)

Natural Daughter, The. Wm. Dunlap. (Park, Feb. 8, 1799.)

Nature and Art. H. J. Conway. In Prompt Books, II, N. Y. Public Library. (Olympic Theatre, N. Y., Sept. 25, 1848.)

Nature and Philosophy. Anon. From Auguste Duport's opera *Le Frère Philippe* (1818), from La Fontaine's *Les Oies de Frère Philippe*, from *Decameron*, Fourth Day. Richmond, 1821. (Richmond Theatre, July 30, 1821.)

Nature's Nobleman. H. O. Pardey. N. Y., 1854. (Burton's Theatre, N. Y., Oct. 7, 1851.)

Nature's Nobleman; or, The Ship Carpenter of New York. Harry Watkins. (National Theatre, N. Y., Dec. 2, 1850.)

Naval Glory; or, Decatur's Triumph. Anon. (Walnut, March 11, 1844.)

Neighbor Jackwood. J. T. Trowbridge. Boston, 1857. (Boston Museum, March 16, 1857.)

Neill, the Rebel. L. H. Medina. (Bowery, May 11, 1835.)

Neptune's Defeat; or, The Seizure of the Seas. John Brougham. N. Y., [1858]. Prompt Copy, Harvard. (Wallack's Theatre, N. Y., Oct. 5, 1858.)

Nervo Vitalics; or, The March of Science. J. M. Field. (Olympic Theatre, N. Y., Sept. 19, 1842.)

New Comedy of Errors, A. Anon. (Arch, May 18, 1855.)

New England Coquette, The. J. H. Nichols. Salem, n. d.

New England Drama, The. Perkins Howes. Dedham, 1825.

New Orleans Assurance. Anon. (St. Charles Theatre, New Orleans, Feb. 13, 1842.)

New Park, The. Anon. (Burton's Theatre, N. Y., Oct. 21, 1831.)

New President, The. W. E. Burton (?). (National Theatre, Phila., March 24, 1841.)

New Scene . . . to . . . Columbus, A. Alex. Martin. Phila., 1798. (Chestnut, Jan. 30, 1797.)

Newsboy of New York, The; or, Mose in Town. G. J. Arnold (National Theatre, N. Y., Sept. 8, 1852.)

News of the Night; or, A Trip to Niagara. R. M. Bird. *A. L. P.*, 1941.

468

A LIST OF AMERICAN PLAYS

MS. in University of Pennsylvania Library. (McMillan Theatre, N. Y., Nov. 2, 1929.)

New World Planted, A; or, The Adventures of the Forefathers of New England. Joseph Croswell. Boston, 1802.

New World, The; or, The Home of Liberty. A. Allen. (Olympic Theatre, N. Y., Nov. 25, 1840.)

New York and Brooklyn; or, The Poor Sewing Girl. Anon. (Bowery, Oct. 25, 1858.)

New York as It Is. B. A. Baker. (Chatham Theatre, N. Y., April 17, 1848.)

New York by Gas Light. G. C. Foster. (Bowery, Nov. 20, 1856.)

New York Directory; or, The Cockney in America. W. E. Burton. (Burton's Theatre, N. Y., Oct. 10, 1849.)

New York Fireman and Bond Street Heiress. S. D. Johnson. MS. Brown Univ. (National Theatre, N. Y., July 22, 1850.)

New York Girls and Brooklyn Boys. Anon. (National Theatre, N. Y., March 1, 1858.)

New York in 1860; or, A Hit at the Times. Anon. (New Bowery, June 12, 1860.)

New York in Slices. Anon. (Burton's Theatre, N. Y., Oct. 9, 1848.)

New York Merchant and His Clerks, The. By author of *Satanas.* (Park, April 12, 1843.)

New York Milliners. Anon. (Chatham Theatre, N. Y., Feb. 14, 1848.)

New York Patriots; or, The Battle of Saratoga. H. J. Conway. (Barnum's Museum, N. Y., June 2, 1856.)

New York Printer, The. Harry Watkins. (National Theatre, N. Y., Jan. 20, 1851.)

New York Volunteers; or, Who's Afraid. Anon. (Olympic Theatre, N. Y., July 14, 1812.)

Nicaragua; or, General Walker's Victories. E. F. Distin (?). (National Theatre, N. Y., July 21, 1856.)

Nice Young Man, A. J. E. Durivage. (Burton's Theatre, N. Y., Dec. 25, 1854.)

Nicholas Nickleby. Anon. (Park, Jan. 30, 1839.)

Nicholas Nickleby. Dion Boucicault. (Winter Garden, N. Y., Nov. 1, 1859.)

Nick of the Woods. G. W. Harby. Dram. of novel by R. M. Bird. (Natchez Theatre, Feb. 6, 1838.)

Nick of the Woods. L. H. Medina. N. Y., n. d. (Bowery, Feb. 5, 1838.)

Nick of Time. Anon. (Arch, May 8, 1843.)

A LIST OF AMERICAN PLAYS

Night and Morning. John Brougham. N. Y., [1856]. Dram. Bulwer's novel. (Wallack's Theatre, N. Y., Jan. 15, 1855.)

Night of Expectations, A. Charlotte Barnes Conner. (Chicago Theatre, Sept. 6, 1848; Arch, April 9, 1850.)

Nina. Wm. Dunlap. (Park, Feb. 4, 1805.)

1940; or, Crummels in Search of Novelty. A. Allen. (Olympic Theatre, N. Y., Oct. 15, 1840.)

Noble Exile, The. W. I. Paulding. In *American Comedies*, Phila., 1847.

Nolens Volens; or, The Biter Bit. Everhard Hall. Newbern, 1809. (Petersburg, by amateurs.)

Norah; or, The Girl of Erin. J. H. Payne (?). (Covent Garden, London, Feb. 1, 1826.)

Norman Leslie. W. R. Blake. Dram. novel by T. S. Fay. (Walnut, Dec. 28, 1840.)

Norman Leslie. L. H. Medina. (Bowery, Jan. 11, 1836.)

Norman Leslie. F. C. Wemyss. (Walnut, March 14, 1836.)

Norman Maurice; or, The Man of the People. W. G. Simms. In *Southern Literary Messenger*, 1851. Also Richmond, 1851.

North American, The. Mrs. W. B. Wood. (Chestnut, April 30, 1823.)

North Point; or, Baltimore Defended. G. W. P. Custis. (Balt. Theatre, Sept. 12, 1833.)

Not at Home. Farce "by a gentleman of New Orleans." (American Theatre, New Orleans, June 8, 1827.)

Nothing to Nurse. C. M. Walcot. N. Y., n. d. (Laura Keene's Theatre, N. Y., Sept. 28, 1857.)

Nowadays. G. C. Foster. (Burton's Theatre, N. Y., Sept. 25, 1854.)

Nullification. Anon. (Richmond Hill Theatre, N. Y., Jan. 29, 1833.)

No. 333 Locust Street. Anon. (Chestnut, May 29, 1850.)

Nydia. G. H. Boker. MS. dated 1885. Phila., 1929.

Oath of Office, The. C. J. Cannon. N. Y., 1854. (Bowery, March 18, 1850.)

Oatman Family, The. C. E. Bingham. (American Theatre, San Francisco, Sept., 1857.)

Oberon; or, The Siege of Mexico. J. D. Burk. Norfolk Theatre, March 23, 1803.)

Occurrences of the Times; or, The Transactions of Four Days. Anon. [Boston, 1789.]

Octavia Bragaldi. Charlotte Barnes Conner. In *Plays, Prose and Poetry*, Phila., 1848. (National Theatre, N. Y., Nov. 8, 1837; Surrey Theatre, London, May 9, 1844.)

A LIST OF AMERICAN PLAYS

Octoroon, The; or, Life in Louisiana. Dion Boucicault. Full original version, Harvard, rep. in *Representative American Plays.* (Winter Garden, N. Y., Dec. 5, 1859.)

O'Dowd, The. Dion Boucicault. N. Y., [1909]. (Booth's Theatre, N. Y., March 17, 1873 as *Daddy O'Dowd;* as *The O'Dowd,* revised, (Adelphi, London, Oct. 21, 1880); as *Suil-A-Mor,* (Boston Museum, Feb. 6, 1882.)

O'Grady, the Irish Guardsman. George H. Andrews. (Walnut, Sept. 13, 1849.)

Oh Yes; or, The New Constitution. M. M. Noah. Cf. Rees.

Old Brewery, The. Anon. (Barnum's Museum, Feb. 27, 1854.)

Old Clock; or, Here She Goes and There She Goes. Anon. (Franklin Theatre, N. Y., March 25, 1839.)

Old Continental, The; or, The Veteran of '76. Anon. (National Theatre, N. Y., March 1, 1851.)

Old Hickory; or, A Day in New Orleans. Anon. (Chatham Theatre, N. Y., Feb. 11, 1825.)

Old Homestead, The. G. L. Aiken. (National Theatre, N. Y., Nov. 3, 1856.)

Old Ironsides. N. H. Bannister. (American Theatre, New Orleans, May 16, 1835.)

Old Job and Jacob Gray. J. S. Jones. (Boston Museum, Jan. 8, 1849.)

Old Jonathan and his Apprentices. W. Barrymore. (Bowery Theatre, Sept. 12, 1832.)

Old New York; or, Democracy in 1869. Elizabeth Oakes Smith. N. Y., 1853. (Broadway, 1853?; New Orleans Theatre, 1854.)

Old Plantation, The; or, The Real Uncle Tom. George Jamieson. (Old Bowery, March 1, 1860.)

Old Waggoner of New Jersey and Virginia, The. N. H. Bannister, (Arch, Feb. 10, 1847.)

Oliver Twist. Dram. by F. C. Wemyss (?). (Walnut, Jan. 1, 1839.)

Oliver Twist. Dram. by James Rees. (St. Charles Theatre, New Orleans, March 24, 1839.)

Oliver Twist. Dram. by Joseph Jefferson. (Winter Garden, Feb. 2, 1860.)

O'Neal the Great; or, The Hag's War. N. B. Clarke. MS., Brown Univ. (National Theatre, N. Y., Feb., 1853.)

One Coat for Two Suits. C. M. Walcot. N. Y., [1857]. (Wallack's Theatre, N. Y., 1857.)

One Thousand Milliners Wanted for the Gold Diggings of California. N. Y., n. d., as by J. S. Coyne. (Burton's Theatre, N. Y., Nov. 8, 1852.) [Maybe same play as that produced at Olympic Theatre, London, Oct. 2, 1852].

A LIST OF AMERICAN PLAYS

Onoleetah. Anon. (Arch, Feb. 23, 1846.)

Oolaita; or, The Indian Heroine. Lewis Deffebach. Phila., 1821.

Opera Mad. F. S. Hill. (American Theatre, New Orleans, Jan. 12, 1836.)

Oralloossa, Son of the Incas. R. M. Bird. In C. E. Foust, *Life and Dramatic Works of Robert Montgomery Bird*, N. Y., 1919. (Arch, Oct. 10, 1832.)

Orange Girl of Venice, The. N. H. Bannister. (Bowery, Feb. 18, 1846.)

Orange Girl of Venice, The. C. W. Taylor. (National Theatre, April 7, 1856.)

Oregon; or, The Emigrant's Dream. J. M. Field. (Arch, June 6, 1845.)

Origin of the Feast of Purim, The; or, The Destinies of Haman and Mordecai. Royall Tyler. *A. L. P.*, 1941. See Bib., chap. III.

Orion the Gold Beater. G. L. Aiken. MS., The Players, N. Y. (National Theatre, N. Y., Jan. 15, 1851.)

Orion the Gold Beater. John Brougham. See *False and True*.

Orlando: or, A Woman's Virtue. Horatio N. Moore. Phila., 1835.

Orlando; or, Parental Persecution. W. C. White. Boston, 1797. (Federal St. Theatre, Boston, March 10, 1797.)

Oronaska; or, The Chief of the Mohawks. J. B. Phillips. (Bowery, June 27, 1834.)

Orphan of Prague, The. J. Hutton. Phila., 1808.

Orphan's Dream, The. Anon. (Barnum's Museum, Aug. 30, 1852.)

Orphans, The. M. Pinckney (?). Charleston, 1818.

Osceola. John H. Sherburne. (National Theatre, Phila., Oct. 15, 1841.)

Ossawattomie Brown; or, The Insurrection at Harper's Ferry. Mrs. J. C. Swayze. N. Y., n. d. (Bowery, Dec. 16, 1859.)

Oswali of Athens. J. H. Payne. (Chatham Garden Theatre, N. Y., June 13, 1831.)

Othello Travestie. Anon. (Bowery, Aug. 19, 1836.)

Otho. John Neal. Boston, 1819.

Oua Cousta; or, The Lion of the Forest. N. H. Bannister. (Arch, Phila., Nov. 9, 1850.)

Our Best Society. O. E. Durivage. (Burton's Theatre, N. Y., Jan. 21, 1854.)

Our Clerks. Anon. (Burton's Theatre, N. Y., April 23, 1852.)

Our Clerks; or, Suppose War Was Declared. Anon. (Laura Keene's Theatre, N. Y., Sept. 5, 1859.)

Our Country's Sinews. Harry Watkins. (Chambers St. Theatre, N. Y., Feb. 23, 1857.) Same play as *Nature's Nobleman*.

Our Female American Cousin. Charles Gayler. (Burton's Theatre, Jan. 31, 1859.)

Our Flag. C. H. Saunders. (North River Opera House, N. Y., April 2, 1845.)

Our Flag is Nailed to the Mast. Anon. (Arch, July 8, 1845.)

Our Flag; or, Nailed to the Mast. "By a Gentleman of Portland." (Union Hall, Portland, Monday, July 8, 1844.)

Our Gal. S. D. Johnson. N. Y., [1856]. (National, N. Y., May 2, 1850.)

Our Jedidah; or, Great Attraction. Anon. (Chicago Theatre, May 6, 1848; Olympic Theatre, N. Y., Feb. 28, 1849.)

Our Jemimy; or, Connecticut Courtship. H. J. Conway. N. Y., n. d. (Chestnut, May 9, 1853.)

Our National Defences. See *National Defences.*

Our Revolutionary War; or, The Patriots of '76. Anon. (Arch, Nov. 1, 1851.)

Our Set; or, The Vacant Consulship. Morris Barnett. (Burton's Theatre, N. Y., Jan. 24, 1855.)

Outallissi. Anon. (Bowery, Sept. 29, 1834.)

Out of Place; or, The Lake of Lausanne. [William Turner.] New York, 1808.

Paddy's Trip to America; or, The Husband with Three Wives. C. S. Talbot. N. Y., 1822. (Washington Hall, N. Y., 1821-2?)

Paddy the Piper. James Pilgrim. N. Y., n. d. (National Theatre, N. Y., Nov. 6, 1850.)

Painter of Brienne, The. "By a gentleman of Philadelphia." (Walnut, March 22, 1852.)

Paint King, The; or, The Fairies' Claim. C. H. Saunders. Dram. Washington Allston's poem. (Boston Museum, June 2, 1845.)

Palo Alto. Anon. (St. Louis Theatre, Sept. 11, 1846.)

Paoli. J. H. Payne (?). (Surrey Theatre, London, Oct. 27, 1823.)

Partisan, The. Anon. Dram. of Simms' novel. (St. Louis Theatre, Oct. 31, 1837.)

Pathfinder, The; or, The Inland Seas. J. B. Phillips. MS., Harvard. (Bowery, April, 1840.)

Patrick Lyon; or, The Philadelphia Locksmith. J. Rees. (Arch, Aug. 26, 1843.)

Patriot, The; or, Union and Freedom. G. L. Stevens. Boston, 1834.

Patriot Chief, The. Peter Markoe. Phila., 1784.

Patriots, The. Robert Munford. Phila., 1776. In *Plays and Poems,* Petersburg, 1798.

Patriots of '76, The; or, The Jersey Blues. Anon. (Arch, Nov. 27, 1851.)

Paul and Alexis; or, The Orphans of the Rhine. See *Wandering Boys.*

Paul Clifford. J. D. Phillips. Dram. of Bulwer's novel. (Bowery, Sept. 28, 1830.)

Pauline. Dion Boucicault. Prompt Book, New York Public Library. See *Spell-bound.*

Paul Jones. Trans. from Dumas by W. Berger. Phila., 1839. (St. Charles, New Orleans, Jan. 31, 1840.)

Paul Jones; or, The Pilot of the German Ocean. W. H. Wallack. N. Y., 1828. (Chatham Theatre, N. Y., March 21, 1827.)

Paul Revere and the Sons of Liberty. J. S. Jones. (Boston Museum, March 13, 1876.)

Paul Ulric. ?Matson. (Walnut, April 30, 1836.)

Pauvrette. Dion Boucicault. [N. Y., 1858]. (Niblo's Garden, N. Y., Oct. 4, 1858.)

Pawnee Chief, The. G. W. P. Custis. Before 1830. See p. 272.

Paxton Boys, The. Anon. [Phila.], 1764.

Pearl Diver, The. S. S. Steele. (Boston Museum, July 5, 1847.)

Pedlar, The. Alphonso Wetmore. St. Louis, 1821. (St. Louis Theatre by the Thespian Soc., 1820-26.)

Peep from a Parlour Window, A. John Brougham. (Burton's Theatre, N. Y., March 10, 1857.)

Peeping In at 6 P.M. "Joe Jefferson." (Charleston Theatre, Jan. 15, 1852.)

Pelican, The. R. P. Smith. MS. dated 1825 in Hist. Soc. of Penna.

Pelopidas; or, The Fall of the Polemarchs. R. M. Bird. In C. E. Foust, *Life and Dramatic Works of Robert Montgomery Bird*, N. Y., 1919.

People's Candidate, The. J. S. Robb. (Howard Athenaeum, Boston, Nov. 22, 1847.)

People's Lawyer, The. J. S. Jones. N. Y., n. d. (National Theatre, Boston, May 6, 1839.)

Percy. Jane Wilson. (American Theatre, New Orleans, April 18, 1825.)

Percy's Masque. J. A. Hillhouse. London, 1819. N. Y., 1820.

Peter Smink: or, The Armistice. J. H. Payne. London, n. d. (Royal Surrey Theatre, London, July 8, 1822; Park, Oct. 14, 1826.)

Peter the Great; or, The Russian Mother. Wm. Dunlap. N. Y., 1814. (Park, Nov. 15, 1802.)

Phelles, King of Tyre; or, The Downfall of Tyranny. Reuben Potter. N. Y., 1825. (Park, June 13, 1825.)

Philadelphia as It Is. Anon. (Walnut, Jan. 8, 1841.)

Philadelphia Assurance. S. S. Steele. (Arch, Dec. 6, 1841.)

A LIST OF AMERICAN PLAYS

Philadelphia Directory. Anon. (Arch, Dec. 29, 1849.)

Philadelphia Fireman, The; or, The Chesnut Street Heiress. Anon. (Chestnut, Jan. 19, 1850.)

Philadelphia in Spots. Anon. (Arch, Dec. 25, 1848.)

Philadelphia Lawyer, The; or, A Week at the Springs. W. E. Burton. Act I, MS., Seymour Collection. Princeton.

Philadelphia Volunteers; or, Who's Afraid? Anon. (Olympic, Phila., Oct. 5, 1912.)

Philo: An Evangeliad. Sylvester Judd. Boston, 1850.

Phryne; or, The Romance of a Young Wife. Dion Boucicault. Printed Copy in Fitzhugh Greene Coll. (Baldwin Theatre, San Francisco, Sept. 13, 1887.)

Pilgrim of Love, The. James Pilgrim. (Arch, Nov. 12, 1851.)

Pilot, The. Anon. Adap. of Cooper's novel. (Park, Oct. 29, 1824.)

Pioneer Patriot, The. Harry Watkins. Dram. Cobb's Story. (Barnum's Museum, N. Y., Jan. 18, 1858.)

Pioneers, The. Anon. (Park, April 21, 1823.)

Pirates' Legacy; or, The Wrecker's Fate. C. H. Saunders. Boston, n. d. (Bowery, Dec. 8, 1843.)

Pirates of the Mississippi, The. John Brougham. MS., Brown Univ. (Bowery, July 21, 1856.)

Pizarro in Peru; or, The Death of Rolla. Wm. Dunlap. Adap. of Kotzebue's *Die Spanier in Peru.* 1800. (Park, March 26 1800.)

Plattsburgh; or, The Battle of Lake Champlain. Anon. (Bowery, Sept. 11, 1840.)

Player's Plot, The. Anon. (Burton's Theatre, N. Y., Feb. 6, 1855.)

Playing with Fire. John Brougham. London, n. d. (Wallack's Theatre, N. Y., Oct. 2, 1860.)

Plymouth Rock. J. S. Jones. (Warren Theatre, Boston, Nov. 24, 1834.)

Pocahontas. S. H. M. Byers. N. p., n. d.

Pocahontas. R. D. Owen. [N. Y.], 1837. (Park, Feb. 8, 1838.)

Pocahontas; or, The Gentle Savage. John Brougham. N. Y., [1856]. (Wallack's Theatre, N. Y., Dec. 24, 1855.)

Pocahontas; or, The Settlers of Virginia. G. W. P. Custis. Phila., 1830. (Walnut, Jan. 16, 1830.)

Podesta's Daughter, The. G. H. Boker. Phila., 1852.

Poetus [sic] *Caecinna.* Isaac C. Pray. (Astor Place Opera House, N. Y., Oct. 2, 1850.)

Polish Wife, The. J. B. Phillips. (Bowery, Nov. 25, 1831.)

Politian. Edgar A. Poe. In *The Raven and Other Poems.* N. Y., 1845 Ed. complete from MS. by T. L. Mabbott, Richmond, 1923.

A LIST OF AMERICAN PLAYS

Politician Outwitted, The. Samuel Low (?). N. Y., 1789.

Politicians, The. Cornelius Mathews. N. Y., 1840.

Politicians, The; or, A State of Things. J. Murdock. Phila., 1798.

Poltroonius. E. F. Head (?). Boston, 1856.

Pomp of Cudjo's Cave. T. B. De Walden. Dram. of *Cudjo's Cave* by J. T. Trowbridge. (Bowery, April 9, 1864.)

Ponteach; or, The Savages of America. Robert Rogers. London, 1766.

Pontiac; or, The Siege of Detroit. Alexander Macomb. Boston, 1835. (National Theatre, Wash., 1838.)

Poor Lodger, The. W. C. White. Boston, 1811. (Federal St. Theatre, Boston, Dec. 17, 1810.)

Poor of New York, The. Dion Boucicault. N. Y., [1857]. (Wallack's Theatre, N. Y., Dec. 8, 1857.)

Pope of Rome, The. Dion Boucicault. Extensive revision of *Sixtus V; or, The Broken Vow,* by Boucicault and John Bridgeman. Adap. of *L'Abbaye de Castro,* by Dinaux and Lemoine. (Niblo's Garden, Oct. 27, 1858.)

Post-Chaise, The. J. H. Payne (?). (Park, April 21, 1826.)

Prairie Bird; or, A Child of the Delawares. Walter Leman. (Walnut, Jan. 3, 1846.)

Prairie Girls. Anon. (St. Charles Theatre, New Orleans, 1836.)

Preparing for the Convention. Anon. (Charleston Theatre, April 19, 1860.)

Preservation; or, The Hovel in the Rocks. J. B. Williamson. Charleston, 1800. (Federal St. Theatre, Boston, Feb. 27, 1797.)

Priestess, The. Epes Sargent. Boston, 1854. (Boston Theatre, March 21, 1855.)

Prince and the Patriot, The. Anon. In *Poems, Moral and Divine,* "By an American Gentleman." London, 1756.

Prince of Parthia, The. Thomas Godfrey. In *Juvenile Poems,* Phila., 1765. (Southwark Theatre, April 24, 1767.)

Printer of New York, The. Anon. (National Theatre, N. Y., Jan. 20, 1851.)

Procrastination. J. H. Payne. (Haymarket Theatre, London, Sept. 21, 1829.)

Prophecy, The; or, Love and Friendship. M. B. Fowler. N. Y., 1821. (Washington Hall, N. Y., Oct. 8, 1821.)

Prophet of St. Paul's, The. D. P. Brown. Phila., 1836. (Walnut, March 20, 1837.)

Proverb, The; or, Conceit Can Cure, Conceit Can Kill. Wm. Dunlap. (Park, Feb. 20, 1804.)

A LIST OF AMERICAN PLAYS

Psammetichus; or, The Twelve Tribes of Egypt. N. H. Bannister. Quotation in Rees, 36–7.

Putnam. George Hielge. (Burton's Theatre, Phila., Sept., 1844.)

Putnam, the Iron Son of '76. N. H. Bannister. Boston, [1859]. (Bowery, Aug. 5, 1844.)

Putty-man; or, The Iron Pot of '49. D. G. Robinson. (San Francisco Theatre, Jan., 1853.)

Quadroone, The. Anon. (Chatham Theatre, N. Y., April 12, 1841.)

Quadroone, The; or, St. Michael's Day. J. S. Jones. Dram. from novel of same name by J. H. Ingraham. (Tremont Theatre, Boston, April 19, 1841.)

Queen's Heart, The. John W. Palmer. Boston, 1858. (Howard Athenaeum, Boston, June 30, 1858.)

Quite Correct. R. P. Smith. In *Gentleman's Vade Mecum*, I, No. 8, (Feb. 24,) 1835, 1ff. Also Phila., 1835. (Chestnut, May 27, 1828.)

Rachael is Coming. Dion Boucicault. (St. Louis Theatre, Nov. 8, 1855.)

Rafael. Dion Boucicault (?). Adap. of *Les Filles des Marbres*, by Barrière and Thiboust, 1853. (Wallack's Theatre, April 10, 1875.)

Rag Picker of New York, The. Anon. (National Theatre, N. Y., Dec. 2, 1858.)

Railroad, The. G. W. P. Custis. (Walnut, May 16, 1830.)

Rake Hellies. S. E. Glover. Dramatization of *Lionel Lincoln*. (Camp St. Theatre, New Orleans, March 24, 1831.)

Rathenemus. N. H. Bannister. (Camp St. Theatre, New Orleans, March 24, 1835.)

Ravenswood. J. W. Simmons. (Charleston Theatre, April 12, 1824.)

Rebellion in Canada, The; or, The Burning of the Caroline. S. S. Steele. (National Theatre, Balt., 1841.)

Rebels and Tories; or, The Shoemaker of New York in 1774. N. B. Clarke. (National Theatre, N. Y., June 21, 1852.)

Recess, The; or, The Masked Apparition. Revision by "A gentleman of Philadelphia," of Bickerstaff's Adap. Calderon's *El Escondido y la Tapada.* (Southwark Theatre, Phila., April 27, 1791.)

Recollection of O'Flannigan and the Fairies, A. John Brougham. N. Y., [1856]. (Broadway, July 9, 1855.)

Reconciliation, The; or, The Triumph of Nature. Peter Markoe. Phila., 1790.

Red and Black, The; or, The Fates at Faro. Printed for the author. Phila., 1796.

A LIST OF AMERICAN PLAYS

Red Branch Knight, The; or, Ireland Triumphant. George Pepper. (Arch, April 10, 1831.)

Red Mask, The; or, The Wolf of Lithuania. John Brougham. N. Y., [1856]. (Bowery, Nov. 3, 1856.)

Red Rover, The. S. H. Chapman. Phila., 1828. (Chestnut, Feb. 21, 1828.)

Redwood. J. P. Addams. (St. Louis Theatre, Sept. 25, 1843. First ?)

Reformed Drunkard, The. D. G. Robinson. Later revised and renamed *Ten Nights in a Bar Room.* (Dramatic Museum, San Francisco, August 17, 1850.)

Regent's Daughter, The. Anon. New York, 1854.

Reign of Reform, The; or, Yankee Doodle Court. Anon. [Margaret Botsford?] Balt., 1830.

Remorse. See *Richelieu.*

Removal of the Deposits, The. Anon. (Bowery, June 25, 1834.)

Removing the Deposits. H. J. Finn. (Bowery, Sept. 7, 1835.)

Renegade, The; or, France Restored. Dr. Cooper and Dr. Gray. Prompt Books, N. Y. Public Library. (Park, Sept. 26, 1823.)

Reparation; or, The School for Libertines. T. P. Lathy. Boston, 1800. (Boston Theatre. ?)

Rescue, The; or, The Villain Unmasked. Rinaldo D'Elville. N. Y., 1813.

Rescued; or, A Girl's Romance. Dion Boucicault. MS., Lord Chamberlain's office, London. (Booth's Theatre, Sept. 4, 1879; Adelphi Theatre, London, Sept. 30, 1879.)

Restoration; or, The Diamond Cross. John A. Stone. (Charleston Theatre, April 14, 1825.)

Retribution; or, Blackbourne the Avenger. George Bennett. (Walnut, Aug. 28, 1850.)

Retribution; or, The Drunkard's Wife. Anon. (Barnum's Museum, Phila., Aug. 19, 1850.)

Retrospect, The. Wm. Dunlap. (Park, July 5, 1802.)

Return from a Cruise, The. Anon. (Chestnut, Dec. 11, 1812.)

Return from the Camp. Mary Carr. (Chestnut, Jan. 6, 1815.)

Return of the Volunteers. Anon. (Chatham Theatre, N. Y., Aug. 14, 1847.)

Revolt of the Sextons, The. John Brougham. (Burton's Theatre, N. Y., Aug. 24, 1848.)

Revolution. Charles Burke (?). (Bowery, Nov. 15, 1847.)

Revolution, The; or, The Yeomanry of '76. Anon. Prompt Copy, Harvard. (Bowery, Nov. 18, 1844.)

Revolutionary Soldier, The; or, The Old Seventy-Sixer. George Jaimson [sic]. Boston, n. d. (Federal St. Theatre, Boston, 1847.)

Rhode Island; or, Who's the Governor? S. S. Steele. (Walnut, 1842.) Cf. Rees.

Ribbemont; or, The Feudal Baron. Wm. Dunlap. N. Y., 1803. (John St., Oct. 31, 1796, as *The Mysterious Monk.*)

Rich and Poor of Boston, The. "By a Gentleman of this City." (Boston Museum, Feb. 8, 1858.)

Richard Savage. "Trans. and adapted to the Eng. stage by M. Morton Dowler." (St. Charles Theatre, New Orleans, Dec. 6, 1840.)

Richelieu; a Domestic Tragedy. J. H. Payne. N. Y., 1826. (Covent Garden, London, Feb. 11, 1826; Chestnut, 1829.)

Richmond Hill. N. H. Bannister. (Greenwich Theatre, N. Y., May 11, 1846.)

Rienzi. L. H. Medina. (Bowery, May 23, 1836.)

Right of Search, The; or, Freedom and Unity. S. S. Steele. MS. Harvard. (National Theatre, N. Y., June 21, 1858.)

Rights of Man, The. O. S. Leland. Adap. of *Les Droits de l'Homme* by J. De Premary. N. Y., 1857. (Wallack's Theatre, N. Y., May 23, 1857.)

Rinaldo Rinaldini; or, The Great Banditti. Wm. Dunlap (?). N. Y., 1810.

Rinaldo Rinaldini. Anon. (Pennsylvania Theatre, Nov. 16, 1836.)

Rio Grande, The. Anon. (Greenwich Village Theatre, N. Y., July 4, 1846.)

Rip van Winkle; or, The Spirits of the Catskill Mountains. Anon. (Pearl St. Theatre, Albany, May 26, 1828.)

Rip Van Winkle; or, The Demons of the Catskill Mountains!!! John Kerr. Phila., [1830-5]. (Tottenham St. Theatre, London; Walnut, Oct. 30, 1829.)

Rip Van Winkle, A Legend of the Catskills. Charles Burke. N. Y., n. d. (National Theatre, N. Y., Jan. 7, 1850.)

Rip Van Winkle, A Legend of Sleepy Hollow. Revision by T. H. Lacy of two preceding plays. London, n. d., as by John Kerr.

Rip Van Winkle. J. H. Wainwright. N. Y., 1855. (Niblo's Garden, N. Y., Sept. 27, 1855.)

Rip Van Winkle. Revision by Dion Boucicault. MS., Lord Chamberlain's office. (Adelphi Theatre, London, Sept. 4, 1865.)

Rip Van Winkle. Revision by Joseph Jefferson. N. Y., 1895. See text.

Rise of the Rothschilds, The. W. E. Burton. (National Theatre, Phila., Jan. 27, 1842.)

Rising Glory of America, The. H. H. Brackenridge and Philip Freneau. Phila., 1772. (College of New Jersey, 1771.)

Rival Chieftains of Mexico, The; or, A Yankee Right Side Up. Silas S. Steele. (Arch, Dec. 3, 1852.)

A LIST OF AMERICAN PLAYS

River Driver, The; or, The Raftsman's Oath. A Tale of the Penobscot and Rio Grande. Anon. (Concert Hall, Portland, Maine, Sept. 29, 1847.)

Rizzio. C. J. Cannon. In *Poems, Dramatic and Miscellaneous*, N. Y., 1851.

Road to Fortune, The. Eugene Raux. Phila., 1846.

Robber Chieftain, The. "By a gentleman of Philadelphia." (Walnut, March 24, 1837.)

Robbers, The. J. H. Payne (?). (Sadler's Wells Theatre, London, Sept. 20, 1820.)

Robbery, The. Wm. Dunlap. (Park, Dec. 30, 1799.)

Robert Emmet. Dion Boucicault. *A. L. P.*, 1940. (McVickar's Theatre, Chicago, Nov. 5, 1884.)

Robert Emmet. James Pilgrim. N. Y., [1857]. (St. Charles Theatre, N. Y., Aug. 29, 1853.)

Robert Emmet, the Irish Patriot. N. H. Bannister. 2 acts in prompt copy, Brown Univ. (New Chatham Theatre, N. Y., Jan. 6, 1840.)

Robespierre. Wm. Dunlap.

Rokeby. By "Mr. Kilty, Chancellor of Maryland." (Baltimore, Nov. 19, 1816.)

Rokeby; or, A Tale of the Civil War. William Cox. (Park, May 17, 1830.)

Roman Captive, The. Anon. (Bowery, Oct. 21, 1839.)

Romance after Marriage; or, The Maiden Wife. F. B. Goodrich and F. L. Warden. Adap. of *La Clef d'Or*, by Octave Feuillet. N. Y., n. d. (Wallack's Theatre, N. Y., Nov. 17, 1857.)

Romance and Reality; or, Silence Gives Consent. John Brougham. N. Y., [1856]. (Princess Theatre, London, June 1, 1847; Broadway, April 17, 1848.)

Romance of a Poor Young Man, The. Lester Wallack and Pierrepont Edwards. N. Y., [1859]. Adap. of Feuillet's novel. (Wallack's Theatre, N. Y., Jan. 24, 1860.)

Roman Tribute, The; or, Attila the Hun. Elizabeth Oakes Smith. N. Y., 1850? (Arch, Nov. 11, 1850.)

Romanzo; or, The Conscience Stricken Brigand. John N. Smith. N. Y., 1840. (Walnut, Aug. 19, 1839.)

Romulus, the Shepherd King. J. H. Payne. MS. in Harvard Univ. Library. *A. L. P.*, 1940.

Ronmore. O. B. Bunce. MS. Harvard Library, n. d.; c. 1850.

Rookwood. [N. H. Bannister?] Dram. novel by W. H. Ainsworth. Phila., 1849. (Bowery, June 17, 1839.)

Rosa. W. G. Hyer. N. Y., 1822.

A LIST OF AMERICAN PLAYS

Rose Elmer; or, A Divided Heart and a Divided Life. G. L. Aiken. Adap. of a novel by Mrs. Southworth. (New Bowery, Oct. 29, 1860.)

Rose Gregorio; or, The Corsican Vendetta. Mrs. Sidney F. Bateman. (Winter Garden, N. Y., May 21, 1862.)

Rose of Arragon, [sic] *The; or, The Vigil of St. Mark.* S. B. H. Judah. N. Y., 1822. (Park, April 18, 1822.)

Rosina Meadows, the Village Maid. C. H. Saunders. N. Y., n. d. Prompt Copy, Harvard. (National Theatre, Boston, March 21, 1843.)

Row at the Lyceum, A. John Brougham. (Brougham's Lyceum, N. Y., April 22, 1851.)

Royal Poetaster, The. Epes Sargent. In *The New World*, III, (1841,) 33-34. Reprinted as *The Candid Critic* in *Songs of the Sea*, Boston, 1847.

Rudolph; or, The Robbers of Calabria. J. D. Turnbull. Boston, 1807. (Bedlow St. Theatre, N. Y., Dec. 8, 1804.)

Ruling Passion, The. John Brougham. (Wallack's Theatre, Oct. 19, 1859.)

Rural Felicity. John Minshull. N. Y., 1801. (Bedlow St. Theatre, N. Y., Jan. 15, 1805.)

Sabotier; or, The Fairy and the Wooden Shoemaker. J. S. Wallace. (Franklin Theatre, N. Y., Oct. 2, 1837.)

Sack of Rome, The. Mercy Warren. In *Poems, Dramatic and Miscellaneous*, Boston, 1790.

Sailor's Joy, The; or, Commerce Restored. Anon. (Charleston Theatre, April 25, 1808.)

Sailor's Return, The; or, The Constitution Safe in Port. Anon. (Boston Theatre, 1815.)

St. Dollar, and the Monster Rag. S. S. Steele. (National Theatre, Balt., June 7, 1841.)

St. Vallier's Curse; or, The King's Fool. W. E. Burton. Prompt Copy, dated Providence, Feb. 29, 1852, in Brown Univ. Adap. *Le Roi S'Amuse.* (Bowery, June 2, 1855 as *The King's Fool.*) Prob. revision of Burton's earlier *Court Fool.*

Sam Patch; or, The Daring Yankee. E. H. Thompson. (Buffalo Theatre, 1836-37; Bowery, May 1, 1837.)

Sam Patch in France; or, The Pesky Snake. J. P. Addams. (Walnut, May 11, 1843.)

Sans Souci, alias Free and Easy; or, An Evening's Peep Into a Polite Circle. Anon. Boston, 1785.

A LIST OF AMERICAN PLAYS

Santa Anna; or, The Liberation of Texas. Anon. (Bowery, June 20, 1836.)

Santa Claus; or, A Christmas Dream. J. B. Phillips. (Burton's Theatre, N. Y., Dec. 24, 1849.)

Sara Maria Cornell; or, The Fall River Murder. Mary Clarke. N. Y., 1833. (Richmond Hill Theatre, N. Y., August, 1834.)

Saratoga Springs; or, The Dangers of an Alias. Anon. (Olympic Theatre, N. Y., Dec. 2, 1841.)

Sassacus; or, The Indian Wife. W. Wheatley (?). Quotations in Rees, 16. (Park, July 8, 1836.)

Saul. A. C. Coxe. N. Y., 1845.

Saul Sabberday, the Idiot Spy. Dram. of Ned Buntline's story. Anon. (Bowery, June 21, 1858.)

Saw Mill, The; or, A Yankee Trick. Micah Hawkins. N. Y., 1829. (Chatham Garden Theatre, N. Y., Nov. 29, 1824.)

Scarlet Letter, The. G. L. Aiken. Dram. of novel. (Barnum's Museum, Feb. 24, 1858.)

Scarlet Letter, The. G. H. Andrews. Dram. of novel. (Boston Theatre, Dec. 28, 1857.)

Scenes at the Fair. Anon. Boston, 1833.

School for Citizens, The; or, The Choice—Love or Honour. Anon. (John St., May 14, 1796.)

School for Politicians, The; or, Non Committal. Anon. Adap. of Bertrand et Raton, by Scribe. N. Y., 1840.

School for Prodigals, The. J. Hutton. Phila., 1809. (Chestnut, Feb. 20, 1809.)

School for Soldiers, The. Wm. Dunlap. (Park, July 4, 1799.)

School for Soldiers, The. John Henry. Kingston, Jamaica, 1783. (John St., April 24, 1788.)

School of Ten Quakers, The. F. S. Hill. (American Theatre, New Orleans, April 16, 1838.)

Sckaggs Family. J. M. Field. (American Theatre, New Orleans, Jan. 24, 1842.)

Scott and Pierce; or, The Champion of Freedom. Anon. (National Theatre, Phila., Aug. 26, 1852.)

Scourge of the Ocean, The. Henry Coleman. (American Theatre, New Orleans, Jan., 1837.)

Scourge of the Ocean, The. W. A. Fenno. MS., University of Pennsylvania Library. (Chatham Theatre, N. Y., Aug. 3, 1846.)

Sculptor's Daughter, The. C. J. Cannon. In *Dramas*, N. Y., 1857.

Seamstress of New York, The. Anon. (National Theatre, N. Y., Feb. 17, 1851.)

A LIST OF AMERICAN PLAYS

Sea of Ice, The; or, A Thirst for Gold, and The Wild Flower of Mexico.
Anon. N. Y. and London, n. d. Adap. of *La Prière des Naufragés*
by Dennery and Dugué. (Chatham Theatre, N. Y., April 17,
1854 as *The Child of Prayer*.)

Search after Happiness. Anon. Catskill, 1794.

Sea Serpent, The; or, Gloucester Hoax. William Crafts. Charleston,
1819. (Anthony St. Theatre, N. Y., July 14, 1814.)

Seeing the Elephant. (Burton's Theatre, N. Y., Sept. 15, 1848); an
adaptation by D. G. Robinson, *Seeing the Elephant; or, Seth
Slope's First Visit to San Francisco*, was played at Dramatic
Museum, San Francisco, July 4, 1850.

Self. Mrs. Sidney F. Bateman. N. Y., [1856]. (Bateman's St. Louis
Theatre, June 18, 1856.)

Semiramis; or, The Queen of Assyria. J. T. Trowbridge. Adap. from
play by Voltaire. (National Theatre, Phila., Sept. 25, 1857.)

Señor Valiente. G. H. Miles. Baltimore, 1859. (Holliday St. Theatre,
Balt., 1859; Niblo's Garden, N. Y., April 18, 1859.)

Sentinels, The; or, The Two Serge[a]nts. R. P. Smith. Adap. of *Les
deux Sergents*, by M. D'Aubigny. MS. in Hist. Soc. of Penna.
A. L. P., 1941. (Walnut, Dec. 18, 1829.)

Sertorius; or, The Roman Patriot. D. P. Brown. Phila., 1830. (Chestnut, Dec. 14, 1830.)

Servants by Legacy. James Pilgrim. N. Y., n. d. (National Theatre,
N. Y., Feb. 19, 1851.)

Seth Slope, or Done for a Hundred. Anon. (Walnut, Oct. 26, 1839.)

1777; or, The Times That Tried Us Americans. Anon. (Walnut,
April 5, 1844.)

Shadow on the Wall, The. Anon. (Chestnut, Oct. 3, 1835.)

Shaker Lovers, The. S. D. Johnson. N. Y., n. d. (National Theatre,
Boston, Feb. 10, 1851.)

Shakespeare in Love. R. P. Smith. MS. in Hist. Soc. of Penna.
A. L. P., 1941.

Shakespeare's Dream. John Brougham. N. Y., n. d. (Academy of
Music, N. Y., Aug. 2, 1858.)

Shandy Maguire; or, The Bould Boy of the Mountains. James Pilgrim.
N. Y., n. d. (Bowery, Aug. 18, 1851.)

Sharratah; or, The Last of the Yemassees. Anon. (Walnut, Nov. 18,
1842.)

Shaughraun, The. Dion Boucicault. London, [1875]. (Wallack's
Theatre, N. Y., Nov. 14, 1874.)

Shelty's Travels. Wm. Dunlap. (John St., April 24, 1794.)

Shepherdess of the Alps. Anon. N. Y., 1815.

A LIST OF AMERICAN PLAYS

She Would Be a Soldier; or, The Plains of Chippewa. M. M. Noah. N. Y., 1819. (Park, June 21, 1819.)

Ship's Carpenter of Kensington, The. Anon. (Arch, Aug. 13, 1850.)

Shocco Jones; or, Southern Assurance. By "a Mississipian." [J. G. Stearns?] (City Theatre, Natchez, March 26, 1842.)

Shoemaker of Toulouse, The; or, The Avenger of Humble Life. F. S. Hill. Adap. of *Le Savetier de Toulouse* by Pierre Cadmus and Francis Cornu. Boston, n. d. (Warren Theatre, Boston, Oct. 27, 1834.)

Siam Light Guard, The. E. G. P. Wilkins. (Laura Keene's Theatre, Sept. 28, 1857.)

Siege of Algiers, The; or, The Downfall of Hadgi-Ali-Bashaw. J. S. Smith. Phila., 1823.

Siege of Boston, The; or, The Spirit of 1776. J. S. Jones. (National Theatre, Boston, March 11, 1839.)

Siege of Charleston, The; or, The Battle of Fort Moultrie. Anon. (Charleston Theatre, Feb. 22, 1843.)

Siege of Monterey, The. J. Foster. (Arch, Oct. 31, 1846.)

Siege of Tripoli, The. M. M. Noah. (Park, May 15, 1820.)

Siege of Yorktown, The. M. M. Noah. (Park, Sept. 8, 1824.)

Signor Marc. J. H. Wilkins. *A. L. P.*, 1941. (Broadway, Sept. 3, 1854.)

Silver Knife; or, The Hunters of the Rocky Mountains. James Pilgrim. (National Theatre, N. Y., March 3, 1856.)

Silver Spoon, The. J. S. Jones. Boston, 1911. (Boston Museum, Feb. 16, 1852.)

Simon Solus; or, Just Paid Off from the "Dale." Charles Clewcaring. N. Y. Priv. Print., 1843. (By amateurs, on board the U. S. Sloop-of-war "Dale," Valparaiso Harbor, July 22, 1843.)

Siren of the Sea, The. Anon. (Bowery, July 15, 1844.)

Sister, The. Charlotte R. Lennox. London, 1769. (Covent Garden, London, Feb. 18, 1769.)

Sisters, The. Fitz James O'Brien. Adap. *Ange ou Diable.* (Wallack's Lyceum, Dec. 27, 1854.)

Six Degrees of Crime, The. F. S. Hill. Adap. of *Les Six Degrés du Crime* by Theodore Nezel and Benjamin Antier. (Tremont Theatre, Boston, Jan. 15, 1834.)

Skeleton Robber, The. H. E. Stevens. (Walnut, Oct. 1, 1836.)

Slave Actress, The. Elizabeth F. Ellet. (Burton's Theatre, N. Y., Dec. 10, 1856.)

Slaves in Algiers; or, A Struggle for Freedom. S. H. Rowson. Phila., 1794. (Chestnut, Dec. 22, 1794.)

A LIST OF AMERICAN PLAYS

Slaves in Barbary. David Everett. In *The Columbian Orator*, 1810.

Smike, or Scenes from Nicholas Nickleby. See *Nicholas Nickleby.*

Snow Fiend, The. Anon. (Franklin Theatre, N. Y., Nov. 13, 1837.)

Snow Flower, The. Dion Boucicault. (Windsor Theatre, N. Y., Nov. 22, 1880.) Same as *Pauvrette*, slightly revised.

Socialism; or, Modern Philosophy Put in Practice. Anon. Adap. from *Fourierism.* (Burton's Chambers Street Theatre, N. Y., April 9, 1849.)

Soldier of '76, The. Wm. Dunlap. (Park, Feb. 23, 1801.)

Soldier of the Revolution, The. W. Barrymore. (Walnut, Feb. 4, 1832.)

Soldier's Dream, The. C. L. Stone. (Park, Jan. 3, 1840.)

Solitary, The; or, The Man of Mystery. R. P. Smith. MS. in Hist. Soc. of Penna.

Solitary of Mount Savage, The; or, The Fate of Charles the Bold. J. H. Payne. Adap. of Pixerécourt's *Le Mont Sauvage.* Auto. MS., Luquer Coll. *A. L. P.*, 1940. (Surrey Theatre, London, May 27, 1822.)

Solitary of Mount Savage, The. "Trans. by a gentleman of this city." (American Theatre, New Orleans, June 2, 1824.)

Solon Shingle; or, The People's Lawyer. N. Y., 1890. See *The People's Lawyer.*

Some Things Can Be Done as Well as Others. H. H. Paul. (Peale's Philadelphia Museum, May 16, 1848.)

Son and Father; or, The Dutch Redemptioner. J. Kerr and S. Chapman. (Walnut, April 26, 1830.)

Son of the Night, The. Charles Gayler. Adap. of *Le Fils de la Nuit* by Victor Sejour. N. Y., [1857]. (Broadway, May 4, 1857.)

Son of the Wilderness, The. Charles Edward Anthon. Translated from a dramatic poem by Friedrich Halm. New York, 1848.

Sons of the Cape; or, Life's Lee Shore, J. S. Jones. (Boston Museum, Jan. 29, 1866.)

Spae Wife, The. Dion Boucicault. Dram. of *Guy Mannering.* MS. Lord Chamberlain's Office, MS. fragment, Princeton. (Copyright perf., Elephant and Castle, Lond., March 30, 1886.)

Spanish Castle, The. See *The Knight of Guadalquiver.*

Spanish Husband, The; or, First and Last Love. J. H. Payne. MSS., Harvard and Lord Chamberlain's Office. *A. L. P.*, 1940. (Drury Lane, London, May 25, 1830; Park, Nov. 1, 1830.)

Spanish Pirates; or, A Union of the Flag. H. J. Conway. (Walnut, Nov. 14, 1835.)

Spanish Rover, The. J. N. Barker.

Spanish Student, The. H. W. Longfellow. Cambridge, 1843.

485

A LIST OF AMERICAN PLAYS

Sparring with Specie. Anon. (Olympic Theatre, N. Y., Sept. 7, 1840.)

Spell-bound. Dion Boucicault. Adapted by Grangé and Montepin from *Pauline*, by Dumas *père*. (Wallack's Theatre, Feb. 24, 1879.)

Spirit of Air, The; or, The Enchanted Isle. John Brougham. (Brougham's Lyceum, N. Y., April 7, 1851.)

Spirit of '76, The; or, Washington. Anon. Prompt Copy, Brown Univ. (Walnut, Sept. 23, 1835.)

Splendid Misery. C. T. P. Ware. (Laura Keene's Theatre, October 19, 1857.)

Sprightly Widow, The; or, A Speedy Way of Uniting the Sexes by Honorable Marriage. John Minshull. N. Y., 1803. (Bedlow St. Theatre, Aug. 7, 1805.)

Spy, The; A Tale of the Neutral Ground. C. P. Clinch. *A. L. P.*, 1941. MS. in N. Y. Public Library, 1822. (Park, March 1, 1822.)

Spy in New York, A. Anon. (Chatham Theatre, N. Y., Nov. 6, 1843.)

Spy in Washington. J. S. Wallace. (Franklin Theatre, N. Y., Dec. 25, 1837.)

Squatter, The. J. Rees. (St. Charles Theatre, New Orleans, March 31, 1838.)

Squire Hartley. C. S. Talbot. Albany, 1827. (York, Upper Canada, March, 1825.)

Stage Struck Yankee, The. O. E. Durivage. In *New York Drama*, IV, 1878, 250-256. (Chatham Theatre, N. Y., Dec. 14, 1840.)

Star of Seville, The. Frances Kemble (Butler). N. Y., 1837. (Walnut, Aug. 7, 1837.)

Star of the West, The. Anon. (Arch, Phila., Dec. 10, 1852.)

Star-Spangled Banner, The. Anon. (Bowery, May 8, 1846.)

Star Spangled Banner, The; or, The American Tar's Fidelity. Anon. (Bowery, Feb. 13, 1837.)

Stars and Stripes, The; or, The Patriot's Dream. Charles Gayler. (New Bowery, April 29, 1861.)

Sterne's Maria; or, The Vintage. Wm. Dunlap. (Park, Jan. 14, 1799.)

Stewart's Capture; or, The Captive's Ransom. S. S. Steele. (Bowery, Aug. 22, 1841.)

Stewart's Triumph. Anon. (Arch, Aug. 3, 1842.)

Stranger, The. Wm. Dunlap. (Park, Dec. 10, 1798.)

Stranger's Birthday, The. Wm. Dunlap. (Park, April 23, 1800.)

Strike for Wages, The. Anon. (Bowery, Sept. 7, 1850.)

Struggle for Life and Death, The. Dion Boucicault. (Arch, April 27, 1850.)

Student of Morlaix, The. E. Forrester. (Arch, Oct. 10, 1851.)

Such as It Is. J. M. Field. (Park, Sept. 4, 1842.)

A LIST OF AMERICAN PLAYS

Suicide, The. Thos. Day. Litchfield, [1797]. (Yale College, Sept. 13, 1797.)

Sultana, The; or, A Trip to Turkey. Anon. N. Y., 1822.

Superstition. J. N. Barker. [Phila., 1826]. (Chestnut, March 12, 1824.)

Superstition. Anon. MS., Harvard. [Circa 1815.]

Surgeon of Paris, The. J. S. Jones. N. Y., [1855]. (National Theatre, Boston, Jan. 8, 1838.)

Swamp Fox, The; or, Marion and his Merry Men. Anon. (Arch, April 1, 1846.)

Swamp Steed, The; or, Marion and his Merry Men of 1776. H. H. Paul. Dram. of *The Partisan* by Simms. (National Amphitheatre, Phila., April 28, 1850.)

Sweet Lips; or, The Magic Deer. James Pilgrim. (National Theatre, N. Y., March 2, 1852.)

Sybil. John Savage. N. Y., 1865. (St. Louis Theatre, Sept. 6, 1858.)

Sylla. Anon. N. Y., 1827. Adap. of *Sylla* by E. Jouy. (Chatham Theatre, N. Y., Jan. 15, 1827.)

Syracusan Brothers, The. N. H. Bannister. (Walnut, Jan. 15, 1836.)

Tailor in Distress, The; or, A Yankee Trick. Sol. Smith. (Globe Theatre, Cincinnati, July 17, 1823.)

Take Care of Little Charley. John Brougham. N. Y., [1858]. (Wallack's Theatre, N. Y., Nov. 26, 1858.)

Take That Girl Away. Anon. (Burton's Theatre, N. Y., May 15, 1855.)

Taking the Chances. Charles Gayler. (Burton's Theatre, March 19, 1855.)

Tale of a Coat, The. Dion Boucicault. MS., Lord Chamberlain's office, as *Jimmy Watt.* (Daly's Theatre, N. Y., Sept. 14, 1890.)

Tale of Lexington, A. S. B. H. Judah. N. Y., 1823. (Park, July 4, 1822.)

Tale of the Crusades. "By a Gentleman of New York." (Park, June 25, 1827.)

Talisman, The. "By a gentleman of this City." (American Theatre, New Orleans, April 7, 1826.)

Tammany. Anne Kemble Hatton. (John St., March 3, 1794.)

Tam O'Shanter. J. S. Jones. (Warren Theatre, Boston, May 26, 1834.)

Tancred; or, The Rightful Heir of Rochdale Castle. G. R. Lillibridge. Providence, 1824.

Tancred; or, The Siege of Antioch. John A. Stone. Phila., 1827.

Tancred, King of Sicily. John A. Stone. Fourth Act, in *A. L. P.*, XIV, 1941. (Park, March 16, 1831.)

Tangorua. Anon. Phila., 1856.

Tantalization; or, The Governor of a Day. Royall Tyler. MS. See *The Island of Barrataria.*

Tars from Tripoli. J. D. Turnbull. Adap. Dibdin's *Naval Pillar.* (Park, Feb. 24, 1806.)

Tears and Smiles. J. N. Barker. Phila., 1808. (Chestnut, March 4, 1807.)

Tecumseh; or, The Battle of the Thames. Richard Emmons. Phila., 1836. (Tremont Theatre, Boston, June 4, 1834.)

Telemachus; or, The Enchanted Isle. J. B. Phillips. (National Theatre, N. Y., Jan. 15, 1838.)

Tell Truth and Shame the Devil. Wm. Dunlap. N. Y., 1797. (John St., Jan. 9, 1797.)

Telula; or, The Star of Hope. C. H. Saunders. Prompt Copy, Brown Univ. (Boston Museum, Feb. 7, 1845.)

Temple of Independence, The. Wm. Dunlap. (Park, Feb. 22, 1799.)

Temptation; or, The Irish Immigrant. John Brougham. N. Y., [1856]. (Burton's Theatre, N. Y., Sept. 10, 1849.)

Ten Nights in a Bar Room. William W. Pratt. Dram. of novel by T. S. Arthur. N. Y., n. d. MS. copy of original MS., Harvard. (National Theatre, N. Y., Aug. 23, 1858.)

Ten Years of a Seaman's Life. J. B. Phillips. (Bowery, May 21, 1831.)

Teresa Contarini. Elizabeth F. Ellet. In *Poems, Translated and Original*, Phila., 1835. (Park, March 19, 1835.)

Thérèse, the Orphan of Geneva. J. H. Payne. London, 1821. (Drury Lane, London, Feb. 2, 1821; Anthony St. Theatre, N. Y., April 30, 1821.)

There's Nothing in It. Dion Boucicault. (Walnut Street Theatre, Phila., June 29, 1855.)

Thirty Years; or, The Life of a Gamester. Wm. Dunlap. MS. in Yale Univ. *A. L. P.*, 1940. (Bowery, Feb. 22, 1828.)

This House to be Sold, the Property of the Late William Shakespeare! John Brougham. (Olympic, N. Y., Nov. 15, 1847.)

Three Brothers; or, Crime Its Own Avenger. N. H. Bannister, Buffalo, 1840. (Chatham Theatre, N. Y., 1839-40?) [Cast given in printed play, but not in Odell.]

Three Degrees of Banking. J. S. Jones. (National Theatre, Boston, March 12, 1838.)

Three Dukes, The; or, The Lady of Catalonia. See *Isadora.*

Three Eras of Washington's Life. Anon. (Walnut, Jan. 1, 1849.)

Three Experiments of Living, a Tale of Boston. J. S. Jones. (National Theatre, Boston, Feb. 20, 1837.)

Three Fast Men; or, Female Robinson Crusoes. (Bowery, March 29, 1858.)

Three Guardsmen, The. Lester Wallack. (Bowery, Nov. 12, 1849.)

Three Milanese. In *Two Tragedies*, "by an American," N. Y., 1835.

Three Years After. B. A. Baker. (National Theatre, N. Y., June 4, 1849.)

Times, The; or, Life in New York. J. H. Hackett (?). (Park, Dec. 10, 1829.)

Times that Tried Us; or, The Yankee in 1777. J. H. Conway. (Caldwell's New Theatre, Mobile, Feb. 1, 1841.)

Time Tries All. Anon. (Bowery, Nov. 6, 1848.)

Tippecanoe; or, The Hunter of the West. Anon. (Bowery, May 8, 1840.)

'Tis Ill Playing with Edged Tools. Anon. (Burton's Theatre, April 16, 1856.)

Tohopeka; or, The Heroes of the South. Anon. (Bowery, Dec. 24, 1830.)

Tom and Jerry in America. John Brougham. (Niblo's Garden, Nov. 13, 1844.) Played at Chatham Theatre, Nov. 30, as *Life in New York.*

Toodles, The. W. E. Burton. N. Y., n. d. (Burton's Theatre, N. Y., Oct. 8, 1848.) Revision of Burton's *The Broken Heart* (Park, Dec. 26, 1842.)

Toothache, The. John Bray. Phila., 1814. (Park, March 21, 1813.)

Tortesa the Usurer. N. P. Willis. N. Y., 1839. (National Theatre, N. Y., April 8, 1839.)

Tourists in America. J. M. Field. (American Theatre, New Orleans, May 7, 1833.)

Tower of Nesle, The. "Adapted from J. Haynes' translation of Victor Hugo by George Farren." (American Theatre, New Orleans, May 22, 1835.)

Tragedians, The. Rawlinson, "A gentleman of this city." (American Theatre, New Orleans, May 24, 1831.)

Tragedy of Superstition, The. See *Superstition.*

Traitor, The; or, The Battle of Yorktown. Anon. (Bowery, May 4, 1846.)

Traveller Returned, The. Mrs. Judith Sargent Murray. In *The Gleaner*, III, (1798,) 116-163. (Federal St. Theatre, Boston, March 9, 1796.)

A LIST OF AMERICAN PLAYS

Travellers, The. J. N. Barker. Adap. of Andrew Cherry's *Travellers, or Music's Fascination.* (Chestnut, Dec. 26, 1808.)

Trial of Effie Deans, The. Dion Boucicault. See *Jeanie Deans.*

Trial without Jury; or, The Magpie and the Maid. J. H. Payne. Auto. MS., Harvard. *A. L. P.*, 1940. (Covent Garden, September 15, 1815?.)

Tripolitan Prizes; or, The Veteran Tar. (Chestnut, March 7, 1804.)

Trip to Niagara. Anon. (Burton's Theatre, N. Y., Dec. 25, 1855.)

Trip to Niagara, A; or, Travellers in America. Wm. Dunlap. N. Y., 1830. (Bowery, Nov. 28, 1828.)

Trip to the California Gold Mines, A. Charles Burke (?). (Arch, Jan. 10, 1849.)

Triumph at Plattsburg, The. R. P. Smith. In Quinn, *Representative American Plays*, 165-180. See Bibliography. (Chestnut, Jan. 8, 1830.)

Triumph of Liberty, The; or, Louisiana Preserved. J. B. White. Charleston, 1819.

Triumph of Texas, The. Anon. (Bowery, Dec. 31, 1835.)

Triumphs of Love, The; or, Happy Reconciliation. J. Murdock. Phila., 1795. (Chestnut, May 22, 1795.)

Triumphs of Rough and Ready, The; or, The Past, Present, and the Future. Anon. (Welch's Amphitheatre, Phila., Nov. 24, 1848.)

True Blue; or, The Sailor's Festival. (John St., April 24, 1788.)

Trust, The. Charles Breck. N. Y., 1808.

Truxtun's Victory; or, The Captive of the Mine. S. S. Steele. (Front St. Theatre, Balt., Nov. 24, 1840.)

Tuckitomba; or, The Obi Sorceress. (Park, May 16, 1831.)

Tutoona; or, The Battle of Saratoga. G. W. Harby. (American Theatre, New Orleans, Feb. 21, 1835.)

'Twas All for the Best; or, 'Tis All a Notion. R. M. Bird. MS. dated 1827 in Univ. of Pennsylvania. *A. L. P.*, 1941.

'Twas I; or, The Truth a Lie. J. H. Payne. London, 1825. N. Y., 1827. (Covent Garden, London, Dec. 3, 1825; Park, May 19, 1826.)

Two Galley Slaves, The; or, The Mill of St. Aldervon. J. H. Payne. Adap. of *Les deux Forçats* by Boiré. London, n. d. (Covent Garden, London, Nov. 6, 1822; Park, Oct. 27, 1823.)

Two Gregories, The; or, Luck in a Name. Anon. New York, n. d.

Two Sons-in-Law, The. J. H. Payne. MS. in Harvard Univ., dated London, March 26, 1824. *A. L. P.*, 1940.

Two Spaniards, The. N. H. Bannister. (Franklin Theatre, N. Y., Aug. 31, 1838.)

A LIST OF AMERICAN PLAYS

Two to One; or, The King's Visit. Lester Wallack. (Wallack's Theatre, N. Y., Dec. 6, 1854.)

Tycoon, The; or, Young America in Japan. Joseph Jefferson (?). (Laura Keene's Theatre, July 2, 1860.)

Tyrant's Victims, A. M. Pinckney (?). Charleston, 1818.

Tyrolese Peasant, A. J. H. Payne (?). (Drury Lane, London, May 8, 1832.)

Ugolino. J. B. Booth. Phila. and N. Y., [1840]. (Chestnut, April 20, 1825.)

Una. Dion Boucicault. (Gaiety Theatre, New Orleans, Feb. 6, 1856.)

Uncle Pat's Cabin. H. J. Conway. (Burton's Theatre, N. Y., May 23, 1853.)

Uncle Tom's Cabin; or, Life Among the Lowly. G. L. Aiken. N. Y., n. d. (Museum, Troy, Sept., 1852.)

Unknown, The; or, The Demon's Gift. J. Rees. MS., Harvard. (St. Charles Theatre, New Orleans, March 2, 1837.)

Upper Ten and Lower Twenty, The. T. B. DeWalden. (Burton's Theatre, N. Y., Nov. 16, 1854.)

Ups and Downs of New York Life. George L. Aiken. (National Theatre, N. Y., June 8, 1857.)

Upside Down; or, Philosophy in Petticoats. J. Fenimore Cooper. (Burton's Chambers St. Theatre, N. Y., June 18, 1850.)

Usef Caramalli. See *The Siege of Tripoli.*

Usurper, The. James McHenry. Phila., 1829. (Chestnut, Dec. 26, 1827.)

Usurper, The; or, Americans in Tripoli. J. S. Jones. Revision of Ellison's *American Captive.* MS. in Beck Collection, New York Public Library. *A. L. P.*, 1941. (Boston, 1840-41?.)

Valdemar; or, The Castle of the Cliff. J. W. Simmons. Phila., 1822.

Valeria; or, Love and Blindness. Adap. by "an American Author" from *Valérie*, by Scribe and Mélesville. Albany, n. d.

Valeria; or, The Roman Sisters. Anon. (Chestnut, Sept. 19, 1851.)

Vanity Fair. John Brougham. (Burton's Theatre, N. Y., Jan. 25, 1849.)

Vanity Fair; or, Vain of their Vices. Dion Boucicault. Adap. of *Les Fanfarons de Vice* by Dumanoir. Orig. MS. in Fitzhugh Greene Coll. (Laura Keene's Theatre, N. Y., March 12, 1860.)

Velasco. Epes Sargent. Boston, 1837. (Tremont Theatre, Boston, Nov. 20, 1837.)

A LIST OF AMERICAN PLAYS

Venetian Bride, The. "By one of the literati of New York." (Bowery, June 6, 1834.)

Venetian, The. R. P. Smith. Holograph MS. dated 1836. Harvard. (Arch, March 24, 1849.) [This play was first called *The Bravo.*] See Bibliography, Chap. VIII.

Venetian Buccaneers, The; or, The Prophet of the Bohmer Wald. J. F. Poole. Prompt Copy, Harvard. (Bowery, Aug. 20, 1859.)

Venice Preserved. Revised by Dion Boucicault. (Booth's Theatre, Sept. 14, 1874.)

Venison Preserved; or, a Pot Uncovered. J. S. Jones. (Tremont Theatre, May 19, 1829.)

Vermont Wool Dealer, The. C. A. Logan. N. Y., n. d. (Bowery, April 11, 1840.)

Very Age, The. E. S. Gould. N. Y., 1850.

Veteran, The; or, France and Algeria. Lester Wallack. N. Y., [1859]. Dram. of *Frank Hilton; or, "The Queen's Own,"* by James Grant. (Wallack's Theatre, N. Y., Jan. 17, 1859.)

Vice Versa. Dion Boucicault. Adap. *Le Truc d'Arthur* by Alfred Duru and Henri Chivot. Orig. MS. in Fitzhugh Greene Coll. (Wollock's Theatre, Springfield, Mass., March 21, 1883; Star Theatre, N. Y., March 26, 1883.)

Victim, The. D. G. Robinson. (Dramatic Museum, San Francisco, Aug. 13, 1850.)

Victoire; or, A Tale of the American Camp. Anon. (Tremont Theatre, Boston, Sept. 7, 1835.)

Victor; or, The Independents of Bohemia. J. D. Turnbull. Charleston, 1806 ?. (Providence Theatre ?.)

Victoria. J. M. Field. (St. Louis Theatre, Oct. 19, 1838.)

Victory upon Victory; or, Triumphs on Land and Sea. Anon. (The Circus, Phila., April 24, 1847.)

Virginia. John Parke. Phila., 1786.

Virginia; or, Love and Bravery. Albert M. Gilliam. (Richmond Theatre, May 29, 1829.)

Virginia; or, The Patrician's Perfidy. J. H. Payne. (Park, Feb. 19, 1834.)

Virginius. W. K. Northall. Burlesque of Knowles' play. (Olympic, N. Y., Dec. 14, 1844.)

Virgin of the Sun, The. Wm. Dunlap. Adap. *Die Sonnen Jungfrau,* N. Y., 1800. (Park, March 12, 1800.)

Virtue Triumphant. Mrs. Judith Sargent Murray. In *The Gleaner,* III, (1798,) 15-87. (Federal St. Theatre, Boston, March 2, 1795, as *The Medium.*)

A LIST OF AMERICAN PLAYS

Vision of the Bard, The. William Barrymore. (Tremont Theatre, Boston, Jan. 22, 1833.)

Voice of Nature, The. Wm. Dunlap. N. Y., 1803. (Park, Feb. 4, 1803.)

Volunteers, The. S. H. Rowson. (Chestnut, Jan. 21, 1795.)

Volunteers' Departure and Return. Anon. (Walnut, July 24, 1848.)

Votary of Wealth. J. G. Holman. (Charleston Theatre, Feb. 14, 1816.)

Wacousta; or, The Curse. N. H. Bannister (?). (Arch, Feb. 19, 1849.)

Wacousta; or, The Curse. ?. Jackson. (Walnut, April 8, 1834.)

Wacousta; or, The Curse. R. Jones (?). MS. in New York Public Library.

Wacousta; or, The Curse. L. H. Medina. (Bowery, Dec. 30, 1833.)

Wag of Maine, The. C. A. Logan. (Park, April 16, 1834.)

Waldimar. J. J. Bailey. N. Y., 1834. (Park, Nov. 1, 1831.)

Wall Street. T. B. De Walden. (Burton's Theatre, Mar. 23, 1857.)

Wall Street as It Now Is. ?. Mead. N. Y., 1826.

Wall Street; or, Ten Minutes Before Three. ?. Mead. N. Y., 1819.

Walter Brandt; or, The Duel in the Mist. Anon. (Walnut, Sept. 24, 1836.)

Walter Raymond; or, The Lovers of Accomac. Anon. (Walnut, March 8, 1849.)

Wandering Boys, The; or, The Castle of Olival. M. M. Noah. Boston, 1821. (Charleston, 1812, as *Paul and Alexis;* Covent Garden, London, Feb. 24, 1814; Park, March 16, 1820.)

Wandering Jew, The. N. H. Bannister. (St. Charles Theatre, New Orleans, Jan., 1837.)

Wanted—A Widow. Dion Boucicault and Charles Seymour. N. Y., [1857]. Adap. of *Touch and Take,* (London, Dec. 11, 1827) from *Monsieur Jovial; ou, L'huissier chansonnier,* by Theaulon and Choquart. (Wallack's Theatre, N. Y., Nov. 9, 1857.)

Washington and Napoleon; or, The Conqueror's Dream. S. S. Steele. (1841.) Cf. Rees.

Washington; or, The Hero of Valley Forge. James Rees. (Walnut, Jan. 9, 1832.)

Washington; or, The Orphan of Pennsylvania. "By a Charleston Gentleman." ("Old" Charleston Theatre, Jan. 8, 1824.)

Washington; or, The Path to Fame and Glory. Anon. (Bowery, Feb. 17, 1851.)

Washington; or, The Retaliation. John Dumont. Adap. of *Washington; ou, Les Représailles,* by Henri de Lacoste. (Walnut, Jan. 9, 1832.)

A LIST OF AMERICAN PLAYS

Washington Preserved. James Rees. (American Theatre, New Orleans, Jan. 8, 1836.)

Washington's Birthday; or, The New York Boys. (Greenwich Village Theatre, July 4, 1846.)

Washington's Challenge. S. S. Steele. Cf. Rees.

Washington, the Savior of His Country. Anon. (Arch, May 22, 1831.)

Water Witch, The. C. W. Taylor. (Bowery, March 21, 1830.)

Water Witch, The. J. S. Wallace. (Arch, 1831-32.)

Water Witch, The; or, The Skimmer of the Seas. R. P. Smith. Dram. Cooper's novel. (Chestnut, Dec. 25, 1830.)

Weeds Among the Flowers. "By an American Gentleman." (Wallack's Lyceum, Nov. 21, 1854.)

Wept of Wish-Ton-Wish, The. Anon. N. Y., 1856. (Bowery, Dec. 1, 1834.)

Werdenberg; or, The Forest League. Caroline Lee Hentz. (Park, March 24, 1832.)

Western Heir, The. Anon. (Chatham Theatre, N. Y., June 15, 1846.)

West Point; or, A Tale of Treason. Joseph Breck. Balt., 1840.

West Point Preserved. Wm. Brown. (Haymarket Theatre, Boston, April 17, 1797.)

Westward Ho. J. S. Wallace. (National Theatre, Boston, Feb. 7, 1833.)

Wheat and Chaff. D. W. Wainwright. N. Y., 1858. (Wallack's Theatre, N. Y., Oct. 30, 1858.)

Wheel of Truth, The. James Fennell. (Park, Jan. 12, 1803.)

Wheelwright, The; or, Boston Pride. J. S. Jones. (Boston Museum, Jan. 13, 1845.)

Where Is He? Wm. Dunlap. (Park, Dec. 2, 1801.)

Where's Barnum? W. E. Burton. (Burton's Theatre, N. Y., Dec. 11, 1848.)

Which Shall I Marry; or, Who Loves Best? James McHenry. MS.

Whigs and Democrats; or, Love of No Politics. J. E. Heath. Richmond, 1839. (Walnut, Oct. 12, 1839.)

White Lies. Mrs. E. F. Ellet. N. Y. *c.* 1858, as by "Cyril Turner." Adap. of Reade's novel. (Laura Keene's Theatre, Jan. 30, 1858.)

White Maid [or Lady], The. J. H. Payne. (Covent Garden, London, Jan. 2, 1827; Park, May 21, 1832.)

Who's Got Macready?; or, A Race to Boston. Anon. (Olympic Theatre, N. Y., Oct. 6, 1848.)

Who's Got the Countess?; or, The Rival Houses. D. G. Robinson. (San Francisco Theatre, June 20, 1853.)

Wicomiket; or, The Indian's Curse. H. J. Conway. (New Bowery, Feb. 27, 1860.)

A LIST OF AMERICAN PLAYS

Widow of Malabar, The; or, The Tyranny of Custom. David Humphreys. In *Miscellaneous Works*, Phila., 1790. (Southwark Theatre, Phila., May 7, 1790.)

Widow's Curse, The. J. B. Phillips. (Franklin Theatre, N. Y., Jan. 5, 1837.)

Widow's Marriage, The. G. H. Boker. In *Plays and Poems*, Boston, 1856.

Widow's Son, The; or, Which is the Traitor? Samuel Woodworth. N. Y., 1825. (Park, Nov. 25, 1825.)

Wife at a Venture, A. R. P. Smith. MS. in Hist. Soc. of Penna. *A. L. P.*, 1941. (Walnut, July 25, 1829.)

Wife of Two Husbands, The. Wm. Dunlap. N. Y., 1804. (Park, April 4, 1804.)

Wigwam, The; or, Templeton Manor. Anon. Dramatization of *The Pioneers.* (Park, July 3, 1830.)

Wild Goose Chace, The. Wm. Dunlap. N. Y., 1800. (Park, Jan. 24, 1800.)

Wild Indian, The. W. T. Thompson. (Burton's Lyceum, N. Y., Jan. 10, 1851.)

Wild Irish Girl, The. N. Y. and London, n. d., (Holliday St. Theatre, Balt., April 1, 1858.)

Wild Steed of the Prairie, The. Anon. Adap. of Simms' *Yemassee.* (Bowery, Dec. 7, 1845.)

William Penn. R. P. Smith. Holograph MS., Prompt copy, Harvard. *A. L. P.*, 1941. (Walnut, Dec. 25, 1829.) See Bibliography. Chap. VIII.

William Tell; or, The Archers. See *The Archers.*

Wissahickon; or, The Heroes of 1776. Anon. (National Theatre, N. Y., Jan. 17, 1857.)

Wissmuth and Company; or, The Noble and the Merchant. Elizabeth F. Ellet. Adap. novel by Franz Dingelstadt. (Park, April 13, 1847.)

Witch, The; or, A Legend of the Catskill. H. B. Mattison. (Chatham Theatre, N. Y., May 24, 1847.)

Witch, The. R. P. Smith. Holograph MS. dated Oct. 1, 1837. Harvard.

Witchcraft; or, The Martyrs of Salem. Cornelius Mathews. London, 1852. N. Y., 1852. *A. L. P.*, 1941. (Walnut, May 5, 1846.)

Wives Pleased and Maids Happy. William Milns. (Park, May 16, 1798.)

Wizard of the Wave, The. Anon. (Bowery, Jan. 19, 1846.)

Woman of the World, A; or, A Peep at the Vices and Virtues of City Life. J. B. Howe. N. Y., n. d. (National Theatre, N. Y., Dec. 13, 1858.)

A LIST OF AMERICAN PLAYS

Woman's Revenge. J. H. Payne. Auto. MS., Harvard. *A. L. P.,* 1940. (Olympic Theatre, London, Feb. 27, 1832.)

Wood Dæmon, The; or, The Clock Has Struck. J. D. Turnbull. Boston, 1808. (Boston Theatre, 1808; Park, May 9, 1808.)

World a Mask, The. G. H. Boker. MS. dated 1851. *A. L. P.,* 1941. (Walnut, April 21, 1851.)

World's Fair in London, The. John Brougham. (Brougham's Lyceum, N. Y., Feb. 10, 1851.)

World's Fair, The; or, London in 1851. W. E. Burton. (Burton's Chambers St. Theatre, Feb. 15, 1851.)

World's Own, The. Julia Ward Howe. Boston, 1857. (Wallack's Theatre, N. Y., March 16, 1857, as *Leonora.*)

Wounded Hussar, The; or, Rightful Heir. J. Hutton. N. Y., 1809. (Chestnut, March 29, 1809.)

Wreck of Honor, The. Lemuel Sawyer. N. Y., 1824.

Wrong Passenger, The; or, Secrets of the Cotton Market. Anon. (Park, Sept. 20, 1847.)

Xerxes the Great; or, The Battle of Thermopylæ. Anon. Phila., 1815.

Yankee Chronology; or, Huzza for the Constitution! Wm. Dunlap. N. Y., 1812. (Park, Sept. 7, 1812.)

Yankee Naval Chronology. Continuation of above. N. Y., 1812.

Yankee Duelist; or, Bunker Hill's Representative. N. H. Bannister. (Walnut, Oct. 3, 1838.)

Yankee Duelist; or, The Steamboat Excursion. A. Newton Field. Prompt Copy. Brown Univ. (Arch, Dec. 3, 1852.)

Yankee in Spain, The. See *Knight of the Golden Fleece.*

Yankee in Time, The. J. P. Addams? (Park, Aug. 9, 1838.)

Yankee Jack; or, The Buccaneers of the Gulf. James Pilgrim. MS., N. Y., Public Library. Also Brown Univ. (National Theatre, N. Y., Feb. 9, 1852.)

Yankee Land. C. A. Logan. N. Y., n. d. (Penna. Theatre, Phila., Jan. 4, 1837.)

Yankee Peddler. Anon. (Park, Sept. 6, 1834.)

Yankees in China. Anon. (Bowery, July 20, 1840.)

Yankee Tar, The; or, The Storming of the Derne. Anon. (Bowery, Jan. 8, 1835.)

Yankey in England, The. David Humphreys. N. p., n. d. [1815]. (Humphreysville, Conn., by amateurs, Jan., 1814?)

Yelva; or, The Orphan of Russia. Said to be trans. from the French by Lola Montez. (American Theatre, San Francisco, May 27, 1853.)

A LIST OF AMERICAN PLAYS

Yemassee, The. Anon. (Bowery, Aug. 17, 1835.)
Yemassee, The. A. G. Fenno (?). Dram. of Simms' novel. (Charleston Theatre, Jan. 6, 1845.)
Yorker's Stratagem, The; or, Banana's Wedding. J. Robinson. N. Y., 1792. (John St., April 24, 1792.)
You Can't Open. "Mr. Shands of St. Louis." (Varieties Theatre, St. Louis, May 10, 1852.)
Young Actress, The. Dion Boucicault. Revision of *The Manager's Daughter*, by E. Lancaster. MS. Prompt Copy, Fitzhugh Greene Coll. (Burton's Theatre, N. Y., Oct. 22, 1853.)
Young America in London. Anon. (New Theatre, Charleston, April 22, 1774.)
Young Carolinians, The; or, Americans in Algiers. M. Pinckney (?). Charleston, 1818.
Young Man About Town, The. L. B. Chase (?). N. Y., 1854.
Young New York. E. G. P. Wilkins. N. Y., n. d. (Laura Keene's Theatre, N. Y., Nov. 24, 1856.)
Youthful Days of Harrison, The. Anon. (American Theatre, New Orleans, Nov. 29, 1840.)
Yuseff Caramalli. See *The Siege of Tripoli.*

Zafari, the Bohemian. J. S. Jones. (Boston Theatre, Feb. 25, 1856.)
Zamba; or, The Insurrection. Mrs. Elizabeth Ricord. Cambridge, 1842.
Zamira. J. B. Phillips. N. Y., 1835.
Zamor. J. G. Percival. In *Poems*, New Haven, 1821. (Yale College, 1815.)
Zanthe; or, The Fatal Oath. William Barrymore. Adap. of Kenney's version of *Hernani*. (Walnut, Jan. 28, 1835.)

INDEX

INDEX

INDEX

Armand, 316-317.
Armourer's Escape, The, 144-145; scenario, 145.
Arnold, 278.
Arnold, Benedict, 52, 88, 127, 157, 278.
Arnold; or, The Treason of West Point, 278.
Arrah-na-Pogue, 380.
Aston, Anthony, 5.
Athenia of Damascus, 266.
Aurungszebe, influence of, 26.
Autobiography of an Actress, 318, 319.
Aylmere, 251.

B

Babo, J. M., influence of, 101.
Bailey, J. J., his *Waldimar,* 254-255.
Baker, B. A., 336; his *Glance at New York,* 305-307; *New York as It Is,* 306, 307; *Three Years After,* 306; *Mose in China,* 307.
Ballou, M. M., his *Miralda,* 302.
Baltimore Theatre, 61, 143, 201.
Balzac, H. de, 220.
Banker's Daughter, The, 382.
Bankrupt, The, 356-357, 362.
Bannister, N. H.: his *Putnam,* 265, 278-279; *Gaulantus,* 265; *England's Iron Days,* 265; *The Three Brothers,* 265; *The Gentleman of Lyons,* 265; *The Maine Question,* 284.
Bare and Ye Cubb, Ye, 5.
Barker, James N., 136-151, 159, 161, 205, 269, 270, 294, 309, 336; birth, 136; a Democrat, 136; military service, 136; public career, 136-137; death, 137; his *The Spanish Rover,* 137; *America,* 137; *Tears and Smiles,* 137; *The Embargo,* 138; *The Indian Princess,* first Indian play performed, and first original American play performed in London, 139, sources of, 139; *Marmion,* 140-144, announced as foreign play, 140, 141, sources of, 141-142, used as medium to express patri-

otic views during War of 1812, 142-144, quotations from, 143-144; *The Armourer's Escape,* concerning the Northwest Boundary, 144-145; *How to Try a Lover,* 145-147, its French sources, 146-147; *Superstition,* on Colonial themes, 147-151, quotations from, 149, 150; his skill, 150-151; bibliography of, 409.
Barnes, Charlotte (Mrs. Conner), 170, 184, 282; her *Octavia Bragaldi,* 260-261; *La Fitte,* 261; *A Night of Expectations,* 261; *Charlotte Corday,* 261; *The Forest Princess,* 273, 282; bibliography of, 414.
Barnes, Mrs. John, 273.
Barrett, Lawrence, 349, 355.
Barrière, Théodore, influence of, 382.
Bateman, Mrs. Sidney F.: her *Self,* 321; *Golden Calf,* 322; *Geraldine,* 322; *Rose Gregorio,* 322; *Evangeline,* 322.
Battle of Brooklyn, The, 57-58.
Battle of Buena Vista, 286.
Battle of Bunker's Hill, The, 50-53, 405; analysis of, 50-53; quotations from, 50-52; reprint of, 396.
Battle of Eutaw Springs, The, 155.
Battle of Lake Champlain, The, 333.
Battle of New Orleans, The (Dunlap), 107.
Battle of New Orleans, The (Grice), 154.
Battle of Stillwater, The, 282.
Baudouin, J. M. T., influence of, 168.
Bayard, Alfred, influence of, 377.
Beatrice, 323-324.
Beauchampe, 260.
Beauchamp-Sharpe murder, 260.
Beaumont and Fletcher, influence of, on Godfrey, 4, 26.
Beaux Stratagem, The (Farquhar), 11.
Beaux Without Belles, 160.
Beete, John, his *Man of the Times,* 133.
Beggar's Opera (Gay), 11.
Belle Lamar, 382-383.

INDEX

INDEX

INDEX

Brisebarre, Edouard, influence of, 308, 370.

British soldiers in drama, 59.

Broadway Theatre, closing of, 389.

Broker of Bogota, The, 239-243, 267; remarkable character study, 240-243; quotations from, 241, 242; letter from Forrest concerning, 243; vitality of, 243; financial returns of, 245; Forrest prevents publication of, 246; first publication of, 412-413.

Brougham, John, 217n., 275, 335; his *Pocahontas,* 273; *Franklin,* 279; his version of *Dred,* 289; *Life in New York,* 307-308; *The Musard Ball,* 322; *Temptation,* 376, 377.

Brown, Charles Brockden, 80, 85, 119, 175, 254.

Brown, D. P.: his *Sertorius,* 249; *Prophet of St. Paul's,* 250.

Brown, Jacob, 151, 152.

Brown, John, 290, 372.

Brown University Library, 96

Brutus (Voltaire), influence of, 171-174.

Brutus; or, The Fall of Tarquin, 170-174, 178, 219, 220, 254; actors in title rôle, 170; sources of, 171-174; quotations from, 174; played at testimonials, 184, 185; influence in later tragedy, 187; reprints of, 397, 410.

Bryant, W. C., 271, 363.

Bulwer, influence of, 360.

Bunce, O. B.: his *Love in '76,* 279; *The Morning of Life,* 280-281; *Marco Bozzaris,* 281; *Fate; or, The Prophecy,* 364; bibliography of, 415.

Bunker Hill, reprint of, 408.

Burgoyne, General, 46, 51, 59, 152.

Burk, J. D., 117-120, 126; his *Bunker Hill,* 117, 119, 126; *Female Patriotism,* 117-119, quotations from, 118; relation of *Female Patriotism* to *Henry VI,* 117; his conception of Joan of Arc, 117-119; *Bethlem Gabor,* 119; *The Innkeeper of Abbeville,* 120n.; *Oberon,* 120n.; bibliography of, 408.

Burke, Charles, 287, 300, 301, 328-331; his *Rip Van Winkle,* 328-331.

Burnett, J. G., 369; his *Blanche of Brandywine,* 281.

Burney, Fanny, influence of, 116.

Burton, W. E., 206, 208, 229, 307, 322, 332, 335, 390; his *Toodles,* 332; *Ellen Wareham,* 332.

Butler, Fanny Kemble: see Kemble, Fanny.

Byers, S. H. M., 273.

Byron, Lord, 188, 192, 220, 310.

C

Caigniez, L. C., influence of, 102, 168, 220.

Caissier, Le, influence of, 209.

Caius Marius, 213-215, 218, 219, 267; quotations from, 214-215.

Calavar, 247.

Calaynos, 338-340, 341, 364; London performance of, 338; laid in Spain, 339; revisions of, 339, 340n., 362; receipts from, 363n.

Caldwell, J. H., 263.

California plays, 287.

Camillus, 253.

Canadian characters, in drama, 156.

Candidates, The, 54-55; first Negro character in, 55.

Cannibals, The, 158.

Cannon, C. J., his *Oath of Office,* 364, 376.

Caprice, 323.

Captain Kyd, 301.

Captain Morgan, 283.

Captured Slave, The, 290n.

Careless Husband, The (Cibber), 11.

Caridorf, 224.

Carleton, General Guy, 52.

Carpenter of Rouen, The, 299n.

Cato, 7, 8, 60.

Cerro Gordo, 286.

505

INDEX

Cervantes, influence of, 137, 266.
Champions of Freedom, The, 282.
Chanfrau, F. S., 304-307.
Chapman, Mrs. S., 326n., 327n.
Chapman, S. H., 161n.; his *Son and Father*, 275-276.
Chapman, William, 327.
Chapman, W. A.: his *Mose in California*, 306; *Mose in a Muss*, 306.
Charles the Second, 164, 178-181; Payne's collaboration with Irving in, 179-181; source of, 180-181; played at testimonials, 184; reprints of, 396, 410.
Charles II, roi d'Angleterre, 180.
Charleston group of playwrights, 187-193; bibliography of, 411.
Charleston theatres, 61, 135; first, in Dock Street, 8; new theatre, 15; histories of, 400.
Charlotte Corday, 261.
Chase, L. B., his *Young Man About Town*, 324.
Chatham Garden Theatre, opening of, 200.
Chaucer, influence of, 337.
Chester, Leonard, his *Federalism Triumphant*, 131.
Chestnut Street Theatre: built, 82; description of, 82; fine company in, 201; decline of, 201.
Chippewa, Battle of, 151, 152, 155.
Chivers, T. H., his *Conrad and Eudora*, 260.
Christy Minstrels, 335.
Cid, The, 262.
Circuit, theatrical, 62.
City life, plays of, 225, 303-309.
City Looking Glass, The, 225.
Civil War: play dealing with, 383; effect of, upon drama, 389.
Clapp, W. W., 154.
Clara; ou, Le Malheur et la Conscience, influence of, 215.
Clara Wendell; ou, La Demoiselle Brigand, influence of, 215.
Clari, 178.

Clarissa Harlowe, 386.
Clarke, Mary, her *Fair Americans*, 154.
"Classic," definition of, 221.
Clay, Henry, 142.
Clifton, Josephine, 255, 261.
Clinton, Sir Henry, 49, 51, 87, 157.
Cockings, George, 29.
Coleman, William, 165.
Colleen Bawn, The, 377-380; circumstances of composition of, 377; sources of, in fact and fiction, 377-379; reality of characters in, 379; vitality of, 380; performances in Great Britain, 380; adaptation into French, 380; basis for first travelling company, 388.
College drama: effect of, on Godfrey, 4, 18; at William and Mary, 5, 7, 28; at University of Pennsylvania, 18-20, 27; at Princeton, 27-28; at Yale, 62, 134; at Dartmouth, 134; as origin of American play writing, 391.
College of Philadelphia: see University of Pennsylvania.
College student satirized, 160.
Collegians, The, influence of, 377-379.
Colman, George, influence of, 296.
Colonial history, in drama, 147-151, 208, 275-277.
Colonial period, bibliography of, 403-405.
Columbian Daughter, The, 123.
Comedy: first, 61; social, 53-54, 63-70, 76-77, 109, 111, 137-138, 178-181, 188, 206, 279-280, 309-324, 344-346, 386, 391; romantic, 145, 257-259, 316-317, 324, 341-343, 368, 369, 377-382, 383-385; domestic, 91, 96, 99-100, 114-115, 159-160, 166, 294-303; American types of, 292-336; mixture of types of, 324-325; bibliography of, 415-417.
Comet, The, 133.
Commercial Crisis, A, 362.
Committee, The (Howard), 11.

506

INDEX

INDEX

Day, Thomas, his *Suicide*, 134.
Dean (Hayne), Julia, 263, 277, 346, 356.
Death of General Montgomery, The, 52-53.
Decatur, Stephen, 154.
Deed of Gift, The, 156.
Deformed, The, 211-213, 218, 219; quotations from, 212-213; reprint of, 411.
Dekker, Thomas, influence of, 93-95, 211-212.
De Lara, 204, 264-265.
Democracy and Aristocracy, 308.
Democratic ideas: in *Prince of Parthia*, 27; in later drama, 63, 185, 267.
Democratic party, 284-285.
Désaugiers, influence of, 206.
Deseret Deserted, 287.
Deserteur, Le, 95.
De Soto, 274-275.
De Walden, T. B., his *Upper Ten and Lower Twenty*, 321.
Dialogue Between a Southern Delegate and his Spouse, 56-57; quotations from, 56-57.
Dialogue Between the Ghost of General Montgomery and an American Delegate, 53; reprint of, 405.
Dickens, Charles, combination of classic material and idealistic treatment in, 221.
Diderot, 90.
Disappointment, The, 29, 160.
Disowned, The, 209-210.
Distant Relations, 291.
Distressed Mother, The (Ambrose Philips), 11, 24-25, 26, 162.
Divorce, The, 206, 211, 218.
"Dixie," 335.
Dixon, G. W., his "Coal Black Rose" and "Old Zip Coon," 334.
Doctor in Spite of Himself, The, 72.
Dolman, John, 287.
Domestic comedy, 91, 96, 99-100, 114-115, 159-160, 166, 294-303.

Domestic drama, 89-91, 93-94, 110-111, 211-213, 215-216, 325-331, 371-372; relations of, in England, France, Germany and America, 90.
Domestic tragedy, 62, 89, 115-116, 120, 181-183, 189-190, 239-243, 372-374.
Don Carlos, 95.
Don Quixote, influence of, 72, 122.
Dot, 371-372.
Doubts and Fears, influence of, 206.
Douglas, Payne's début in, 165.
Douglass, David, manager of the American Company, 13; plays in New York, 13, 15; in Philadelphia, 13; in New England, 14, 15; in Williamsburg, 15; in Charleston, 15; goes to England, 16; builds theatre in Philadelphia, 16; plays in *Prince of Parthia*, 16, 23; builds theatre in New York, 30; in Annapolis, 31; in Charleston, 31; departs for West Indies, 32.
Down East, 297.
Downman, Hugh, influence of, 171-174.
Drama, early, significance of, 391-392.
Dramatic criticism: first, 14; in New York, beginning of, 80.
Dred: Taylor's version, 289; Brougham's version, 289; Conway's version, 289.
Dresser, Marcia van, 350.
Drew, John, 388.
Drew, Mrs. John, 287.
Drink, 387n.
Drummer, The (Addison), 11.
Drury Lane, first American play produced at, 139.
Dryden, John, influence on Godfrey, 26.
Ducange, Victor, influence of, 175.
Duché, Jacob, epilogue by, 27.
Duff, John, 140, 141.
Duff, Mary Ann, 147, 161.
Duke's Wager, The, 253.

INDEX

INDEX

510

INDEX

INDEX

INDEX

Historical tragedy, 62-63, 86-88, 97-98, 109, 110, 111, 116-118, 147-151, 170, 174, 213-215, 224-239, 249, 255, 265-266, 270, 274, 276-277, 340-341, 346-360.

Histories of the American Theatre, 398-402.

Hodgkinson, John, 79, 82, 83, 86, 88, 96, 99, 101, 132, 135; death, 105.

Hoffman, C. F., 260.

Holcroft, Thomas, 90, 102.

Holland, E. C., his *Corsair*, 192.

Holland, E. G., his *Highland Treason*, 278.

Holland, George, 374.

Holmes, O. W., 363.

"Home, Sweet Home," 178.

Honest Whore, The, influence of, 93-95, 211.

Honor, motive in drama, 222.

Hook, Theodore, influence of, 206.

Hooke, N., his *Roman History*, a source for *The Gladiator*, 230.

Hopkinson, Francis: first poet-composer, 18; takes part in *Masque of Alfred*, 19; ode by, 27.

L'Hôtel garni, ou la Leçon singulière, 206.

Howard, Bronson, 336, 382.

Howard, Cordelia, 288.

How to Try a Lover, 145-147; sources, 146.

Howe, General, 47, 49, 51, 59, 281.

Howe, Julia Ward, 267, 365-367, 391; birth, 365; her *Leonora*, 365; *Hippolytus*, 365-367; quotations from, 366; bibliography of, 414-415.

Hoyt, Charles, 287.

Hubbell, Horatio, his *Arnold*, 278.

Hue and Cry, 301.

Huger, Francis, 158.

Hugo, Victor, influence of, 216, 218, 219, 220, 354.

Humphreys, David, 122; his *Widow of Malabar*, 113-114; *Yankey in England*, 113, 114-115; bibliography of, 408.

Hunt, Leigh, 351-352.

Hunter, Governor Robert, 6.

Hurlbert, W. H., his *Americans in Paris*, 323.

Hutchinson, Foster, satirized: in *The Adulateur*, 36; in *The Group*, 41.

Hutchinson, Thomas, satirized: in *The Adulateur*, 34-38; in *The Group*, 41, 44; in *The Fall of British Tyranny*, 48.

Hutton, Joseph: his *School for Prodigals*, 196; *Wounded Hussar*, 196; *Orphan of Prague*, 196; *Fashionable Follies*, 196.

Hutton, Laurence, 333, 399, 410, 411.

I

"Idealistic," definition of, 221.

Inchbald, Mrs., 91, 92, 166, 167.

Inconstant, The (Farquhar), 11.

Independence; or, Which Do You Like Best?, 188.

Indian characters, 131, 138-140, 145, 208, 244, 251, 269-275.

Indian plays: motive first treated in *Ponteach*, 28; first to be performed, 139; vogue of, 269-270, 270-275; the Pocahontas theme in, 272-273; list of (1825–1860), 275n.; burlesqued, 275; bibliography of, 415.

Indian Princess, The, 138-140, 270, 272; first Indian play performed, 139; first original American play performed in London after performance in America, 139; reprints of, 396, 405.

Indian Prophecy, The, 270.

Indian Wife, The, 156n., 274, 297.

Indians in England, The, 95.

Infidel, The, novel dramatized, 247.

Ingersoll, C. J., 116-117; his *Edwy and Elgiva*, 116-117; *Julian the Apostate*, 117; bibliography of, 408-409.

Inquisitive Yankee, The, 297.

Ioor, William: his *Battle of Eutaw Springs*, 155; *Independence*, 188.

INDEX

Ireland: plays laid in, 249, 364, 375, 376, 377-380, 381, 386.

Ireland and America, 376.

Irish Assurance and Yankee Modesty, 376.

Irish characters in American drama, 104, 108, 249, 287, 375-381; conventional types of, 375-377; reality of, in Boucicault's plays, 377-381.

Irma, 263.

Irving, Washington, 164, 165, 168, 255, 267, 296, 325, 330, 332; collaboration with Payne, 179-181, 182-183.

Is She a Brigand? 215.

Isidora, 224.

Island of Barrataria, The, 72; manuscript and publication of, 406.

Italian Bride, The (Levy), 364.

Italian Bride, The (Payne), 186.

Italian Father, The, 93, 95, 109, 111, 112, 211.

Italy, plays laid in (including Roman historical plays), 93, 95, 100, 110, 111, 112, 170-174, 178, 185, 186, 187, 188, 190-191, 192, 205, 211-215, 224, 229-237, 251, 252, 253, 255, 256-259, 260, 261, 264, 265, 267, 341-344, 348-356, 364, 371.

J

Jack Cade, 205, 251, 267.

Jackson, Andrew, 154, 207-208, 267, 283.

Jackson, Stonewall, 383.

Jacob Leisler, 276-277.

James IV of Scotland, 142-144.

Jamieson, George, 291.

Jane Shore (Rowe), 11.

Jefferson, John, 145, 326-327.

Jefferson, Joseph, 1st, 89, 94, 137, 145.

Jefferson, Joseph, 2d, 330.

Jefferson, Joseph, 3d, 281, 288, 330-332, 371, 372, 374; his revision of *Rip Van Winkle,* 330-332; commissions Boucicault to rewrite

play, 330-331; alterations by, 331-332.

Jefferson, Thomas (actor), 145.

Jefferson, Thomas (President), 33; drama attributed to, 57; as character, 130.

Jefferson and Liberty, 130.

Jérôme Pointu, 84.

Jessie Brown; or, the Relief of Lucknow, 371.

Jeunesse de Henri V, La, influence of, 180-181.

Jeunesse du Duc de Richelieu, La, influence of, 181.

Jewitt, John, 144, 145.

Jilt, The, 386.

"Jim Crow," song of, 334.

Joan of Arc, in the drama, 117-119.

John Street Theatre, 71; built, 30; reopened, 61.

Johnson, S. D., 376; his *The Fireman,* 307.

Jonathan in England, 296.

Jones, Hugh, 6-7.

Jones, J. S., 153, 298-301; his *Adventure,* 282; dramatization of *Eugene Aram,* 298; *The Liberty Tree,* 298; *The Green Mountain Boy,* 298; *Moll Pitcher,* 298, 299n.; description of the conditions of the playwright, 298-299n.; *The People's Lawyer,* 299-300; *The Silver Spoon,* 300; *Captain Kyd,* 301; *The Surgeon of Paris,* 301; *The Carpenter of Rouen,* 301; bibliography of, 416. See also the List of Plays.

Joseph and His Brethren, 72; manuscript and publication of, 406.

Judah, S. B. H.: his *Tale of Lexington,* 155; *Mountain Torrent,* 197; *Rose of Arragon,* 197.

Judgment of Solomon, The, 72; manuscript and publication of, 398.

Jugement de Salomon, Le, influence of, 102.

Julia, 165.

Junius Brutus, influence of, 171-174.

515

INDEX

INDEX

Liberty in Louisiana, 135.
Liberty Tree, The, 298.
Libraries containing collections of American plays, 403.
Life in London, influence of, 303.
Life in New York (Anon.), 304.
Life in New York (Brougham), 307.
Life in Philadelphia, 304.
"Light of the Lighthouse, The," 311.
Lighting by gas introduced, 201.
Lillo, George, influence of, 90, 120-121.
Lily of Killarney, The, 380.
Lincoln, Abraham, 288.
Lindsley, A. B., his Love and Friendship, 160, 294.
Lion of the West, The, 205, 293-294, 319.
Lippard, George, influence of, 281.
Live Woman in the Mines, A, 287.
Logan, C. A., 301-302; his Yankee Land, 301; The Vermont Wool Dealer, 301; Chloroform, 301.
London, first original American play produced in, 139.
London Assurance, 368.
Longfellow, H. W., 205, 266-267, 363; his Spanish Student, 266-267.
Lord, W. W., his André, 278.
Louis XII, 250.
Louis XV, 316.
Louis XVI, 134, 279.
Love and Friendship, 160, 294.
Love for Love (Congreve), 11
Love in Humble Life, 177, 184.
Love in '76, 279; reprint of, 396, 415.
Love of country, motive in drama, 222.
Love of sex, motive in drama, 222.
Lovers' Vows (Dunlap), 91-92.
Lovers' Vows (Payne), 166, 169; comparison of versions, 166-167.
Low, Samuel, his Politician Outwitted, 129-130.
Lowell, J. R., 287, 363.
Lucius Junius Brutus, Father of His Country, influence of, 171-174.

Lucius Junius Brutus; or, The Expulsion of the Tarquins, influence of, 171-174.
Luck of Roaring Camp, The, 387.
Lucy Sampson, 89.
Ludlow, N. M., 325, 326, 328.
Lying Valet, The (Garrick), 11.

M

"Macedonian, The," 154.
MacKaye, J. S., 176.
Macomb, Alexander, his Pontiac, 274.
Macready, W. C., 203, 220.
Madame du Barry, 186n.
Mademoiselle de Belle Isle, 253.
Madison, James, 50.
Madmen All, 320.
Mahomet, 167.
Mahomet II, 194.
Maid and the Magpie, The, 168.
Maid's Tragedy, The, 26.
Major André, 278.
Man of Fortitude, The, 85, 132, 133.
Man of the Black Forest, The, 186n.
Man of the Times, The, 133.
Man of the World, The (McKenzie), influence of, 115.
Manfredi, 192.
Marble, Dan, 295, 301, 302, 303.
Marchand de Jouets d'Enfant, Le, influence of, 371.
Marco Bozzaris, 281.
Marcos Farfán de los Godos, Captain, 4.
Marion, Francis, 277.
Marion; or, The Hero of Lake George, 152.
Marion; or, The Reclaimed, 324.
Marius, Caius, 213-214.
Markoe, Peter: his The Patriot Chief, 62; The Reconciliation, 63.
Marmion, 140-144; its production, 140-141; great popularity, 141; relation to Scott, 141-142, to Holinshed, 141-142; quotations from, 143-144; expresses national feeling, 142-144.

INDEX

INDEX

on John St., 30; Park Theatre, 86; general condition of, in 1805, 135; in 1822-25, 200; Chatham Garden Theatre, 200; Lafayette Theatre, 200; Bowery Theatre, 200; rise of Park Theatre, 202; strong company at Park, 202; Niblo's Garden, 202; foreign stars in, 203; histories of, 399.

News of the Night, 225.

Niblo's Garden, opening of, 202.

Nicholas Nickleby, 372.

Nichols, J. H.: his *Essex Junto*, 130; *Jefferson and Liberty*, 130n.; *The New England Coquette*, 130n.

Nick of the Woods, novel, 247; dramatization of, 247, 274.

Night of Expectations, A, 261.

Nina, 104.

Noah, M. M., 151-153, 154, 161, 198; birth and death, 151; his early efforts in Philadelphia, 151; his *Fortress of Sorrento*, 151; *Paul and Alexis*, 151, 193-194; *She Would be a Soldier*, 151-152, 154; *Marion*, 152; *The Grecian Captive*, 152-153, 194; *The Siege of Tripoli*, 153, 154; comparison with Payne, 177; *The Wandering Boys*, 193-194; bibliography of, 409.

Noble Exile, The, 319.

"Noble savage," the, in drama, 98.

Nodier, Charles, influence of, 368.

Norah, 186n.

Northeastern Boundary dispute, 284.

Northwestern Boundary dispute, 145, 284.

Nunes, J. A., his *Fast Folks*, 287.

Nus, Eugène, influence of, 308, 370.

Nydia, 360, 362.

O

Oath of Office, The, 364, 376.

O'Brien, Fitz-James, his *Gentleman from Ireland*, 377.

Octavia Bragaldi, 260-261, 273.

Octoroon, The, 290, 291, 335, 372-374; risk of presentation, 372; sources of, 373-374; skillful changes by Boucicault, 373; appeals to both North and South, 374; reprint of, 396, 421.

"Ode to America," 358.

Odell, George C. D., 95, 97, 237n., 296n., 304n., 309n., 328n., 349n.

O'Dowd, The, 381-382; source of, 381.

O'Keeffe, John, 70, 77, 375.

"Old Block," his *Live Woman in the Mines*, 287.

Old Guard, The, 368.

Old Heads and Young Hearts, 368.

Old New York, 277.

Old Plantation, The; or, The Real Uncle Tom, 291, 374n.

Oldest surviving theatre, 13.

Oliver, Andrew, satirized in *The Adulateur*, 34.

Oliver, Peter, satire of, 43.

Oralloossa, 215, 238-239, 267, 274; sources of, 238; noble savage motive in, 238; financial returns of, 245; publication of, 246.

Orchestra, beginnings of, 86.

Oregon, 284.

Origin of the Feast of Purim, The, 72; manuscript and publication of, 406.

Orlando; or, Parental Persecution, 115.

Orphan of Prague, The, 196.

Orphans, The, 192.

Orton, J. R., his *Arnold*, 278.

Ossawattomie Brown, 290.

Oswali of Athens, 184.

Othello, 11.

Otho, 196-197.

Otis, James, 33, 35, 42.

Our Best Society, 321.

Our Flag is Nailed to the Mast, 286.

"Our Heroic Themes," 358.

Owen, R. D., his *Pocahontas*, 273.

Owens, J. E., 300, 321, 372.

P

Paddy's Trip to America, 375.

Paine, Thomas, 53.

INDEX

INDEX

Power of Sympathy, The, 76.
Powhatan, 140.
Preservation, 120.
Preuss, H. C., his *Fashions and Follies of Washington Life*, 324n.
Price, Stephen, 105.
Prince of Parthia, The: production of, 16; revival of, 17; plot of, 20-21; criticism of, 22, 23; quotations from, 22, 25, 27; comparison with British drama, 23; sources in Parthian history, 24; sources in British plays, 24-26, 28; representative play of its period, 30; priority to *Leicester*, 78; progress from, to *Francesca da Rimini*, 367; reprints of, 396, 405.
Princeton College, 27-28, 50, 338.
Prize plays, 263, 264, 265, 270-271, 296, 302, 309.
Procrastination, 183.
Prophet of St. Paul's, The, 250.
Proverb, The, 103.
Providence theatres, histories of, 400.
Provoked Husband, The (Vanbrugh), 11; influence of, on *The Contrast*, 70.
Puritan intolerance, 161, 276.
Putnam, 265, 278-279.
Putnam, Israel, 49, 50, 58, 277, 278-279.

Q

Quadroon, The, influence of, 373.
Quaker, the, on the stage, 124, 281.
Quite Correct, 206.

R

Radcliffe, Mrs. Anne, 80.
Räuber, Die, influence of, 89.
"Realistic": definition of, 221; not antithetic to romance, 221.
Realistic plays of city life, 303-309.
Receipts of the theatre: in 1754, 12; in 1761, 15; in 1798, 89; comparison of British and American plays, 152n.
Recruiting Officer, The (Farquhar), 11.
Red Branch Knight, The, 376.
Red Rover, The, 161.
Rede, Leman, his *Hue and Cry*, 301.
Reid, Mayne, influence of, 373.
Religious feeling, motive in drama, 222.
Remorse, 183.
Removing the Deposits, 284.
Remuneration to the dramatist, 161, 363.
Reparation, 120n.
Retrospect, The, 101.
Return from a Cruise, The, 154.
Revolution, the, 33-60, 95, 126, 127, 155-158, 161, 264, 277-281; bibliography of drama of, 405-406.
Ribbemont, 83-84, 109; quotation from, 84.
Rice, T. D., 334; his "Jim Crow" song, 334; *Bone Squash*, 334; *Virginny Cupids*, 334.
Richelieu, a Domestic Tragedy, 181-183; its source, 181-182; collaboration with Irving, 183; difficulties with the censor, 183; reappearance of character in later play, 316.
Richings, Peter, 277, 338.
Richmond Theatre, burning of, 167.
Rienzi, 221.
Rifle, The, 334.
Rights of Man, The, 323.
Rinaldo Rinaldini, 106.
Rip Van Winkle, 384.
Rip Van Winkle, 205, 325-332; first dramatization in America, 325; version by Kerr, 326-328; casts of London and Philadelphia performances, 326-327; relation to Irving's story, 327; Bernard's version, 328; Burke's version, 328-329; Lacy's revision of Kerr, 329-330; Boucicault's version for Jefferson, 330-332, 380; Jefferson's

523

INDEX

alterations, 331-332; as an opera, 332; reprints of, 396, 417.

Rip Van Winkle (opera), 332.

Rip Van Winkle, a Legend of Sleepy Hollow (Lacy version), 329.

Rip Van Winkle, a Legend of the Catskills (Burke), 320.

Rip Van Winkle; or, The Demon of the Catskill Mountains!!! (Kerr), 326-328.

Rising Glory of America, The, 50.

Rittenhouse, David, 89.

Robber plays, 116.

Robbers, The (Payne?), 186n.

Robbers, The (Schiller), 197.

Robbery, The, 96.

Robert Emmet (Boucicault), 386.

Robert Emmet (Pilgrim), 364, 376.

Robertson, Agnes, 368, 371, 372, 374, 385.

Robespierre, 108.

Robineau, A. L. B., 84.

Robinson, J., his *Yorker's Stratagem*, 131, 294.

Robinson, Solon, his *The Rifle*, 334.

Rogers, Robert: his *Ponteach*, 28; appears in *Pontiac* as a character, 29, 274.

Rolfe, John, 140.

Roman historical plays: See Italy.

Romance: not opposed to realism, 221; essence of, freedom from restraint, 221.

Romance After Marriage, 324.

"Romantic," definition of, 221.

Romantic comedy, 145-147, 210-211, 257-259, 316-317, 324, 341-343. See also Romantic play.

Romantic dramatist, choice of material and treatment, 221-222.

Romantic movement in France and America, 220.

Romantic play, (first), 20-27; 78-80, 80-82, 83-84, 92-95, 97-99, 100-102, 107, 109, 111-112, 113-120, 138-146, 170-174, 178-180, 188-195, 211-219, 220-267, 271, 337-367, 368-369, 371, 377-382, 383-385; decline of the type, 390.

Romantic tragedy, (first), 20-27; 78-80, 117-118, 188-192, 213-215, 216-219, 220-267, 271, 337-367; progress of, from 1767 to 1855, 367. See also under Romantic play, esp. 170-174.

Romeo and Juliet, 11, 14; influence of, 224, 259.

Romulus, 185; quotation from, 185.

Rose Gregorio, 322.

Rose of Arragon, The, 197.

Rowe, Nicholas, 4; influence on Godfrey, 24.

Rowson, Mrs. S. H., 121-123, 153, 181; joins American Company, 82; her *Slaves in Algiers*, 121-123, quotation from, 122-123; *The Volunteers*, 123; *The Female Patriot*, 123; *Americans in England*, 123; *Columbia's Daughters*, 123; bibliography of, 409.

Royalties, dramatic, 161, 363.

Rudolph, 196.

Ruggles, Timothy, satire of, 43.

Rural Felicity, 133.

Ryan, Dennis: reorganizes American Company, 61; plays in the South, 61.

S

Sack of Rome, The, 46.

Sagamore, The, 270.

St. Leon, influence of, 119.

Salle, J. de la, influence of, 209.

Sans Souci, 63.

Saratoga Springs, 310.

Sargent, Epes, 261, 291, 311, 317; his *Bride of Genoa*, 261; *Velasco*, 262-263, Marylebone Theatre opened with (1849-50), 262, quotation from, 262; *The Candid Critic*, 263; *The Lampoon*, 263; *The Priestess*, 263; bibliography of, 414.

Satire, social: See Social comedy.

Savage, John, his *Sybil*, 260.

INDEX

INDEX

INDEX

INDEX

Trumbull, John, 113, 114.
Trust, The, 160.
Tunbridge Walks (Baker), 11.
Turnbull, J. D.: his *Rudolph*, 196;
  The Wood Dæmon, 197.
'Twas All for the Best, 224.
'Twas I, 183.
Twin Rivals, The (Farquhar), 11.
Two Galley Slaves, The, 177, 178.
Two Sons-in-law, The, 183n.
Tyler, J. S., 115.
Tyler, Moses Coit, 21.
Tyler, Royall: birth, 64; military
  career, 64; admitted to bar, 64; en-
  gagement to Abby Adams broken,
  64; marriage to Mary Palmer, 64;
  visit to New York, 64; writes *The
  Contrast*, 64; *May-Day in Town*,
  71; *A Georgia Spec*, 71; *The Farm
  House*, 72; *The Doctor in Spite of
  Himself*, 72; *The Island of Barrataria*, 72; *The Origin of the Feast of
  Purim*, 72; *Joseph and His Brethren*, 72; *The Judgment of Solomon*,
  72; a novel, *The Algerine Captive*,
  73; a satire, *The Yankey in London*,
  73; Chief Justice of Vermont, 73;
  death, 73; influence of, 121, 294,
  269; manuscripts of, and bibliography of, 406.
Tyrant's Victims, A, 192.
Tyrolese Peasants, The, 186n.

U

Ugolino, 252-253.
Uhland, J. L., 351.
Uncle Tom's Cabin, 287-289, 335, 372;
  American versions of, 288; British
  versions of, 288; French versions
  of, 288.
Under the Gas Light, 308.
Union College, 165.
"United States, The," 154.
Upper Ten and Lower Twenty, The,
  321.
Usurper, The (Jones), 282.
Usurper, The (McHenry), 249, 375.

V

Valdemar, 192.
Valentine; ou, la Séduction, influence
  of, 176.
Vanbrugh, Sir John, 70.
Vanity Fair, 375.
Velasco, 262-263; Marylebone Thea-
  tre opened with (1849), 262, 317.
Venetian, The, 213.
Vermont Wool Dealer, The, 301.
Very Age, The, 324n.
Veteran, The, 324.
Veuve de Malabar, La, 113.
Vice Versa, 386.
Victoria, 284.
Victoria, Queen, 284.
Victory Upon Victory, 286.
Vie de Bohème, La, influence of, 382.
Vining, Fanny, 262.
Virgin of the Sun, The, 97.
Virgin Unmasked, The (Fielding), 11.
Virginia (Parke), 62.
Virginia (Payne), 174.
Virginia Company, 9.
Virginia theatres, 135.
Virginius, 254, 272.
Virginny Cupids, 334.
Virtue Triumphant, 126.
Voice of Nature, The, 102.
Vol, Le, influence of, 169.
Voltaire, influence of, 167, 171-174,
  310.
Volunteers, The, 123.

W

Wainwright, D. W., his *Wheat and
  Chaff*, 322.
Wainwright, J. H., his version of *Rip
  Van Winkle*, 332.
Waldimar, 254-255.
Wallack, J. W., 141, 170, 195, 213,
  257, 287, 324, 335, 367.
Wallack, Lester, 257; his *Veteran*,
  324.
Wallack's Lyceum Theatre, closing
  of, 389.
Walnut Street Theatre: built (1809),

INDEX

Winter's Tale, The, influence of, 259.
Witchcraft, 276.
Witchcraft, theme of, 147-151, 276.
Woman's a Riddle (Bullock), 11.
Woman's Revenge, 183.
Wood, Mrs. William, 137, 147, 149.
Wood, William, 88, 92, 93, 134, 137, 140, 144, 147, 161, 162, 194, 203, 224, 249, 304, 398.
Woodworth, Samuel, 156-159, 161, 164, 336; his *Widow's Son,* 156; a transition writer, 156; birth, 156; collaboration with Payne in newspaper work, 156; death, 156; his *Deed of Gift,* 156; *Forest Rose,* 156, 294, 295; *The Widow's Son,* a drama of the Revolution, significance of it, 157-158, 159; *La Fayette,* inspired by visit of Lafayette, 158; *Blue Laws,* 158; *The Cannibals,* 158; *King's Bridge Cottage,* 158; *The Foundling of the Sea,* 296; bibliography of, 409, 416.
Workman, James, 135.
World a Mask, The, 344-345, 362; quotation from, 345-346; receipts from, 363n.
Wounded Hussar, The, 196.
Wreck of Honor, The, 160-161.
Wright, Frances (Darusmont): her *Altorf,* 194-195; her comparison of

British and American stages, 195; bibliography of, 411.

Y

Yale College, 62, 131.
Yankee characters: first on the stage, 64; in scene from *The Contrast,* 67-69; in other plays, 108, 114-115, 131, 137, 153, 155, 156, 160, 205, 274, 281, 289, 294-303, 336, 376.
Yankee Chronology, 106, 154.
"Yankee Doodle," air indicated in 1767, 29.
Yankee Land, 301.
Yankee plays, 294-303; significance of, 302-303. See also Yankee characters.
Yankey in England, The, 113, 114-115.
Yankey in London, The, 73.
Yorker's Stratagem, The, 131, 294.
Yorktown, Battle of, 159, 277.
Young, Brigham, 286, 287.
Young, Mrs. Charles, 193.
Young America in London, 31.
Young Carolinians, The, 153.
Young Man About Town, The, 324n.
Young New York, 322.
Yuseff Caramalli, 153.

Z

Zschokke, J. H. D., influence of, 100.

(5)

530